CENTRAL TO THEIR LIVES

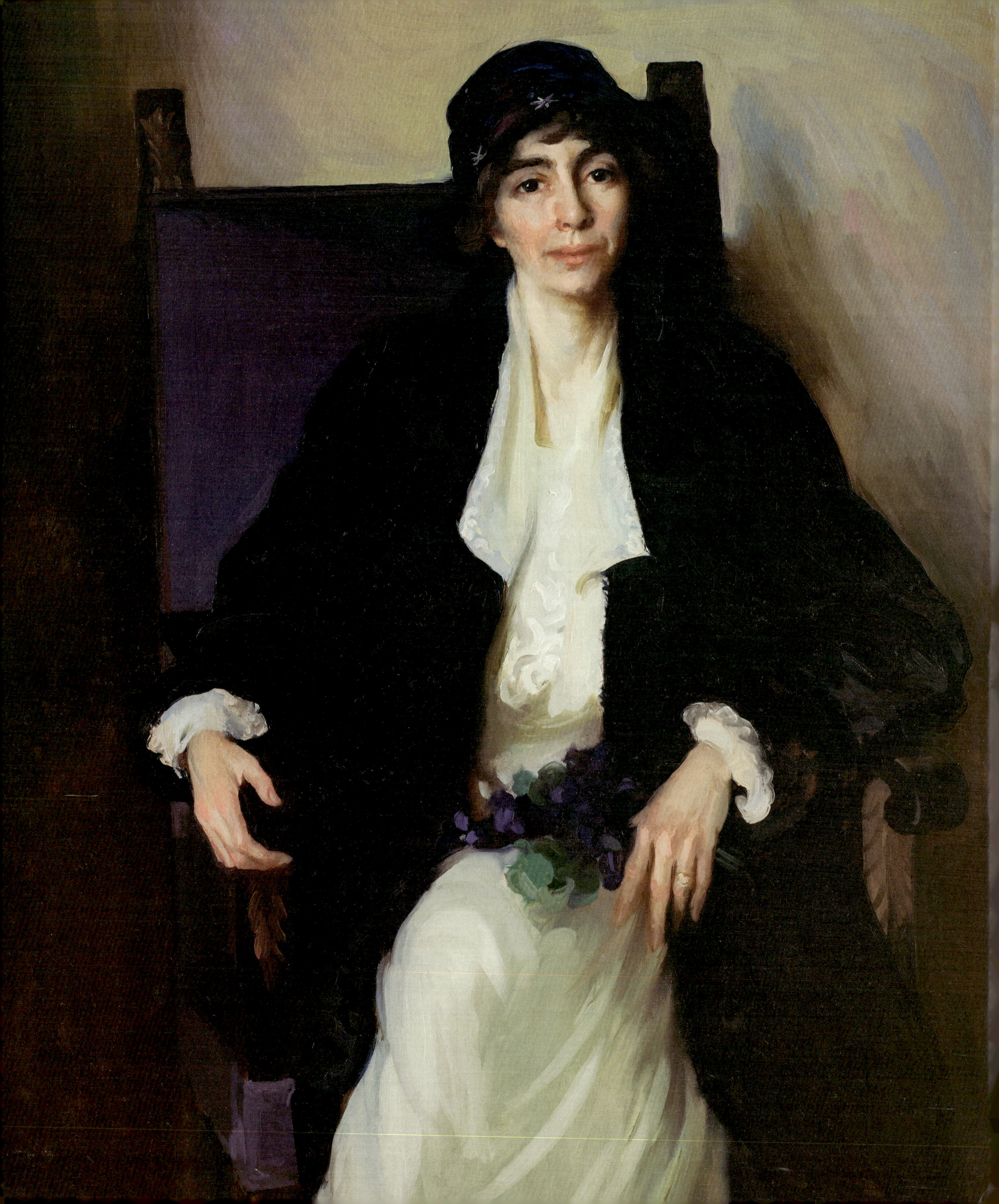

CENTRAL TO THEIR LIVES

SOUTHERN WOMEN ARTISTS
in THE JOHNSON COLLECTION

Edited by LYNNE BLACKMAN

Foreword by SYLVIA YOUNT

Essays by

MARTHA R. SEVERENS

DEBORAH C. POLLACK

EVIE TERRONO

KAREN TOWERS KLACSMANN

ERIN R. CORRALES-DIAZ

and DANIEL BELASCO

THE JOHNSON COLLECTION in association with

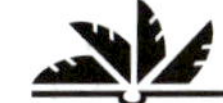

THE UNIVERSITY OF SOUTH CAROLINA PRESS

© 2018 University of South Carolina
Published by the University of South Carolina
Press
Columbia, South Carolina 29208

www.sc.edu/uscpress

Manufactured in Canada

27 26 25 24 23 22 21 20 19 18
10 9 8 7 6 5 4 3 2 1

Library of Congress Cataloging-in-Publication Data
can be found at http://catalog.loc.gov/.

ISBN: 978-1-61117-954-5 (cloth)
ISBN: 978-1-61117-955-2 (ebook)

Unless otherwise noted, all images are property of
the Johnson Collection, LLC.

Frontispiece: Ella Sophonisba Hergesheimer (1873–1943), *Portrait of Madeline McDowell Breckinridge*, 1920, oil on canvas, 48¼ × 37 inches

This volume accompanies the exhibition of the same title.
Exhibition venues include

Georgia Museum of Art, Athens
June 30–September 23, 2018

Mississippi Museum of Art, Jackson
October 6, 2018–January 20, 2019

Huntington Museum of Art, West Virginia
March 2–June 30, 2019

Dixon Gallery and Gardens, Memphis, Tennessee
July 28–October 13, 2019

Gibbes Museum of Art, Charleston, South Carolina
January 17–May 3, 2020

Cummer Museum of Art and Gardens, Jacksonville, Florida
June 23–November 29, 2020

Taubman Museum of Art, Roanoke, Virginia
January 30–June 13, 2021

Contents

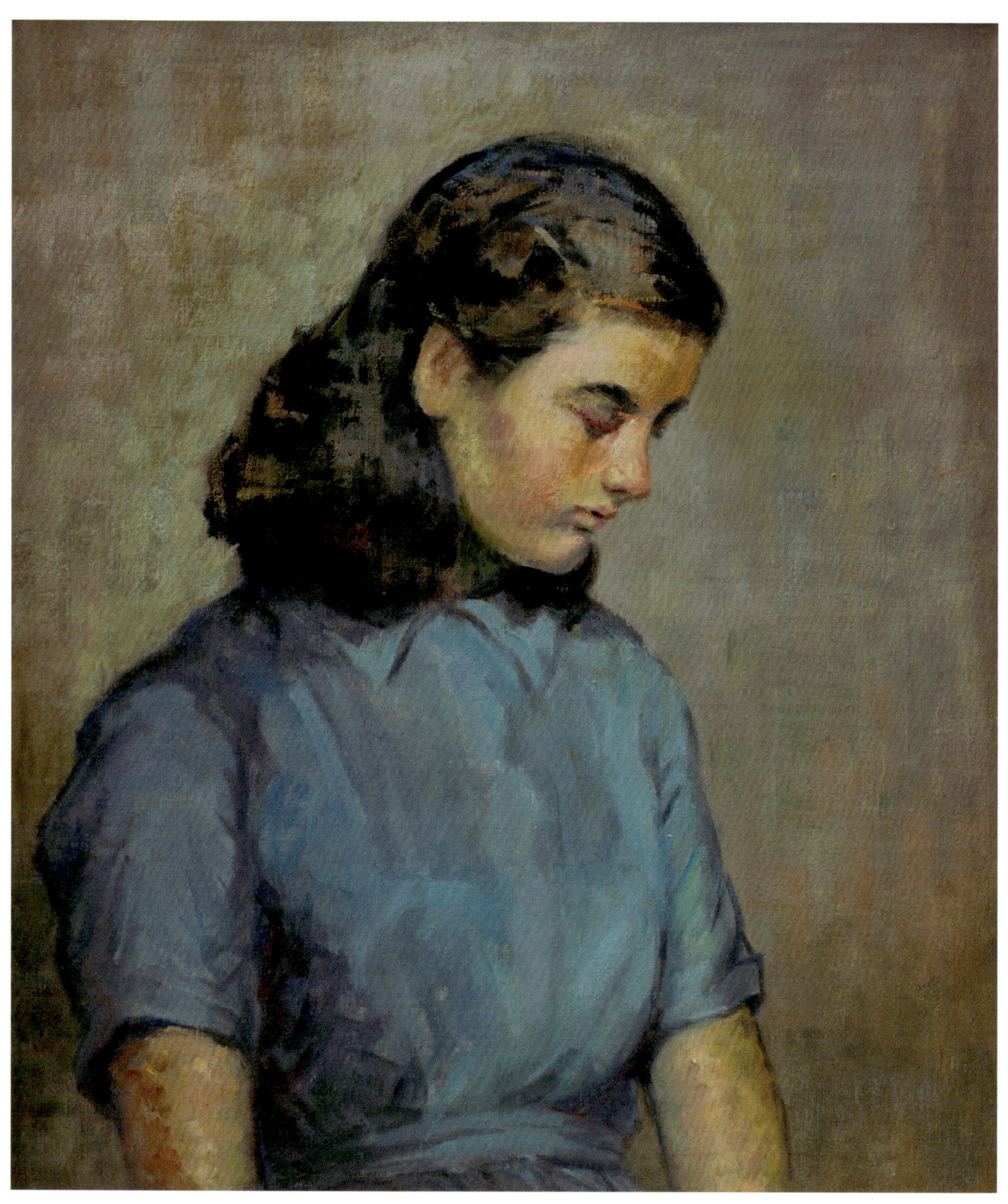

Anne Mauger Taylor Nash (1884–1968), *Portrait of a Young Girl*, oil on canvas, 23⅞ × 19⅞ inches

Foreword

Central to Their Lives: Southern Women Artists in the Johnson Collection is the third survey exhibition and publication to be organized by the Johnson Collection, marking another exciting contribution to the overdue investigation of a critical dimension of American art history—artistic production and reception in the American South. Having long been concerned with regional art worlds as well as women artists and artists of color in my own scholarship, I am particularly cheered by the expanding interest of academy- and museum-based scholars in these lesser-known figures of our discipline.

Stronger literary traditions in the region have allowed many Southern women writers of the period covered by this catalog—late 1890s to early 1960s—to flourish on a national, even international stage, from Kate Chopin to Zora Neale Hurston to Harper Lee. While visual art had a later start in the South, in the eighteenth century there were "face paint-ers"—for example, Henrietta Johnston and Mary Roberts, based in Charleston, South Carolina—who pioneered profes-sional careers, among the first in the nation.

Conservative gender norms and biases embraced through-out nineteenth-century America created challenging obsta-cles for women intent on pursuing careers in the arts, but many persisted. Education was key, and in the post–Civil War decades, more art schools opened their doors to women. Philadelphia's Pennsylvania Academy of the Fine Arts and New York's Cooper Union and Art Students League were leading institutions that inspired Southern women to leave their homes and head north in pursuit of art studies from the 1880s through the early decades of the twentieth century. Artist-educators Thomas Eakins, William Merritt Chase, Cecilia Beaux, Robert Henri, and others served as influential mentors to a generation of women from the South—painters, sculptors, and photographers, as well as teachers, patrons, and museum founders. That many of these women congre-gated in both year-round and summer art colonies in the North and South—Shinnecock, Long Island; Cos Cob, Con-necticut; Blowing Rock and Tryon, North Carolina, to name a few—suggests a more complex picture of social and cultural cross-fertilization than has often been acknowledged. Colleges in the region, such as Converse, Newcomb, Randolph-Macon, and Spelman, also nurtured the growth of artists and inde-pendent women in both the so-called fine and applied fields. Progressive clubs and suffrage organizations were as critical to creating networks of support and opportunity for women in the South as they were throughout the United States. In the thoughtful and revealing essays that follow, these and other subjects are given well-deserved attention in the context of works in the Johnson Collection.

How do we define an artist's Southern identity, whether she is native-born or transplanted, a permanent resident or a seasonal visitor? Does an iconic figure like Georgia O'Keeffe—who attended boarding school at Virginia's Chatham Hall and spent some of her twenties in Charlottesville, then taught in South Carolina at Columbia College—bear traces of that experience? What about the internationally acclaimed Massachusetts-born sculptor Anna Hyatt Huntington, who married into an established family with Virginia roots and lived the latter half of her life in South Carolina; or the Flor-ida-raised Harlem Renaissance sculptor and teacher Augusta Savage, who struggled to overcome the challenges of her Southern past?

The Johnson Collection is to be commended for casting a wide net in its formation of holdings that reflect a range of socioeconomic, racial, and stylistic differences among women artists associated with the region—trained and untrained, professional and amateur, working in a variety of media. Moreover, the consequential scholarship that the Johnson Collection is supporting will serve as an important comple-ment and corrective to the greater emphasis that has hereto-fore been placed on women active in the larger art centers of Boston, New York, Philadelphia, and Cincinnati.

Having descended from generations of inspiring Southern women, grown up in the North as well as the South, and worked in art museums from Boston and Philadelphia to Atlanta, Richmond, and New York, I have both personal and professional interest in seeing the art historical record of women's achievements—across America—recovered and shared. Only then will we all be able to appreciate more inclusive narratives and enriching cultural experiences in our classrooms, galleries, and museums. It is high time.

SYLVIA YOUNT
LAWRENCE A. FLEISCHMAN CURATOR IN CHARGE OF THE AMERICAN WING
THE METROPOLITAN MUSEUM OF ART

Introduction

"Art is central to my life. Not being able to make or see art would be a major deprivation."
Nell Blaine, quoted in Roy Proctor, "Green Thumb"

Nell Blaine's assertion about the centrality—the essentiality—of art to her life has a particular resonance. The Virginia modernist painter was seventy years old when she made this comment in 1992 during an interview about her fifty-first solo exhibition. Blaine's creative path began early, informally, and academically, and over the course of her life, she would overcome significant barriers in her quest to make and see art, including the premature death of her mother, serious vision problems, polio, and paralysis. And then there was her gender. Nearly four decades prior, Blaine had been hailed by *Life* magazine as someone to watch, profiled along with four other emerging painters whom the journalist praised "not as notable women artists but as notable artists who happen to be women."

We are, as a species, wired for creativity. Scrawls on cave walls gave way over the ages to museum masterpieces. In the eons between, men and women have recorded their experience and expressed their ideas in countless formats. And throughout history, women gifted with the instinct to "make art" have had to scrape and squeeze and salvage the space—literal, temporal, and emotional—to pursue it. In many aspects, Blaine's struggle is not singular, but rather typical, especially in the conservative American South in the late nineteenth and nascent twentieth centuries. Whether constrained by family responsibilities, societal expectations, or a narrow menu of professional tracks, women have perpetually needed a sustained and sturdy sense of purpose when it comes to composing, studying, or selling art.

I was born into what is popularly labeled the millennial generation, and my entrée to art—its production and its appreciation—has been comparatively easy and unquestionably rewarding. A fervent feminist, my mother, Susu Johnson, enrolled in women's history classes as a graduate student in the 1970s, and she's been studying, teaching, and preaching

women's history ever since. Susu's understanding of the obstacles women working in all spheres have faced—and still face—was a lesson she shared early and often, along with the reminder to be grateful to the trailblazers. As the proud graduate of a women's college, she believes deeply and vocally in the enormous value of female capacities and contributions in

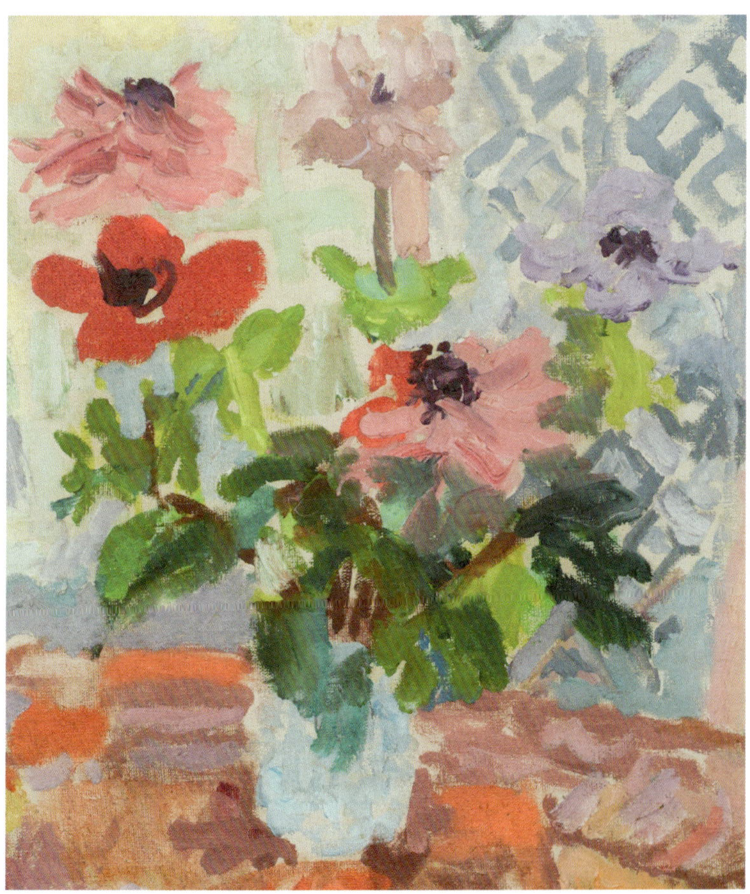

Nell Blair Walden Blaine (1922–1996), *Anemones with Red Cloth*, circa 1961–1962 (detail), oil on canvas, 30 × 18¼ inches

every endeavor. A generation down the line, I see her curriculum being administered anew with my two-year-old daughter, her first grandchild.

My childhood was infused with art, enlivened by art. That exposure—and the joy it inspired—led me to pursue an art history major at Washington and Lee University. It was around that time that my parents' collecting habit began to outpace the available wall space. While the growing inventory provided me with excellent inspiration and resources for a senior thesis devoted to female painters from South Carolina, it also gave me pause. These treasures and their legacies deserved—demanded—to be shared. My parents generously credit my observation of this as the spark for the Johnson Collection's formalization. But in truth, our family's pledge to preserve and promote Southern art was a four-way pact.

After college one of my first real jobs was as a fundraiser for Cooper Union in New York, an institution at the forefront of women's art education during the years considered in this book, in terms of both accessibility and affordability. Two of the women featured within—Augusta Savage and Helen Turner—were Cooper Union alumnae. This line of work reflected my parents' influence and example as well. They instructed us in the importance of stewardship, and I have priceless memories of running among the sculptures at Brookgreen Gardens with my brother, Geordy, on the visits we made there while our mother attended trustee meetings. Art has long been important to Geordy too, and that interest has been nurtured not only by his engagement with the collection, but also by his marriage to Carter Lee, herself a student of art history at Southern Methodist University and since. Coincidentally, their wedding took place at St. Philip's Church in Charleston, where between 1708 and 1716 the rector's wife, Henrietta Johnston, supported the family financially with her pastel portraiture and earned recognition as the first professional female artist in this country.

Life comes full circle, again and again. When I look back—and when I look ahead—I see strong women and I see art, not only at the center, but also in the radiating spokes. What a privilege it is for my entire family circle to support the scholarship this volume encompasses and to shine a light on the wondrous and frequently overlooked achievements of these fine women artists.

SUSANNA JOHNSON SHANNON

Editorial Note

The heavy editorial lifting of *Central to Their Lives* took place in the late autumn of 2016 and early winter of 2017. The surprising defeat of the first female major-party nominee for US president had robbed our work of a certain serendipity. In the wake of this political milestone, millions of women galvanized in marches and meetings across the wide, diverse, curious, and beautiful idea called America. Fifty percent of the population was jolted, it seemed, out of a comfortable complacency, having grown all too accustomed to the progress and protections earlier generations of women had secured on our behalf.

The genesis of this publication that focuses on the achievements—some heralded, most comparatively unnoticed—of Southern women artists reflects the foundational underpinnings of the Johnson Collection. In its specific emphasis on art of the American South, the collection's aim is not to divide and conquer, but instead to pinpoint and promote, in the hope of drawing overdue attention to the import and scope of the region's rich artistic history. As with the examination of African American artists—within the collection and the national canon—full credit accrues only when we highlight the distinction, with an eye toward eventually eliminating categorizations that have the capacity to marginalize rather than magnify. Great Southern art and great art by women connected to the South is simply great American art. Operating with the belief that a rising tide lifts all boats, we ultimately aim to make the modifiers unnecessary.

The collection's staff is a small crew of women who are rowing a boat captained by a woman who has long championed women's history, talents, rights, and responsibilities. Since the collection's inception, Susu Johnson has prioritized the acquisition of objects created by female artists. As we established our publication agenda, the study of these works was not merely intuitive, but insistent. Working in concert with Susu, the collection's founding director, David Henderson, devised the framework for this volume and its companion exhibition. David's remarkable breadth of knowledge about Southern art and artists—the makers and the market—had its ideal complement in Martha Severens, a respected author whose prolonged scholarship on the topic helped shape the project. David and Martha's curatorial contributions to *Central to Their Lives* were critical to its organization and execution. Under Martha's guidance, University of North Carolina graduate intern Russell Gullette compiled a sizeable database of native-born Southern women artists and others who came south for the purposes of teaching, seasonal residencies, or commission work. This inventory was subsequently disseminated to twenty regional professionals for distillation, and their feedback helped us narrow the list to three hundred names. In the end, a more manageable number was selected to represent a diversity of styles and subjects, proffered here with caveats. This volume is neither exhaustive nor definitive, and it does not attempt to address photography or decorative arts and crafts created by women. While deserving of attention, these areas are not a collection focus, and therefore they are not part of the project.

The collaborative nature of our work on *Central to Their Lives*, both in intellectual and practical terms, meant that the entire art suite played a critical role in the book's premise, refinement, advancement, and manufacture. Our first on-staff curator, Erin Corrales-Diaz, brought a fresh academic sensibility to the plan and spearheaded the call for papers, the fruit of which is found in an insightful essay by Daniel Belasco, as well as several catalog entries by outside writers. This initiative allowed us to support the scholarly efforts of emerging art historians who are eager to publish, not unlike their respected veteran counterparts—Karen Klacsmann, Deborah Pollack, Evie Terrono, and Martha Severens—all of whom contributed thoughtful, engaging chapters indicative of their expertise. Chief operations officer Sarah Tignor offered critical input into the book's content and compilation and, as usual, served as a benevolent tyrant when it came to issues of image fidelity and business protocol. In keeping with our determination to leave documentary breadcrumbs for future scholars' investigations, registrar Holly Watters took charge of the biographical directory that now indexes more than two thousand women who were artistically active in the South between the late 1880s and 1960. Painstaking is too mild an adjective to describe Holly's efforts on this registry, and her dogged attention to detail has produced an invaluable resource.

Amid the gender conversations of the first quarter of 2017, State Street Global Advisers, a Manhattan financial firm, commissioned Delaware sculptor Kristen Visbal to execute a statue that would, as the firm reported on its website "raise awareness and drive a conversation around the need to improve gender diversity in corporate leadership roles." In conjunction with International Women's Day, the bronze sculpture, titled *Fearless Girl,* was installed on Wall Street, strategically positioned across from the massive, iconic charging bull. Hands on hips, the *Fearless Girl* defiantly faces into—and faces down—a totem associated with a traditionally male-dominated, testosterone-fueled industry. Measuring only fifty inches tall, *Fearless Girl* is petite and pony-tailed, but powerful in her depiction and in the message she conveys to other young girls, fearful or not. During the countless hours of final preparations for this manuscript, I have distracted myself with alternative versions of *Fearless Girl*. In my imagination, she sometimes stands with arms not akimbo, but at work, a palette in one hand, paintbrush in the other. Surveying the city skyline, she contemplates the artistic imprint she might make on the country's cultural landscape. In that way and to my mind, she is another silent sentinel in the proud line of women artists and changemakers.

LB

"THE PEDESTAL HAS CRASHED"

ISSUES FACING WOMEN ARTISTS IN THE SOUTH

MARTHA R. SEVERENS

The pedestal has crashed....It was only an image after all....In its place is a woman of flesh and blood, not a queen, or a saint, nor a symbol, but a human being with human faults and human virtues.[1]

For women artists working in the closing years of the nineteenth century and the first several decades of the twentieth, the pedestal image had double meaning. Long the object of the male gaze—especially when undraped—women had provided artistic fodder since ancient times. Thus it was particularly hard for women artists to assert themselves in an environment dominated by men—to move, as it were, to a place behind the easel instead of in front of it.

By the 1950s, however, women artists had made significant inroads and were gaining wider representation in museum collections, exhibitions, and academe. Those from the South and working there faced additional challenges, as the region clung to conventional beliefs about the role of the fairer sex. Painter and poet Maria Howard Weeden of Huntsville, Alabama, dropped her first name in her signature, even on works bound for international gallery shows. In an interview published in 1904—just a year before her death—she offered a nostalgic reflection on her life: "Happy women have no histories it is said—and perhaps it is because I have been so happy that I have nothing to tell you. I live in the old house in which I was born, here in the loveliest old town in the world, with my friends, my books, and my pictures, and this is my history."[2] While Weeden was evidently content with her situation, other women artists suffered alienation from families, never married, and lived a bare-bones existence. The essays and catalog entries in this volume tell the fascinating stories of women dedicated to their art, willing to make sacrifices, and—while still not household names—deserving of greater study.

Although notoriously conservative, the South reigns supreme in historical terms and can claim America's earliest professional female artist: Henrietta de Beaulieu Dering Johnston. Of French Huguenot descent, she arrived on this side of the Atlantic in 1708, a financial helpmate to her second husband, the Reverend Gideon Johnston, rector of St. Philip's Church in Charleston, South Carolina. The cleric acknowledged his wife's invaluable contributions to their household, writing to his supervisors in London that "were it not for the Assistance my wife gives me by drawing of Pictures....I shou'd not have been able to live."[3] Despite the challenges of obtaining supplies from abroad, the delicacy of her materials, and limited patronage, Johnston frequently created delightful likenesses, such as that of Henriette Charlotte de Chastaigner, age eleven, shown with a marvelous red ribbon.

In the ensuing decades, Southern women frequently conducted drawing schools for girls who aspired to be accomplished exemplars of their sex. The instructors were typically either spinsters in need of income or the wives of artists. Lessons for genteel young women were conducted in domestic settings in larger cosmopolitan cities like New Orleans and Charleston, and traditional subjects for depiction were portraits, still lifes, and occasionally landscapes copied from engravings. The pursuit of art, along with music and needlework, was considered proper for women whose destiny was marriage and motherhood. In 1825 Mrs. William Brown, the wife of an artist who painted miniatures and portraits, advertised in a Charleston newspaper: "Lessons to Ladies on the Piano Forte, and painting on black or white Velvet, Satin, etc. without theorems."[4]

In her iconic retrospective, *Gone with the Wind,* author Margaret Mitchell described Scarlett O'Hara's talents in flirtation: "She knew how to smile so that her dimples leaped, how to walk pigeon-toed so her wide hoop skirts swayed

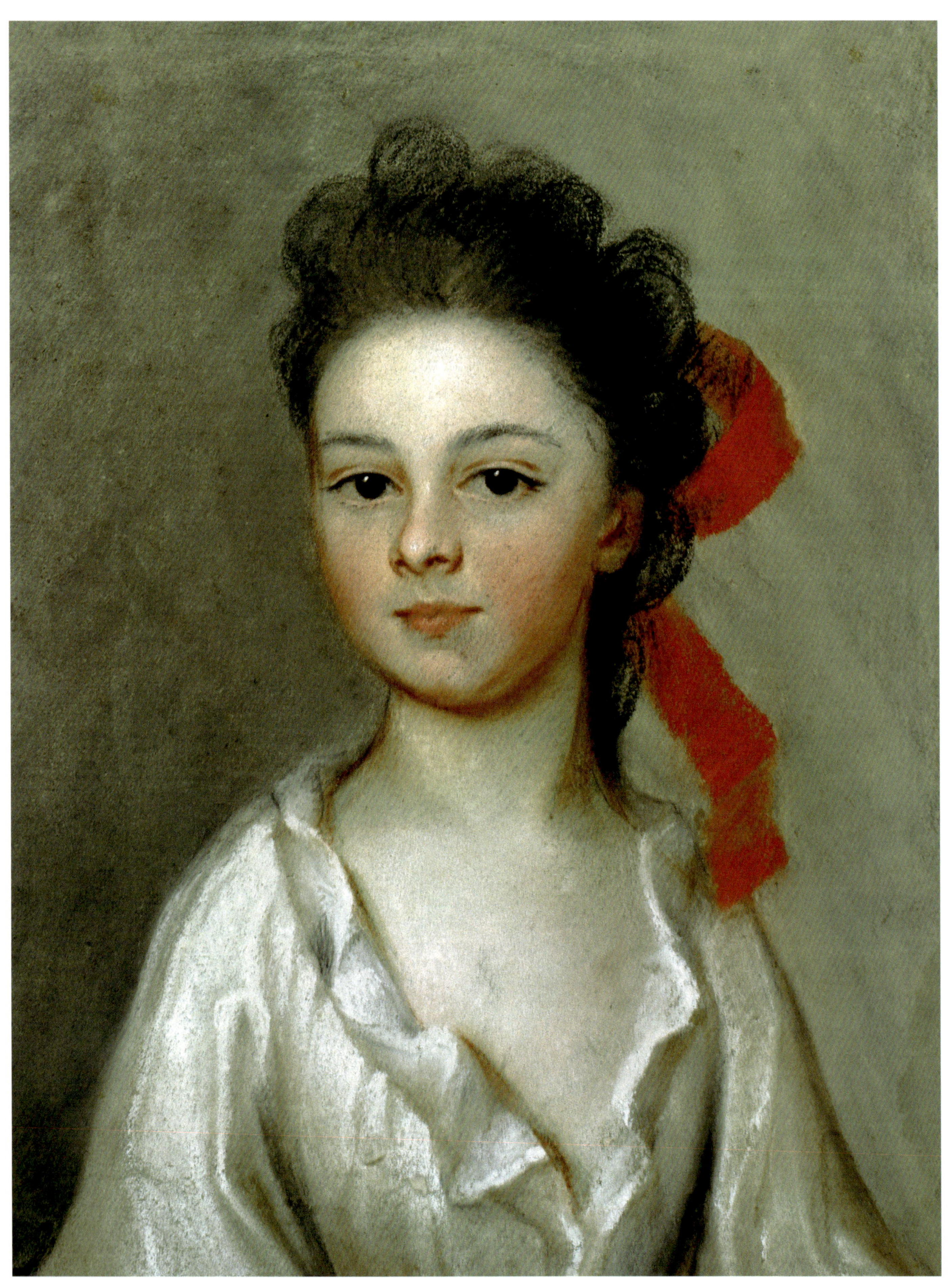

Henrietta de Beaulieu Dering Johnston (circa 1674–1729), *Henriette Charlotte Chastaigner* (Mrs. Nathanial Broughton, 1700–1754), 1711, pastel on paper, 11¾ × 9 inches; 1938.020.0004; image courtesy of the Gibbes Museum of Art/Carolina Art Association, Charleston, South Carolina

entrancingly, how to look up into a man's face and then drop her eyes and bat the lids rapidly so that she seemed a-tremble with gentle emotion. Most of all she learned how to conceal from men a sharp intelligence."[5] The Civil War, as Mitchell portrayed so dramatically, was a turning point for the South and for women. Scarlett took charge of her destiny, used her brain, became a success in business, and emerged as a woman of the New South. But prejudice against women persisted. For example, Harvard Medical College professor Edward H. Clarke contended that reproductive organs would be damaged by mental overexertion, proclaiming in his best-selling 1873 text *Sex in Education: Or, A Fair Chance for the Girls* that the "identical education of the sexes is a crime before God and humanity."[6] Nevertheless, in the postbellum period, women's colleges were established, some land-grant universities embraced coeducation, and gradually women began to move into the workforce as teachers, nurses, and store clerks.

Female artists had several possible pathways: they could remain single, marry and continue their art, or marry and abandon it. Although known mainly as an abolitionist and feminist, the Pennsylvania artist Jane Swisshelm spoke for many women when she lamented: "A man does not marry an artist, but a housekeeper [which] fitted my case, and my doom was sealed. I put away my brushes and resolutely crucified my gift, and while it hung writhing on the cross, spent my best years and powers cooking cabbage."[7] In South Carolina, Josephine Sibley Couper managed to balance being a wife and an artist, albeit on a limited scale. While her husband was alive, she produced family-oriented subjects and portraits. Following his death in 1913 she flourished, furthering her studies under the aegis of Elliott Daingerfield and Hugh Breckenridge, and in Paris with André Lhote. Willie Betty Newman, who had displayed an early talent for drawing, married at age seventeen and gave birth to a son a year later. Still ambitious for a career in art, she left her young son behind in Tennessee and enrolled at the Art Academy of Cincinnati. She prospered there and received a three-year scholarship to study in Paris, then remained abroad for a decade. When she returned to the United States, Newman continued to prefer the role of artist over that of wife and mother.

Marriage to a fellow artist was common. Sarah Blakeslee wedded one of her instructors from the Pennsylvania Academy of the Fine Arts, Francis Speight. They lived and painted in Bucks County, Pennsylvania, although her exhibition activities were diminished somewhat after the birth of two children. When the couple moved to Greenville, North Car-

olina, she resumed her career with a renewed focus. In New Orleans, Marie Seebold, the precocious daughter of a gallery owner, grew up to be a devoted protégé to Andres Molinary, a fixture in the city's art scene. He taught her drawing and painting, and she became proficient with portraits and still lifes, as well as restoration. After many years together, they finally married shortly before Molinary's death. Corrie McCallum and William Halsey were another artist couple who juggled art, matrimony, and parenthood. They met at the University of South Carolina, where she had matriculated a year before he arrived; when he went off to the Boston Museum School in 1935, she joined him there. Following their return to his native Charleston after years in Mexico and Savannah, they painted very similar streetscapes. By the 1950s, however, their art diverged significantly as Halsey moved toward abstraction and collage, and McCallum painted more decorative pieces and took up printmaking—an obvious attempt on her part to distance her aesthetic output from his.

Alabama debutante Zelda Sayre and Jazz Age author F. Scott Fitzgerald had a volatile relationship whose turbulence may have contributed to her mental instability. The belle of the ball in her native Montgomery, she fell in love with the young lieutenant during World War I. Together they lived a glamorous and itinerant lifestyle in the United States and abroad. Zelda was creative as a dancer, writer, and painter, taking her first art lesson at age twenty-five. In their abstract and surreal qualities, many of her delicate watercolors display the influence of European modernism. In 1932 she published *Save Me the Waltz,* a heavily autobiographical novel, which her husband severely criticized. Ironically, he drew heavily on Zelda's characters in his next volume, *Tender Is the Night,* which appeared two years later.

Many artists remained single, out of either preference or the paucity of sympathetic men. Blanche Lazzell wrote defensively to a friend, "I am going to be an independent maiden lady and I can show people I can be as happy as anyone."[8] Although Mississippi-born Kate Freeman Clark apparently had one fleeting romance, she never married. In true Southern fashion, she was heavily chaperoned by her mother, who with reservations supported her daughter's artistic aspirations and agreed to relocate north. Clark attended a New York finishing school before enrolling at the Art Students League, where William Merritt Chase became her mentor.

The League was the preferred destination for many aspiring artists. Inaugurated in 1875 when its founders broke away from the National Academy of Design, it prided itself in having active practitioners like Chase and Robert Henri as instructors. The school's motto, *Nulla Dies Sine Linea*—no day without a line—exhorted students to practice their craft daily,

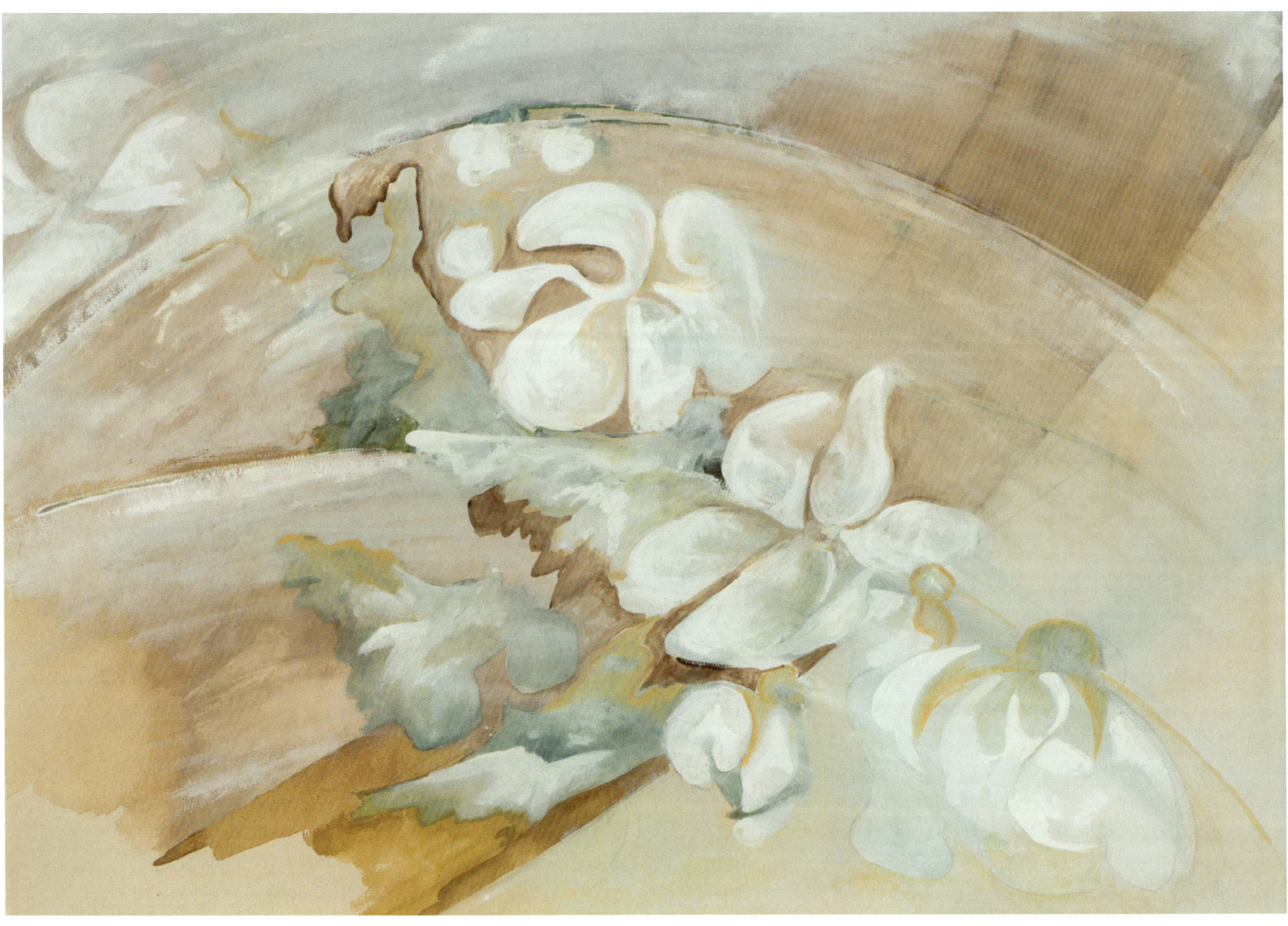

Zelda Sayre Fitzgerald (1900–1948), *Still Life with Cyclamen*, gouache, pastel, and graphite on paper, 16¾ × 23¼ inches

even if it meant drawing only a single line. Chase also offered summer sessions at Shinnecock on Long Island emphasizing plein air painting, which Clark attended six years in a row, again accompanied by her mother. For generations, painting outdoors had been considered inappropriate for women, but by the 1890s, it had become more commonplace for them to leave the studio behind and explore nature. Photographs of Chase's Shinnecock classes show women dressed in long full skirts, white blouses, and bonnets standing in front of easels scattered across the dunes. Under his tutelage, Clark thrived and exhibited at notable venues like the National Academy, listing herself as "Freeman Clark" to disguise her gender. Clark's mother strictly prohibited her from selling any paintings, an enterprise she considered unladylike. When the

artist's mentor, grandmother, and mother died in quick succession, Clark retreated home to Holly Springs, Mississippi, never to paint again.

Chase was a popular instructor and welcomed female students, who provided him with a healthy income. After the termination of the Shinnecock summer school, he escorted groups of students—again, mostly women—to Europe, where he challenged them to improve their technique and planned museum, gallery, and studio visits. During one of Chase's tours to London during the summer of 1904, South Carolinian Anna Heyward Taylor saw James McNeill Whistler's famed Peacock Room and, to her great delight, met the expatriate American master John Singer Sargent. She wrote to her sister: "Now for the best news of all! I have seen 'S a r g e n t.' . . . Sargent is just as easy and unaffected as if he were nobody at all." In Venice, Chase encouraged another student, Dixie Selden, to relax her concerns about being a voyeur and to paint spontaneously. She recalled how he instructed his students to "hold up a card with a square hole in it and put what you see through the opening on your canvas.... Let the edges of your picture lose themselves."[9]

One major hurdle for women pursuing art education was the matter of drawing from nude models, a well-established practice at institutions that followed the custom of European academies. American students, both male and female, had gravitated to Paris for the advanced study of art, creating an industry that supported not just the schools, but also boardinghouses and cafés. Women were admitted to such august places as the Académie Julian, and although their tuition was twice that of their male counterparts, the instruction was equitable. In the nineteenth century sessions with unclothed models were segregated, but by 1900 such restrictions were relaxed. In the United States, Thomas Eakins became a cause célèbre at the Pennsylvania Academy of the Fine Arts, where he taught anatomy and figure drawing. In 1886—four years into his directorship of the prestigious institution—Eakins audaciously removed the loincloth from a male model in front of a coeducational class. A controversy ensued, and he was asked to resign.

Southern women wishing to study art had few choices close to home. While some engaged private tutors, the large majority went to New York or Paris. There were a few exceptions; for example, Alice Ravenel Huger Smith attended classes in Charleston conducted by a young French woman, Lucie-Louise Féry, who taught the fundamentals of watercolor—invaluable lessons for Smith, who made it her primary medium. For many years Elliott Daingerfield was an instructor at the Philadelphia School of Design for Women, which encouraged art as a career rather than a hobby. During the summer Daingerfield taught at his studio in Blowing Rock, North Carolina, where his students, including Josephine Couper, became known locally as the "painting ladies."

The most successful Southern institution of higher learning for women interested in art was H. Sophie Newcomb Memorial College in New Orleans. The generosity of Josephine Le Monnier Newcomb, who established the school in memory of her daughter, provided the school with a financial security few other women's colleges in the region could boast. As the women's coordinate of Tulane University, Newcomb offered a liberal arts education, but its greatest strengths were the physical education department and the art school. While the college as a whole emphasized preparation for domestic success, the art department was committed to equipping students with the skills necessary to support themselves in the realm of arts and crafts. Newcomb pottery became nationally recognized for the high quality of its distinctive green-blue matte glaze and pictorial motifs derived from local flora and fauna. Other instructional subjects included book design, silversmithing, jewelry, and textiles—all aimed to make women self-supporting artists. Newcomb's mission paralleled a statement made by President William Howard Taft in a 1909 address at Mississippi University for Women: "A girl has the right to demand such training that she can win her own way to independence, thereby making marriage not a necessity, but a choice."[10]

The South's other major art school was Black Mountain College, an avant-garde institution located near Asheville, North Carolina. Founded in 1933 by several instructors who had been released from Rollins College in Florida, the small and persistently underfunded school attracted impressive global talent both as faculty and students. However, few native Southerners went there, perhaps because its curriculum was considered too experimental. Under the inspired leadership of Josef Albers, collaborative and innovative interdisciplinary projects took place. Anni Fleischmann Albers, a graduate of Germany's Bauhaus, taught courses in weaving that integrated her husband's color theory and implemented new ways to use a variety of common items, most vividly seen in her jewelry made from paper clips, sink drains, and simple chains. Many of her textile designs, incorporating such modern materials as plastic, were influenced by Mexican and pre-Columbian prototypes, which she translated into more contemporary wall hangings and room dividers. She also translated her motifs to silkscreens, such as *Triangulated Intaglios.*

Another German, Edith Caspary London, attended the University of Berlin, then studied in Rome and Paris. Like the Alberses, as Nazism advanced London and her husband immigrated to North Carolina. They settled in Durham, where she became the slide librarian at Duke University and painted Cubist-derived compositions that evolved into collages and collage-like pieces.

Two South Carolina women's colleges—Columbia College in Columbia and Converse College in Spartanburg—had respected art programs. The most notable aspect of the former was the employment of Georgia O'Keeffe for six months during the 1915–1916 school year. Although there is little evidence that she influenced her students to any great extent, it was a crucial period in her aesthetic development. Isolated

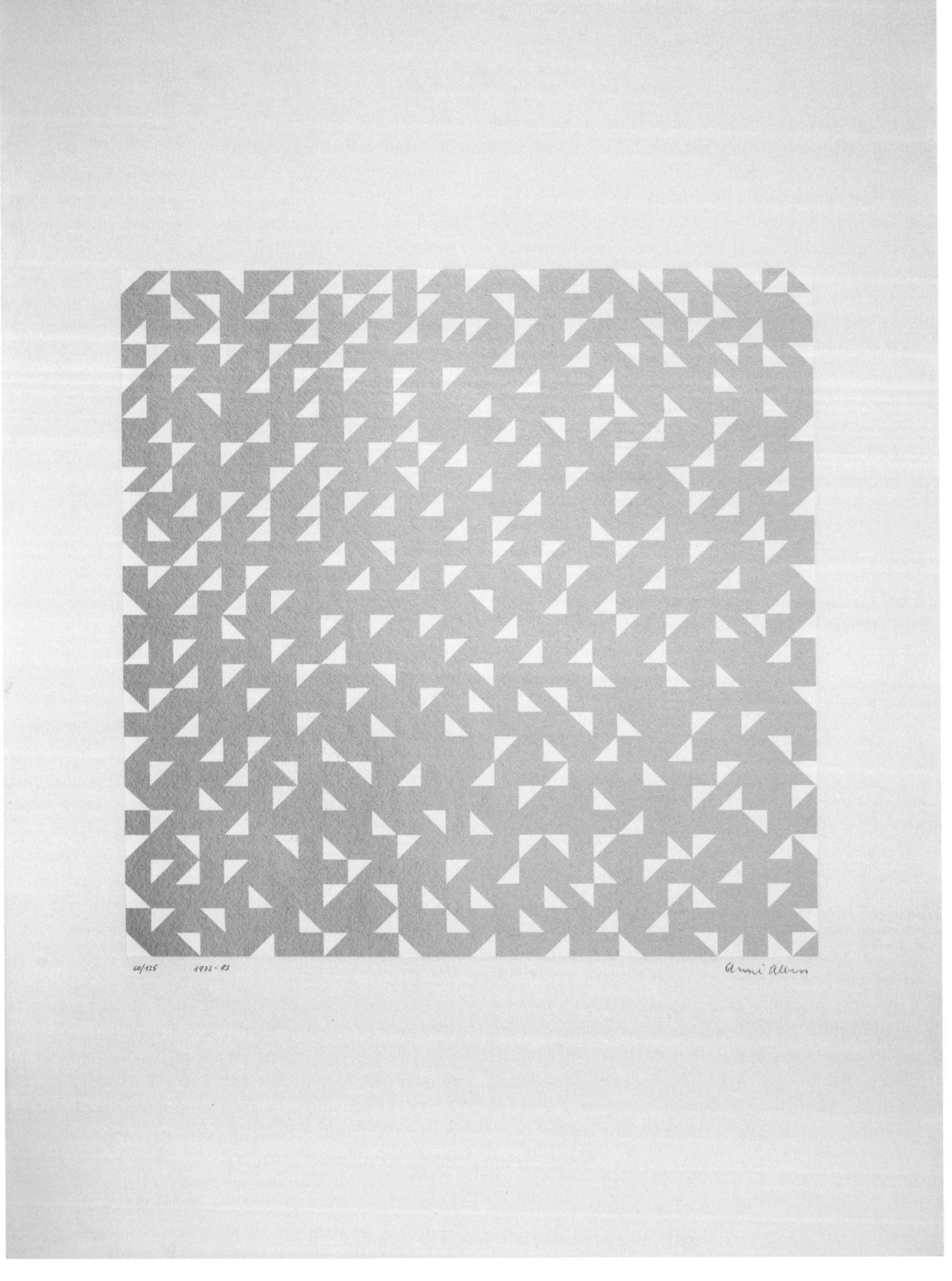

Annelise Elsa Frieda Fleischmann Albers (1899–1994), *Triangulated Intaglios*, 1972/1983, silkscreen on paper, 27½ × 19¾ inches (sheet size); 14¼ × 14¼ inches (image size)

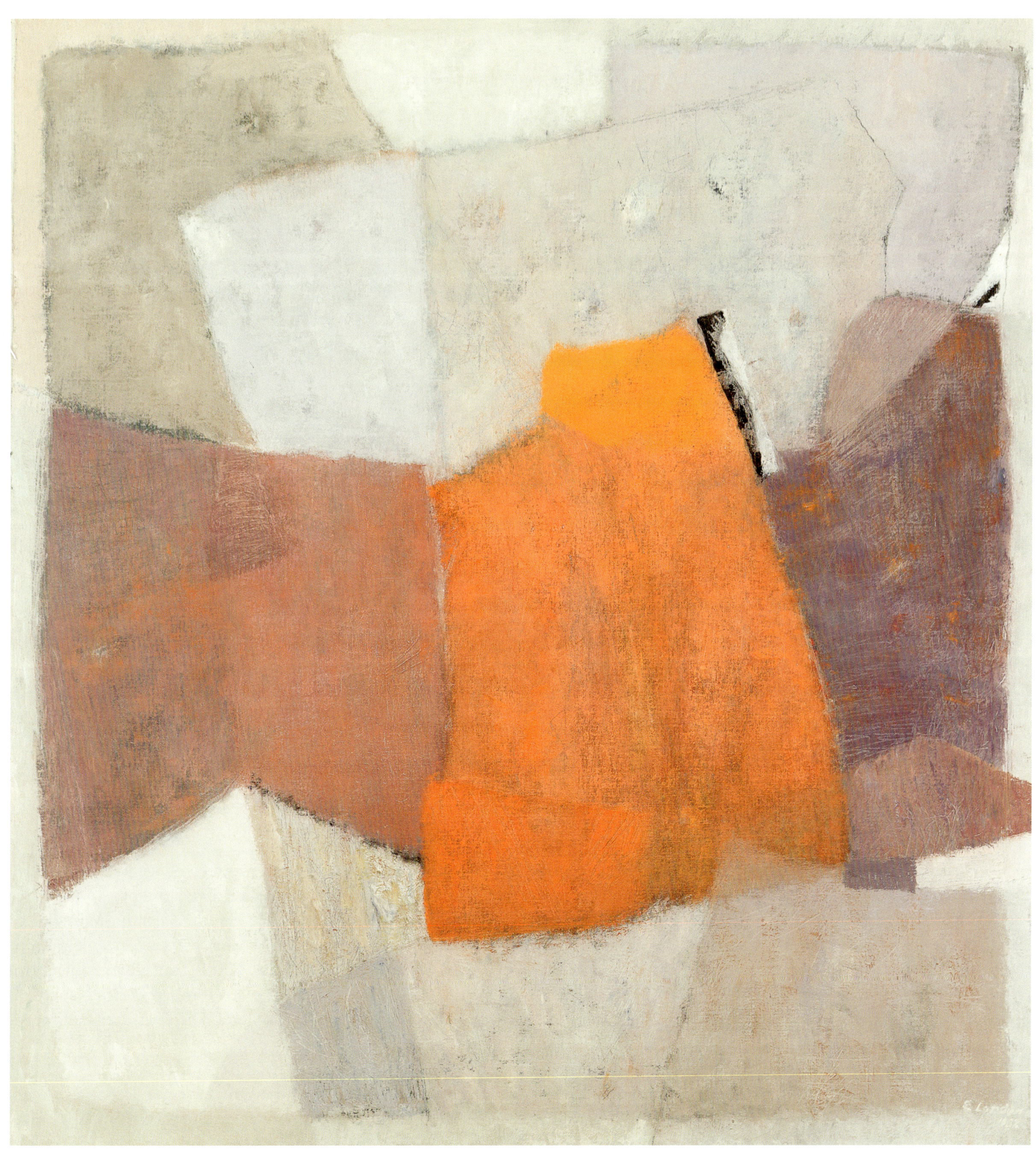

Edith Caspary London (1904–1997), *Tension and Harmony*, 1983, oil on canvas, 40 × 35⅞ inches

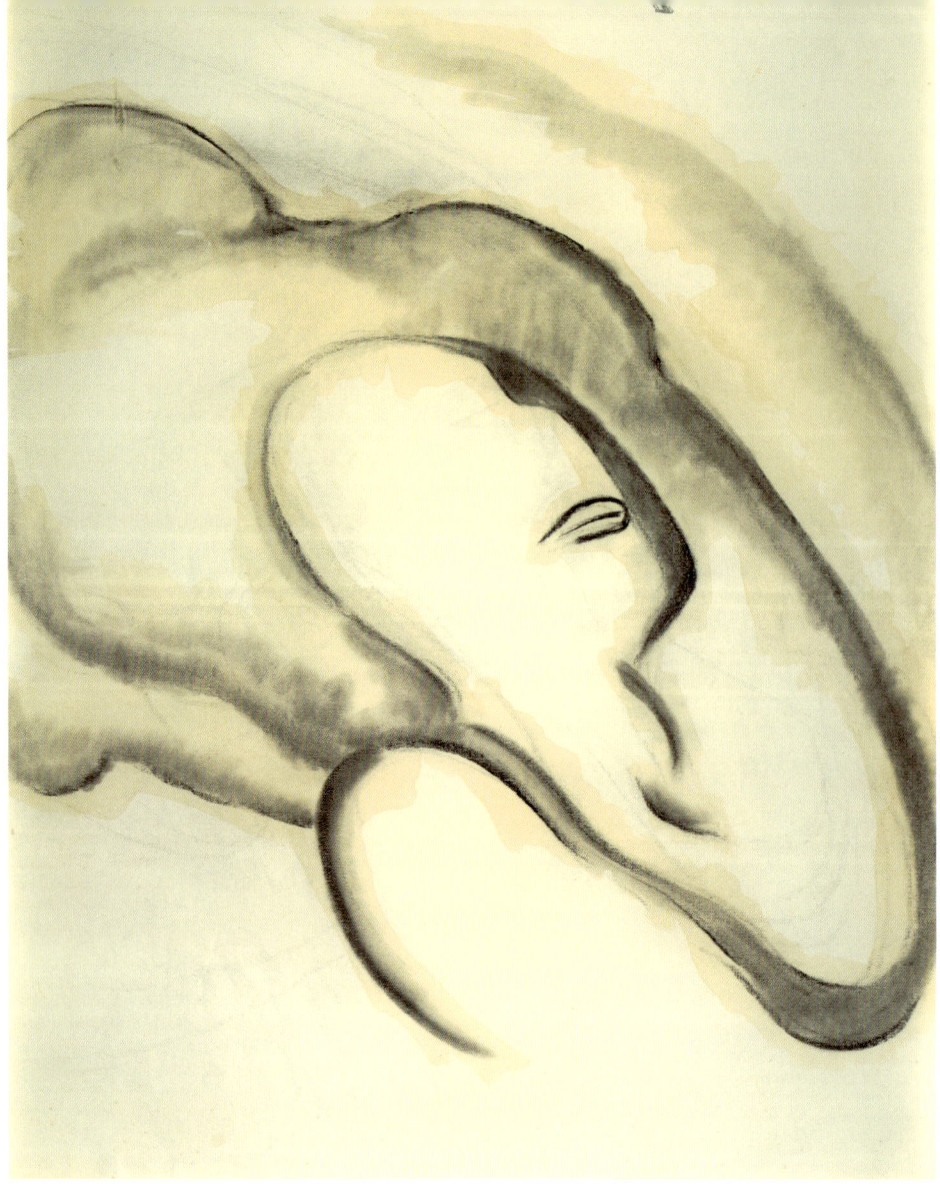

Georgia Totto O'Keeffe (1887–1986), *Abstraction*, 1916, charcoal and wash on paper, 24⅞ × 19 inches; Greenville County Museum of Art, Greenville, South Carolina; museum purchase with funds donated by the Museum Association, Mr. and Mrs. Thomas Howard Suitt Jr., Rich's Department Store, and Mr. and Mrs. C. H. Abbe

from friends, family, and the stimulation of colleagues, O'Keeffe turned inward to create a pivotal body of abstracted imagery rendered in black and white. She later acknowledged the importance of this Southern sojourn: "Hibernating in South Carolina is an experience I would not advise anyone to miss—The place is of so little consequence—except for the outdoors—that one has a chance to give one's mind, time and attention to anything one wishes."[11] She sent her drawings to her friend Anita Pollitzer in New York, who in turn showed them to the gallerist Alfred Stieglitz, who was known for his discerning eye. A highly successful promoter of photography and modernist artists, Stieglitz was enthralled by the drawings and placed ten on exhibit without O'Keeffe's permission, thus igniting a contentious and dynamic relationship that led eventually to marriage.

Converse College, a small private college in Spartanburg regarded for its music and theater departments, became the alma mater of three important South Carolina painters. In 1895 Margaret Law earned a diploma with a concentration in art and went on to study with Chase, initially at the Pennsylvania Academy of the Fine Arts and then in New York at the Art Students League, where Henri was her mentor. A passionate learner, she also received instruction from Charles Hawthorne in Provincetown, Massachusetts, André Lhote in Paris, and Lamar Dodd at the University of Georgia in 1946, more than forty years after her graduation from Converse. Law's eagerness to continue her education may reflect her dedication as a teacher, first at the Bryn Mawr School in Baltimore for twelve years, followed by her appointment in 1936 as superintendent for art in Spartanburg. That same year

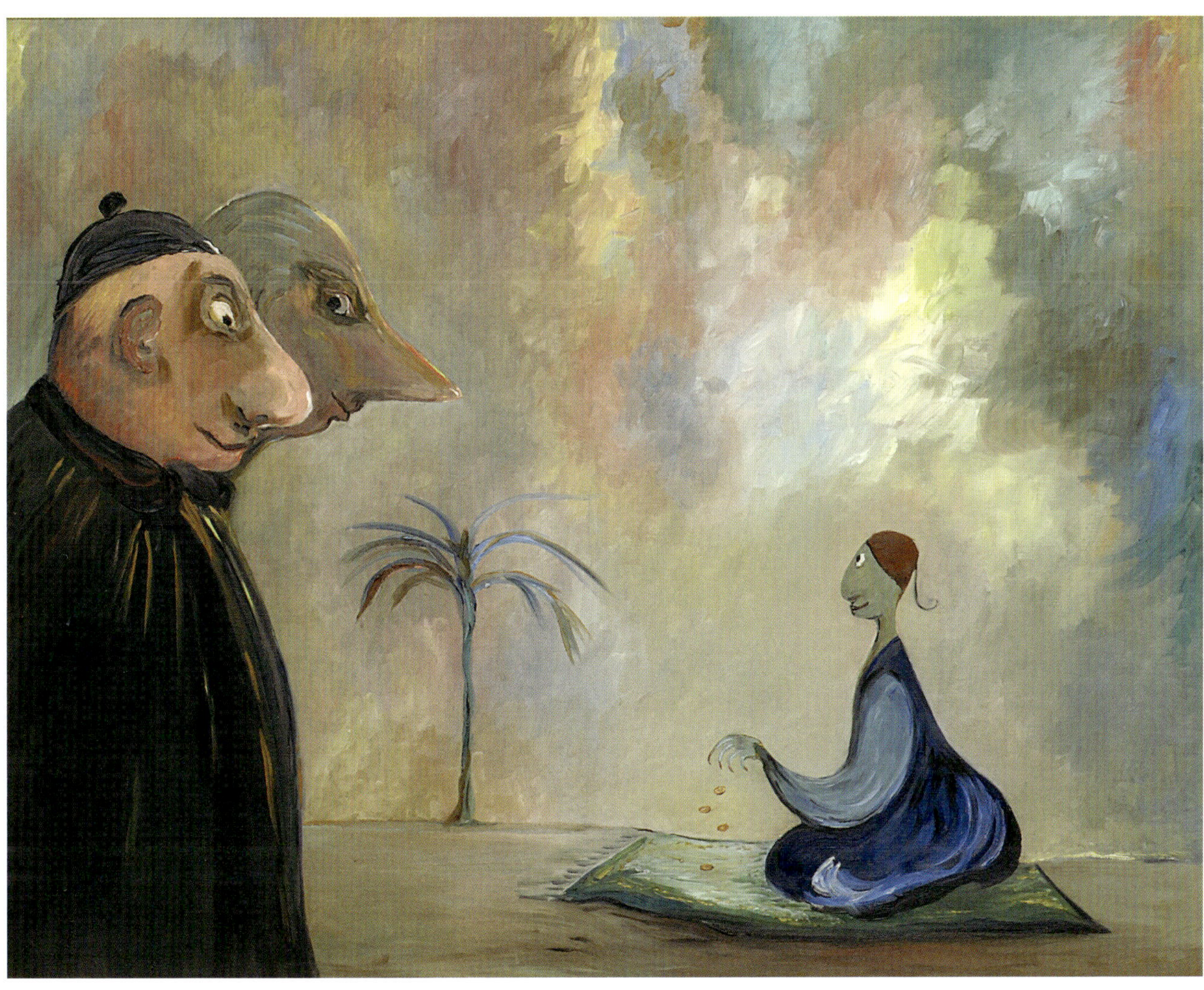

Helen Allston DuPré Moseley (1887–1984), *Untitled*, oil on canvas, 28¼ × 34⅛ inches

she assembled an exhibition of her students' drawings at the Brooklyn Museum, which Henri lauded: "I congratulate you on the life and humor of your children's drawings. It is a big thing you are doing for them, and you must have great pleasure in the doing of it.... This freeing of children will eventually revolutionize the world. You are much more a revolutionist than the man with a gun." The reference to the gun-wielding male is ironic, as Henri once advised his students, "Be a man first, be an artist later."[12]

At age fifteen Blondelle Malone enrolled at Converse to study French and music, an academic track she may have selected because her father owned a piano showroom in Columbia, South Carolina. Soon, however, she became enamored with the visual arts, which she pursued for three years before going to New York City. She wrote her parents: "I have finally decided on art as a profession and I mean to work at it as hard as I can and see if I can be an artist some day. Think this way of girls going to school and getting married

nonsense." Malone matriculated at the recently established New York School of Applied Design for Women, where the mission mirrored that of Newcomb College: to provide practical instruction in book and wallpaper design, illustration, and stained glass so women could support themselves. She also began studies at the Art Students League with John Twachtman and with Chase, who once said: "Women are usually more sensitive and easily taught than men. They do better when guided, but when thrown on their own resources, they usually show less strength."[13] Malone proved the exception: while in France she wrote letters asking advice of Mary Cassatt and even managed to wrangle an interview and critique from Claude Monet, the reclusive Giverny master known for his antagonism toward American artists.

A member of the class of 1907 at Converse College, Helen DuPré Moseley did not set out to be an artist; indeed, it wasn't until forty years later that she took the notion to paint. Following the sudden death of her husband, she needed to earn an income to support their three children. From 1934 to 1956 Moseley successfully ran Spartanburg's post office. In a speech at the time of her retirement, Governor James F. Byrnes paid her the following tribute: "She served longer (and I am going to say more efficiently) than any Postmaster in the history of the office. Of course, she was confronted with many problems, but I suspect the gravest was the men who had been running the post office—like all men—did not like the idea of having a woman in charge of the office.... But they were true sportsmen. They gave her a chance, and those men soon learned what her personal friends knew—here was a very wise woman."[14] Moseley also had a keen sense of humor, which is vividly reflected in her habitually untitled paintings of "creatures," images rich with social commentary based on *New Yorker* cartoons or photographs in *National Geographic*.

Discrimination and sexism were pervasive in the art world as well as the post office. While many women studied art and contributed significantly to the incomes of their male instructors, they often encountered prejudice and severe competition at exhibitions, where men dominated juries and controlled the awarding of prizes. For example, of the 1,300 works of art displayed at the famed 1913 Armory Show, only 16 percent were created by women. Alabama native Anne Goldthwaite's *The House on the Hill/The Church on the Hill*, a Cézannesque landscape, was one of that select number, on view in the same gallery space as paintings by Leon Kroll and G. Ruger Donoho. Alluding to the bias against female exhibitors, O'Keeffe, who regularly showed at Stieglitz's 291 and Intimate galleries, complained: "They have objected to me all along; they have objected strenuously. It is hard enough to do the job without having to face discrimination too. Men do not have to face these discriminations."[15]

Women persisted, however, by banding together, forming their own clubs, and being active in other arts organizations. The National Association of Women Painters and Sculptors was founded in 1889 as the Woman's Art Club of New York, but soon transitioned into a national organization dedicated to offering educational programs and showcasing work by its female members. By 1922 six hundred women from across the country had participated in the association, remitting an annual fee of ten dollars. A fair number of Southern-born artists were members, including several who spent the majority of their careers in the South: Josephine Couper, Dixie Selden, Anna Taylor, Margaret Law, and Marie Atkinson Hull. Southerners who had moved north were also members, including Goldthwaite, Clara Weaver Parrish, and Helen Turner. Kentuckian Maud Mason served as the organization's president from 1913 to 1917, and in

1934 Augusta Fells Savage became the first African American elected to the membership. Beginning in 1939 Blanche Lazzell was a regular exhibitor, and Adele Gawin Lemm, a Memphis, Tennessee, modernist painter, won the Grumbacher Watercolor Prize in 1954 for *Regatta* and the same prize five years later for a watercolor titled *Monhegan and Manana*.

Patronage in the South was hampered by long-standing preconceptions, as Nell Blaine observed: "There was a certain notion in Virginia about 'culture': that art was a genteel thing, prissy, and somewhat bland."[16] The Southern States Art League, established in 1921, set out to address this bias with exhibitions that celebrated the region's heritage and charm. Although one-third of its members were men, the association served as a vehicle for women to assert themselves and gain visibility. Elizabeth O'Neill Verner was active in organizational aspects of the league, and her mentor Alice Smith annually funded a cash prize for the best watercolor.

Women sought exhibition opportunities for the same reasons men did: to elevate their professional profiles and to promote sales. For portraitists, exhibitions were less critical, as these artists worked on commission, with business often generated by word of mouth and occasionally by advertisement. Selden maintained a successful career in Cincinnati by painting likenesses of local officials and members of high society. These she executed during the winter, which liberated her to travel during warmer months to such favorite locales as the northern coast of France. In Charleston, Leila Waring sustained an active clientele of individuals wanting miniature portraits, a traditional medium long popular in the South. Her account book records 210 names—a testament to her success. Waring had a delicate palette and technique, and she knew how to flatter her sitters. She studied at the Art Students League in 1902 and exhibited the following year with the Pennsylvania Society of Miniature Painters, but it was in her native city that she met with success.

Waring's *Afternoon Tea* is as much a social statement as it is a portrait of her relative Dorothy Waring. In depicting the accoutrements associated with a tea service, the miniature evokes gentility and hospitality—attributes that Waring and other women artists shrewdly employed as a sales technique for the many tourists flocking to Charleston during the 1920s. Waring's studio was located on Atlantic Street near those of Smith, Verner, and Taylor, the proximity creating an art district that obviated the need for galleries. Verner's daughter recalled: "On Sundays in March and April the four artists would be At Home, each serving tea. Visitors would go from house to house. Charleston confections, rolled wafers, cheese straws, bennie biscuits, [and] peach leather were served. Tea was poured from silver teapots and steaming silver kettles.... Of course, being Sunday nothing was offered for sale, but

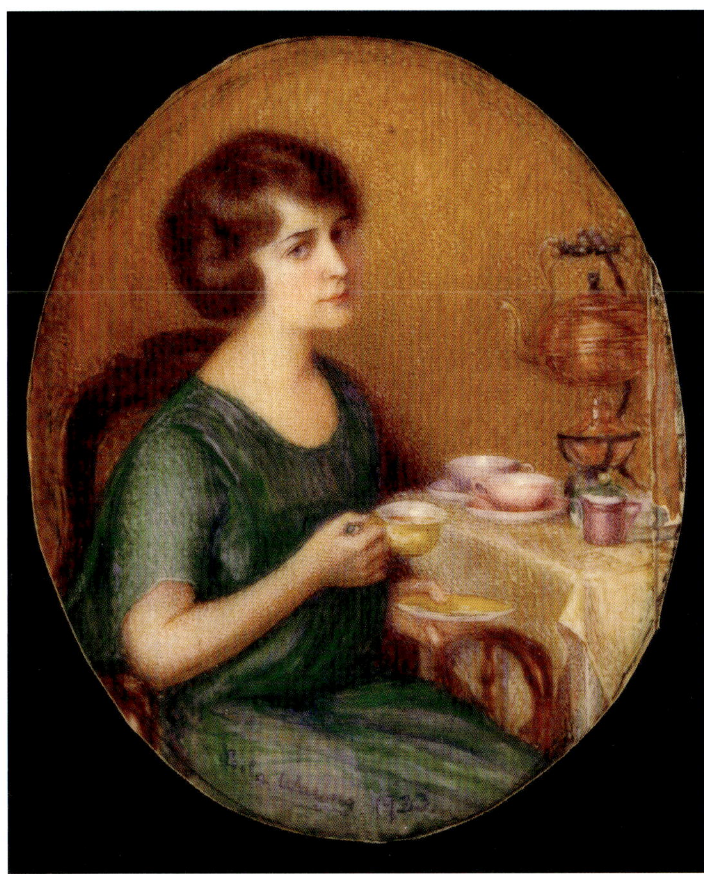

Leila Waring (1876–1964), *Afternoon Tea* (A Cup of Tea, Dorothy Thomson Waring), 1923, watercolor on ivory, 3 × 2½ inches; 1980.005.0004; image courtesy of the Gibbes Museum of Art/ Carolina Art Association, Charleston, South Carolina

there was a warm feeling in the community that Atlantic Street was a very interesting place to visit."[17]

Teaching provided women artists with another opportunity to support themselves in a profession deemed respectable for women of all disciplines. Many artists taught privately in their own studios, while others, like Law, were instructors in local school systems. Lemm taught for twenty-three years at the junior school of the Memphis Academy of Arts (now the Memphis College of Art), her alma mater. Although she had taken courses at the rival National Academy, Goldthwaite joined the faculty of the Art Students League in 1922 after having spent seven years in Paris before the war. Like Henri Matisse and Pablo Picasso, she had been a frequent visitor to Gertrude Stein's salons. In the mid-1920s Goldthwaite was the only female instructor listed in the League's catalog, a reality that probably fueled her activism. In a 1934 radio interview, she acknowledged the increased attention women artists had

been receiving: "The best praise that women have been able to command until now is to have it said that she paints like a man. . . . We want more—to speak to eyes and ears wide open and without prejudice—an audience that asks simply—is it good, not—was it done by a woman."[18]

After two years at the Art Students League, Catherine Wiley returned to her alma mater, the University of Tennessee, and became an art instructor in the home economics department, well before art departments became commonplace at universities. Most of her students were female, and many served as models for her lushly painted canvases. Wiley had matriculated at the university in 1895—four years after women were first admitted—and had studied there for two years before leaving for New York. She pursued an early interest in illustration and even took a course at the League with Howard Pyle, the so-called father of American illustration. As a contributor to various university publications, Wiley produced stylized illustrations of women in black and white that emphasized line and sinuous curves resembling the then-popular fashion of Art Nouveau design.

Teaching and illustration work also proved critical to Helen Turner's career. She grew up in diminished circumstances following the Civil War, but managed to secure a teaching certificate from Louisiana State Normal School in New Orleans in 1878. During the next decade she took free Saturday classes with Ellsworth Woodward at the art school of Tulane University, and the Artists' Association of New Orleans selected her for lessons at no cost. In a later interview she bemoaned the limitations imposed on members of her sex: "Ladies in those days did not go out in the world to make money, so there only remained for me the tasks of making paper flowers, doing charcoal sketches, and painting palmetto fans, to make money."[19] Turner wanted more, so she took a teaching job at St. Mary's College in Dallas, Texas, and taught there for two years, during which she saved sufficient funds to enable her relocation to New York. Like Kate Clark, who was accompanied by her mother, Turner arrived in the city properly chaperoned by her sister. Turner studied at the Art Students League and availed herself of tuition-free classes at the Cooper Union School of Design for Women. In 1902 she started a seventeen-year stint as an instructor at the art school of the Young Women's Christian Association in Manhattan, where she prepared students to enter the workforce as designers of wallpaper, textiles, and greetings cards, and as illustrators for books and magazines.

As Turner recounted, even within the field of art, certain arenas were judged less appropriate for women, but gradual

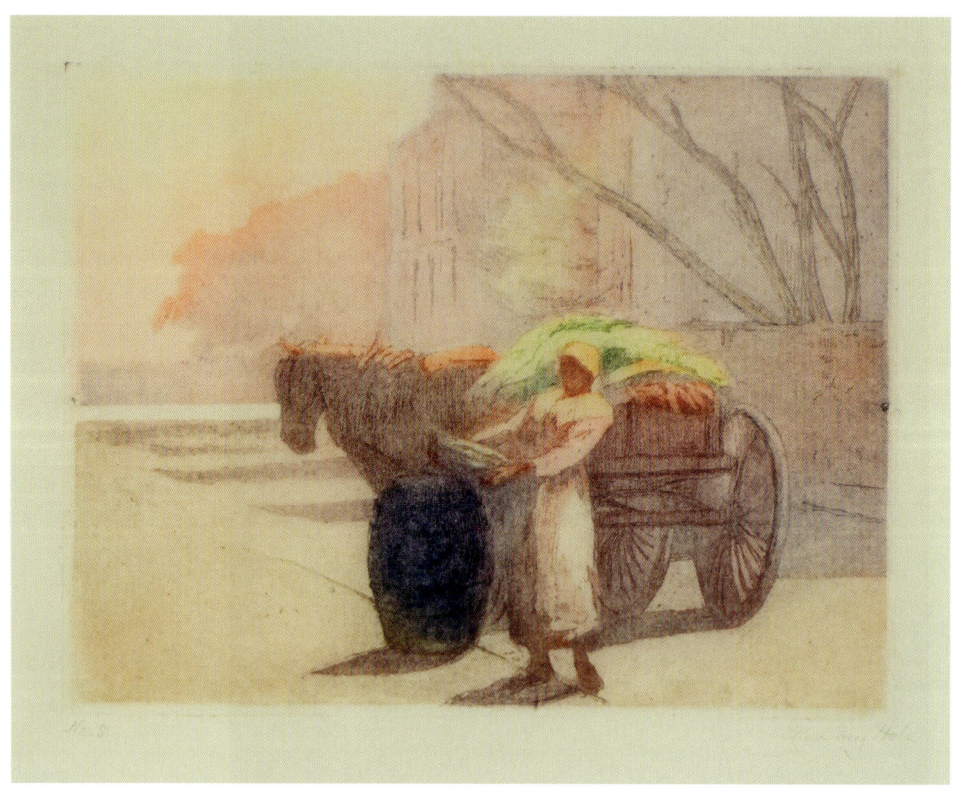

Ellen Day Hale (1855–1940), *Early Vegetables, Charleston, S.C.*, circa 1918, soft ground color etching on paper, 7¾ × 10 inches

inroads were made against these prejudices. Despite the success of a coterie of women such as Harriet Hosmer and Edmonia Lewis, who worked in Italy in the nineteenth century, sculpture was generally viewed as men's work, given the medium's physical demands. Even though the press referred to her as a "bachelor maid," Kentucky sculptor Enid Yandell created a forty-foot statue of Athena for the 1897 Tennessee Centennial in Nashville.

The myriad challenges facing African American sculptor Augusta Savage were particularly significant. Her father opposed her interest in art; she later recalled that he "licked me four or five times a week and almost whipped all the art out of me."[20] Nevertheless, she left her home state of Florida and worked menial jobs in New York City so that she could attend the Cooper Union. She modeled portrait busts of the leading figures of the Harlem Renaissance, but it was her popular depiction of a young street urchin that paved her way for a Julius Rosenwald Fellowship to study in Paris. Regrettably, Savage frequently lacked funds to cast her sculptures in bronze, although she made many plaster versions of her most recognized piece, *Gamin.* Over the course of her career, Savage became a powerful force for the art education of African Americans, nurturing the creative talents of such nationally recognized individuals as Jacob Lawrence, Gwendolyn Knight, and Norman Lewis at the Savage Studio of Arts and Crafts, which evolved into the Harlem Community Art Center. It is estimated that over 1,500 people participated in her classes and workshops, some of which were underwritten by the Works Progress Administration.

While Savage lived very modestly, Anna Hyatt Huntington enjoyed a high-profile career and privileged existence. The daughter of a Harvard University professor, she later married a wealthy philanthropist. These advantages aside, she was extremely industrious; by 1912 she was reportedly among the best paid professional women in the United States, earning more than $50,000.[21] Huntington began by making small bronze sculptures of lions, tigers, and elephants, whose anatomy she studied at the Bronx Zoo. She sold these pieces through prestigious metal and jewelry firms, such as Gorham and Company and Shreve, Crump, and Low. Her signature work was *Joan of Arc,* the first New York City monument created by a woman, and the city's first public statue of a real woman, as opposed to an allegorical one. A nationalist icon for France, the saintly heroine was a symbol of women's rights internationally. Coincidentally, Joan of Arc was canonized in 1920, the same year American women won the right to vote. At the age of forty-seven, the sculptor married Archer M. Huntington, the stepson of railroad magnate Collis P. Huntington, after which she made sculptures with less frequency. Her energy and focus were redirected toward the transformation of four coastal South Carolina plantations into Brookgreen Gardens, a sculpture museum and wildlife

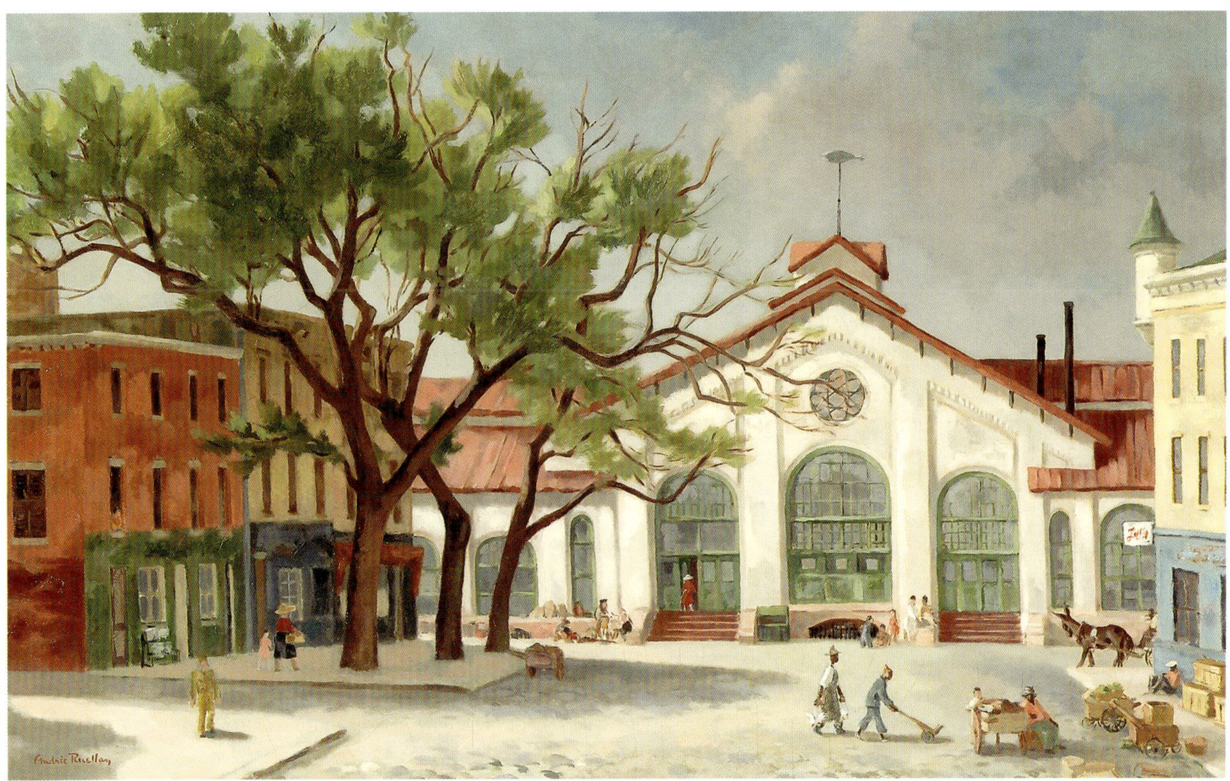

Andrée Ruellan (1905–2006), *Savannah Landscape, The City Market,* circa 1943, oil on canvas, 26¼ × 40¼ inches

preserve of more than nine thousand acres. It was the first outdoor sculpture park in the country, and an ideal site to showcase Huntington's work alongside a comprehensive survey of American figurative sculpture.

Huntington was not a native of the South, but she spent extended periods in South Carolina and left an indelible mark. When World War I and its aftermath made European travel impractical, many artists explored the region and had an impact as well. Ellen Day Hale and Gabrielle Clements were in Charleston around 1918 and discussed with Alice Smith a collaborative printmaking enterprise: "We'd like to teach the artists how to etch. Get together a group so you can buy a press and we will show you how to use it, where to buy the copper plates, the wax ground, the varnish, the stylus, the handmade paper, the etcher's ink. We'll teach you, so you can teach them."[22] Thus was founded the Charleston Etchers' Club, an enterprise that reflected a national fervor for prints. The organization's initial brochure listed nine inaugural members, seven of whom were women: Hale, Clements, Smith, Leila Waring, Minnie Mikell, Antoinette Rhett, and Elizabeth Verner, who was dutifully noted in the literature as "Mrs. E. Pettigrew Verner."

The making and selling of etchings was an ideal match for Charleston artists, and especially for Verner. Although etchings were laborious to create, artists produced them in multiples, thereby reducing cost and increasing profit. Gener-

ally measuring no more than twelve by fifteen inches, etchings were also easily transported, an advantage for the city's many seasonal visitors. Along with books and articles, these small artworks captured the area's picturesque charm and fueled the Charleston Renaissance. Artists of national renown such as Edward Hopper, Childe Hassam, and Thomas Hart Benton were among the many travelers who made their way south, but few interacted with locals as closely as Hale and Clements did.

Andrée Ruellan and her husband Jack Taylor visited Charleston in 1936, then five years later had a longer stay in Savannah. At times, Ruellan felt discriminated against because of her gender; she recounted that "critics were sometimes putting me down, patronizing me, as [they did] many women of the time, by using phrases like feminine, charming, pretty, nice, gentle, delicate, etc."[23] Ruellan's modus operandi was to place her sketchpad inside a newspaper so passersby would not disturb her. Typically she took the sketches back to her studio near Woodstock, New York, and developed them into oil paintings. The end results often appear staged and frozen in time, and many of her paintings resemble murals—a quality that made Ruellan an ideal choice for New Deal–sponsored post office commissions in Emporia, Virginia, and Lawrenceville, Georgia.

During the 1930s and early 1940s, the United States Treasury Department's Section of Fine Arts commissioned large-scale wall paintings and sculptures across the country. Although the Section selected almost three hundred federal buildings in small Southern towns for decoration, few local artists were chosen for the work. The reasons are many. One seems to have been Southerners' lingering reluctance to apply for federal assistance, a practice reminiscent of Reconstruction. More significantly, parochial administrators in Washington were largely ignorant about artists beyond the Northeast. In the South there was also a dearth of art schools and museums, two resources that promoted the program. Furthermore, the director of the Section, Edward Rowan, found it more conducive to work with established artists who were familiar to him. As might be expected, he appointed fewer women than men, reflecting a Depression-era prejudice that favored men. Rowan encouraged—but did not require—artists to make on-site visits, or at the very least to communicate with the local citizenry. When the artists did so, the results were usually sympathetic and well received; when they did not, the reaction was often fraught with controversy. Artists sent small paintings, usually oils, to Washington for preliminary review of subject matter and style, and Rowan rarely hesitated to make emphatic suggestions.

For commissions in two towns in Alabama, Tuskegee and Atmore, Rowan fortuitously assigned Goldthwaite, a native of the state who returned home to Montgomery every summer from her residence in New York. Her mural *The Road to Tuskegee* portrays both the old and the new South with overt references to the postal system. The overall setting is agrarian: a white-columned plantation house sits on a distant hill, and an African American woman drives a pair of cows in the left foreground. However, a train bifurcates the scene, an airplane flies overhead, and an automobile stops in the right foreground as a man in a uniform delivers mail. The mural in Atmore, *The Letter Box*, also addresses postal history in a positive way. Once again the scene is agricultural, although telegraph poles in the distance punctuate the landscape. Well-dressed girls gather around a mailbox, while a barefoot boy accompanied by two dogs eagerly watches them.

Laura Glenn Douglas was another post office muralist whose career was centered outside the South. A native of Winnsboro, South Carolina, Douglas pursued her art education in New York and Paris, spent the Depression in her home state, and then taught painting at the Phillips Collection in Washington, DC, for twenty years. Her 1942 mural for the post office in Camilla, Georgia, displays a colorful, Cubist style and is aptly called *Theme of the South*. It depicts an integrated scene of agricultural workers using familiar stereo-

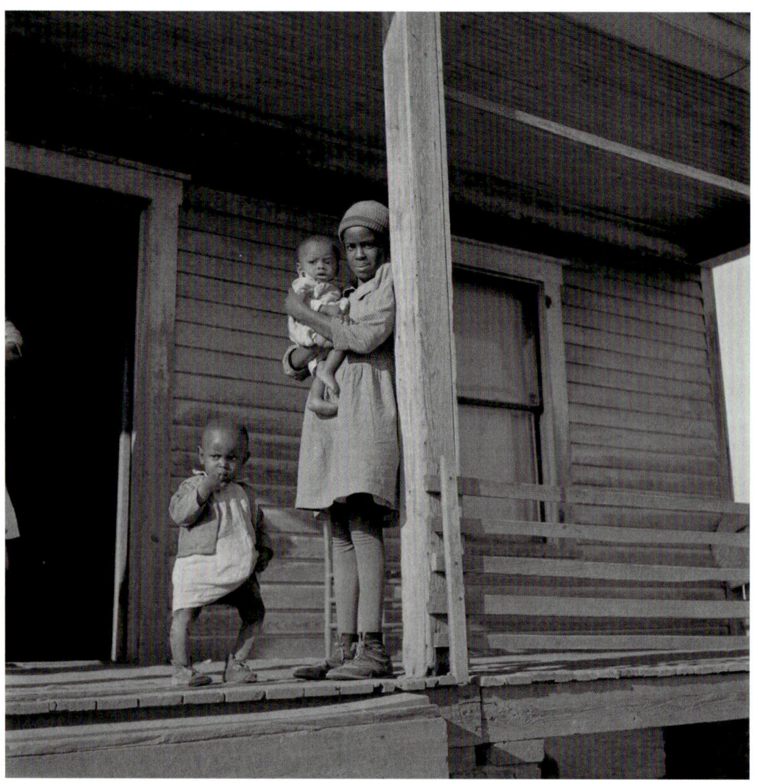

Marion Post Wolcott (1910–1990), *Negro children near Wadesboro, North Carolina*, 1938, digital file from original nitrate negative; Library of Congress, Washington, DC, Prints & Photographs Division, FSA/OWI Collection, LC-DIG-fsa-8c29971

types; dark-skinned women pick cotton and tend chickens, while white figures supervise or inspect products. In a lecture at the Phillips, Douglas declared: "I seek to put the poetry and history of the South in paint, but with vigor, creativeness and not sentimentalism."[24]

Blanche Lazzell's mural for the Morgantown, West Virginia, courthouse is exceptional for its lack of figures and for the stylized nature of its buildings and smoke stacks. In contrast, Sarah Blakeslee's down-to-earth *Apple Orchard*, at the post office in Strasburg, Virginia, shows lush rolling hills probably inspired by her life in Bucks County, Pennsylvania, a topography that resonated well with the residents of the small town nestled in the Shenandoah Valley. Landscape dominates the composition, which is carefully structured with figures at work in the foreground, a horse-drawn wagon in the middle ground, and a vista toward mountains in the distance.

Between 1935 and 1944, the federal government, under the auspices of the Farm Security Administration (FSA), dispersed photographers across the country to document living

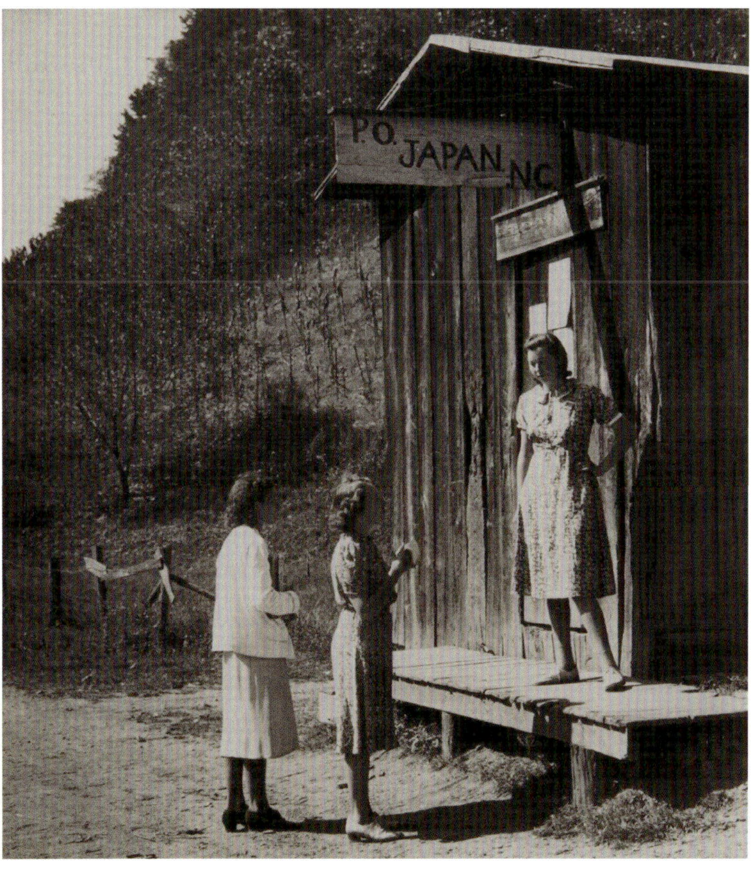

Mary Bayard Morgan Wootten (1876–1959), *Post Office, Japan, NC*, silver gelatin print, 10 × 8 inches

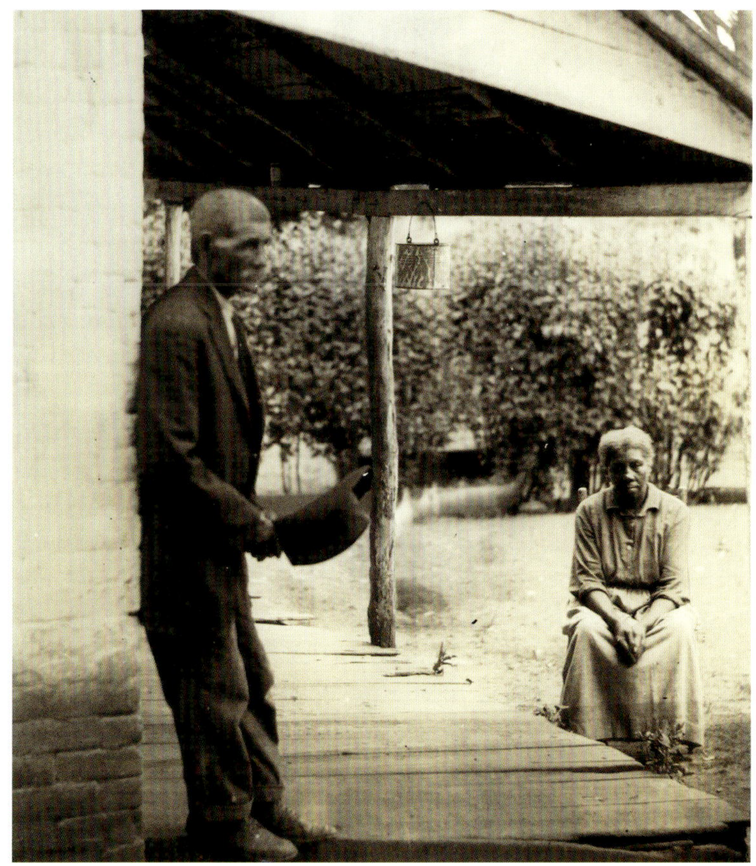

Doris May Ulmann (1882–1934), *African-American woman and man on porch*, 1920/1934, photographic print. Doris Ulmann Album No. 14, PH038–14–1641, Special Collections & University Archives, University of Oregon Libraries, Eugene, Oregon

and working conditions. Photography had been invented in the mid-nineteenth century and was used initially to record people's faces, and occasionally places. The Civil War was the first military engagement to be broadly captured by a camera for posterity, but it was not until the late years of the century that an effort was made to promote photography as an art form. Edward Steichen, Clarence White, and Alfred Stieglitz labored to give precedence to the aesthetic merits of the process. The purpose of the government's Depression-era project was true to photography's roots and ultimately produced 250,000 black and white prints, which humanized the Great Depression while cataloguing the extent of rural poverty, particularly in the South. Today these images are valued for their aesthetic qualities as well as for the contribution they made toward ameliorating the effects of economic privation.

One of a small coterie of female photographers, Marion Post Wolcott traveled throughout the region in search of imagery. No stranger to hardship or discrimination, Wolcott often went on dates to ensure that she got one meal a day. When she was hired by the *Philadelphia Evening Bulletin*, male staff members objected; they frequently urinated in her chemicals and extinguished cigarettes in her developing trays. Although some bias continued during her employment by the FSA, Wolcott managed to create photographs that revealed in stark detail the suffering of poor African American sharecroppers. Photographs by Margaret Bourke-White were also compelling visual records of life in the South during the Depression. A selection of these images appeared in the book *You Have Seen Their Faces* in 1937, accompanied by Erskine Caldwell's potent text, which begins with the following: "The South has always been shoved around like a country cousin. It buys mill-ends, and it wears hand-me-downs. It sits at second-table and is fed short rations. It is the place where the ordinary will do, where the makeshift is good enough."[25]

The photographs of Bayard Morgan Wootten are less severe and are populated by white figures. A native of New Bern, North Carolina, Wootten took up portrait photography after her husband abandoned her and their two children, working first in New Bern and then in Chapel Hill. She also did commission work as illustrations for books about the South, but her biggest claim to fame was that she was probably the first woman to take an aerial photograph. In contrast to the sharply focused work of Wolcott and Wootten, Doris Ulmann's images are far more pictorialist, with subjects typically bathed in sepia-toned light. While visiting Lang Syne Plantation in South Carolina around 1930, Ulmann found the local population challenging. In a letter to a friend, she recounted: "It is difficult to get the studies I am interested in here. The place is rich in material, but these Negroes are so strange it is almost impossible to photograph them. So this is a rather strenuous affair and I do not feel satisfied."[26] Nevertheless, ninety of her poetic photographs were published in the book *Roll, Jordan, Roll*, a collaboration she undertook with the 1928 Pulitzer Prize winner Julia Mood Peterkin, her hostess at Lang Syne.

Simultaneous with the New Deal programs, greater opportunities emerged in the 1930s and 1940s for art education in the Southern states. At the University of Georgia in Athens, the art program was initially assigned to the College of Agriculture, but it was eventually transferred to the university proper in 1932. Three years later bachelor of fine arts degrees were being offered. At the University of South Carolina, Katherine Bayard Heyward led the art department, which was inaugurated in 1925 to appeal to prospective women students. At the time Heyward was one of two female faculty members at the university; during her first year, she taught sixty students in nine separate courses. She modeled the art department on those at Vassar, Wellesley, and Randolph-Macon—all distinguished colleges for women. "Art," she said, "is not a question of painting pictures only, or of making statues, but it touches almost every phase of life."[27] Elizabeth White, an artist from Sumter, South Carolina, who had studied at the Pennsylvania Academy of the Fine Arts, and Catharine Phillips Rembert, a 1927 graduate of the University of South Carolina's art department and a student of Hans Hofmann, were the first to join Heyward on the art faculty. Rembert taught until 1964 and is perhaps remembered best as Jasper Johns's enlightened mentor, responsible for encouraging him to leave South Carolina and pursue his passion for art in New York.

Having studied with these women at the University of South Carolina between 1932 and 1936, Corrie McCallum spoke glowingly of Heyward: "As a teacher, she was fair, clear, tireless and inspired confidence," qualities McCallum emulated in her own teaching.[28] Following her graduation, McCallum oversaw a community gallery space in Columbia's City Council chamber under the auspices of the Works

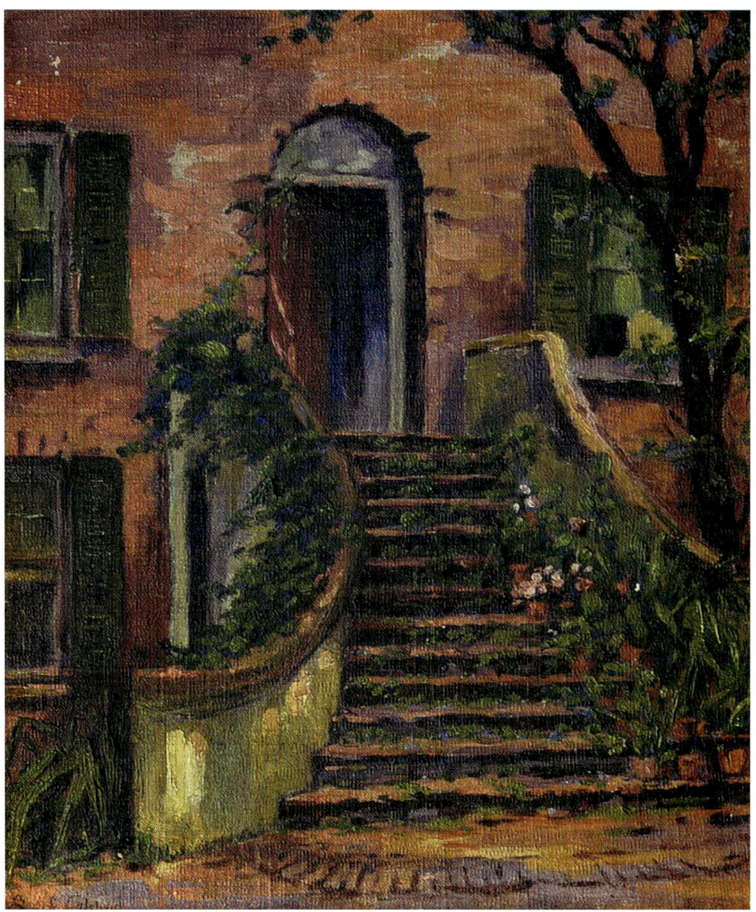

Emma Susan Gilchrist (1862–1929), *The Glebe Mansion, 1770*, 1925, oil on canvas board, 13⅛ x 11 inches

Progress Administration's federal art program. The National Exhibition Service provided traveling exhibitions, and McCallum, recognizing that administrators in Washington liked quantity, cleverly enhanced her attendance records by bringing large numbers of high school students through the gallery. The experience prepared her well for her post as curator of education at the Gibbes Art Gallery in Charleston.

The genesis of many Southern art clubs and prestigious museums can be credited to the advocacy and generosity of female artists and art patrons. For the first six decades of its existence (1858 to circa 1920), the Carolina Art Association, housed at the Gibbes Art Gallery, excluded women from its governing body, over the objections of several outspoken artists led by Emma Gilchrist. In 1912 Gilchrist founded the Sketch Club, whose mission was to encourage professional and amateur artists to interact. The club's largely female membership met during the daytime and only reluctantly sold their work. The Carolina Art Association provided funds for workshops and hired male directors from away for its school until females lobbied for local women to administer it.

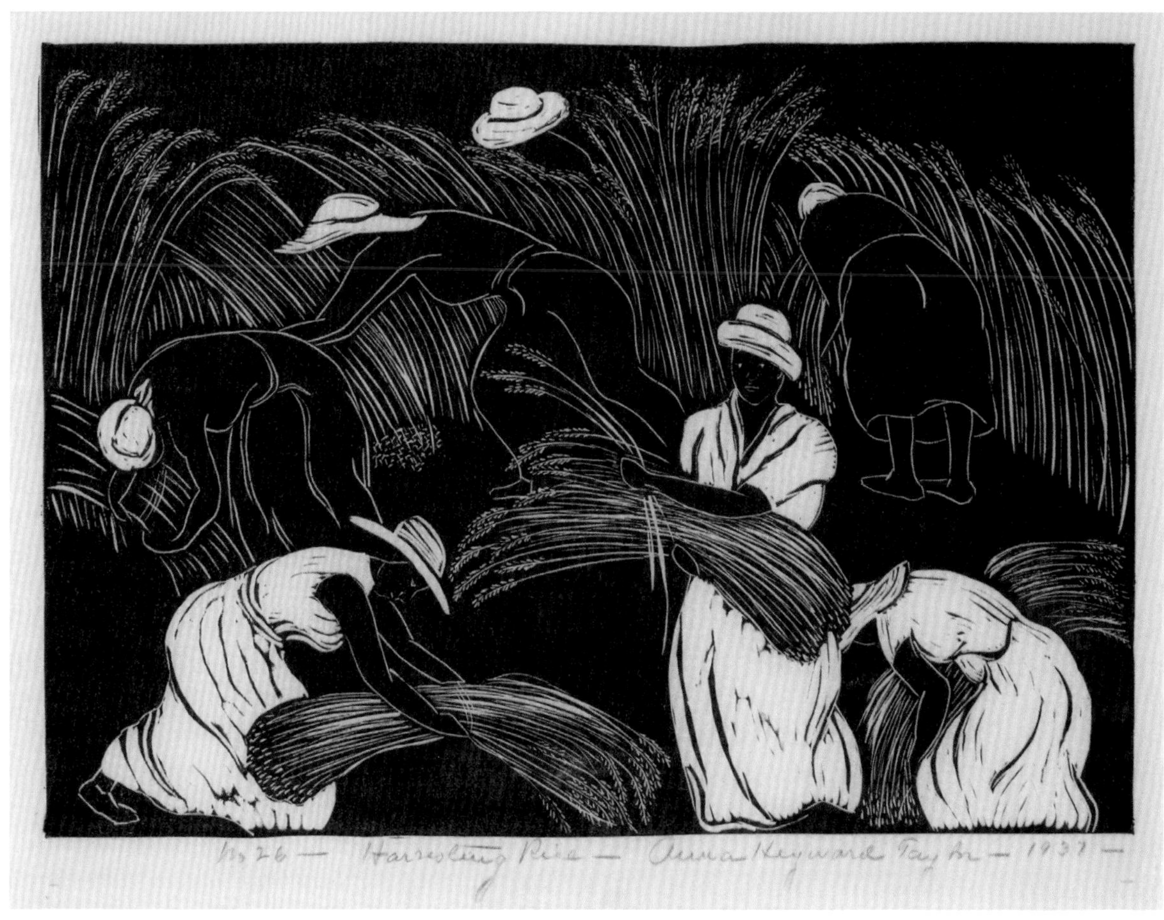

Anna Heyward Taylor (1879–1956), *Harvesting Rice*, 1937, linoleum print on paper, 11⅛ x 13⅛ inches

In Jackson, Mississippi, Marie Hull was a charter member and president of the Mississippi Art Association, which not only organized exhibitions for local artists, but also lobbied the state legislature to incorporate art into schools. In 1912 Hull suggested that the association start collecting—a commitment that led eventually to the founding of the Mississippi Museum of Art.

Savannah can boast the first public art museum building in the South, the result of Mary Telfair's bequest of her Regency-style home to the Georgia Historical Society for an academy of arts and sciences. In Birmingham women took an active role in the Art Club, established in 1908, and purchased paintings and sculptures for a future museum three decades before it opened in 1951. The Atlanta Art Association, founded in 1905, acquired a permanent home in 1926 when Harriet Harwell Wilson High donated her mansion on Peachtree Street to be used as a museum, which is still known as the High Museum of Art.

In Charlotte, North Carolina, women under the leadership of Mary Myers Dwelle were largely responsible for establishing the Mint Museum in 1936, the first art museum in the state. In the years prior, the city had enjoyed exhibitions mounted in the studio of Eugene Thomason, a New York–trained artist, and the response was so enthusiastic that when the old United States Mint building was about to be demolished, a grassroots effort led to the acquisition of the structure and its reconstruction in an upscale neighborhood. That same year Richmond gained its own museum with the opening of the Virginia Museum of Fine Arts. One of its earliest benefactors was Lillian Thomas Pratt, who gave the museum her magnificent collection of objects fabricated by Peter Carl Fabergé.

In addition to championing museums, women also promoted historic preservation through such entities as the Mount Vernon Ladies' Association, the Ladies' Hermitage Association, the Colonial Dames of America, and the Daughters of the American Revolution. In Charleston women artists spearheaded and fueled the preservation movement. Working in collaboration with her historian father, Alice Smith wrote and illustrated the first study of the city's residential architecture, *The Dwelling Houses of Charleston, South Carolina*, in 1917. This landmark study was complemented by Elizabeth Verner's later volumes *Prints and Impressions* (1939) and *Mellowed by Time* (1941), as well as Anna Taylor's evocative block prints for *This Our Land* (1949). These books, which inspired Charlestonians to take pride in the city's architectural heritage, were also read by outsiders who came to enjoy the area's scenic treasures. Illuminated by sensitive illustrations, these publications also furthered the artists' respective careers. The synergetic endeavors of artists, writers, and civic leaders in Charleston—a movement known as the Charleston Renaissance—led to the 1931 passage of the nation's first historic district preservation ordinance.

During the pervasive scarcity of the Depression era, American women from all walks of life and in every profession were often overlooked in deference to men, who, as family breadwinners, were accorded top priority for jobs. A decade later women across the country willingly stepped up to fill unfamiliar roles left vacant by their male counterparts who had been called to military service, a trend immortalized by Norman Rockwell's depiction of Rosie the Riveter. With the emergence of Abstract Expressionism in the late 1940s, men reasserted themselves as the dominant force in the sphere of art.[29] Having gained a more secure foothold in the country's larger socioeconomic and cultural arenas, however, women artists forged ahead. In the 1950s, art education expanded at all levels, requiring more instructors, both male and female. The increased number of museums led to extended offerings by small and large institutions, where women were employed as educators, exhibition preparators, and occasionally curators. Commercial galleries proliferated, especially in larger metropolitan areas, and magazines devoted to art and artists became plentiful. But there was still room for improvement.

With the rise of the feminist movement of the 1960s, women artists advocated for more visibility, participation in exhibitions, lucrative commissions, and expanded opportunities. Perhaps the most strident and outspoken feminist statement came in 1974 when Lynda Benglis—a native of Louisiana and a student of Ida Rittenberg Kohlmeyer—posed nude for a provocative photo in *Artforum*, calling attention to the male-dominated art world. "I saw it as a macho game, a big heroic, Abstract Expressionist macho sexist game. It's about territory."[30] By the time of the new millennium, Benglis's efforts and those of others had led to a more enlightened and equitable climate for skilled women artists in the South and elsewhere. Their advances fulfill—at least in part—portraitist Cecilia Beaux's century-old forecast: "I predict an hour when 'Women in Art' will be as strange sounding a topic as the title 'Men in Art.'"[31]

SISTERHOODS OF SPIRIT

SOUTHERN WOMEN'S CLUBS AND EXPOSITIONS

DEBORAH C. POLLACK

From the late nineteenth through mid-twentieth centuries, entrepreneurial female artists in the South relied on local women's clubs and regional expositions to earn income and advance their professional reputations. In turn, exposition organizers and energetic clubwomen of the era counted on female artists to help their respective events and corporate ambitions flourish. This symbiotic dynamic—grounded in economic realities, aesthetic aspirations, personal connections, and feminist values—created a sisterhood of shared purpose that enhanced the landscape of Southern art then and continues to do so today.

Inspired by national precedents, women in many Southern communities, both large and small, formed clubs to engage female citizens in meaningful activities. The origins and goals of these affiliations varied widely in terms of their service orientation, political agenda, social component, and exclusivity. Some organizations were branches of sizeable American federations, while others were strictly parochial. For many the visual arts were a core focus, while other clubs approached the subject more casually. No matter their makeup or mission, these clubs—and their support of art and artists—were culturally consequential, as noted by one state chairperson in 1926: "Unthinking people sometimes rate art a luxury, a concern of the few, a matter merely of 'old masters and museums.' The work of the women's clubs for art is to aid in the creation of a truer public opinion, a saner valuation of art—by every possible means, to make more people realize that art is an essential to happy and successful living for everyone, holding besides an important place in the business and social fabric of the nation."[1]

Turn-of-the-century women's clubs' efforts to promote arts awareness and appreciation can be traced in part to the wave of Aestheticism that swept through America in the wake of Irish writer Oscar Wilde's 1882 nationwide lecture tour.[2] As a proponent of Aestheticism and the Arts and Crafts movement, Wilde believed that art's value resided solely in its beauty, rather than in its capacity to instruct or persuade. This credo—that utility should be imbued with art and decoration in all aspects of life—became a popular and enduring philosophy, especially among women. Accordingly, many women's clubs were motivated to inculcate a democratic, aesthetic enlightenment in hopes of improving members' communities and the lives of their families, while simultaneously providing revenue for enterprising creative women. Southern organizations devoted to Aestheticism and the fine arts were founded as early as 1883 in Little Rock, Arkansas, and burgeoned in the following decade in Louisville, Kentucky; Atlanta, Georgia; and Wilmington, North Carolina.[3]

The inclusion of women's departments at Southern expositions followed the example set by the Women's Pavilion at the 1876 Centennial Exhibition in Philadelphia. Organized by an all-female committee, the pavilion's exhibitions showcased women's traditional fine and decorative arts, as well as remarkable scientific, industrial, literary, practical, and other creative achievements and inventions. Like their national and international counterparts, Southern expositions of the era attracted global audiences, and their designated buildings featured fine art submissions from both sexes. The fairs thus afforded women artists the chance to display their works alongside those of some of the most acclaimed painters and sculptors of the period. Many women maximized the income potential of these exhibitions and other exposition-related activities. For instance, the Southern Exposition, held for five consecutive years between 1883 and 1887 in Louisville, Kentucky, offered painter Patty Thum—a member of the Woman's Club of Louisville and the Louisville Art Association—an exhibition platform and the opportunity to write articles for major newspapers praising the fair, her hometown, and other exposition artists.[4]

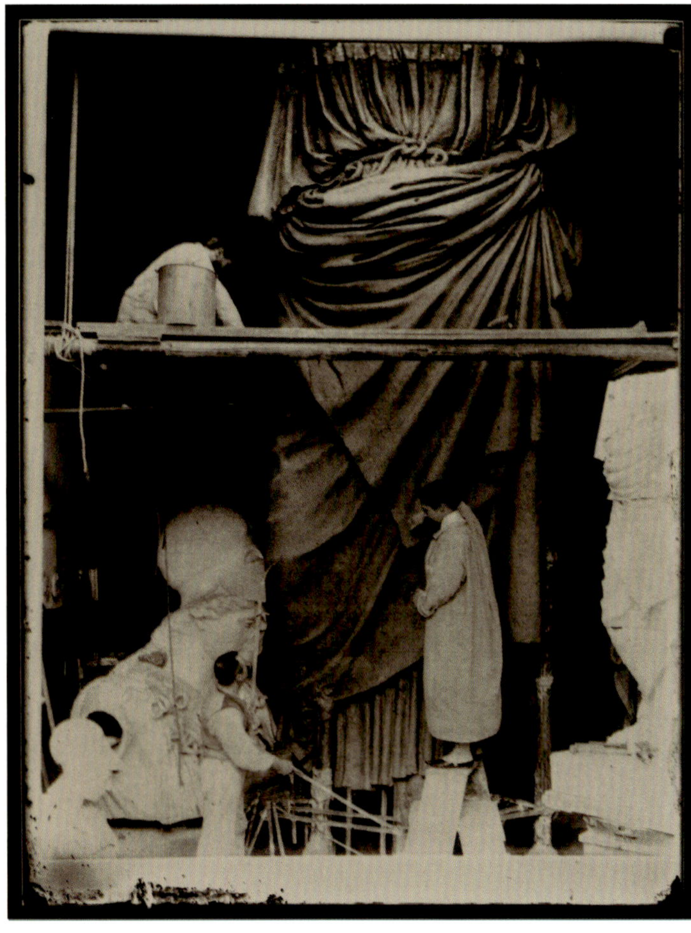

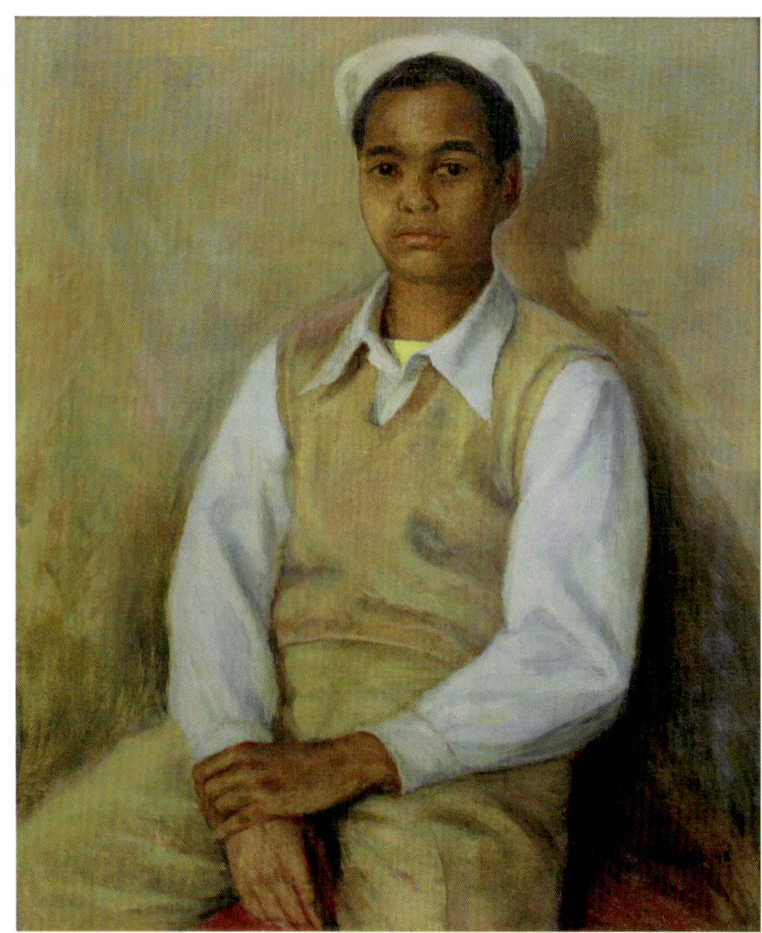

Enid Yandell at work on her sculpture of Pallas Athena, 1896, photographic print, 26 × 21 centimeters; Enid Yandell Papers, 1878–1982; Archives of American Art, Smithsonian Institution, Washington, DC; Digital ID: 8014

Emma Cheves Wilkins (1870–1956), *Young Sailor,* 1948, oil on canvas, 30 × 24¼ inches

Held in commemoration of the one hundredth anniversary of Tennessee's statehood, the 1897 Tennessee Centennial Exposition included a women's department that eventually led to the formation of Nashville's Centennial Club. The event was a major milestone in the career of Louisville, Kentucky, sculptor Enid Yandell. A copy of a Greco-Roman antiquity, Yandell's forty-foot-tall *Pallas Athena* was installed at the entrance to the Fine Arts Building, which had been modeled on the Parthenon. When exposition officials circulated a photo of the young artist at work on the piece, the story made international news. The image was used repeatedly in promotional materials, and an illustration of the completed sculpture appeared on souvenirs, posters, and other fair ephemera.[5] Another Yandell work at the Nashville fair, *Allah-Il-Allah,* earned a silver medal and was deemed a "serious and most excellent piece of work and were not the standards by which this exposition is being judged so high, it might be worth an even higher award."[6]

A few years later Yandell exhibited at the South Carolina Interstate and West Indian Exposition, held in Charleston from December 1901 through June 1902. Charleston resident, painter, and author Eola Willis showed monotypes and paintings there as well.[7] Willis knew how to thrive as a creative professional. The Dalton, Georgia, native had studied in Europe and at the Art Students League in New York with William Merritt Chase and Helen Smillie. Upon her return to the United States, she settled in Charleston and joined Southern art associations—often serving in leadership positions—and participated in Southern expositions. Diminutive in stature but stalwart in spirit, Willis aligned herself with a network of like-minded women to share her passion for art with the world. She was the chair of the South Carolina Interstate and West Indian Exposition Woman's Department fine arts committee, served on the women's administration board, and headed the decoration and arrangement committee of the Daughters of the American Revolution exhibition installed

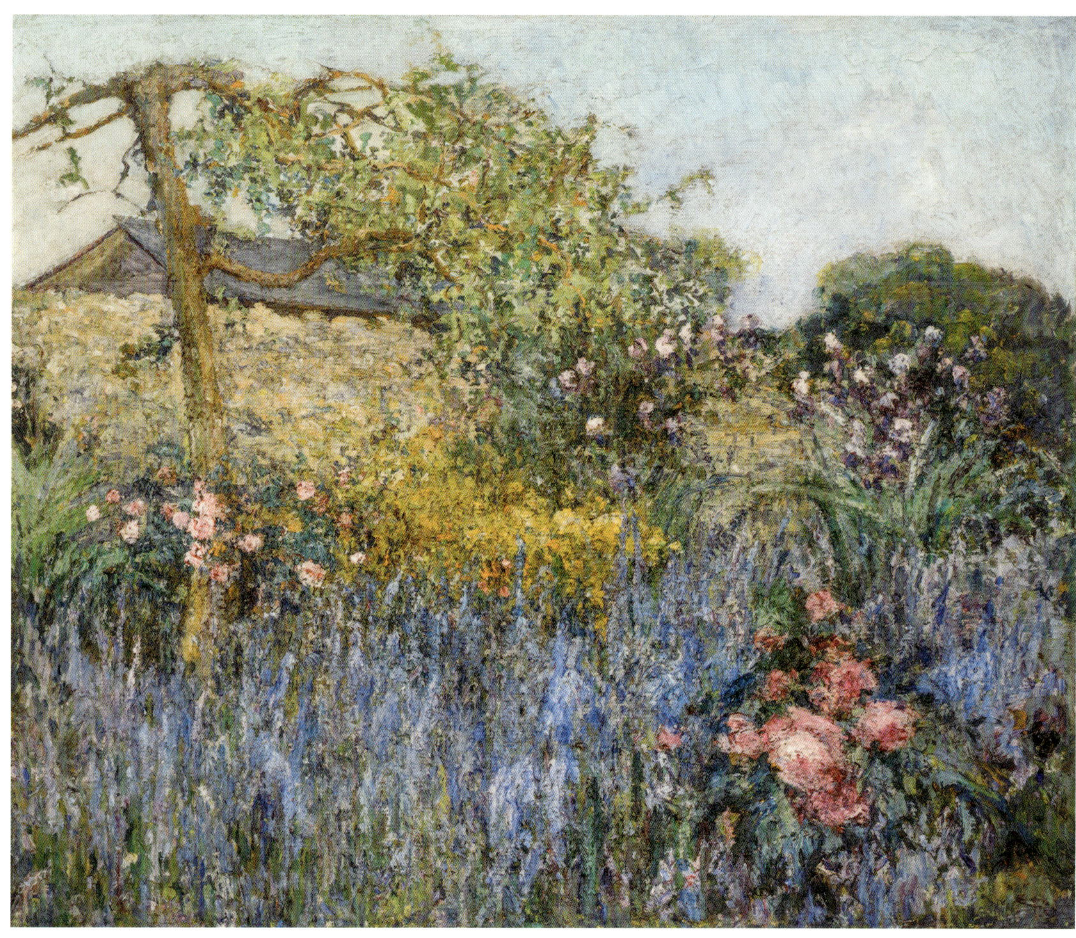

Blondelle Octavia Edwards Malone (1877–1951), *Garden Scene*, oil on canvas, 26⅛ x 30⅛ inches

within the Woman's Building. As a member of the exposition's press committee, she wrote articles publicizing the fair, just as Thum had in Louisville. Willis asserted in the *New York Herald* that the exposition would mark a defining moment in Charleston's reawakening to a "new order of things." She also touted the event's "Negro exhibit," proclaiming it to "be the most complete and satisfactory of any yet made." To raise funds for the fair, she instructed socialites in the art of bridge whist, a popular card game.[8]

Like countless other artistic women of fortitude, Willis was not afraid to express her opinion. In a letter to the exposition's director general, John H. Averill, Willis lobbied for the inclusion of women on the fine arts jury: "As the art spirit in Charleston had in latter years been almost entirely fostered by women, . . . it would seem only fair that they should be appointed to work upon the art committees with the men for the art collection proper."[9] Fortunately, New Yorker James B. Townsend, director of the fine arts department, and his

committee accepted several entries created by women in addition to works by Willis and Yandell. For example, Savannah, Georgia, artist Emma Cheves Wilkins, who relied on exhibitions and portrait commissions for her livelihood, showed a *Study from Life*. She had taken classes with Carl Brandt domestically, had attended the Académie Colarossi in Paris, and would teach art to several Savannah women artists, including Hattie Saussy.[10]

Throughout the South, ever-popular annual state fairs provided another opportunity for professional women artists to exhibit. By 1902 Columbia native Blondelle Malone had spent time studying with Harry Stuart Fonda in California, visited art galleries in San Francisco, and toured Chinatown there. She would soon embark on an extended trip to Japan. In October 1902 her handicraft designs for buttons, medals, and other items were exhibited at the South Carolina State Fair, which took place in her hometown. A local journalist complimented Malone's book covers,

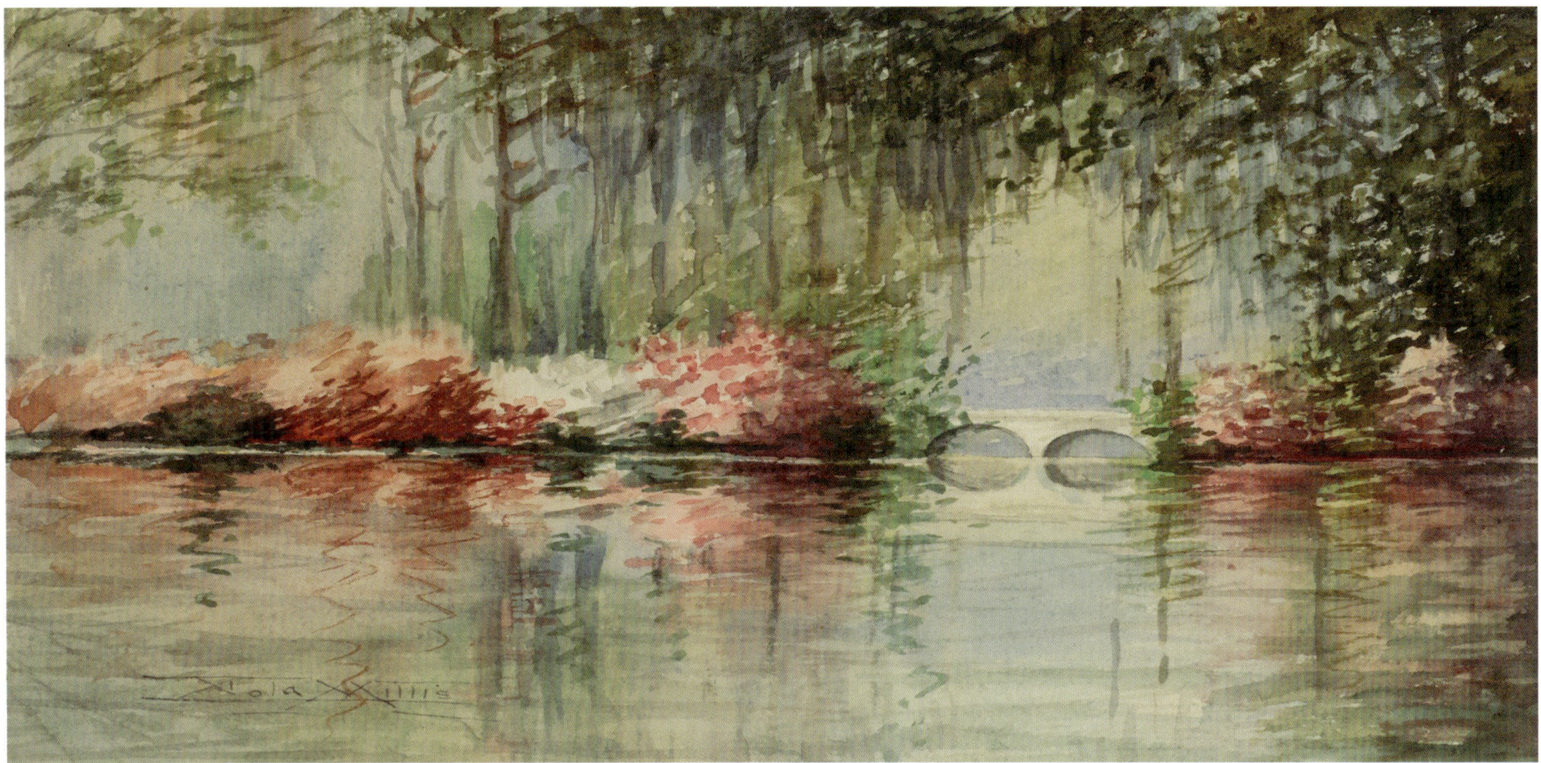

Eola Henley Willis (1856–1952), *Magnolia on the Ashley*, watercolor on paper, 6⅝ × 13¼ inches

writing that she possessed "rare talent in this direction not only on the designs themselves but on her combinations of colors."[11]

All the while, African American women's groups in the South, largely ostracized from national women's club affiliations, pursued parallel artistic goals. At a board of directors meeting held just prior to the 1900 biennial conclave of the General Federation of Women's Clubs in Milwaukee, Southern members vigorously protested the admission of integrated clubs, but were thwarted in their attempt to legislate that the word "white" be stipulated in the organization's bylaws.[12] Faced with this kind of racism, women of color formed their own societies. The National Association of Colored Women's Clubs, organized in 1896, elected the indefatigable Mary Church Terrell as its first president. Born in Memphis, Tennessee, the college-educated feminist and art lover wrote that her first trip to the Louvre in Paris "opened up an entirely new world" and that she had studied its masterpieces avidly.[13] Terrell collaborated with Margaret Murray Washington—principal of Tuskegee Normal and Industrial Institute, founder of the Tuskegee Woman's Club, and Booker T. Washington's wife—to compile objects, including fine art, for the woman's department within the South Carolina Interstate and West Indian Exposition's Negro Building.

Terrell explained the impetus behind the establishment of the National Association of Colored Women's Clubs: "Colored women have always had high aspirations for themselves.... They have often struggled single handed and alone against the most desperate and discouraging odds, in order to secure for themselves and their loved ones that culture of the head and heart for which they had hungered and thirsted so long in vain. But it dawned upon them…that individuals working alone…would…accomplish little compared with the…achievements of many individuals, all banded strongly together,…with heads and hearts fixed on the same high purpose, and hands joined in united strength." Under her leadership, the association quickly formed a department of art. At its first convention, representatives debated the subject of arts in education, and they regularly discussed arts and crafts at subsequent meetings. New chapters planted in Alabama, Florida, Georgia, Kentucky, Mississippi, South Carolina, and Virginia studied art at their gatherings and submitted members' work to state fairs.[14]

At the dawn of the new millennium, women's clubs throughout the South continued to cultivate an appreciation of arts and crafts, and provide exhibition opportunities for both. In Nashville clubwoman Elizabeth "Lizzie" Lee Bloomstein promoted art and artists in her many lectures; at the 1897 Tennessee Centennial Exposition, she delivered a well-received keynote address titled "The Decorations of the Parthenon." Having worked as a college professor and university librarian, Bloomstein was an ardent suffragist, and her membership in a number of local clubs reflected her belief "that the women's-club movement is the consciousness of a desire for larger relations of life. The home with the broadest culture is that which articulates most largely with the world. Culture humanizes, develops, and broadens sympathy, and thus stimulates and enables one to be helpful to others."[15]

Northern art journalists were beginning to recognize Southern women's organizations as influential cultural forces. At the 1910 American Federation of Arts convention held in Washington, DC, the editor of *Century Magazine* encouraged the federation to rely on Southern women to establish art museums in their communities: "If one or two cities of a state like Alabama or Tennessee, which we will take for granted have no art museums, would take the initiative, the pride of the citizens would secure the exhibits and provide that they should be of a high standard. I believe that the Federation could set on foot a movement by which, let us say, the city of Mobile could be induced to establish an art museum. I should go at it by first enlisting the interest of the prominent ladies of that city, and I should have them put under tribute all the rich men of Alabama for this purpose."[16] As if following this suggestion, the Woman's Club of Richmond, Virginia, eventually helped establish the Virginia Museum of Fine Arts, and the Atlanta Woman's Club assisted the Atlanta Art Association in reaching its museum goals.[17]

Also in 1910, six Mississippi women's clubs held art shows, and several North Carolina women's clubs "gave exhibitions of original water-colors by well-known artists…and pictures painted by North Carolina artists." The chair of North Carolina's Federation of Women's Clubs art department noted that "this effective work for art should prove inspiring, and give a hint to the clubs that have done nothing along those lines."[18] In her capacity as president of the South Carolina Federation of Women's Clubs, Sarah Bentschner Visanska encouraged women to "cultivate crafts peculiar to their section, and… [employ] native material" in hopes that the organization's efforts would bring the state's "residents of rural districts a knowledge of the world's artistic masterpieces through the medium of a traveling stereopticon."[19] By 1917 branches of the State Federation of Women's Clubs located in Alabama, Arkansas, Florida, Georgia, Kentucky, Louisiana, Mississippi,

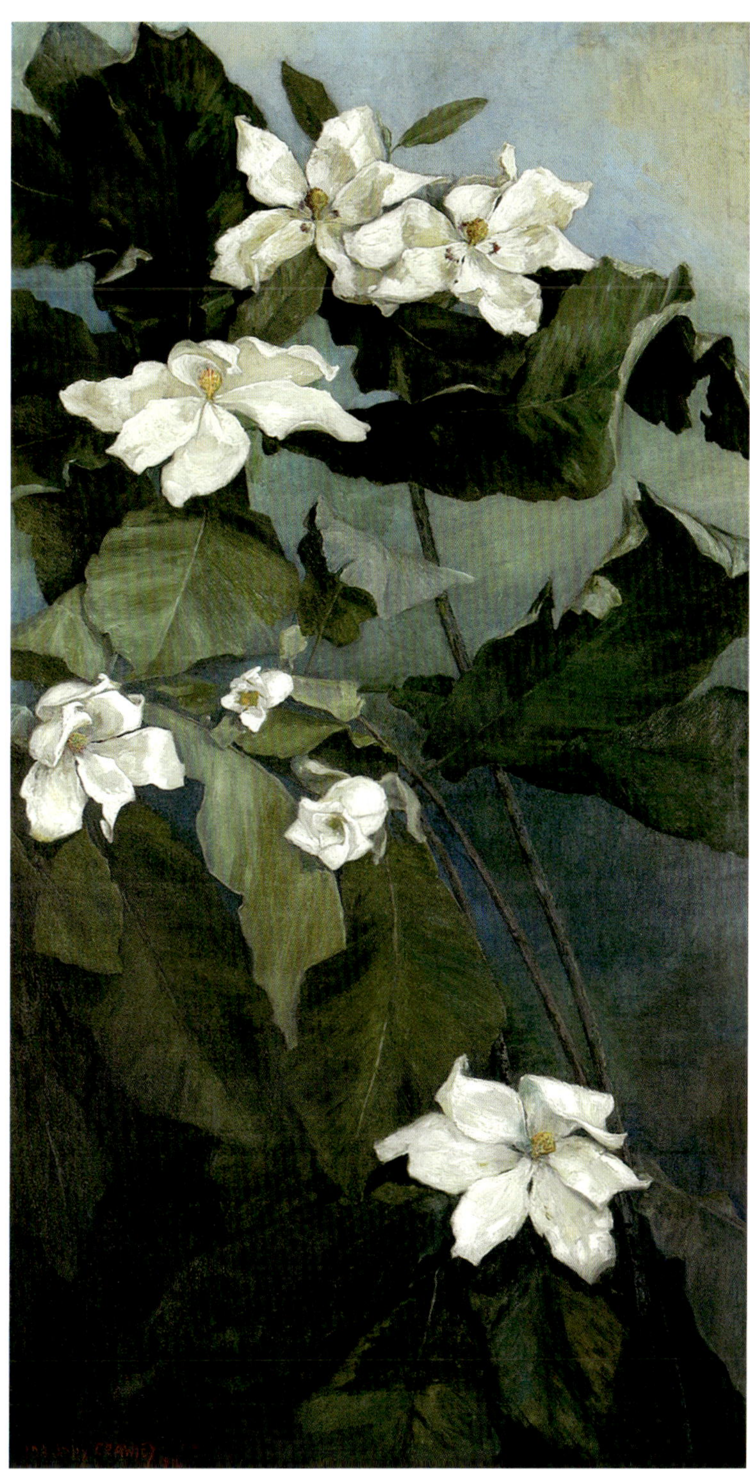

Ida Jolly Crawley (1867–1946), *Magnolia Macrophylla*, 1916, oil on canvas, 94 × 42 inches

North Carolina, South Carolina, Tennessee, Virginia, and West Virginia contained art committees.[20]

Regional and state-sponsored expositions continued to thrive well past the turn of the twentieth century, affording women artists even more venues to display their work. Malone exhibited in the fine arts department at the 1910 Appalachian Exposition (forerunner of the National Conservation Exposition), held in Knoxville, Tennessee, as did Alice Smith of Charleston, South Carolina, with a painting titled *Meeting Street.* Willis showed a Catskill Mountain landscape and *The Lake and Azalea Beds,* which relates to several Charleston garden scenes she painted, including *Magnolia on the Ashley.* Clara Weaver Parrish also submitted work to the Appalachian Exposition, winning a silver medal for her genre painting *The Green Lamp.* Ida Crawley displayed several of her works, as did her fellow Tennessean Catherine Wiley, who won a gold medal for "the most meritorious group in Appalachian territory."[21]

Bolstered by hometown support, Wiley received other honors at the 1910 event: the art committee illustrated one of her figural works, *The New Story,* in the exposition catalog, and the arts and crafts department of the Woman's Building awarded her the Hope Medal. At the 1911 Appalachian Exposition, Nashville artist Ella Sophonisba Hergesheimer received a gold medal for "the best group by a Southern artist." Both Hergesheimer and Wiley served on the art jury of the 1913 National Conservation Exposition, and Wiley was named the fine art department's chair. After listing male and female Northern and Southern artists who participated in the fairs from 1910 to 1913, Wiley concluded that "the display of work such as this cannot help but be of inestimable benefit to the public." Hergesheimer went on to win prizes at the 1924, 1926, and 1933 Tennessee State Expositions, and Willie Betty Newman displayed her paintings at the 1920 Tennessee State Fair.[22]

Partnerships between artists, art clubs, and women's clubs seemed to multiply in the South in the early 1920s. At the decade's outset, the Alabama Federation of Women's Clubs recommended the study of art in public schools and instituted an annual Celebration of Art Week to be observed by women's clubs throughout the state. Furthermore, they vowed to work in cooperation with the Alabama Art League so "individual clubs of the State may secure exquisite little exhibitions together with reference material for study…and large exhibitions may be sent to Districts and Counties."[23] In another instance, the Lexington, Kentucky, Woman's Club organized exhibitions of works by artists of both genders, earning

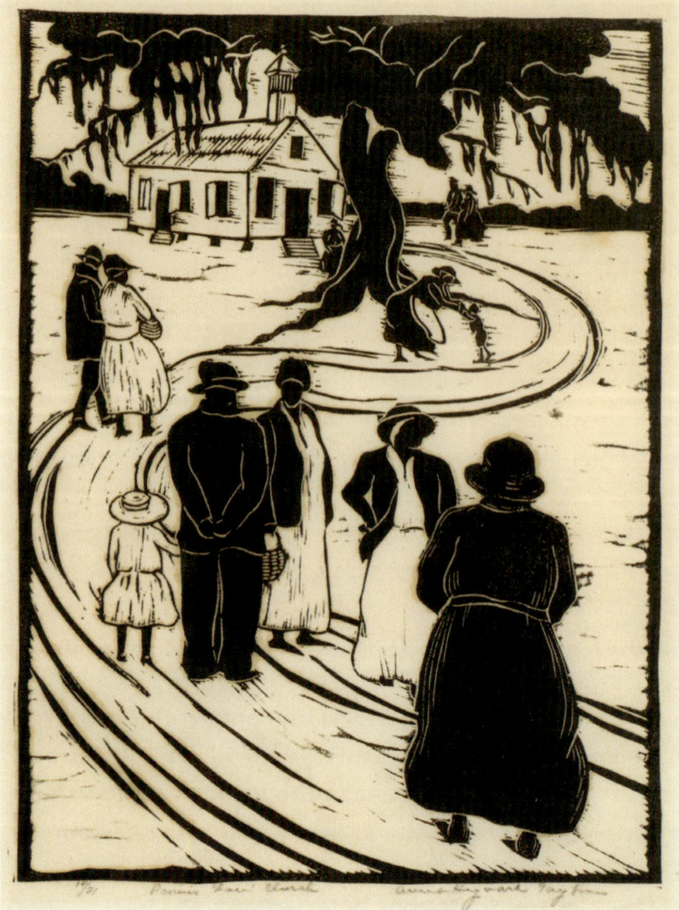

Anna Heyward Taylor (1879–1956), *Promis Lan' Church,* **1930, linoleum print on paper, 11⅜ × 8¼ inches**

praise from the director of the University of Kentucky's art department in 1921: "the tireless efforts of these ladies in the interest of art have not only been of inestimable value to the art department, but to the entire community as well."[24]

Most Southern women's clubs maintained memberships in the Southern States Art League. A 1925 exhibition sponsored by the Woman's Club of Charlotte, North Carolina, showcased works for sale by male and female members of the League. South Carolina painters Margaret Law, Alice Smith, and Elizabeth O'Neill Verner participated in the November event, as did Hergesheimer and Emma Gilchrist.[25]

During that same decade, artist Elisabeth Chant lectured on art before the Wilmington, North Carolina, chapter of Sorosis.[26] At the 1929 Biloxi, Mississippi, Woman's Club exhibition, Marie Atkinson Hull of Jackson was awarded third prize for her entry titled *California Hills.* Three years earlier the same group had enlisted the renowned New Orleans artist and teacher William Woodward to help them establish an art colony—an effort that led to the founding of the Mississippi

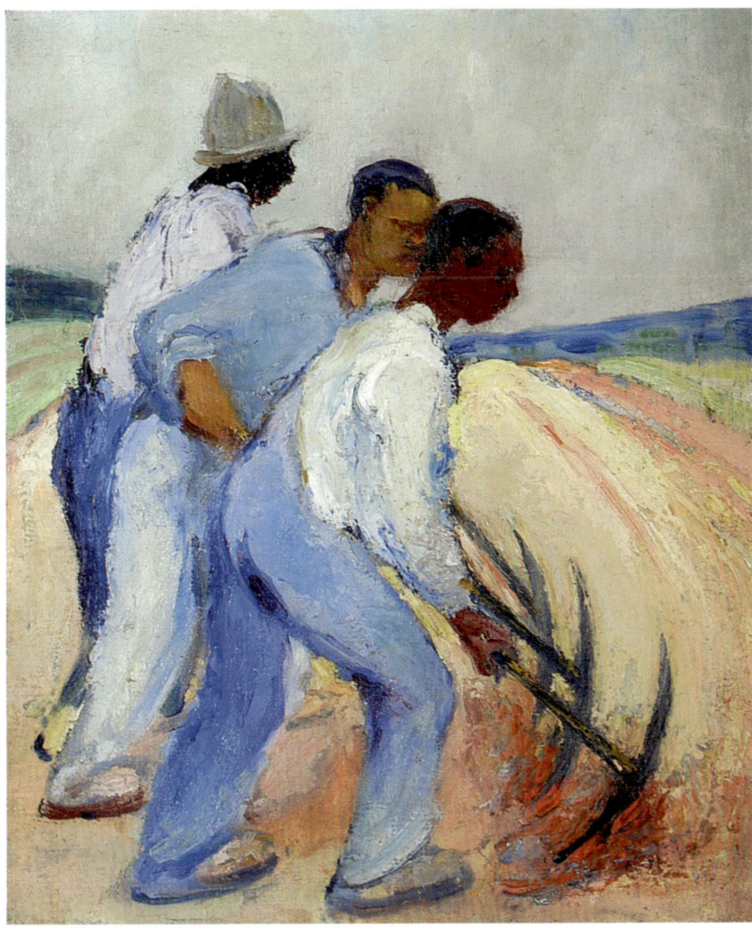

Margaret Moffett Law (1871–1956), *Laborers,* **oil on canvas, 21⅝ × 17¾ inches**

Gulf Coast Association in November 1929.[27] Further north in the state, the Cleveland Woman's Club hosted a 1927 showing of South Carolina artists' work, including woodblock prints by Anna Heyward Taylor. Following study with William Merritt Chase and travel throughout Europe and in Asia, Taylor had spent time at the art colony in Provincetown, Massachusetts, mastering printmaking. For the rest of her career, she employed it with great success to portray African American culture in the South, as seen in *Promis Lan' Church.*[28] These club-sponsored exhibitions led many organizations to establish permanent art collections. State pride spurred members of the Paducah, Kentucky, Woman's Club to purchase a painting by Helen Turner. Born in Kentucky, Turner was only the fourth woman elected to full membership in the prestigious National Academy of Design.[29]

By the 1930s recently established fine arts museums and federal and city art centers had begun to fill the need for exhibition space across the South. Founded in 1924, the New Orleans cultural club Le Petit Salon, elected Angela Gregory a "courtesy," or honorary, member representing art in 1930. The club's first president, author Grace King, had championed the young sculptor, praising her architectural relief for a New Orleans criminal courthouse as a "great historical work." King described Gregory's bronze plaque of Sophie Newcomb College president Brandt Van Blarcom Dixon as "strong and truthful," saying that it "goes straight to the mark."[30]

In North Carolina members of the Charlotte Woman's Club thought so much of Margaret Law that in 1931 they hosted her one-woman show, accompanied by music and tea. Their exhibition garnered attention from the press, which described Law as a nationally known "southern artist who has furnished such typical and distinctive interpretations of color and character to American art." The Willis article also noted that Law's depictions of African Americans were "full of sympathy and appreciation."[31]

That same year, Law's friend and relative by marriage Josephine Sibley Couper was on the planning committee for an exhibition held at the South Carolina Federation of Women's Clubs' state convention in Charleston. Law and Couper had established the Spartanburg, South Carolina, Arts and Crafts Club in 1907, which paved the way for the eventual founding of the city's art museum.[32] It was precisely that sort of local advocacy that their colleague Willis extolled in her role as art chair of the South Carolina Federation of Women's Clubs. In a letter made public at the 1931 state convention, Willis proposed:

> to found an Art Society in every South Carolina community which has a federated club. The collections…will be the exhibits for the first year. They can start in a very small way in somebody's parlor; …the main thing is to enlist the sympathy and cooperation of an enlightened public opinion and the appreciation of beauty in all things. With an Art exhibit held once a year, bringing together the townspeople with a more ambitious outlook for the future when a loan collection may be engaged is a high privilege for each of us to contemplate. This…will help remove the reproach that southern women are indifferent to the collection and preservation of source material.

She asked every convention attendee to join her, "heart and soul," in this endeavor. Furthermore, she requested that individual clubs throughout the state read her proposal aloud and take an "art survey" to secure resources for exhibitions.[33]

The North Carolina branch of the Federation of Women's Clubs partnered with the Southern States Art League to sponsor an exhibition at their 1931 state convention. Mabel Pugh's charming painting *Little Carolina Bluebonnet* was

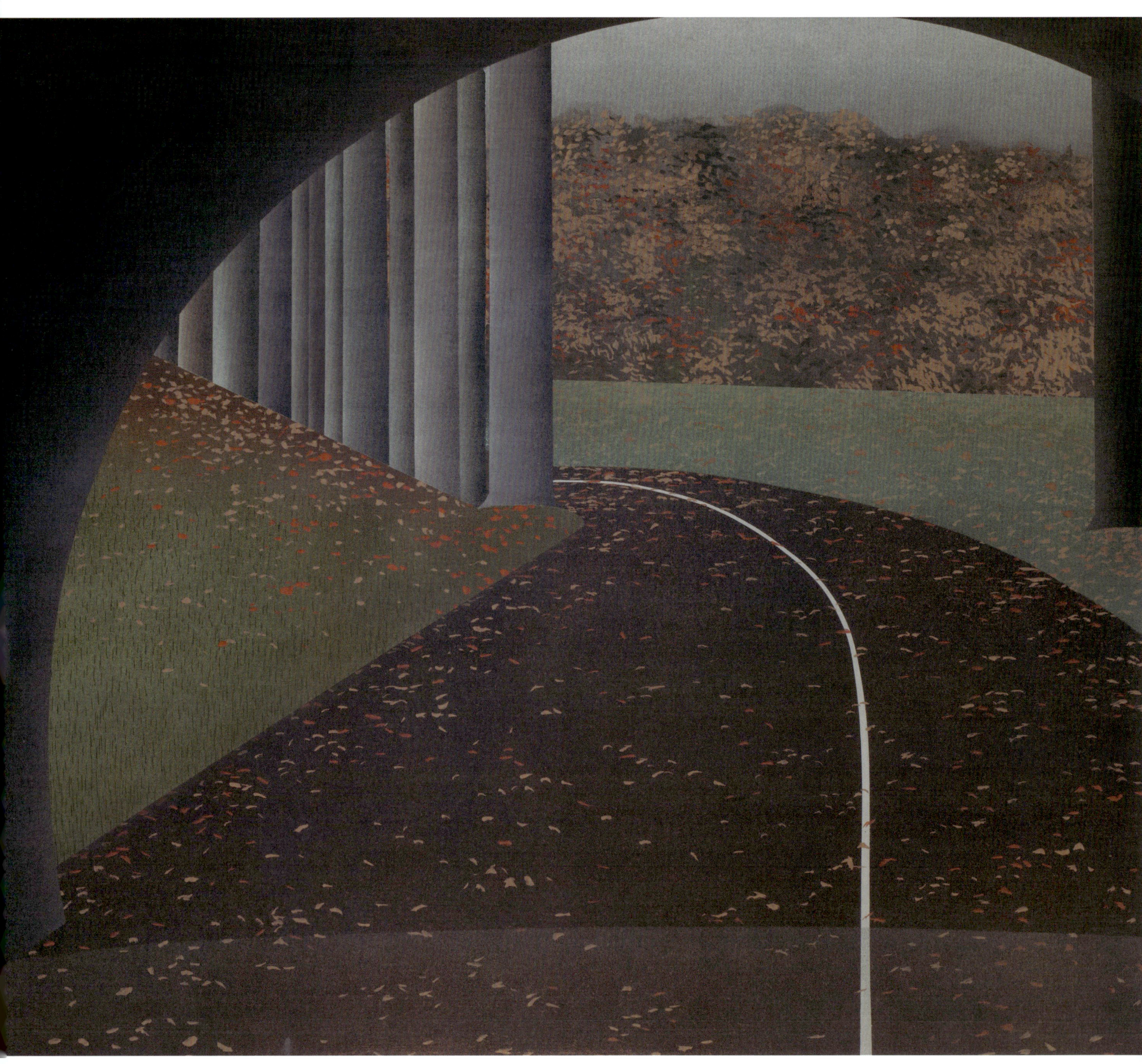

Maud Florance Gatewood (1934–2004), *Autumn Tunnel*, 1975, acrylic on canvas, 50 × 56 inches

commended as a highlight of the show. Two years later, that image—featuring a child sitting outside wearing a lavender smock and blue sunbonnet—graced Pugh's book of the same title. Pugh depended on illustration and writing for the bulk of her income; as she noted, "artists must live." The Greensboro, North Carolina, Woman's Club helped supplement Pugh's revenue by exhibiting her block prints in 1932, as did the North Carolina General Federation of Women's Clubs, which mounted another Pugh print show at its state assembly in Winston-Salem.[34]

African American women were equally intent on enhancing the cultural vibrancy of their communities through the establishment of local clubs in the 1930s. Both the Elite Art and Social Club of Charleston, South Carolina, and the Agnes J. Lewis Federated Club of Montgomery, Alabama—founded in 1936 and 1939, respectively—sponsored art exhibits.[35] The National Association of Colored Women's Clubs also continued its critical support of female African American artists during this time.

Throughout the 1940s state fairs—particularly in Louisiana, Virginia, and Georgia—included art exhibitions in which women won prizes for painting and sculpture. The extensive network of women's clubs remained loyal to the cause as well. In 1940 clubs across Virginia participated in twenty traveling exhibitions of watercolors, a joint initiative of the Virginia Museum of Fine Arts and the state's Art Alliance.[36] A 1941 exhibition sponsored by the Columbus, Georgia, Woman's Club in cooperation with the Columbus Art Association featured works by members of the Southern States Art League, including Hull.[37]

The nation's entrance into World War II did not diminish club support for art and women artists. Following Zelda Sayre Fitzgerald's 1942 exhibition at the Montgomery, Alabama, Museum of Fine Arts, the Montgomery Woman's Club mounted a show of her watercolors and drawings that December. The success of these public exhibitions encouraged Fitzgerald, who passionately pursued art in spite of her mother's vocal disdain. The woman's club display included a controversial self-portrait, as well as floral still life paintings reflecting a Chinese influence.[38] In January 1943 the Charleston, South Carolina, City Federation of Women's Clubs presented three significant gifts to a female colonel who spoke at the South Carolina group's annual meeting: the organiza-

tion's official pin, designed by Willis; an etching by Verner; and Verner's book *Mellowed by Time*.[39] Clubs in Miami, Florida; Shreveport, Louisiana; Charlotte, North Carolina; and Nashville, Tennessee, also hosted exhibitions in the war years.[40]

In 1948 the *American Art Annual* cited the General Federation of Women's Clubs as a prominent national organization that boasted 3 million members and had held 251 art exhibitions in forty-four states, including many in the South, between 1944 and 1948.[41] As the century entered its second half, women's clubs adapted to meet contemporary artists' needs and popular cultural interests. Lecture topics included modern painting and sculpture. In April 1951 the Windsor, North Carolina, Woman's Club mounted a joint exhibition of Sarah Blakeslee's work and paintings by her husband, Francis Speight, in a downtown commercial space.[42] In 1953 the North Carolina Federation of Women's Clubs granted a scholarship to a promising young artist named Maud Gatewood to attend the state's Woman's College (now the University of North Carolina at Greensboro). Gatewood later became one of North Carolina's most important modernist painters. In *Autumn Tunnel*, she strips away embellishment to convey the essential feeling of the season and effectively juxtaposes fabricated and natural objects.[43]

Southern women artists relied primarily on gender-neutral art clubs, commercial galleries, museums, and other cultural centers to display their work during the 1960s, diminishing the importance of Southern expositions and women's clubs to professional artists' careers. However, that did not stop clubs from supporting fine artists through local exhibitions and the conferring of accolades. In 1962 the National Association of Colored Women's Clubs added abstract artist and consummate colorist Alma Thomas to its honor roll of distinguished women in recognition of Thomas's "outstanding achievement in club and community activities."[44] Ten years later Thomas became the first African American to receive a one-woman show at the Whitney Museum of American Art.

Commending Thomas's remarkable accomplishments—as both a preeminent artist and an active clubwoman—is just one illustration of the significant role women's clubs played in advancing the careers of female artists during the late nineteenth and twentieth centuries. The unflagging efforts of enthusiastic women who united in a sisterhood of spirit to support artists and promote art in its myriad forms is inextricably woven into the South's complex historical tapestry, a fabric made far more beautiful by their legacies.

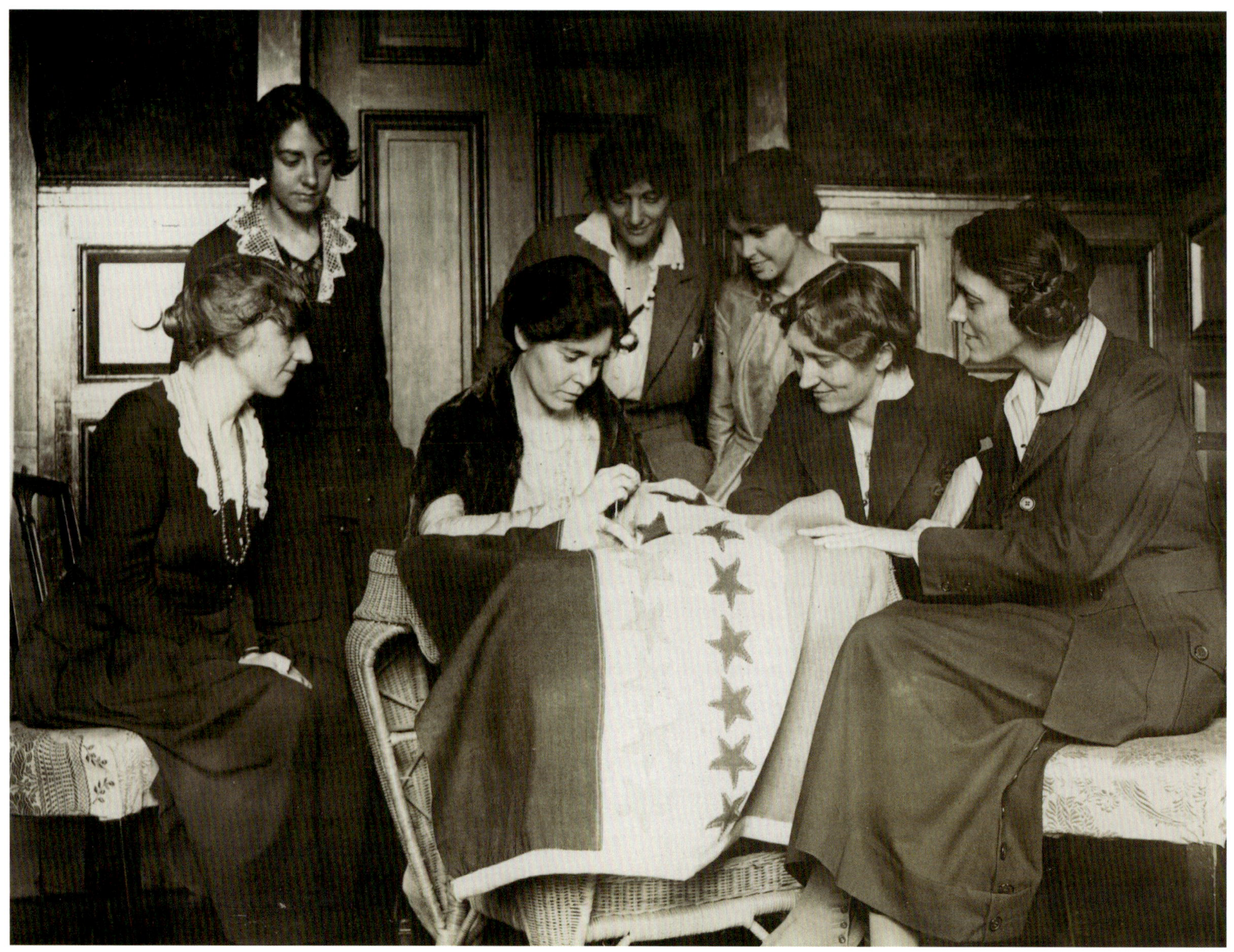

National Photo Company, Washington, DC, National Woman's Party activists watch Alice Paul sew a star onto the NWP Ratification Flag, representing another state's ratification of the 19th Amendment, circa 1919–1920; image retrieved from the Library of Congress, www.loc.gov/item/mnwp000263; Anita Pollitzer is shown standing, third from right

SUFFRAGE, SOCIAL ACTIVISM, AND WOMEN ARTISTS OF THE SOUTH

EVIE TERRONO

Writing in 1916 to her friend the artist Georgia O'Keeffe, equal rights champion Anita Pollitzer confided, "I am working like the Devil for Suffrage. The Pickets telegraphed me to come on to Washington."[1] The Pickets had indeed called, and Pollitzer was deeply involved in the ensuing battles. Born in Charleston to a German-Jewish family whose members were committed to communal activism, Pollitzer had embraced suffrage in her youth when she, along with her two sisters, founded the South Carolina branch of the Congressional Union for Woman Suffrage, later part of the National Woman's Party.[2] She recalled that in 1918, while protesting at the United States Senate Office Building, she "was banged around" and detained in the Capitol basement until Congress adjourned for the day.[3]

Drawing on the example of their British counterparts, American suffragists early on adopted confrontational strategies to apply political pressure, a practice that increased throughout the 1910s. On March 3, 1913, they organized a massive parade in Washington, DC, to coincide with Woodrow Wilson's presidential inauguration, and their fervor increased thereafter.[4] Throughout 1917 and 1918 the Silent Sentinels, "mute, but resolute," demonstrated at the White House, identifying Wilson as the chief opponent of women's enfranchisement.[5] Despite threats of incarceration, these suffragists persisted, and on July 14, 1917, they were arrested for unlawful assembly and obstruction of traffic. Among them was Detroit painter Betsy Graves Reynau, granddaughter of a chief justice of the Michigan Supreme Court.[6] The sixteen women were sentenced to sixty days in jail; when offered a fine in lieu of their sentence, they unanimously refused.[7]

Even though many Americans questioned the wisdom of agitating for suffrage following the nation's entry into World War I in April 1917, its advocates persevered. In a change of course, Wilson proposed the Nineteenth Amendment as an emergency war measure, arguing before Congress in September 1918 that women who had served the country in "a partnership of sacrifice and suffering and toll" could not be denied "a partnership of privilege and of right."[8] The president's endorsement was both tepid and overdue, and the amendment failed in the Senate that year by a margin of two votes.[9] Escalating their activism on February 9, 1919, suffragists—including influential New York art patron Louisine Waldron Elder Havemeyer—marched to the White House and burned Wilson in effigy, prompting their arrest and imprisonment. When a pardon was offered, the group chose to serve their three-day sentence rather than capitulate to the president, for whom, according to Havemeyer, "the thought of mobilized woman-power was as a red flag to an infuriated bull." Within weeks Havemeyer, along with many who had been incarcerated, boarded the "Prison Special" train on its national tour.[10] Pollitzer was responsible for organizing the tour and designated Charleston, her birthplace, as its first stop.

As these episodes illustrate, the women engaged in the campaign for suffrage were united by mission regardless of geographic roots. They came largely from middle- to upper-middle-class families, were trained in the arts in the United States and abroad, and as adults had become full participants in the civic life of their communities.[11] Seminal in their ideological formation was the emergence of the "New Woman," a

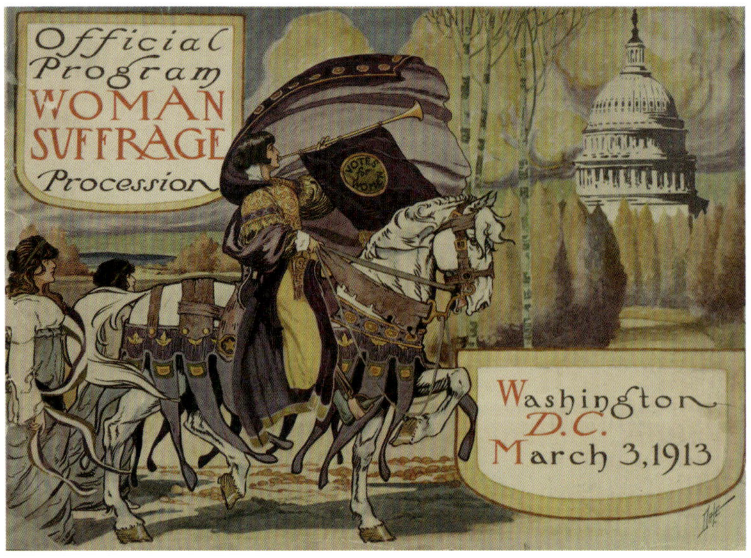

Dale, Benjamin M. (died 1951), Artist, and U.S. Records League of Women Voters, *Official Program—Woman Suffrage Procession, Washington, DC, March 3, 1913/Dale*; image retrieved from the Library of Congress, www.loc.gov/item/94507639

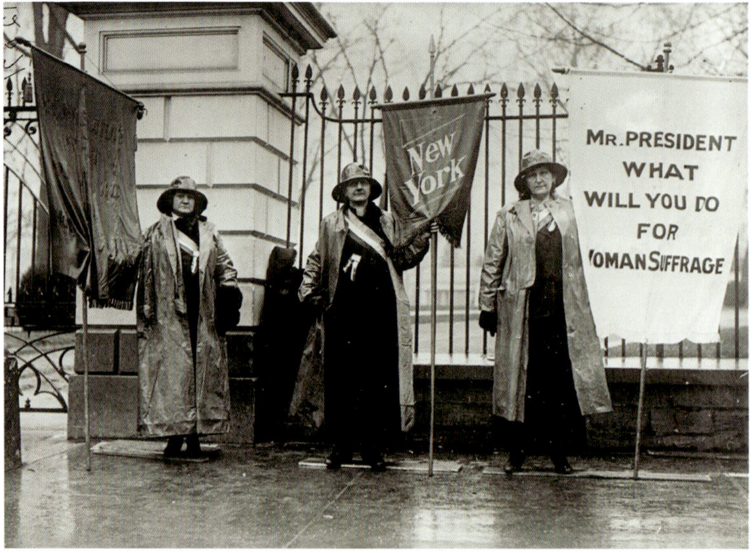

Harris and Ewing, photographer, *Woman Suffrage Picket Parade*, 1917; image retrieved from the Library of Congress, www.loc.gov/item/hec2008007306

term used to describe an independent and empowered female who sought to redefine her place in the American polity by challenging well-established notions of her subjectivity, docility, and propriety. By the 1910s the New Woman was often associated with leftist radicalism and was striving toward equal rights and sexual liberation.[12]

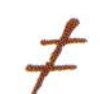

The Southern artists discussed here rarely matched the militant activism of their Northern counterparts.[13] Many aligned themselves philosophically with suffrage, recognizing the urgency of women's struggles toward economic and social agency, but remained fully cognizant of the negative impact such insurgent beliefs might entail for their patronage, still predominantly male and largely inimical to feminist ideals.[14] Representative in this respect were the attitudes of German-born sculptor Elisabet Ney, who spent her mature career in Texas, settling in the countryside in 1872 prior to a move to Austin in 1892.[15] Unconventional in thought and dress, Ney did not subscribe to the archetype of Southern womanhood—a stance that contradicted her romance with life on Liendo, a pre–Civil War cotton plantation, as well as her popularization of Lost Cause myths through her monuments to the Confederacy. A generation older than Pollitzer and O'Keeffe, Ney reflected in 1886: "My life has been a protest against the subjection to which women were doomed from their birth."[16]

In 1898 Ney sent a letter to reformist Mariana Thompson Folsom, who had invited her to lend her influence to women's voting rights at Austin's city council. Ney wrote: "My wishes are in accord with yours, and my conviction on the subject you judge right. Woman [*sic*] ought to be permitted not to feel any longer curtailed if they have ambitions & the desire to judge for herself." She went on to recommend fellow Texas artist Nannie Zenobia Carver Huddle as an advocate for suffrage because, according to Ney, Huddle's "feelings & thoughts" were "decidedly in favor of the subject."[17] Ney had taken a motherly interest in Huddle, who had studied in New York at the Art Students League with William Merritt Chase, befriending the young widow and training her without compensation. The two women became very close friends and worked together in Ney's studio until her death in 1907. Although not very vocal in her activism, in 1904 Ney would appear at the Texas House of Representatives in support of the state ballot for suffrage.[18]

Southern women artists—including Huddle, Kate Freeman Clark, Josephine Sibley Couper, and Margaret Law—were often exposed to suffrage during their advanced studies at progressive urban schools in the Northeast, such as the Art Students League and William Merritt Chase's school, where the faculties included luminaries like Chase and Robert Henri. The latter's support of his female students prompted "their own autonomy and self-determination" and might have provided them with the confidence not only to embrace suffrage, but to pursue future cultural initiatives as well.[19]

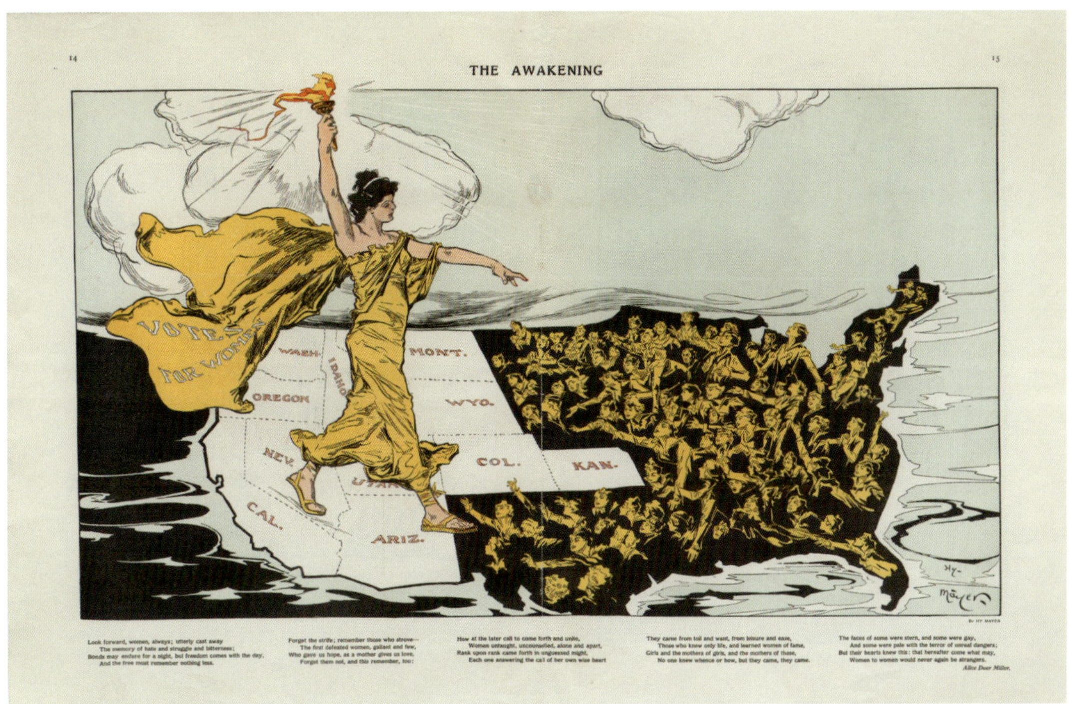

Henry Mayer (1868–1954), *The Awakening*, 1915, as published in *Puck Magazine*, February 20, 1915, 14–15; Cornell University, PJ Mode Collection of Persuasive Cartography, Ithaca, New York

In late 1913 the *New York Times* sponsored a competition titled "Girl of To-Day," issuing a call for readers to submit photographs of candidates who represented the "typical American girl." Commenting in the newspaper on the qualifications for such an exemplar, Henri acknowledged that "revolution has affected women very much, and to-day women are doing their part in furthering this revolution. They are becoming conscious of their right to claim recognition as human beings…and of taking an active part in the defense of woman against established prejudices and laws."[20] Standing at the forefront of this revolution, women artists were instrumental in mounting benefit art shows that were held the same year as the landmark 1913 Armory Show, where female artists were woefully underrepresented.[21] Two years later, as feminists were waging the Empire State Campaign—leading up to a referendum on a suffrage amendment on November 2, 1915, and just prior to the largest suffrage parade in New York City—women organized the *Exhibition of Painting and Sculpture by Women Artists for the Benefit of the Woman Suffrage Campaign*. Held from September 27 to October 16 at the Macbeth Gallery in New York City, it was the most significant exhibition devoted to the issue. Participants included Anne Goldthwaite (who served on the steering committee), Mary Tannahill, Helen Turner, and sculptors Edith Barretto Parsons and Enid Yandell—all born in the South. The exhibition's aesthetic and thematic pluralism led a critic to remark that the show was "held together by the tie, not of artistic affinity, but of political conviction."[22]

Descended from a prominent Alabama family involved in local and national politics, Goldthwaite came of age during a period of remarkable activism for suffrage. She studied first in New York City and then from 1906 to 1913 in Paris.[23] Goldthwaite lived at the American Girls' Club in the French capital, as did New York sculptor and suffrage activist Alice Morgan Wright.[24] Although Goldthwaite noted that her conduct at the club was "somewhat exemplary," she also remarked, "We knew all that went on around us."[25] Correspondence between Southern women artists and their families during this time clearly reveals the anxiety these foreign sojourns generated. As Goldthwaite recalled in her journal on her way back to New York, "Uncle Henry…tried to protect me with good advice."[26]

Freed from parental surveillance and the restrictions of a Southern upbringing that still maintained that marriage and motherhood were the obligatory paths to adulthood, women artists who pursued studies at large urban centers were acculturated to liberal, and sometimes radical, perspectives that prompted them to interrogate normative boundaries and challenge gendered responsibilities. Parental admonitions about the deleterious impact of suffrage emerged early and were expressed persistently. Suffragism's shifting paradigms were often antagonistic to the Southern proprieties that their families aimed to inculcate and reinforce. Although committed to providing their girls with a worldly education, Southern families steadfastly retained their allegiance to social decorum.

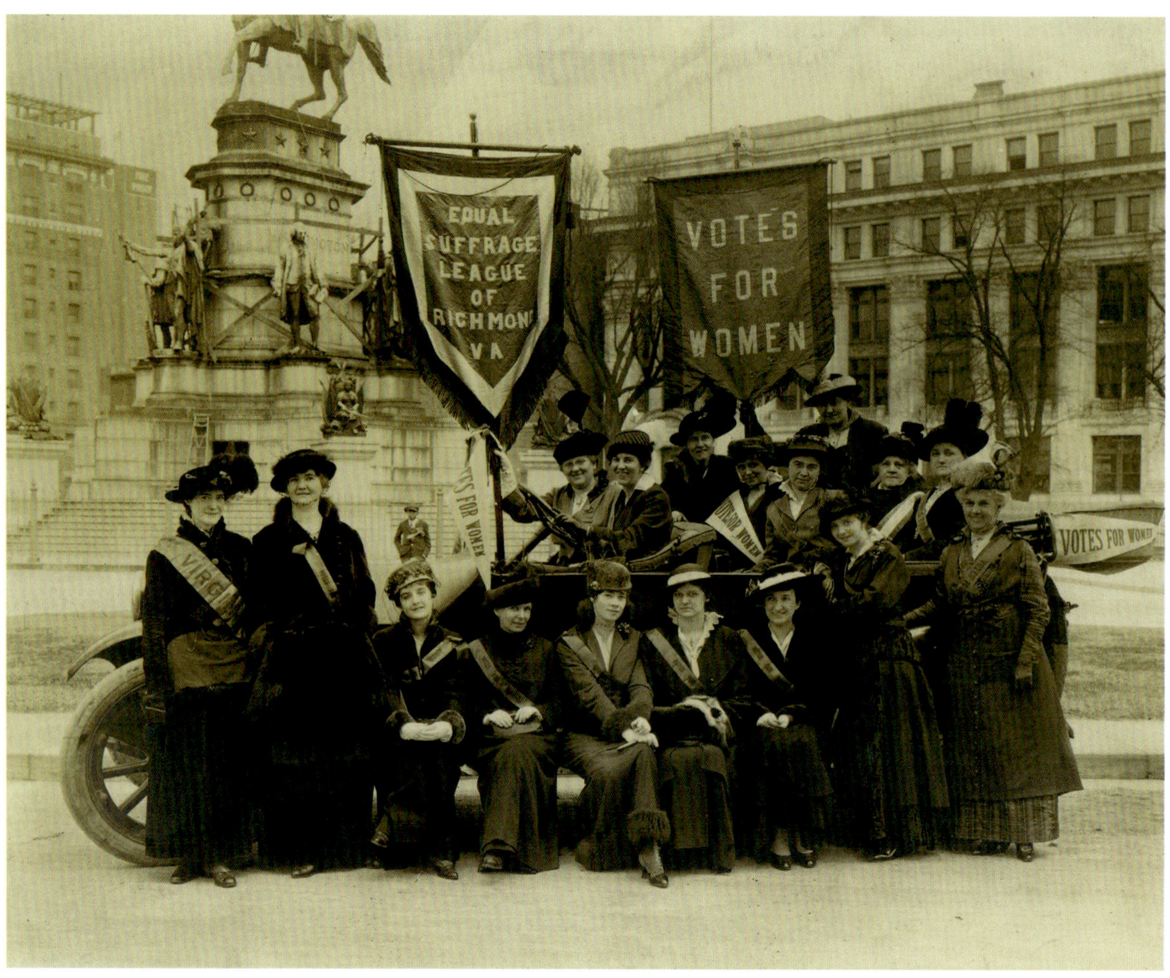

Equal Suffrage League of Richmond, Virginia (2001.230.1925), photographic print, 1915; Virginia Historical Society, Richmond, Virginia

Mary Poppenheim's matriculation at Vassar College in 1882 at the impressionable age of sixteen exposed the native Charlestonian to liberal ideas and nurtured the activist spirit she would later employ to advance the arts in her South Carolina hometown. Poppenheim, who served as president of the school's art club, wrote enthusiastically about her art studies, noting in 1884 that she "drew from the life model," a fact she revealed only to her sister Louisa, who would follow her at Vassar, and not to her conservative mother. Mrs. Poppenheim, on the other hand, constantly alert to the danger of progressive ideas, advised her young daughter to "be very retiring and ladylike whenever there is any voting to be done, and avoid having any thing to do with a party that savors of woman's rights....For you know a Lady...should avoid the *appearance* of evil."[27]

Equally concerned was William Lewis Stanton, the father of Georgia artist Lucy Stanton, who expressed his reservations over her "spiritual welfare," a condition he feared was jeopardized by the "change in regard to keeping the Sabbath–Lord's day, and worldly amusements" that occurred while she was studying abroad.[28] Born in Atlanta to a comfortable middle-class family whose ancestors had fought for the Confederacy, Stanton was exposed to European culture during her family's Grand Tour in 1889 and subsequent studies in Paris.[29] Familial admonitions aside, Stanton later declared that "no harm comes to a good girl from contact with men in coeducational colleges or from living and working in ateliers in Paris."[30]

Enthusiastic about her artistic talents while she was safely ensconced in her hometown of Holly Springs, Mississippi, Kate Freeman Clark's family similarly sought to circumscribe her activities while she was studying in New York. Accompanied by her widowed mother and grandmother, Clark left the Mississippi Delta and enrolled at the Art Students League in 1894, where her instructors included Chase and John Henry Twachtman. She then studied at the Corcoran School of

Art in Washington, DC, in 1895–1896, and again with Chase at Shinnecock until 1902.[31] Though Clark was perennially chaperoned by her surviving parent, the family's underlying concerns lingered. An 1897 letter from her uncle exhorted Clark to retain the values of ideal femininity, asserting that the "women of our land…are decidedly the superior sex in all that is cherished and refined." He also warned the young artist not to engage with feminists, who were "only working to disturb this most desirable state of things when they seek to operate in spheres of life which belong to men."[32]

Involvement with suffrage often equipped women artists with the necessary skills to trespass on the distinctly masculine boundaries of the marketplace, thus upsetting gendered allocations of authority. In her memoirs, Virginia-born painter Marietta Minnigerode Andrews described in detail the benefits that accrued from her studies at Chase's Shinnecock art colony, as well as the liberal attitudes of other female artists. Andrews maintained her career following her marriage to her teacher, the successful portraitist Eliphalet Andrews. When a cousin denounced her as an "active Suffragette" and an embarrassment to her family, Andrews angrily retorted that "my father must know that I did a man's work in providing for his large family after he was gone and perhaps he would approve of my having a man's opportunity and recognition."[33] Her allegiance to suffrage placed her in a liminal space, forcing her to mediate between her female sensibilities, conservative Southern environment, and professional choices. Andrews was exceptional among the artists discussed here because she put her art to the service of suffrage, contributing many drawings to the *Suffragist*, the publication of the National Woman's Party.

Many female artists who were devoted to suffrage did not marry and either lived alone or maintained lifelong relationships with other women, thus challenging heteronormative expectations. Stanton addressed the incompatibility of an artistic life with a domestic life for women, noting that "the artist…lives a lonely life—often dies in poverty, desolation, having no children to carry forward his personality."[34] Dedicated to expanding access for women, Stanton formed a suffrage club in her Athens, Georgia, studio in 1906 that later became the local chapter of the League of Women Voters. In 1913 she was one of the founding members of the Athens Art Association, a hub of professional opportunities for women artists.[35]

The Virginia artists Adèle Clark and Nora Houston shared Stanton's commitment to public service and were tire-

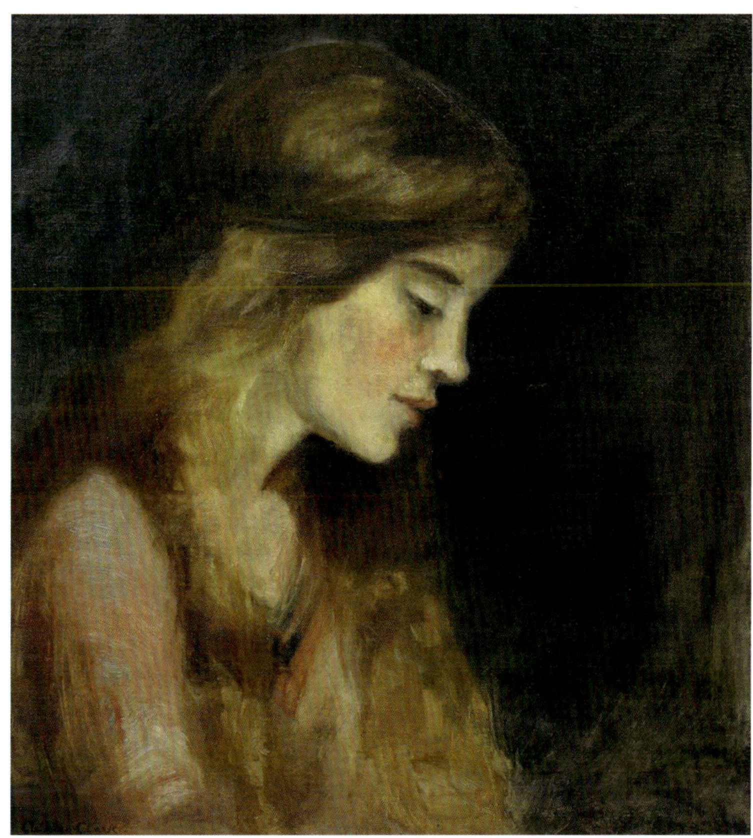

Adèle Goodman Clark (1882–1983), *Adeline*, circa 1932, oil on canvas, 20⅛ × 18 inches

lessly devoted to the Equal Suffrage League from 1909 until the passage of the Nineteenth Amendment.[36] Referencing her election as the organization's secretary, Clark remarked that she was qualified only because of "two accidents": she "had been active in art work in Richmond…and…didn't have any husband."[37] Clark and Houston were inseparable as adults; they shared their home-studio as professionals who agitated for social change in Jim Crow Virginia, pioneered art organizations, and successfully sustained themselves through the challenges of World War I and the Great Depression.[38]

Clark and Houston began their art training at the Art Club of Richmond under the tutelage of portraitist and illustrator Harriotte Lee Taliaferro Montague. It was through Montague—who had lived in Wyoming, where woman suffrage had been legal since 1869—that Clark became aware of the suffrage movement. Thanks to Montague's intervention, Houston and Clark studied with Chase and Henri at the Chase School in 1905 and 1906.[39] Upon Houston's return to Richmond, following her studies in Paris from 1907 to 1909, the two women focused their artistic aspirations on the Art Club, where they also nurtured their political awakening.[40] It was at the Art Club in 1909 that Sophie Meredith, Virginia

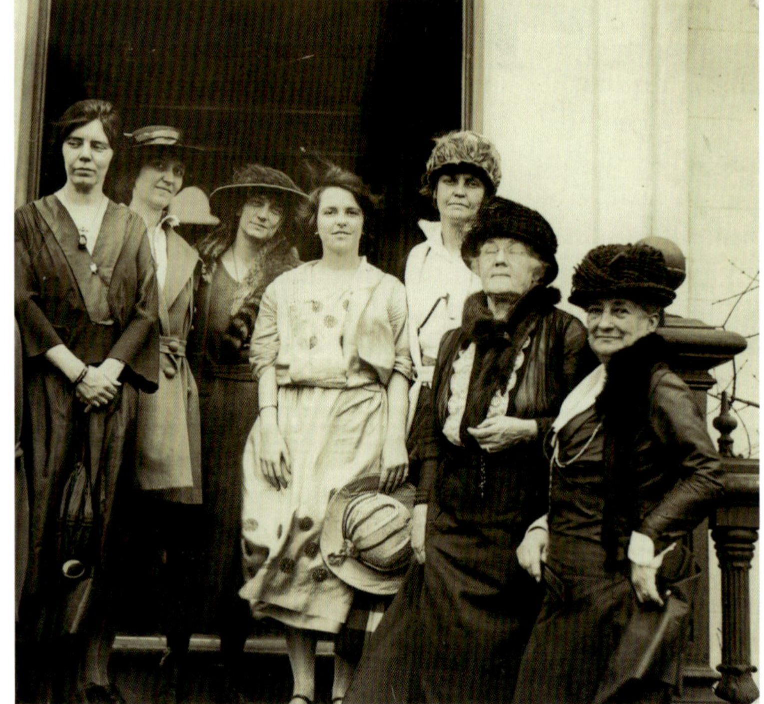

National Photo Company, Washington, DC, Officers of the National Woman's Party meeting in Washington to complete the plans for the dedication ceremonies on May 21st of the Party's new national headquarters opposite the Capitol. Alice Paul, New Jersey, vice president; Miss Sue White, Tennessee Chairman; Mrs. Florence Boeckel, executive committee; Miss Mary Winsor, member of the Council; Miss Anita Pollitzer, South Carolina, legislative secretary; Sophie Meredith, Virginia chairman; and Mrs. Richard [Wainwright], District of Columbia, member of the Council, 1922; image retrieved from the Library of Congress, www.loc.gov/item/mnwp000318

chair for the National Woman's Party, came to advocate for suffrage, and Clark signed the petition.[41] Clark and Houston later crusaded for black women's rights.[42] On Election Day in 1920, riding in a car that Houston's mother had rented, they "visited all the Negro polling places just to see if everything was going quietly.... In spite of the fact that there had been threats of bloodshed and riot and everything else, there wasn't any rioting. The Negro women went up quietly and voted, but I think they were very much heartened by the fact that... white women... went to the polls to give them their backing."[43]

Operating within the shifting boundaries of Southern female propriety while combating essentialist definitions of their duties and responsibilities, the women artists discussed here subverted stringent opposition and effected seminal social change. That courage was not mirrored in their largely conservative artistic endeavors. Most maintained their attachment to figuration, and although some pursued unconventional themes—in particular, documenting the lives of African Americans in the South—they did not challenge stylistic and aesthetic boundaries. Outside the studio, however, their professional status and networks facilitated and buttressed their activism. With the passage of the Nineteenth Amendment on June 4, 1919, these artists' political priorities diverged. Anita Pollitzer would later advocate for the Equal Rights Amendment, but Adèle Clark would oppose it, as did many other female Southerners who feared that it would compromise hard-earned legal protections for women. Having secured the right to vote, many of these women artists applied their remarkable organizational and advocacy skills to social justice initiatives such as children's education, regulation of child labor, and interracial cooperation.

"OF THE SOUTH, FOR THE SOUTH AND BY THE SOUTH"

THE SOUTHERN STATES ART LEAGUE

KAREN TOWERS KLACSMANN

In the wake of the 1920 passage of the Nineteenth Amendment, which granted American women the right to vote, women's access, autonomy, and authority grew in every sector of the nation's society and economy, including the arts. Across sixteen Southern states and the District of Columbia, one particular arts organization found its strength—and much of its success—in the contributions of its female members. Founded in 1921, the Southern States Art League had a threefold purpose: to promote the work of artists with ties to the South, to encourage local arts education, and to expose area visitors and residents alike to original works of art.[1]

During the course of its twenty-nine–year existence, from 1921 to 1950, the League held twenty-seven annual exhibitions, sponsored numerous circulating exhibitions between 1923 and 1946, and had an active membership of more than 1,200 *professionally* trained artists with strong ties to the region.[2] Over two-thirds of the League's ranks were female. These women members worked tenaciously to instill a sense of regional pride and an air of sophistication by endorsing both the distinctive character of Southern art and an appreciation of the newest trends in contemporary aesthetics. They attended to logistics by maintaining lines of communication and meaningful connections with local arts groups and with their friends, families, instructors, and colleagues throughout the nation. And while these women were artists first and foremost, they were also engaged in teaching, advocacy related to child welfare, and the first-wave feminist movement that fought for women's suffrage.

In a region still stinging from the aftermath of the Civil War and Reconstruction, Southern customs and culture were pilloried from all sides in the early decades of the twentieth century. In a scathing 1917 essay social critic and journalist H. L. Mencken described the South as "almost as sterile, artistically, intellectually, culturally, as the Sahara Desert," lending credence to a commonly held notion of a backward, poverty-stricken province.[3] Jim Crow laws had created extreme disparity between the races. The class system was based on an agrarian lifestyle that had not yet recovered economically, and there were relatively few major cities.[4] The result was a society made up of a very few wealthy citizens, a small middle class, and a large population living below the poverty line. In addition, the relative dearth of museums and institutions of higher learning forced those with means to travel far afield for higher education and edifying cultural experiences. In this atmosphere the Southern States Art League was established through the collaboration of women from Memphis, Tennessee, and Charleston, South Carolina. For nearly three decades the League's work to enhance the South's cultural climate was crucial to aligning the region with the rest of the nation in the arena of visual arts.

The majority of artists in this volume were active members of the Southern States Art League who engaged in the full range of participation—as artists, officers in the organization, community leaders, and activists. Representing three distinct generations of membership, they all espoused the cause of developing a homeland exposed to and appreciative of the finest American art currently in production. The earliest generation—which includes Josephine Sibley Couper, Anne Goldthwaite, Ella Sophonisba Hergesheimer, Margaret Law, Willie Betty Newman, Clara Weaver Parrish, Dixie Selden,

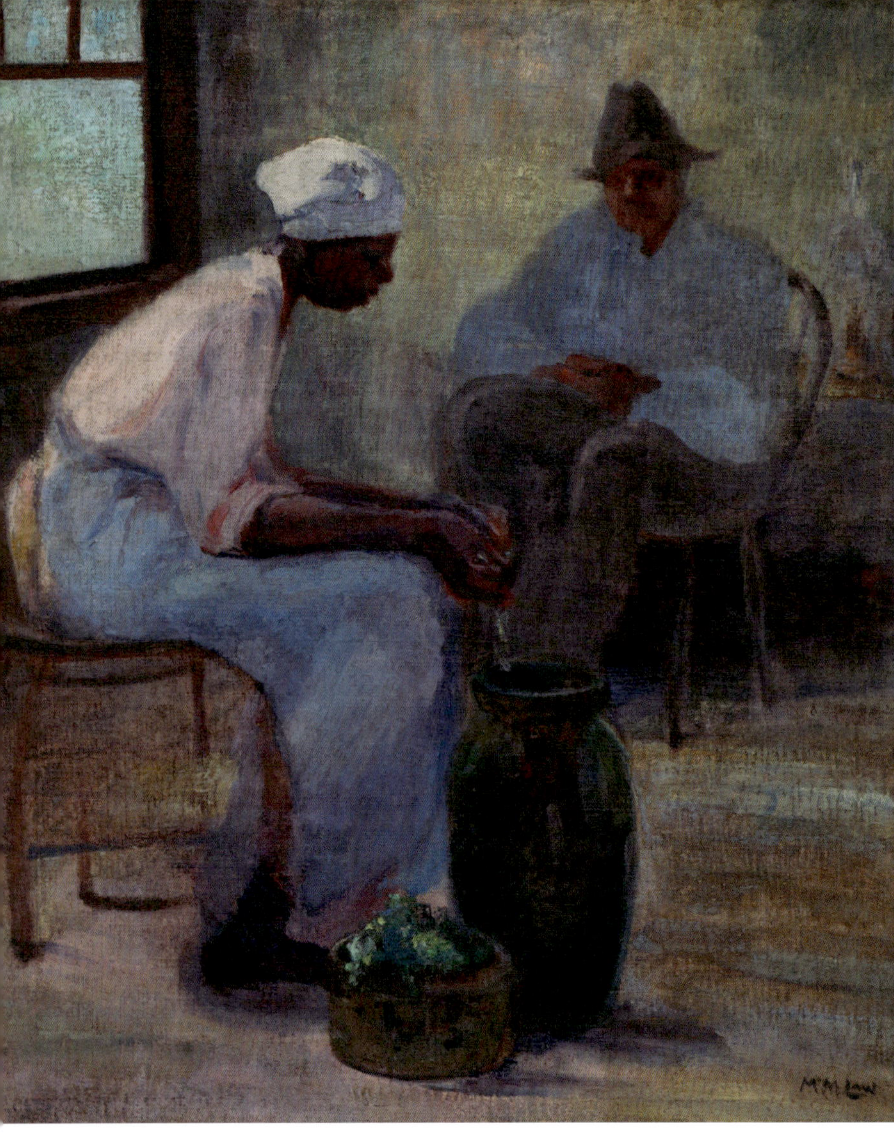

Margaret Moffett Law (1871–1956), *Making Grape Wine*, oil on canvas, 29 × 24⅛ inches

Alice Smith, and Helen Turner—was born in the nineteenth century, and many of its members were well-established practitioners when the League was formed. Working in a wholly different social climate, Wenonah Bell, Marie Atkinson Hull, Nell Choate Jones, Mabel Pugh, Hattie Saussy, and Elizabeth O'Neill Verner constituted a second generation. These women, born in the final quarter of the nineteenth century, had careers that spanned the entire length of the League's activity and beyond. Born in the twentieth century, a final generational cohort—Angela Gregory, Adele Gawin Lemm, Corrie McCallum, and Augusta Oelschig—benefited from increased access to college-level fine art instruction, but nevertheless faced modern obstacles in their quest to fulfill their artistic dreams.

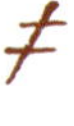

The Southern States Art League's origins can be traced to the American Federation of Arts, a national coalition formed in 1909 to bring the visual arts to the public through traveling exhibitions, educational programs, and publications. When the federation's Memphis and Charleston delegates expressed a mutual interest in mounting an exhibition of Southern art, it was decided that the Carolina Art Association would take the organizational lead in the endeavor. The ambitious plan commenced in 1919 when four thousand letters were mailed in a call for artists who were born in the South or had deep ties to it (defined as residence in the region for at least five years). Operating under the aegis of the All-Southern Art Association, the effort culminated in the All-Southern Exhibition, which opened at the Gibbes Memorial Art Gallery (now known as the Gibbes Museum of Art) in Charleston on March 21, 1921. Paintings by Couper, Hull, Law, Newman, Parrish, and Smith were displayed at that first exhibition.[5]

Writing in the *American Magazine of Art*, Birge Harrison proclaimed the inaugural exhibition a successful experiment that had realized "the most sanguine hopes of the originators." A respected artist teacher, and the director of the Woodstock summer colony of the Art Students League, beginning in 1908 Harrison was a frequent winter resident in Charleston who participated in the city's artistic life. Harrison's review praised the exhibition's "very high level of artistic performance" as well as the "distinct southern flavor, … which was most interesting and which called forth the enthusiastic encomiums of the hundreds of Northern visitors who saw the show." This warm reception, he contended, was confirmation that Southern art's unique character had its place within the larger domain of American art.[6]

Plans were immediately made for a second exhibition to be held in Memphis at the Brooks Memorial Art Gallery (now the Memphis Brooks Museum of Art) in April 1922. Once again the crowds were large and the reviews favorable. Georgia native Lucy Stanton was living in Boston when her miniature paintings were featured in that year's exhibition and again in 1924. Although out of favor in many parts of the country by this time, miniatures were still a medium much beloved by Southerners; they were included in the annual shows through 1940. Stanton's self-portrait highlights her unusual technique of "puddling"—applying loose washes of watercolor to the ivory. The method brings a freshness and vitality to the painting, making it more impressionistic than most portrait miniatures. In 1926 Stanton returned permanently to Georgia, where she later cofounded the Georgia

Peace Society and remained active in the visual arts and the women's suffrage movement.[7]

At the 1922 convention—a business conclave held in conjunction with the annual exhibition—provisional committees were created, delegates chosen, and organizational meetings held to ratify a constitution and bylaws. The organization's new name, Southern States Art League, was adopted at this time, and New Orleans was selected as its headquarters. The League's first president, Ellsworth Woodward, resided in the city as a member of Tulane University's faculty. Woodward was a brilliant choice for the office. He had come to the South during the New Orleans World's Industrial and Cotton Centennial Exposition of 1884–1885 with his brother and fellow artist, William. Both men were proponents of the Arts and Crafts movement and had trained at the Rhode Island School of Design. When H. Sophie Newcomb Memorial College was established in 1886 as the women's coordinate of Tulane, Ellsworth joined its art department and was named director of the art school four years later. The college, endowed by Josephine Le Monnier Newcomb in memory of her daughter, was a degree-granting institution that stressed the liberal arts as well as pragmatic handicraft training to ensure graduates a ready means of support. It was the only college of its kind in the South. The inclusion in the League's annual exhibitions of both fine arts and handmade works of art—the latter often relegated to the category of "craft" or "women's work"—reflected Woodward's philosophy and Newcomb's mission.

With geographic boundaries far more expansive than the area considered the South by current standards, the League's commitment to collaborative governance over a large section of the country, inclusion of many art forms, and broad public exposure to original art of high quality was implicit from the start.[8] Annual exhibitions were juried, and only active, dues-paying members of the organization were allowed to submit objects for consideration. The exhibitions were held on a rotating basis in the major cities of the region. The lack of formal art museums in many of the major cities in the early years did not impede the organizers. They used available venues, and several League members served on committees that would later develop art museums.

Additionally, selections culled from the annual exhibition rotated to smaller cities throughout the region. These extracts circulated to locations including women's clubs, libraries, school auditoriums, college and civic art galleries, and—during the 1940s—military bases. The circuit exhibitions were also offered in venues that had hosted previous annual exhibitions in an effort to keep residents and tourists in major Southern cities engaged in the League's activities. Sales generated by these touring displays were instrumental

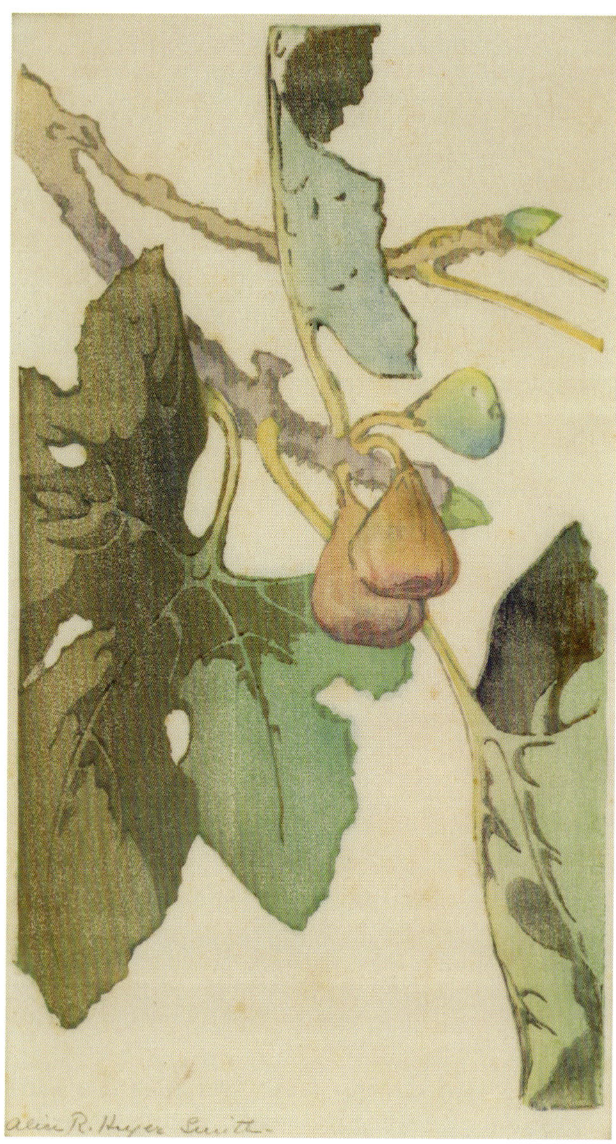

Charlestonian Alice Smith was represented in Southern States Art League shows numerous times during the organization's existence, including the 1922 exhibition that featured this print; Alice Ravenel Huger Smith (1876–1958), *Celestial Figs*, circa 1917, color woodblock print on paper, 11½ × 6½ inches

in promoting participating artists' reputations and advancing sales. Artists received the bulk of the proceeds, and the League retained between 10 and 20 percent of the sales price.

In the twenty-seven annual exhibitions the Southern States Art League held from 1921 to 1947, approximately 1,200 artists showed their work—and women artists predominated. The prevailing medium in each exhibition was two-dimensional work. Unsurprisingly, the number of participating artists and works on exhibit varied widely in a period that encompassed the Great Depression and World War II. Membership records in the League's archives are incomplete, but

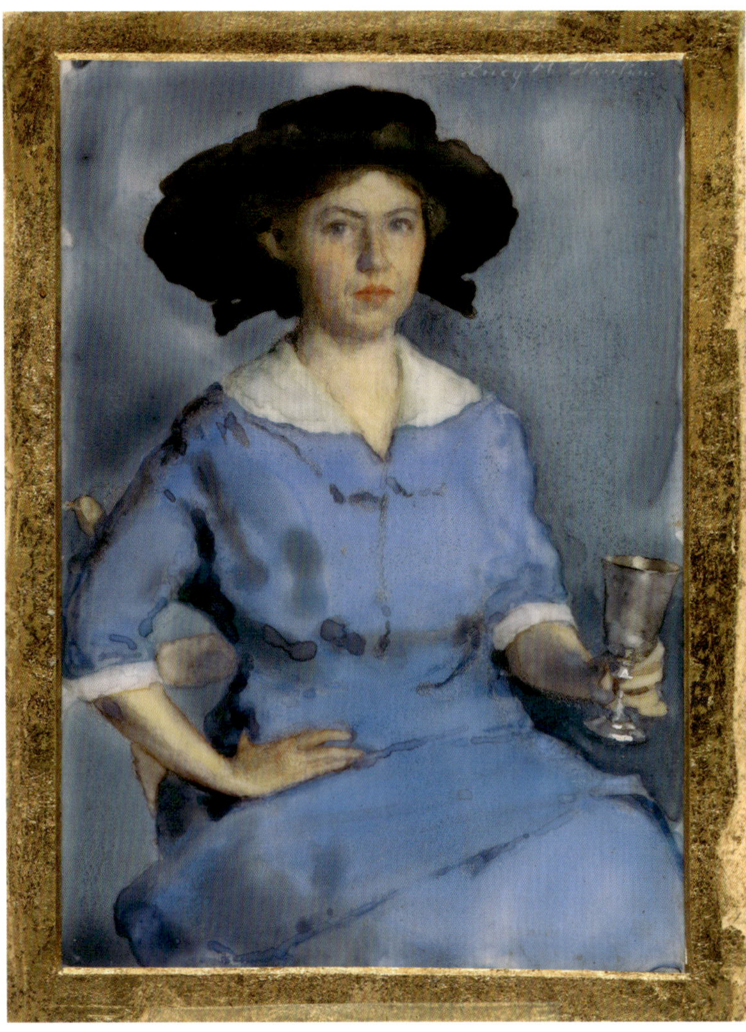

Lucy May Stanton (1875–1931), *Lucy May Stanton Self-Portrait*, 1912, water-color on ivory, 5⅜ x 3¾ inches; National Portrait Gallery, Smithsonian Institution, Washington, DC; gift of Mrs. Edward C. Loughlin

in 1988 a list of 425 members included in the archives was compiled and published.[9] Dues-paying members of the League never exceeded 597 at any one time.[10] However, it is possible to compile a list of active members over the existence of the organization by using the catalogs for the annual exhibitions. When these two types of lists are combined, an idea of the strength and breadth of the organization emerges. Paintings, watercolors, etchings, drawings, prints, and sculptures—all considered fine arts—were considered for exhibition, as were pottery, textiles, jewelry, metalwork, and bookbinding. Photography was featured only once and by a single artist, Mississippi native Martha "Matsy" Wynn Richards, during the second annual exhibition, in 1922.[11]

In addition to remitting dues of five dollars, each applicant for membership completed a registration card that was designed by Ethel Hutson in 1925. The card recorded the member's name, place of birth, Southern residence (location and duration), art school, instructors, preferred artistic medium, exhibition history, awards, affiliation with other art organizations, and representation in permanent art collections. Neither gender nor race was noted on the membership card. Membership categories included sustaining members, patrons, and, during wartime, honorary members who were artists in military service.[12]

New Orleans was the site of the third annual exhibition, as well as the home of Ellsworth Woodward, who governed as League president from 1923 until his death in 1939. A founder of the exclusively male Art Association of New Orleans at the turn of the century, Woodward served in many leadership capacities within the Southern visual arts community, in addition to his academic duties and League responsibilities. An elegant and eloquent gentleman, Woodward was a perfect spokesperson for the fledgling organization: "The movement is not centralized in any city or around any group of artists," he proclaimed; "it is of the South, for the South and by the South, and its ultimate aim is to form in the South an appreciation for what the South can and will create in the fine arts."[13]

Although Woodward held the League's top position, it was the organization's women—usually named to secondary offices—who creatively and tenaciously kept the unwieldy organization functioning smoothly. Memphis painter and charter member Florence McIntyre was elected as the first vice president and stressed a commitment to quality, writing that the League sought to include "artists who have studied art, and judges who will only hang such work as will be a credit to the South." She continued: "This is the time to strike a certain standard."[14]

The unsung hero of the organization was Hutson, who held the title of secretary-treasurer from 1924 until her retirement in 1947.[15] During her tenure all League correspondence emanated from her home on Panola Street in New Orleans, where the organization's records were stored. Hutson was very active in the women's suffrage movement, worked as an administrator at the Isaac Delgado Museum of Art (now the New Orleans Museum of Art), and exhibited her work in ten annual exhibitions of the League. She routed the circuit exhibitions, communicated with the membership via a monthly bulletin, and promoted the activities and aims of the League by writing articles that were placed in local and national publications. The League, she wrote, sought "to interest Southern people in the art of the South" and continually strove "to make them see that their own artists are today doing work comparable to that of other parts of the country, and that they need no longer feel that it is necessary to go North, East, West or abroad to find pictures, sculptures, and crafts worth buying and preserving."[16] It is no coincidence that the final annual exhibition coincided with Hutson's retirement.

Whether working in formal League roles or independently, women members labored tirelessly to increase education, awareness, and appreciation of the visual arts in a region with few art schools, museums, or large urban art markets. By shrewdly accessing the existing network of conventional social and cultural gatherings of women, they were able to advance the League's mission. On the whole, female members were attuned to the compelling social and political issues of the day. Ella Hergesheimer's portrait of Madeline McDowell Breckinridge is a case in point. An activist for feminist causes her entire adult life, Breckinridge lobbied for child welfare and women's rights, and is credited with ensuring the ratification of the Nineteenth Amendment by the Kentucky legislature.[17] Breckinridge embraced the causes she held dearly despite her fragile health. Ironically, after decades of campaigning for suffrage, she participated in a single election, in November 1920, just weeks before her death. The forthright gaze and use of purple throughout Hergesheimer's painting—in the chair, the hat, and the violets—conveys a regal but not imperious affect. Although her subject is elegantly clad in a fur-trimmed coat and a dress adorned with lace, Hergesheimer endows Breckinridge with an air of respectful authority.

The 1920s were a prosperous time for the League. Exhibitions rotating between major Southern cities highlighted a diverse array of work by its members. Although the first four annual exhibitions were held in established art museums, the 1925 installation took place at the Biltmore Hotel Arcade in Atlanta.[18] This multipurpose building housed a hotel, residential apartments, the Atlanta Historical Society, and the WSB radio tower, which became a distinctive element of the city's skyline. The following year the Museum of Fine Arts in Houston was chosen as the first exhibition venue west of the Mississippi River.

A designated art gallery within the Birmingham Public Library made it a logical destination for the League's circuit exhibitions and for the annual juried show in 1928. Two Alabama artists whose careers flourished in Northern locales were loyal supporters of the visual arts in their home state. With art studios in New York and Paris, Clara Parrish dreamed of creating an art museum in her hometown of Selma but did not live to see that hope fulfilled.[19] Parrish's use of a dark pal-

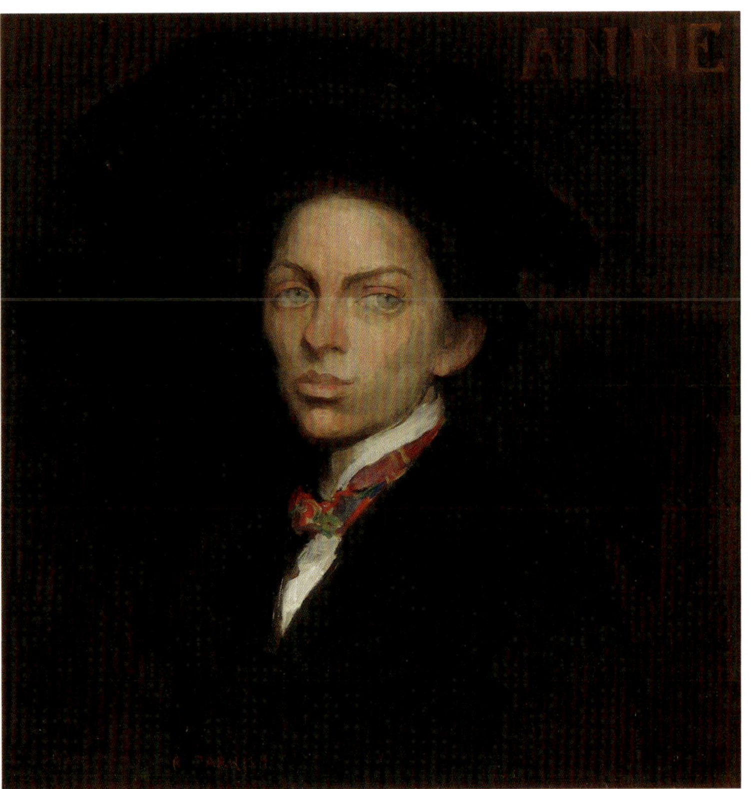

Clara Minter Weaver Parrish (1861–1925), *Portrait of Anne Goldthwaite*, circa 1895, oil on canvas, 20¾ × 19½ inches; Montgomery Museum of Fine Arts, Montgomery, Alabama, Association Purchase, 1963.50

ette favored by one of her Munich-trained teachers, William Merritt Chase, adds a layer of mystery to her pensive portrait of fellow artist and League member Anne Goldthwaite. Born in Montgomery, Goldthwaite spent her professional life in urban art centers and was one of the few female artists whose work was included in the seminal 1913 New York Armory Show.

The final exhibition of the decade was held in San Antonio, Texas. At the companion annual meeting, League leaders expressed a need to redefine the organization's policies, and the constitution and bylaws were subsequently revised in advance of the 1930 gathering. The League's objective was made more succinct: "To encourage and promote art and its appreciation throughout the South by any and all practical means."[20] Three distinct membership categories—active, sustaining, and patron—were retained, but guidelines for active membership now required artists to be over eighteen years old, born in the South, or resident in the South for five consecutive years.[21] As before, only active members could submit work for exhibition, and an additional caveat was put into place to address the quality of work: "Before election to active membership, candidates must submit to the officers of the

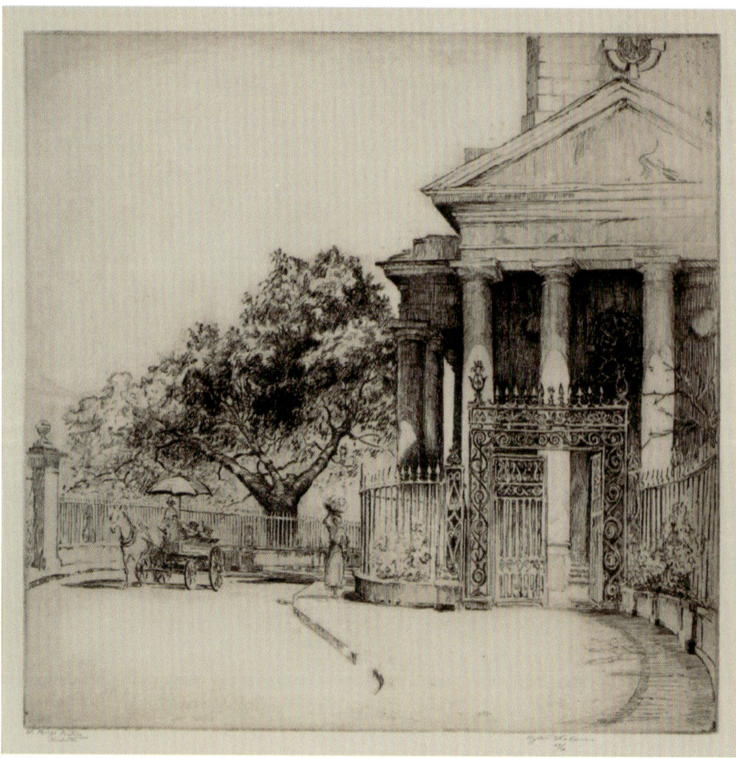

This print depicting an iconic Charleston, South Carolina, landmark was featured in the 1932 annual exhibition; one of the original Southern States Art League members, Verner held various leadership positions and was regularly represented in annual exhibitions; Elizabeth Quale O'Neill Verner (1883–1979), *St. Philip's Portico, Charleston*, etching on paper, 10 × 9¾ inches

League evidence that they have fulfilled the requirements,… and further, must submit for approval to an authorized Jury of the League one or more examples of their work."[22]

With new prerequisites in place, annual and circuit exhibitions continued to be robust in participation and attendance during the 1930s.[23] Between 1930 and 1938 more than twice as many women displayed their work as their male counterparts. These successes could not, however, immunize the League— whose financial stability had been vulnerable since its onset— from the economic challenges of the Great Depression. Exhibits were strategically routed in order to save on shipping and traveling costs. Local judges were increasingly engaged, and at times no monetary awards accompanied juries' recognition of outstanding work. To retain active members, certain requirements were relaxed to admit younger artists with less professional training. At the midpoint of its organizational life, survival of the League was deemed more important than stringent membership rules and quality standards.

As the century progressed, more artists had access to training at regional colleges and universities. Many had left the South to seek instruction at prestigious academies in the Northeast or abroad and returned with impeccable credentials that were put to use in the newly developing art departments of Southern schools. North Carolinian Mabel Pugh exhibited in eleven annual exhibitions from 1922 to 1933, submitting work from her studio on West 57th Street in New York City. A graduate of Peace Institute in Raleigh, she had pursued additional instruction in New York, Pennsylvania, and Europe—a familiar trajectory for Southern artists. Pugh was a successful commercial artist in New York, working chiefly for magazines, and also wrote and illustrated children's books. In 1936 she returned to her alma mater as the head of the art department as the institute transitioned into a junior college.[24]

Some artists returned home reluctantly. Sculptor Angela Gregory's work was accepted in five annual exhibitions during the 1930s. Born in New Orleans, Gregory was a graduate of Newcomb College, as was her mother, Selina, and her father was a professor at Tulane University. After spending several years in Paris, she returned with misgivings to New Orleans in 1928. She lamented that the city offered "no music, no art. It was hot as Hades. There was nothing. I thought I would go out of my mind. But after a while I realized that if you don't have it inside you, it doesn't matter if you are here or in Paris." Gregory acknowledged the cost of her commitment to a creative life: "Too often a woman is torn by conflicting obligations, as a mother, a wife, sister, daughter. Unless she can stay on the track, she becomes a dilettante. To be an artist sometimes requires sacrifice, yet I have found it thrilling."[25]

Following Ellsworth Woodward's death in 1939, James Chillman Jr. assumed the League's presidency. A professor in the architecture department of Rice Institute (now Rice University), the first director of the Museum of Fine Arts in Houston, and a practicing artist, Chillman had served as one of the League's vice presidents since 1925. Hutson continued as secretary-treasurer, and the headquarters remained based at her home in New Orleans. New venues were worked into the well-established rotation cycle: the Mint Museum in Charlotte, North Carolina (1940); the Louisiana State Exhibit Building in Shreveport (1941); the fine arts building at the University of Georgia in Athens (1942); the Dallas Museum of Fine Arts (1944); the Birmingham Public Library (1945); the High Museum of Art in Atlanta (1946); and the Virginia Museum of Fine Arts in Richmond (1947).

As part of the wartime effort, military bases were added to the circuit exhibition roster, and the yearly business meeting was cancelled beginning in 1942. The League kept members apprised of civil service opportunities for artists. Invitations to membership were extended to artists serving in the military, and an honor roll of their names was displayed at annual exhibitions during the war years. Prizes were awarded in war bonds during this period.

As midcentury neared, Southern States Art League exhibitions featured fewer artists, fewer objects, and a diminished range of works, a decline counterbalanced by an increase in the number of regional art schools, university art departments, summer artist colonies, and art museums. While participation in the League's annual exhibitions declined during the 1940s, many of its members found a new platform for their work outside the South, thanks to the efforts of the Southern Women's National Democratic Organization. Based in New York City, the organization first hosted an exhibition of Southern art in 1934, and it joined the League as a sustaining member in 1937. Though the New York exhibitions were not confined to League members, the majority of participating artists were League affiliates, half of whom were women.

Buoyed by the swell of national pride and a return to normalcy after the Allied victory, the League's 1946 annual exhibition marked a major turning point. The presentation was more robust than it had been during the war years, and the annual convention was reinstated. Much of the meeting agenda concerned recommendations for making the League more effective within the region and throughout the nation. This year also marked the final time that circuit exhibitions were culled from the larger annual exhibition for rotation throughout the region.

In January 1947, Southern States Art League membership totaled 597, the highest in its history. This expanded roster, however, did not reflect the organization's strength or durability. Proposals adopted at that year's annual convention included holding quadrennial exhibitions in four venues simultaneously and transferring the League's headquarters to Atlanta. Both Chillman and Hutson resigned their leadership positions, and first vice president Edward Shorter ascended to the presidency. That winter critical administrative tasks were abandoned: no newsletters were sent to members, no membership dues were collected, and no annual exhibitions were held.[26]

Having outlived its original purpose, the Southern States Art League was officially dissolved in 1950. By then the visual arts enjoyed a much greater presence in the region, and American nationalism had supplanted the partisan animosity that had lingered in the South since the Civil War. While segregation and other pressing sociopolitical issues would continue to define parts of the sixteen-state League territory, fiscal disparities between North and South narrowed during the post–World War II economic boom.

From its inception, the women members of the Southern

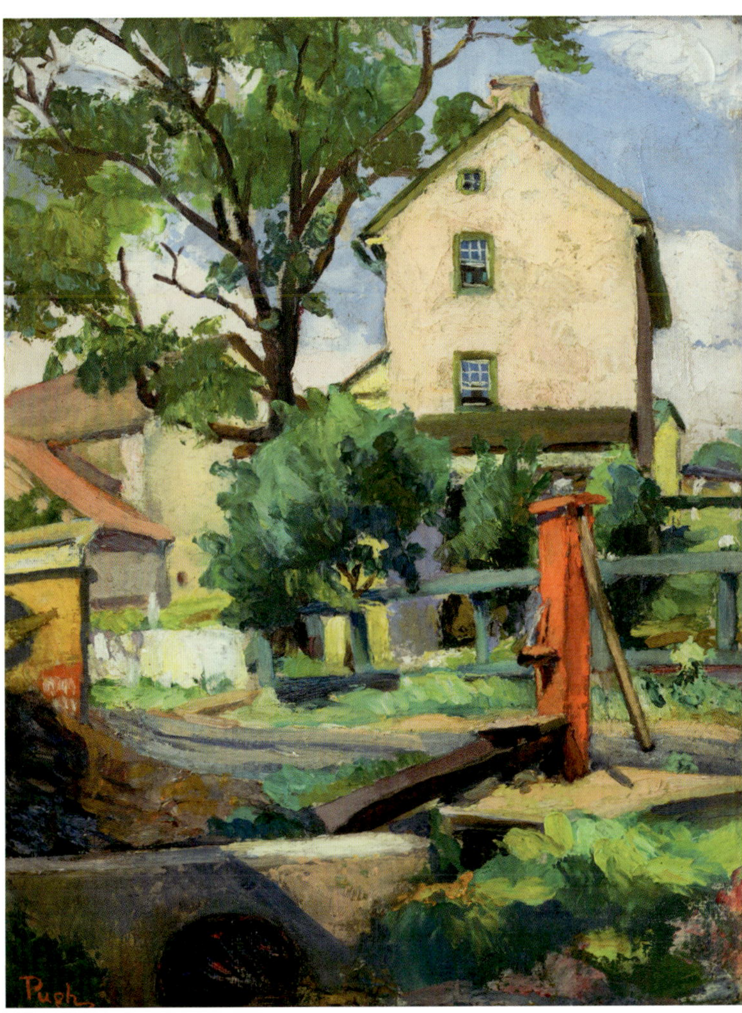

Sarah Mabel Pugh (1891–1986), *Red Pump*, oil on canvas board, 16 × 12 inches

States Art League played a seminal role in creating the armature necessary for building up the visual arts in the region. Many of these members enjoyed critically and commercially successful careers, but their shared legacy as advocates for Southern art surpasses their individual achievements as artists, teachers, and activists. Their creative collaborations reaped widespread cultural benefits. They championed the importance of art education and art appreciation for all ages and at all levels of society. By lending the League's imprimatur to both fine arts and traditional crafts, they engaged new participants and patrons. They leveraged their family ties, education, professional relationships, and personal resources to establish an influential network within and beyond the South. Their collective diligence and dedication to the League's mission ensured its advancement and represents yet another illustration of why women artists of the South deserve a place in the larger conversation about twentieth-century American art.

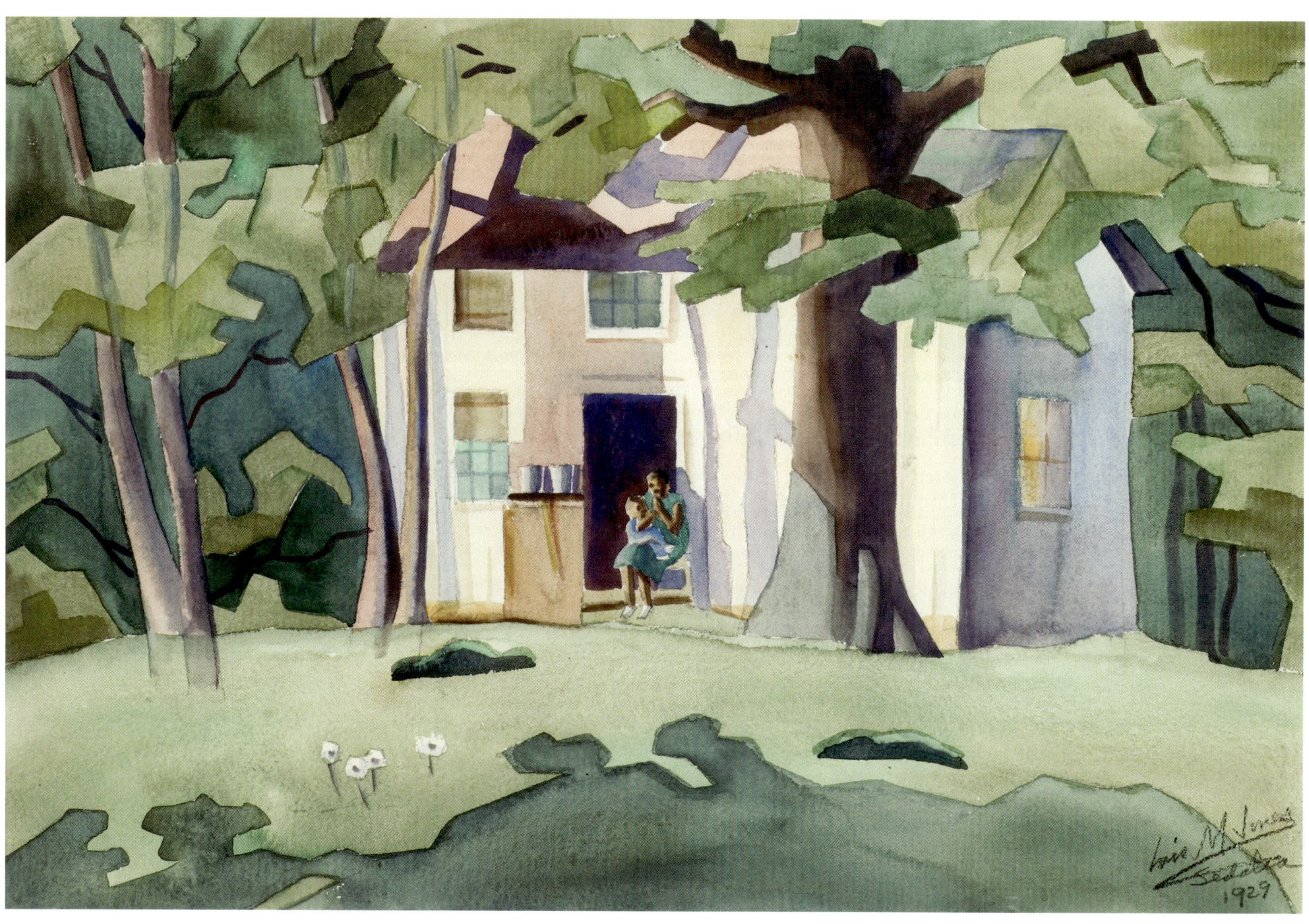

Loïs Mailou Jones (1905–1998), *Sedalia, North Carolina*, 1929, watercolor on paper, 13¾ × 19¾ inches; promised gift of Drs. Chris and Marilyn Chapman, PG2009.92; collection of the Mint Museum, Charlotte, North Carolina

CONTRARY INSTINCTS

ART HISTORY'S GENDERED COLOR LINE

ERIN R. CORRALES-DIAZ

In 1928 African American painter Loïs Mailou Jones applied for a teaching post at her alma mater, the School of the Museum of Fine Arts in Boston.[1] Despite her distinguished student record there, the school's administration rejected her application and advised her to instead "go South to help your people."[2] Having been raised in a middle-class Boston household, Jones had no experience with or connection to the American South. Yet finding few opportunities in the Northeast, Jones did indeed go south, relocating that same year to provincial Sedalia, North Carolina. There, she was tasked with starting an art department at the Palmer Memorial Institute, a preparatory school for African Americans, at the height of the Jim Crow era. During her two-year tenure at Palmer, Jones witnessed African Americans' unflagging strength and spirit in the face of overt racism and debilitating poverty—emotions and experiences she channeled into her work of that period. While hardly uncommon, this pivotal episode in Jones's life illustrates the racism that pervaded American society, regardless of region, and underscores the assumption that modern African American art must address the American South and the legacy of slavery. Jones's time in the rural South served as a catalyst, propelling her to Paris, Haiti, and Africa in an effort to forge visual "links on the diaspora trail" that began, for her, in North Carolina.[3]

During the social and cultural movement known as the Harlem Renaissance (1920–1940), intellectual black leaders like Alain Locke and W. E. B. Du Bois, as well as philanthropic institutions like the Harmon Foundation, advocated that African American art, as an expression of racial identity, be used to elevate the African American community and to combat negative stereotypes.[4] Immersed in these ideologies and other philosophies inherent to the parallel New Negro movement, Jones embraced an artistic style that balanced European modernism and African imagery, as exemplified by her painting *Africa*. Her female contemporaries Meta Warrick Fuller and Augusta Fells Savage similarly felt compelled to use their art as a vehicle to promote the dignity of their race—an obligation that may have at times constricted their creative impulses. While the larger realm of Western art was experimenting with abstraction, Jones and her peers lingered on the cusp of conservative, but politically radical realism. As a result, their art has been isolated as "black art" rather than being integrated into the established art historical canon.[5]

Jones valiantly surmounted the immense social hurdles her race and gender decreed. Even as Aaron Douglas designed powerful covers for *The Crisis*—the official magazine of the National Association for the Advancement of Colored People—to rally support for black artists, female artists of color remained sidelined. As writer Elise Johnson McDougald noted, New Negro movement initiatives were "directed chiefly toward the realization of equality of the races, the sex struggle assuming the subordinate place."[6] As a member of the faculty at Howard University in Washington, DC, Jones confronted institutional sexism when the chair of the art department asked her to paint in the "ladylike" medium of watercolor instead of the more "masculine" oils.[7] In spite of her prolific output, impressive exhibition record, and decades-long career as both artist and educator, Jones has been largely ignored.

The invisibility of a trained African American female artist like Jones is all the more puzzling given the art world's increased interest in Southern self-taught African American artists.[8] The hypnotic, symmetrically patterned drawings of Minnie Jones Evans have caught the eye of collectors and museums in the modern marketplace.[9] Evans drew vibrant designs inspired by the verdant surroundings of Airlie Gardens, the historic Wilmington, North Carolina, public park where she was employed as a gatekeeper. Upon Evans's "discovery" by friend, advocate, and dealer Nina Howell Starr, her work appeared in New York galleries and eventually headlined an exhibition at the Whitney Museum of American Art in 1975.[10] At that time her intellectual and experiential remove from art historical traditions suggested a kind of "authentic naïf, an undisturbed and breathtakingly gifted primitive" or a more "genuine" black art, untainted by outside influences.[11] Her drawings appealed to the predominantly white art establishment precisely because of her lack of formal art training. Evans overcame her financial disadvantages, maternal responsibilities, and racial bias to produce captivating art free from imposed hierarchies of power. But critical regard for these objects stems first and foremost from Evans's status as "outsider"—an artist celebrated but marginalized, appreciated less for the quality of her work than for the narrative of her life.

Does American art institutions' increased interest in art by Evans and other self-taught artists come at the expense of the work produced by trained artists like Jones? What are we to make of the lack of recognition of Jones and Savage in public collections? Art historian Kinshasha Conwill expressed concern over this discrepancy in her seminal 1991 essay "In Search of an 'Authentic' Vision," then revisited her inquiries a decade later, offering a more nuanced review of the state of self-taught African American art.[12] Yet contention regarding institutional approval and differentiation of self-taught over trained artists persists.[13] It is the plight of the academically trained artist to be evaluated against prevailing standards that dismiss them, while self-taught artists circumvent such appraisal due to their peripheral status. Contemporary artist Kerry James Marshall noted this disparity, calling it a catch-22 for African American artists: "Whom should they emulate—the academics or the folk?"[14] In either instance, as Conwill concludes, the black artist is discounted—either deemed too educated to qualify as avant-garde or too original to be examined as a mainstream artist.[15] There is more to be gained if, rather than position self-taught artists against trained artists in a binary equation, we recognize their mutual marginalization and appreciate how their fluid creative dialogues transcend traditional art education and institutions.

The challenges posed by Jones and Evans's race were complicated by an additional and perhaps steeper barrier: gender. As limited as the opportunities were for African American male artists in the early twentieth century, their female counterparts had far fewer choices and faced immense prejudice when attempting to study, practice, and exhibit their art.[16] For many African American women living in the South at that time, an artistic career seemed unattainable,

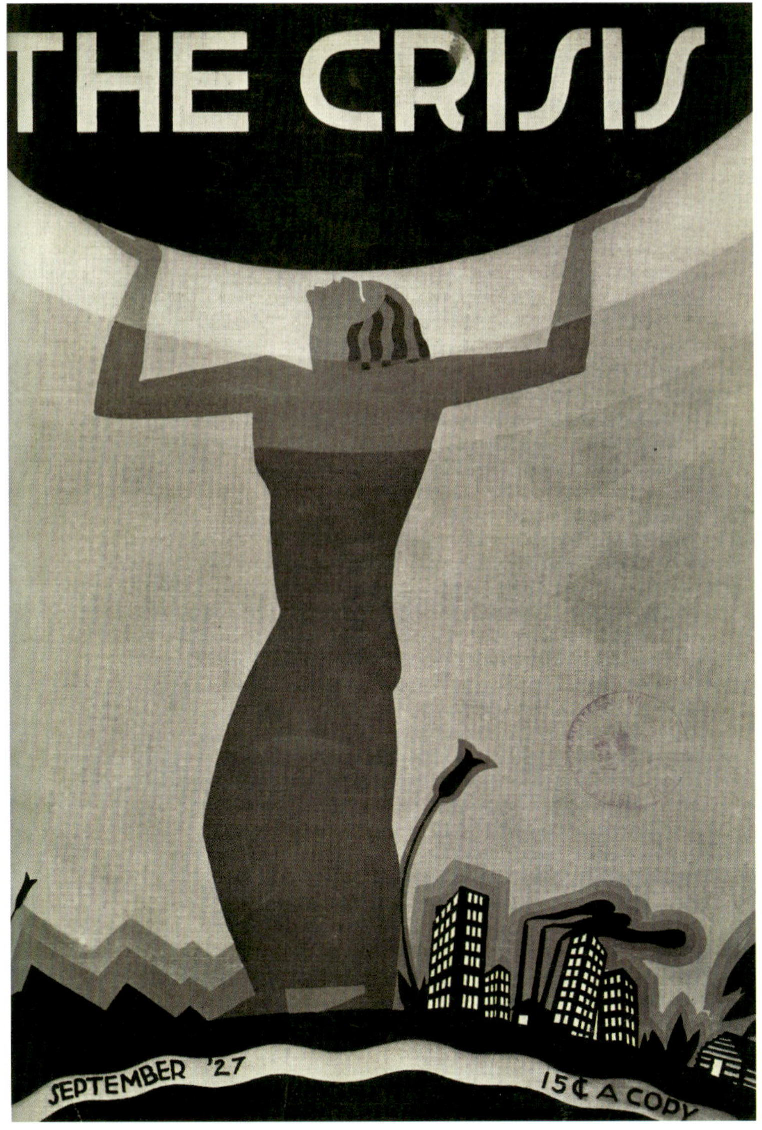

Aaron Douglas (1899–1979), *The Burden of Black Womanhood, The Crisis,* 1927; photograph courtesy of the Library of Congress, Washington, DC. The Johnson Collection wishes to thank the Crisis Publishing Co., Inc., publisher of the magazine of the National Association for the Advancement of Colored People, for the use of this image, which was first published in the September 1927 issue.

as their "contrary instincts" dictated that they set aside their aesthetic aspirations in deference to societal constraints and domestic duties. This suppression of artistic self-expression was the focus of Alice Walker's eloquent essay, "In Search of Our Mothers' Gardens." In her study of the lives of African American women, Walker laments the loss of unrealized creative potential but exalts women's private, anonymous production of stories, quilts, and gardens as vehicles of artistic exploration.[17] Bearing Walker's argument in mind, the fact that Evans was able to gain recognition, even as an outsider

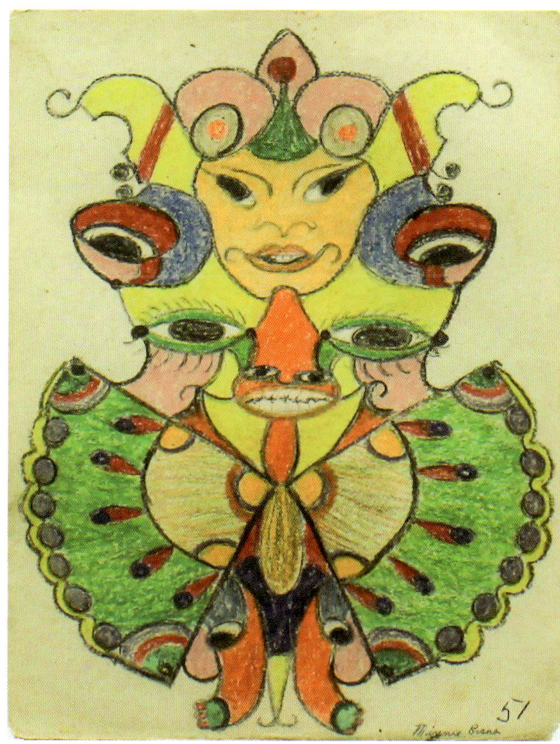

Minnie Eva Jones Evans (1892–1987), *Untitled*, 1951, crayon and pencil on paper, 12 × 9 inches

artist, is remarkable. But how many artists like Evans have existed and are simply unnoticed in art history because we were not looking in the right places?

Nomenclature may be part of the problem. Self-taught innovators often do not identify themselves as artists, as illustrated by Clementine Reuben Hunter's assertion: "I'm not an artist, you know, I just paint by heart."[18] Nonetheless, these individuals' creative production deserves consideration by art critics, collectors, and historians. When we examine the work of trained artists—Jones, Alma Thomas, and Selma Burke—alongside that of untrained practitioners—Evans and Hunter—it is apparent that they all challenged sociocultural expectations of African American women and female artists through their range of creative expression and their transgressive achievements. They need not be viewed as rivals competing for a prized place in the mainstream art world. Rather, these artists can be appreciated as allies in a capricious market, each demonstrating the vast scope of American art and increasing the exposure of an African American art presence. All of which begs the question: does the semantic distinction between self-taught and trained artists really matter?

While education and social class have tended to separate self-taught African American artists from those who received formal instruction, the American South acts as a unifying element in their artwork: the complex cultural and historical dynamics of Southern life are manifested in subject matter, medium, and critical reception. Stigmatic descriptions of the South as "intellectually backward," "impoverished," and "culturally isolated," mirror pervasive stereotypes of African Americans and loom large over these artists' bodies of work. Of course, there are many Souths—New, Old, Deep, rural, urban, black, white, etc.—and African American artists across the generations represent this multiplicity. What connects them all are their attempts to express or interpret the American South as a charted or imagined place.[19]

In the early twentieth century few African American women pursued artistic careers, let alone worked in the more traditionally masculine medium of sculpture. With a persistence and determination evident from childhood, Augusta Savage broke through the barriers of prejudice and became an advocate for racial and gender equality. Her deeply religious father disapproved of her "graven images" and nearly "whipped all the art out" of her—only changing his tune after her clay models were exhibited to great acclaim at a Palm Beach county fair in 1920.[20] This small success was enough to convince Savage to move to New York and advance her education.

While studying at the Cooper Union in 1923, Savage applied for and received a summer scholarship to attend the Fontainebleau school in Paris. But once the advisory committee became aware of her race—one member felt it would not "be wise to have a colored student"—they withdrew the award.[21] Devastated by the retraction, Savage publicly appealed the decision to the committee and to the press: "I wanted to go so badly that I worked night and day and bought new clothes so that I would look all right. I was much surprised when they told me that I was a little too dark. I am the only colored girl in my class at Cooper Union and the others look on me as though I were a freak. If I accomplish anything that is worth while they pat me on the back as though I were a little child."[22] Despite her protestations, the committee's decision held. In speaking out, Savage fought not only for her "own sake now, but for colored girls in the future."[23] Her courageous refusal to accept racism positioned her as a pioneering political and artistic activist.

Her resolve to champion her own merit and capacity and that of future generations led Savage to teaching, first at the eponymous Savage Studio of Arts and Crafts and later at the Harlem Community Art Center, which she eventually directed. "I have created nothing really beautiful, really lasting," Savage contended, "but if I can inspire one of these

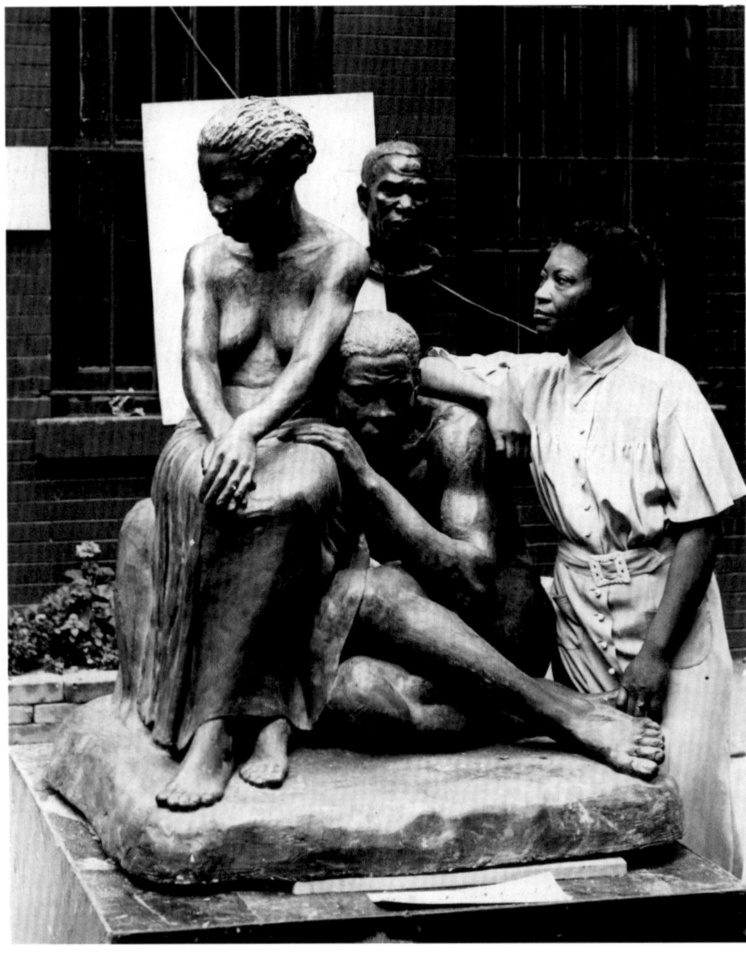

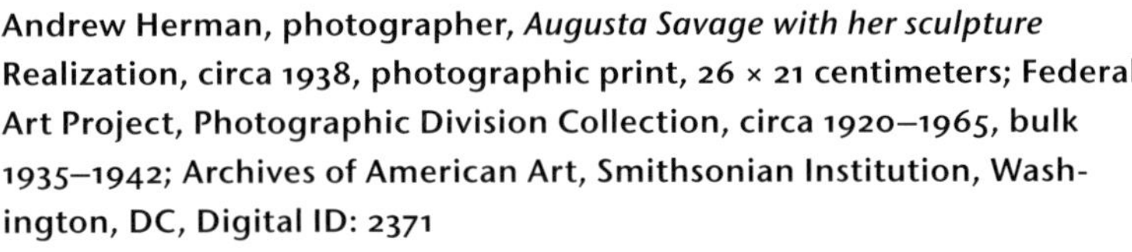

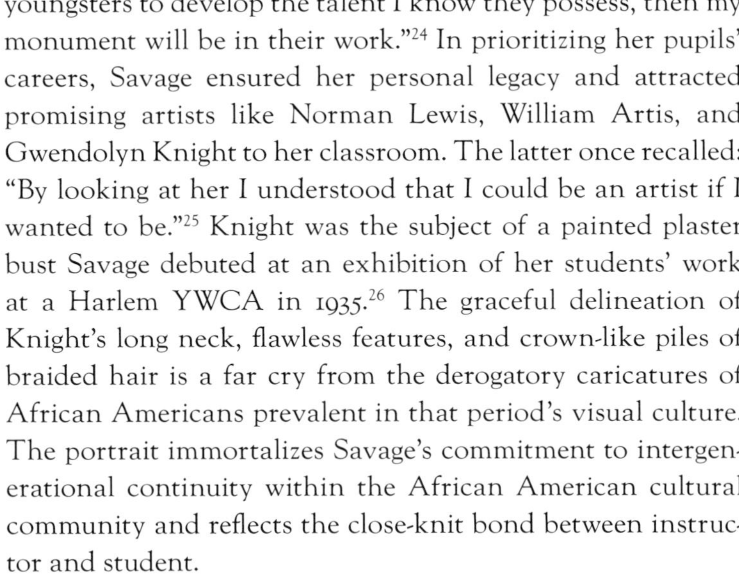

Andrew Herman, photographer, *Augusta Savage with her sculpture Realization*, circa 1938, photographic print, 26 × 21 centimeters; Federal Art Project, Photographic Division Collection, circa 1920–1965, bulk 1935–1942; Archives of American Art, Smithsonian Institution, Washington, DC, Digital ID: 2371

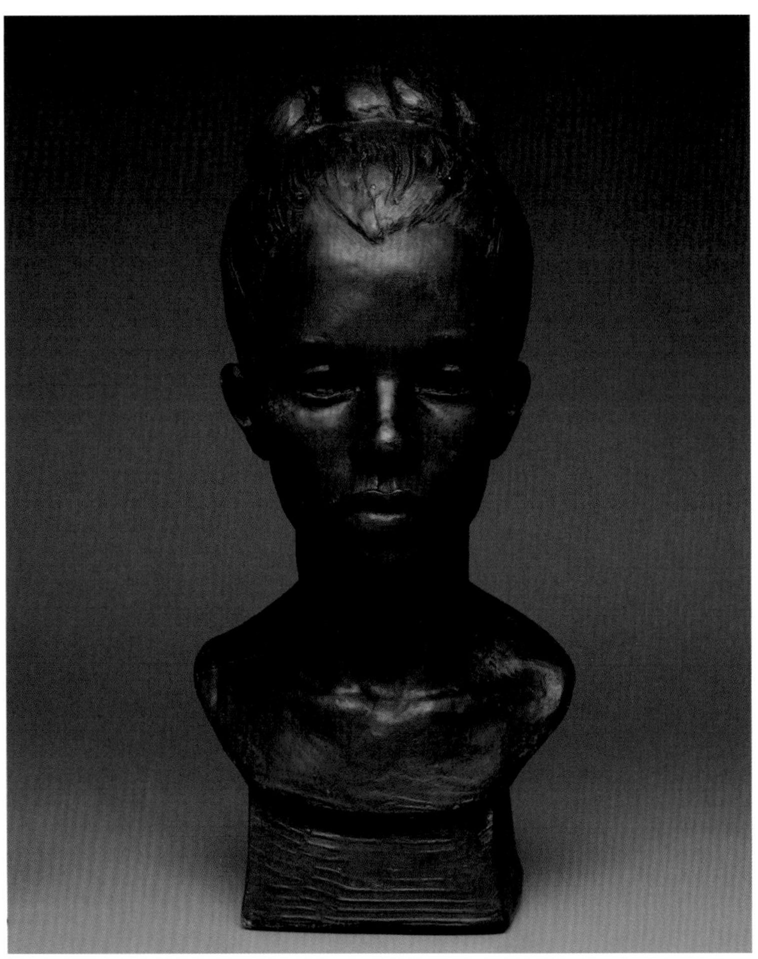

Augusta Christine Fells Savage (1892–1962), *Gwendolyn Knight*, circa 1938, painted plaster, 18½ × 8½ × 9 inches; Seattle Art Museum, Seattle, Washington; gift of Gwendolyn Knight Lawrence (2006.86)

youngsters to develop the talent I know they possess, then my monument will be in their work."[24] In prioritizing her pupils' careers, Savage ensured her personal legacy and attracted promising artists like Norman Lewis, William Artis, and Gwendolyn Knight to her classroom. The latter once recalled: "By looking at her I understood that I could be an artist if I wanted to be."[25] Knight was the subject of a painted plaster bust Savage debuted at an exhibition of her students' work at a Harlem YWCA in 1935.[26] The graceful delineation of Knight's long neck, flawless features, and crown-like piles of braided hair is a far cry from the derogatory caricatures of African Americans prevalent in that period's visual culture. The portrait immortalizes Savage's commitment to intergenerational continuity within the African American cultural community and reflects the close-knit bond between instructor and student.

As Savage devoted more time to arts education, her production dwindled. One art historian estimated that Savage created around seventy works, but only a few are extant.[27] This scarcity is partially due to the fragile nature of her sculptures, many of which were composed of cheaper materials such as plaster, soap, and wax, the routine casting of bronze being cost-prohibitive.[28] Savage's best known work, *Gamin*, earned her a coveted Julius Rosenwald Fellowship, which enabled her to finally study abroad in Paris. The small bust takes its title from the French word for "street urchin" and depicts a jaunty—albeit slightly disheveled—young boy. Long thought to be a portrait of the artist's nephew, *Gamin* exists in a liminal space between individual portrait and generic type. Exhibited in 1930 at the Harmon Foundation, *Gamin* embodied Alain Locke's call for the artistic representation of modern African Americans, rather than outdated stereotypes.[29] At the same

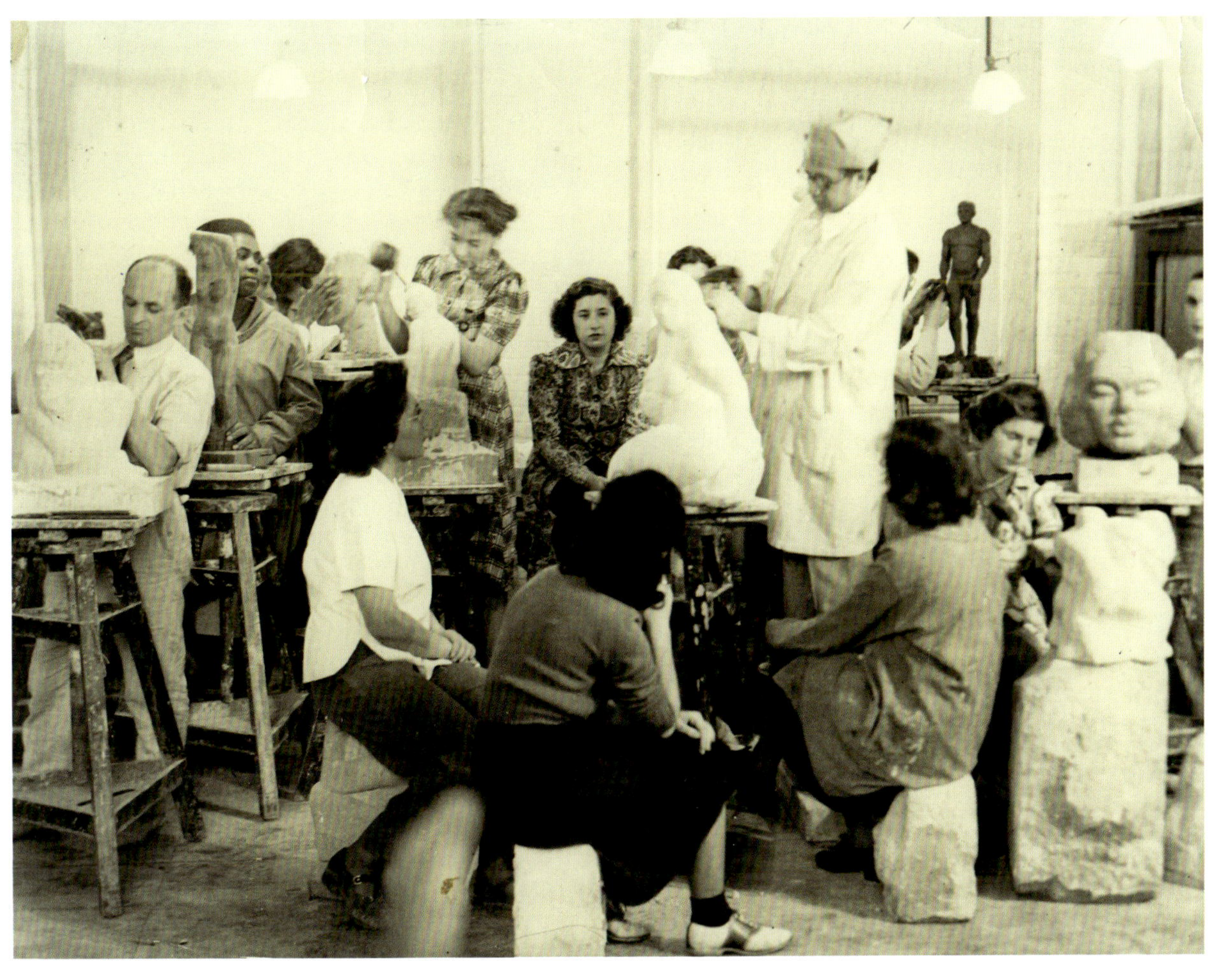

Selma Burke, Columbia University, 1939, photographic print; University Photograph Collection, Winston-Salem State University Archives at C. G. O'Kelly Library, Winston-Salem, North Carolina

time, however, *Gamin* reflects Savage's formal training and emulation of Western art. She disagreed with Locke's notion that African American artists should look for an artistic legacy in African art, stating in 1936: "We have had the same cultural background, the same system, and the same standard of beauty as white Americans."[30] Although Savage claimed that nurturing the creativity of young African Americans would be her greatest achievement, her own artwork, like *Gamin*, offered the black community—and the predominately white art market—positive portrayals of African Americans.

Education was paramount to Selma Burke's life and work as well. The North Carolina sculptor taught with Savage at the Harlem Community Art Center before founding her own schools in New York and Pittsburgh. The color of her skin and the objections of her parents precluded an arts education in the South; it was only after obtaining a nursing degree that she enrolled at Columbia University for graduate studies in fine arts. Burke declared that she "wanted to be a lady but also an artist," an acknowledgment of the male bias in her new field.[31] Favoring wood and limestone, Burke relied on her chosen materials' intrinsic shape to release a subject from its confinement. This is apparent in *Woman Holding Sheaf of Wheat*, in which the grain and form of the wood flows organically into the figure's contrapposto stance.

While the emotional intensity of Burke's art drew critical acclaim, she strove to become "a shining beacon" for African American children and to rectify the educational inequity she had endured in the segregated South.[32] Firmly believing that art is "a great leveller of class and race lines," Burke advocated arts education as a path to racial equality; at her New York academy, the student population was over two-thirds white.[33] When the Women's Caucus for Art developed an annual award for artistic excellence, Loïs Jones nominated Burke, not only to endorse Burke's achievements, but in a deliberate effort to see women of color represented. Disheartened by the entrenched institutional racial bias she had experienced in the arts, Jones did not think that "the people at the Metropolitan Museum had ever heard of" Burke.[34] Burke received the inaugural award alongside Georgia O'Keeffe, Louise Berliawsky Nevelson, and Isabel Bishop in 1970.

Loïs Jones, Augusta Savage, and Selma Burke overcame staggering odds to succeed as students, educators, and practicing artists in the nation's most sophisticated urban art centers. Though they enjoyed the benefits of formal art training, the disadvantages of race and gender were inescapable impediments to commensurate participation in the complex economic market—a plight they shared with their self-taught counterparts. Southern self-taught artists of both sexes were frequently exploited by unscrupulous "benefactors," patrons, and promoters who ostensibly sought to advance these artists' creative careers and improve their practical circumstances.

At Melrose Plantation in Louisiana, Clementine Hunter initially gave away her paintings, but later wisely began charging visitors an admission fee "to look." She eventually started selling her "pictures" to the scores of curious, insistent customers who refused to "go away unless I would."[35] In North Carolina, Minnie Evans's job as gatekeeper at a popular tourist attraction provided a steady flow of buyers for her drawings, priced at a mere fifty cents.[36] Instances like these demonstrate how enterprising self-taught artists gradually came to realize their art's economic worth. Hunter was reluctant to charge visitors for her paintings, believing them to be gifts from God, and she came to understand the inherent hypocrisy and profiteering of the commercial marketplace. Elite consumerist desire for an "authentic" or "original" work of art—ideally acquired on the cheap—eliminates living makers from the equation, discounting their need to earn a decent wage or be fairly compensated for their talents. Many of the earliest collectors of self-taught African American art were "white, educated, and affluent," connoting an imbalance rooted in race.[37] Yet when asked about their white patrons or collectors, the artists readily acknowledged their dependence on advocates with marketplace expertise. Furthermore, they valued the personal relationships such partnerships generated. Evans introduced her friend and representative Nina Starr as "president of my pictures in New York," and Hunter is buried in a mausoleum next to her champion Francois Mignon, in testament to their lasting friendship.[38]

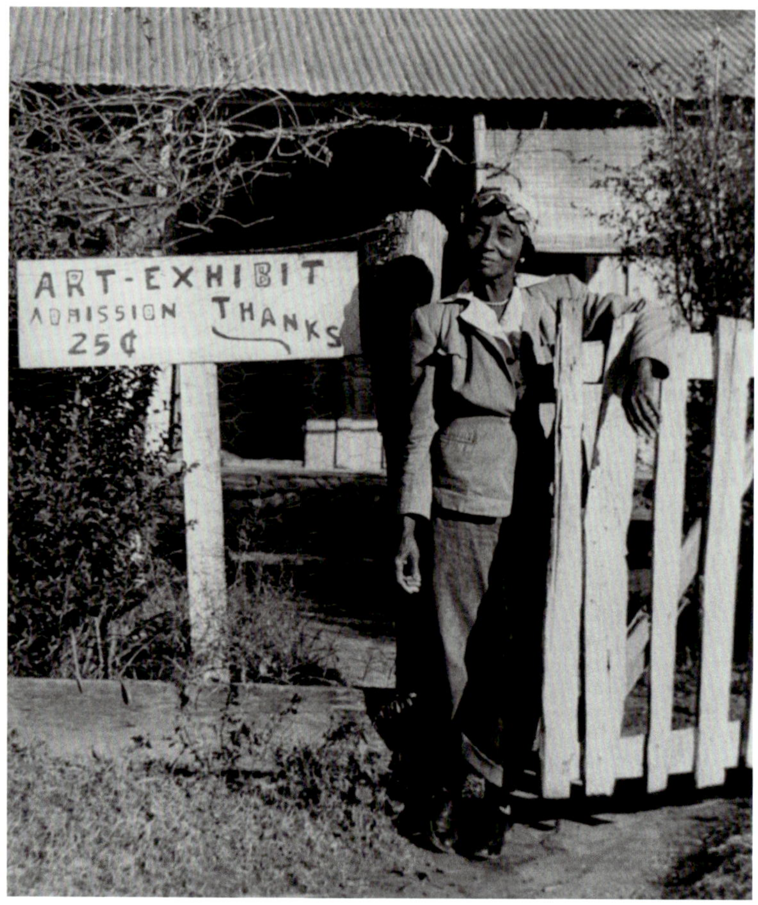

Clementine Hunter, photographed outside her studio, Melrose, Louisiana; Northwestern State University of Louisiana, Watson Memorial Library, Cammie G. Henry Research Center (Mildred Hart Bailey Collection, Scrapbook 1), Natchitoches, Louisiana

This dynamic is further complicated when galleries and museums impose their standards on self-taught artists. Monographic exhibitions tend to leverage such artists' marginalization, emphasizing their works' "naive" essence and production outside conventional traditions. Critics reviewing Hunter's first major exhibition, held in 1952 at the Saturday Gallery in St. Louis, described the painter as "an authentic primitive" and praised her works' "child-like charm."[39] A press release for the same show recast Hunter's trajectory, exaggerating the role that Carmelite "Cammie" Garrett Henry, the white owner of Melrose Plantation, had played in Hunter's development.[40] This type of semantic segregation under the guise of celebration is further heightened when race inhibits artists' full participation in the marketplace.[41] When Louisiana's Northwestern State College mounted a solo show of her work in 1955, the institution prohibited Hunter from viewing the exhibition during public operating hours.[42]

Conversely, exhibitions of works by self-taught African American artists can signify a rupture in the canonical status quo.[43] The 1975 Whitney Museum of American Art presentation of fifty-six pieces by Evans marks such a schism. As art historian Katherine Jentleson has noted, the show coincided with the Whitney's ongoing reevaluation of its holdings, an examination aimed at increasing diversity in light of burgeoning interest in works by self-taught artists.[44] Evans's exhibition challenged the contemporary institutional preponderance of white male artists by highlighting deficits in an established museum's collection.[45]

Formally trained African American female artists encountered similar racial barriers when attempting to break into museums. When the Rhode Island School of Design invited alumna and sculptor Nancy Elizabeth Prophet to participate in a local exhibition with the proviso that she decline attending the whites-only opening reception, she refused and withdrew her piece.[46] During her time on the faculty of Dillard University in the 1940s, Loïs Jones's former pupil Elizabeth Catlett tried to take her students to the Isaac Delgado Museum (now the New Orleans Museum of Art), but a segregated park barred the way to the institution. Undeterred, Catlett bused her students to the museum's front door when the museum was closed to the public.[47]

Well into the twentieth century, the bifurcation of race and gender continued to hinder African American women's artistic elevation. Gwendolyn Knight's activity and acclaim were often superseded by the notoriety of her husband, Jacob Lawrence. Although Knight seemed not to resent his fame, she did offer some insight into the complex dynamic: "I think that is the way it is or has been for a lot of women artists.... I don't think that any black woman artist is known the way the black male artists are known."[48] She also proposed that women artists needed a certain "kind of temperament" to succeed, noting that while her peers Catlett and Jones had "that sort of real drive," she did not.[49] Knight echoed early-twentieth-century New Negro movement ideology that privileged racial over sexual equality. Whether the artist is self-taught or trained, when it comes to exhibitions and museum relations, gender tends to be subsumed by race.

In the face of these obstacles, Jones and her contemporaries devised alternative means for countering systemic racism. Inspired by her time abroad in the French ateliers, Jones orchestrated her own art conclave in Washington, DC, the Little Paris Group, comprising African American painters, including Alma Thomas. Every spring beginning in 1946, the

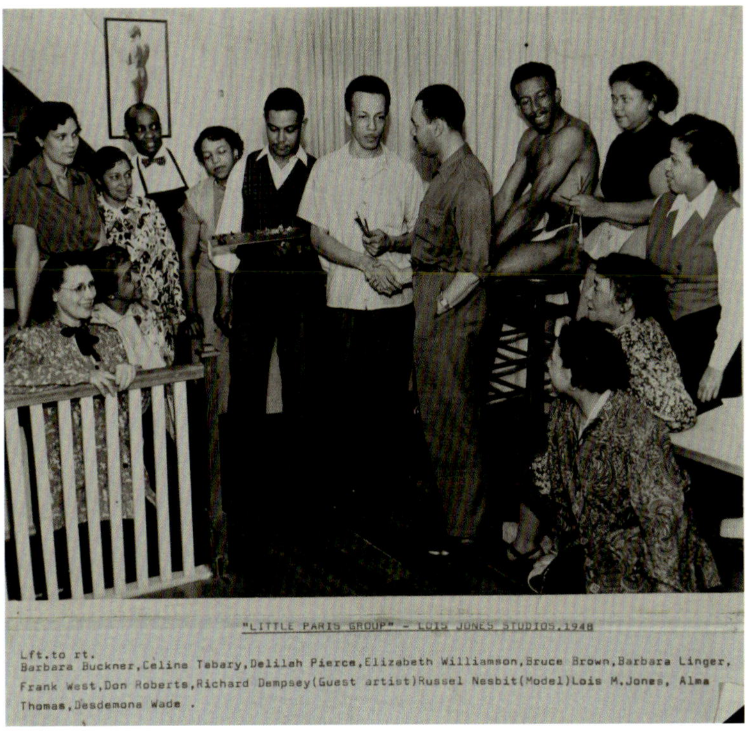

Little Paris Group in Loïs Jones' studio, 1948, photographic print, 21 × 26 centimeters; Alma Thomas Papers, 1894–2000, bulk 1936–1982; Archives of American Art, Smithsonian Institution, Washington, DC, Digital ID: 7393

group hosted an exhibition at Inspiration House, its leased residence, which became one of the few venues in the city where African American artists could showcase their work.[50] Participation in the club's activities encouraged Thomas—who was by then in her sixties—to continue painting, and ultimately motivated her to enroll in classes at American University. Exposure to new aesthetic philosophies and techniques, such as Cubism and Abstract Expressionism, led Thomas to abandon her early realistic style in favor of more modern expression, as evidenced in the Cubist-inspired *Still Life with Mandolin*.

The year 1972 marked a milestone in Thomas's life—and in the history of American art—when the Whitney Museum mounted a solo show of the eighty-year-old painter's work, making her the first African American woman to achieve such an honor. Empowered by the civil rights and women's liberation movements, Thomas rebelled against expectations that her work reflect both her race and gender.[51] She believed that "creative art is for all time and is therefore independent of time…of age, race, and nationality," and found freedom in abstraction. Influenced by Color Field and minimalist painting, she developed "her own personal style," characterized by sublime washes or quivering dabs of color.[52] This was

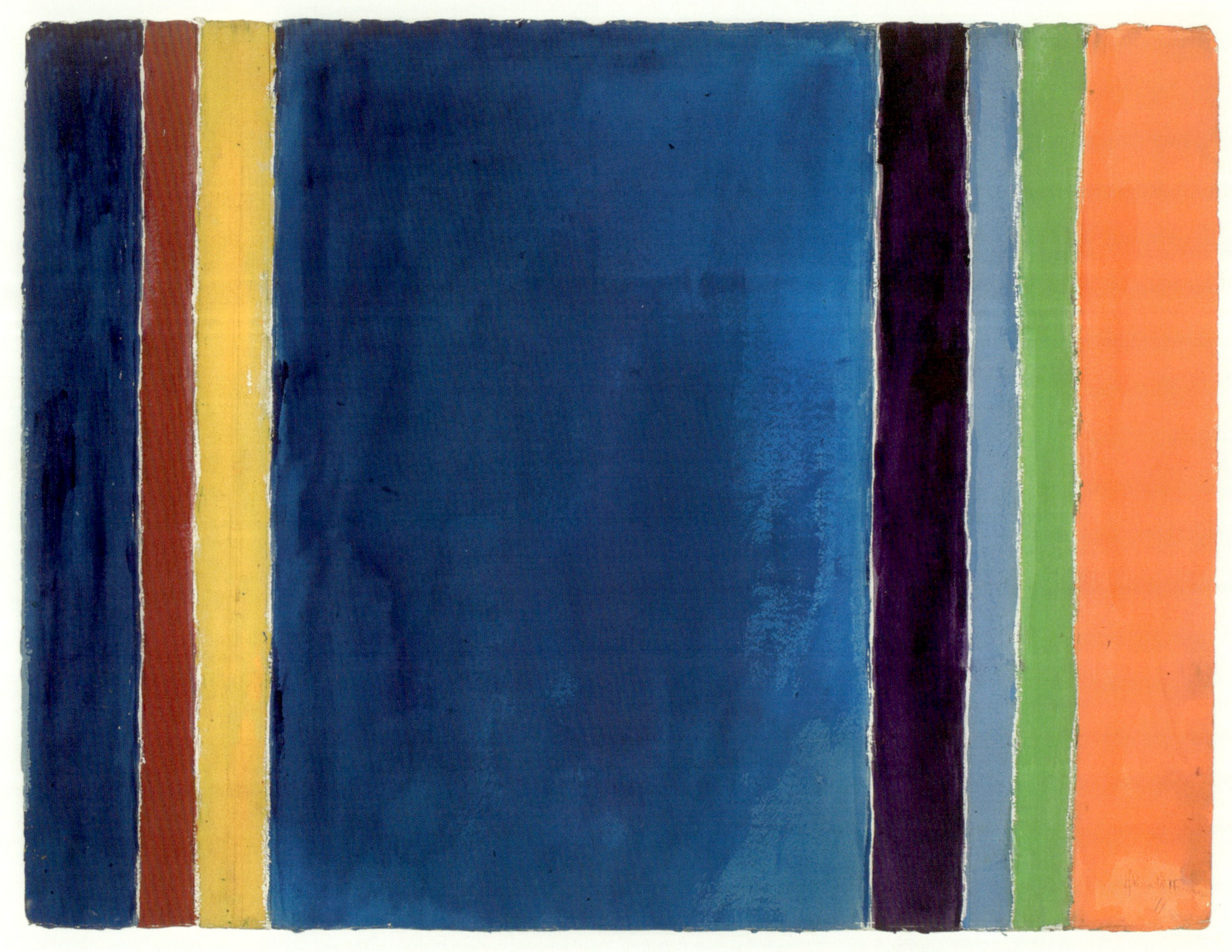

Alma Woodsey Thomas (1891–1978), *Blue Ground Stripe*, 1971, acrylic and watercolor on paper, 22½ × 29⅞ inches

a bold move for the equally bold artist at a time when the global audience was in thrall to the machoism of Abstract Expressionism. Such gender bias did not dissuade Thomas, who recounted that "everybody says I paint like a man anyway."[53]

Thomas's long-standing connections to Howard University and her principal role in the establishment of the integrated Barnett-Aden Gallery helped her succeed where other African American artists had failed. Prior to Thomas's 1972 Whitney exhibition, members of the Black Emergency Cultural Coalition met with the museum's director, John I. H. Baur, to discuss ways to promote African American contributions in an institution devoted to the entirety of American art. However, the coalition's rhetoric prioritized black men over black women, reiterating earlier incarnations of gender exclusionary practices for the benefit of advancing race. Around the same time African American multimedia artist Faith Jones Ringgold began protesting the Whitney's persistent omission of women of color in exhibitions, in the collection, and on the curatorial staff. As a result of these growing cultural pressures, leading museums like the Whitney acknowledged—and sought to amend—the predominance of urban, white, male artists in their holdings. The attention accorded to Thomas and Evans, in 1972 and 1975, respectively, was a direct result of institutional assessments that offered—if only for a moment—the possibility of professional equality. It is impossible to overstate the significance of Thomas's exhibition. Recalling her childhood in segregated Georgia, she noted that "one of the things we couldn't do was go into museums, let alone think of hanging our pictures there. My, times have changed. Just look at me now."[54] Sadly, Thomas's hard-won ascendancy waned for thirty years following her death. It was only after the nation's first black president selected two of her paintings to hang in the White House that interest in her work was resurrected.[55]

Thomas's relative obscurity after a triumphant major exhibition underscores the perseverant prejudices that have impeded countless African American female artists' advancement. While present-day rediscoveries of artists like Thomas can bear witness to these women's marginalization, they have little power to remedy the root of the problem: the critical registers that shape reception.[56] To do that would require acknowledgment of the fallacies and biases inherent in the mainstream art world. Should the canon of American art be rewritten to incorporate artists such as Loïs Jones, Augusta Savage, Selma Burke, Minnie Evans, Clementine Hunter, and Alma Thomas? Would such a revision diminish the power of their work or the remarkable circumstances of its creation? Would it threaten the legacies of their male or white counterparts? The women artists examined here, whether self-taught or trained, refused to let hegemonic hierarchies revoke or dictate their creative output. And in so doing, they rebelled against their "contrary instincts" to forge alternative avenues of self-expression.

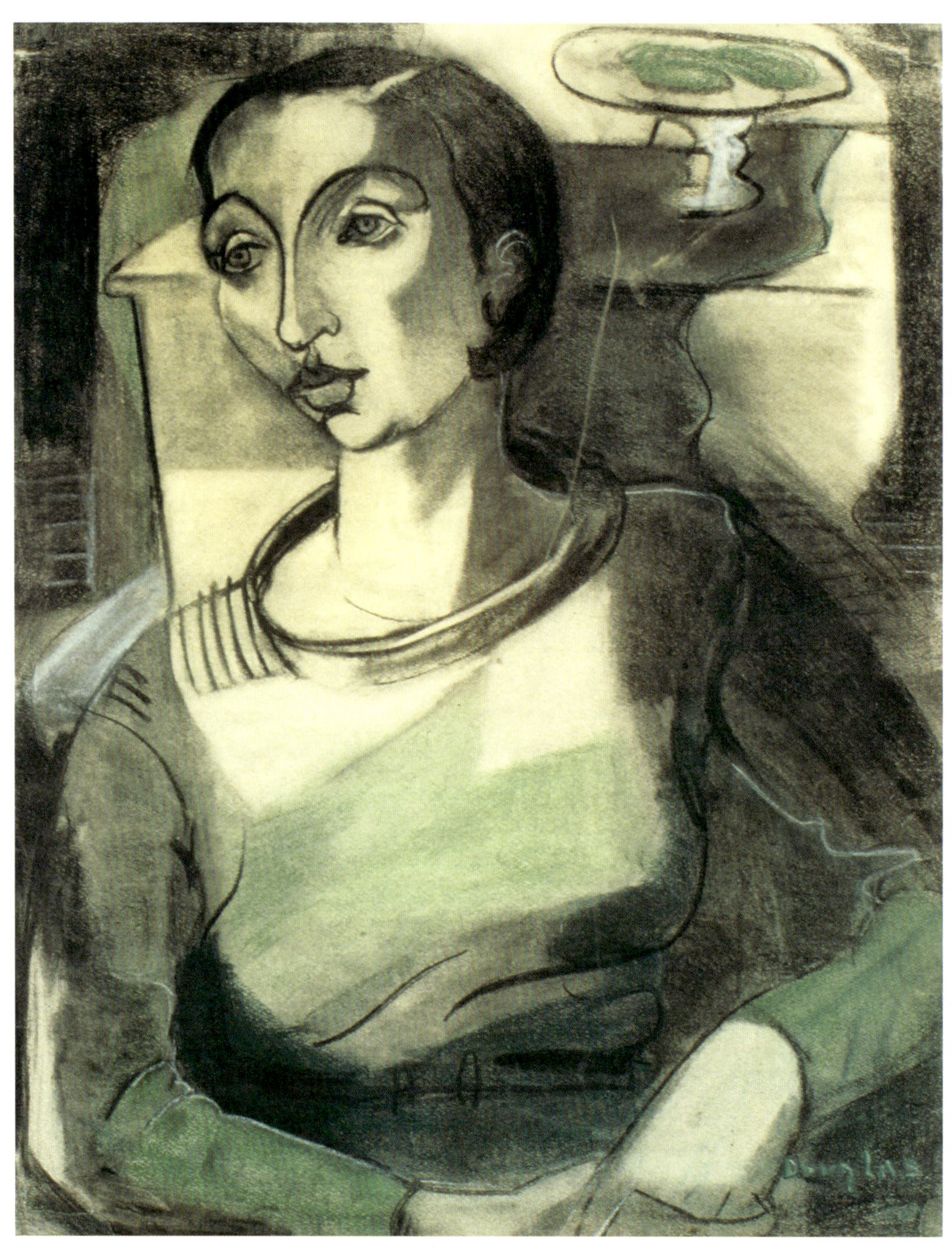

Laura Glenn Douglas (1896–1962), *Woman in Green*, circa 1933, charcoal and pastel on paper, 24⅝ × 19 inches; courtesy of the South Carolina State Museum, Columbia, South Carolina

EYES WIDE OPEN

MODERNIST WOMEN ARTISTS IN THE SOUTH

DANIEL BELASCO

Like Henry Miller, Vladimir Nabokov, and Jack Kerouac, French philosopher Simone de Beauvoir journeyed across a rapidly modernizing mid-twentieth-century America. During her four-month coast-to-coast lecture tour in 1947, Beauvoir kept a detailed journal, paying special attention to the lives and images of American women she met. Her observations were published in the travelogue *America Day by Day* and partly inspired her monumental study *The Second Sex*. The intellectual architect of second-wave feminism, Beauvoir provides a critical position from which to begin an evaluation of female modern artists in the South.

Beauvoir logged hundreds of miles in the region, speaking in Virginia, Louisiana, and Texas, recording her encounters with whites and blacks at bus stations, jazz clubs, and college campuses. She described these experiences in prose stylistically evocative of celebrated writer James Agee, blending journalistic detail and political commentary. An antiracist activist, she dedicated *America Day by Day* to Richard Wright, the Mississippi native and acclaimed African American author of *Native Son* and *Black Boy*, and his wife, Ellen. Beauvoir did not hide her ire toward segregation and its effects; she wrote of the South: "Tragic earth, human earth, where life is a drama and not a social process managed by experts."[1] Her distinction between "drama" and "social process" contrasted nineteenth-century ideals of Southern society with those of modern technocracy. The modernist voice of William Faulkner, the social realist reportage of Erskine Caldwell, the vernacular culture of African Americans, and the flashy urbanism of the New South could not fully portray the internal moral and aesthetic struggle in Southern life and art, Beauvoir asserted. Southern artists—male or female, black or white—who felt a kinship with the universalist values of existentialism and modernism inevitably opposed the constraints of the storytelling culture of their region.

Beauvoir introduced gender into the equation by comparing the widespread anger of middle-class white and poor black women with the aristocratic airs of advantaged college students. She recoiled from the attitude expressed by Randolph-Macon Woman's College undergraduates that being unmarried was a "defect." And she lamented the willingness of young women to adhere to the traditional caste system, as noted by one of the institution's more "democratic" professors. "It is impossible to eradicate such deep-seated prejudice," Beauvoir quoted the teacher. "These young minds are already made up."[2] Beauvoir hardly considered that colleges like Randolph-Macon were havens for open-minded young women in the South seeking an education in the arts. She identified the need for independent voices but did not perceive the diffuse activities of a small number of Southern women who embraced modernism and its promotion of individual subjectivity through abstract art. The topic of modernism and Southern women artists remains little explored to this day. The very category of Southern female modern artists clusters so many marginal identities that it explodes binary thinking. The artists at this intersection, largely invisible to Beauvoir, offer a powerful lens through which to explore the crisis of self-expression faced by all Americans eager to cast off the old myths and develop new forms of transcendent subjectivity.

Southern women modern artists can be principally separated into two generations: those born in the late-nineteenth century, and those born in the first decades of the twentieth. Across these divides, Southern women overcame low expectations of their ability to make fine art of consequence. They were often born to money and benefited from familial status and racial privilege. Yet, as Baltimore Museum of Art director Adelyn Dohme Breeskin explained in a 1955 lecture, they also resented the assumption that "the Southern gentlewoman, generally speaking, prefers to be the power behind the throne rather than the outright acknowledged ruler of the roost."[3] Some women artists lived rather conventional bourgeois lifestyles, while others became bohemian free spirits.[4] Many

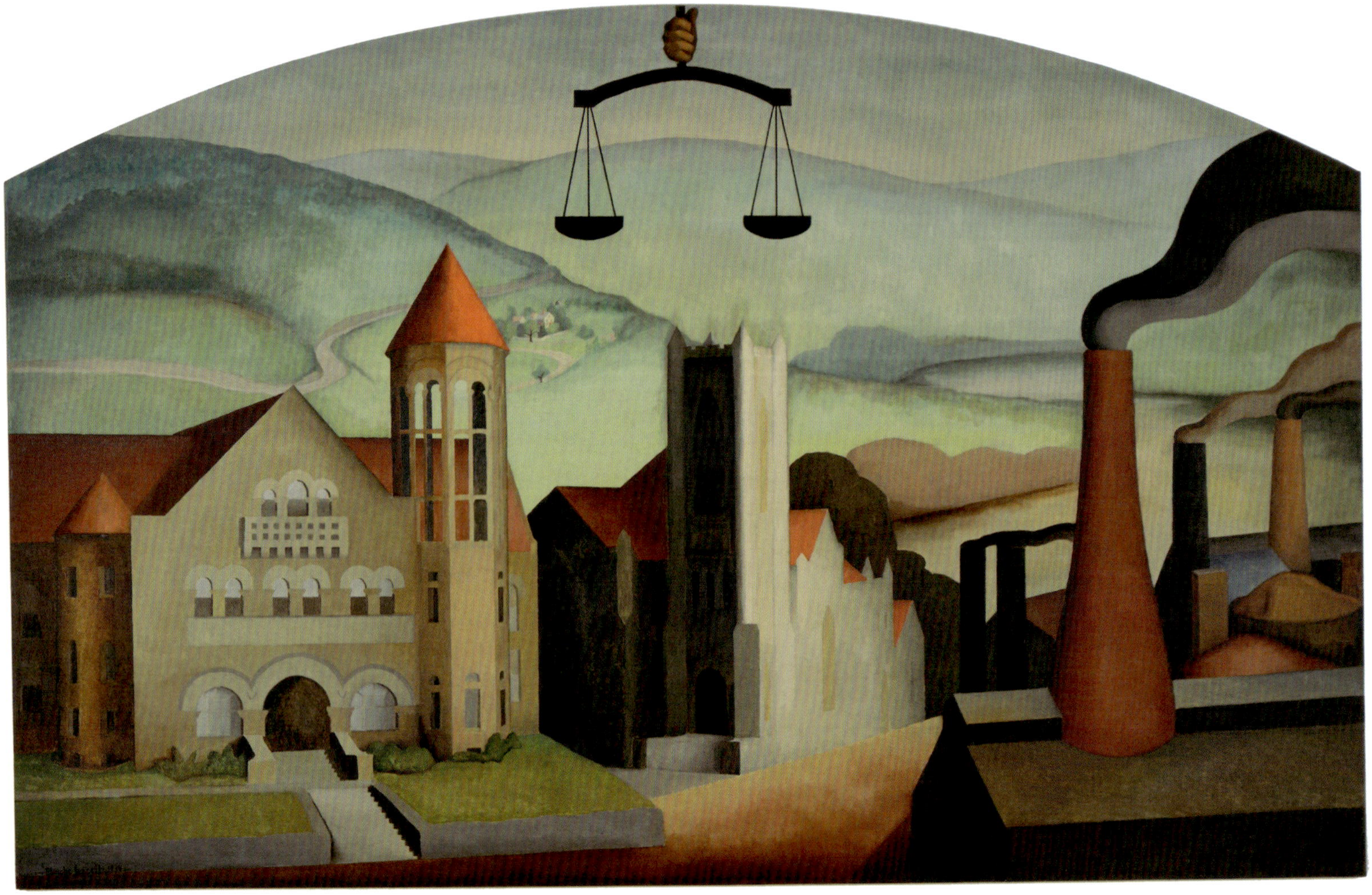

Nettie Blanche Lazzell (1878–1956), *Justice*, 1934, oil on canvas, 95 × 150 inches; courtesy of the Art Museum of West Virginia University, Morgantown, West Virginia

chose to remain unmarried and pursue their art self-sufficiently, though some found supportive husbands.

Above all, aesthetic quality was paramount for achieving equality, and they tirelessly worked to excel as *artists*—not as women artists. "We want to speak to eyes and ears wide open and without prejudice, an audience that asks simply— is it good—not, was it done by a woman?" stated Alabama painter Anne Goldthwaite in 1934.[5] Four decades later the New Orleans modernist Ida Rittenberg Kohlmeyer regretted that women still had to overcome historical and personal sexism resulting from discriminatory practices as well as their own "deficiencies and mediocrity": "With tensions relaxing for women artists, one quickly forgets the Olympian efforts which were required to sustain them against society's unrelenting demands, lack of encouragement and opportunity, unfair competitive treatment, persistent fall-out from male chauvinism plus the energy, dedication, and zeal implicit in a

creative life."[6] Both generations necessarily became feminists, whether by word or by deed.

≠

The first generation of Southern women modern artists participated in the development of the New South. Energized by the quickening of cultural activity in their region, a number of Southern women found their artistic voices in local schools and then sought further professional training at established art schools in the Northeast, studying at the Art Students League in New York City and spending summers at colonies in Old Lyme, Connecticut; Provincetown and Gloucester, Massachusetts; and Shinnecock and Woodstock, New York. The ambitious and affluent also traveled to Paris between the 1890s and the 1920s—the period of the avant-garde and the formation of the School of Paris—learning modernism firsthand in French academies and studios.[7] Many of these artists came to reject Impressionism and Tonalism as too imprecise to capture the new structural vision of contemporary life. Whether or not they ventured abroad, most preferred to live and work in urban centers such as New York, Philadelphia, or Washington, DC, routinely returning to their home states to visit family, gain inspiration, and complete commissions. In so doing, they became apostles for modernism, introducing new styles to the South through their roles as teachers and independent artists.[8]

Born on a farm in West Virginia, Blanche Lazzell graduated from West Virginia University with a degree in fine arts in 1905 before moving to New York in 1907 and enrolling at the Art Students League.[9] She first studied in Paris in 1912 and then worked in Provincetown, where she became an early adopter of modernist woodblock printmaking and oil painting. While spending the summer of 1917 in Woodstock, Lazzell painted *White Peonies and Red Rose*. This still life depiction of three vessels and four flowers on a counter features almost pointillist arrangements of wide brushstrokes. The close tonal harmonies and the modeling of distinct objects evince little of the planar Cubism that she later learned from Fernand Léger, André Lhote, and Albert Gleizes after her return to Paris in 1923. Lazzell was among America's first modern artists and one of a handful of Southern women who painted murals in the federal art programs. Her Public Works of Art Project mural *Justice*—executed in 1934 for the Monongalia County, West Virginia, courthouse—coolly choreographs architectural spaces.[10] Stylistically, Lazzell embodied the first generation's oscillation between representation and Cubist construction.

Anne Goldthwaite can be considered the other major figure of this early generation. A native of Montgomery, Alabama, Goldthwaite became a nationally recognized painter and printmaker. Unlike Lazzell, she never accepted Cubism, despite prolonged encounters with leading modernists. During a 1906 Parisian sojourn, Goldthwaite met Gertrude Stein and studied with Charles Guérin. Upon her return, she spent most of her professional career in New York, teaching at the Art Students League, exhibiting in the Armory Show in 1913, and cofounding the New York Society of Women Artists in 1925. While a fixture in that city's vibrant art scene, she maintained close ties to her home state, returning many summers to paint genre pictures, portraits, and landscapes. She executed two federal Section of Fine Arts murals in Alabama: *The Road to Tuskegee* in Tuskegee (1937) and *The Letter Box* in Atmore (1938). Goldthwaite's *Three Figures*, featuring two women and an infant, displays similar notational brushwork as *The Letter Box*, whereas her elegant portrait of *Frances Greene Nix* appears

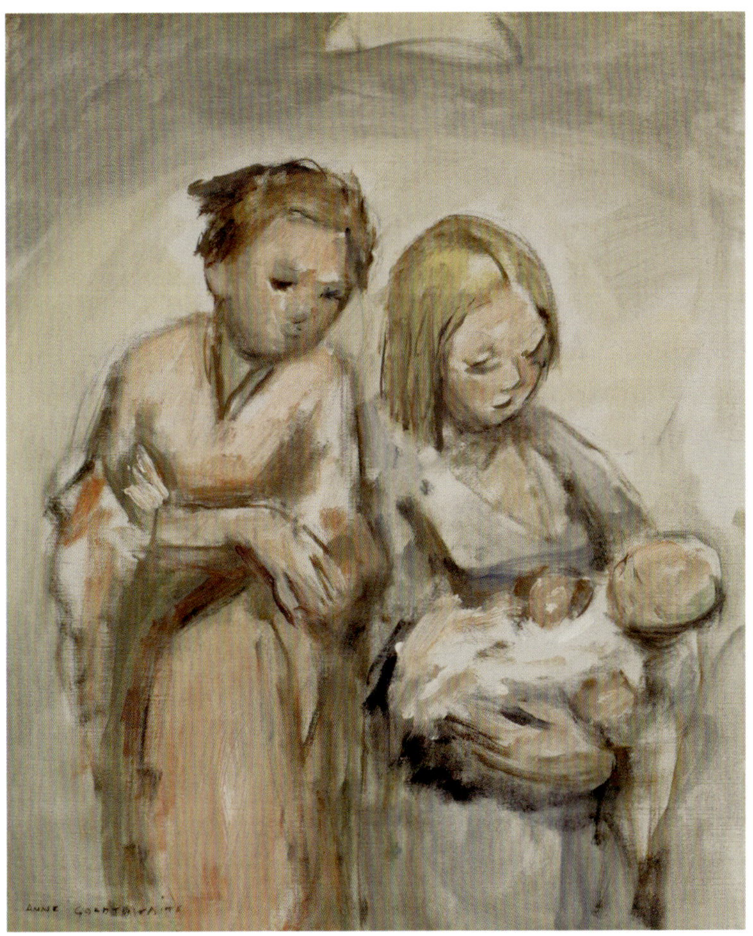

Anne Wilson Goldthwaite (1869–1944), *Three Figures*, oil on canvas, 20 × 16 inches

more finished—and appropriate for a fashionable subject who would later become director of the Montgomery Museum of Fine Arts. Though Goldthwaite did not innovate formally, her advocacy for women's rights and forthright depictions of liberated women made her an important figure in advancing progressive ideals in contemporary art.[11]

Like Lazzell and Goldthwaite, Laura Glenn Douglas studied in Europe and later executed a mural under the auspices of the Federal Art Project. Born in Winnsboro, South Carolina, Douglas matriculated at the Presbyterian College for Women in nearby Columbia and at the Corcoran School of Art in Washington, DC, before moving to New York in 1925 and studying at the Art Students League. From 1927 to 1935 Douglas painted in Paris with Fernand Léger and in Munich with Hans Hofmann. She exhibited widely in France before resettling in South Carolina. Works like *Symphony No. 2, Charleston* demonstrate a hybrid of local subject matter and Expressionist composition. In 1942 Douglas created a Section of Fine Arts mural, *Theme of the South*, depicting stereotypes

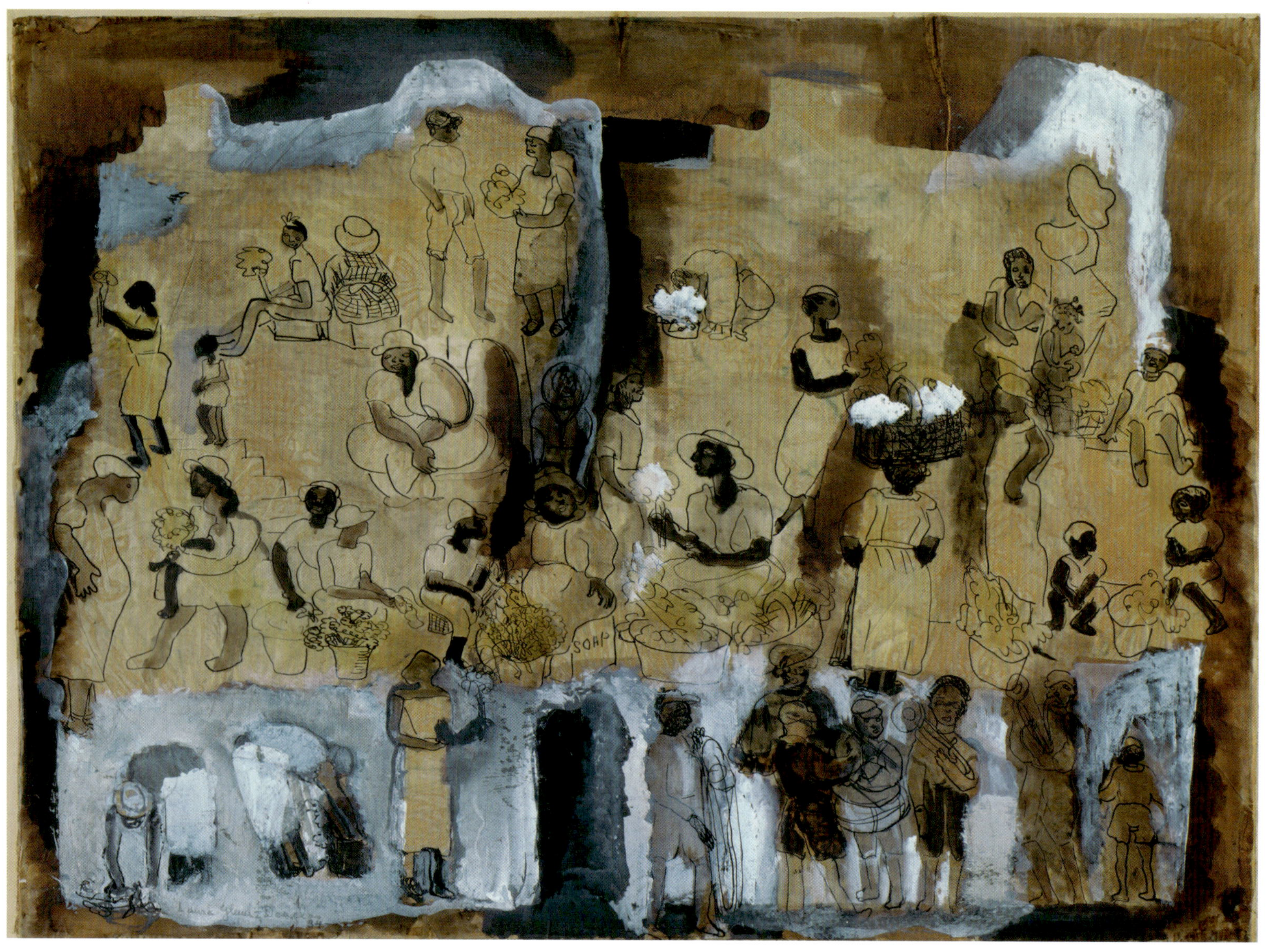

Laura Glenn Douglas (1896–1962), *Symphony No. 2, Charleston*, 1934, gouache and ink on paper, 17¾ × 23⅝ inches; acquired 1942; the Phillips Collection, Washington, DC

of white workers and black laborers, in the post office of Camilla, Georgia. She then moved to Washington, DC, and began teaching at the Phillips Collection, becoming known as one of "the real moderns in Washington," if a somewhat conservative one who continued to paint regionalist subjects on annual trips south.[12]

Josephine Crawford learned Cubism firsthand in Paris before emerging as one of the style's first practitioners in the South in the 1920s.[13] Born in New Orleans, Crawford did not undertake formal instruction until 1926, when, at the age of forty-seven, she began classes at the Arts and Crafts Club in the French Quarter. Following a year's study in Paris with Lhote in 1927, she returned to her hometown. There, she helped consolidate what may have been the first Southern modern art scene. Activity centered on the Arts and Crafts Club, a hub of progressive cultural activity in the city that attracted painters Will Henry Stevens, Paul Ninas, and Jane Smith Ninas; photographer Walker Evans; and other artists who offered subjective alternatives to regionalism. Her own work included Cubist still lifes with flat geometric planes and incisive portraits of diverse members of New Orleans society. Crawford, along with Lazzell, Goldthwaite, and Douglas,

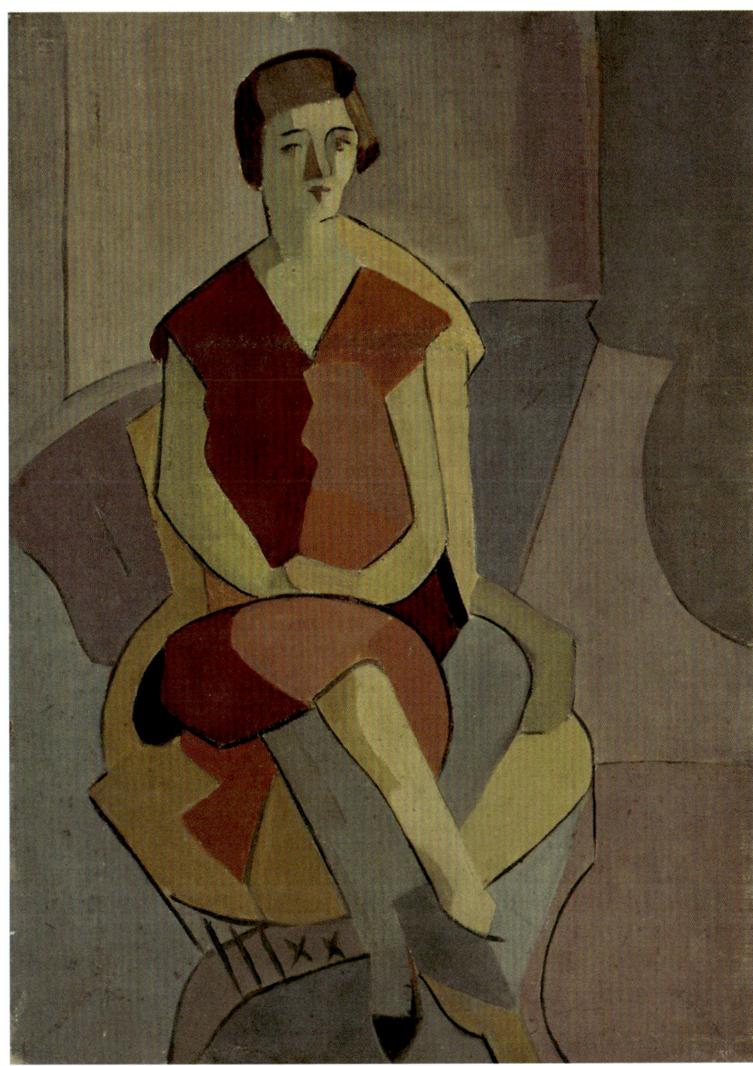

Josephine Marien Crawford (1878–1952), *Full length view of Mrs. Jean Martin seated,* oil on canvas, 19 × 13¼ inches; the Historic New Orleans Collection, New Orleans, Louisiana; bequest of Charles C. Crawford, 1978.23.30

planted the seeds of a homegrown Southern modernism that took root in the 1930s and flowered in subsequent decades.

The second generation of Southern women modern artists—those born in the early twentieth century—was more ethnically diverse than its predecessor and included women of African American, Jewish, and other backgrounds. They came from middle- and upper-class families and did not need to travel to Europe to pursue advanced art education, World War II having made such journeys impossible. The importance of Southern institutions of higher education to this generation cannot be overstated. Little in mainstream culture encouraged women to excel in the visual arts beyond producing practical handicrafts or visionary folk art. Only colleges and universities provided opportunities for professional development in the arts. Once larger numbers of women began teaching in Southern degree-granting art programs in the 1920s, they were able to mentor young women and establish new female-to-female lineages that would expand what was once an exclusively male and white heritage. Thanks in part to the accomplishments of their forerunners, by the 1930s and 1940s several Southern cities—notably Washington, DC, New Orleans, and Charleston—contained the requisite networks of liberal arts schools, risk-taking galleries, and enlightened patrons to incubate local modernisms.

In Washington during the 1940s and 1950s, Laura Douglas exhibited her still lifes and other subjects in exhibitions of contemporary art at the Corcoran Gallery of Art and the integrated Barnett-Aden Gallery alongside works by Loïs Mailou Jones and Céline Tabary. Because of her exposure to European modernism, Douglas perhaps felt some kinship with the younger women. Jones, an African American born in Boston, had also studied in Paris, having spent 1937 at the Académie Julian, where she met the French-born Tabary. Jones and Tabary moved to Washington the next year and in 1945 began leading art classes in a studio located on the top floor of the house they shared.[14] Modeled after French ateliers, the Little Paris Group was a pioneering artist affiliation made up primarily of African Americans and included many women, some of whom were art teachers with ties to Howard University, where Jones had taught since 1930.[15] Jones typically painted in a realist style, but she occasionally negotiated the intersection of Western modernism and African ritual objects, as seen in her paintings *Africa* and *Les Fétiches,* dating to 1935 and 1938, respectively.

After World War II the nation's capital became the Southern center for African American women artists painting in international modern styles. Alma Thomas bridged the Little Paris Group and modernist abstraction. The Georgia native was the first graduate of Howard's art department in 1924 and taught art in a District junior high school for decades. Initially she painted in an accomplished representational style, as in *Still Life with Mandolin,* executed in the 1950s. Eager to advance, Thomas continued her education at American University, taking classes with abstract painter Jacob Kainen and evolving from academic approaches to Abstract Expressionism and then Minimalism. A 1958 *Ebony* magazine article noted that African American artists were moving away from "Negro subject matter" and into abstraction because of greater social integration.[16] Thomas's later work, like the vibrant *Blue Ground Stripe,* successfully blended Fauvism and

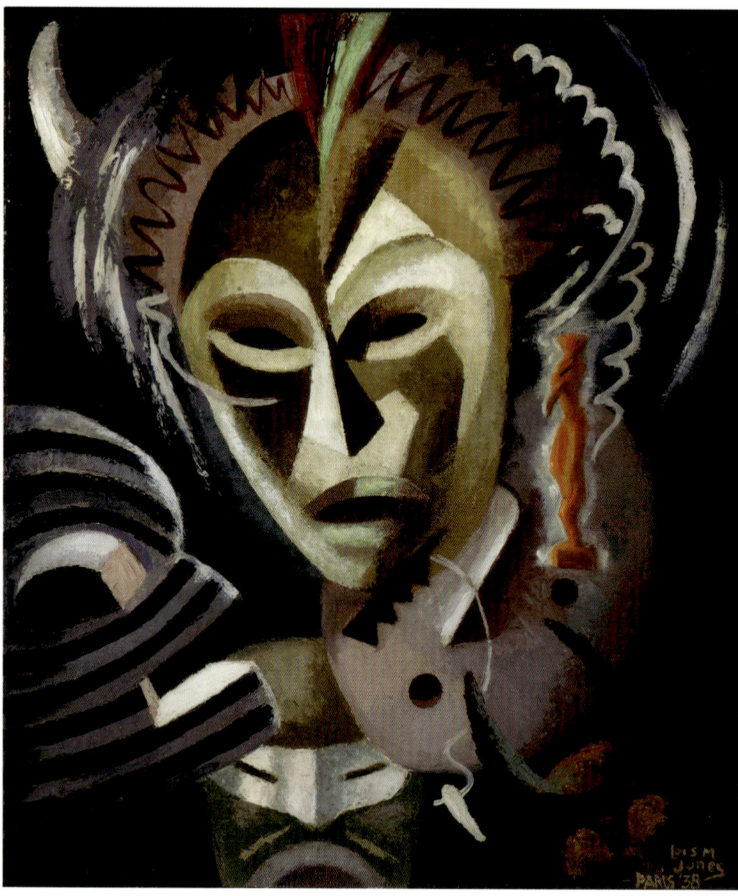

Loïs Mailou Jones (1905–1998), *Les Fétiches*, 1938, oil on linen, 25½ × 21¼ inches; Smithsonian American Art Museum, Washington, DC; museum purchase made possible by Mrs. Norvin H. Green, Dr. R. Harlan, and Francis Musgrave, 1990.56

other leading abstract painters. Critic Lawrence Campbell observed that the theatricality of her Abstract Expressionist work attempted to render emotion into visual form. "That something that the South gives to its writers, its painters take pains to disavow," he wrote.[20] Populated by a series of beige rectangles, *The Family* shows Bongé's ongoing synthesis of Expressionism and symbolic abstraction. The five monolithic shapes crowd the picture plane and assert an elemental force like an Easter Island head or prehistoric pottery.

Ida Kohlmeyer became arguably the most celebrated product of New Orleans's engagement with Abstract Expressionism in the 1950s. Born to Polish Jewish immigrants in that city, Kohlmeyer first took art classes at the John McCrady School of Art 1947 when she was in her late thirties and the mother of two young girls.[21] While earning a master's degree in fine arts at Newcomb College, Kohlmeyer gained exposure to advanced painting from campus visits by David Smith, Jack Tworkov, and—most important to her development—Mark Rothko. She learned how painting could be revelatory and within a year shifted from figural representations of lonely children to abstract fields of color and loosely structured totemic shapes. Kohlmeyer joined the cooperative Orleans Gallery in 1956 and held her first New York show at Ruth White Gallery in 1959. A restless innovator, Kohlmeyer sought to formulate her own personal style in the early 1960s. *Fantasy No. 2*, executed in 1964, depicts a cacophony of suggestive shapes and patterns that foreshadow the symbolic imagery in her work of the following decade.

Charleston, South Carolina, played a pivotal role in the exhibition and interpretation of modern art in the South. Solomon R. Guggenheim first exhibited his collection of nonobjective art at the Gibbes Memorial Art Gallery in 1936. Faith Cornish Murray recalled that "the walls were hung with Kandinskys and Klees. I was one of the guides and when I first went in there and saw all that color tears rolled down my cheeks."[22] Yet few local painters took up the mantle of modern art. The prevailing female painter remained the skilled yet provincial watercolorist Alice Smith. Elsewhere in the state, the University of South Carolina provided opportunities for modernist women to study and teach. Catharine Phillips Rembert, a Columbia native, was the first graduate of the USC art department in 1927 and began teaching there soon afterward. She is best known as the mentor of Jasper Johns. With her deep awareness of modernist ideas and having previously studied with Hans Hofmann, Rembert encouraged Johns, then a talented but unworldly youth, to go to New York in 1948.

The universities of North Carolina also nurtured the development of modern art by women.[23] Mary Leath Thomas,

Southern decorative patterns, her distinctive contribution to the white male–dominated Washington Color School.[17]

Perhaps the most bohemian Southern city, New Orleans became another magnet for female modernists. Dusti Swetman Bongé frequently visited New Orleans in the 1940s and participated in the city's incipient modern art scene in the French Quarter, which had direct links to New York critics and galleries.[18] Born to a prominent Biloxi banking family, she has been called "the first modernist painter in Mississippi."[19] Bongé moved to Chicago to study theater in the late 1920s before switching to painting and returning to Biloxi. Her mark-making was vigorous and her palette vivid, as seen in her 1942 German Expressionist portrait of her friend Hazel Guggenheim McKinley, sister of collector and gallerist Peggy Guggenheim. Bongé started to exhibit in New York in 1939, and in 1947 she first showed at the Betty Parsons Gallery, one of the centers of Abstract Expressionism. The New York art magazines regularly reviewed her exhibitions, and she maintained friendships with Mark Rothko, Kenzo Okada, and

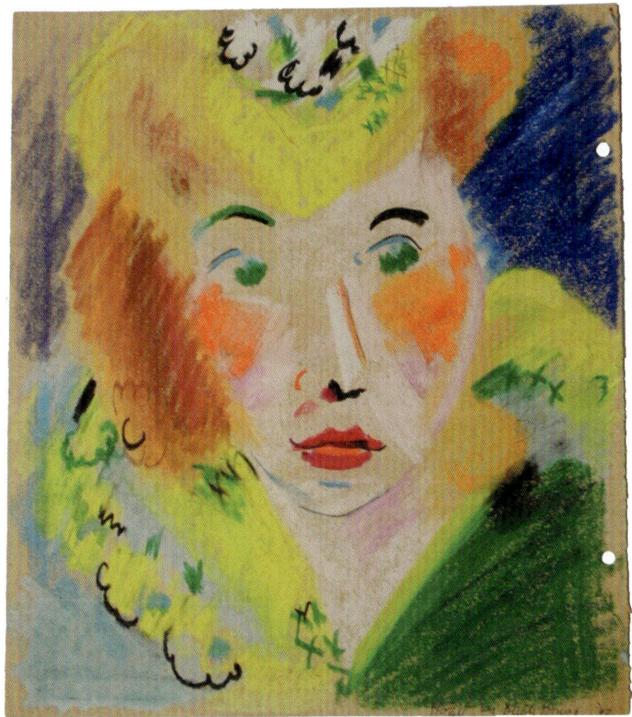

Eunice "Dusti" Lyle Swetman Bongé (1903–1993), *Portrait of Hazel Guggenheim McKinley*, 1942, pastel on paper, 14 × 12 inches; Dusti Bongé Art Foundation, Biloxi, Mississippi

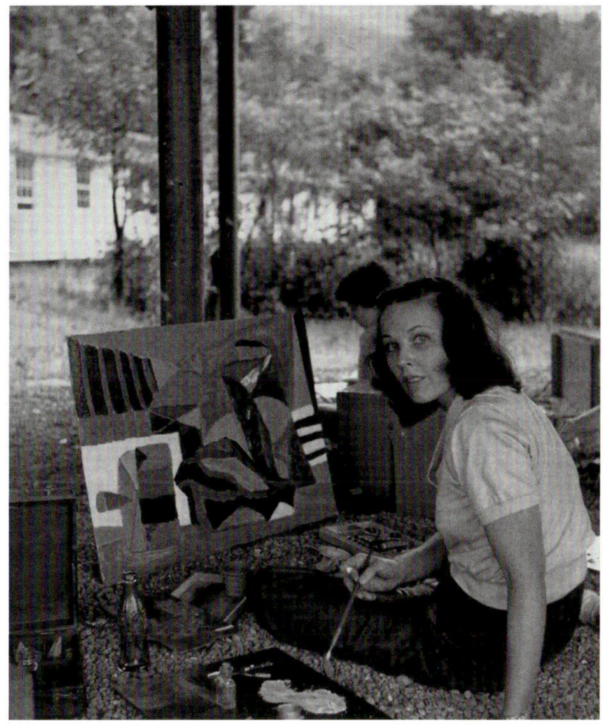

Cora Kelley Ward (1920–1989) in Emerson Woelffer's paint-ing class at Black Mountain College, 1949, photograph; image courtesy of Black Mountain College Museum + Arts Center, Asheville, North Carolina

an assistant professor of art at the Women's College of the University of North Carolina at Greensboro who later served as president of the North Carolina Art Teachers Association, became an abstract artist after encountering work by Paul Klee in 1941. The daughter of a Hazlehurst, Georgia, grocer, she began her career painting watercolor sketches of South-ern landscapes. In the mid-1940s she mixed pigments from local clay and painted "earth-toned, stucco-textured patterns of birds," as in *Birds of the Night*.[24] Thomas's abstract painting *Red, Gold and Black* reveals her continued interest in exper-imenting with the relationships between texture and color. Here, she fully rejected the horizontal orientation of land-scape and celebrated the influence of Klee with asymmetrical shapes and close attention to surface quality. The vibrant contrasting color pattern could be compared to a quilt and seems as much designed as painted.

Edith Caspary London worked in the Duke University art department from 1955 until 1969. A Jewish refugee from Germany, she had studied art in Paris with Marcel Gromaire and André Lhote before moving to Durham in 1939 when her husband, Fritz, took a professorship at Duke. It took several decades for London to find her voice. *Marine Still Life* employs an expressive variant of Cubism. Her work would not become

fully abstract until the 1960s, and she became known for her fragmented color fields in works like *Tension and Harmony*. London and Kohlmeyer were the only women artists working abstractly to be discussed and illustrated in one of the few critical essays on modernism in Southern art. In the ground-breaking 1983 volume *Painting in the South*, Donald Kuspit opined that "their independence is mediated by lyric color."[25] Perhaps their Jewishness as well accounted for their comfort with intuitive and transcendental abstract imagery, as there is no prevailing tradition of figural art in Judaism, which expresses faith through ritual and language.

For many in the South, modernism appeared as an alien force that had little to do with the native culture and land-scape. Nestled in the North Carolina Blue Ridge, Black Moun-tain College exemplified this dialectic. Established in 1933 as a cradle of avant-garde experimentation, the school served pri-marily Northern artists looking for a summer retreat. Never-theless, a few Southern women took advantage of the extraor-dinary faculty and advanced their careers there.[26] Cora Kelley Ward, born in Eunice, Louisiana, attended Newcomb and then studied painting at Black Mountain during the summers of 1949 and 1950. There, she met the powerful critic Clement Greenberg, who became a longtime friend and later organized

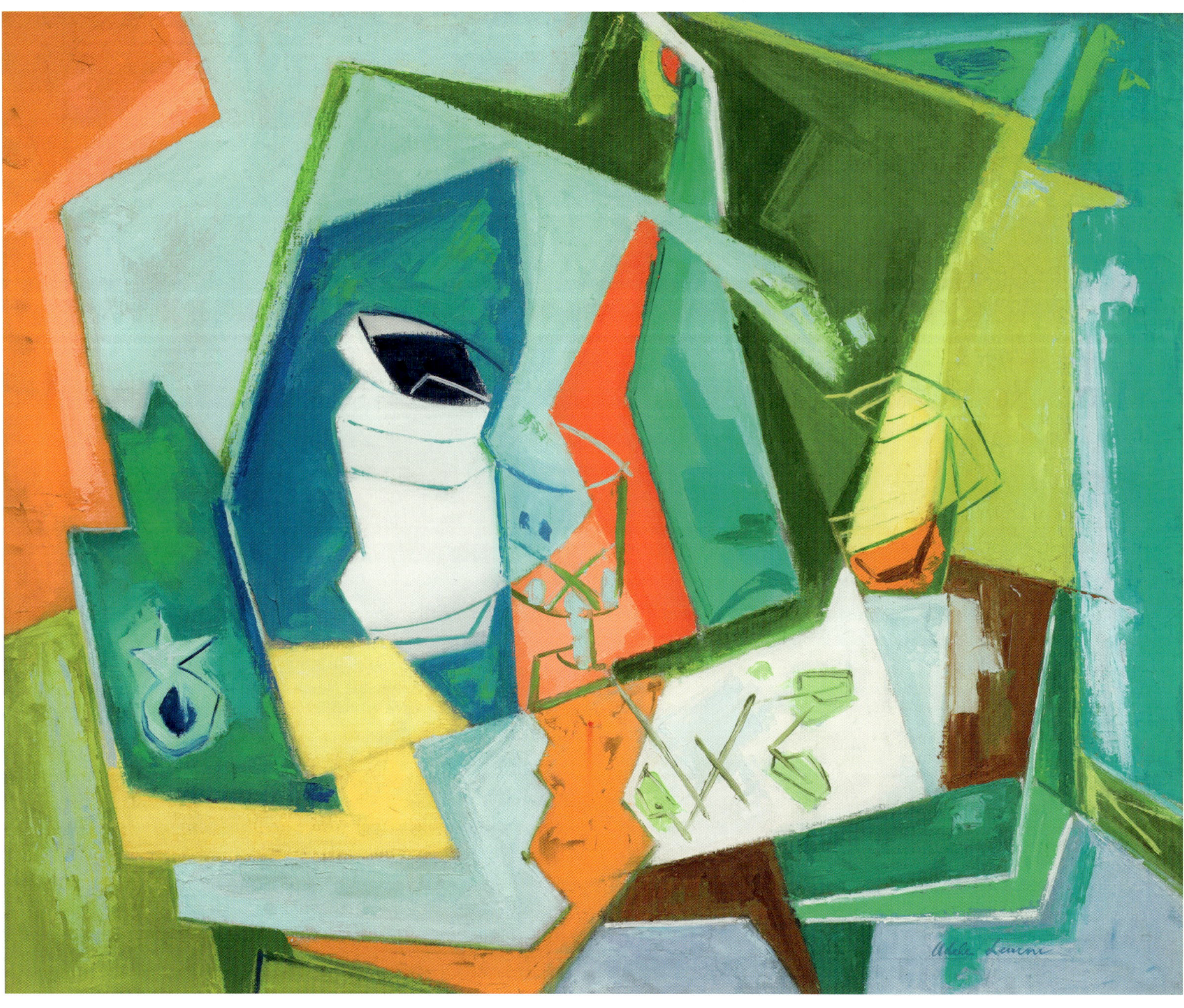

Adele Marion Gawin Lemm (1897–1977), *Still Life,* **oil on canvas, 32 × 38 inches**

a memorial exhibition of her paintings and photography.[27] Additionally, several progressive women already established in the Southern art scene sent their children to Black Mountain. Adelyn Dohme Breeskin brought her daughters Dorothy and Gloria to the summer music institute in 1943 and 1944 while she studied with sculptor José de Creeft.[28] Dusti Bongé's son Lyle Bongé attended the college in 1948 and 1949, which contributed to the development of his photographic practice.[29]

Beyond Black Mountain, some Northerners who studied in the South established long and productive careers in the region as artists and educators. Milwaukee-born Adele Gawin Lemm studied at Siena College in Memphis, Tennessee, and taught for twenty-three years at the Memphis Academy of Art. Her *Still Life* displays the conventions of the fractured picture plane of late Cubism. Lemm exhibited in New York at the Ward Eggleston Galleries in the early 1960s, probably showing works similar to the untitled 1965 Abstract Expressionist canvas featured in this volume, whose fleshy pink central form suggests corporeal experience in motion. Sidney Tillim wrote of Lemm at the time: "Mobile patterns support

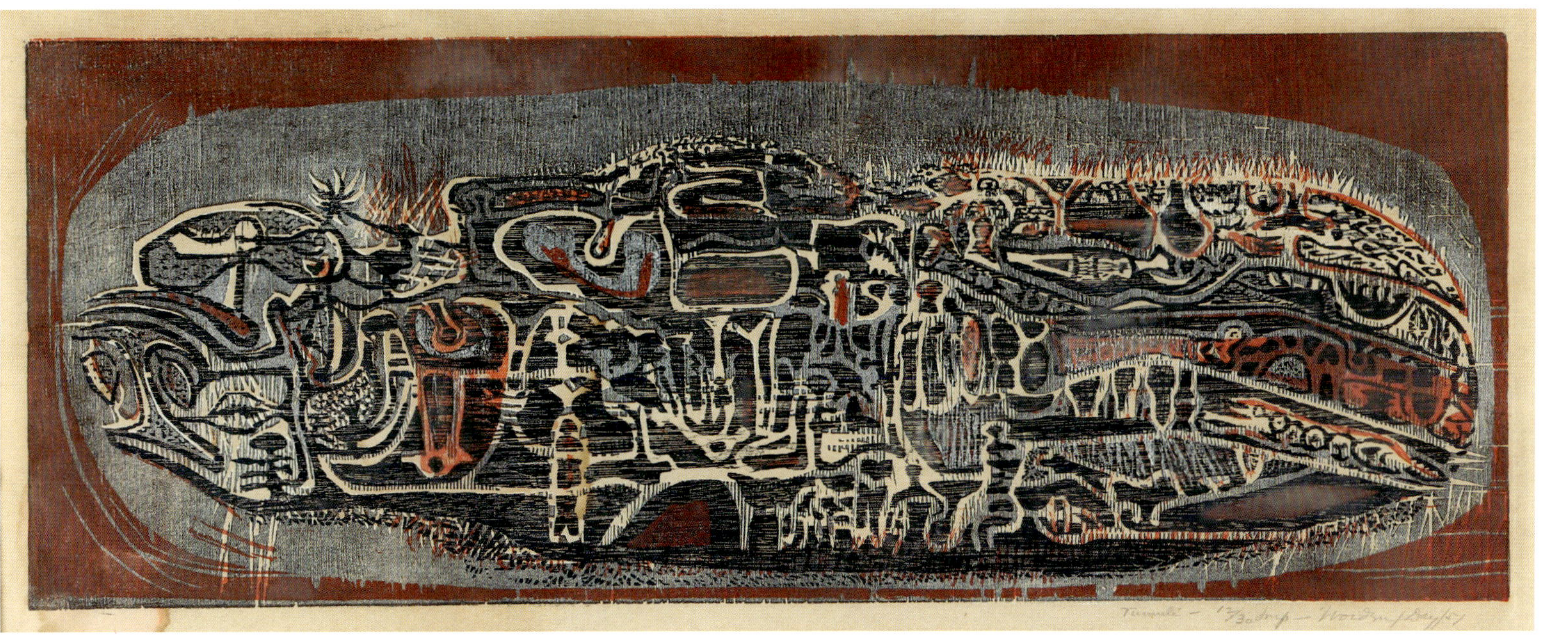

Esther Worden Day (1912–1986), *Tumuli*, 1951, woodcut print, 8⁵⁄₁₆ × 22⅛ inches; Maier Museum of Art at Randolph College, Lynchburg, Virginia

tentative drawing in a cool, figurative style that is otherwise modestly but invitingly direct."[30]

A decade spent studying and teaching in Virginia made a lasting impact on Worden Day's art and reputation. Day left her home state of Ohio to enroll at Randolph-Macon Woman's College. Following her graduation in 1934, she taught at the Richmond Professional Institute (now Virginia Commonwealth University) in the early 1940s. She exhibited at the Virginia Museum of Fine Arts and the avant-garde David Porter Gallery in Washington, DC.[31] Day advocated for women throughout her life. And her woodcut print *Tumuli* visualized her utopian ideals. "Ours is an age of the grey dawning of a new consciousness, requiring a new mental species, a spiritual evolution," Day wrote in 1957.[32] Day, Lemm, Bongé, London, and Kohlmeyer were among the leading Southern practitioners of Abstract Expressionism, embracing its promise of gender-neutral universal values.

Considerably younger than Day, Nell Blaine linked the nascent modernism in the South to the literalist and pop styles that would eventually supplant Abstract Expressionism. A native Virginian, Blaine attended art classes at the Richmond Professional Institute that were taught by Day, who opened her eyes creatively and ideologically. Day encouraged the aspiring artist to read Virginia Woolf's *A Room of One's Own* and to study painting at the Hofmann School and printmaking at Atelier 17.[33] Blaine received essential support from local institutions, winning the Virginia Museum of Fine

Arts Visual Arts Fellowship, and moved to New York in 1942. Her Chelsea loft hosted a popular salon for city bohemians, especially gay men.[34] In the years following her first solo show at the Tibor de Nagy Gallery—the hub of the so-called second-generation Abstract Expressionists—in 1953, critics began to recognize her as one of the leading women in American contemporary art, featuring her work in articles in *Life* and *Cosmopolitan* magazines.[35] When Blaine created *Anemones with Red Cloth* around 1961, she had to paint in a more concentrated manner and scale, the consequence of a nine-month bout with polio. Flowers were a nostalgic connection to her childhood in Richmond, especially her own simple patch of zinnias and bluets.[36]

Throughout the twentieth-century push toward abstraction critics continued to ask, "What is Southern art?" The challenge for many Southern painters—male or female, white or black—was to overcome the bias of critics who perceived the South as a backwater and its artists as unsophisticated and insular. The Southern landscape dominated perception, even of nonrepresentational art. Bongé's paintings "suggest sets for some 'Threepenny Opera of the Levee,'" one critic wrote in 1960.[37] "There is a Southern laziness and a kind of cheerful eroticism," another wrote about Worden Day in 1958.[38] Other critics believed that Southern women personified the authentic position of the modern artist, which is to be properly alienated from bourgeois mass culture in order to tap into the timeless and primitive elements of humanity.

Anthropologist Kenneth Lawrence Beaudoin, who lived in New Orleans before moving to New York in the mid-1940s and founding Galerie Neuf and the short-lived journal *Iconograph*, once exhibited his paintings under the name Galatea Jones, claiming they were created by an African American housekeeper in New Orleans.[39] Larry Rivers, a New York artist who later painted Southern political themes, wrote that his friend Nell Blaine's art possessed outsider authority because she worked in a manufacturing district, was a lesbian, and was a Southerner.[40]

These two generations of female modern artists working in the South, disparate in styles, shared a fierce independence and a faith in the international language of modernism. Modernist women counteracted personal limitations to attain the freedom to paint with their eyes wide open. The rise of abstraction and its universal values, alongside the transformative civil rights movement, managed to eradicate most significant differences between contemporary artists in the South and the rest of the United States by the late 1960s. It took a younger generation of postmodernist artists like Kara Walker, Mary Reid Kelley, Sonya Clark, and Stacy Lynn Waddell to revisit the troubled history and imagery of the South that the abstract modernists worked to transcend. But that's another story.

THE WORKS
OF ART

WENONAH DAY BELL (1890–1981)

Peach Packing, Spartanburg County, 1938

Oil on canvas, 38⅛ × 48⅛ inches

Wenonah Day Bell captured the importance of women to South Carolina's thriving peach industry during the 1930s and 1940s in *Peach Packing, Spartanburg County.* Born in Trenton, a crossroads situated about one hundred miles southwest of the locale depicted, Bell spent much of her youth moving between small towns in the Piedmont region, including Spartanburg. Eventually, the family settled in Gainesville, Georgia, after Bell's father, a Baptist minister, established his ministry there.[1] Not long thereafter, Bell began her artistic education, which took her well beyond her Southern birthplace.

Between 1908 and 1929, Bell attended Brenau College in Gainesville, the Pennsylvania Academy of the Fine Arts in Philadelphia, Académie Colarossi in Paris, and the Hans Hofmann School of Fine Arts on the Italian island of Capri, among other institutions. Such extensive and diverse training provided Bell with a solid foundation on which to cultivate a successful career as a painter, teacher, and author.[2] Her talent was particularly appreciated at the venerable Pennsylvania Academy, where she twice received the William Emlen Cresson Memorial Travel Scholarship to finance studies in Europe; she was also honored in 1925, winning the Charles Tappan Prize for work that emphasized the characteristics of drawing rather than painting.[3]

Bell's hard-edged technique is apparent in *Peach Packing.* Although it is composed in the Realist tradition encouraged at her Philadelphia alma mater, the picture also demonstrates Bell's familiarity with modern art movements in the United States and elsewhere. The expressive use of bright hues, simplified forms, minimal and somewhat arbitrary chiaroscuro, and slightly distorted figures and perspective lend the painting a naive quality that was celebrated among early-twentieth-century artists. No doubt Bell's saturated Gauguinesque coloring and skewed perspective owe something to the landmark exhibitions featuring European Post-Impressionist and Cubist art that occurred at the Pennsylvania Academy while she was enrolled: *Representative Modern Masters* in 1920 and *Later Tendencies in Art* in 1921.[4] In both subject matter and execution, *Peach Packing* is a Southern interpretation of the American Scene painting being contemporaneously explored by Regionalists like Thomas Hart Benton and John Steuart Curry.

Far from abstract, Bell's painting offers documentary insight into a critical agricultural enterprise in the South. A column of women fill peach baskets with ripe fruit while an androgynous worker transports the crates from shed to truck for shipping north. The crates are noticeably marked with a circled B—perhaps a reference to the cooperative of farmers that managed the facility rather than a label denoting a particular brand of produce.[5] Pulley wheels overhead and at the far left of the composition allude to the presence of a mechanism that aided the employees' efficiency. Amid this bustling activity, it is the row of colorfully clothed women aligned before a sorting bench that grabs the viewer's attention.[6] At the time, women were considered particularly proficient at grading peaches and culling fruit that was damaged or overripe. Industry leaders had recently determined that a woman's delicate touch and expertise in choosing produce when shopping for her own family made her ideally suited for classifying peaches and then carefully stacking them in the six-basket carrier crates pictured.[7] This notion undoubtedly intrigued Bell, who would have been well versed in the challenges women faced when working in a male-dominated field.

Like many other women artists, Bell did not limit her oeuvre to so-called feminine subject matter. In addition to painting New York urban scenes, the artist created still lifes and portraits in both oil and watercolor, which she regularly submitted to exhibitions in the Northeast and South.[8] Yet, her most prized compositions are warmly colored Southern landscapes and rural vignettes, such as *Peach Packing.*[9] Indeed, although she taught art at various schools in and around New York City throughout her career—including a lengthy tenure at the Parsons School of Design—Bell periodically returned to the South, the source of her artistic inspiration, to sketch and paint.[10] She also authored a memoir, *The Restless Bells,* which recounts her family's history from the postbellum years through World War II. Shortly after she completed her book in 1973, Bell's health deteriorated, and, in need of her own rest, she returned to the South and spent her final years near relatives in Georgia.[11]

SANDY McCAIN

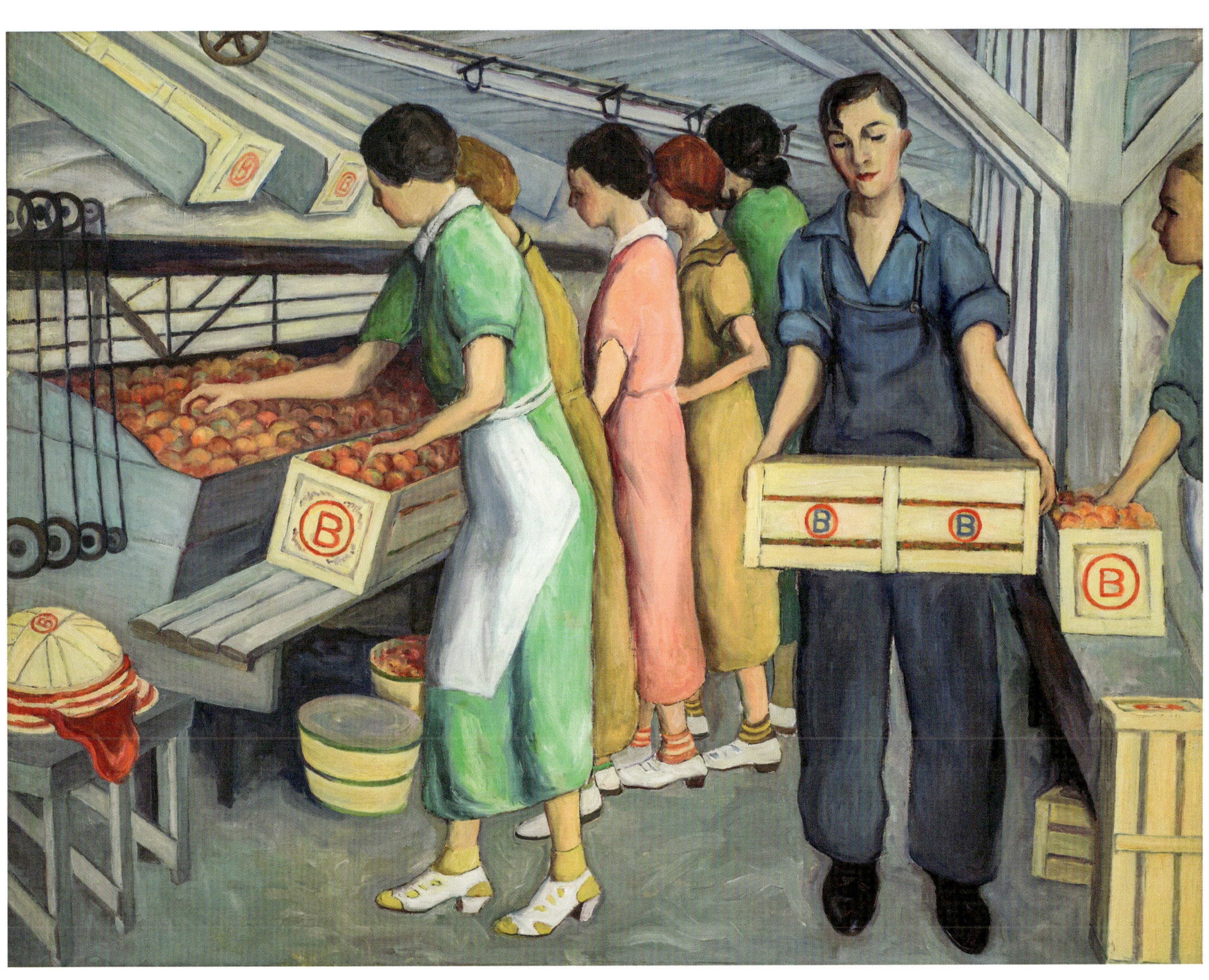

NELL BLAIR WALDEN BLAINE (1922–1996)

Anemones with Red Cloth, circa 1961–1962

Oil on canvas, 30 × 18¼ inches

A May 1957 issue of *Life* magazine recognized five "Women Artists in Ascendance," painters who had "won acclaim not as notable women artists but as notable artists who happen to be women."[1] Photographs of the select group illustrated the article, including one of Nell Blaine sitting in her sunny New York studio surrounded by still lifes and large-scale figural works. Those canvases testify to Blaine's decades of experimentation—from naturalism in her early efforts, to radical abstraction throughout the 1940s, and back to figuration in the 1950s and beyond.[2] This constant search for stylistic renewal characterized Blaine's sweeping, successful career. Her prolific output demonstrated a commitment to devising a personal style grounded in the primacy of nature and the work of Henri Matisse, Piet Mondrian, Hans Hofmann, and others. At the height of her abstract phase, in 1947, Blaine noted that "realism in painting consists of order, rhythms, growth, and shapes, rather than the actual appearance of things"—concepts that were foundational in her art.[3]

The death of her mother at a young age, the volatile temper of her father, and the conservative religiosity of her stepmother marked Blaine's upbringing in Richmond, Virginia, during the Great Depression.[4] Severe vision problems—Blaine was born cross-eyed—further compromised her youthful stirrings toward art. Corrective surgeries liberated her from physical restrictions, and by the age of sixteen she had enrolled in the School of Art of the Richmond Professional Institute (now Virginia Commonwealth University), learning under the tutelage of Theresa Pollak and Worden Day. Day's Surrealist leanings and exposure to Jean Hélion's modernist works at the Virginia Museum of Fine Arts inspired Blaine's interest in abstract art. At Day's urging, Blaine set out for Hofmann's studio in New York in 1942.

Although perpetually constrained by tight finances, Blaine felt like "a bird out of a cage" in New York. Nurtured by Hofmann's emphasis on organic rhythms and the rectilinearity modeled in Mondrian's images—which she came to know intimately during visits to the Dutch innovator's studio—Blaine moved from abstraction to nonfiguration. At the Jane Street Gallery, an artist's cooperative founded in 1942, she adhered to purely formal art and developed an abiding love for jazz. The shared sensibilities between that musical genre and her increasingly progressive aesthetic were not lost on Blaine: "I began to play the drums, and I think handling the drumsticks affected to this day the way I used paintbrushes."[5] In 1944 she joined the American Abstract Artists group, as did many other students in the Hofmann circle.[6]

Blaine's radical investigations attracted the attention of critic Clement Greenberg, who enthusiastically singled out her *Great White Creature* as "best in the show" at the 1945 annual exhibition of the American Abstract Artists.[7] On Greenberg's recommendation, Blaine was invited to participate in *Art of This Century: The Women,* Peggy Guggenheim's second landmark exhibition of women artists, also held in 1945.[8] In appraising her involvement with Abstract Expressionism, Blaine later recalled: "We…were very dogmatic about our program. Now, as I look back on it, I'm a little ashamed.… When you're young you are very sure of yourself."[9]

The closing of the Jane Street Gallery in 1949 and an ensuing trip to Paris in 1950 prompted Blaine's realization that nonfiguration deprived her "of some wonderful sensuous pleasure with painting." While she reconnected with the work of Hélion and visited Fernand Léger's studio there, she gradually reembraced representation.[10] Blaine's paintings of the 1950s track her thematic and stylistic shifts: she focused on studio interiors and portraits, but also produced luminous landscapes in brilliant, animated colors depicting her travels to New England, Mexico, Italy, and Greece.

While working on the Greek island of Mykonos in 1959, Blaine contracted bulbar-spinal polio. The virus paralyzed her and necessitated an arduous rehabilitation and the exertion of enormous will to return to painting. Undaunted, Blaine modified her approach and focused on smaller compositions. As she noted in a 1967 interview, her work prior to her paralysis was "very athletic," demanding strength and physicality. By contrast, her disability required intimate engagement with the canvas. *Anemones with Red Cloth* is representative of this new direction toward light-filled, painterly forms saturated in exuberant colors and activated through dynamic brushstrokes.

Although limited in her mobility, Blaine was by no means confined; she often painted in Gloucester, Massachusetts, and she traveled widely throughout Europe with the help of devoted friends. For the rest of her life Blaine enjoyed an almost frenetic pace of individual and group exhibitions in galleries and museums, fueled by a steady output of small-scale oils and watercolors. In 1992, on the occasion of her fifty-first solo exhibition showcasing intensely colored flower paintings and landscapes, the ever indomitable Blaine proclaimed: "Art is central to my life. Not being able to make or see art would be a major deprivation."[11]

EVIE TERRONO

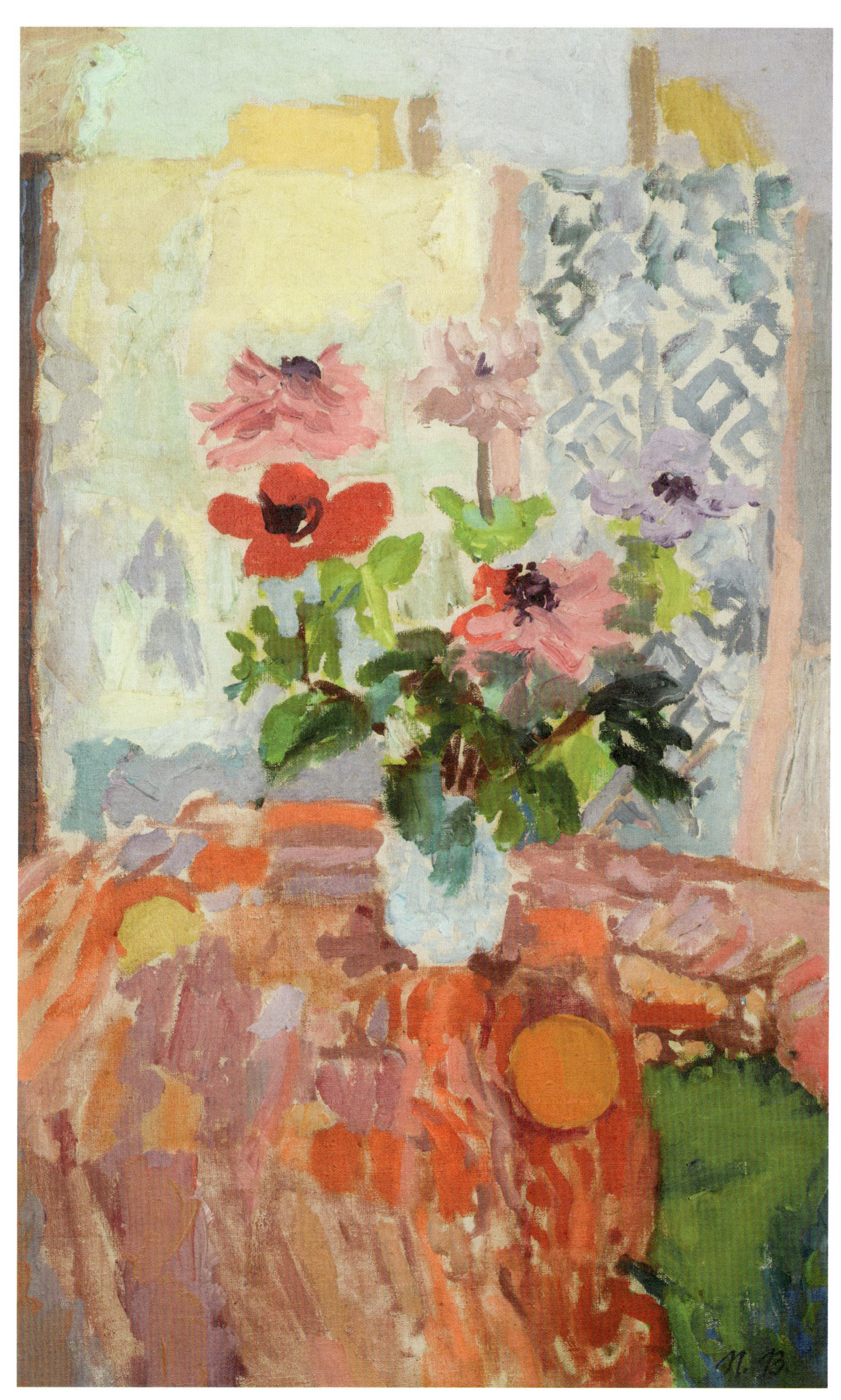

SARAH JANE BLAKESLEE (1912–2005)

Springhouse at Home, Castle Valley

Oil on canvas, 38⅛ × 42⅛ inches

Sarah Blakeslee's pursuit of art began in her teenage years when the Evanston, Illinois, native enrolled in classes at the Art Institute of Chicago. After her family relocated to the Washington, DC, area, she pursued further instruction at the Corcoran School of Art and at a private school operated by Catherine Critcher, an accomplished painter associated with the Taos, New Mexico, art colony. At Critcher's urging, Blakeslee continued her studies at the Pennsylvania Academy of the Fine Arts, where she was awarded two Cresson Traveling Scholarships that enabled her to spend a number of months abroad, time she used to visit museums and learn from firsthand encounters with the work of European masters.

Blakeslee developed into an accomplished and versatile artist using both watercolor and oil with equal dexterity. After her return to the States, she married one of her former Academy teachers, Francis Speight, in 1936. They moved to the bucolic community of Castle Valley in Bucks County, Pennsylvania, where they lived until 1961.[1] Blakeslee painted directly from her subjects—whether she was painting the surrounding landscape or portraits of friends and family. Although it is not unlike many of her other rural landscape scenes, *Springhouse at Home, Castle Valley* is one of Blakeslee's most freely painted and reflects the artist's deft assimilation of both Impressionism and Realism.

The painting depicts the family's homestead, which Blakeslee knew intimately. Her familiarity with the subject's every detail allowed her to eschew specificity for an easy naturalism and painterly approach that favored areas of vivid color and broad, loose brushstrokes. The two-acre plot in Castle Valley included a three-story house built in 1820 and covered in yellow stucco. A springhouse stood near a creek running along the back and one side of the property. Blakeslee painted the property from that perspective in another canvas, *Snow Scene,* dating to the 1940s. *Springhouse at Home, Castle Valley* may depict the scene in late summer, and the view is from the front. The house—with its overhanging roof and

front porch—is typical of others in the area recorded by both Blakeslee and Speight; it is positioned in the upper left of the painting, while the shadowed springhouse balances the composition on the right. Blakeslee's chosen vantage point offers a sense of spatial depth, even as it is countered by the lively brushwork on the surface of the canvas. Two children, the artist's son and daughter, are at the spring's edge, an area where they likely often played. The spring itself seems still compared to the turmoil of gestural brushstrokes in the trees above and behind the structure. Blakeslee's contrasting treatment of the two areas draws the viewer into the space and invites exploration of the painting's highly active surface.

During the busiest years of motherhood, Blakeslee's domestic responsibilities slowed her career, yet she found time to produce still life paintings, figure studies, and interior scenes that were exhibited and won awards. Her impressive exhibition record dates back to 1937, when the twenty-five-year-old painter's entries were accepted to the forty-eighth annual exhibition at the Art Institute of Chicago and the fifteenth biennial exhibition at the Corcoran Gallery of Art. She frequently showed her work at the Pennsylvania Academy of the Fine Arts and participated in the 1939 and 1940 Golden Gate International Expositions in San Francisco and at the 1939 New York World's Fair. In 1937 the United States Treasury Department's Section of Fine Arts commissioned her to paint a mural for the post office in Strasburg, Virginia. Blakeslee's work was the subject of solo exhibitions at the Greenville, North Carolina, Museum of Art, in 1937 and 1963.

Always independent-minded, Sarah Blakeslee retained her maiden name as her professional moniker throughout her career. Recognition in the Southeast added to both Speight and Blakeslee's reputations elsewhere in the country, although by mid-century their work was falling out of fashion in the art market. Blakeslee continued to paint and teach at various regional art centers in North Carolina through the 1960s and 1970s until she retired to Pennsylvania in 1998 to be near her daughter for the rest of her long life. NANCY M. DOLL

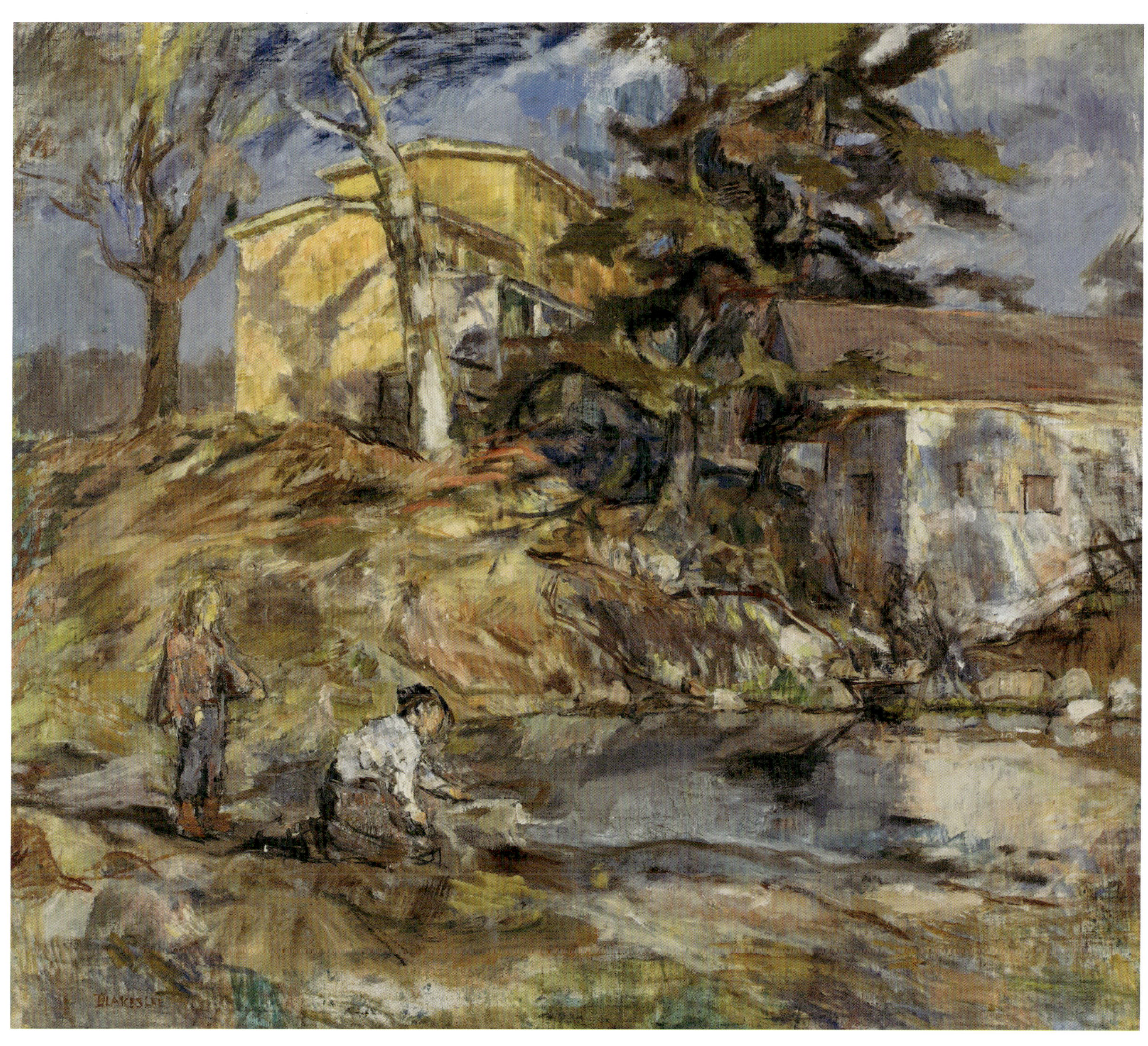
BLAKESLEE

EUNICE "DUSTI" LYLE SWETMAN BONGÉ (1903–1993)

The Family, 1965

Oil on canvas, 54¼ × 86¼ inches

Dusti Bongé had childhood dreams of becoming an actress and an artist, aspirations she successfully realized on the stage and on canvas. Later in life vivid dreams would lead her to create dynamic nonrepresentational paintings and to become the first artist in Mississippi to fully embrace modernism. Reflecting on her creative evolution, Bongé recalled, "As I changed my style from realistic to the abstract, dreams formed a bridge between the two."[1]

Bongé was born Eunice Lyle Swetman, the youngest of three children in a well-to-do Biloxi, Mississippi, family. Her early inclination toward visual art was matched by an enthusiasm for drama, and she regularly involved neighborhood children in performances of her own plays. With her sights set on acting, she graduated from Blue Mountain College in northeastern Mississippi, then studied at the Lyceum Arts Conservatory (later known as the Bush Temple Conservatory of Music and Dramatic Art) in Chicago. While there she won small roles, and friends gave her the nickname Dusti because she always washed her face after traveling home from theaters through the city's dirty streets.[2]

Bongé moved to New York in 1924 to further her career and appeared in musical comedies, vaudeville acts, and dramas. In 1928 she married Arch Bongé, a charismatic Nebraska painter and Art Institute student whom she had met in Chicago.[3] The challenges of raising their young son Lyle in Manhattan prompted the couple to move to Biloxi in 1935. Arch recognized Dusti's talent and encouraged her to resume painting. Her early output included still lifes and local genre scenes rendered in both realist and Cubist modes. Following her husband's tragic death in 1936, Dusti took solace in her work, painting in the studio Arch had built in their backyard.

Grief fueled Bongé's production. By the end of the 1930s, she had mastered a Surrealist style and had exhibited in New York. "As time passed," she recalled, "I became more comfortable with my work and my pictures became more and more abstract."[4] An early association with Betty Parsons proved significant to Bongé's aesthetic advancement. Established in 1946, Parsons's eponymous 57th Street gallery championed a group of progressive artists known as the New York School, who spearheaded Abstract Expressionism. Using an abstract vocabulary, they produced large-scale images that radiated with pure emotion, spontaneity, and improvisation. Bongé's friendships with other artists in Parsons's stable—including Willem de Kooning, Kenzo Okada, Mark Rothko, and Theodoros Stamos—offered exposure to avant-garde philosophies and techniques that were slow to reach coastal Mississippi. Perhaps more meaningfully, the Abstract Expressionists' ideals echoed Arch's early advice to Dusti. Having felt constrained by academically rigid instructors, Arch had dissuaded Dusti from formal training: "He did not want me to be restricted by rules;…he wanted me to have the freedom to be creative."[5]

Bongé began experimenting with Abstract Expressionism in the 1950s. In contrast to the rich, saturated hues of her initial investigations, Bongé's palette darkened over the next decade, a change that attracted the notice of a *New York Herald Tribune* critic in 1960: "Dusti Bongé, artist of the deep south, appears at the Betty Parsons Gallery with forceful and determinedly non-objective paintings. Having her third show here, Miss Bongé is perhaps more dramatic at this moment than she has ever been. Her canvases are extremely vigorous, dark-keyed and spacious."[6] Dating to that period, this untitled example is executed in what the artist would have termed "dull" colors—a term that was not negative to her—and is as compelling a composition as any of her more vibrant works. A series of irregular rectangles, each imbued with a distinctive personality, marches across the space. Bongé enlivened the surface by alternating the thick and thin application of paint and by gouging away the medium in linear strokes. Dreams continued to play a part in Bongé's artistic expression, influencing the configuration of works like this: "I see, in my dreams, not only the feeling that I want to convey, but the colors that I want to use and their exact location on the canvas."[7]

KRISTEN MILLER ZOHN

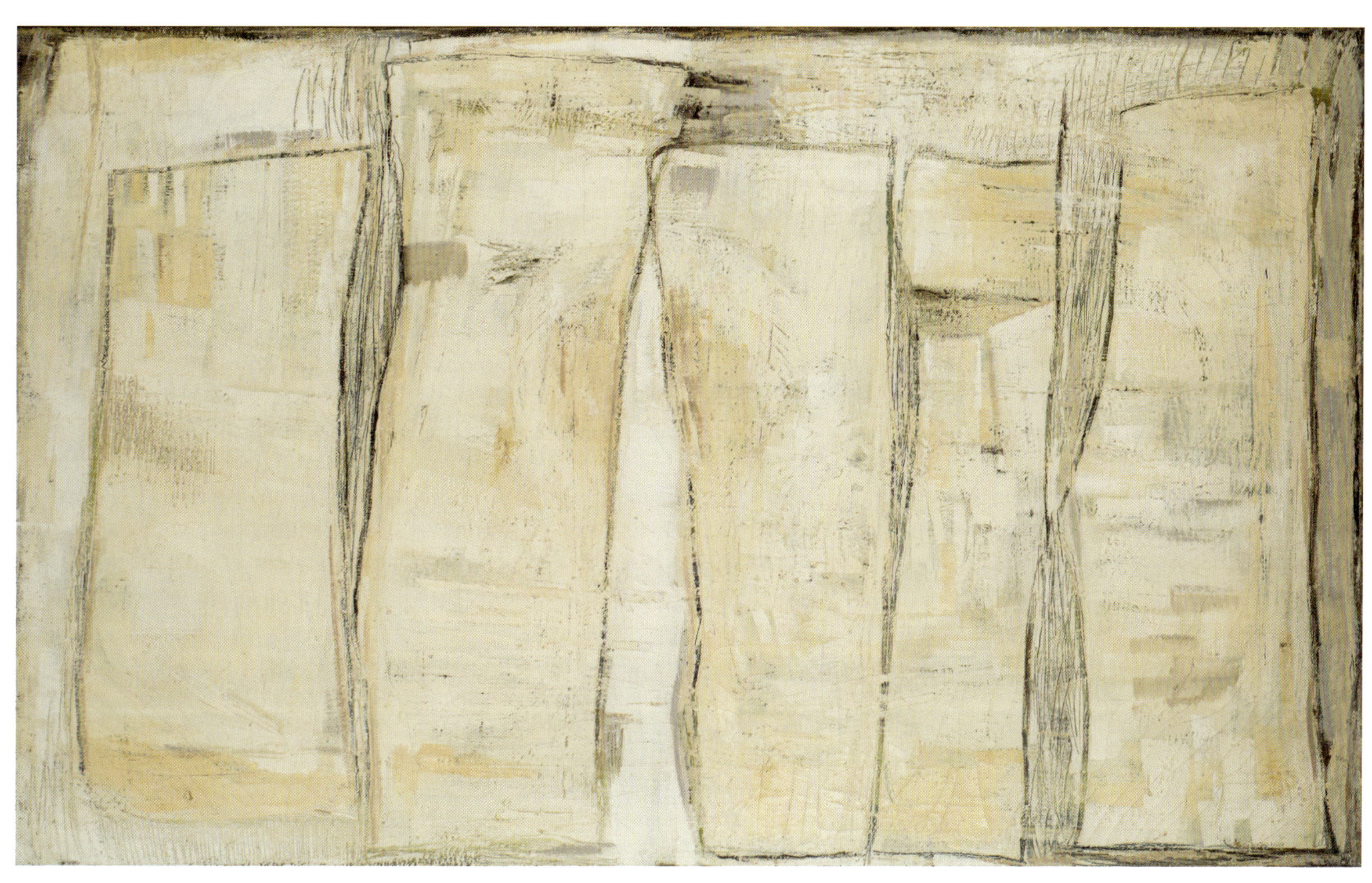

SELMA HORTENSE BURKE (1900–1995)

Woman Holding Sheaf of Wheat, circa 1940

Wood, 31¾ × 7⅛ × 8 inches

In recalling her childhood fascination with sculpture, Selma Burke remembered: "One day, I was mixing the clay and I saw the imprint of my hands. I found that I could make something,…something that I alone had created."[1] From the riverbeds of North Carolina to the urban environments of New York and Philadelphia, Burke remained a lifelong devotee of the three-dimensional form as both an artist and an art educator. Favoring wood and limestone as materials, Burke crafted her sculptures from the materials' intrinsic shape, releasing the subject from its confinement.

Incorporating the wood's whorls and knots into folds of fabric or suggestions of body parts, Burke masterfully leveraged the organic imperfections in *Woman Holding Sheaf of Wheat.* Created during the height of her career, the sculpture portrays a young woman standing in contrapposto, a stance that accentuates the sensuous curves of her body. The slightly exaggerated hands, neck, and ear of wheat offer a stylistic interpretation of the human figure and nature's bounty. Although the work appears to embrace modern abstraction, the figure's features simultaneously evoke African sculpture, which was prevalent in the Burke household. At a time when black intellectuals like Alain Locke encouraged African American artists to look to Africa for inspiration, Burke had "known African art all of [her] life."[2] The sculpture's enigmatic, symmetrical face and pupil-less eyes mask any expression, allowing the figure to stand in for every woman and no woman in particular. Her stoicism and resolute composure offer a positive depiction of black womanhood—a sharp contrast to the negative stereotypes so prevalent in the period's visual culture. One critic described Burke's woodcarvings as achieving "an almost Gothic feeling in the emotional intensity of her work."[3]

The artist's best-known work can be found in most American pockets or coin purses, on the dime. Burke's bronze profile portrait of Franklin Delano Roosevelt was selected as the winning entry in a national competition. When she unveiled the sculpture to Eleanor Roosevelt in 1945, the first lady declared that the artist had made her husband "too young."[4] Aware that the presidential image would be circulated in perpetuity, Burke replied: "I've not done it for today, but for tomorrow and tomorrow." Burke's likeness captured Roosevelt's fortitude, with a "jutting chin and steeply sloping forehead and nose,…which she believed gave the president 'that wonderful look of going forward.'"[5] The United States Mint adapted her composition for the coin but credited the work to John Sinnock, the mint's former chief engraver. For the rest of her life Burke would contest the misattribution.[6]

Despite Burke's early aptitude for art, her mother encouraged her to find a more financially stable and socially respectable career. Accordingly, the North Carolina native pursued nursing at the St. Agnes school of nursing in Raleigh and in 1929 accepted a position as a private attendant to a wealthy heiress in Philadelphia.[7] Nursing enabled Burke to survive the Great Depression relatively unscathed and underwrote her artistic aspirations. As a first step, she relocated to New York City in 1935.[8] Arriving at the height of the Harlem Renaissance, she immersed herself in the vibrant arts community and diligently honed her artistic skills. These efforts were rewarded with a scholarship to attend Columbia University; subsequent awards from the prestigious Rosenwald Fund and Boehler Foundation funded study abroad in Vienna and Paris.[9] After Burke earned a master's degree in fine arts from Columbia in 1941, her sculpture was included in significant exhibitions at important venues, including the Pennsylvania Academy of the Fine Arts and several notable commercial galleries in New York.[10] Although she was encouraged by this success, her truer ambition took a longer view, and she devoted her energies to making the arts more accessible to future generations, establishing eponymous art schools in New York and Pittsburgh. For Burke, art had the potential to transcend racial boundaries: "Art didn't start black or white, it just started.…Why do we label people with everything except 'children of God'?"[11]

ERIN R. CORRALES-DIAZ

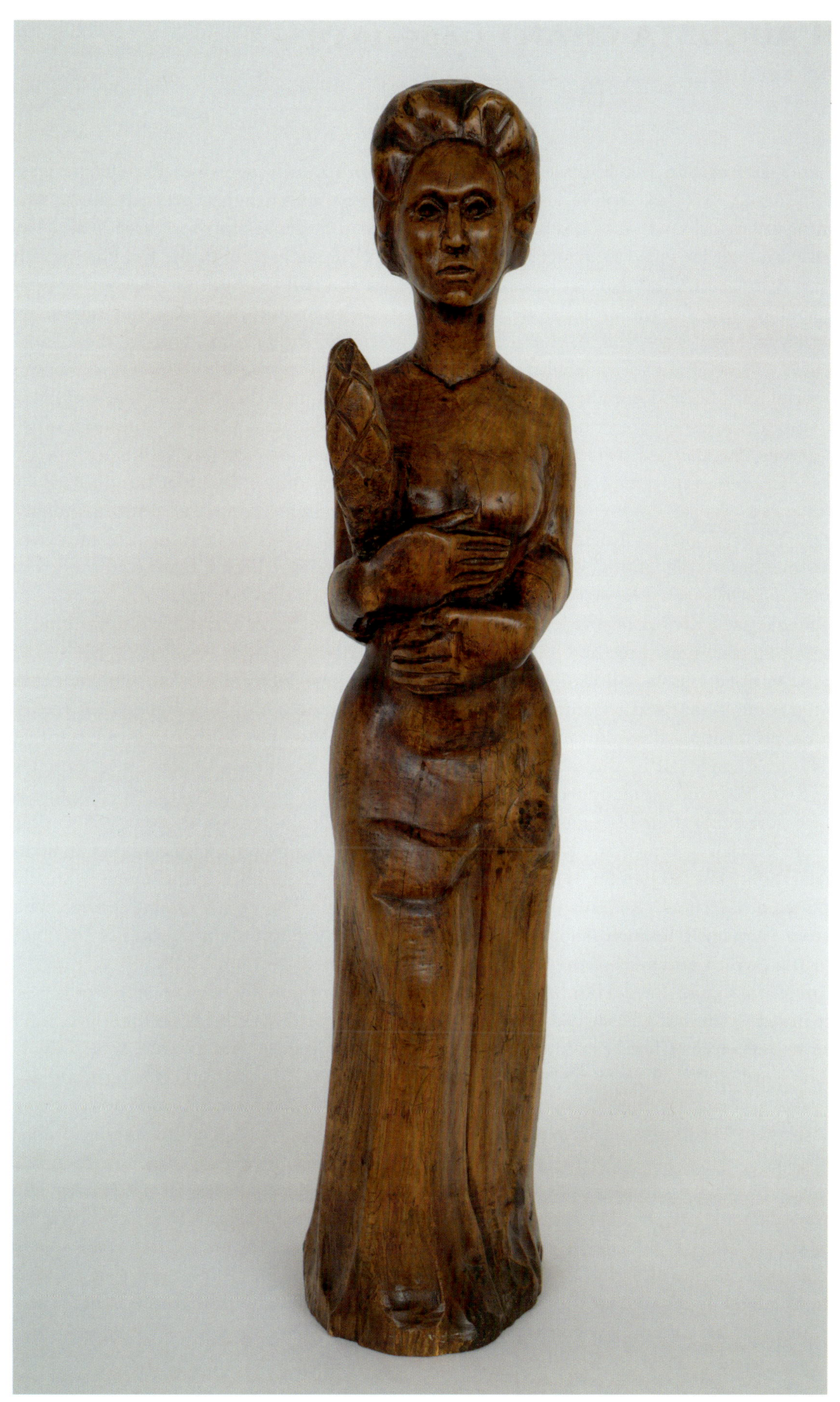

ELISABETH AUGUSTA CHANT (1865–1947)

Spring Landscape, circa 1927

Oil on canvas, 18 × 21 inches

Eclectic in her art and eccentric in her lifestyle, Elisabeth Chant moved to Wilmington, North Carolina, in 1922 with the hope of establishing an art colony that would bring noted artists to the port city. Although she failed to attract a national audience, she became a force in the local art community, teaching classes and advocating for the establishment of a museum. A former student, Henry MacMillan, characterized her approach to art thus: "Miss Chant's strong belief was that drawing was the essential foundation for an art education.... She instilled in her students a respect for complete sincerity of purpose. The portraits she painted were never popular because of her honesty and refusal to compromise in order to achieve a flattering likeness."[1]

Chant was born in Yeovil, Somerset, England. Her father was the captain of a merchant ship and took his wife and young daughter along on his voyages. The artist claimed that she had "sailed the seven seas by the age of seven."[2] While she was still a child, the family immigrated to the United States, eventually settling in Minneapolis, a culturally ambitious metropolis. As a young adult, Chant was encouraged to study nursing, one of the few professional disciplines then open to women. Although she was employed in the field for a time and served with the Red Cross in Georgia during the Spanish-American War, she never abandoned her passion for art.

At the Minneapolis School of Fine Arts, Chant studied under founder Douglas Volk, a noted painter of figures. From 1899 to 1910 she supported herself as a painter of decorative panels and murals that frequently featured subjects derived from the legends of King Arthur and tales of the Druids. She also became very involved in the local Handicraft Guild, which regularly met in her studio. She described the organization in glowing terms reflective of her keen interest in the medieval period: "The word 'guild' carries with it a flavor of the middle ages. It takes us back to those sumptuous times when men, as well as women, wore gorgeous raiment and went plumed and bejewelled."[3]

Until she settled in North Carolina, Chant led a peripatetic and sometimes difficult life. From 1901 to 1903 she enjoyed an extended trip to England, where she explored her ancestry and took classes at the Royal School of Art Needlework in Kensington. She later spent six years in Springfield, Massachusetts, working with an interior design firm. In 1917

Chant's family determined that she was mentally unstable and committed her to an institution, where she was treated for manic depression for three years. Upon her release she traveled extensively in the Far East, revisiting places she had seen as a child.

In the realm of art Chant's talents were diverse and appreciable; she pursued pottery, batik, and Japanesque prints in addition to painting. *Spring Landscape* was probably done in the Wilmington area and may portray the Cape Fear River. On its front and verso is a monogram she used during her late career, consisting of an inverted V on top of two others underscored by a line. Her handling of paint is impressionistic, with areas of impasto defining grasses and foliage. In the foreground tall trees reminiscent of the works of Post-Impressionist painter Paul Cézanne frame a vista of water and of buildings in the distance.

When Chant arrived in Wilmington, she made an immediate impression, as recalled by her student, Claude Howell: "A strange looking woman with enormous plaits of chestnut hair over each ear stepped off the Atlantic Coast Line train.... Miss Elisabeth Augusta Chant was an artist by profession.... She was a force to be reckoned with.... No one ever knew much about her past life. She had no visible means of support."[4] She tended to wear voluminous embroidered garments of her own making and had an attraction to the occult, which furthered her exotic image. A steady stream of students found their way to her quaint cottage, where she lived simply, if unconventionally, surrounded by objects and fabrics she had crafted.

Chant quickly became active in her adopted community, championing art education for youth and helping to establish the Wilmington Art League, which evolved into the Wilmington Art Association. Her ultimate goal, however, was to establish an art museum, and she devoted considerable energy to its realization. Appealing to civic pride, Chant wrote to the editor of the local newspaper in 1938: "In the life of cities a time comes for cultural development. The drama, music, art each in turn filling a place in the civic fabric....[A museum] will mean: Wider horizons for the young. New interest for the mature. For visitors and tourists, a place of intellectual enjoyment. For Wilmington, a decided step-up in culture."[5]

MARTHA R. SEVERENS

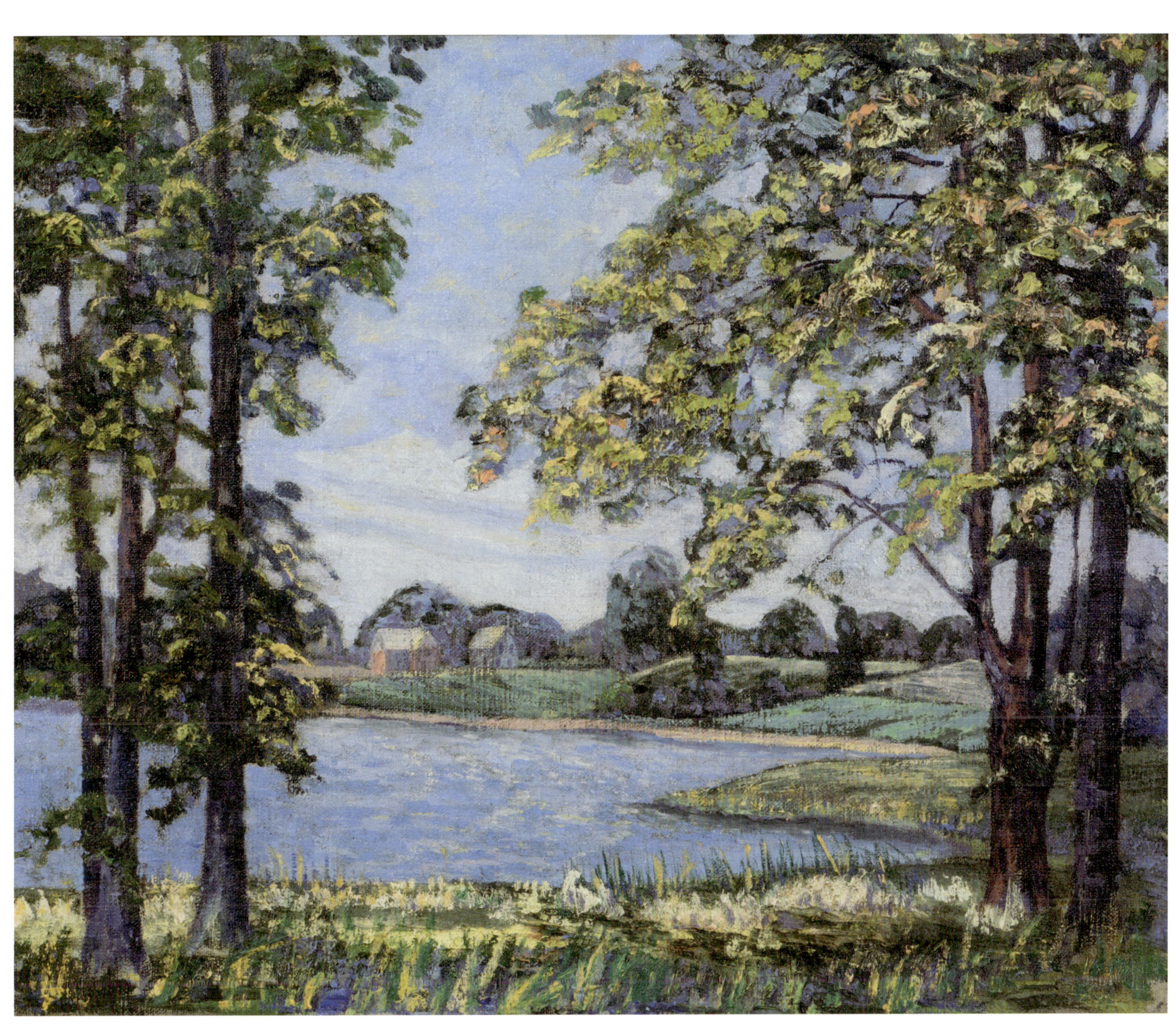

KATE FREEMAN CLARK (1875–1957)

Summer Landscape, circa 1909

Oil on canvas, 26 × 30 inches

Kate Freeman Clark was born in Holly Springs, Mississippi, to a powerful family that included the first mayor of the city, several attorneys, and a Confederate general who later was elected a US senator. Her own father, Edward Donaldson Clark, was appointed Assistant Secretary of the Interior during President Grover Cleveland's administration but died of pneumonia on the day of his confirmation. An only child, Kate was given a typical young Southern woman's upbringing. After the war and a yellow fever epidemic, however, Holly Springs fell on hard times, and Kate's widowed mother agreed to travel north in search of better educational opportunities for her daughter.

They moved to New York City, where Kate, who had displayed an aptitude for art, enrolled at the Art Students League in 1894. She took the standard curriculum and, the following summer, studied with Irving Wiles at Peconic, Long Island. It was a transformative experience for the nineteen-year-old, who began painting *en plein air.* On a visit to the summer art school operated by Wiles's close friend William Merritt Chase, Clark was mesmerized by a Chase critique.[1] When she returned to the city, she immediately enrolled at Chase's school, and for the next six summers attended his Shinnecock Hills Summer School of Art.

During the first decade of the new century, Clark practiced what she had learned from Chase, painting mostly landscapes as well as still lifes and portraits. She intermittently submitted her paintings for juried shows and exhibitions, and when she did, she signed her work as "Freeman Clark," disguising her feminine identity. "Freeman Clark" was represented in several of the most prestigious exhibitions of the day, including those held at the National Academy of Design, the Pennsylvania Academy of the Fine Arts, the Corcoran Gallery, and the 1915 Panama-Pacific International Exposition. Despite these successes Clark never sold any of her work, in deference to her mother and uncle, who both strongly disapproved of ladies conducting business.

An outstanding example of Clark's plein air technique, *Summer Landscape* presents a beautiful seasonal scene: lush green trees grow atop a hill, and wispy clouds adorn a bright blue sky. The canvas is organized on a diagonal; the rock wall on the left leads the eye uphill to the dense grove of trees on the right. Mountains in the distance are skillfully framed on either side by trees and rocks in the front. The brushstrokes are primarily thick, but slender tree trunks are easily visible throughout.

Between 1916 and 1922 Clark lost the three most important people in her life: her mentor, Chase; her grandmother; and her mother. This was a difficult period, during which Clark acted as a caregiver and painted little. In 1923 she returned to her ancestral home, known as Freeman Place, in Holly Springs, adding an upstairs studio to the property. Although this renovation suggests an intention to either paint or give lessons, Clark never did. Neither did she bring any of her finished pieces back to Holly Springs. It was not until after her death that her entire oeuvre—totaling over one thousand objects—was discovered in a New York City warehouse and transported to Mississippi. The artist's will endowed the construction of a gallery to store and exhibit her legacy, and in 1963 the Kate Freeman Clark Art Gallery opened next door to Freeman Place.[2]

CAROLYN J. BROWN

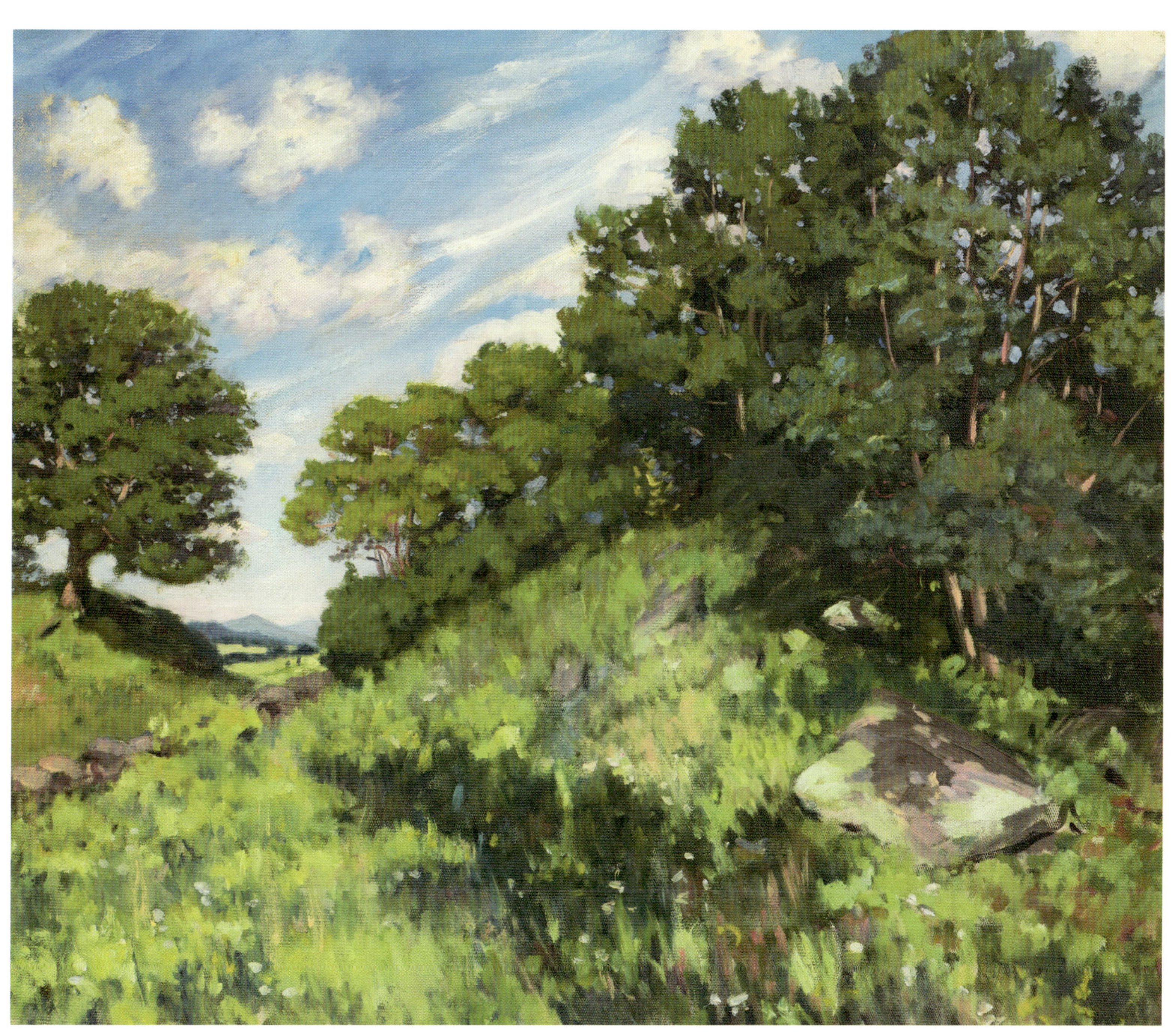

EMMA JOSEPHINE SIBLEY COUPER (1867–1957)

Yellow Dahlias

Pastel on paper, 24½ × 20½ inches

Despite the ravages of the American Civil War, the Sibley family of Augusta, Georgia, retained their fortune, which provided a comfortable childhood for Josephine. Her early passion for art was nurtured by a trip abroad at the age of twelve, and when she returned, her father hired an instructor and equipped a studio for her use. While he was supportive of his daughter's burgeoning talent, Josiah Sibley also hoped these provisions would keep her safely ensconced at home. That paternal control went with him to the grave in 1888; the very next year, Josephine enrolled at the Art Students League, a move that was funded by the sale of some property he had left her.

At the League, William Merritt Chase was her mentor, although she took the standard classes in drawing antique casts from other instructors. Chase was noted for having a large number of female students and for his exacting painting exercises, which focused on still lifes. An admirer of the French painter Jean-Baptiste-Siméon Chardin, Chase once famously declared: "If you can paint a pot, you can paint an angel."[1] The boldness that had propelled Sibley to New York City was often at odds with deeply ingrained Southern mores. When a necessary League course in composition was scheduled for seven o'clock in the evening, Sibley refused to attend on the grounds that "no lady could be on the streets unescorted" at night.[2] In 1890 Sibley made a second grand tour of Europe, where she sketched genre scenes and copied old master paintings. The following year she returned home and married a widower sixteen years her senior.

For women artists, marriage raised certain issues. Balancing household and child-rearing responsibilities with a desire to be creative was a daily challenge. Developing a professional identity in the public arena was complicated too. In the South these dilemmas were aggravated by traditional, conservative values. Like her father, Couper's husband encouraged her creativity: he constructed a studio as an "integral part" of their residence, "not an addition."[3] During their fourteen-year marriage, Couper was a dutiful wife and mother of two children, and she primarily painted likenesses of family members and friends. Over her long career she was frequently listed in exhibition brochures as "Mrs. B. King Couper," although she regularly signed her work "J. S. Couper," which did not divulge her gender.

Couper was also active in the art community of her adopted home of Spartanburg, South Carolina. In 1907, along with Margaret Law, a distant relative and fellow student at the Art Students League, she cofounded the Spartanburg Arts and Crafts Club. Its greatest accomplishment was the mounting of an exhibition that showcased Couper and Law's paintings alongside works by Chase, Robert Henri, and Elliott Daingerfield. The effort was a great success and included a contest in which attendees voted on their favorite painting. The popular choice was Henri's *Girl with Red Hair,* now a prized possession of the Spartanburg Art Museum.

Once her children came of age, Couper broadened her subject matter as well as her style. She studied under Daingerfield in Blowing Rock, North Carolina, and spent several summers in Gloucester, Massachusetts, where her instructor was Hugh Breckenridge. Both teachers are known for their landscapes, and while Daingerfield is recognized for his glazing techniques, Breckenridge gained his reputation as a vivid colorist who painted with broad strokes. In 1929 and 1930 Couper spent time abroad, living in Paris and taking classes under the French Cubist André Lhote, probably at the suggestion of Law, who had studied with him earlier. Couper attempted some abstract paintings but did not embrace the style wholeheartedly. Most of her career she pursued a conventional form of realism, though by the 1920s the influence of Impressionism had become more evident.

Given her financial security, Couper never felt compelled to sell her work, even though she exhibited widely with such entities as the Southern States Art League, the National Association of Women Artists, and the 1930 Salon d'Automne in Paris. In 1927 the High Museum of Art in Atlanta hosted a solo exhibition in her honor. When Couper happened to make a sale, she donated the proceeds, after expenses, to her church or to missions in Africa. The artist rarely dated her work, which makes placing *Yellow Dahlias* problematic, but Chase's impact is unmistakable: his dedication to still life, his admiration for Chardin, and his use of pastel. Yet *Yellow Dahlias* also reflects Breckenridge's propensity for intense colors. The pastel reveals a remarkable freshness, and the composition's drooping blossoms exude a certain sweetness.

MARTHA R. SEVERENS

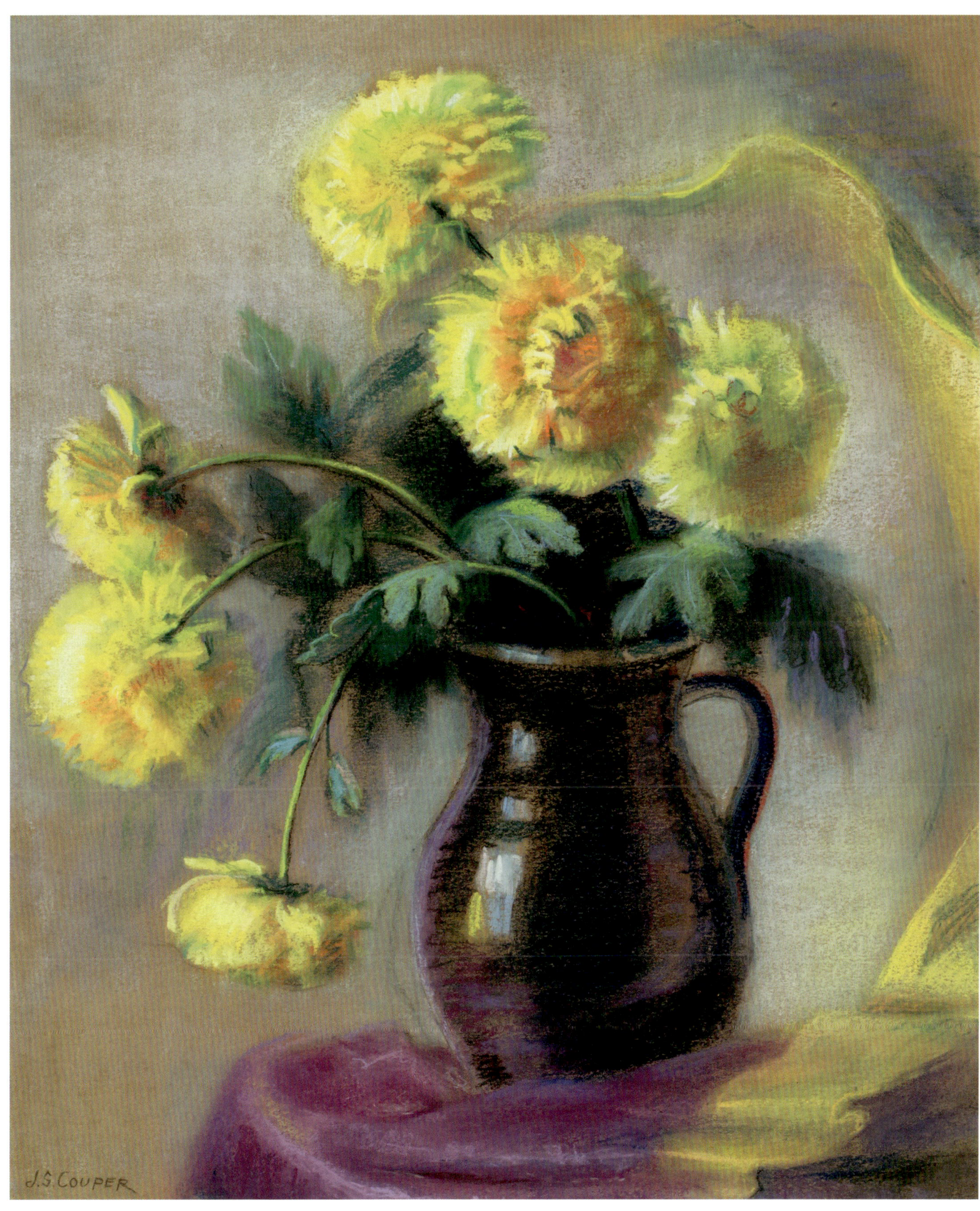
J.S.COUPER

MINNIE EVA JONES EVANS (1892–1987)
Untitled

Crayon and pencil on paper, 12 × 9 inches

This untitled drawing represents Minnie Evans's characteristic visual vocabulary from the mid-1940s to the 1960s. Contained within sensuous, curvilinear forms reminiscent of classical amphorae, or two-handled Grecian vases, the work visualizes a liminal realm between dreams and consciousness. Hypnotic, repetitious patterns made up of flower petals, leaves, horns, and reptilian scales mirror in perfect symmetry on the vertical axis. Scrolls interlace to construct elaborate, kaleidoscopic arabesques, paisleys, and filigrees. A colonnade of frontal faces emerges from a swirl of colorful headdresses to reveal multiple noses, pairs of eyes, and vibrant red lips frozen in archaic smiles. Between the top and middle heads, a clearing in the vegetation reveals a landscape with a setting sun on the horizon. An additional pair of disembodied eyes float beneath the vignette, imbuing the work with an omniscient undertone.

Born in Long Creek, North Carolina, Evans embraced her creative sensibility late in life. On Good Friday in 1935, Evans had a vision in which a divine voice told her to "draw or die."[1] The result was two of her first drawings; they were filled with "ancient writing," repeating lines, and distinct visual registers.[2] It was not until five years later, in 1940, that she rediscovered the drawings while cleaning her home. From that moment on, Evans conscientiously produced her signature chromatic, mythical drawings, sometimes executing as many as seven in one day as a form of religious discipline.[3] The incessant instruction to draw guided her hand over the page and receded as she worked—only to recur at night in her dreams. Deeply tied to her faith, Evans considered these messages gifts from God and approached her art through the lens of Christian belief.[4]

Evans's output represented to her a holy partnership of sorts, the result of an intense collaboration between herself as vessel and the Lord she worshiped.[5] Yet the artist was quick to note that her work was not a literal translation of her visions, but rather "a memorandum" or impression of its archetype: "We can get the imitation, but we can't paint the real angel."[6] Her drawings became recursive exercises where she would revisit and contemplate her visual language over and over again, repeatedly addressing the same themes and motifs anew. Replete with facial features, flora, and fauna, Evans's work rarely diverged from these symmetrical abstractions; however, no two drawings are identical. In some instances, as here, Evans cut out the drawing and pasted it on a new piece of paper because she wanted the background to be unsullied.[7]

Evans refused to provide interpretations of her work, readily acknowledging her own mystification at its process and portent: "They are just as strange to me as they are to anybody else."[8] This disjuncture between creator and object is unusual in the history of art and has therefore led scholars to seek evidence of her source material. Indeed, Evans may have been subconsciously influenced by her surroundings in coastal North Carolina. From 1948 until her retirement in 1974, Evans worked as the gatekeeper of Airlie Gardens, a public garden in Wilmington, the historic port city situated between the Cape Fear River and the Atlantic shoreline. Collecting admission tickets year in and year out afforded Evans ample opportunity to observe the park's shifting seasonal splendor, including the annual festival display of azaleas.[9] Certainly her dense, ornate drawings suggest organic forms of leaves and flowers, yet none includes exact replicas from nature.

Additional possible references for Evans's enigmatic drawings range from the Oriental rugs and decorative arts she regularly encountered in her employer's house to Kongo cosmograms and Greco-Roman mythology.[10] Evans could have been referencing all or none of these. Because her work was created outside of the academic mainstream, it cannot readily be explained or interpreted through conventional art historical means. Simply put, Evans's art transcends fixed iconographic interpretation. Rather than limit her drawings to the particular, it is best to think of them in terms of the universal, taking into consideration how her art defies academic categorization.

ERIN R. CORRALES-DIAZ

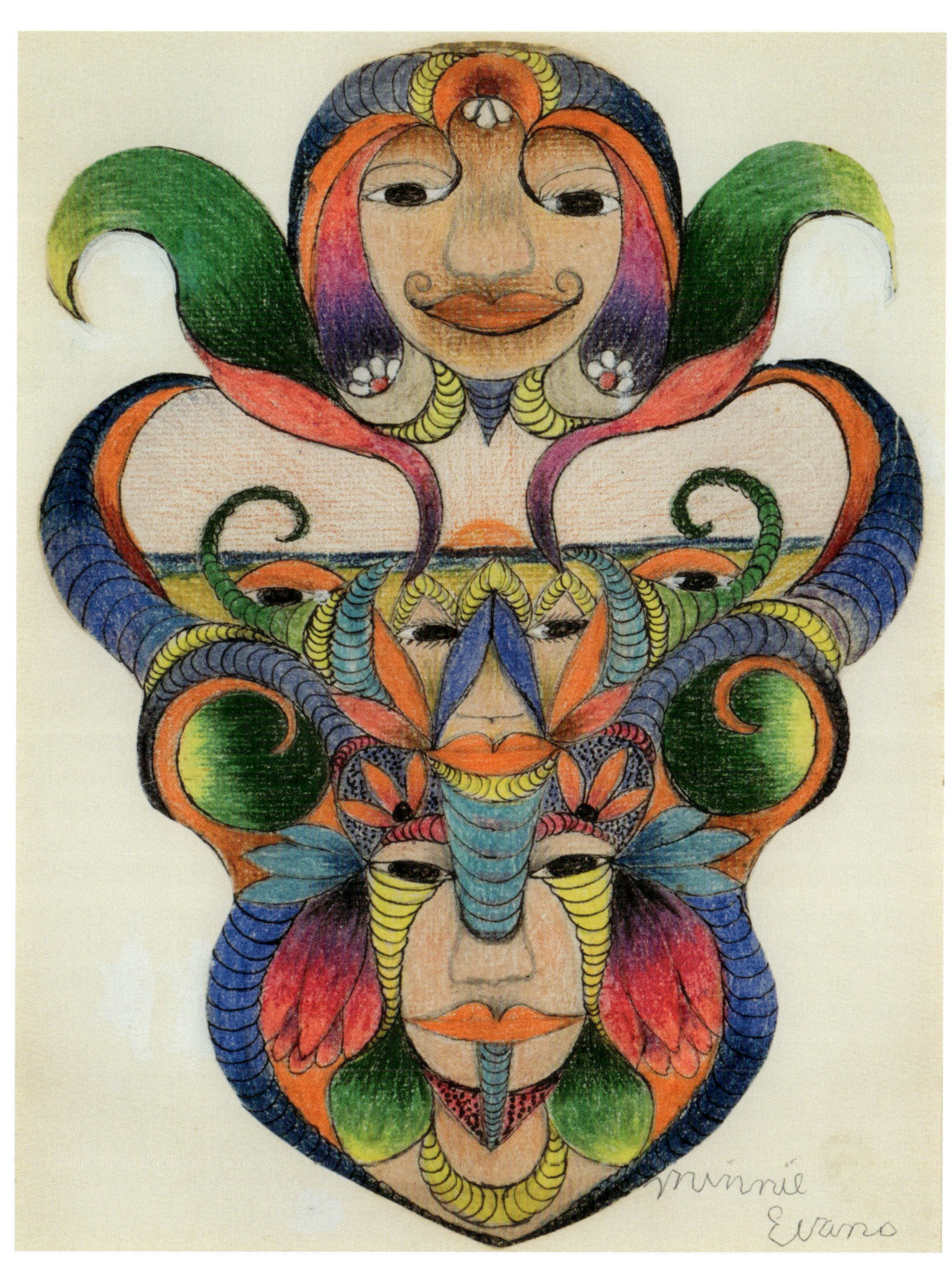

VIRGINIA BARGER EVANS (1894–1983)

Gloucester Garden

Oil on canvas, 24⅛ × 26¼ inches

A gifted painter, teacher, and glass designer, Virginia Evans was one of the leading artistic figures in West Virginia during the twentieth century. A native of Moundsville, she received early instruction in art at Wheeling's Mount de Chantal Visitation Academy, a Catholic all-girls school that boasted one of the finest secondary-level arts education programs in the region. After graduating in 1914, she continued her studies at the Carnegie Institute's School of Fine Arts in nearby Pittsburgh, at the Pennsylvania Academy of the Fine Arts summer school at Chester Springs, and at the Louis Comfort Tiffany Foundation on Long Island. Evans visited Europe four times between 1926 and 1931. Her initial destination was Fontainebleau, France, where she spent a summer at the fine art conservatory for American students. Subsequent excursions included working travels through Portugal and Spain, Great Britain, and the Netherlands and Germany.

Evans exhibited her work to great acclaim both regionally and nationally during the 1920s and 1930s. Finely executed impressionistic paintings entered in the annual exhibitions of the Associated Artists of Pittsburgh were perennial favorites with critics, as were her plein air gouaches, which were accorded multiple solo exhibits in Wheeling and Pittsburgh during this period. Her work was also exhibited regularly in New York City. In addition to solo shows at the city's Studio Guild and the New York Public Library, she participated regularly in the yearly expositions mounted by the Tiffany Foundation Fellows, as well as those of the Society of Women Painters and Sculptors, to which she was elected in 1931.

The course of Evans's career took a turn in 1942 when Imperial Glass Corporation engaged her to develop designs based on traditional Chinese motifs for a new line of glassware. Thanks to Evans's painstaking studies and expansive aesthetic vision, what was initially intended as modest dinnerware evolved into Imperial Cathay crystal, a distinctive selection of vases, bowls, and other functional and decorative items that included some of the finest pieces of molded crystal made in the United States. Embossed with Evans's signature, the Cathay crystal line was represented in the exhibition *Twentieth Century Glass, American and European* at the Metropolitan Museum of Art in New York in 1950 alongside pieces by Tiffany and Lalique.

Following additional ventures in glass and ceramic design, Evans moved to Florida in 1957. She spent a year in Orlando before moving south to Naples, where she became a leading member and teacher at the budding Naples Art Association and returned to painting in earnest. Her output during this period was highly eclectic, ranging from abstract works—often bearing titles suggestive of musical themes—to both traditional and experimental landscapes. In 1972 Evans was one of five West Virginia artists commissioned to create a work for the state's newly created permanent art collection, to be housed at the West Virginia State Museum.[1] She returned to the Mountain State permanently two years later and spent her final years in her hometown of Moundsville.

In a 1934 review, the noted Pittsburgh art critic Penelope Redd hailed Evans as one of the "best trained and most gifted painters" in her region and "in a far greater radius."[2] Works such as *Gloucester Garden* attest to the validity of such praise. Flower gardens, a subject that lends itself so naturally to the techniques and spirit of Impressionism, drew the attention of painters on both sides of the Atlantic. Evans was no doubt familiar with the innumerable renderings of Claude Monet's gardens at Giverny, and with American examples like Childe Hassam's popular paintings of Celia Thaxton's gardens on New Hampshire's Isles of Shoals, just a few miles north of Gloucester.

Evans first visited the New England coast during the summer of 1920 and returned many times thereafter, traveling nearly its entire length. In *Gloucester Garden* she explores the colors and contrasts of two of her favorite themes, botany and the sea. Her depiction of the foreground's lush beauty is bright, bold, direct, and brilliant in its communication of the texture and feel of species that are easily identifiable despite the economy of their rendering via spontaneous but orderly dashes and dabs, blobs and strokes of buttery pigment. The pure joy of painting is in evidence here. The muted depiction of the harbor in the painting's background, in which wharves and vessels are merely suggested, enhances the garden's dazzling aura. An architectural form, possibly a trellis or arbor, dissects the composition in its middle. Its geometric white lines provide an interesting counterpoint to the natural forms of this engaging picture, which is perhaps as much a still life as it is a landscape.

JOHN A. CUTHBERT

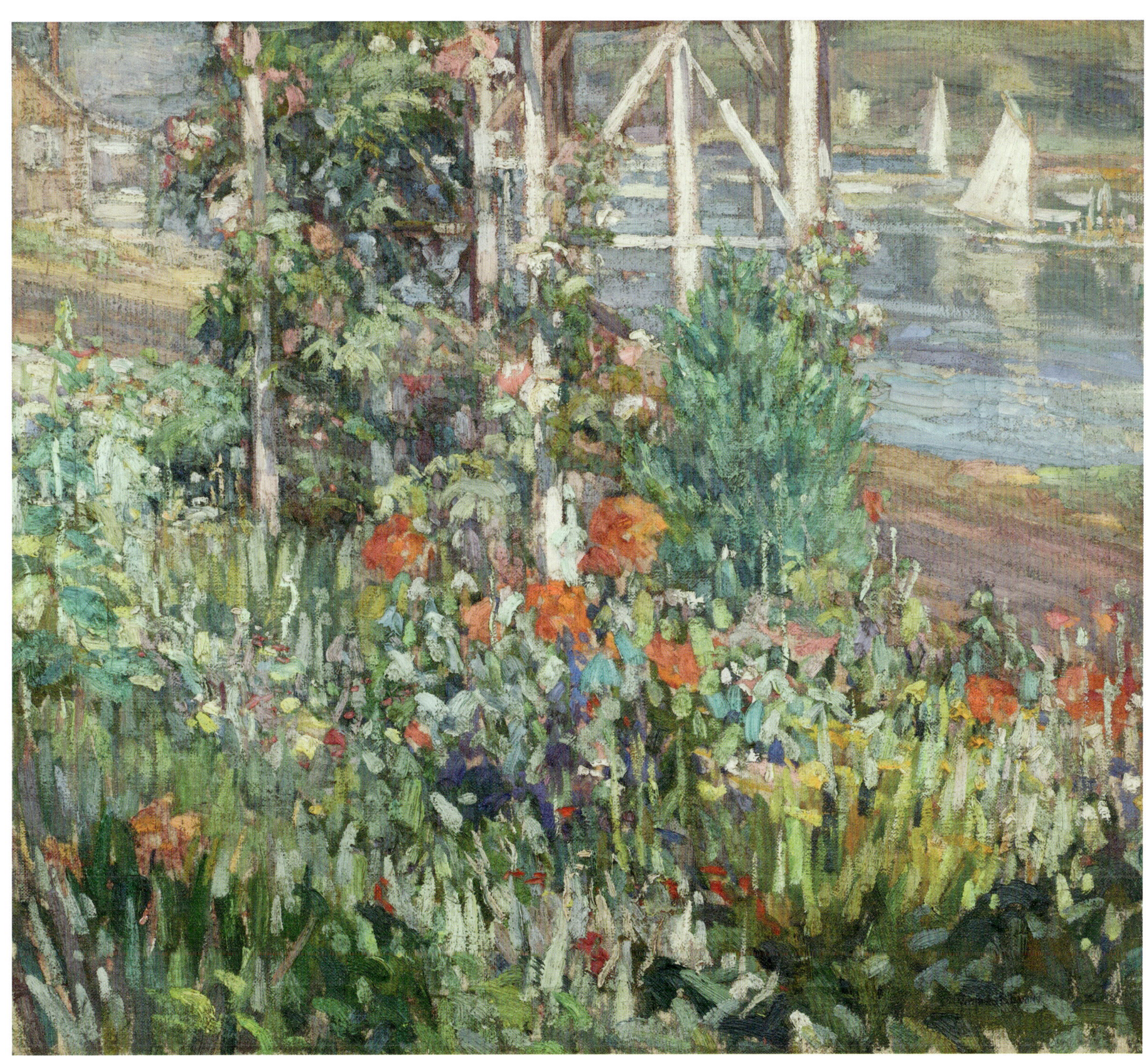

ANNE WILSON GOLDTHWAITE (1869–1944)

Frances Greene Nix, circa 1935–1940

Oil on canvas, 49⅜ × 39½ inches

In a 1934 radio interview, Anne Goldthwaite characterized the status of women artists by noting that "the best praise that women have been able to command until now is to have it said that she paints like a man. But that women have a valid place as women artists is both obvious and logical.... We want to speak to... an audience that asks simply—is it good, not—was it done by a woman."[1] The Alabama painter had come of age during an era when intrepid American women increasingly contested gendered barriers in the art world as well as in the wider sociopolitical realm.[2] Her participation in these struggles belied her conservative Southern upbringing in Montgomery as the daughter of a former Confederate officer. After her parents' untimely deaths, Goldthwaite was placed in the care of her aunt, Molly Arrington. Arrington had certain nuptial aspirations for her niece, admonishing young Anne that "it is better to marry badly than not at all." Goldthwaite recalled: "I was brought up to believe that matrimony was the desired end of a woman's life and a woman's career."[3] But her life and career would be different. At eighteen, Goldthwaite came out in society as a debutante, marking her eligibility as a bride. She failed to find a husband by twenty-three, however, and her family suggested she move to New York to pursue her interest in art.

Goldthwaite arrived in New York around 1898, and for the next six years she studied at the National Academy of Design with Henry McBride and Frank Mielatz, and took lessons with Walter Shirlaw, a founder of the Society of American Artists.[4] In 1906 she moved to Paris, where she cofounded the Académie Moderne and lived at the American Girls' Club.[5] A fellow club member introduced her to Gertrude Stein, through whom Goldthwaite was exposed to the works of modernists like Paul Cézanne, Henri Matisse, and Pablo Picasso. Under their influence the academicism of her earlier work loosened, and her brushwork grew more fluid. Yet Goldthwaite never fully abandoned representation; although she exhibited at the 1913 Armory Show alongside abstract modernists, her own paintings remained in the Realist mode.

On the eve of World War I, Goldthwaite returned to New York, where she would live for the rest of her life, although she visited Montgomery nearly every summer.[6] She quickly gained a reputation for portraiture. "You forget all the portraits you have seen before when you see this easy and fluid style," raved one early critic, who was also compelled to note that Goldthwaite's works "seem to satisfy what I am looking for in portraiture better than most male painters and better than any other women."[7] Goldthwaite resisted this kind of gendered criticism. She fought adamantly for the political rights of women, producing the design for a suffrage banner unfurled at a 1916 New York Giants baseball game, and co-organizing the 1915 Exhibition of Painting and Sculpture by Women Artists for the Benefit of the Woman Suffrage Campaign.[8] Her participation in the suffragist cause reveals how far she had come since her debutante days and points to the deep divide between her personal political leanings and her relatives' anti-suffragist stance.[9]

In 1922 Goldthwaite became an instructor at the Art Students League, a position she would hold for over twenty years. She also continued to teach during her summer sojourns in Alabama, offering advice to students at the Dixie Art Colony. Established near Montgomery by painter John Kelly Fitzpatrick in 1933, this enclave is where Goldthwaite may have met Frances Greene Nix, who is known to have studied with both Goldthwaite and Fitzpatrick.[10] Like Goldthwaite, Nix was a native of Montgomery and a practicing portraitist; she later served as director of the Montgomery Museum of Fine Arts.[11] Goldthwaite's likeness of her shows a softly striking woman, presumably in her mid-thirties, seated in a space reminiscent of Mary Cassatt's Impressionist domestic interiors. Nix's decorous attire, jewelry, and what appears to be a mirror or a watch dangling from her left hand are akin to the feminine accouterments frequently featured in Cassatt's vignettes, while the limited palette, visibly fluid brushstrokes, and slightly indeterminate spatial relations evince Goldthwaite's absorption of Post-Impressionist painterly strategies.

Goldthwaite's sitters were often other women artists. In New York she painted Katherine Dreier, an ardent suffragist and cofounder of the Société Anonyme, as well as future first lady Ellen Axson Wilson, a Georgia-born painter who had studied at the Art Students League.[12] Goldthwaite's portrait of Nix should be seen in the context of these depictions of strong, independent women who insisted on pursuing professional careers in the arts at a time when the art world was still seen as a man's world.

ELIZABETH S. HAWLEY

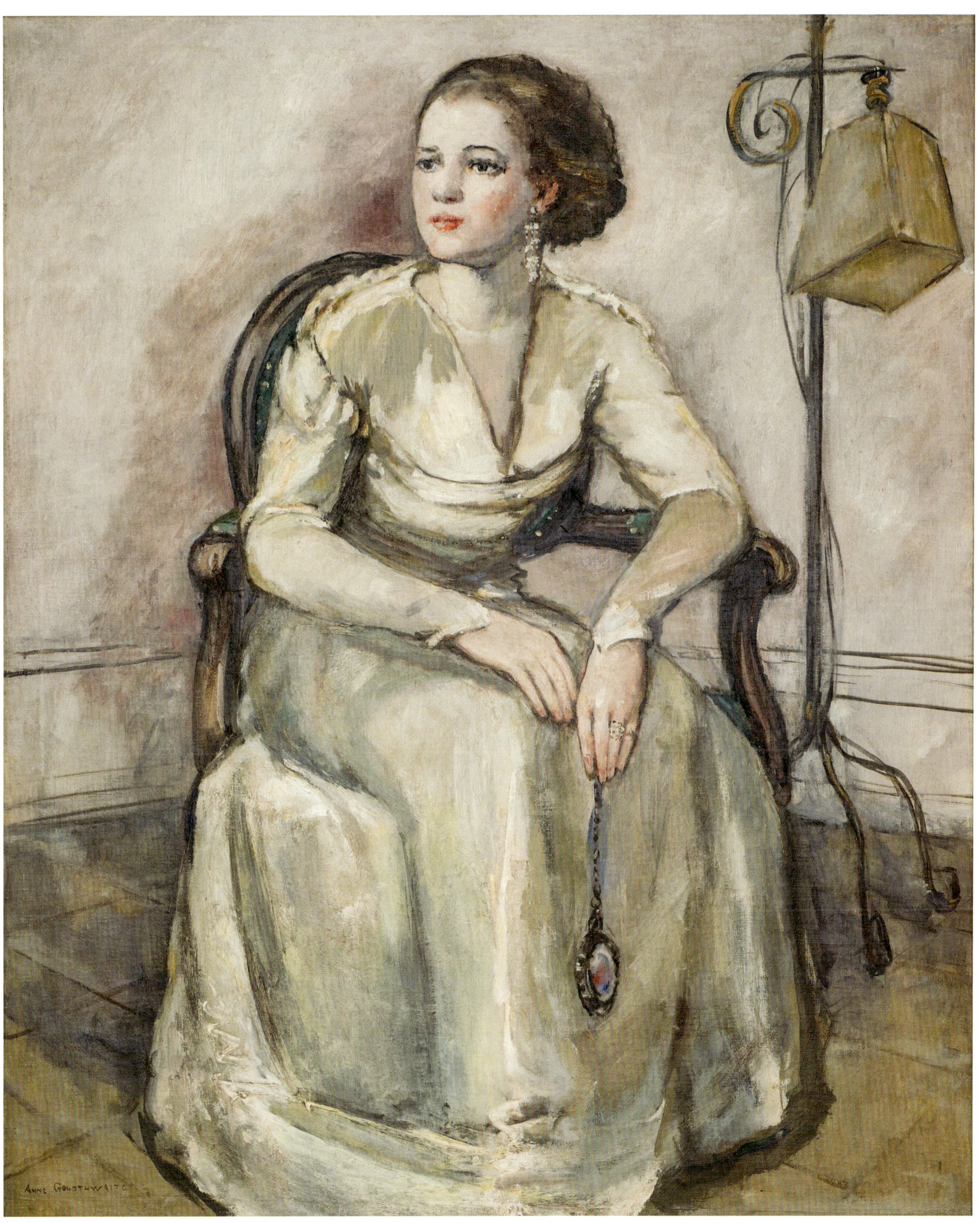

ANGELA GREGORY (1903–1990)

Head of a Woman

Bronze, 9⅞ × 5¾ × 3½ inches

"I have decided to become a sculptor. How do you like that? I made up my mind long ago to be an artist and I think I will like that best of all."[1] With this proclamation, made to her father at the age of fourteen, Angela Gregory determined her life's path—early on and with confidence. Having grown up in an artistic household on the Tulane University campus in New Orleans—her mother, Selina Bres Gregory, was a painter and potter associated with the Newcomb College school of art and a founding member of the Arts and Crafts Club—Gregory was all too familiar with both the joys and challenges of a creative life.[2] Her course set, she spent the summer of 1917 studying clay modeling and relief casting, and in 1921 she enrolled as an undergraduate at Newcomb, where her professors included Ellsworth Woodward and Will Henry Stevens. She undertook additional studies in sculpture at the Arts and Crafts Club and later in New York.

Upon her graduation from Newcomb in 1925, Gregory earned a scholarship to study illustrative advertising at the Paris branch of the Parsons School of Design. While she was honored by the award, Gregory's true objective was realized a year later when she was admitted to the teaching studio of sculptor Antoine Bourdelle, whose expressive style reflected his tenure as an assistant to Auguste Rodin.[3] Keenly aware of the obstacles she would encounter in a "notoriously masculine field," Gregory asked Bourdelle: "Do you think I have enuf [sic] talent to go on with sculpture or do you think I should develop my interest in painting?" The French artist answered with a question of his own: "Did anyone tell Joan of Arc she should rid France of the English? She wanted to do it and she did. It is your decision."[4] Her unconventional professional path was matched by her equally unconventional resolve to remain single. Having watched her mother subordinate her own artistic ambitions to domestic responsibilities, Gregory recognized that "too often a woman is torn by conflicting obligations, as a mother, a wife, sister, daughter. Unless she can stay on the track, she becomes a dilettante."[5]

When her European sojourn ended after three years, Gregory regretfully returned to New Orleans. Although she complained of the city's relative lack of culture and its oppressive heat, she resolutely set to work in her Pine Street studio, building friendships along the way with other artists in the community, including Helen Turner and Josephine Crawford.[6] One of her first undertakings was the "Negro Project," in which she studied African American residents of Port Gibson, Mississippi. The project resulted in some of her most admired works. When selections from this series were exhibited in 1933, one critic commented that they revealed "the influence of her teacher…and the strength of her gift. They are strong, well modeled, vital works that are essentially plastic and full of character."[7] Like her French master, Gregory favored irregular and tactile surfaces, but her subject matter was truly American.

Comparable to these Port Gibson works, *Head of a Woman* portrays a serene, mask-form head of a sitter with contemplative, downcast eyes and softly pursed lips.[8] The surface is smooth in the rounded areas of her forehead, cheeks, and chin, while the hair and neck are depicted with crevices and folds. Imbued with what Gregory termed "quiet dignity," *Head of a Woman* conveys the artist's insistence on emotional authenticity, as well as her sensitivity to African American culture in the region: "I appreciate more each day the rich artistic back-ground [sic] of the South, and the important part the Negro has had in its history."[9]

Gregory built a national and international reputation, and her body of work includes large-scale architectural decoration, bas-relief portraits, plaques, and medals. Over her long career she was employed as a state supervisor for the Works Progress Administration Federal Art Project, as an assistant architectural consultant to the Army Corps of Engineers, and as a camouflage designer; she also taught at both Newcomb and St. Mary's Dominican College. In one of the many eulogies given at her memorial service, the dean of Newcomb College remembered Gregory's vision and courage, traits that enabled her to forge a pioneering "life that was full of compassion and ribbed with experience and art."[10]

KRISTEN MILLER ZOHN

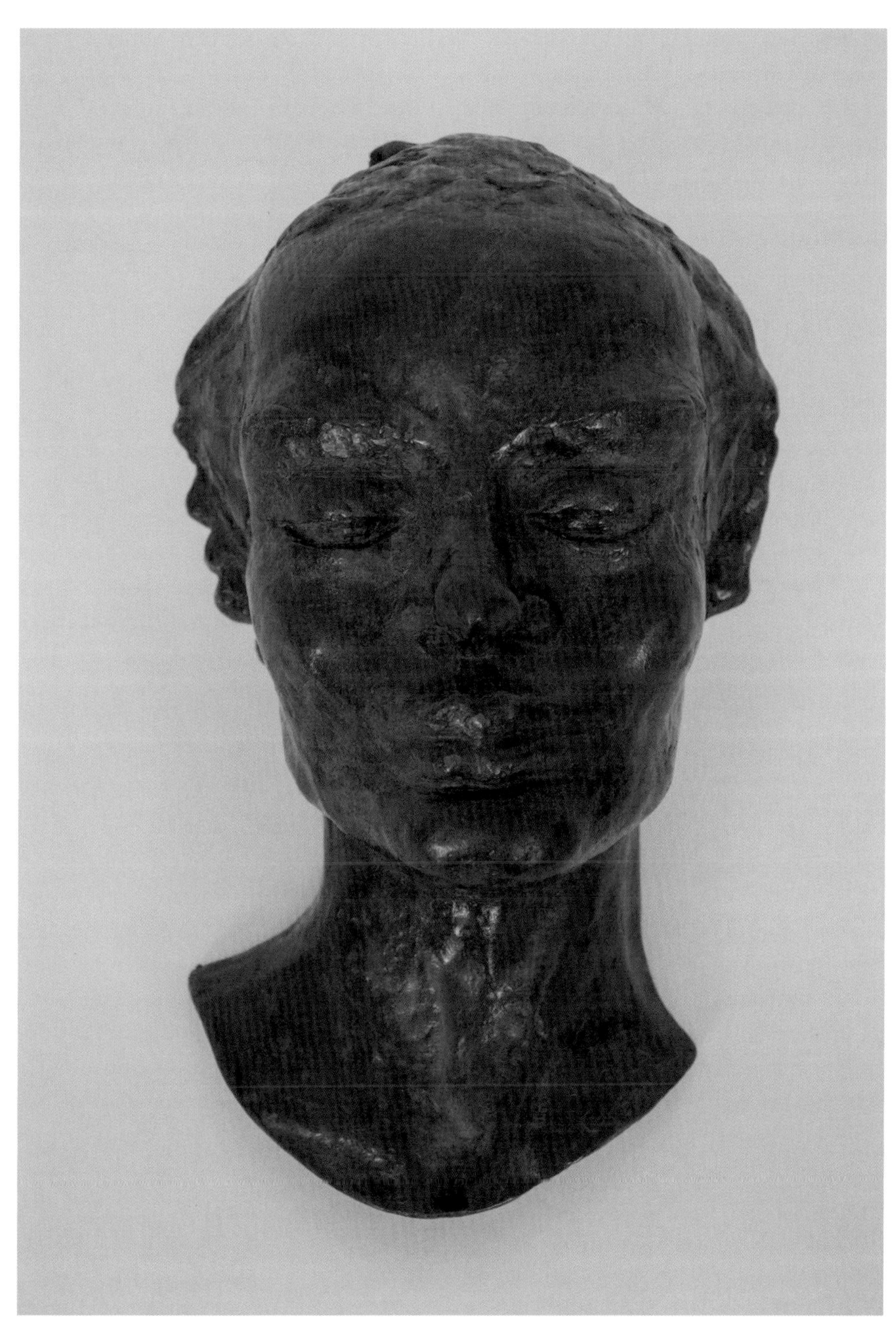

ELLA SOPHONISBA HERGESHEIMER (1873–1943)

Portrait of Madeline McDowell Breckinridge, 1920

Oil on canvas, 48¼ × 37 inches

"With the paint smeared on her thumb," the Pennsylvania-born Ella Sophonisba Hergesheimer "captivated the South and was in turn captivated by it."[1] A descendent of Charles Willson Peale, Hergesheimer took after her famous relative and pursued a career in the visual arts. Her middle name and preferred professional moniker, Sophonisba, pays homage to Peale's own daughter, who was named after another famous female artist, the Italian Renaissance painter Sofonisba Anguissola. Hergesheimer enrolled at the Pennsylvania Academy of the Fine Arts in 1900, studying under William Merritt Chase and Cecilia Beaux, and regularly won prizes for her artistic achievements, including the coveted Cresson Traveling Scholarship—a three-year award for study.[2] While in Europe she became enamored with the work of Diego Velázquez, whose sensuous handling of paint left a profound impact on the burgeoning artist. In Paris she took courses at the Académie Colarossi and exhibited her paintings at the prestigious Salon.

By chance, Hergesheimer submitted several of her paintings to an international traveling exhibition cosponsored by the Nashville Art Club and the Atlanta Art Association in 1905.[3] These works caught the attention of Methodist bishop Holland N. McTyeire, one of the founders of Vanderbilt University, who would thereafter commission the artist to paint his portrait.[4] Executed upon the artist's return to the United States in 1907, the portrait's success led to subsequent commissions; Hergesheimer soon found herself limning "many of the wealthiest and most beautiful women of the South."[5] To her delight, she discovered an abundance of possible subjects in the region: "The country around Nashville is, some of it, the most beautiful I have ever seen—a large and bounteous field for the landscape painter. There are hosts of beautiful women and children and strong, fine men to inspire great portraits."[6] So assured of the possibilities available in the region, she declared Nashville a future art center of the South.[7] Flush with success, Hergesheimer resided in the state until her death in 1943.

While Hergesheimer experimented with other painting genres and even dabbled in printmaking alongside fellow artist Blanche Lazzell, portraiture was her primary source of income.[8] Lauded for their ability to convey "poetic feeling in addition to mere physical form," Hergesheimer's portraits reveal as much about the artist as they do about the sitter.[9] Such is the case with her 1920 *Portrait of Madeline McDowell Breckinridge,* a work that alludes to the challenges both women confronted in that era. Breckinridge was a prominent leader of the women's suffrage movement and a tireless advocate for children's welfare in her home state of Kentucky and on the national stage.[10] The Nineteenth Amendment, which granted women the right to vote, was ratified in Kentucky on January 6, 1920, the same year Hergesheimer completed Breckinridge's portrait. Although Hergesheimer was not known to be active in the suffrage movement, her defiance of conventional gender roles—she never married and was self-supporting—suggests a certain kinship between artist and sitter.

Using broad strokes of rich color, Hergesheimer presents a mature woman of quiet authority—composed, assured, and at ease. Sitting askew in a chair with decorative gilded fluting and deep blue fabric—details evocative of an elegant throne—Breckinridge confidently meets the viewer's gaze. Attired in a loose, diaphanous dress, she also wears a heavy overcoat and cloche hat embellished with stars. In her lap, her left hand holds a dense bouquet. These flowers may have had period iconographic connotations, but they are more symbolic due to their color. Traditionally associated with royalty and fidelity, Hergesheimer's purple may be signaling loyalty to the suffrage cause and a belief in the glory of womanhood. The painting reflects the courage and resolve of all women fighting for equal rights in the early twentieth century.

Aware of a growing enthusiasm for photography over painted portraits, Hergesheimer addressed the distinction between the two mediums in a 1913 public lecture: "The camera is faultless.…The picture is real. But the portrait painter does not make this kind of a picture. He sees his subject as a living, breathing human being with an atmosphere, a kind of aurora as it were, about him, and without hesitancy the artist sacrifices straight, literal lines in order to give life to his picture."[11] Despite her considerable professional achievements by this time, Hergesheimer curiously refers to the "portrait painter" as male, revealing a latent gender bias in the art world.

Hergesheimer strove to communicate her sitters' essential natures, imbuing these likenesses with a quality she believed unobtainable through a mechanical apparatus. Here she portrays her subject with palpable sensitivity, perhaps aware that Breckinridge was succumbing to tuberculosis, which would cause her death mere months later.

ERIN R. CORRALES-DIAZ

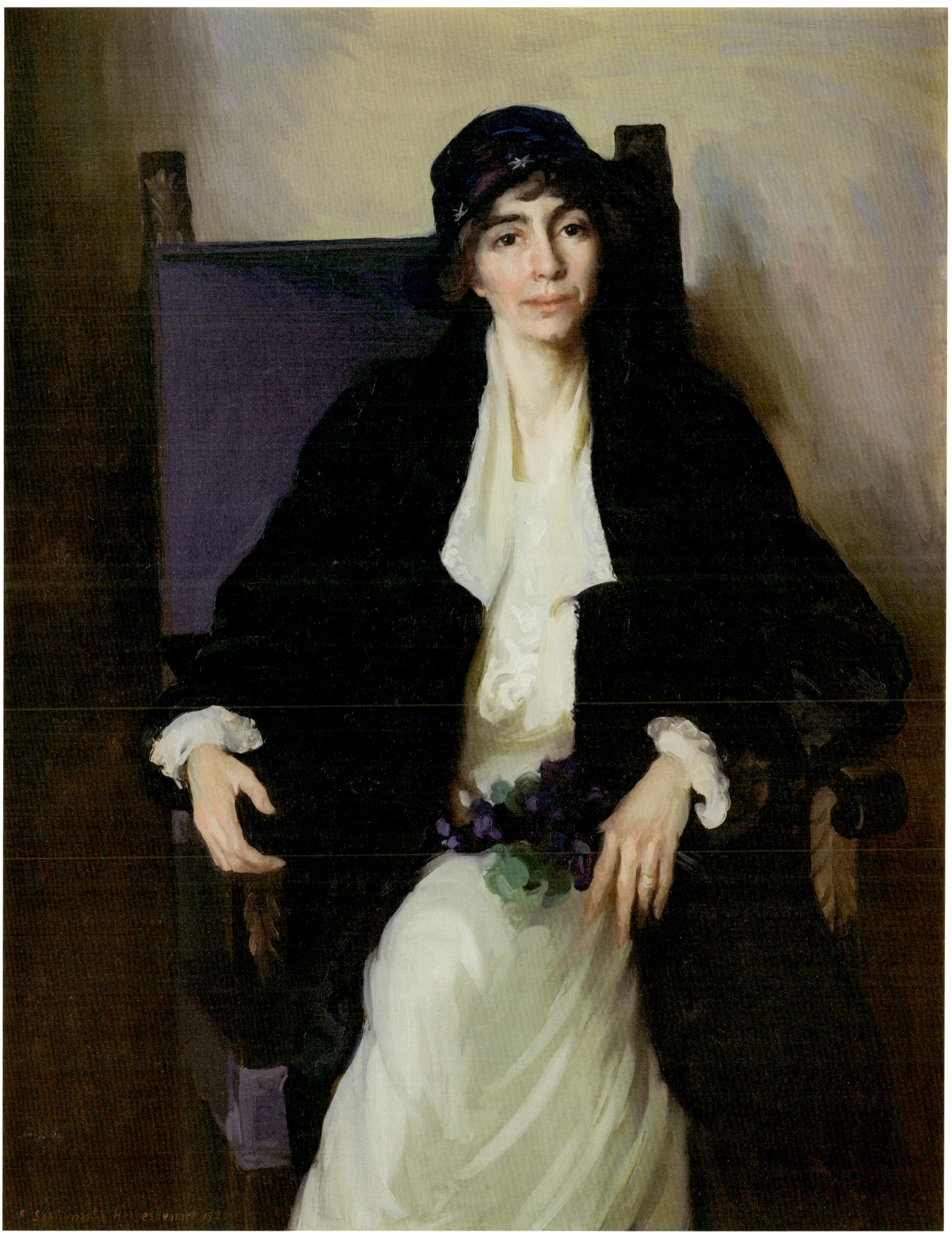

EMILY MARIE ATKINSON HULL (1890–1980)

Red Parrots, circa 1926

Oil on canvas, 25⅛ × 25⅛ inches

Marie Hull was one of Mississippi's most beloved artists and teachers, probably more popular and better known during the course of her ninety years than since her death. Longevity, productivity, and an indefatigable constitution gave her the extended runway needed to build up a national reputation. She made two lengthy trips to Europe, one in 1913 and another in 1929, and thereafter had dozens of exhibitions and entered scores of competitions across the country, bringing home a bounty of accolades, prizes, and awards. Subsequent generations have been deprived of direct contact with the extraordinary self-confidence and extroverted personality that fueled her achievement, and today her name is a household word only in the Deep South.

Hull was extremely prolific, but no more than sixty-five of her oil paintings are in museum collections, with perhaps another 250 in private hands. Throughout her very social life, Hull both sold and gave away an untabulated number of works and frequently traded her paintings for those by other artists, such as Georgia O'Keeffe and Ida Rittenberg Kohlmeyer. There are very few records of these hundreds of transactions, and when Hull died without immediate heirs, no inventory was made of the contents of her house and studio at 825 Belhaven Street in Jackson, Mississippi.[1]

It was not until about 1920 that Hull's stylistic personality began to emerge. The gestation had been protracted because her artistic education (at prestigious institutions such as the Pennsylvania Academy of the Fine Arts, the Colorado Springs Fine Arts Center, and the Art Students League in New York) had been episodic—interrupted by other personal and professional pursuits—and multivalent, influenced by the contradictory forces of traditional academic training and the more avant-garde strategies of European modernism, as represented in the Armory Show of 1913. A handful of small but highly accomplished floral still lifes and landscapes dating to the years 1919–1929 survives, executed in a vibrant divisionist technique most clearly reliant on the Neo-Impressionism of French painters Henri-Edmond Cross, Maximilien Luce, and Paul Signac.

The artist was working in this vein in late 1925 when the Hulls arrived in St. Petersburg, Florida, where Emmett (whom Marie had married in 1917) opened an architectural practice.

For unknown reasons the venture was a short one, lasting less than a year, during which time Hull made only a handful of captivating paintings of beaches and fishing boats. On the other hand, she produced hundreds of drawings and watercolors of the exotic birds to be seen in a subtropical Eden—as the Gulf Coast of Florida must have seemed in those days. The pages of at least one intact sketchbook, as well as troves of loose-leaf portfolio sheets, are filled with studies of wild pheasants, peacocks, pelicans, cranes, egrets, herons, parrots, macaws, and flamingos. These are typically annotated with the specific name of the species depicted or detailed descriptions of the size, shape, and pigments of each bird's plumage, eyes, skin, talons, and bill or beak, obviously made as points of reference for later use in the studio, where Hull created a limited number of portraits of her favorite specimens.

The finished paintings in gouache or oil—on canvas, compressed fiberboard, and wood—are of exceptional rarity in the artist's oeuvre: only a dozen or so can be accounted for today, including this example.[2] A theoretical companion work of identical format and dimensions, *Blue Parrots, Florida,* complements *Red Parrots.*[3] Whether considered individually or as a pair, these paintings embody Hull's stylistic progression from the divisionist brushwork of Signac to the *cloisonnisme* of Émile Bernard. In both pictures she combines the technique of brush and palette knife with solid black outlines, applies gem-like fields of color resembling stained glass, and dramatically asserts the surface plane by means of flattened floral blossoms; the backgrounds are only vaguely illusionistic in character. The result is highly decorative and represents the nearest Hull came to working in the fashionable, contemporaneous style of Art Deco.

None of the artist's paintings of exotic birds is dated. It is possible that many were made after the Hulls had returned to Mississippi. At the top left corner of the original stretcher appears an inscription in the artist's hand: *Red Parrots/Marie A. Hull/Jackson, Miss.* If it was not created during the Florida sojourn, *Red Parrots* was likely executed soon thereafter, before the Hulls departed on an automobile trip across Texas and the southwestern deserts, and on to the Pacific Coast.

ROGER WARD

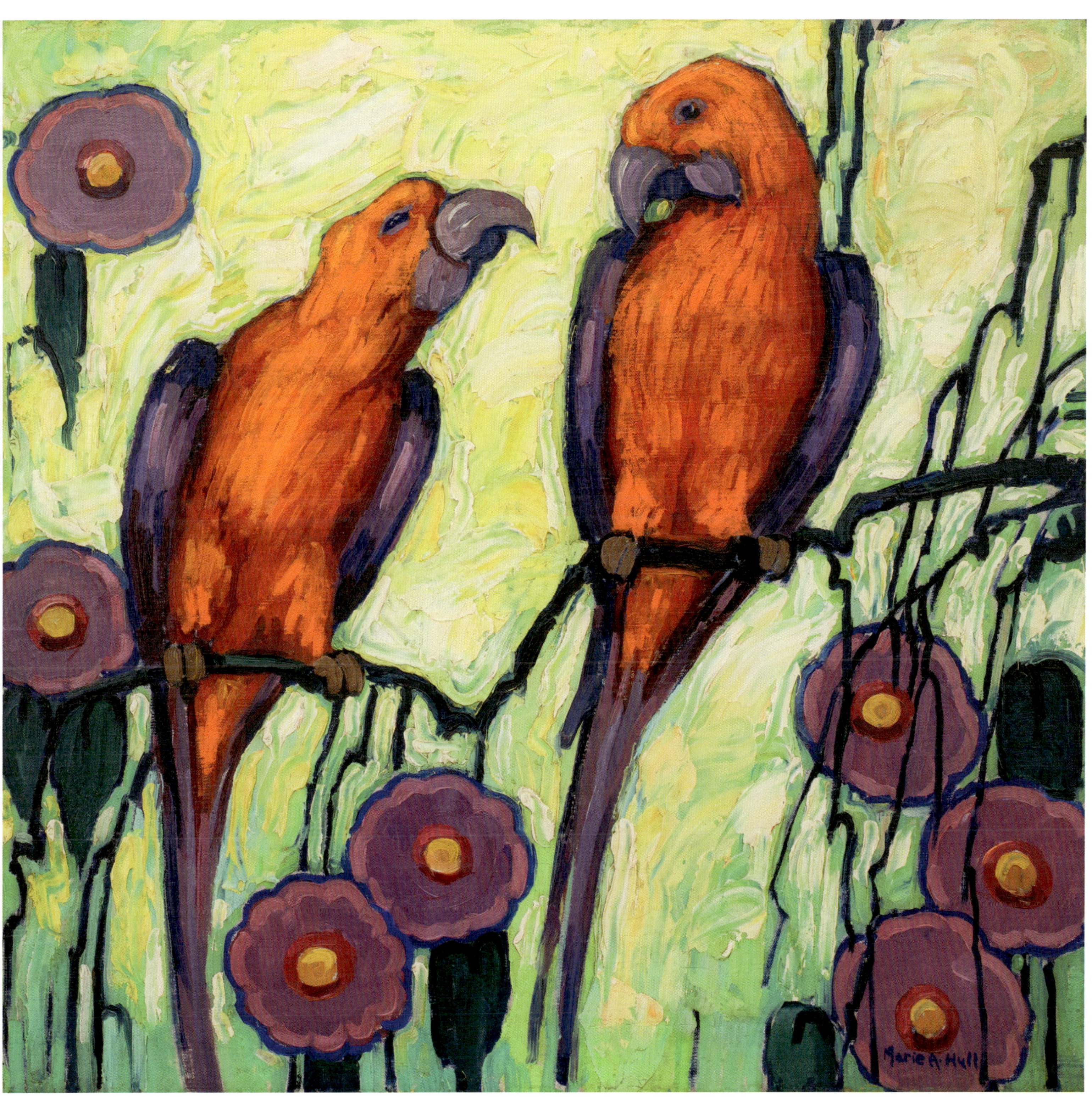

CLEMENTINE REUBEN HUNTER (1886–1988)

Cane River Baptism, circa 1950–1956

Oil on paper board, 19 × 23⅞ inches

When asked about her work, Clementine Hunter said: "I tell my stories by marking pictures. The people who lived around here and made the history of this land are remembered by my paintings. I like that. I'm glad the young people of today can look at my paintings and see how easy and uncomplicated things were when we lived off the land. I wanted to tell them. I paint the history of my people. The things that happened to me and to the ones I know."[1] Painted from memory, *Cane River Baptism* fuses Protestant and Roman Catholic traditions during a sacramental rite that would have been both familiar and meaningful to the artist. Here Hunter compresses time and space, organizing the ceremonial procession into three horizontal sequences, or registers, with each figure or object firmly resting on a ground line. At the top of the painting a deacon rings a bell, while priests, white-robed baptismal candidates of various skin tones, and the congregation wind toward the Cane River. To the right a white church reminiscent of St. Augustine, the nearby Catholic parish, is surrounded by verdant overgrowth and vibrant flowers. In the lower right-hand corner two partially immersed priests or deacons anoint one of the baptismal candidates in the water. At once visual storyteller and vernacular historian, Hunter illuminates the complex racial and religious diversity of her homeland.

Born on Hidden Hill Plantation in rural Louisiana, Hunter spent the majority of her life as a resident laborer and domestic worker on the neighboring Melrose Plantation. Melrose's owner, Carmelite "Cammie" Garrett Henry, an avid patron of the arts, fostered an informal creative colony on the property, frequently hosting various authors, poets, and artists. Regular interaction with this community inspired Hunter to pick up a paintbrush in her fifties.[2] Hunter's artistic origins are shrouded in myth, but her friend and advocate Francois Mignon recounted a moment when Hunter found discarded paint tubes and, with his assistance, gathered an old window shade, brushes, and turpentine. The following morning Hunter completed a painting.[3] With Mignon's support, Hunter achieved national recognition for her depictions of the Southern African American experience, and critics heralded her work for its idealized and picturesque representation of post–Civil War plantation life.[4] Yet although Hunter was self-taught and geographically isolated, she was steeped in the artistic atmosphere of Melrose and familiar with popular culture motifs such as Catholic prayer cards and Sunbonnet Sue.[5] Hunter's art was not produced in an aesthetic vacuum, but rather should be attributed to her innate originality, sharp intelligence, and keen perceptive powers.

Hunter repeatedly transcribed river baptisms—scenes she had witnessed "a-many a time"—in addition to other routine religious liturgies.[6] Given the repetitious nature of her subject matter, Hunter's work can be divided into categories: plantation life, recreational scenes, religion and spirituality, flora and fauna, and abstractions. Identifiable by their richly saturated colors, sometimes applied straight from the paint tubes, these paintings offer an optimistic view of a life that was filled with hard labor, poverty, and tragedy. Within the compositions, scale acts as a barometer for the artist's regard for featured individuals or as an indicator of their importance to the narrative. Despite the lack of perspective and skewed scale, Hunter achieves balance through the use of repeating patterns, motifs, and figures, the latter notable for their minimal, reductive features. In *Cane River Baptism,* Hunter painted the background first with gradations of pinks and blues, lending an ethereal aura to the scene.

For Hunter baptisms, funerals, and wakes represented a transitional stage between the heavenly and earthly realms, between sin and salvation.[7] In focusing on this liminal space, Hunter alludes to the symbolic connection between African American emancipation and the biblical flight for freedom through the passage of water.[8] The ceremonial procession and presence of a consecrated structure suggest the importance of journey and ritual to the quest for redemption. Although she had been baptized as an infant in the Catholic Church and was a registered communicant at St. Augustine's, Hunter attended the local Baptist church, where she joined its congregation in exuberant singing.[9] As a result, her theological paintings reflect the fluidity of a deeply personal faith unconstrained by denominational dogma.

ERIN R. CORRALES-DIAZ

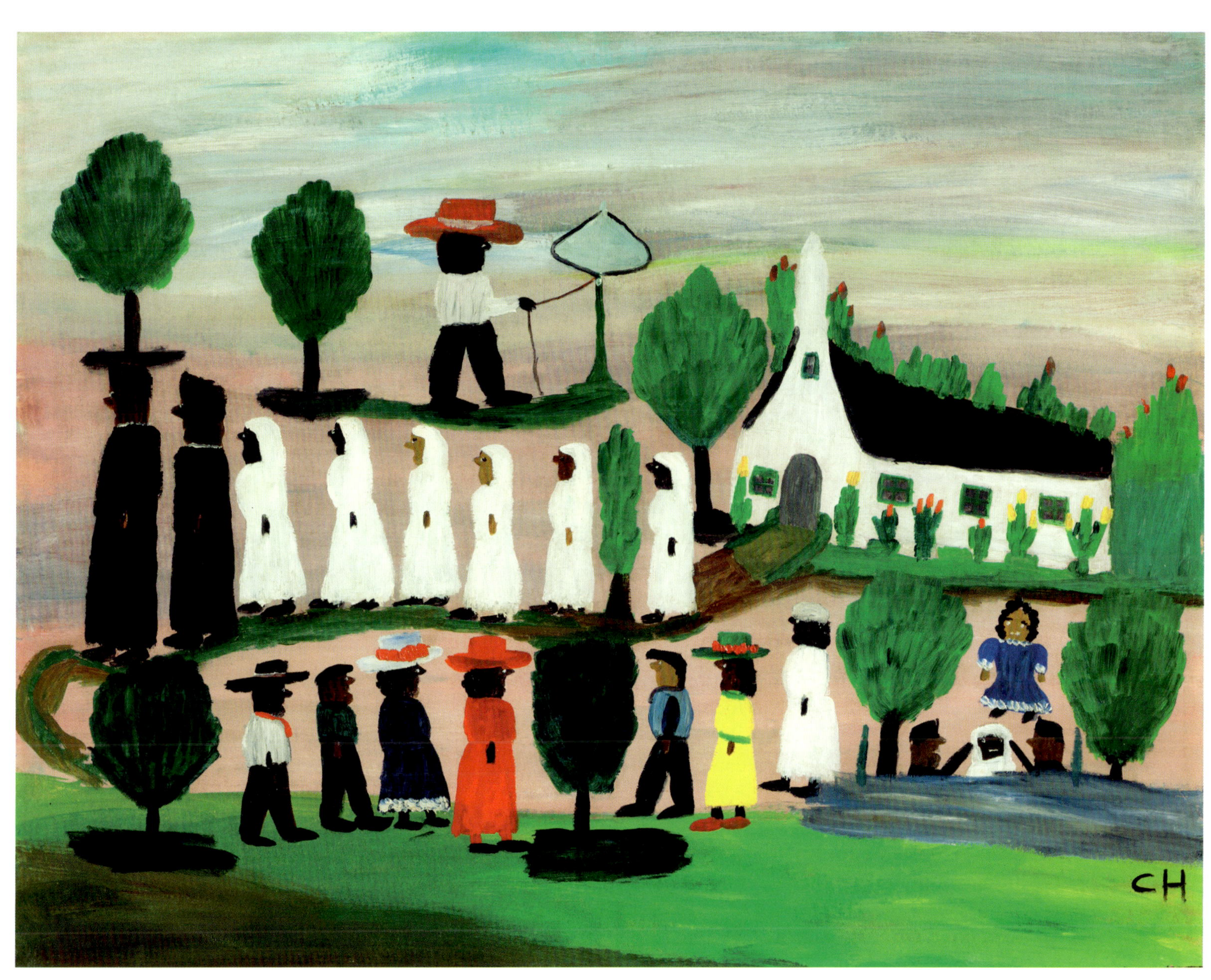

ANNA VAUGHN HYATT HUNTINGTON (1876–1973)

Yawning Tiger

Bronze with brown patina, 8½ × 7 × 28⅞ inches

Anna Hyatt's initial creative interest was the violin, and she devoted several hours each day to practice in hopes of a professional career in music. In her early teens, however, Anna put down the violin and began modeling animal figures in clay, following the example of her older sister, Harriet. Her knowledge of animal anatomy was the result of a keen power of observation honed during field trips with her father, a renowned paleontologist and professor, and on visits to her brother's farm near Leonardtown, Maryland: "As soon as she could crawl, she headed for horses' hoofs to examine them, and long before she could swim, peered so intently at minnows that she toppled off our dock.... All her life she understood how to control animals, caressing dangerous dogs without being bitten and breaking colts without breaking her bones."[1]

These experiences provided the inspiration and foundation for the largely self-taught artist's development. Hyatt studied briefly with Boston sculptor Henry Hudson Kitson and collaborated with her sister on a few small projects. In 1902 she relocated to New York City and enrolled for a short time at the Art Students League, where her instructors included Gutzon Borglum. She befriended a fellow League student, Abastenia Eberle, with whom she executed several well-received pieces, including *Men and Bull*, which won a bronze medal at the 1904 Louisiana Purchase Exposition, held in St. Louis. Hyatt's bronze *Winter Noon*—a composition of two work horses, one with a trailing blanket—was also shown, and national attention soon followed.

Hyatt's other New York classroom was the Bronx Zoo, where she spent countless hours modeling the great cats and other exotic animals. In 1905 a *New York Times* reporter observed her at work and wrote about the "tall, young woman in tailor made frock and red-plumed hat...doing a clay study." He referred to the young woman's plans to travel abroad, but only after she felt "perfectly independent" in her own work and "above outside influence."[2] By 1907 Hyatt felt sufficiently prepared and rented a studio in Auvers-sur-Oise, France. Over that summer she worked on enlargements of her studies of "Señor Lopez," a jaguar at the Bronx Zoo. Two resulting pieces, *Reaching Jaguar* and its companion, *Jaguar*, were exhibited in 1908 at the Paris Salon, where they were widely acclaimed as powerful yet elegant depictions of feline grace, and helped to launch Hyatt as an important animal sculptor.

For the next few years Hyatt alternated her time between Paris and New York. Her masterful and historically accurate equestrian monument *Joan of Arc* was installed in Riverside Park in 1915; it was New York City's first public monument executed by a woman. Around that time Hyatt earned more than $50,000 a year through her work—becoming one of the country's highest paid women—and was recognized with prestigious awards.[3] In 1923, at the age of forty-seven, she married Archer Milton Huntington, a philanthropist in the arts and humanities, and member of one of the wealthiest families in the country. Their union created and supported a vast string of museums, organizations, educational facilities, and cultural initiatives.

Hoping to escape the cold and relieve Anna's respiratory difficulties, the Huntingtons purchased four former coastal rice plantations in South Carolina in January 1930. Captivated by the haunting beauty of the land and its native plants and animals, they initially planned to use the nine-thousand-acre property as a winter home. They established Brookgreen Gardens on July 13, 1931, creating the first public sculpture garden in the United States. Determined to acquire the best figurative works by the best American artists, Anna Hyatt Huntington made curatorial choices that reflected her own aesthetic inclinations and traditional personal taste. Works by women sculptors, though not a deliberate focus, were acquired throughout the 1930s.[4]

The Bronx Zoo's jaguars, tigers, and lions served as a catalyst for Huntington's work for decades, and her careful study of the powerful feline anatomy found repeated expression, as evidenced by *Yawning Tiger*. Modeled in 1917, this popular subject was created in two sizes, the example featured here being the larger version. The languorous, sinewy tiger—portrayed on its stomach in mid-stretch with tail lifted—is yawning broadly. Its front and back paws reach outward with claws extended. Huntington captured the essence of the animal with minimal detail, a trademark of her oeuvre. In response to a 1929 exhibition of her work, a critic opined that Huntington's "living animals are surpassed only by the great Hellenistic masters of animal life. Every beast seems to have waited for this American lady to give it soul."[5]

ROBIN R. SALMON

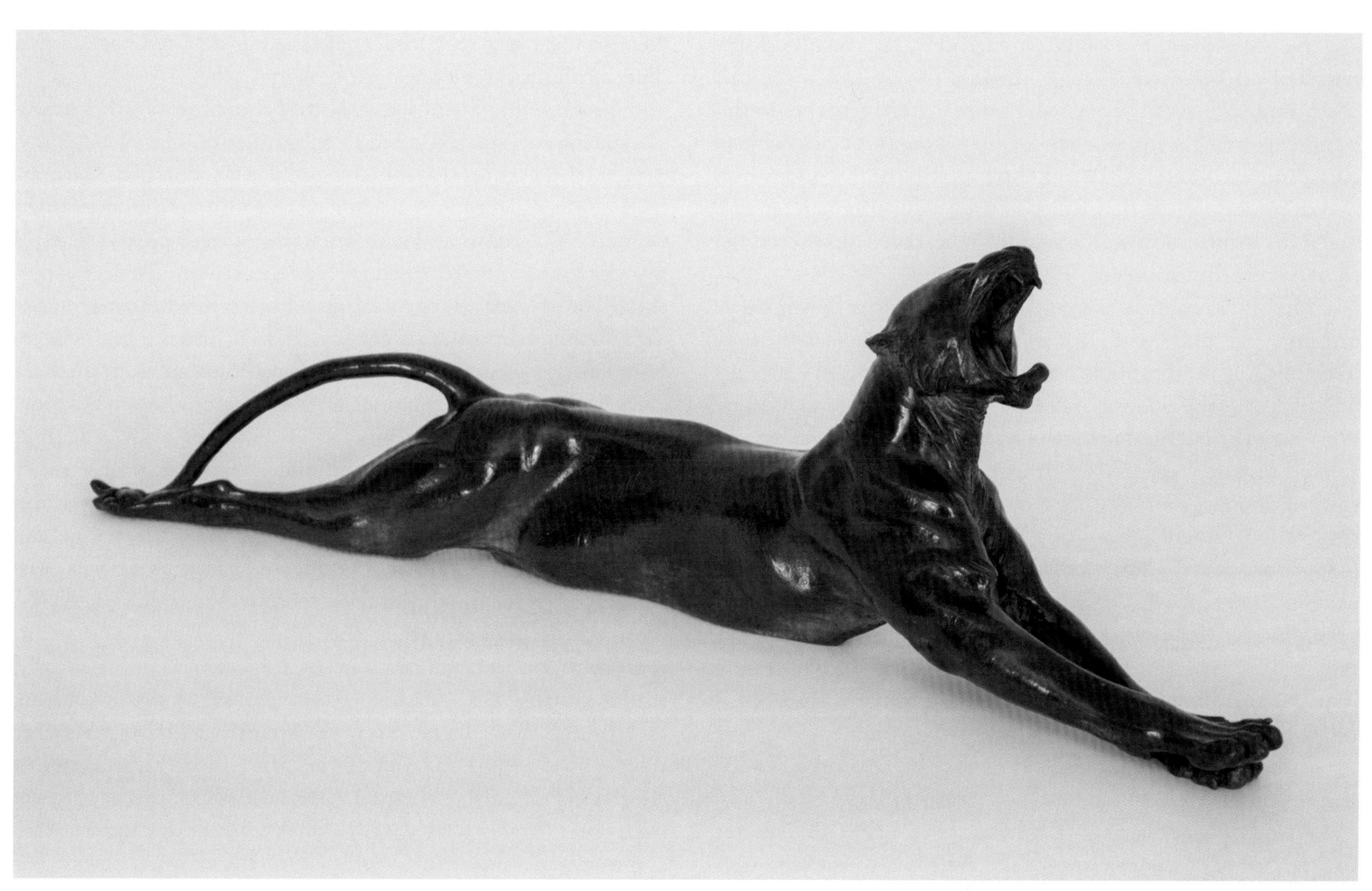

LOÏS MAILOU JONES (1905–1998)

Africa, 1935

Oil on canvas board, 24 × 20 inches

On the occasion of her ninetieth birthday, Loïs Mailou Jones reflected on her artistic longevity and the obstacles she had confronted. "It wasn't easy," she said. "There was the double handicap: being a woman and being a woman of color. I kept going on, with determination. As I look back, I wonder how I've done it."[1] Jones had indeed faced daunting gender and racial discrimination, yet her stalwart resolve empowered her to persevere and succeed.

The Boston-born artist displayed creative promise at an early age and, with her parents' encouragement, began her training at the High School of Practical Arts in 1919, advancing to the School of the Museum of Fine Arts in 1923.[2] Although the curriculum at the Museum School included life, freehand, and perspective drawing courses, she gravitated toward design as a major. She enrolled in graduate studies at the Designers Art School of Boston and eventually became a freelance textile designer.[3] Work from this period reflects Jones's preference for bold, pulsating colors and flattened graphics of Caribbean-inspired flora and fauna. On a family trip to Martha's Vineyard, Jones spotted some of her designs in a shop window and was distressed by the omission of her name on the printed cloth: "As I wanted my name to go down in history, I realized that I would have to be a painter. And so it was that I turned immediately to painting."[4]

Armed with new resolve, Jones applied to her alma mater, the School of the Museum of Fine Arts, for a teaching position. Her request was denied, the rejection tendered with the director's suggestion that she "go South to help your people."[5] Initially Jones balked at the notion, but after attending a lecture delivered by pioneering educator Charlotte Hawkins Brown at a local community center, she began to reconsider.[6] Jones convinced Brown of the necessity of art instruction at Palmer Memorial Institute, a preparatory school for African American youth in Sedalia, North Carolina. Jones's two-year residency in the rural community, from 1928 to 1930, was her first encounter with the sort of segregation and racism particular to the American South.[7] She established a thriving art department at Palmer, which soon attracted the attention of another artist-educator, James Herring, who recruited her to Howard University.[8] Jones would remain at Howard for forty-seven years, teaching exceptional students such as Alma Thomas, Elizabeth Catlett, and David Driskell.

In 1968 an article in *Ebony* magazine remarked on Jones's creative curiosity, reporting that "she has devoted her life to a quiet exploration—a quest for new meanings in color, texture and design."[9] That innovative spirit is borne out in this example, dating to 1935. Executed in vibrant jewel-like hues, *Africa* depicts three sharply-defined figures with chiseled features. In the lower right-hand corner of the foreground, a profiled woman's lifted chin and gaze draw the viewer's eye to a second woman to the left. Adorned with gold earrings and neck rings, these women buttress an androgynous figure whose placement defines the composition's vertical axis. While the high cheekbones and arched brows suggest a feminine character, the bare chest with prominent rectangular pectorals reads as masculine. Rather than depict a specific individual—or even a distinct gender—this figure conveys the multiplicity and universality of the African continent. A warm, gradient background and oversized foliage recall Jones's early work in textile design.

This trio's symmetrical, elongated features and expressionless eyes recall similar visages found in African masks. Throughout Jones's career, the mask was a vital and recurrent aesthetic component; it is the subject of her well-known 1938 painting *Les Fétiches.* Alain Locke, Jones's collegue at Howard, had urged African American artists to create images that would contradict pervasive racial stereotypes of the period. He also exhorted African Americans to connect with their "ancestral legacy."[10] Jones's incorporation of African-inspired masks into her oeuvre began well before her tenure at Howard or the execution of this canvas. While still in high school, she had worked with Grace Ripley, a costume designer, to fabricate African-style masks and clothing.[11] As part of her personal investigation of ancestral legacy, she produced a watercolor precursor to *Africa* that graced the August cover of *Opportunity* magazine in 1928.[12] And in 1934 Jones attended summer school at Columbia University to study masks from non-Western cultures, including African tribes and indigenous peoples of the Americas.[13] *Africa* grew out of these explorations and offers a dynamic tribute to her heritage. Jones remarked on her tendency to "combine motifs from various regions in Africa, which result in a composition which tends to unify Africa."[14] By stressing their shared origins, Jones used art to unify African Americans. Ultimately she hoped that race and gender would no longer circumscribe her art or achievements, asserting, "I'm an American painter who happens to be black."[15]

ERIN R. CORRALES-DIAZ

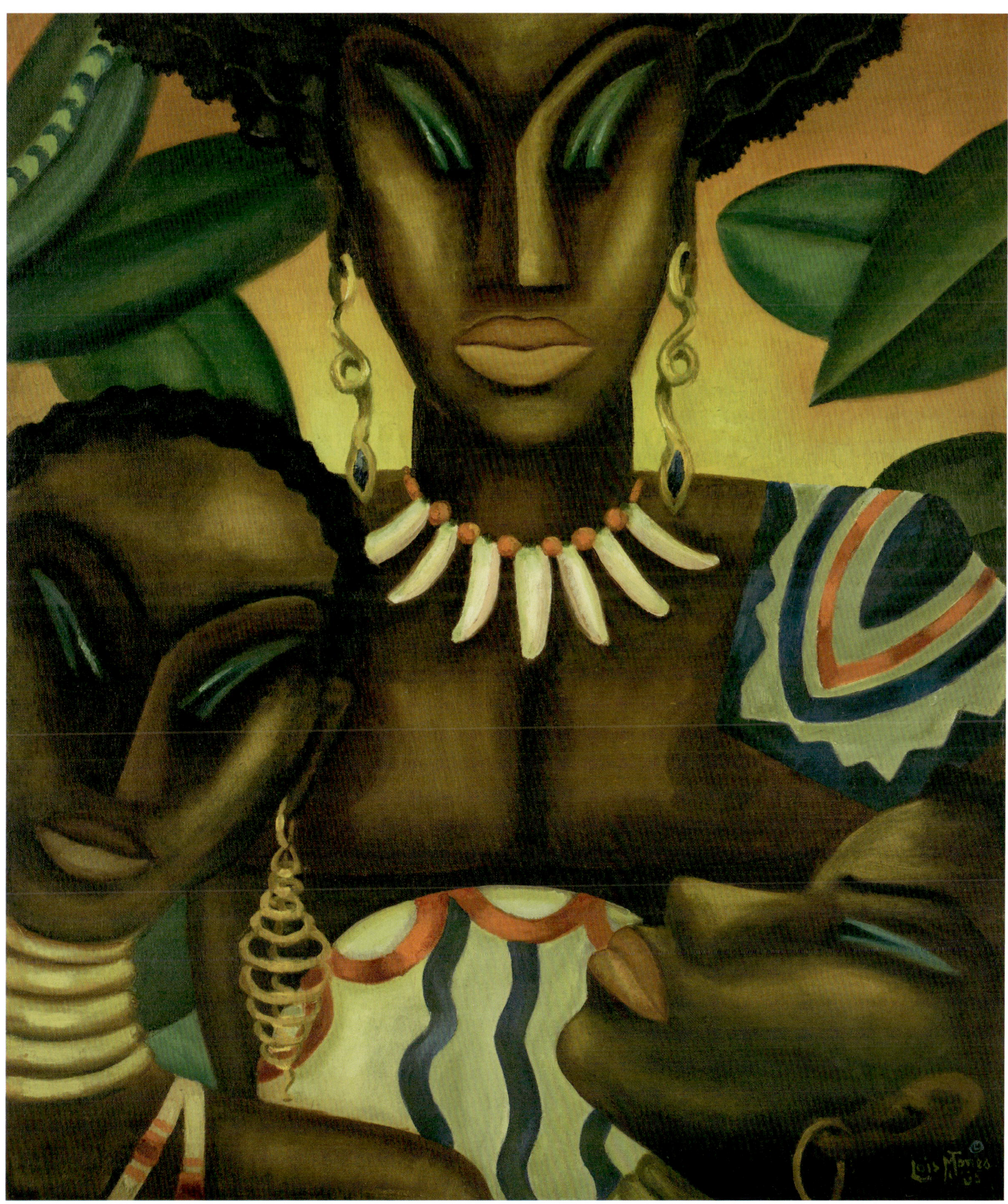

NELL HINTON CHOATE JONES (1879–1981)

The Fortune Teller

Oil base and gouache on tracing paper, 23½ × 17⅞ inches

It was not until the early twentieth century that professional women artists began to receive critical recognition in the American South. Nell Choate Jones, the daughter of a former Confederate captain, was among the first to earn such acclaim, especially for her dignified portrayals of both black and white Southerners.[1] Born in Hawkinsville, Georgia, young Nell lived in her birthplace for only a few years until her father died, prompting the family's relocation to Brooklyn, New York. Although she would reside there for the remainder of her life, Jones's Southern roots proved strong, drawing her back to Georgia for annual visits and providing the picturesque subject matter that dominated her work.

The artist's inspiration may have been distinctly Southern, but her formal education occurred on an international scale. She had a late start and only began to hone her skills in her forties, at the behest of her husband, the artist Eugene Arthur Jones. What started as leisurely painting excursions to Brooklyn's Prospect Park quickly evolved into exhibitions at the Southern States Art League in 1925 and at New York's Holt Gallery in 1927. In 1929 Jones received a scholarship to study at Fontainebleau School of Fine Arts outside Paris, which she followed with a trip to England and subsequent summers at the art colony in Woodstock, New York. At Fontainebleau—a region made famous by its Barbizon associations—Jones developed her painterly application of pigment. Instructors in the United States were influential in her maturation as well. John Fabian Carlson, a Swedish-born Impressionist living in Woodstock, reinforced her practice, while Frederick J. Boston introduced her to genre painting. Another early mentor, Ralph Johonnot, encouraged simplification of forms and limited shading, consistent with abstract art.

Jones's training was briefly interrupted in 1936 when her sister's untimely death necessitated a trip to Hawkinsville. Captivated by the verdant landscape and unassuming inhabitants, she resolved to return regularly thereafter. Georgia became the artist's muse and the provenance for numerous paintings created over the next two decades. In Jones's own words, "I've been wanting to come back to Georgia. I was born here. I'm a Southerner and that's all there is to that."[2]

The Fortune Teller exemplifies Jones's fascination with the ethnic diversity of Southern towns. Framed by an illegible sign at left and an abstracted tree at right, the scene depicts a clutch of women gathered in a market stall. At the composition's center, a white-bloused figure stares down, presumably into the palm of a paying customer. A cloaked character standing behind the circle appears to attract the attention of the woman at left, whose red attire is accentuated by a basket of similarly toned flowers. Shrouded in aubergine fabric with head bowed and a curve of grey hair, this woman appears to represent an older generation of Romani people—or gypsies, as they were colloquially known. Traveling throughout the rural South during the 1930s and 1940s, Romanis often concealed their ethnicity because of the intolerance they encountered.[3] Significant Roma populations had occupied parts of South Carolina and Georgia as early as the mid-nineteenth century. Jones's interest in this outlying group is unsurprising, given her long history of volunteering with poor immigrant populations in New York, visiting tenement homes and assisting mothers in need.[4] In contrast to women in Northern immigrant communities who primarily worked in the home, Roma women in the South routinely ventured to markets and county fairs to sell goods and tell fortunes.[5]

Traditionally the otherness of such women has been emphasized in American art. Despite their ethnic ties to the Balkan states, Roma tend to be portrayed as aged, turbaned, dark-skinned figures, as in Harry Roseland's popularly reproduced late-nineteenth-century painting *The Bride and the Fortune Teller*, in which he blurs the black mammy archetype with that of the gypsy seer.[6] To her credit, Jones did not advance this stereotype. Instead, she created an unsentimental, densely populated composition in which the title figure is not prioritized. Rich, saturated colors and expressive brushwork faithfully convey the bustling atmosphere of a marketplace. The skewed perspective—which conflates frontal and aerial views—in conjunction with the application of black contour lines to block in large areas of vibrant colors, attests to the artist's familiarity with contemporaneous art movements, particularly Fauvism.

Memorable paintings like *The Fortune Teller* earned Jones a national reputation, setting the stage for representation at the 1939 New York World's Fair and in exhibitions at prestigious venues such as the National Academy of Design. An active member of the Southern States Art League and other peer organizations, Jones was particularly supportive of women artists. In 1951 she was elected president of the National Association of Women Artists, and she also served as the first female president of the Brooklyn Society of Artists. Jones lived the majority of her 101 years in New York, but following her death in 1981, her ashes were interred in Georgia.

SANDY McCAIN

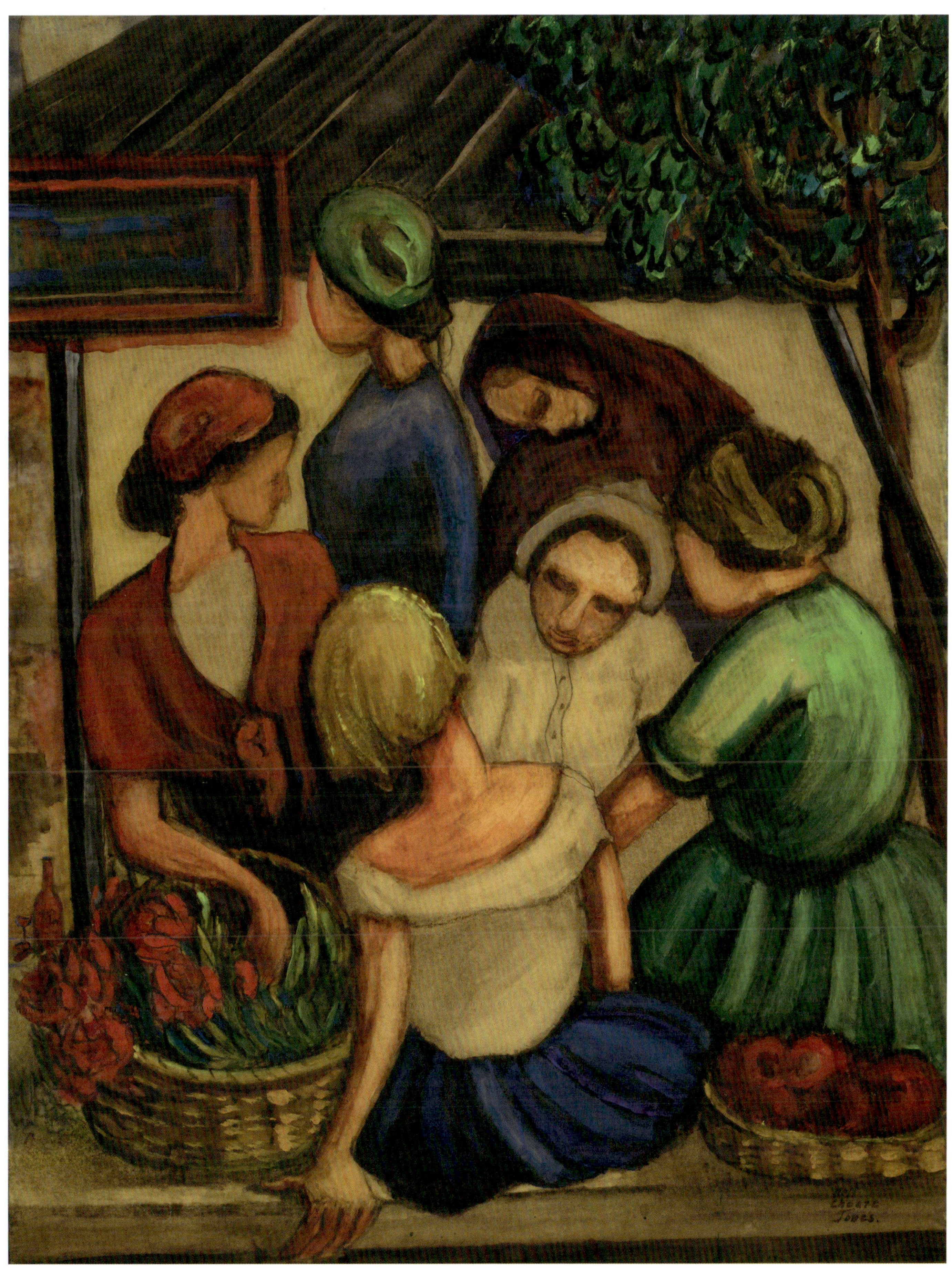

IDA RITTENBERG KOHLMEYER (1912–1997)

Fantasy No. 2, 1964

Oil on canvas, 58 × 50½ inches

Ida Kohlmeyer was a distinguished voice in American art, best known for brightly hued symbolic paintings and sculptures created during the 1970s and 1980s that blended Abstract Expressionism and postmodern design. An outspoken woman who espoused the importance of personal transformation, Kohlmeyer operated in a wide frame, incorporating cultural, social, and aesthetic themes into her conceptually rigorous art. She left a lasting legacy as an artist, educator, feminist, and cultural leader.

Rebecca and Joseph Rittenberg, the artist's Polish-Jewish immigrant parents, had prospered in their adopted home of New Orleans, Louisiana, and Ida, born on November 3, 1912, initially followed the expected path of a bourgeois daughter. She graduated from H. Sophie Newcomb Memorial College in 1933 with a bachelor of arts in English and married Hugh Kohlmeyer, a local food broker. Their honeymoon in Mexico exposed her to the ritual masks, folk art, and pre-Columbian figurines that later formed the core of an impressive personal collection. Kohlmeyer ran a small gift shop before giving birth to two daughters in the mid-1940s and devoting her energies to motherhood. Seeking a new means of personal expression, Kohlmeyer first studied art at the John McCrady School of Art, an independent art academy in the bohemian French Quarter, then returned to Newcomb in 1950 to take evening classes with painter Pat Trivigno. There she was exposed to contemporary abstract art by George Rickey and by visiting lecturers David Smith and Jack Tworkov. She earned a master's degree in fine arts in 1956 with a thesis show of figural paintings depicting anxious children. At the age of forty-three, Kohlmeyer improbably launched her illustrious career and quickly attained commercial gallery representation, major museum sales, and lasting influence as a teacher and organizer.

Kohlmeyer's paintings evolved rapidly because of the acknowledged influence of Hans Hofmann and Mark Rothko, both of whom instructed her. These textbook Abstract Expressionist compositions, replete with totems, color fields, and gestures, displayed overt interest in spirituality and universality. Her eighty-one-inch-high painting *Opposed* won the Ford Foundation Purchase Prize at the *Twenty-Eighth Biennial Exhibition of Contemporary American Painting* at the Corcoran Gallery of Art. As a fervent individualist, Kohlmeyer felt increasingly troubled by the irony that she had established her reputation in a borrowed style. "For seven or eight years I would have a Rothko-like painting on my canvas, and I couldn't rid myself of it until finally I deliberately drew a huge circle on one painting and that broke the spell," Kohlmeyer recalled.[1] As a mother Kohlmeyer may have wished to reclaim the circular womb as a symbol of women's creativity.

Fantasy No. 2 is a further exploration of the circle as a generative and narrative form. The light-colored background is similar to that in other works from the previous few years, including a smaller horizontal work titled *Fantasy No. 1.*[2] However, broad shapes and fields had given way to more linear representational imagery. The circular motifs resemble fruit, perhaps pears or dates. Leaning slightly to the right, their positions suggest movement or volition. Elsewhere, strokes that resolve into shapes and images seem to float in richly painted space. With this painting and similar works, Kohlmeyer began to formulate the pictographic vocabulary of crosses, clouds, grids, and vessels that would become her signature style in the 1970s. "I remember the feeling of emancipation I felt with these paintings of dancing fragments. They looked more personal, gay and feminine, quite a change in mood and treatment from their predecessors," she wrote.[3] She called these paintings "calligraphic," a literary metaphor that asserted her desire to insert narrative into abstract painting. In this regard, Kohlmeyer's paintings can be compared to contemporaneous abstract symbolic paintings by younger artists like Eva Hesse and Joan Snyder.

Kohlmeyer painted *Fantasy No. 2* at a transitional moment in her career. She left her position as painting instructor at Newcomb College in 1964 and built her own studio in her suburban Metairie backyard. Her sense of professional and personal contentment was evident in a letter she wrote to her New York City art dealer Ruth White: "I am working steadily now in my wonderful studio, and the work reflects my happiness. It is very colorful, sometimes fanciful and gay; other times, strong in form and color....It's a marvelous feeling to feel confidence in your work."[4] As both artist and teacher, Kohlmeyer hit her stride in the mid-1960s and became one of the few Southern women abstract artists to establish a national reputation, which she enjoyed until her death in 1997.

DANIEL BELASCO

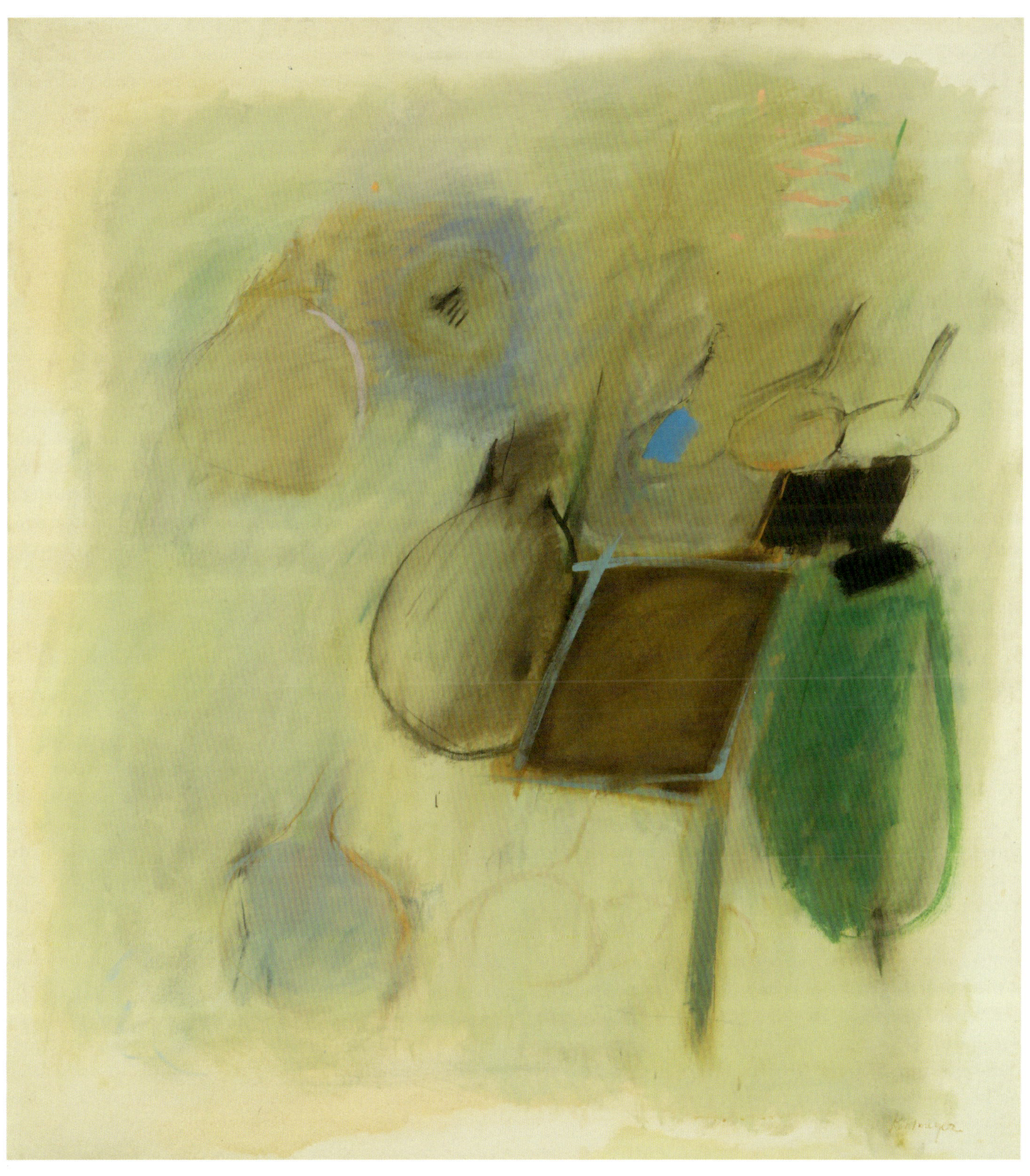

MARGARET MOFFETT LAW (1871–1956)

Peachshed Inman, South Carolina

Oil on canvas, 24⅛ × 30¼ inches

Georgia may be known as the Peach State, but the Piedmont region of South Carolina is also a major producer of the fruit, at times dominating the East Coast market. Within the region, peach production is most prevalent in Spartanburg County, which includes Inman, a small town just northwest of the city of Spartanburg and the setting for Margaret Law's *Peachshed Inman, South Carolina*.[1] This canvas—along with the artist's other paintings, etchings, and lithographs depicting laborers, mill villages, and countryside vistas—are lauded for providing a historical perspective of upstate South Carolina during the early twentieth century.[2]

At a time when few women were able to navigate social and professional barriers to pursue formal training in the arts, the ever-adventurous Law managed to do just that, in New York and in Europe, after graduating from Spartanburg's Converse College in 1895. She studied in the Paris atelier of French Cubist André Lhote in 1923 and worked diligently with American painter Charles Hawthorne at his Cape Cod School of Art in Massachusetts. But the instruction that would most profoundly influence Law's artistic development was her classes with renowned Impressionist William Merritt Chase—first at the Pennsylvania Academy of the Fine Arts and later at the New York School of Art—and with Ashcan School leader Robert Henri at the Art Students League. As popular and revered educators, both Chase and Henri encouraged their female students to seek educational and exhibition opportunities on par with their male counterparts.[3] From Chase, Law learned about vibrant colors and the expressive use of line, while Henri urged her to turn away from academic subject matter and instead seek inspiration from everyday life.[4]

Farmers in Spartanburg County began planting peaches around 1921 and built sheds to store their harvested crops soon thereafter. By the time Law returned to Spartanburg permanently in 1936, production was booming, and the Piedmont had become the largest grower of peaches and busiest loading point in the country.[5] *Peachshed Inman, South Carolina* captures this thriving enterprise in motion. Having picked the ripe fruit, placed the orbs snuggly into sturdy baskets, and hauled them to the packing shed, the workers are grading and tightly packing the peaches to prevent bruising during transport across the country. Known for her truthful, unsentimental portrayals of African Americans, Law here presents an all-white workforce that attests to the prevalence of segregation in every aspect of society at that time.[6]

In accordance with her training under Chase, who advocated painting *en plein air,* Law probably composed this image on-site. The artist routinely drove down winding rural roads in search of scenery to translate onto canvas, her supplies stored neatly in her Ford. She painted several works related specifically to peaches, and this example is by far the most vibrantly colored.[7] Painting outdoors on a sunny day can naturally brighten any color palette, as Chase and other Impressionists knew well. Without the luxury of constant, even light, Law likely executed the painting rather quickly. Her swift brushwork articulating the horizontal band of a basket or a worker's sun-touched forearm—as well as the slightly disproportionate appearance of her figures—demonstrates her adoption of Henri's method of directly experiencing a scene and recording it with great speed. Like her mentor, she sought to capture the essence of the moment, rather than worry about the faithful rendering of particular elements. Instead of creating a documentary account that both Chase and Henri would have found tiresome, Law used fluid line and rich color to convey the larger ramifications of the tasks at hand—namely economic prosperity and communal engagement.

Community was important to the artist. After resettling in Spartanburg, Law served as superintendent of art for the city's school district, implementing a curriculum that gave student "originality full play." She also became an outspoken proponent of progressive art education across the state, citing its potential to "fit [children] for life."[8] In 1907, Law cofounded the Spartanburg Arts and Crafts Club with her distant relative Josephine Sibley Couper, which led to the eventual establishment of the Spartanburg Art Museum. Throughout these years she enriched her own aesthetic maturation by working alongside muralists in Mexico City and studying with Lamar Dodd at the University of Georgia. Law's health declined sharply in 1953, and she died three years later, just two months after her alma mater, Converse College, hosted a celebratory exhibition of thirty of her oils and watercolors.   SANDY McCAIN

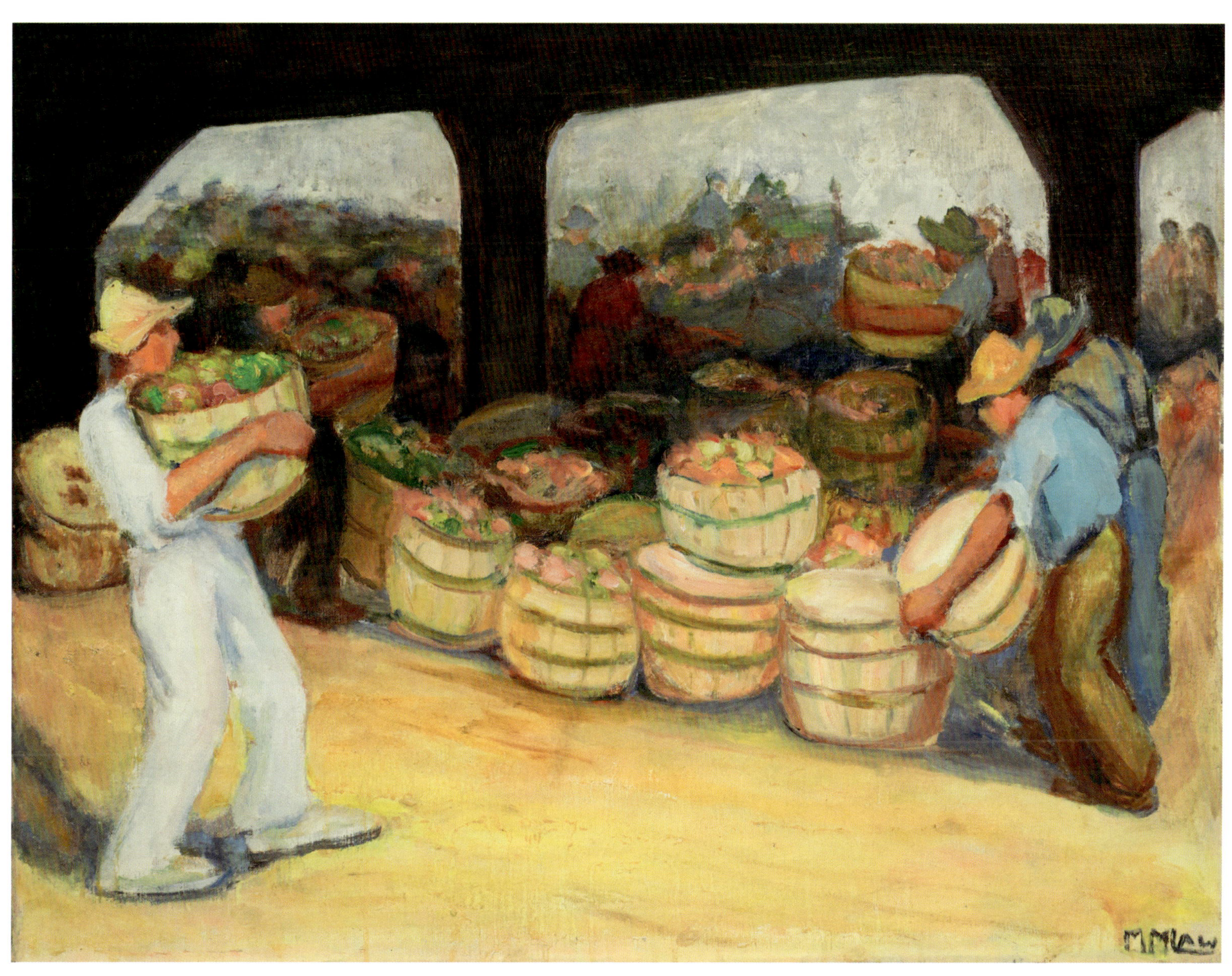

NETTIE BLANCHE LAZZELL (1878–1956)

White Peonies and Red Rose, 1917

Oil on canvas, 19⅛ × 17⅛ inches

Blanche Lazzell's *White Peonies and Red Rose* is an exuberant foray into modernism. Realized through a series of mosaic-like color patches, this painting pulsates with the visual energy, simplified forms, and color theories of late-nineteenth- and early-twentieth-century modernism. Completed after Lazzell's first extended stay in Paris and subsequent studies at the Byrdcliffe Arts Colony in Woodstock, New York, it is one of several similar paintings from this period that demonstrate her shift from a traditional, prescribed aesthetic to a more avant-garde approach.[1]

Lazzell's path toward modernism began in 1913 during studies with Charles Guérin at the Académie Moderne in Paris. Guérin, a follower of Paul Cézanne, urged his students to paint people and objects as they saw them and not necessarily as those subjects appeared in nature. For Lazzell this proved to be a liberating maxim. Back in the United States, these ideas were further advanced through studies with William Schumacher in New York City during the winter of 1916–1917 and the following summer at the Byrdcliffe Arts Colony, where she focused on color analysis.[2]

The artist's exposure to these various influences comes together in *White Peonies and Red Rose.* In the foreground and placed on a tabletop slightly tilted toward the picture plane, a glass filled with liquid rests on a blue and cream saucer. The transparency of the glass and a vase of flowers to its left reveals Lazzell's impasto brush strokes. The overlapping of these objects and the use of diagonal perspective point to conventional spatial constructs, while the combination of warm and cool colors and the planarity suggest a familiarity with Cézanne. The bright red rose pushes forward as the blue and mauve hues in the background recede in the implied space. With the eye of an early modernist, Lazzell again breaks with academic convention by defining the flowers with strong blue lines, a technique that references the white-line woodcuts she had begun to explore by that time.

A native of Maidsville, West Virginia, the artist was the eleventh of twelve children born to Cornelius Carhart Lazzell and Mary Prudence Pope Lazzell. She completed her secondary studies at West Virginia Conference Seminary in Buckhannon, graduating in 1898. On the advice of a doctor treating her for pronounced hearing loss, Lazzell traveled to a warmer climate. She spent a semester at the South Carolina Co-Educational Institute in Edgefield, then accepted a teaching position in nearby Ramsey. Wanting to further her education, she enrolled at West Virginia University in Morgantown and majored in the fine arts between 1901 and 1905. In the fall of 1907 she matriculated at the Art Students League in New York City, where her instructors included Kenyon Cox and William Merritt Chase.

In July 1912 she sailed for Europe and settled in Paris. That fall she immersed herself in the city's rich cultural milieu: taking classes at the Académie Julian, attending lectures at the Louvre, visiting modern art galleries, and seeing the latest manifestations of modernism at the Salon d'Automne. By January 1913 she was studying with Guérin and David Rosen at the Académie Moderne.[3] The transformation in Lazzell's work that began then was solidified when she lived again in Paris from 1923 to 1924, studying with the pioneers of Cubism: Fernand Léger, André Lhote, and Albert Gleizes. It was under Gleizes's influence that she painted a number of Cubist oils, several of which were accepted into the Salon d'Automne between 1923 and 1930.

Apart from these Cubist paintings, Lazzell is well known as one of the founding members of the Provincetown Printers, a group that favored the single-block, white-line woodcut. She studied this technique with Oliver N. Chaffee during the summer of 1916 in Provincetown, Massachusetts, and soon became one of its leading practitioners. She eventually made Provincetown her home, working steadily and offering classes in her studio by the sea. The Depression forced Lazzell to return to Morgantown in 1934. One of two artists from West Virginia employed by the Public Works of Art Project, she completed realistic white-line woodblock prints of local scenes and painted a mural for the Monongalia County courthouse. By 1937 she was back in Provincetown. Drawing lessons taken with Hans Hofmann reignited Lazzell's passionate and prolific pursuit of abstraction, which she believed to be the ideal means for conveying an "artist's inner thought—yes, the artist's very soul. The expression of this spiritual thought, design, or pattern should be in such simple form that we realize the beauty and truth of the abstract rather than the form of expression."[4]

MARY LOUISE SOLDO SCHULTZ

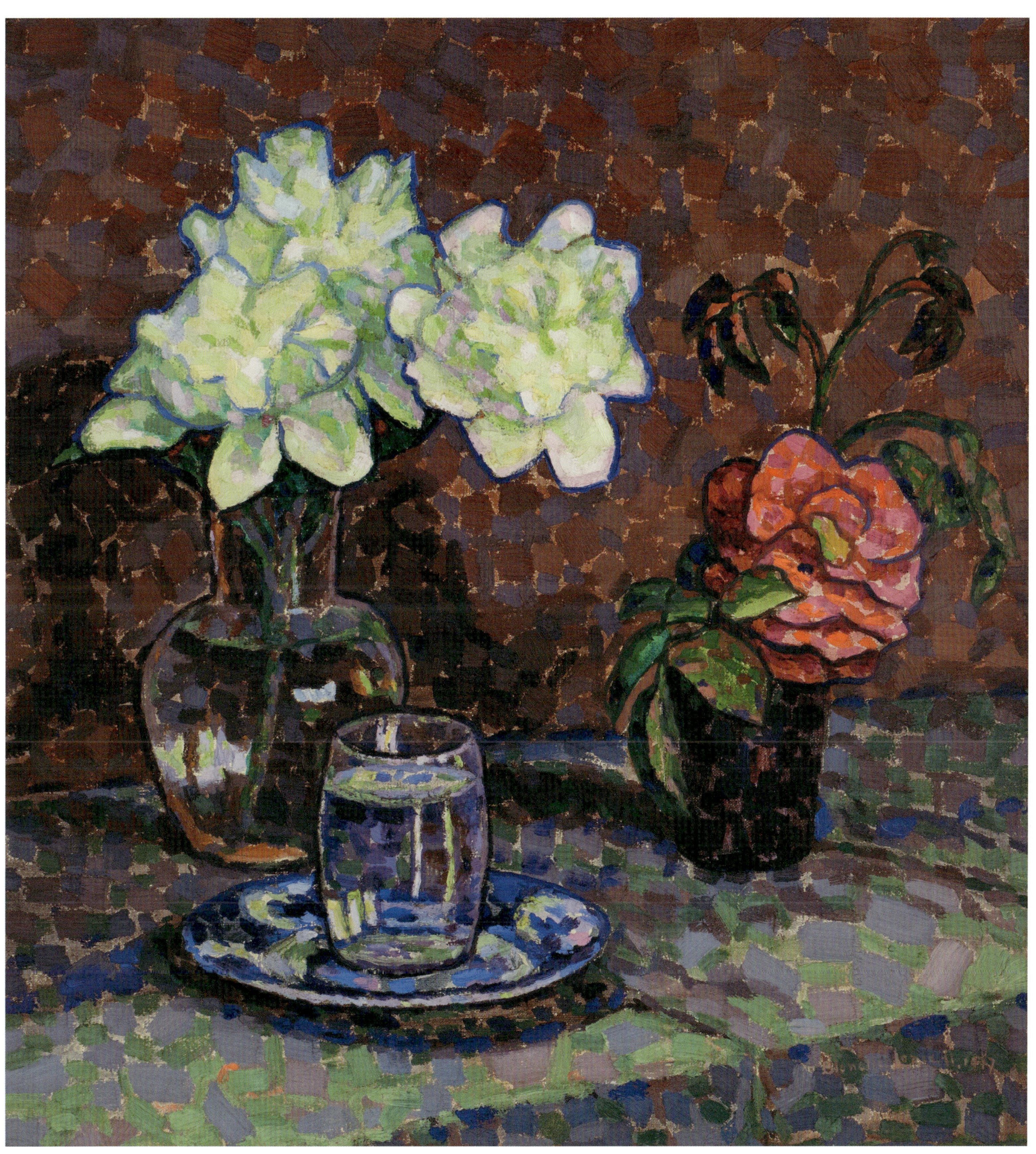

ADELE MARION GAWIN LEMM (1897–1977)

Untitled, circa 1965

Oil on linen, 24⅛ × 30⅛ inches

Artistry ran in Adele Gawin's family.[1] Upon his 1872 arrival in the United States from the Prussian province of Posen, her father, August Gawin, listed his employer as a Milwaukee art glass studio.[2] It remains unclear when or under what circumstances Adele arrived in Memphis, but it is known that she attended St. Agnes College there for one year before marrying Paul Lemm in 1920 and starting a family.[3] Paul Lemm's success as an executive with the Newburger Cotton Company afforded his wife the opportunity to travel and pursue a creative career. Following the opening of the Memphis Academy of Arts (now Memphis College of Art) in 1936, Lemm enrolled and began her art education in earnest, studying under the highly regarded painters Henriette Amiard Oberteuffer and George Oberteuffer. The Oberteuffers, particularly George, worked in a modernist style, and their instruction likely led their eager student to embrace a more avant-garde aesthetic.

Lemm's work quickly found acceptance at juried exhibitions throughout the South and in urban markets like Philadelphia and New York. Seeking a change of climate, her family began spending summers at New England art colonies, first on picturesque Martha's Vineyard and later in Provincetown, Massachusetts, and on Maine's Monhegan Island. She probably met pioneering American abstract painter Vaclav Vytlacil on Martha's Vineyard. Vytlacil would come to have a profound impact on Lemm's development, steering her toward the semi-abstract articulation that characterizes her strongest works. While vacationing in Provincetown, Lemm befriended Hans Hofmann, the German-born Abstract Expressionist whose summer school became a mecca for emerging modernists. Hofmann's bold use of color clearly informs Lemm's output of the early 1950s. From that point onward, her paintings feature a more vivid palette with deliberately strident contrasts, whether they depict coastal views or form complete abstractions. That same decade Lemm spent three summers pursuing advanced training at the Colorado Springs Fine Arts Center at Colorado College, where she used pastels to produce striking Cubist vistas of the surrounding rugged mountain terrain.

In ways that parallel the investigations other American artists were conducting at midcentury, Lemm's work of the 1940s and 1950s vacillated between representation and abstraction. Many of her best paintings portray favorite summer retreats and reveal a keen awareness of and appreciation for the forms, colors, and textures that make up coastal New England. Other preferred subjects include the horse farms that populate West Tennessee and the occasional garden scene. As the 1960s dawned, Lemm increasingly turned to complete abstraction, and by the time she executed this example, she had resolved her approach. The painting exudes the saturated, sun-drenched hues typical of her harbor subjects, but in an effort to thoroughly examine those shades and their relationships to one another, she has eliminated nearly all narrative detail. Only a quickly dashed section of black lines in a herringbone pattern—reminiscent of a fish skeleton—suggests marine life. Alive with movement and color harmony, this untitled work uses tone and texture to their full potential and represents the artist's total realization of the possibilities of abstract expression. Eschewing both descriptive title and realism, Lemm subtly and convincingly communicates the essence of summer, the season so inextricably tied to her artistic identity.

Having enjoyed close associations with her own instructors, Lemm found great satisfaction as an educator; she taught creative painting and drawing at the junior school of the Memphis Academy of Arts, a position she would hold for twenty-three years. All the while she steadily submitted her work to exhibitions across the country; on six occasions prizes were conferred on her entries to the prestigious National Association of Women Artists show.[4] Although she continued to travel for as long as she was able, Lemm remained based in Memphis for the rest of her life, serving as a vital member of the city's arts community. And while today she is included in discussions of Southern art of the twentieth century, her paintings transcend regional compartmentalization. Rather, it is the Tennessean's deep love of the New England coast— and the memorable way that affection manifested itself in her oeuvre—that places Lemm in a larger conversation within the history of abstract art in the United States.   JULIE PIEROTTI

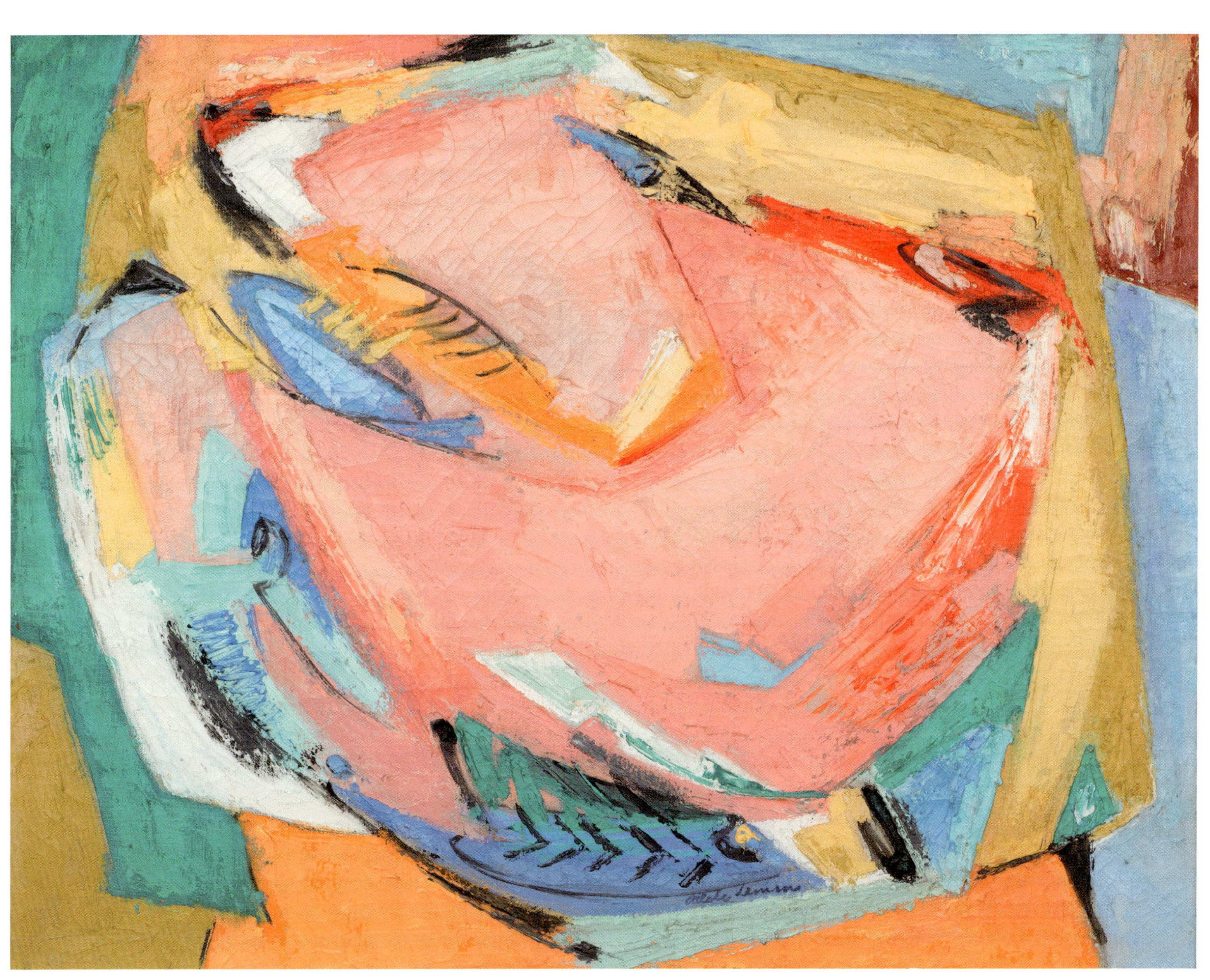

EDITH CASPARY LONDON (1904–1997)

Marine Still Life, 1953

Oil on canvas board, 24⅛ × 36⅛ inches

For many twentieth-century artists, Cubism was a powerful and pervasive influence, and this is especially true for artists who lived and studied abroad. Edith London first embraced the style during her years in Paris when she was a student of André Lhote, an influential practitioner who also taught Josephine Sibley Couper, Margaret Law, and Blanche Lazzell. Painted in 1953, well after London's time in Paris, *Marine Still Life* demonstrates Cubism's main tenets: a flattened, nonperspectival handling of space, overlapping angular shapes, and a penchant for abstracting objects. The composition is further defined by heavy black lines and enlivened by textures ranging from unprimed canvas to restrained impasto. Even London's ambiguous title reflects the avant-garde emphasis on a subject's essence rather than its specificity.

London's exposure to art began when she was a child in Berlin; her extended family included writers and sculptors who enjoyed the lively cultural milieu of the Weimar Republic in the interwar period. Between 1929 and 1931, London attended the University of Berlin and came in contact with two internationally recognized authorities on the philosophy of art: Heinrich Wölfflin and Carl Stumpf. She also took classes at Berlin's Federation of Women Artists and was introduced to the work of Henri Matisse. Matisse's impact on her developing aesthetic was "enormous," as London recounted toward the end of her career: "This is what I have learned from Matisse: that color and form can be created independently of the object."[1]

The artist married a noted theoretical physicist, Fritz London, in 1929, and together they spent a year in Rome—Fritz conducting research with Enrico Fermi on behalf of the Rockefeller Foundation, and Edith enrolled in rigorous training at the British Academy.[2] With the ascendancy of Nazism, the Londons, who were Jewish, fled Germany in 1933 and moved to Oxford, England, followed by nearly three years in Paris, from 1936 to 1939. As Hitler's religious and intellectual persecution escalated, Fritz became one of many refugee scientists who emigrated to the United States, departing in 1939 ahead of his wife and newborn son, who followed soon after. The young family settled in Durham, North Carolina, where he joined the faculty at Duke University. Fritz was nominated for the Nobel Prize in chemistry on five occasions. For many years Edith London attended to responsibilities at home and had limited time for artistic pursuits; the instinct, however, "was in me constantly," she recalled.[3] A year after her husband's death at the age of fifty-four, she became the slide librarian for the art history department at Duke, a position she held from 1955 to 1969.

Around 1960 London began working with paper collage, an extension of her interest in Cubism. These largely abstract works made from handmade and Japanese paper, sandpaper, and wrapping paper, complement her earlier output, which consisted primarily of cubistic seascapes. Interlocking, often transparent planes and compressed space characterize her oeuvre, as seen in *Tension and Harmony,* dating to 1983. Paper had fascinated London since her childhood: "From an early age I learned to love the materials with which artists work. My attitude toward paper is twofold: I have learned to respect it deeply, and I treat it like a mystical possession. But I have also learned to waste. To economize on paper means to economize on one's own creativity, and who wants that!"[4]

At a 1963 Duke University symposium, "Crosscurrents in Contemporary Life: A Commentary by Women," London took the stage with such luminaries as the cultural anthropologist Margaret Mead and Anne Firor Scott, an expert on Southern women's history. During a panel presentation titled "The Artist in the Crisis," she remarked: "In comparing the arts of our time with those of a hundred years ago, we observe that they have become more deeply personal; the attitude to the medium has become much freer, there is an ever present readiness to search further, to RISK experiments which in the past would have been inconceivable."[5]

London achieved local and statewide recognition, including the North Carolina Award in Fine Arts. The North Carolina Museum of Art mounted an exhibition of her collages in 1988, followed by a retrospective organized by the Durham Art Guild four years later. London's passion for her chosen profession never waned: "My artistic work allows me to follow one of the most lofty pursuits in the field of human endeavor. Through it I am privileged to venture carefully into a most noble preserve of the human mind in which my spiritual being is purged and purified and in which each effort made is rewarded with profound enrichment."[6]

MARTHA R. SEVERENS

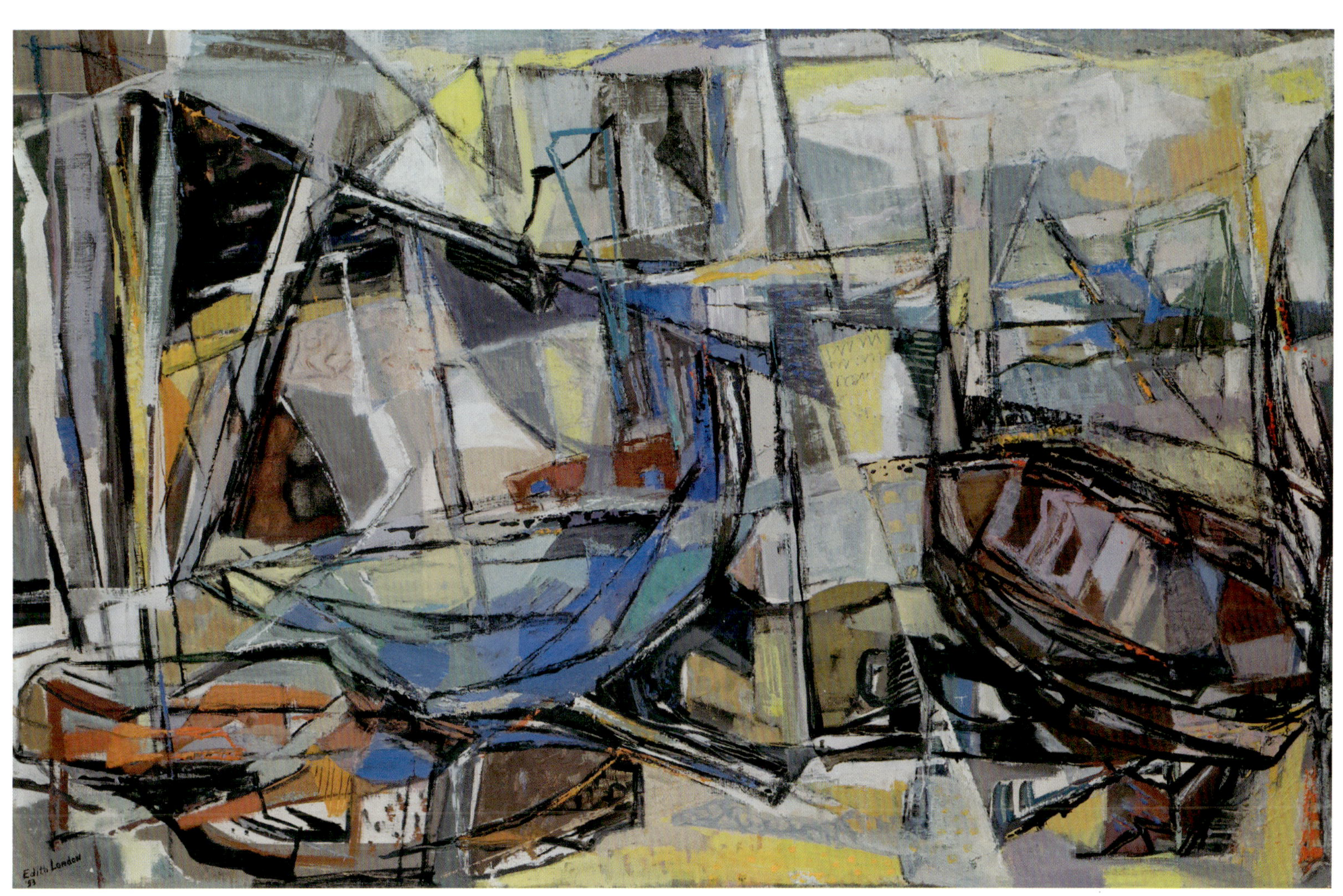

BLONDELLE OCTAVIA EDWARDS MALONE (1877–1951)

Newport, 1907

Oil on canvas, 12⅛ × 20⅛ inches

Inscribed *Newport/Sept 23 1907*, this small plein air painting featuring a field of lavender wildflowers was painted while South Carolina artist Blondelle Malone was visiting her friend and fellow artist, Anna Trimble Swinburne, in Newport, Rhode Island. Classmates at the Art Students League in New York a decade earlier, the two women had also spent the summer of 1899 at the Cos Cob summer art colony, where American Impressionist John Twachtman encouraged his students to paint outdoors.[1] Malone may have traveled to Newport to escape both the heat of a Southern summer and the banality she associated with society in her hometown of Columbia. Always eager to further her social connections, she probably relished the idea of a season spent in the fashionable Gilded Age resort, where Swinburne's husband Henry, an architect and decorator, had family.

After attending Converse College in Spartanburg, South Carolina, Malone studied briefly in New York with two prominent American Impressionists: at the New York School of Art with William Merritt Chase and at the Art Students League with Twachtman. She then embarked on a four-year sojourn, traveling first to California in 1901. For six months she painted landscapes, mostly in watercolor and pastel, her preferred media. Eventually Malone—the only child of a successful music business owner—was able to convince her father to finance an extended overseas tour as a way to broaden her horizons and improve her skills. The attractive, vivacious redhead, who often claimed that she "made friends everywhere," soon persuaded a couple she met on the West Coast to chaperone the next phase of her explorations: a voyage to Japan, where she stayed for almost a year.[2]

From Asia, Malone journeyed on to Europe, arriving in Italy in the spring of 1904. There she encountered Walter Sickert, a protégé of James McNeill Whistler and already a successful, if controversial, artist in his own right.[3] She met another Englishman as well, Henry Simpson, who became a lifelong admirer and correspondent. Flattering company aside, Malone had grander ambitions. Armed with a series of introductions to artists in France, many provided by Sickert, she left Venice for Paris. After a few weeks there, she moved on to the summer art colony at Dieppe and finally to Giverny, home of the reclusive Impressionist master Claude Monet. Surprisingly she managed to arrange an invitation to visit the artist in his iconic garden.[4] Malone also became intimate with the area's circle of American expatriate artists.[5]

Although Malone was popular with her fellow artists, she found few buyers for her pictures, and the resulting lack of income left her entirely dependent on the allowance she received from her parents. Her participation in exhibitions was modest, and she was unable to establish an enduring relationship with any commercial gallery. With her funding and her parents' patience depleted, Malone reluctantly returned to South Carolina in December 1905. The elder Malones were delighted to welcome their sophisticated daughter home, but she was dissatisfied with Columbia's provincialism. She actively corresponded with acquaintances in the Northeast and Europe, and it was through those letters that she eventually received Anna Swinburne's invitation to Newport.

Newport has a conventional horizon line of trees that is anchored by two cottages in shades of gray and blue on the viewer's right; a low stone wall and thin row of trees on the left create a strong diagonal in the otherwise horizontal composition. Pale sunshine illuminates the tree line, and a hazy gray sky reveals the sun peeping from behind the clouds, suggesting that Malone painted it in the early morning or evening. Both the loose brushwork and the artist's attempt to capture the weather are characteristic of Impressionist landscape painting. The field flowers that take up over half the canvas are probably wild asters, purple loosestrife, or wild blue phlox, all of which are native to the region.[6] The numerous floral scenes Malone created over the course of her career led one critic to label her "the garden artist of America."[7]

Despite Malone's enthusiasm for the Swinburnes and Newport, a few months later she left again for Europe, where she remained until the outbreak of World War I in the summer of 1914. Her mother's death the following year put an end to her travels, but the fiercely independent artist continued to paint during her extended residencies in New York and then Washington, DC. Ironically Malone died back home in Columbia—the place she had avoided for much of her life.

JANE W. FAQUIN

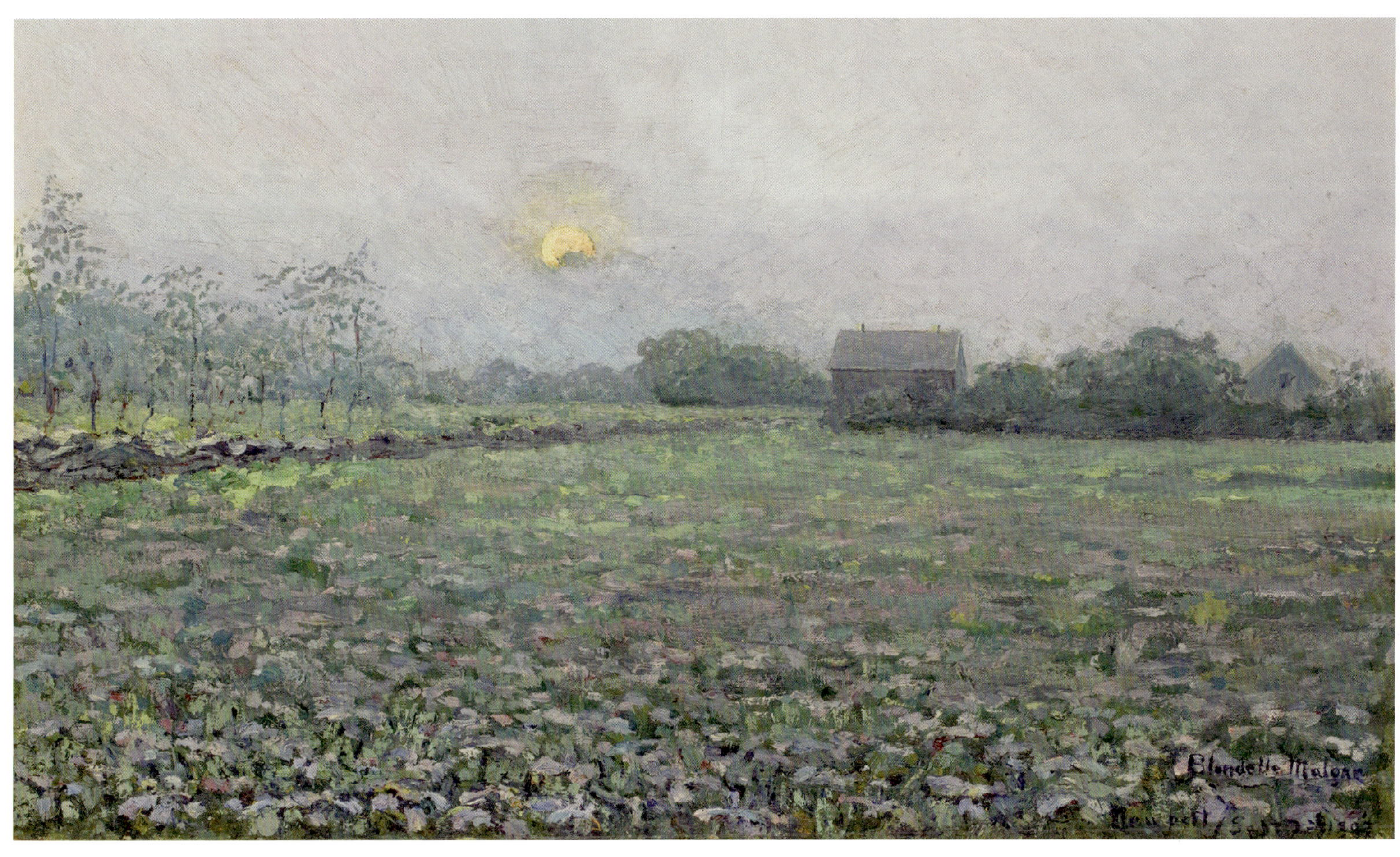

MAUD MARY MASON (1867–1956)

Still Life

Oil on canvas, 25 × 30¼ inches

Maud Mason's youth in rural Russellville, Kentucky, gave scant indication of the distinguished career she would later enjoy in New York's elite art circles. Having little in the way of formal education, she and her two sisters likely began decorating china blanks during their teenage years as a way to supplement the family's income.[1] This "opportunity for making money as well as a love for beautiful things" probably precipitated Mason's pursuit of an artistic path, first in ceramics and later as a painter.[2]

By 1895, after a time spent working as a china decorator in Toronto, Canada, Mason was living in New York and taking classes at the Art Students League with William Merritt Chase, whom she credited with sparking her interest in still life and floral subjects.[3] Although he is most closely identified with American Impressionism and plein air, Chase was also a fine still life painter who worked in the tradition of the seventeenth-century Dutch masters, a practice he had developed during his student days in Munich in the 1860s. There is some evidence that Mason studied briefly in England with the multifaceted artist, Frank Brangwyn, when he operated the London School of Art.[4] Brangwyn was largely self-taught and shared Mason's interest in an array of media, including painting, murals, stained glass, textiles, and prints. Another League instructor, Arthur Wesley Dow, had a profound influence on Mason's aesthetic as well. A seminal figure in the Arts and Crafts movement and an esteemed educator, Dow stressed the importance of color and composition and—like Mason and Brangwyn—believed in the transformative power of art.

Like Dow, Mason became a teacher and leader in the arts community and was especially influential among the growing number of professional female artists. In a 1917 interview with the ceramicist Adelaide Alsop-Robineau, Mason discussed her habit of varying her artistic pursuits. While she often spent the winter teaching design or creating ceramics—in her own studio or at the New York Studio of Ceramic Art and the Fawcett School of Industrial Art in New Jersey—she regularly devoted the warmer months to painting, executing watercolors and still life works in oil. This pattern of alternating activities invigorated the artist, who appreciated the "renewed and refreshed interest" she felt following "the change of work and thought."[5] Mason enjoyed active membership in a number of significant arts organizations, including the National Arts Club, the Society of Ceramic Artists, and the National Association of Women Painters and Sculptors, which she served as president from 1912 to 1917.[6] As an associate member of the National Academy of Design, she regularly participated in its annual exhibitions from 1914 through 1950.[7]

Mason never married. She lived most of her life with her sister Elizabeth, whom she praised as her "right hand and… greatest help and inspiration." Elizabeth and her wealthy husband, Benjamin J. Vanderhoof, divided their time between New York and New Canaan, Connecticut, where they owned a historic home with beautiful gardens. In 1932 Elizabeth became the president of the New Canaan Garden Club, one of the oldest in the United States.[8] As a member of the Vanderhoof household, Maud too became an avid gardener, flower arranger, and flower show judge. It was through the Garden Club of America that Mason became friendly with a prominent Memphian, Frances Rozelle Abston, who seems to have facilitated the painter's relationship with the Brooks Memorial Art Museum. Now known as the Memphis Brooks Museum of Art, the institution hosted two exhibitions of Mason's flower paintings during her lifetime, as well as a memorial exhibition in 1957.[9]

Depicting a large bowl of dahlias from the sisters' garden, *Still Life* was probably painted in the 1920s or early 1930s, and reflects Mason's diverse artistic interests. White blooms with deep yellow centers dominate the composition and are reflected in the shiny surface of the circular ebony table that supports the container. In the background, an open window is filled with loosely painted green foliage, while three brown branches create a strong diagonal. Another piece of ceramic art stands on the window sill and, like the flower bowl, was probably one of Mason's own designs. Behind the flowers to the right hangs a navy and white textile, a reference to another of Mason's collections. In the right foreground a book with a blue cover and red pages provides a rectangular contrast to the flowers, focusing the viewer's eye on the table. The foreshortening mirrors Japanese art and heightens spatial awareness, lending the traditional still life a modern twist. This colorful and soothing painting is typical of Mason's work, which continued to find favor with audiences long after most artists had embraced more avant-garde styles.

JANE W. FAQUIN

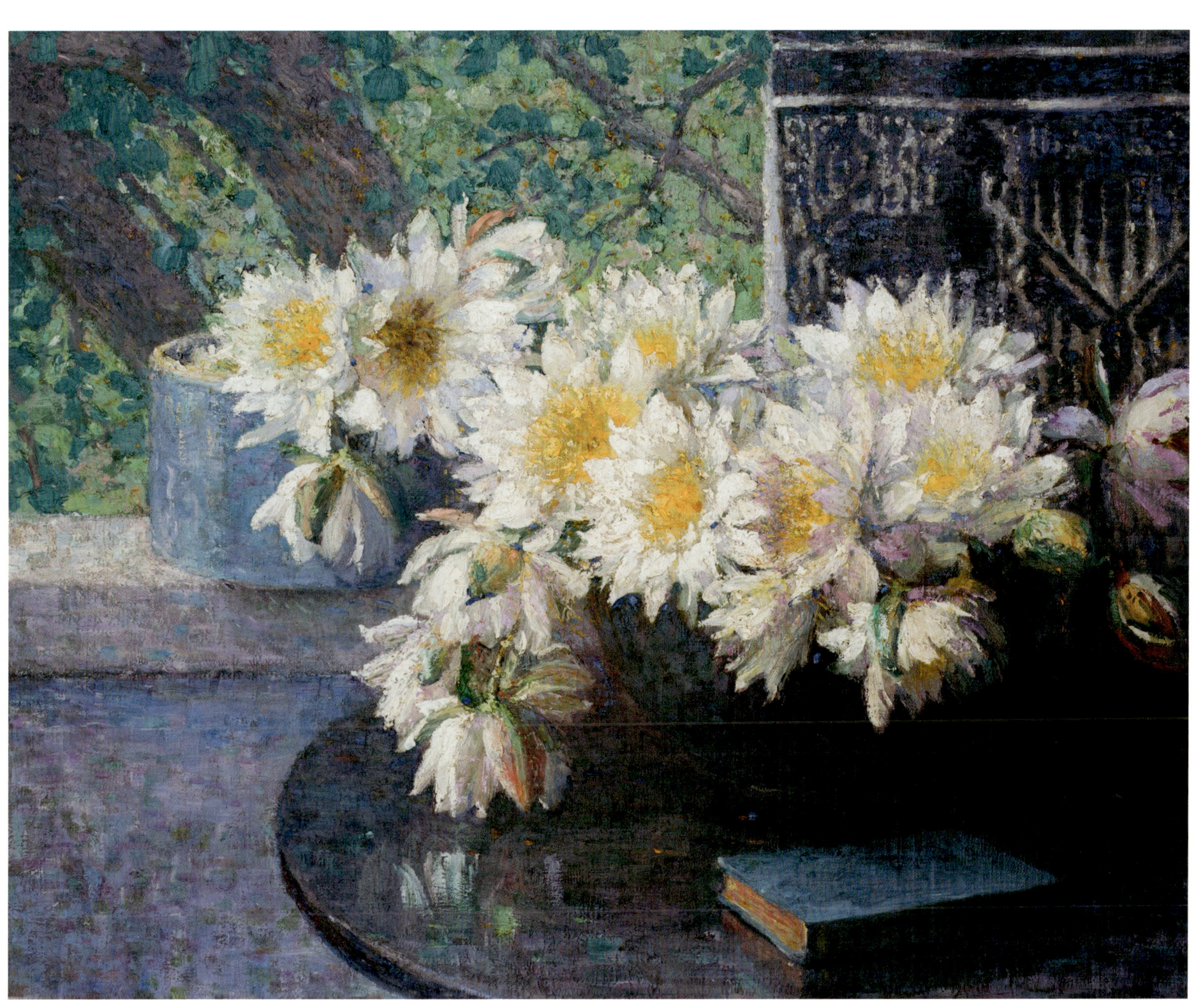

CORRIE PARKER McCALLUM (1914–2009)

Demolition of … Hotel, circa 1957

Casein and ink on board, 23½ × 29⅜ inches

Midway through a very productive career that had seen her combating sexism and working hard to find her own voice, Corrie McCallum made this statement in 1976: "I am against the isolation of art groupings such as 'black art' exhibitions or 'women artists.' What's wrong with variety.… The uniqueness of the individual is most important."[1] As the wife of the acclaimed modernist William Halsey and the mother of three children, McCallum knew what it took to carve out a professional identity that transcended race, gender, and domestic roles. A fierce determination to chart her own course—as woman, creator, spouse, and parent—defined both her personal life and artistic trajectory.

A native of Sumter, McCallum enrolled at the nearby University of South Carolina in 1932; three years later, she received a certificate in fine arts. She chafed against the conservative curriculum, which did not allow drawing from nude models. It was there that she met Halsey, who soon left to attend the prestigious School of the Museum of Fine Arts in Boston, where she eventually joined him. After earning a scholarship at the school for two years of study, she married Halsey in 1939. McCallum retained her maiden name, an unusual step at the time, subsequently explaining: "I kept my name because I did not want to get mixed up with who was what."[2]

When Halsey was awarded a fellowship to study abroad that same year, war was raging in Europe. The pair's decision to travel instead to Mexico was a fortuitous choice, liberating them from the old masters and inviting them to embrace a less familiar culture. Before returning to South Carolina, McCallum wrote to her mother: "I was amused to read some speech of Eleanor Roosevelt's where she said, 'Now that women have been freed from housework and the full care of children, they have time for their activities.' What women???"[3] During World War II the young couple lived in Savannah, where McCallum worked at the Telfair Academy. When they returned to Charleston in 1945, she became a part-time instructor for youth art classes at the Gibbes Art Gallery. She worked there until 1953, when she, Halsey, and sculptor Willard Hirsch established the Charleston Art School. By then McCallum had three children. She recalled: "I liked my kids—enjoyed them. We were buddies, but raising them stole another part of my life."[4]

Much of McCallum's work from the 1940s resembles that of her husband, as exemplified here by the compressed space, reliance on geometric shapes, and use of earth colors. The curious title, *Demolition of … Hotel,* derives from an inscription on brown paper backing, which also bears her bold signature. Might these words have been written later—perhaps when she had the piece framed and had forgotten the Charleston property's name? The subject is probably the four-story Renaissance-style Argyle Hotel, once known as the Pavilion and then as the St. Charles. Demolished in 1957, it was located on Meeting Street at the northwest corner of Hasell Street. The imposing structure in the background with the bright red mansard roof and iron railings was the Elks Lodge, situated on the north side of Wentworth Street between Meeting and King Streets.

Beginning in the late 1950s, McCallum developed a talent for printmaking—a direction that distanced her from Halsey's output. She became proficient in creating woodblock and linoleum prints, lithographs, and monotypes. While Charleston was the primary inspiration for her early work, her horizons were broadened by extensive travel, generally alone, to such far-flung places as Guatemala, Ecuador, Peru, Morocco, Portugal, Cambodia, and Thailand. Ever energetic, from 1959 to 1968 McCallum was curator of art education at the Gibbes Art Gallery, a position that called her to give presentations on art appreciation at area schools at a time when art instruction was absent from the district's curriculum. From 1971 through 1979 she continued her teaching career in the studio art department at the College of Charleston.

McCallum and Halsey collaborated on the 1971 publication of *A Travel Sketchbook,* which reproduced drawings from their journeys and juxtaposed the talents of the two artists. Six months after Halsey passed away in 1999, his eighty-five-year-old widow commented: "It's been so long since I did anything. Now I'm anxious to move on. I'm somebody else and I wonder who. I have to paint to find out."[5] In moving on, McCallum painted a vivid series filled with bold, flattened shapes that became known as her "WOW!" paintings. After decades of making distinctive art, teaching all ages, and supporting community causes, in 2003 McCallum received South Carolina's Elizabeth O'Neill Verner Award for lifetime achievement, an honor named for another strong Charleston female artist.

MARTHA R. SEVERENS

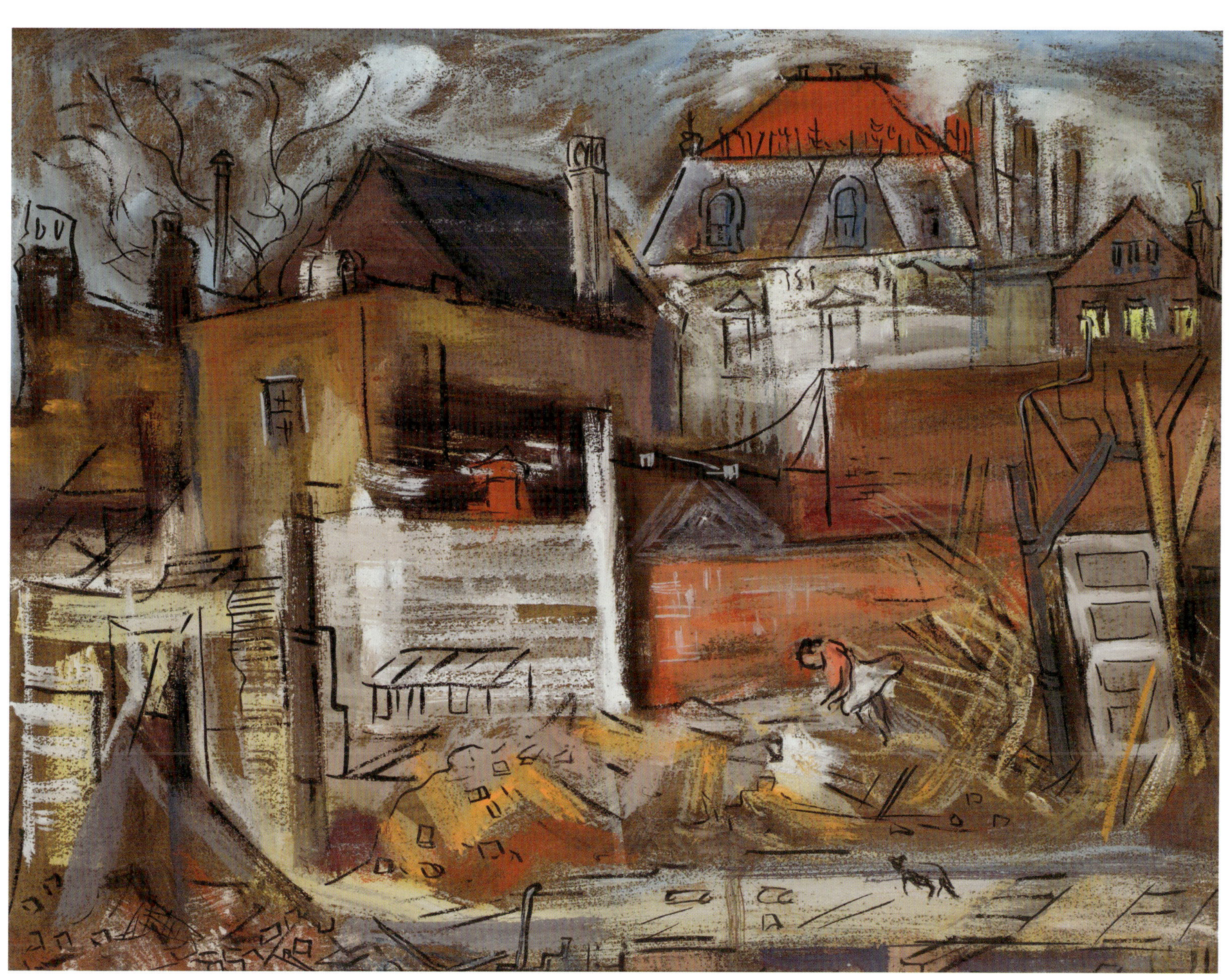

WILLIE BETTY NEWMAN (1863?–1935)

French Poplar Trees in the Mist, circa 1900

Oil on canvas, 20 × 12⅛ inches

To be self-supporting in the opening decades of the twentieth century was challenging for any artist, but especially daunting for a woman. After a decade spent studying and working abroad, Willie Betty Newman achieved self-sufficiency as a popular portraitist in Nashville, Tennessee. Her earlier success in Paris—where she showed annually in the prestigious Salon between 1891 and 1900—bolstered her reputation, although the taste of Tennesseans was far less sophisticated than that of their French counterparts. Nevertheless, Newman praised the South's cultural climate as superior: "I believe the South is the natural and logical home of all true art and that God so intended it to be. Not only on account of the temperament of the people, but all of the environments of 'Dixie' are artistic. Nowhere do the flowers bloom more beautifully, the trees and grass more luxuriant, nor the sunlight more healthful than in this fair southland."[1]

The artist was born during the Civil War on her mother's family plantation near Murfreesboro, Tennessee. She was named for her father, William Betty, a second lieutenant in the Twenty-Eighth Regiment of the Army of Tennessee. In 1881, at the age of seventeen, she married Warren Newman, and the following year gave birth to a son; soon afterward, she left her husband.[2] Her passion for art won out over marriage and motherhood. In 1885 she began formal training at the Art Academy of Cincinnati. Thomas Satterwhite Noble, a widely respected history painter who would later serve as the school's director, was especially significant to Newman's development. She flourished there, eventually earning a three-year scholarship for study in Paris. As a student at the Académie Julian, she worked under noted academicians of the time: William-Adolphe Bouguereau, Jean-Paul Laurens, and Jules-Joseph Lefebvre. There too Newman excelled, finding favor with her instructors and with jurors at Parisian exhibitions.

Paintings from Newman's time in France—including those submitted to the Paris Salon—were generally depictions of peasants rendered in earthy tones and often imbued with a spiritual quality. In search of subject matter, Newman occasionally traveled to Brittany, a picturesque region known for the preindustrial lifestyle of its residents. She also painted fresh landscapes of the countryside that resemble the work of Claude Monet, the archetypal French Impressionist. Hailing him as an "innovator," Newman described how "Monet, who followed nature, God's work, has given birth to a delightful school, a school of painters who bow humbly before nature for inspiration and knowledge and expressing it in their own original way, have created a delightful new school."[3] As *French Poplar Trees in the Mist* attests, Newman herself was very much an Impressionist at times. The association was heightened by her selection of the tall trees that lined the country's fields and roads—hallmarks of many canvases by Monet. Contradictory French legends trace the ubiquitous poplar columns to Napoléon Bonaparte, who hoped that their canopies would shade marching troops, and to victory celebrations in the wake of the French Revolution, when the trees were transplanted to Parisian plazas as "Trees of Liberty."[4]

After returning to Tennessee, Newman established a studio in Nashville and became a driving force for art; in the 1910 edition of *Who's Who in America*, she was the only artist listed for the entire state. For a short while she operated the Newman School of Art in accordance with the teaching methods of French academies. Unfortunately this endeavor did not thrive, and she turned instead to portraying prominent local citizens. Recording these likenesses provided a comfortable living and safeguarded Newman's independence.

There is little documentation—personal or scholarly—that details Newman's decision to surrender her son in the pursuit of creative fulfillment, but the choice cannot have been made lightly or without consequence. A 1905 article in the *Nashville Banner* noted the complexity and courage of her path: "There are few people who are in a position to realize what it means for a woman to exile herself from her own country and alone, in her devotion to her life-purpose, subordinate all things else to the one end in view. With Mrs. Newman this meant a life of strenuous labor and often times of hardship. She was ever ready to sacrifice comfort and convenience to her art. There were days when she went hungry in order that she might have more days to pursue her art studies."[5]

MARTHA R. SEVERENS

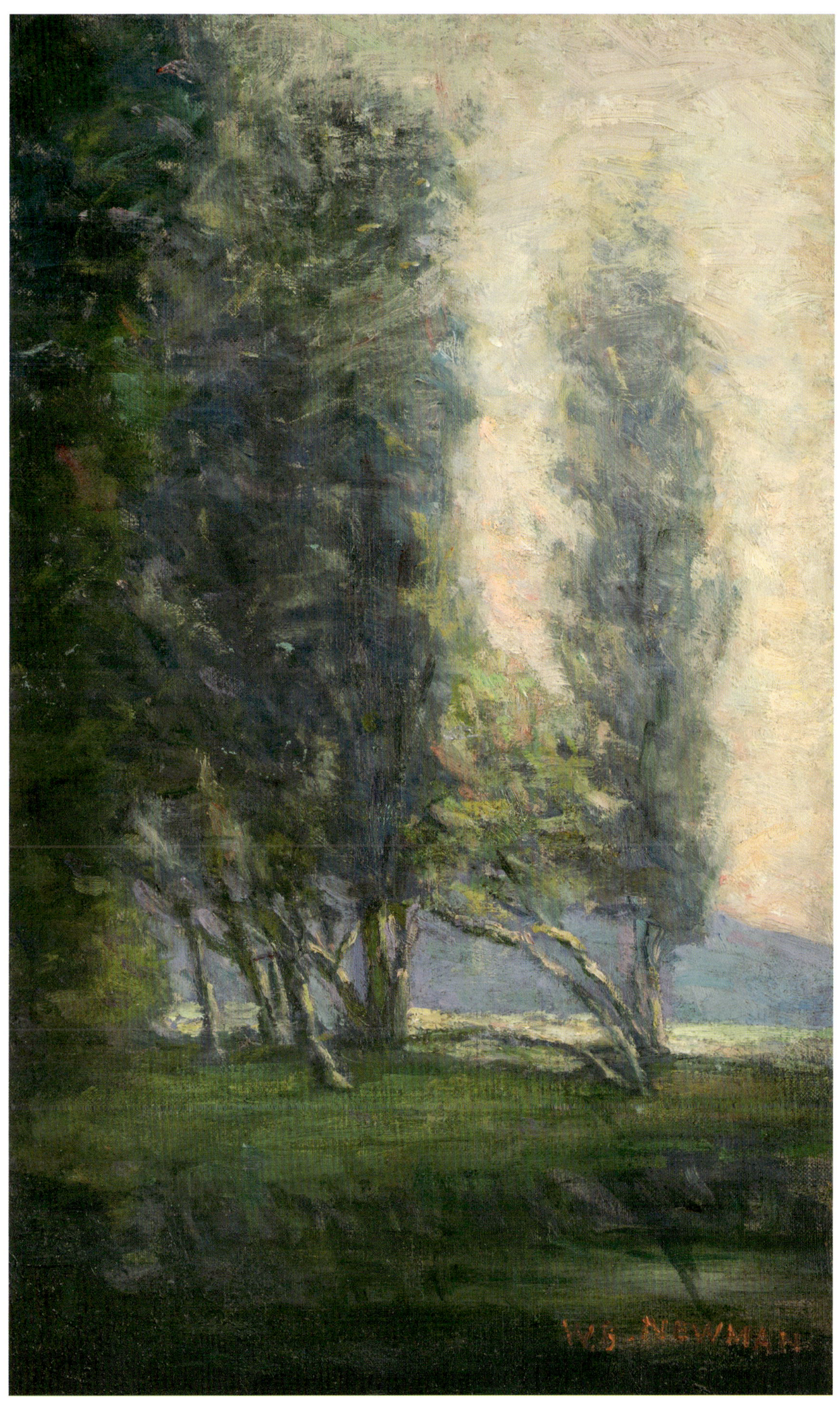

W. B. NEWMAN

AUGUSTA DENK OELSCHIG (1918–2000)

Portrait of a Young Man

Oil on masonite, 32 × 26⅝ inches

Savannah native Augusta Oelschig is known as an American Scene painter who also created politically charged commentaries, and later, highly personal experiments in abstraction. Her lengthy career spanned the time from her entrance to college through the late 1970s, when declining health slowed her production. Although her education and career path have much in common with those of other Southern artists of her generation, Oelschig stands out for incorporating social criticism and themes of racial injustice into her work.

As a young girl Oelschig benefited from the Savannah public schools' strong art curriculum, pioneered by Lila Cabaniss, and then took private lessons with highly regarded painter Emma Cheves Wilkins. Following two years at a local junior college, in 1937 she transferred to the University of Georgia, where the art department was directed by the renowned instructor Lamar Dodd.[1] An iconic figure in the history of art instruction in Georgia, Dodd was a tremendous inspiration to Oelschig and her fellow students. Later in life she reminisced that "all of us kids were in awe of him....One day a preacher leaned over and asked me, 'Is this man's name Mr. God or Mr. Dodd?'"[2] Dodd would become a great advocate of Oelschig's work and prophesied her future success in the catalog for her first solo museum exhibition, held in 1941 at Savannah's Telfair Academy: "The progress that she has made in recent years has been most gratifying. Her creative urge and vision should lead her to even greater heights."[3] After graduation Oelschig returned to Savannah, where she studied with Henry Lee McFee and earned particular acclaim for paintings depicting contemporary African American life. Local critics remarked at the time that her work "shows a distinctly modern approach and a skilful [*sic*] handling of form and color," and that "there seems to be no doubt of Miss Oelschig's talent."[4]

An extended trip to Mexico in 1947 marked a turning point in Oelschig's career. While there, she interacted with noted muralists Diego Rivera and José Clemente Orozco. She later recalled spending hours observing Rivera paint and listening to him pontificate: "I sat for numerous mornings at his feet while he explained his thoughts and the fresco technique in which he worked."[5] Inspired by the political and social content of the Mexican artists' work, Oelschig returned to Savannah in 1948 with plans for a mural documenting the history of Georgia, slated for installation at Savannah High School. Her proposal studies—which included searing depictions of Ku Klux Klan members whipping writhing African American figures—were rejected by school officials. Disheartened by this decision and her home state's seeming unwillingness to embrace the progressive and challenging work she sought to create, Oelschig moved to New York City later that same year. Ironically, Oelschig's mentor Dodd had earlier predicted a more welcoming cultural climate for emerging Southern artists, writing: "I am a firm believer in the future of art in the state of Georgia and the South at large. In years past many of our most talented young artists were obliged to go elsewhere for their art training and consequently many of them were lost to the communities where they rightfully belonged. Today, I am happy to say, that is not so much the case."[6]

Oelschig remained in New York for fourteen years, painting and exhibiting work in a realist style despite the widespread popularity of abstraction in the city at that time. After her return to Savannah in 1962 she offered private art instruction and experimented with abstraction, but primarily continued to produce the American Scene images for which she is best known. A review of a career-spanning exhibition of Oelschig's work that opened just weeks after the artist's death described her aesthetic as having "a distinctive style that is both steeped in the Southern Gothic tradition and remarkably unique. Like the stories of Flannery O'Connor, Oelschig's paintings often juxtapose the grotesque and the spiritual to striking, prophetic effect."[7]

Portrait of a Young Man does not contain the type of social commentary that so sharply distinguishes Oelschig's work from that of her peers, but it does demonstrate her skills as a sensitive portraitist and effective colorist.[8] She enlivens the canvas by using complementary colors as her accents, with the bright yellow of the fruit in the figure's hands playing off the purple flowers in the vase just behind him. At the same time, the ochre shade of the figure's jacket is repeated in the background of the far right of the canvas. The boy's high, chiseled cheekbones and full lips give him a seductive beauty, and his elongated arms and fingers are in keeping with Oelschig's tendency to lengthen her subjects' forms.   COURTNEY A. McNEIL

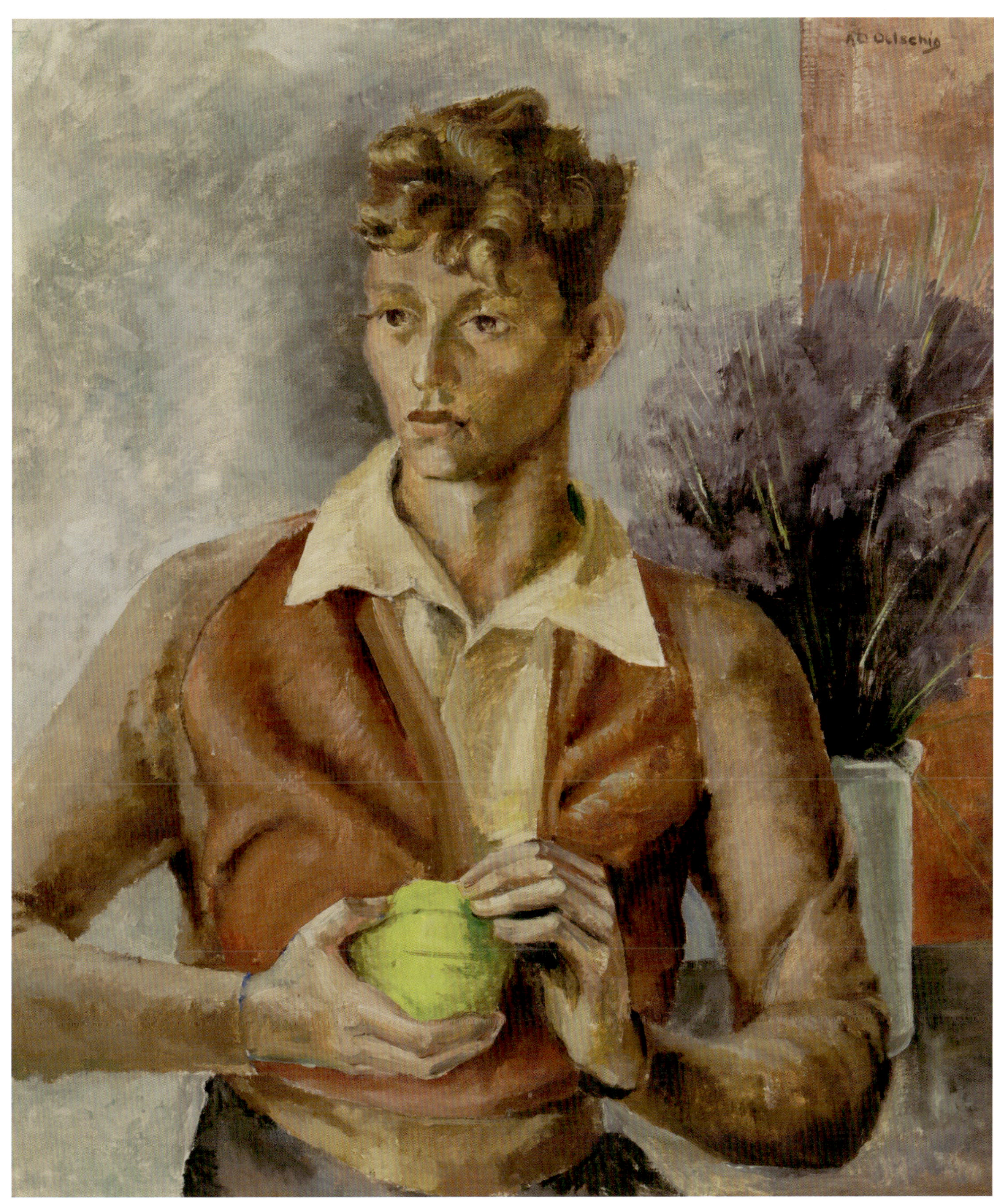

CLARA MINTER WEAVER PARRISH (1861–1925)

Isolde

Pastel on paper, 23¼ × 18½ inches

From the medieval to the modern, human tragedy has been a powerful fuel for art of all disciplines. Rooted in Arthurian legend, the tragic figure of Isolde has been the focus of Celtic folklore, Germanic poetry, operatic masterpiece, and here, Southern interpretation. Of royal descent, the Irish princess Isolde serves as a romantic archetype, a character defined by loyalty, love, and loss—to the point of death.[1] Clara Weaver Parrish's life was also marked by privilege, great love, and grief—grief that deeply influenced her personal and professional endeavors and found elegant expression in her oeuvre. As an artist who could "feel the tragedy," Parrish channeled her sorrow as "inspiration for art of the highest sort."[2]

In her hometown of Selma, Alabama, the artist's father had once been regarded as one of the state's wealthiest men. And while the family fortune suffered in the aftermath of the Civil War, young Clara and her sisters received a typically genteel education for the day. The Weaver household was an especially creative one, where the arts were heartily encouraged and pursued.[3] In light of her considerable talent, the Weavers supported their daughter's aspirations and underwrote her enrollment at the Art Students League in New York. The League was a relatively new institution at the time of her matriculation, and Parrish flourished in its atelier-style curriculum under the instruction of leading American Impressionist William Merritt Chase and classical painter Kenyon Cox. Her portraits' "soulful and introspective quality, with their dark backgrounds and controlled use of color" can be traced to these teachers' influence.[4]

In particular, the women in Parrish's portraits are indeed "soulful and introspective." Whether the model was a living person—as in the likeness she executed of her friend and fellow artist Anne Goldthwaite—or a fictional character, her subjects rarely smile, and in many cases appear to be reflective, resigned, or morose. Rendered in pencil, pastel, and oil, these sober compositions are at once descriptive and contemplative, suggestive of a strong, even if imaginary, connection between artist and model. Parrish's portrayal of Isolde in profile is a wash of rich tonality, the subtly diffused blues and greens accented by golden highlights. The undated work is reminiscent of one of Parrish's best-known paintings, *The Red Lily*, which also depicts a classical figure and reflects her familiarity with Pre-Raphaelitism and the Art Nouveau movement.[5]

In 1887 the artist married William Peck Parrish, a Selma native and successful financier who soon thereafter obtained a seat on the New York Stock Exchange. Living in New York then and later, Parrish exhibited widely, both in and beyond the city, at prestigious venues such as the 1900 Paris Exposition Universelle, the 1893 World's Columbian Exposition, and the 1915 Panama-Pacific International Exposition, as well as at the Pennsylvania Academy of the Fine Arts and the Art Institute of Chicago.[6] The couple's daughter, born in 1889 and christened Clara Weaver Parrish, died before her second birthday. Just a year later, William Parrish suffered a fatal heart attack.[7] Not long before these devastating losses, Parrish had begun working in the stained glass studios of Louis Comfort Tiffany. In this capacity, she designed massive biblically themed window panels for prominent churches in New York, as well as for her home parish of St. Paul's Episcopal Church in Selma, which she dedicated to her family's memory.[8] The characteristic jewel tones and religious iconography of stained glass are evident in Parrish's efforts in other media.

Untethered from domestic responsibilities, Parrish traveled and painted extensively. For a time she kept a Paris studio on the Boulevard du Montparnasse and studied with Gustave Courtois at the Académie Colarossi. Whether they were inculcated by Chase or her French mentors, her adoption of plein air techniques is apparent in the vibrantly colored diminutive oil, *The Flower Garden*, also in the Johnson Collection. While abroad Parrish produced picturesque portrait etchings—"considered very chic in Paris"—as well as scenes of charming French villages and historic landmarks.[9] When World War I interrupted her foreign sojourn, Parrish returned to New York, where her studio was located in the fashionable Van Dyke Building. She regularly returned to Alabama for visits and submitted works to Southern exhibitions. Over the course of her career, Parrish was active in national women's arts organizations and served as an officer of the Woman's Art Club.[10] The widowed artist never remarried. Like Isolde she was reunited with her dearest ones only after death. She is buried beside them in a Selma churchyard.

LYNNE BLACKMAN

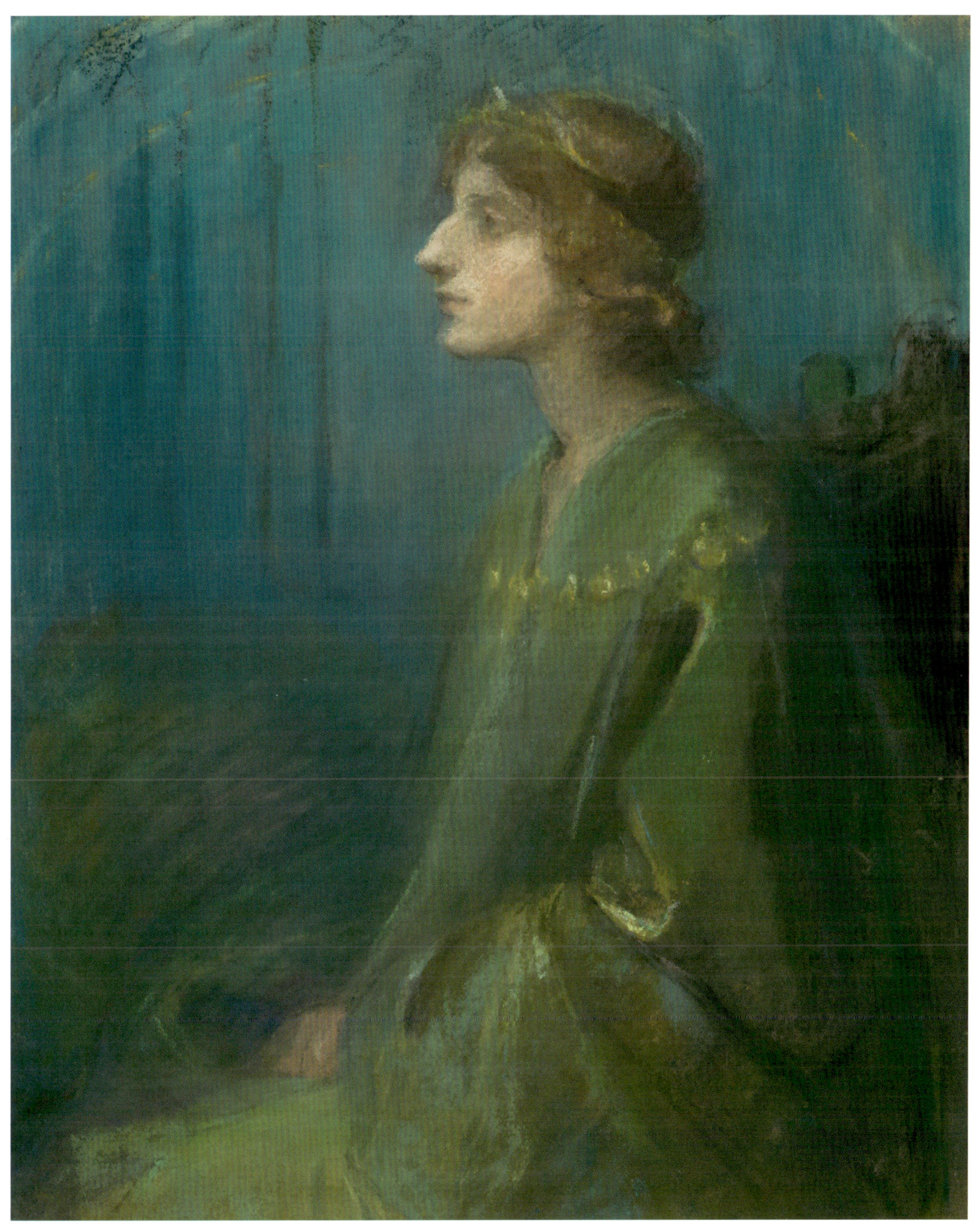

THERESA POLLAK (1899–2002)

Art Studio, 1931

Oil on canvas, 40¼ × 27 inches

A stalwart advocate of the arts in Richmond, Virginia, for over sixty years, Theresa Pollak was as celebrated as a painter as she was as a teacher. Born in Richmond to Hungarian immigrants, Pollak lived a long life that spanned three centuries, making her a witness to enormous cultural, political, and social change in the Virginia capital. Although she sought advanced training in New York City and actively painted during sojourns in New England and Europe, Pollak spent the majority of her life in her hometown, leaving an unprecedented legacy as a teacher and painter.

At the age of thirteen, Pollak attended classes at the Art Club of Richmond and received her first formal instruction in painting from Adèle Clark and Nora Houston, two local painters and suffragists who paired arts education with civic responsibility. This interaction would set Pollak's course, as she later recalled: "I eagerly looked forward to the two afternoons a week,…and these periods began to mean real life to me."[1] Five years later she matriculated at Westhampton College, the recently established women's coordinate of the University of Richmond, from which she graduated in 1921. Having been nominated for a scholarship, Pollak subsequently enrolled at the Art Students League in New York, where her teachers included Allen Tucker and George Bridgman. For Pollak this was a pivotal test, as she gauged her ability and ambition against those of fellow artists from across the country. She was sufficiently encouraged by her experiences that even after a yearlong illness forced her to temporarily return to Richmond in 1924, she was back in New York two years later, participating in her first group show. Success came early on as Pollak regularly showed works and won prizes in important exhibitions in the city. One still life painting, *Sumac,* was included in the Whitney Museum's *First Biennial Exhibition of Contemporary American Painting* in 1932. The following year she was awarded a Carnegie Fellowship, which funded study at Harvard University's Fogg Museum.

In 1928 the dean of the School of Social Work and Public Health (the precursor to what would later become the Richmond Division of the College of William and Mary) offered Pollak a position as the school's instructor of painting and sculpture. That fall Pollak convened her first night class of twenty students in a modest studio housed in a refurbished stable behind the college's original building. Over the next four decades, the institution would be reorganized twice: first as the Richmond Professional Institute and then in 1968 as Virginia Commonwealth University. In the midst of these changes, Pollak was a constant, building an art department that eventually grew to be one of the nation's largest professional art training grounds.[2] Remembered as an exacting yet supportive teacher, Pollak encouraged generations of students to pursue careers in the arts, including painters Judith Godwin and Nell Blaine.

Pollak never stopped maturing as an artist. Writing in the companion catalog to a 1940 exhibition of her work at the Virginia Museum of Fine Arts, director Thomas C. Colt Jr., praised her "freedom gained from technical mastery, happier color, and…gracious emotional quality."[3] At the urging of her students, in 1958 Pollak traveled to Provincetown, Massachusetts, to study with Hans Hofmann. The result was a series of paintings that diverged from her largely naturalistic style and embraced the contemporary manner of Abstract Expressionism.

Although Pollak's style evolved as her career progressed, the depiction of her studio and its environs was a recurring subject, as exemplified by *Art Studio.* A seemingly spontaneous representation, the painting details a small corner of the sunlit room, comfortably furnished with objects related to the study and execution of art. Piled books rest atop an elegant bent-leg side table positioned next to an occupied easel, while a nearby wicker chair is strewn with scattered newspapers. A small maquette of a female torso sits on the window sill. In the background a potential still life composition of fruit and stems is arranged atop a second surface, which partially obscures stacked canvases leaning against the wall. Evidence of the artist's presence and activity is indicated by the indented pillow on the chair, the opened newspaper pages, and a casually discarded blue cloth.

Executed when Pollak was just beginning her extended career as a teacher, *Art Studio* honors the inspirations and elements of artistic production. Pollak's studio seems a place of refinement and refreshment, a creative haven where the instructor retreated to record her "reaction to life."[4] The low-lying rooftops of Richmond's nearby buildings visible outside the window serve to link the artist's cerebral investigations with the community she dearly loved. Often presented in Pollak's compositions as sources of light, open doors and windows also connect to a space external to the insular world of the artist's studio, a place where Pollak thrived as a persistent champion of artistic expression. CHRISTOPHER C. OLIVER

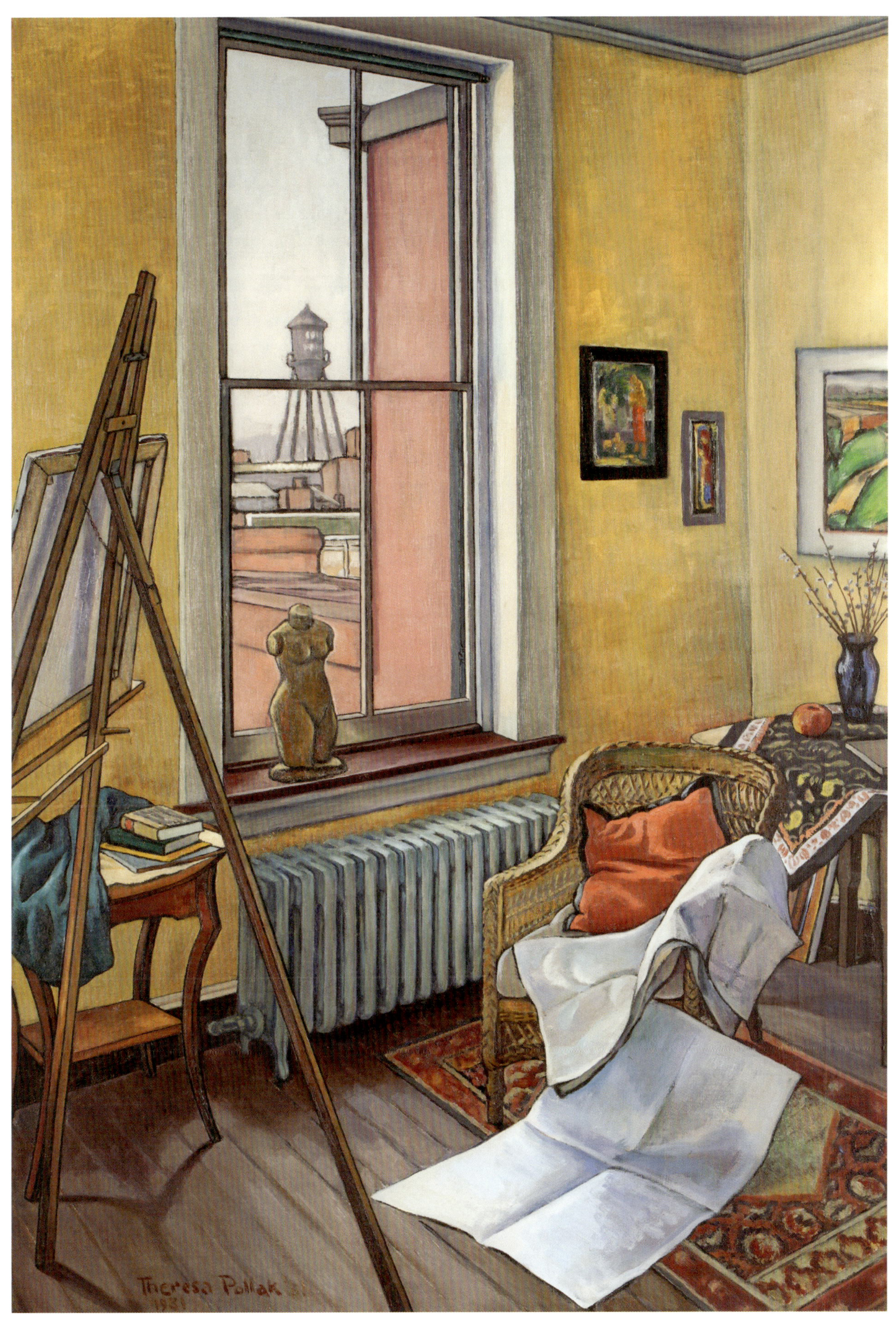

SARAH MABEL PUGH (1891–1986)

The Champion

Oil on canvas, 32⅛ × 26⅛ inches

A versatile artist who was comfortable working in a range of media that included woodblock prints, watercolors, and pen and ink drawings, Mabel Pugh was born in Morrisville, North Carolina, and graduated in 1913 from the nearby women's college, Peace Institute in Raleigh. She moved to New York City to attend classes at the Art Students League and Columbia University before being awarded a four-year scholarship to the Pennsylvania Academy of the Fine Arts in Philadelphia. The esteemed figure painter Charles Hawthorne was among her instructors. Pugh's achievements were recognized in 1919 with a prestigious Cresson Traveling Scholarship to tour and study in Europe.

After returning to New York, Pugh fared well as a professional artist, particularly in the area of book illustration. Her woodblock prints and pen and ink drawings appeared on the covers and within the pages of popular novels and in such widely distributed magazines as *McCall's* and *Ladies' Home Journal.* At the same time, her paintings were included in exhibitions at the National Academy of Design, the National Association of Women Artists, and the Brooklyn Museum, as well as the 1939 World's Fair and in various Southern exhibitions. In 1936 Pugh returned to teach and eventually head the art department at her alma mater, known then as Peace College, where she remained until 1960. She became active in state and Southern arts organizations, as a charter member of the North Carolina Association of Professional Artists, and a member of the Southern States Arts League.[1]

During her tenure at Peace, Pugh began to take on occasional portrait commissions. She created portraits of prominent members of Congress from North Carolina and other states, including Herbert Covington Bonner, Harold Dunbar Cooley, and Clifford Ragsdale Hope. Several of these works hang in buildings in Washington, DC. Pugh's portraits range widely in style. *Woman in Pink,* an oil painting on panel from 1920, and the undated oil on canvas *Señorita* show loose, gestural brushwork and the barest of details, yet succeed in conveying a sense of each sitter's personality. In contrast, two portraits in the collection of the North Carolina Museum of Art in Raleigh—*My Mother,* from 1924, and *Three Sisters,* from 1939—are rendered in a more specific and naturalistic manner.

Among Pugh's portraits, *The Champion* seems to inhabit a world of its own. The painting is of a young, unidentified female golfer who is portrayed with the signifiers of her sport.[2] Seated next to a bag of golf clubs, the figure leans back against what seems to be a chair or stool. In her hands—the left still encased in a supple golf glove—she holds a piece of paper that one might surmise is a scorecard from a match. A possible dating of the painting to the late 1940s or 1950s seems likely, as the sitter's dress suggests athletic wear of that time: a simple red vest, or jerkin, over a white blouse and a gray skirt. A monochromatic background depicts an assortment of trophies arrayed on shelves, and the view through the window is indistinct. This aesthetic device of a pronounced and colorfully clad figure against an imprecise background emphasizes the importance of the sitter in a dramatic way. Whether the trophies in the background are hers or are simply a grouping in a clubhouse, these awards signal her status as a victor. The gray and white setting for the portrait is reminiscent of Renaissance paintings in which the background or, in some cases, the donor panels of an altarpiece triptych, are in similar grisaille.

The clear but not obtrusive outlining of the figure resembles the technique Pugh used in her congressional portraits. The formality of those works, however, is replaced here by a more intimate and casual approach. In comparison to the confident visages of powerful male legislators, the golfer's expression communicates a different sensibility. She appears somewhat timid, even vulnerable—at the very least, humble. While clearly a champion, this young woman seems a bit unsure about claiming or acknowledging her fame.

NANCY M. DOLL

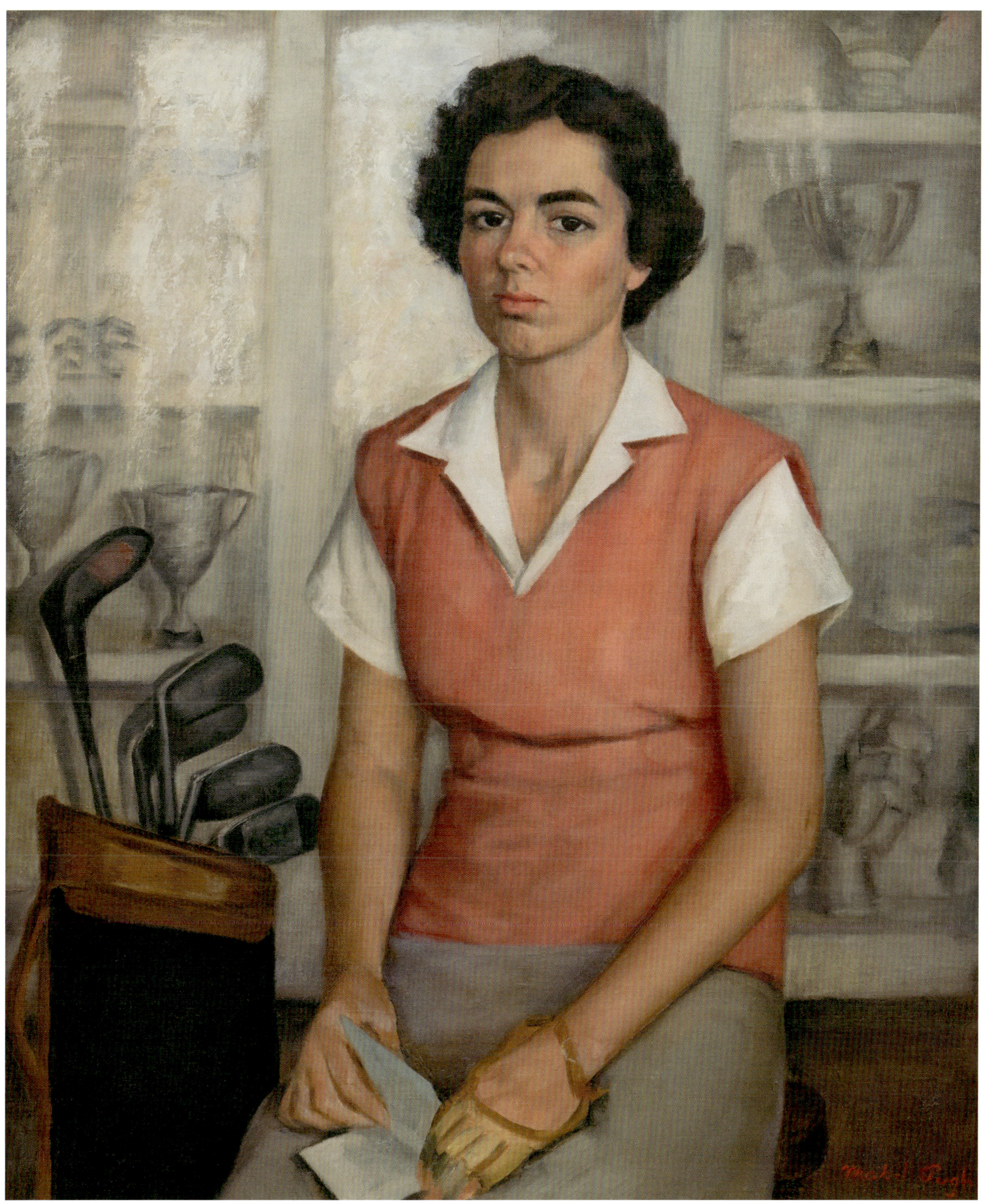

HATTIE SAUSSY (1890–1978)

Wisteria

Oil on canvas, 20⅛ × 24⅛ inches

Known for her sensitive portraits, lush Southern landscapes, and colorful still lifes in both oil and watercolor, Savannah artist Hattie Saussy pursued her passion for painting from the time of her youth until near the end of her long life. Her parents, Joachim Radcliffe Saussy III and Rachel Louise Shivers Saussy, both hailed from prominent local families and granted their daughter the financial independence to study in New York and abroad, and to pursue her artistic practice without having to rely on the sale of her work.

Saussy came of age during a time of dramatic activity and growth in the Savannah art community. She was born on March 17, 1890, just a few years after the Telfair Academy of Arts and Sciences, the South's first public art museum (now Telfair Museums), opened in 1886. In addition to displaying a notable collection of paintings and plaster casts, the museum also offered formal art instruction based on the European academic model. Over the ensuing decades other opportunities for private lessons began to appear in the city, and classes were added to the curriculum of Savannah's public schools in 1915 by artist and teacher Lila Cabaniss. Organizations such as the Savannah Art Association (founded in 1920 as the Savannah Art Club), the Southern States Art League, and the Association of Georgia Artists worked in tandem with the Telfair to enhance the city's cultural vibrancy by organizing exhibitions, providing art education, and hosting visiting artists.

Artistically inclined from a young age, Saussy once described herself as "the little kid on the block who painted paper dolls and made Christmas cards."[1] She was among the first generation of students to benefit from the developments in Savannah's artistic climate, both in the public schools and through private studies with Emma Cheves Wilkins. She recalled that this early instruction placed a strong emphasis on the traditional hierarchy of artistic media and learning through copying: "Of course, back then you had to take classes and do things in a certain order. You would start by copying—you can learn a lot by just copying things—and then you would go into charcoals, water colors, and then start with oils."[2]

After attending Mary Baldwin Seminary (now Mary Baldwin University) in Staunton, Virginia, from 1906 to 1907, Saussy moved with her widowed mother to New York, where she would eventually enroll at the New York School of Fine and Applied Art (founded by William Merritt Chase in 1896 and now known as the Parsons School of Design), the National Academy of Design, and the Art Students League. Her instructors in New York included such luminaries of American art as Eugene Speicher, Frank Vincent DuMond, Eliot O'Hara, and George Bridgman. In 1913 and 1914 she continued her education in Paris under E. A. Taylor. Her European travels and studies were cut short by the onset of World War I. Saussy would later recount her turbulent departure from the French capital: "I had to stand in line for two days and nights to be approved by the police so that I could leave for home.…It was a strange time. It was like a kind of frenzy had gotten hold of people. They didn't know whether they would ever get back home again, and they acted crazy."[3]

Upon her return to the United States, Saussy worked in a government office in Washington, DC. After the war she spent the 1920–1921 academic year teaching at Chatham Episcopal Institute (now Chatham Hall) in Virginia before returning to Savannah permanently. Once she was resettled in her hometown, Saussy taught art and honed her craft, painting *en plein air* to create light-filled landscapes. She immersed herself in the local art scene, was instrumental in founding the Association of Georgia Artists, and held leadership positions in influential regional organizations.[4] Despite her childhood loss of sight in one eye and her advancing years, Saussy continued to paint outdoors until 1972, when she suffered a broken hip on a painting trip and was afterward largely confined to her Savannah home.[5]

Wisteria, an invasive woody vine that can live for up to half a century, is known for simultaneously enchanting Southern gardeners with its abundant bunches of fragrant purple or white flowers and tormenting them with its tenacious tendrils, which can seriously damage the buildings on which it climbs. From her artist's perspective, Saussy found wisteria to be a source of delight and frequent inspiration. Records indicate that she submitted paintings of wisteria in exhibitions in 1932, 1939, and 1940, and wisteria arbors are specifically mentioned as one of her preferred subjects in several published reviews.[6] Saussy's deep and enduring affection for the landscape of Savannah and surrounding regions did not escape the notice of contemporary critics: "Miss Saussy, who has been described as having the gift of capturing her enjoyment of places, paints realistically Savannah's beautiful spring flowers, its wisteria arbors and sometimes the quaint houses around here."[7]

COURTNEY A. McNEIL

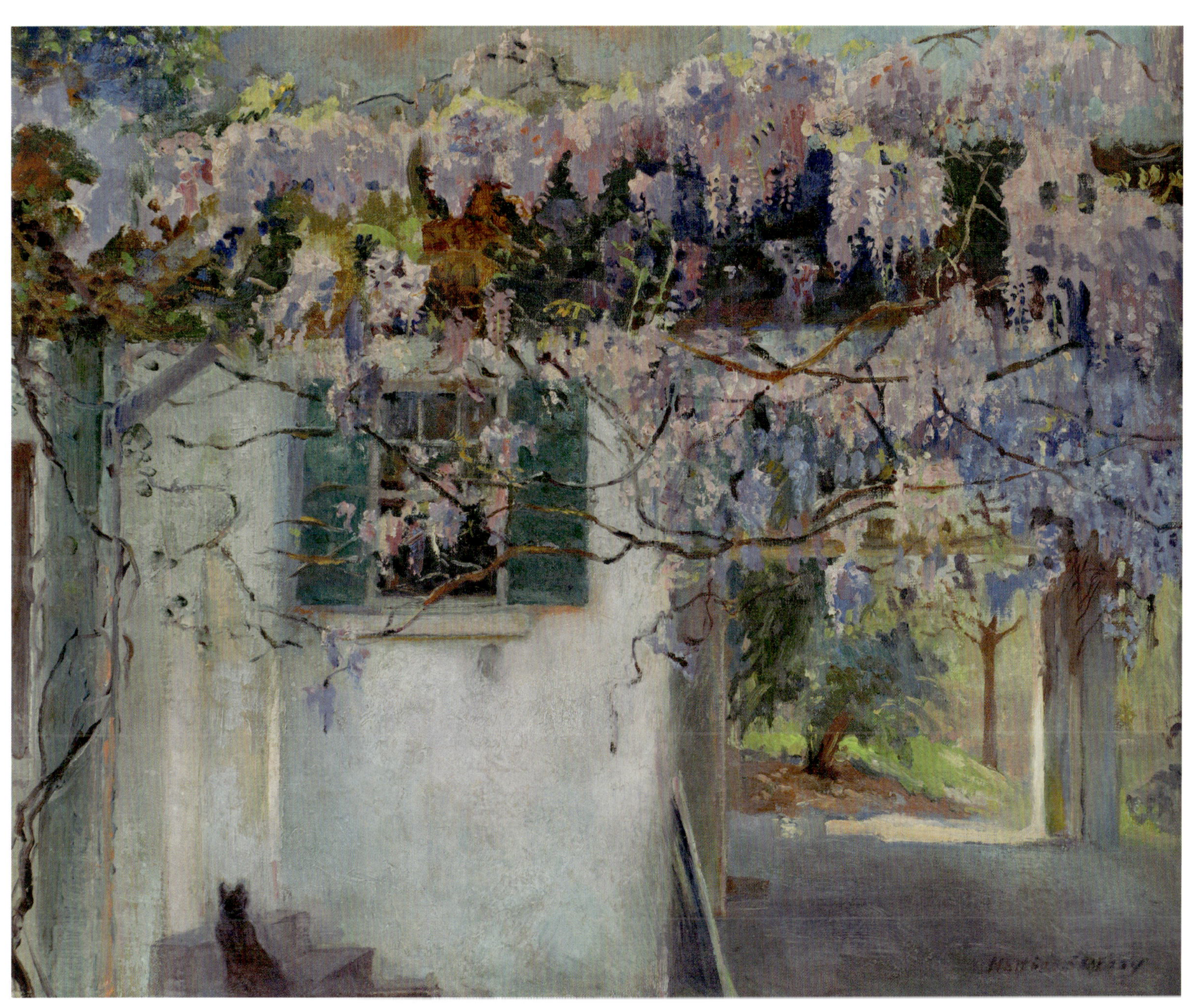

AUGUSTA CHRISTINE FELLS SAVAGE (1892–1962)

Gamin, circa 1930

Painted plaster, 9½ × 6 × 4¼ inches

Augusta Savage was a leading figure of the Harlem Renaissance, a cultural reawakening forged by artists, authors, musicians, and playwrights in the 1920s and 1930s. Ignited in part by the migration of Southern blacks to New York, where a large community settled in Harlem, the leaders of this movement sought to elevate African American culture and society by using visual art, literature, music, and theatre to challenge derogatory racial stereotypes and to cultivate black pride.

Augusta Christine Fells was the seventh of fourteen children (only nine of whom would reach adulthood) born to Edward Fells, a poor rural preacher, in Green Cove Springs, Florida, and his wife, Cornelia.[1] The small town's ancient mineral spring and numerous clay pits were an abundant source of natural materials for young Augusta, who developed an early affinity for shaping forms. The Fells family moved to West Palm Beach when Savage was a teenager, and her interest in sculpture grew with more formal education. As a high school senior, she was paid to teach the modeling of clay to her fellow students.[2]

In the years that followed, Savage took advantage of opportunities to learn and to teach, and also to sell her work, pushing past conventions that would have otherwise kept a black female artist from succeeding in the South—or virtually anywhere else in the United States. At the urging of her Florida mentors, she made the bold decision to leave her family behind. In 1921, with less than five dollars to her name, she moved to New York to more seriously pursue the study of sculpture. Savage enrolled at the Cooper Union, where her extraordinary skill, particularly in creating portrait busts of African Americans, quickly drew praise. Encouraged by this success, in 1923 she applied for a women's summer art program in France. Despite her considerable talent and enormous potential, Savage was denied admission by program officials who believed her race would be "disagreeable to some white students." The controversial decision stirred national headlines. In a letter to the editor of the *New York World*, Savage lamented the prejudice she routinely encountered: "One of the reasons why more of my race do not go in for higher education is that as soon as one of us gets his head above the crowd there are millions of feet ready to crush it back again to that dead level of commonplace."[3] Undeterred, Savage continued to produce art, working in steam laundries to pay the bills.

First created in 1929, *Gamin* was critical not only to Savage's career, but also as an embodiment of the mission of the Harlem Renaissance.[4] The representation of the solemn, sensitive youth expresses the inherent dignity of African American identity that many black artists sought to promote. Here Savage captures an arrested moment and a sense of true immediacy; the child's glance feels natural and uncontrived. While the subject is presumed to be her nephew Ellis Ford, *Gamin* was conceived as a type rather than a portrait, representing one of the city's countless street urchins. With his cap turned to the side and his savvy gaze, this clever gamin would have been instantly recognizable to contemporary New Yorkers.

Savage executed several bronze casts of *Gamin* and continued to make plaster versions of the work into 1930; it is unclear how many she completed or how many survive. She painted assorted plaster casts with bronze dust to simulate the effect of metal. Given the artist's limited means, these painted plasters were a way for her to inexpensively produce large and perhaps multiple editions. As a comparison of any two versions of the sculpture will show, Savage varied the effect from one cast to another. Some mimic the natural, golden color of bronze greened through oxidation; others gleam with the deep brown surface patina favored by certain modern sculptors, including the French master Auguste Rodin, whose work Savage especially admired.

The critical and commercial success of *Gamin* catapulted Savage's reputation far beyond Harlem art circles. The breakthrough sculpture garnered the attention of patrons and at last earned her a fellowship through the Julius Rosenwald Foundation to study in Paris. She arrived there in the autumn of 1929 and connected with fellow African American expatriates like Henry O. Tanner, Nancy Elizabeth Prophet, and Hale Woodruff. In late 1931, in the midst of the Great Depression, Savage returned to Harlem, where she concentrated on teaching and advocacy through neighborhood-based projects funded by the Works Progress Administration. Savage's legacy is inextricably tied to her leadership of these initiatives and specifically to her role as an instructor and mentor to some of the most important African American artists of the postwar era, including Gwendolyn Knight and Norman Lewis. Classes at her eponymous Savage Studio of Arts and Crafts, established in 1932, and later at the Harlem Community Art Center and the Harlem Artists Guild attracted pupils both young and old, and were a beacon of hope for a legion of aspiring African American artists.

JULIE PIEROTTI

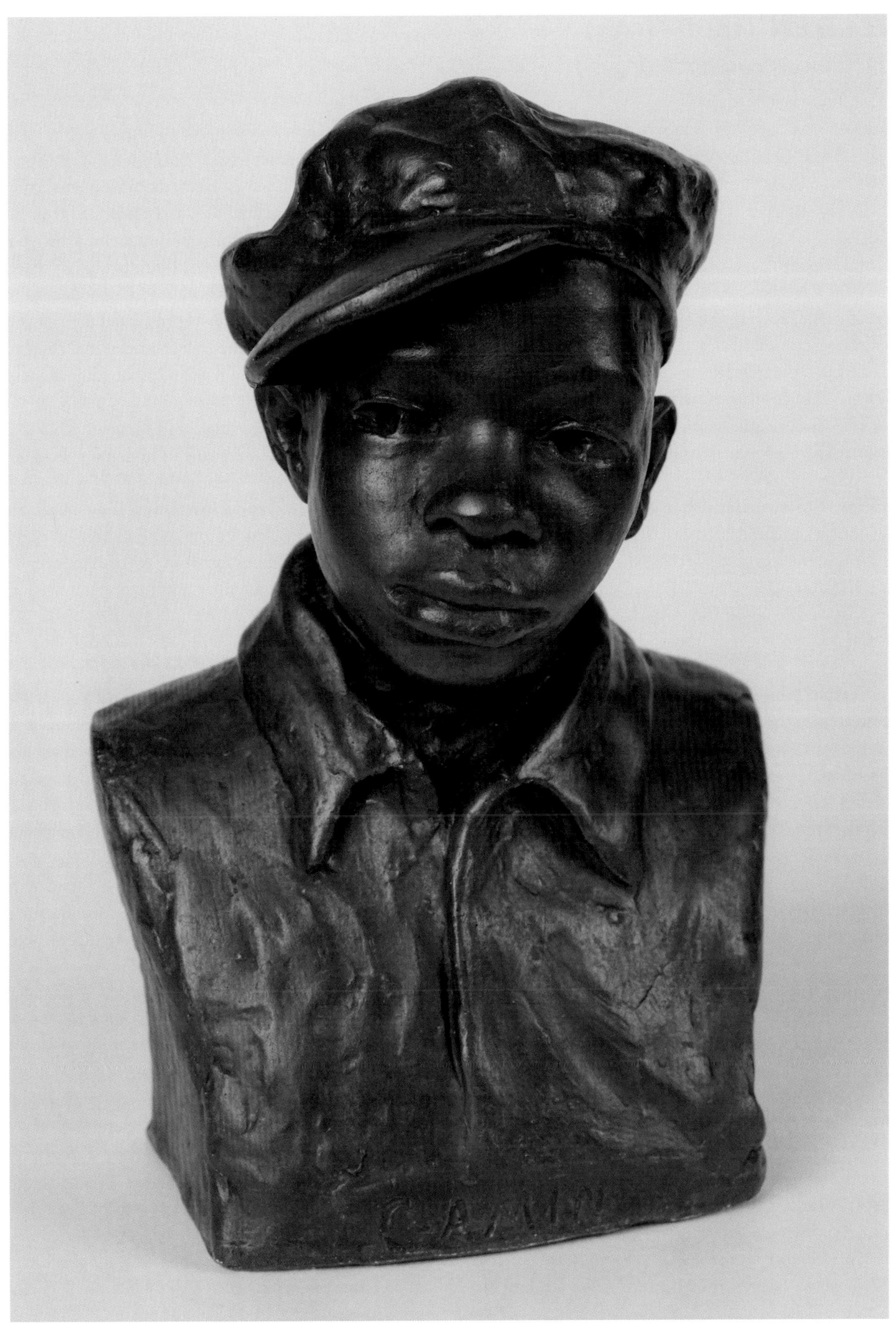

DIXIE SELDEN (1868–1935)

The Blue Sail, Concarneau, 1926 or 1929

Oil on canvas board, 15 × 18 inches

For those states that bordered the lines of demarcation between North and South during the American Civil War, loyalties were deeply divided. Following its initial proclamation of neutrality, the commonwealth of Kentucky ultimately came under Union control, pitting "brother against brother." Just across the Ohio River, the state's leaders also aligned with the federal government, despite the affinity many Ohioans felt with their Confederate neighbors. The Ohio River defined boundaries in Dixie Selden's life as well: a childhood and later years spent in Covington, Kentucky, and art education and midcareer in Cincinnati. Named in honor of both the region and its anthem—notwithstanding her father's service in the Ohio Infantry—Dixie Selden was a study in aesthetic contrasts, working as a successful but conservative portraitist during the winter and exploring foreign lands and new techniques as an adventurous modernist during the summer. Similarly her chief mentors, Frank Duveneck and William Merritt Chase, while colleagues and good friends, represented very different artistic traditions. Contradictions extended to Selden's personal beliefs as well: although she sought recognition for women artists, she refused to be associated with the suffrage movement.

Selden's well-to-do parents first took their only child on a grand tour of Europe in 1878, when the precocious ten-year-old made sketches of what she encountered in continental capitals; a second extended sojourn followed four years later. In 1884 Selden began formal studies at the McMicken School of Drawing and Design, which evolved into the Art Academy of Cincinnati. After six years there she took classes from Duveneck, an accomplished figure painter and a product of the Munich school, which was known for its dark palette and broken brushwork. One of Selden's most impressive portraits was a likeness of Duveneck that was shown at the National Academy of Design and the Pennsylvania Academy of the Fine Arts.

Described as petite and vivacious, Selden had an engaging personality that seems to have infused her creative approach and output. The companion brochure to a memorial exhibition mounted just one year after her death contained the following statement: "She saw life in terms of color yet with clarity of outline, and painting seemed for her a natural medium of expression. Honest and forceful in her art, as in her life, she gave of her best to every undertaking."[1] Her talent and temperament attracted the patronage of her parents' affluent social circle, for both portrait commissions and purchases of her landscapes and still lifes. It is believed that Selden painted several hundred portraits of area bankers, businesspeople, and society women. Independent and single, Selden exhibited with the all-male Cincinnati Art Club in 1891 and occasionally was the sole woman represented in commercial shows. She was also a charter member and twice the president of the city's Woman's Art Club, a forum for female artists that began hosting exhibitions in 1893.

Selden's other mentor was Chase, who was known for his impressionistic plein air landscapes as well as portraits and still lifes. In 1913 she traveled to Venice to participate in his last summer class abroad, an experience that became a stylistic turning point for her. She lightened her palette and—with Chase's encouragement—found greater ease painting outdoor scenes. A local reporter commented that "she was greatly influenced [by him].... This was a phase in which she was absolutely original and one in which her joyous personality came forth unfettered and clear cut."[2] Upon her return Selden exhibited thirty Venetian paintings; within two weeks she had sold ten and received four portrait commissions.

Summers were an opportunity to travel, and Selden's decided preference was for seaside destinations such as Gloucester, Massachusetts; Boothbay Harbor, Maine; and Newport, Rhode Island—along with her French favorite, Concarneau. Located on the Atlantic coast in the northwest corner of France, Concarneau was a charming fishing village with comfortable accommodations and quaint scenery. She spent the summers of 1926 and 1929 there, which accounts for the uncertain dating of *The Blue Sail*. The subject of this small painting—done *en plein air*—is a *thoniér*, a boat used for catching tuna. According to Selden, the harbor was a thrilling sight, with hundreds of small vessels. Though the day she painted *The Blue Sail* was overcast, the painting radiates color, dominated by the sail itself and the roseate tone of the keel. Bright green highlights energize the composition, and the water quivers with reflections rendered with short dashes of paint from her brush. The overall cheerfulness of *The Blue Sail* cannot be disputed and seems to mirror the artist's nature. Selden described her delight in its setting to a reporter: "Concarneau is a marvelous place to paint.... You see pictures everywhere."[3]

MARTHA R. SEVERENS

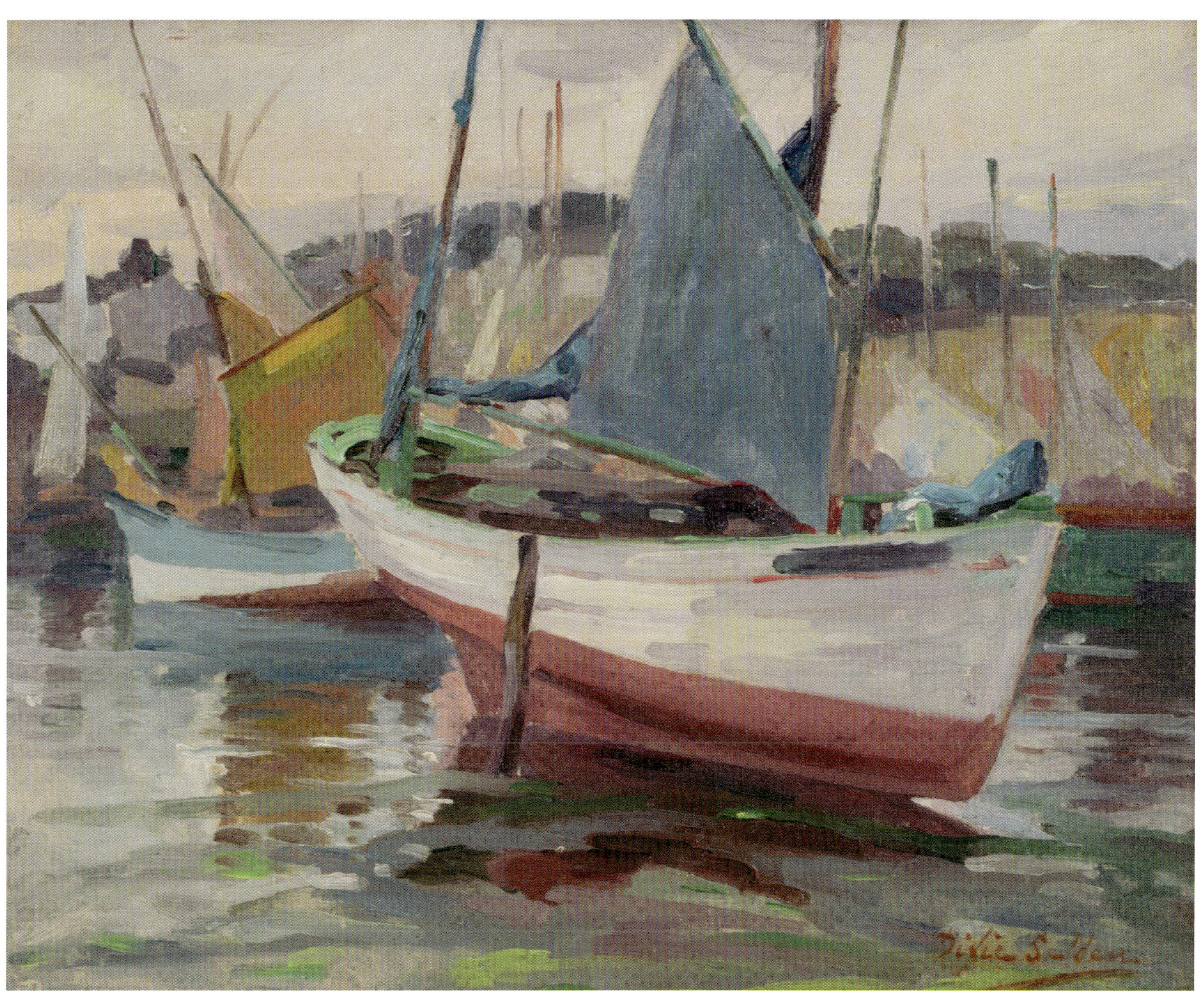

ALICE RAVENEL HUGER SMITH (1876–1958)

Along the Beach, circa 1926

Watercolor on paper mounted on cardboard, 16⅞ × 21 inches

As a key figure in the twentieth-century Charleston Renaissance, Alice Ravenel Huger Smith painted refined watercolors that exalted the natural power and beauty of South Carolina's Lowcountry. Growing up in the postbellum city's highly cultured—if somewhat impoverished—genteel circles, lively young Alice Smith first loved art as girlish play. Her paternal grandmother perceived the child's instinctive gift and advised her to become an artist around age eleven. Alice dutifully "started on the appointed road" in the belief that "a great deal of time is saved by a signpost plainly lettered."[1]

In the wake of her mother's untimely death, Smith enrolled in classes at the Carolina Art Association school, where Lucie-Louise Féry employed "the best French methods of teaching."[2] From about 1888 to 1895, Féry instructed Smith in the fundamentals, including lessons that emphasized the transparency of watercolor—a quality that would define Smith's luminous mature output. She likely joined Féry's "Out-of-Doors Sketching Class," and creating *en plein air* surely appealed to the budding artist, who enjoyed long country walks to sites like Middleton Place Plantation. Initially Smith produced "bright little sketches" in the style of fellow Charlestonian William Aiken Walker, whose work was often showcased in Lanneau's Art Store, a venue she frequented.[3] A study of miniature painting under Cecile E. Payen in New York City during the summer of 1902 expanded her horizons.[4] Between 1902 and 1915, Smith largely concentrated on portraiture—somber, distinguished portraits of male relatives and lighter, spontaneous likenesses of women and children—but also began to execute watercolor landscapes around 1906. These lyrical works were often based on photographs she took of nearby plantations and served as illustrations for two of her many popular publications, *A Woman Rice Planter* (1913) and *A Carolina Rice Plantation of the Fifties* (1936).[5]

Two men who would prove central to Smith's artistic development arrived in Charleston in 1908. Nationally noted painter and writer Birge Harrison used a former kitchen house on the family's property as studio space during his winter visits and informally instructed her on the mood-filled principles of Tonalism. Alston Read, a young scientist who was Smith's beloved cousin and friend, shared his large personal collection of Japanese Ukiyo-e prints with the artist. Read introduced Smith to Asian techniques and, through extensive reading, to Southern Chinese landscape philosophies based on Taoism and Zen Buddhism. Read's influence—as well as her friendship with visiting printmakers Helen Hyde and Bertha Clausen Jaques—led Smith to create a handful of fine woodblock prints that evidenced her total absorption of Japonisme. When a selection of these were included in an exhibition at the Art Institute of Chicago in 1920, the department's curator praised them as "far finer than any other print from wood blocks that I have ever seen that was not made in Japan."[6] Read also helped Smith and her historian father produce *The Dwelling Houses of Charleston* (1917), a seminal architectural history of the city, which the Smiths in turn dedicated to him. Alice Smith credited Read for much of her aesthetic development, writing that "the impetus he had given to my work was incalculable."[7]

Along the Beach reflects Smith's affinity for and mastery of Japonisme. The general composition and the subdued blue-grey colors evoke elements and hues found in several prints in Read's print collection.[8] Smith routinely employed similar dark values in other watercolors. In this example, the artist subtly applied light to these dark tones to direct the viewer's attention. A patch of gold serves as the focal point toward the lower right. Understated highlights draw the eye along the painting's base and onto the trunks of the palmettos framing the work's right and left margins. Rendered here with delicate watercolor strokes, palmetto trees are another recurring element in Smith's oeuvre. These "proud armorial trees" populate South Carolina's fragile maritime forests, gracefully enduring gusts and rain without breaking.[9] Between the palmettos, a wave's movement unifies the major elements.

Tempests may be brewing in *Along the Beach*: although hues appear cool at first glance, a subtle tension permeates the picture. Warm reddish lavenders and cold greenish blues in sea and sky appear primed to explode. Smith appreciated the energy and ethereal drama of coastal Carolina weather: "Whenever I was able to do so I would go out to one of the beaches after a storm. Sometimes there were angry waters;… sometimes there was glorious colour from the clear atmosphere following the winds."[10]

DWIGHT E. H. McINVAILL

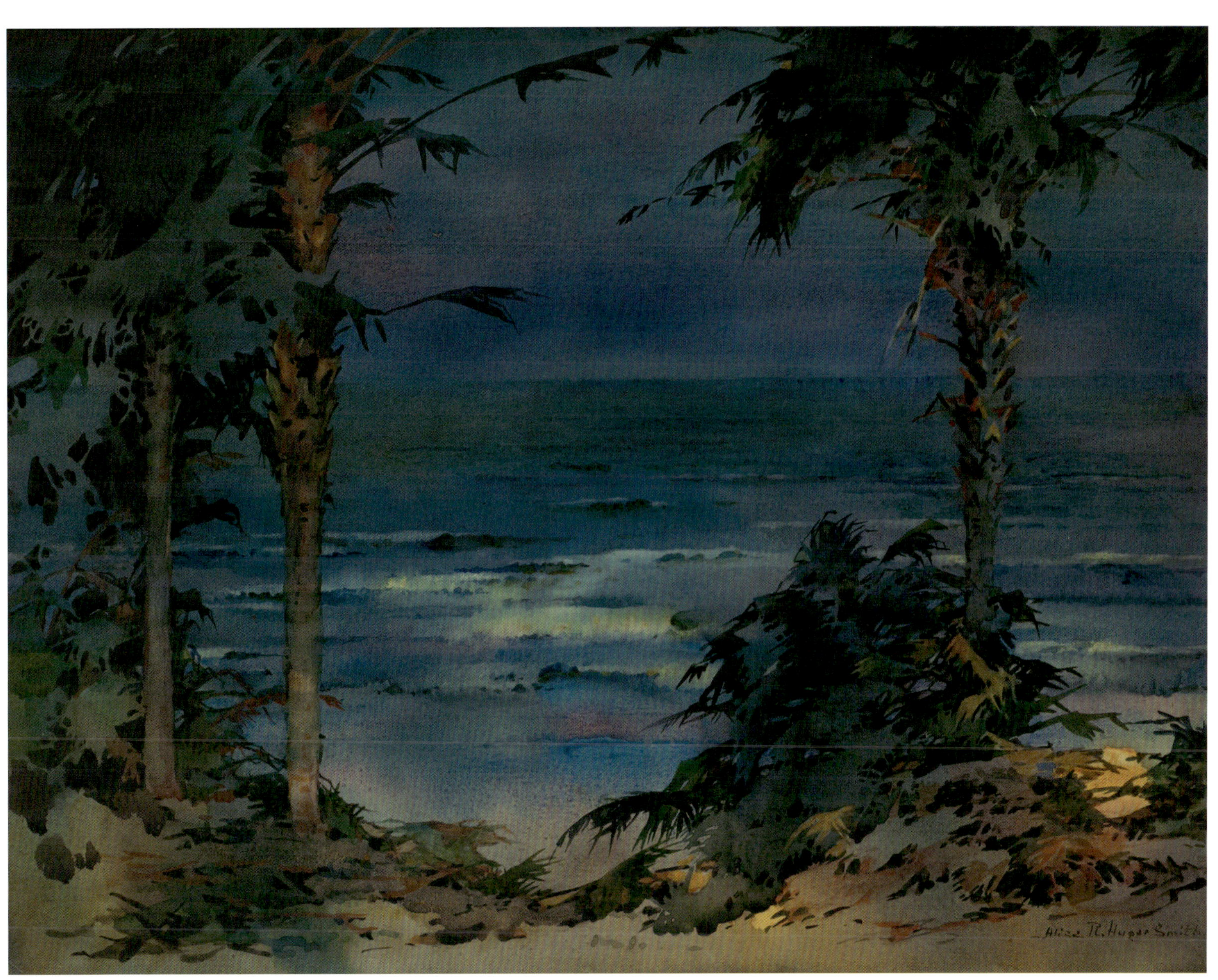

GLADYS NELSON SMITH (1890–1980)

Time Out, circa 1938–1939

Oil on canvas, 42¼ × 38⅛ inches

Little about Gladys Nelson's childhood with nine siblings on a Kansas farm foreshadowed her eventual professional success in the sophisticated art circles of greater Washington, DC. Before finding her niche in the nation's capital, she relocated several times, moves predicated on educational opportunities as well as her husband's job assignments. Through it all, the same early talent that had been nurtured by her parents and that had led her to earn a bachelor's degree in painting from the University of Kansas at Lawrence ultimately gained her entrance to prominent institutions such as the Art Institute of Chicago, the Art Students League in New York, and finally Washington's Corcoran School of Art.

By 1924 Errett Smith's legal career had brought the couple to Chevy Chase, Maryland, and Gladys soon enrolled at the Corcoran School of Art, where she took classes in portraiture and composition through 1930. Edmund C. Tarbell, the noted Impressionist figurative painter from Boston, served as the principal of the school for two of those years. He became Smith's primary mentor, and his interest in seventeenth-century Dutch painters may have influenced her. Beyond the Corcoran, she became active with the prestigious Society of Washington Artists and was elected to the membership of the Arts Club of Washington, a private organization located in the old James Monroe House. She participated in the two exhibitions of the short-lived group known as Twenty Women Painters, an indication of her feminist leanings. At one of those shows her painting titled *The Snob* was noted in the press: it "evidences a pictorial sense and also a command of her medium."[1]

In the mid-1930s, Smith and her husband purchased a sixty-eight–acre farm in rural Frederick County, Maryland. During her time there, Smith—an introvert described as having "marked hypersensitivities"—immersed herself in nature and cultivated a garden.[2] Her inclination toward Impressionism was also nurtured by the bucolic setting, and some of her most colorful and lush paintings—both landscapes and figurative paintings—were probably done in those surroundings. In all likelihood, Smith executed this compelling portrait, *Time Out,* at the farm.[3] The robust iceman, with an endearing half-smile on his face and an upward glance, sits before a narrow opening with a view into the landscape. A very similar character is the subject of an oil held in the collection of the Los Angeles County Museum of Art. Dating to the same period, *The Tippler* is "a pleasant genre scene of a working-class man enjoying a drink. During the 1930s the artist painted several images of elderly people, endowing each figure with a sense of dignity and strength."[4]

Time Out was successfully exhibited in 1940 with the Society of Washington Artists at the Corcoran Gallery of Art. It received an enthusiastic commendation in the local newspaper: "Among the figure paintings shown, outstanding along the lines of tradition is one by Gladys Nelson Smith, of an ice man taking 'Time Out,' seated with his tongs idle beside a cake of ice awaiting delivery. Realistically treated this painting is excellent in tone and technical handling and, more still, as a characterization it carries conviction."[5] What the reviewer failed to mention is how well Smith captured the transparent surface of the ice and the glinting metal of the tongs.

Smith did not always receive such glowing accolades; the year before, the jury for the 1939 Corcoran Biennial rejected her submission. In a scathing letter to her sister, Smith stated that her depiction of an old man was apparently "anathema" to the head juror, Maurice Sterne, a European-influenced modernist. She continued: "My work simply has no chance till this madness [modern art] is over. It is the same madness that makes jitterbugs and politicians eager to barter the people's liberties for personal power.... We are governed by propaganda and the modern art racket has control of this field, completely—such conservatives as do get on juries look timorously to the time when their fate will be decided by similarly dominated juries."[6] Discouraged by the preference for nonobjective art, Smith gave up painting altogether for a while in the 1950s and instead poured her creative energies into poetry. In 1966 she added a studio to her Chevy Chase home and took up her brushes once again until failing eyesight and Parkinson's disease forced her to quit.

MARTHA R. SEVERENS

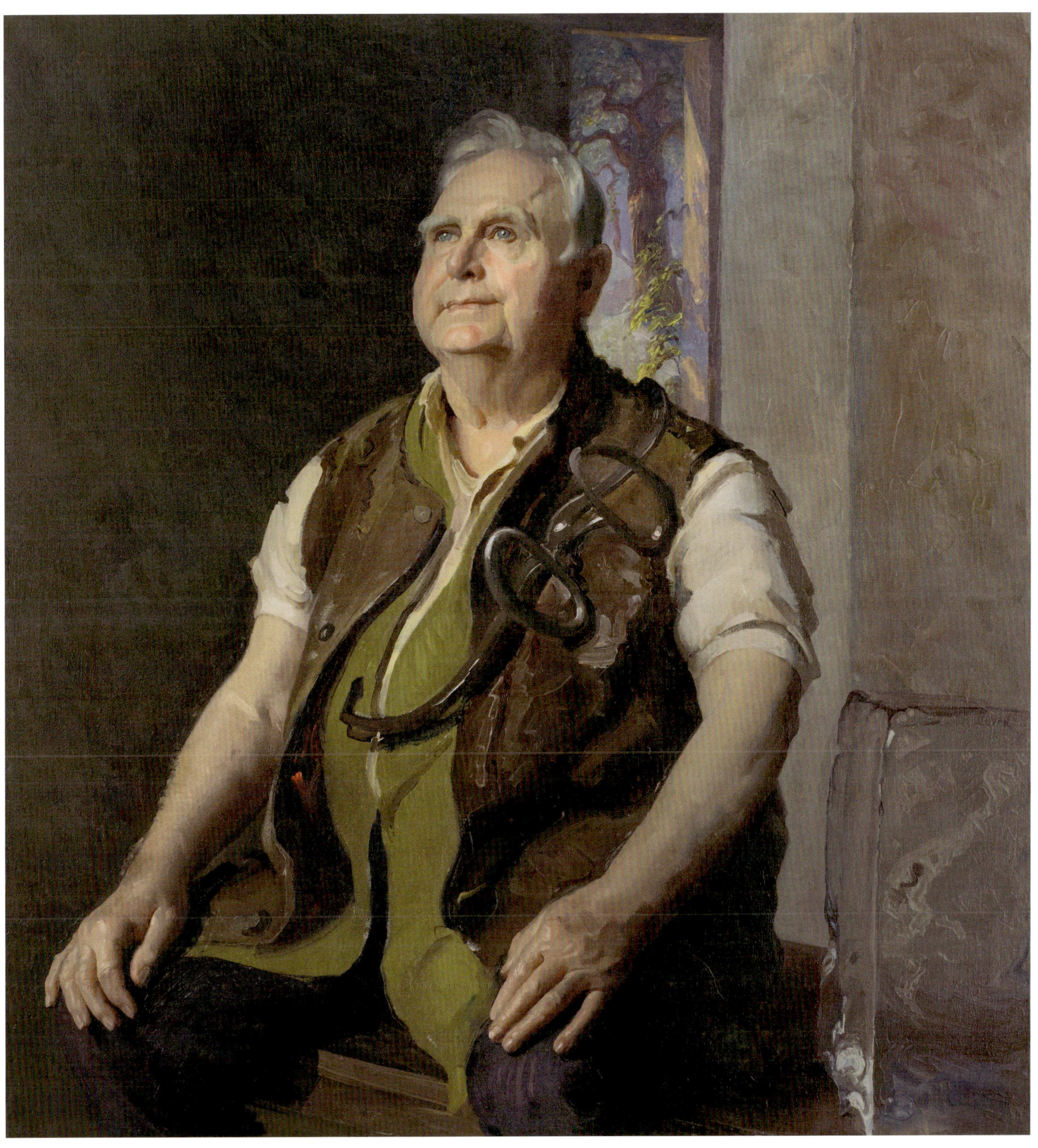

ALMA WOODSEY THOMAS (1891–1978)

Still Life with Mandolin, circa 1955

Oil on masonite, 19⅞ × 35¼ inches

In 1907 the violence against and degradation of black lives in the American South caused John Harris Thomas and Amelia Cantey Thomas to abandon their individual successes in Columbus, Georgia, in order to pursue better educational prospects for their four daughters in Washington, DC. The couple's eldest child, Alma, took full advantage of the educational options set before her. She attended the city's well-regarded historically black college, Howard University, becoming the first graduate of its art program in 1924, and later earned her teaching certification. Throughout her nearly forty-year career as a teacher in the public school system, Thomas remained committed to her artistic ambitions, painting during off-hours. After her retirement in 1960, she devoted herself wholeheartedly to her craft. Although she was often dismissive of her early output, these works document her skillful, sustained negotiation within canonical historical practices, as demonstrated by *Still Life with Mandolin*.

The spatial experimentation seen in *Still Life with Mandolin* preceded the artist's progression toward her signature mature style: full abstractions of the natural world around her. The painting investigates space yet remains firmly rooted in a timeless academic tradition, and reflects Thomas's efforts to master the concepts of depth, color, light, and shadow. As for her avant-garde predecessors Pablo Picasso and Georges Braque, still life provided ideal subject matter for the investigation of form. Both men executed versions of still lifes featuring mandolins in the 1920s at the height of their explorations of Synthetic Cubism. Dating to the 1950s, Thomas's vignette has a Cézannesque quality as it displays the mandolin and the bowl of fruit from different perspectives. The viewer glimpses both the inside of the bowl and the front of the stringed instrument. The red, green, and orange surface on which the arrangement sits provides a similar sense of spatial ambiguity, as the viewer can faintly identify the separation between the horizontal plane and vertical backdrop.

Thomas's participation in Loïs Mailou Jones's Little Paris Group, her association with the Washington Color School painters, and the classes she took with Jacob Kainen and fellow Southerner Ben Summerford at American University in the 1950s galvanized her to create something altogether new for a retrospective exhibition held at Howard University in 1966. She set out to "paint something different from anything I'd ever done. Different from anything I'd ever seen. I thought to myself, that must be accomplished."[1] This trademark adventurous spirit and optimism informed Thomas's paintings from that point forward, as exemplified in her 1971 *Blue Ground Stripe*. Her previous inquiries into color and space carry over to her mature productions, as does her determination to formulate her own techniques and rules.

Thomas's biography is a quintessential American narrative of hope and opportunity. But her story's details also attest to the difficult reality of racial and gender politics in her lifetime. Despite those hardships, Thomas insisted that she "never bothered painting the ugly things in life. People struggling, having difficulty. You meet that when you go out, and then you have to come back and see the same thing hanging on the wall. No. I wanted something beautiful that you could sit down and look at."[2] She played a pivotal role in the 1943 establishment of the Barnett-Aden Gallery, Washington, DC's first gallery to host desegregated art exhibitions, and served as its vice president. In 1972 she became—at the age of eighty—the first African American woman to have a solo exhibition at a major national arts institution, the Whitney Museum of American Art. Even then Thomas lamented that her increasingly frail body did not reflect her brilliant and nimble mind.[3] Alma Thomas died on February 24, 1978, during open-heart surgery, leaving behind an indelible mark on the art world. In her work and in her living she sought to "concentrate on beauty and happiness, rather than on man's inhumanity to man."[4] Inspired by the Apollo lunar missions, Thomas's series of Space Paintings illustrate her Afrofuturistic desires for an existence that transcended earthly bounds, ideas she had been exploring for decades as an innovative artist.

ELIZABETH C. HAMILTON

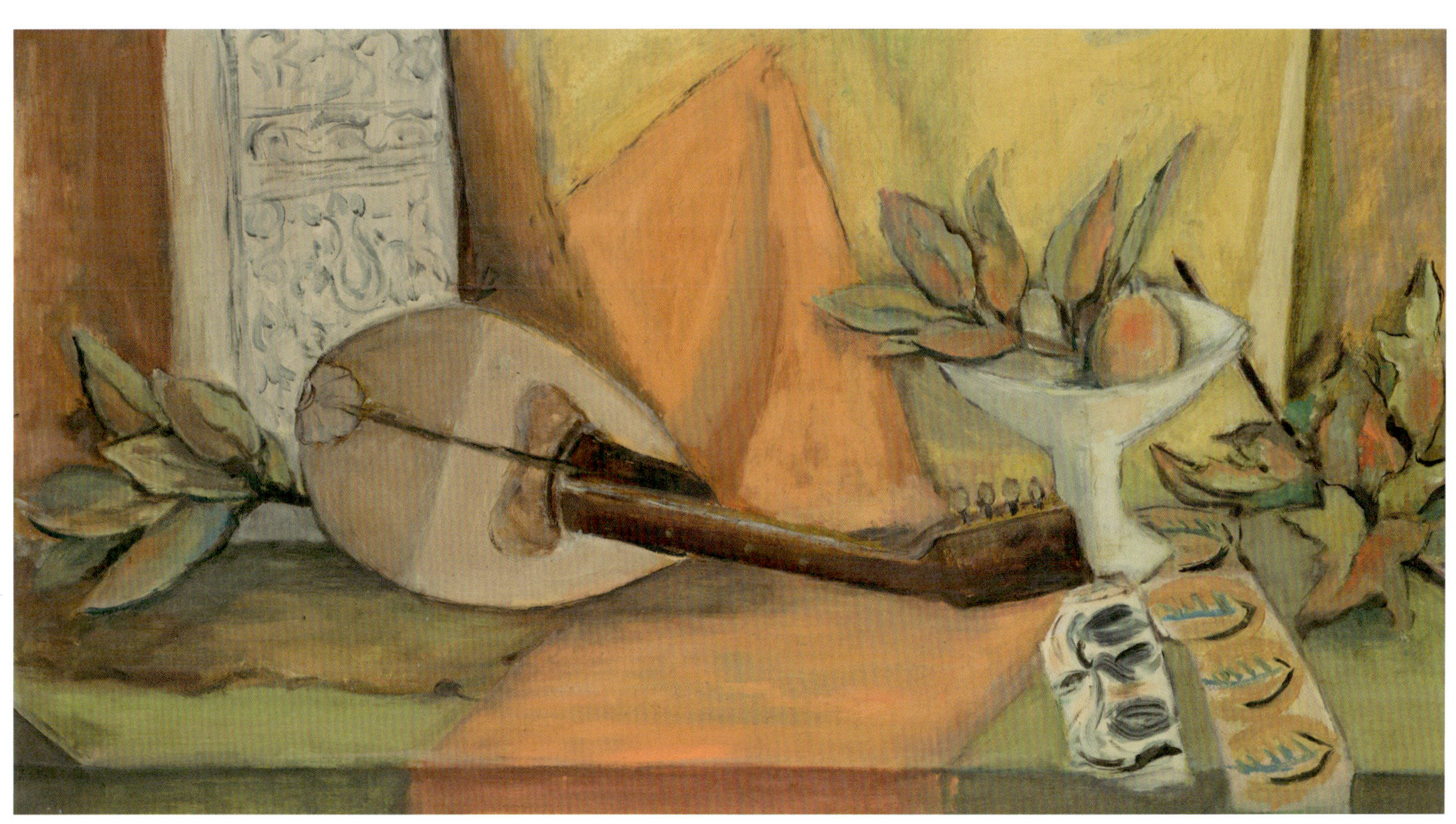

MARY ALICE LEATH THOMAS (1905–1959)

Red, Gold and Black, 1957

Lacquer, gold leaf, and palladium leaf on masonite, 48 × 40 inches

When the University of North Carolina at Greensboro hosted a retrospective exhibition honoring artist and educator Mary Leath Thomas the year following her death, gestural paintings of organic, zoomorphic forms dominated the gallery walls. Dating to 1957, *Red, Gold and Black* stood apart from these images, however, because of its striking geometric abstraction and innovative incorporation of thinly beaten palladium leaf—a medium commonly reserved for sign painters.[1] Upon visiting the exhibition, Thomas's former colleague and the founder of the university's art department, Gregory Dowler Ivy, noted with admiration that his friend's "unexpected use of the precise, yet free geometric shapes achieves a contrast with the color and texture which lends an individual quality of quietness and depth."[2] Ivy's poignant assessment regarding the "quietness and depth" of Thomas's work is equally applicable to the artist herself.

Born into a grocer's family in Hazlehurst, Georgia, Mary Leath had humble beginnings. Little is known about what if any formal art instruction she received as a youth. In 1930 she graduated from Georgia State College for Women (later Georgia College) in Milledgeville and soon began working toward a master's degree at Duke University. In Durham she taught in the public school system and quickly emerged as a leader in art education. Thomas's experiences as president of North Carolina's Art Teachers Association and as an assistant professor of art at the state's women's college (later the University of North Carolina at Greensboro) equipped her to become an effective advocate for art faculty development. She promoted enhanced curricula through her extensive professional networks and in her 1935 publication *Correlating Art with Other School Subjects.* All the while, Thomas worked diligently to hone her own artistic abilities, as borne out in numerous watercolor and gouache sketches of Southern landscapes. The simplified, ethereal forms that populate these works on paper reveal Thomas's familiarity with the beauty and diverse terrains of the Carolinas and Georgia. When examined alongside her *Red, Gold and Black*—painted twenty-five years later—these early efforts also underscore the artist's dedication to her own aesthetic maturation.

It was while studying modern methods at the University of Chicago during the summer of 1940 that the artist met her husband, abstract painter Howard Wilber Thomas.[3] Shortly after marrying in 1945, the couple acquired positions at the University of Georgia. Not only did Mary Thomas teach at the university, she also served as a consultant to Atlanta-area schools and the South Carolina Department of Education. In her own studio she experimented with Abstract Expressionist gestural painting techniques and delved into geometric abstraction in the 1950s. Sharing fellow modern artists' fascination with the expressive quality and formal purity of art produced in so-called primitive cultures, Thomas began reducing images to their basic components. The ephemeral forms of her early landscapes morphed into solid, flatly-painted shapes, and her previously romantic, earthy tones became dramatically bolder. Contemporaries, most notably Paul Klee, deeply influenced the artist's progressively modernist idiom, as well as her pedagogical approach. Indeed, Thomas is known to have distributed reproductions of Klee's work to friends and is said to have frequently referred to the painter's method of instruction at the Bauhaus.[4]

Thomas retired as an art educator in 1956 and had begun focusing entirely on painting by the time she created *Red, Gold and Black,* a spectacular example of her minimalist late style. Here clearly hand-drawn, irregular rectangles of vibrant color extend over slightly crooked columns, creating a quiet visual tension. The composition becomes a spatial study in color relationships, with similarly hued shapes taking on different tones depending on the colored pillar upon which they appear. Thomas's painting calls to mind the work of Josef Albers, a Bauhaus instructor who taught alongside Klee and who famously layered squares of varying tones to explore chromatic interaction and its effect on viewers' perception. Considered in these terms, *Red, Gold and Black* offers a magnificent turnstile of rotating, shimmering colors.

Thomas's modern investigations received mixed responses when they were initially exhibited in Southern venues to a hesitant regional press and skeptical local audiences. Nonetheless, she soon earned a national reputation and a place in the prestigious annual exhibition at the Pennsylvania Academy of the Fine Arts. Just two years after completing *Red, Gold and Black,* Thomas suffered a fatal heart attack. Having juggled multiple responsibilities throughout her career, the artist was robbed of the time she had always coveted. "Time," she had said "is the most valuable possession of the creative person."[5]

SANDY McCAIN

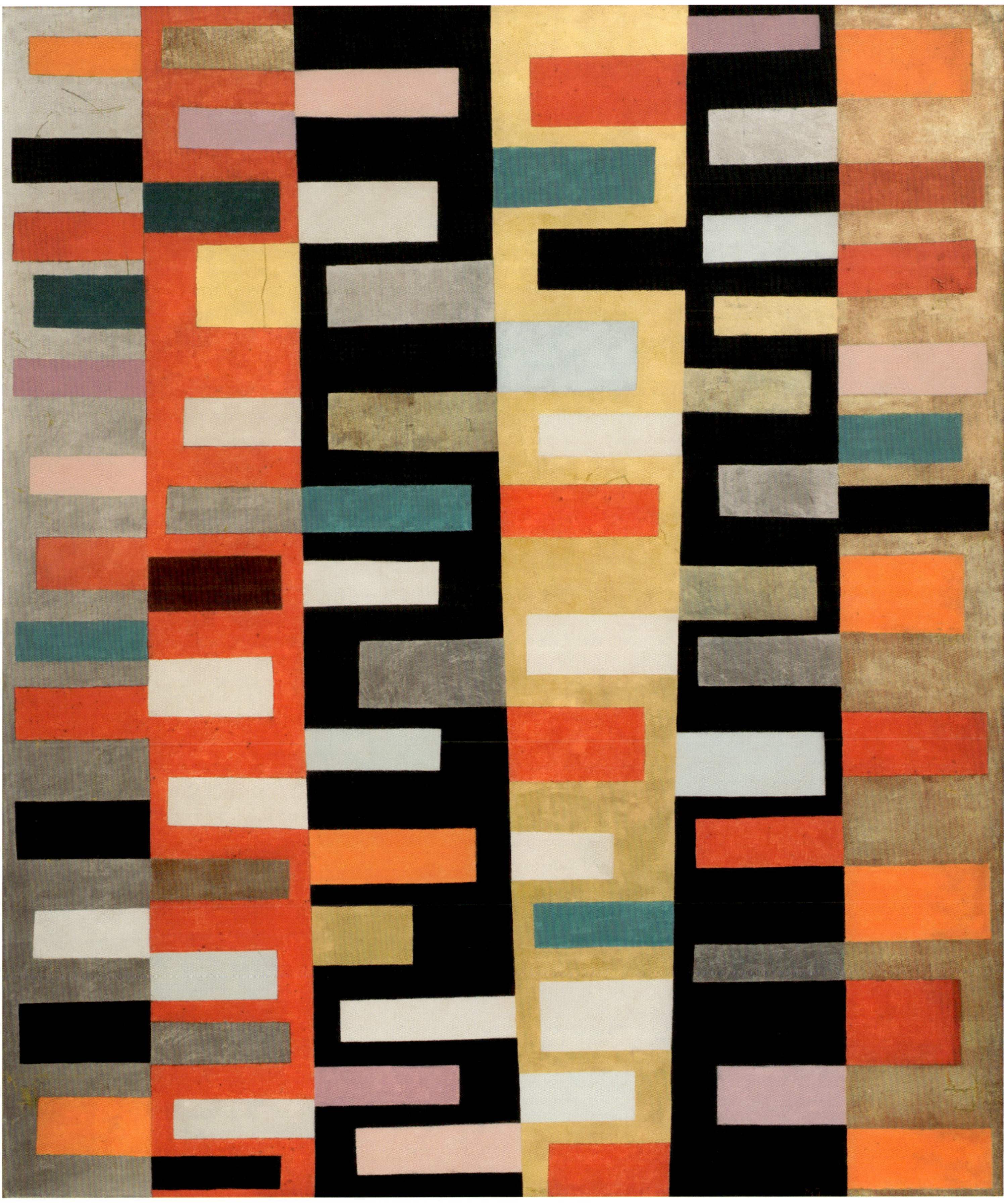

HELEN MARIA TURNER (1858–1958)

A Song of Summer, circa 1915

Oil on canvas, 30⅛ × 40⅛ inches

A Song of Summer captures a moment of reverie as a young woman plays guitar in the artist's woodsy yard at Takusan, her summer home in Cragsmoor, New York. Helen Turner lived mainly in New Orleans and New York City, but Cragsmoor was the setting for the most acclaimed work of her seventy-year career. Between 1912 and 1924, a series of her standout paintings, including *A Song of Summer,* garnered accolades and were sought for exhibitions and purchase by leading museums and discerning collectors.[1] These pieces solidified a stellar career capped by a crowning achievement: Turner's 1921 election as a full academician at the National Academy of Design. She was only the fourth woman to receive this prestigious designation.[2]

Turner's genteel family suffered extreme adversity during the Civil War, including business failures and the deaths of her brother and parents. As a young orphan she spent most of her youth in New Orleans, where she became a member of a loving uncle's household. From girlhood Turner was interested in art. If her family had not lost their fortune, she might have taken a more direct path to study art in New York or abroad, as was the fashion for her contemporaries with means, such as Kate Freeman Clark of Mississippi and Anne Goldthwaite of Alabama. Fortunately for Turner, artistic opportunities existed in New Orleans, and she availed herself of free classes at Tulane University's art school and at the local Artists' Association. Having set her sights higher, Turner was financially able to move to New York in 1895, at the age of thirty-seven.

In New York she refined her skills at the Art Students League under the instruction of Kenyon Cox and Douglas Volk, and later at Cooper Union. She earned a degree from the Teachers College of Columbia University in 1902. From 1902 to 1919 she taught at the art school of the Young Women's Christian Association of New York, training hundreds of women for careers as illustrators and designers. Her teaching salary, supplemented by portrait commissions and sales of her work, funded formative and fulfilling opportunities, such as joining William Merritt Chase's summer trips to Europe in 1904, 1905, and 1911, and building a house in the art colony of Cragsmoor. As Turner's skills matured, she embraced the style and subject matter of Impressionism and contributed to the American Impressionist movement in the United States, exhibiting widely at major venues like the 1915 Panama-Pacific International Exposition in San Francisco.

Dorothea Storey, an art student and a popular model for Turner and for her colleague and Cragsmoor neighbor, Charles Courtney Curran, is likely the subject seen in *A Song of Summer.*[3] The painting was shown at the National Academy's winter exhibition in December 1915 and subsequently traveled down Fifth Avenue to the Macbeth Gallery for inclusion in a January 1916 exhibition that also featured work by Daniel Garber and Emil Carlsen. Gallery owner William Macbeth called Turner an "artist of very serious consideration" whose work "put some of the brethren to their best pace if they are going to be with her at the top of the ladder on which she has a firm hold."[4]

A Song of Summer reveals Turner's expertise in depicting the female figure outdoors. In an impressionistic interplay of light and color, her palette glows with cool verdant green and warm caramel pigments. Thickly applied strokes create energy and vibrancy. Sunlight filters through the trees in bright white patches on the woman's dress and hat. For compositional drama, the woman appears close to the picture plane while loosely painted leafy branches and birch trees create a sense of depth in the background. The guitar's sound hole, just slightly off-center, produces a strong focal point. The eye roams in a triangular direction: from the woman's gaze to her fingers and down the strings to her forearm gracefully aligned with the guitar.

Turner lived to be ninety-nine. Steadfastly committed to her art and career, she was a trailblazer who challenged society's conventions and succeeded in a male-dominated field. Although many women of her generation studied art, few financed their own studies, became self-supporting, or matched Turner's esteemed professional status.   MAIA JALENAK

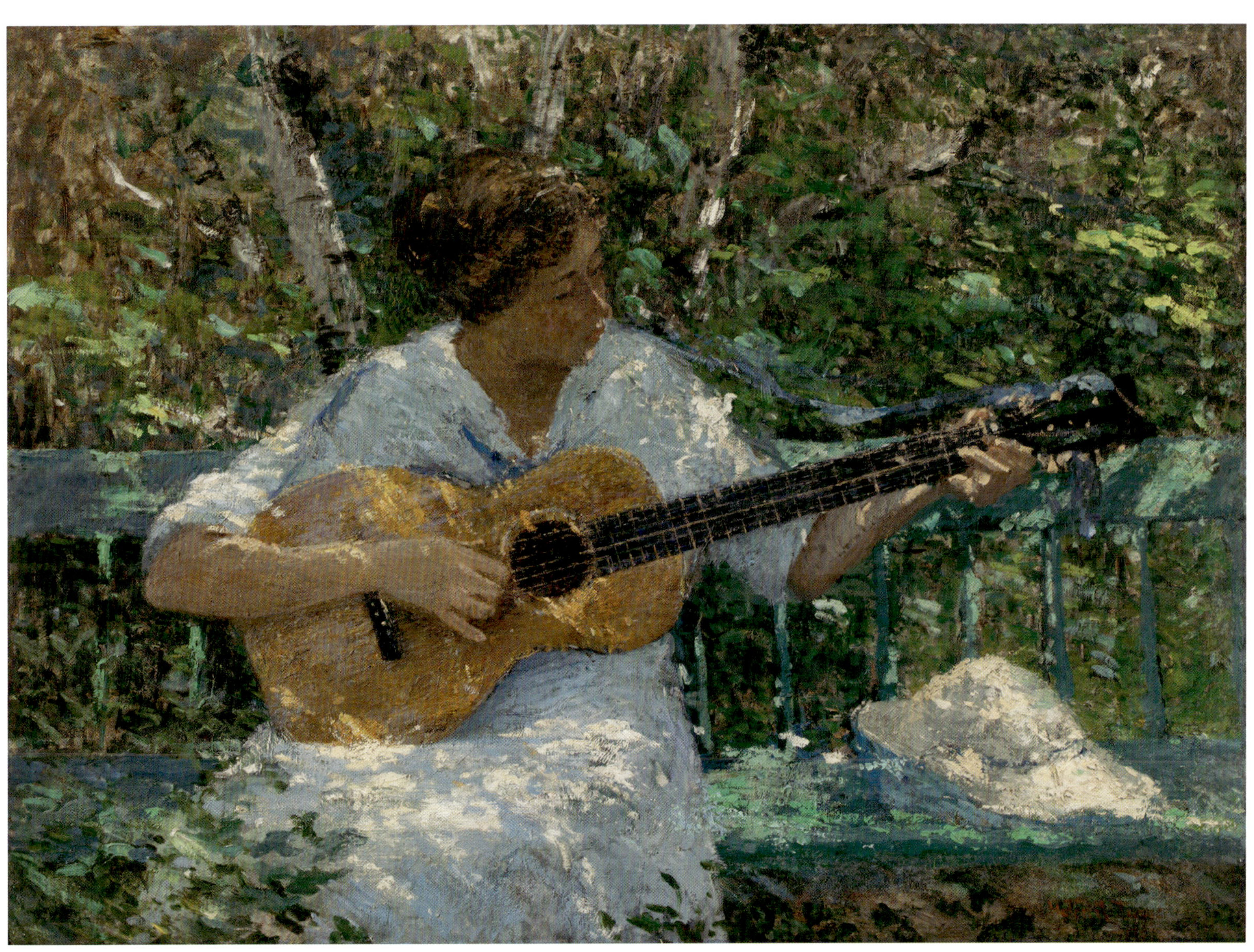

ELIZABETH QUALE O'NEILL VERNER (1883–1979)

Shem Creek, 1954

Pastel on silk mounted on plywood, 23⅛ × 28 inches

In *Shem Creek*, Elizabeth O'Neill Verner pictures the marsh-lined waterways that surround her beloved birthplace. The skyline of the Charleston peninsula looms on the horizon of this westward view overlooking the creek's mouth, where from the banks of Mount Pleasant it empties into Charleston harbor. Verner depicts shrimp trawlers huddled against the docks and seagulls gliding over the channel toward open water. The anchored boats, fading sky, and golden hues of the grasses indicate the shorter days of late fall or early winter in the South Carolina Lowcountry and together frame the view of the distant city. A lone fisherman in the right foreground lends to the subdued seasonal atmosphere, adeptly rendered in pastel.

Shem Creek's sheltered, deep-water channel has long provided important access to Charleston and its harbor, functioning from the early 1700s as a principal site for transportation, shipbuilding, and milling, and since the 1930s as a hub for the local shrimping industry. Its banks also provide a panoramic view of Charleston's eastern shoreline—a vista often depicted in historic engravings of the city. Perhaps Verner was inspired by these early scenes, as scholars have suggested, or maybe visualizing the city from this vantage point represented an attempt to express the abiding connection to her peninsular home that was often roused when she approached it after spending time away: "Every time I cross the Ashley or Cooper rivers and enter the city, whether I come from the North, the West or the South, every time that feeling of rest comes over me; *I am at home.*"[1]

A Charleston native, Verner spent more than half her life interpreting and promoting the city's unique historic architecture, coastal landscapes, and people through her art and writings. In her youth she took art classes at the Carolina Art Association and first met her friend and mentor Alice Smith. Verner later studied at the Pennsylvania Academy of the Fine Arts, where, under the tutelage of Thomas Anschutz, she acquired a solid foundation in drawing.[2] She returned to Charleston in 1907, married, and started a family, but took active roles in community arts organizations and continued to refine her skills.

Following her husband's unexpected death in 1925, Verner began to take her craft more seriously, working full-time to support her two children. Her devotion to her hometown was first evidenced in an extensive body of etchings, which totaled more than 260 over the span of her career. In the mid-1930s she developed an interest in pastel, which engaged her drafting skills and allowed her to work in color. Instead of paper, she chose raw silk mounted on board as the support for these pieces. Unlike her etchings, which primarily focused on cityscapes featuring architectural subjects, Verner's pastels were more often figurative or, as in *Shem Creek*, captured the area's natural landscapes and waterways.[3] In *Shem Creek*, Verner used a limited palette, and her sensibility to architectural line is evident in the vertical masts of the shrimp trawlers and in the subtle formation of the skyline along the horizon.

Verner's Charleston-centric oeuvre exemplifies the pride of place favored by the Regionalist art movement, which gained popularity among American painters and printmakers during the interwar era. The Regionalists eschewed the avant-garde abstract styles being disseminated from Europe and instead celebrated local subject matter. In an era plagued by war, economic depression, and racial violence, Verner's romantic and often placid interpretations of her city stood in stark contrast to the documentation of the practical and political issues of the day by Social Realists.[4] *Shem Creek* embodies Verner's affection for the Lowcountry and exemplifies a perception that she steadfastly promoted to outsiders: "It is impossible for me to enter Charleston from any side, whether by land or by sea, and not feel that here the land is precious; here is a place worth keeping."[5]

SARA C. ARNOLD

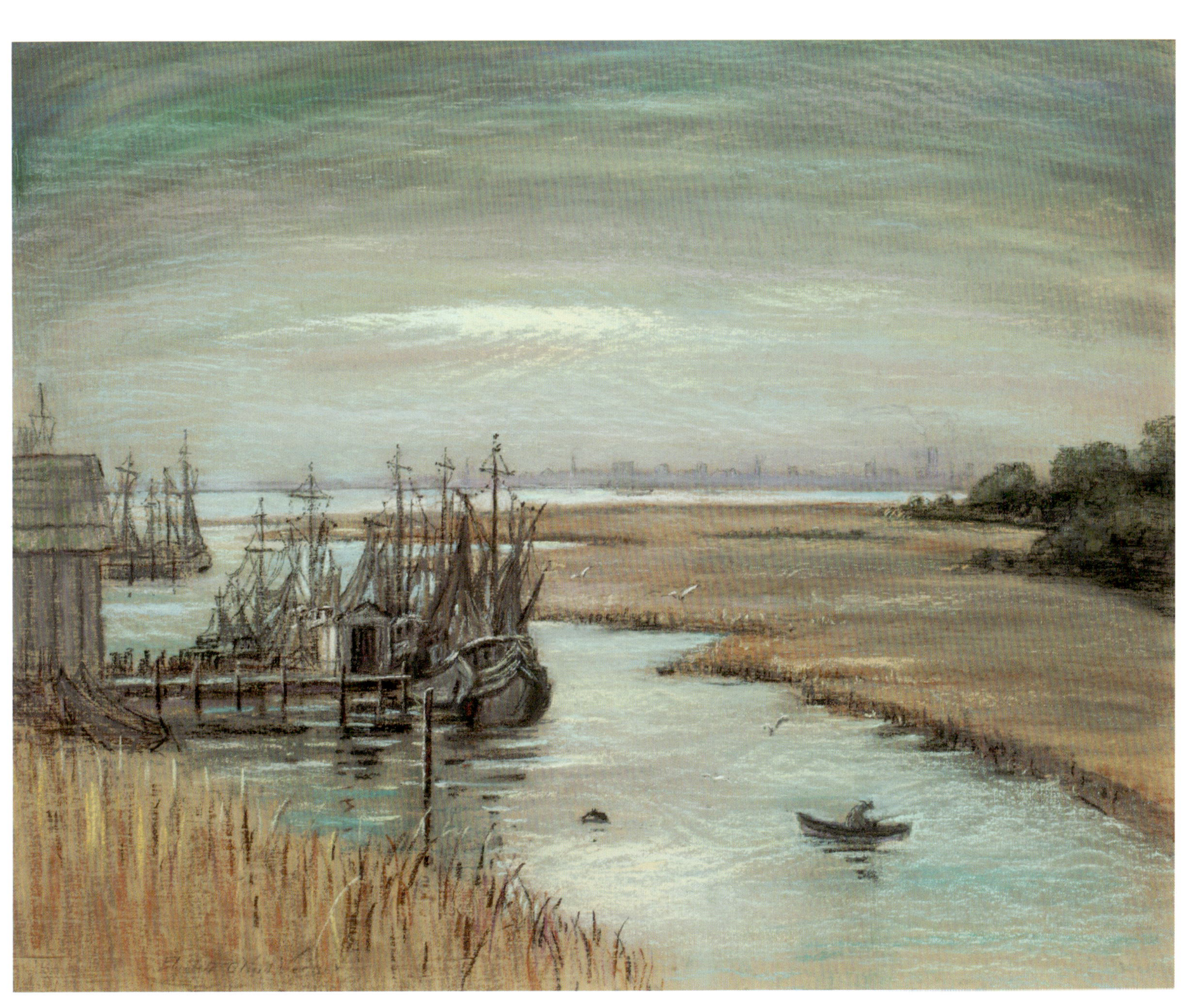

ANNA CATHERINE WILEY (1879–1958)

Lady with Parasol, circa 1915

Oil on canvas, 25⅛ × 20⅛ inches

Impressionist painter Catherine Wiley was perhaps the most active, accomplished, and influential artist in East Tennessee during the early twentieth century. Her artistic path began with undergraduate classes taken at the University of Tennessee between 1895 and 1897, followed by training at the Art Students League in New York from 1903 to 1905, and independent summer sessions in New England with Martha Walter and Robert Reid in 1912.

Upon completing her studies at the League, Wiley returned to Knoxville and soon began to energize the cultural community in a variety of capacities. In addition to her studio practice, she was active as an instructor at the University of Tennessee for thirteen years, 1905 through 1918, a leading member of local art associations, a participant in major art exhibitions for the 1910 and 1911 Appalachian Expositions, and head of the committee charged with organizing the art presentation for the 1913 National Conservation Exposition. These ambitious exhibitions in Knoxville introduced area audiences to hundreds of works by acclaimed artists from around the country, including Cecilia Beaux, Arthur B. Davies, Ellen Day Hale, Childe Hassam, Robert Henri, and Ernest Lawson, and by dozens of prominent Tennessee artists of the day. Although mental illness cut short her career in 1926, Wiley left behind a remarkable and diverse body of work: early Art Nouveau–influenced ink drawings and illustrations (circa 1895–1910), sun-drenched impressionistic canvases (circa 1910–1921), and a small number of late works (circa 1921–1926) whose darker tones and coarse surfaces approach Expressionism and may evince her declining state of mind.

Wiley specialized in outdoor scenes of women amid their daily lives, rendered in jewel-like hues with lively impasto brushwork, as seen in works such as *Lady with Parasol.* Executed around 1915, the painting dates to the height of Wiley's career in a period that included *Willow Pond* (1914) and *A Sunlit Afternoon* (circa 1915), two of the artist's finest and best-known works. It is one of four known compositions by Wiley depicting women with parasols.[1] *Lady with Parasol* features a striking contrast between a radiant seated figure in white and the saturated hues of Asian lilies that surround her. Except for navy cuffs, the sitter's dress appears as an uninterrupted expanse of pure reflected light. Less pronounced, but equally important, are color harmonies connecting the woman and her surroundings—lily blossoms echoing russet hair and crimson lips, and beds of violet-tinged foliage linked by the dark band of a closed parasol lying against her knees. Coarse dabs and angular dashes of textured pigment accentuate clusters of vegetation that appear to flicker in and out of sunlight. The painting reveals the artist's characteristically American adaptation of Monet's Impressionism, one in which she adjusts the gauge of her brush and the application of color to describe atmospheric effects, but without sacrificing narrative details. Blended hues applied with small brushes define the model's delicate facial features, averted glance, and interlocking fingers, and serve to anchor her form in pictorial space.

Beyond her interest in painting light, Wiley sought to capture the inner life of her sitters, a goal she discussed in an essay she composed for the *Woman's Athenaeum* in 1912: "Only when paintings make us realize more acutely the poetry that lies within us all, the romance that we ourselves feel, the power of our own spirit, the 'externalisation' of our own soul, as it were—only then it has a meaning."[2] Viewed within the context of Wiley's statement, *Lady with Parasol* exemplifies the artist's dual objective of representing the effects of outdoor light and conveying the distinct psychological disposition of its central figure. A decade later—in the twilight of her career and under personal circumstances that remain unclear—Wiley's drive to portray the internal reality of her subjects led her to develop emotionally charged compositions in which her own deep-seated turmoil was manifested in the form of urgent brushwork and figures whose hollow-eyed expressions suggest a subliminal burden. One can only wonder at what Wiley might have achieved in this new vein had she triumphed over her illness and continued her artistic journey.

STEPHEN C. WICKS

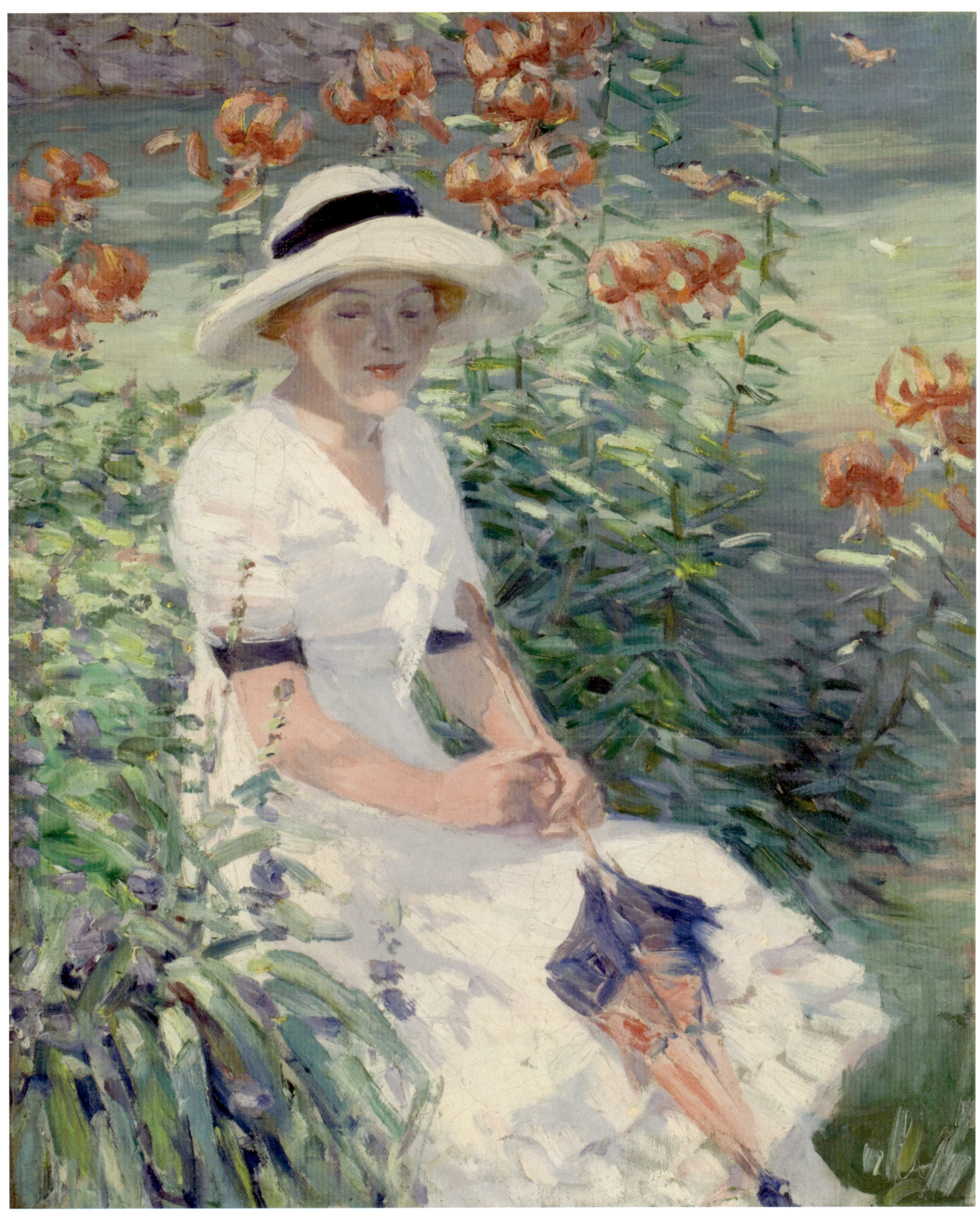

ENID BLAND YANDELL (1869–1934)

Ariadne, 1911

Painted plaster, 8 × 14½ × 6⅛ inches

Within the field of American sculpture, barriers have inhibited women's participation and achievement. The very act of shaping durable substance into aesthetic form is a physically demanding practice—one that since antiquity had been regarded as the purview of muscular male artisans. This was especially true in the American South, where notions of feminine propriety persisted in the antebellum period and the first half of the twentieth century. As critical and commercial success began to accrue to Kentucky sculptor Enid Yandell, a paternal uncle—expressing a sentiment that would have been endorsed by many of his peers—complained that she was "the first woman of the Yandell name who ever earned a dollar for herself" and labeled her "a disgrace to the family."[1]

Growing up in genteel circumstances in Louisville, Yandell began dabbling in mud as early as age three and took to carving by age twelve.[2] She attended Hampton College locally before enrolling at the Cincinnati Art Academy for further study in 1887, an initiative encouraged by her mother, an amateur artist. Following her graduation and a tour of Europe, Yandell accepted a position in 1891 with the World's Columbian Exposition. Held in Chicago in 1893, the world's fair showcased international achievements in arts, science, and industry. During her two-year stay in the Windy City, Yandell labored alongside other female sculptors—a group that came to be known as the White Rabbits—to enlarge statuary designed by male contemporaries, such as Lorado Taft.[3]

Independent commissions came to the artist as well. Louisville's historical society, the Filson Club, engaged Yandell to execute a sculpture of Daniel Boone for the Kentucky State Building at the exposition. The life-size figure and the series of caryatids (carved figural columns) she created for the roof of the Woman's Building were highly regarded. Glowing accolades in the *Louisville Commercial* praised "the genius of a young Kentucky girl" for the depiction of the pioneer.[4]

A few years later a Southern landmark exhibition provided Yandell with a major opportunity to advance her reputation. From her studio in Paris—where she studied with Frederick MacMonnies and sought advice from Auguste Rodin—she executed her monumental *Pallas Athena,* which was shipped in pieces across the Atlantic, then positioned outside the Fine Arts Building at the 1897 Tennessee Centennial and International Exposition in Nashville. Standing over forty feet tall, Yandell's classical figure proved to be one of the fair's leading attractions, garnering extensive news coverage and earning a silver medal.

Yandell pursued advanced training and commissions in both New York and Paris, developing a robust trans-Atlantic practice that crossed many media and was unrestricted in size and subject: her works were constructed in plaster, stone, or bronze, ranged from tabletop to colossal size, and included portraits and mythological representations. In 1913 Yandell was represented in the watershed Armory Show by an allegorical bronze vase titled *The Five Senses,* a sculpture that attested to her aesthetic flexibility and bore witness to modern abstract sensibilities.

Yandell's command of classical subject matter can also be seen in her portrayal of the Greek mythological character Ariadne. The recumbent female figure, shown from the back as if hiding from the viewer, retains realism and physicality, but lacks the individuality that imbued many of the artist's earlier works. Sculptural depictions often expose the prostrated Ariadne's face and body, but Yandell's does not, a creative choice that may signal her debt to Rodin, whose approach emphasized expressive emotion.[5]

At the outbreak of World War I, Yandell pledged herself to humanitarian efforts. She recalled later that "after the war started, there was no art. There was nothing but agony and sorrow and a great striving to help."[6] She was a founding member of Appui aux Artistes, an organization that provided meals for struggling artists and their families, and became involved with La Société des Orphelins de la Guerre, which cared for war orphans. Her efforts were not limited to France; working with the stateside offices of the Red Cross, she established a national indexing system for hospitalized soldiers.[7]

Whether creating enormous public sculptures or interpreting mythological narratives, Yandell challenged the gender norms of early-twentieth-century sculptural practice. Her achievements, though significant, were "hard won" and the collective progress modest, a reality she openly acknowledged both during the height of her career and later, when her record became obscure.[8] Nevertheless, Yandell saw promise for future generations of women sculptors, remarking in 1924: "Yes, I think it is a lovely occupation for women, if they have love for form. It requires much study and is wonderful for developing the mentality. It requires a great deal of physical strength and, of course, one must have talent before entering the field. The field is not overcrowded for art is still much unappreciated in this country, but every year I see it advance."[9] **JUILEE DECKER**

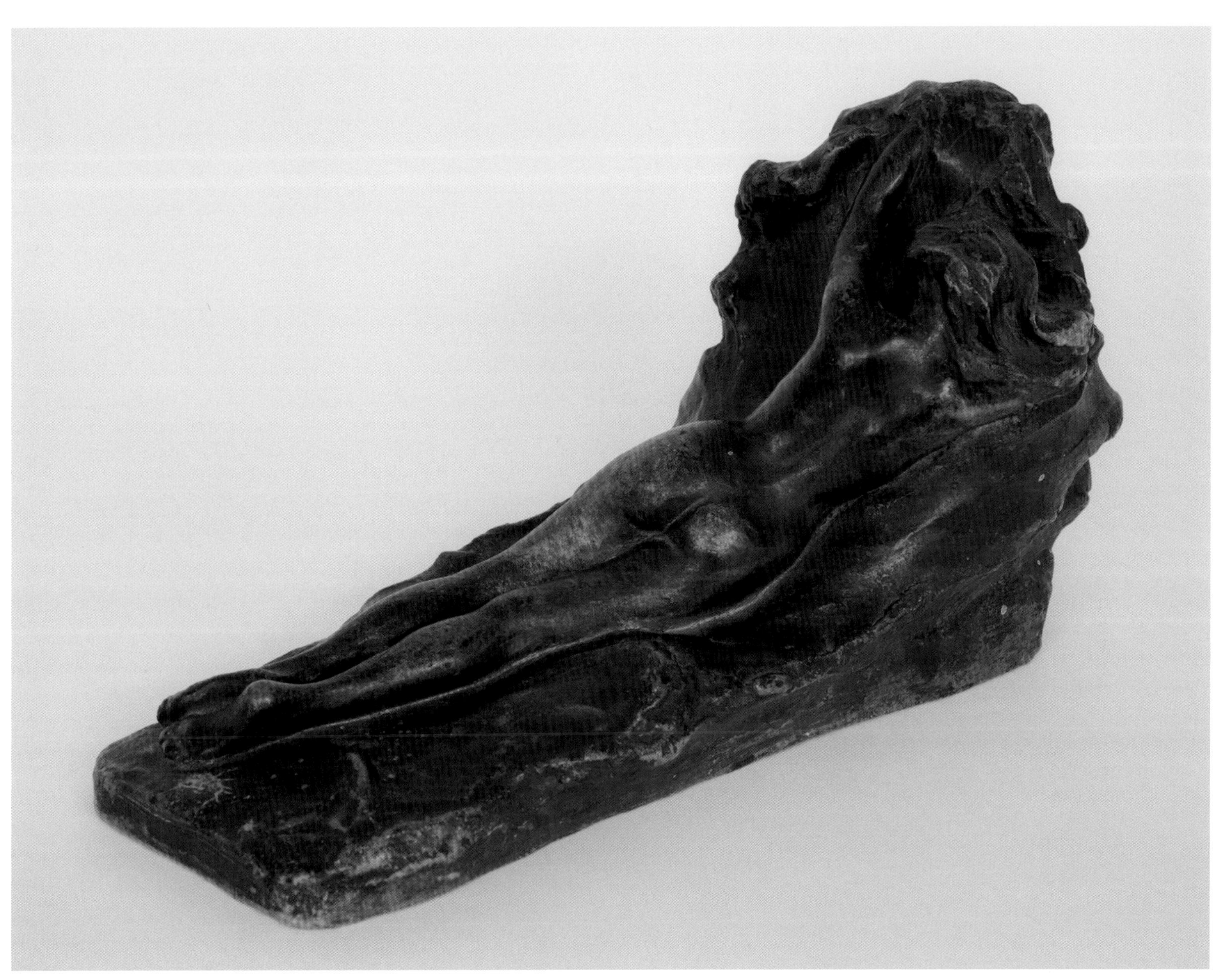

Acknowledgments

While the creation of a single piece of art may be a solitary endeavor, the planning and production of a book that examines forty-two works of art is anything but. The finished piece you are holding and its companion exhibition represent the best efforts of many skilled and dedicated professionals to whom the Johnson Collection owes deep thanks. We are especially grateful to the contributing authors, whose articulate scholarship pays tribute to the singular—and often unsung—achievements of the women artists under consideration.

This project traces much of its inception to the collection's founding director, David Henderson, as well as to consulting curator Martha Severens. From initial concept to final format, the book's scope and style went through several permutations, evolutions traced to long editorial meetings and careful study by David, Martha, and the collection's staff. For his long-held interest in the subject and expert advice, the collection offers thanks to William Eiland, director of the Georgia Museum of Art in Athens. Given Bill's enthusiasm for the topic, it feels more than a little serendipitous for the Georgia Museum to serve as the exhibition's opening venue. A number of other leaders in the field of Southern art—museum curators and directors, university professors, independent scholars, and dealers—provided seminal input as the project developed. Their state-specific expertise and thoughtful consideration are greatly appreciated: Sara Arnold, Margaret Lynne Ausfeld, René Paul Barilleaux, Judith Bonner, Les Christensen, John Cuthbert, Robin Dietrick, Kevin Grogan, Lee Hansley, Amy Moorefield, Julie and Warren Payne, Estill Curtis Pennington, Deborah Pollack, Will South, Kim Spence, Evie Terrono, Janie Welker, Stephen Wicks, and Kristen Miller Zohn.

Museum partners have been critical to the collection's success in advancing its mission of heralding the significance of Southern art, and we value these partners' support. We acknowledge here not only the institutions that will host the *Central to Their Lives* tour, but also those that have collaborated on other exhibitions: Asheville (North Carolina) Art Museum; Blowing Rock (North Carolina) Art and History Museum; Columbus (Georgia) Museum; Cummer Museum of Art, Jacksonville, Florida; Dixon Gallery and Gardens, Memphis, Tennessee; Florence County (South Carolina) Museum; Gibbes Museum of Art, Charleston, South Carolina; Greenville County (South Carolina) Museum of Art; Huntington Museum of Art, Huntington, West Virginia; Jule Collins Smith Museum of Fine Art, Auburn University, Alabama; Knoxville (Tennessee) Museum of Art; McKissick Museum, Columbia, South Carolina; Mint Museum, Charlotte, North Carolina; Mississippi Museum of Art, Jackson; Montgomery (Alabama) Museum of Fine Arts; Morris Museum of Art, Augusta, Georgia; South Carolina State Museum, Columbia; Spartanburg (South Carolina) Art Museum; Taubman Museum of Art, Roanoke, Virginia; and Telfair Museums, Savannah, Georgia.

Under the careful eye of resident image guru Sarah Tignor, the collection works with a handful of talented photographers and conservators to ensure the best possible presentation of objects—on paper and in person—including: Carroll Foster, Hot Eye Photography, Spartanburg, South Carolina; Tim Barnwell Photography, Asheville, North Carolina; Rick Rhodes Photography and Imaging, Charleston, South Carolina; Tipton Gentry, Asheville, North Carolina; Colin Post and Elizabeth Sanchez, Colin Post Painting Conservation, Asheville, North Carolina; Ruth Barach Cox, Painting Conservation, Durham, North Carolina; and Ginny Newell, ReNewell Fine Art Conservation, Columbia, South Carolina.

The Johnson Collection's staff is small, but sturdy. And part of this sturdiness can be attributed to colleagues who make up the extended village we call Team TJC. This village includes the graduate fellows and undergraduate interns who have shared in the exacting work of research, fact-checking, and proofreading: Russell Gullette, Zelle Richardson, and Christa Roberts. TJC staff alumni Alix Refshauge and Jim Creal supported the larger effort during their tenures. Over her four years with the collection, Aimee Wise played a key role in early compilations and object research. Thanks are also due to the art squad at Smith Dray Line—Michael Stumbo, Mitchell Slaton, Zach Slaton, and Bill Turrentine—

and our coworkers at Johnson Development Associates, notably Dan Breeden, Lori Comer, Susan England, Katie Lovell, Tina Mitchell, Michael Russ, Ashley Simpson, Joel Sizemore, Leslie Ann Wesson, Mark Wesson, Tammy Waddell, Shelly Webb, and Mendy Williams.

Scholars, curators, professors, archivists, and librarians around the country lend support, guidance, and accuracy to the collection's publications, especially the professionals on staff at the Smithsonian Archives of American Art and the Library of Congress. Particular thanks are extended to Ray Bonis, James Branch Cabell Library, Virginia Commonwealth University, Richmond; John P. Bowles, University of North Carolina at Chapel Hill; Elizabeth Jones; Leo G. Mazow, Virginia Museum of Fine Arts, Richmond; Holly Tripman, Cameron Art Museum, Wilmington, North Carolina; and the librarians at Spartanburg County Public Libraries and Wofford College in Spartanburg.

Beginning with the collection's inaugural publication, *Romantic Spirits*, the University of South Carolina Press has been a vital partner in a remarkably ambitious publication agenda. For their direction and encouragement, we are indebted to former director Jonathan Haupt and acting director Linda Fogle, as well as to the press's talented editorial and design departments.

LB

Directory of Southern Women Artists

Through its scholarly research over the years—and especially since we began to compile those investigations into published form—the Johnson Collection has worked intently to document and celebrate the achievements of artists associated with the American South. While many of the artists connected to the region are widely known and duly noted in the generally accepted canon of American art history, far more fine artists have thus far been overlooked by the academy. Overlooked, perhaps, because they were far from the Northeast's urban art centers, the epicenter for premier educational institutions and venerable museums. Overlooked, perhaps, because they lacked savvy commercial representation that could facilitate notable exhibition placements, press coverage, or critical sales. Overlooked, perhaps, because they were deemed less consequential due to their dialect, gender, or race.

As its essential mission, the Johnson Collection draws attention to the artists we identify as Southern. And being a Southern enterprise, we are characteristically hospitable when it comes to classifying an artist as Southern and adopting her into the fold. Native-born artists, seasonal tourists, visiting professors, itinerant painters, political refugees, and birds of passage: all are welcome here. Given the gender specificity of this project and its chronological scope—the late 1880s to 1960—we encountered hundreds of women who were influential as teachers and community advocates, and who participated in vital regional arts organizations like the Southern States Art League through regular exhibitions, but who have never been codified as capital-A "Artists," whether by dint of their own modesty, their lack of agency, or the contemporary tendency to marginalize female aesthetic pursuits as decorative, craft, or hobby.

What this directory of more than two thousand names seeks to address—and redress—is the lack of a comprehensive index of Southern women artists working in the period surveyed. However, as vast and detailed as this index is, it is not in any way comprehensive, and it is emphatically not presented as such. Sourced from established scholarly and primary materials, as well as museum archives and sociocultural records, this list is neither exhaustive nor perfect. With those caveats in place, the information presented includes each artist's name (including birth and married names, nicknames, professional monikers, and pseudonyms, where applicable); the artist's life dates (ideally with birth and death locations, and occasionally with place of burial); and the Southern state or states with which the artist was associated (whether by birth, residency, education, or exhibition activity). Within name listings, alternate spellings are noted where we discovered persistent records of such variations. Marital names that were not used as an artist's primary identity are denoted in braces. Artists who achieved significant professional recognition under both a maiden and a married name are cross-referenced.

The Virginia Museum of Fine Art's landmark book and companion exhibition *Painting in the South: 1564–1980* is generally acknowledged as one of the first extensive and credentialed catalogues on the subject. Since its publication in 1983, hundreds of lay and professional art historians have turned to that volume—well-worn and dog-eared, usually—as a sort of codex and, always, as a place to start. It, too, is incomplete and inexact. But like every encyclopedic resource published at a moment in time, its inherent limitations provided space and opportunity for subsequent scholarship, which in turn has created more paths for study.

Art historians' work is aided, every single day, by the thick scholarly tomes that warp library bookshelves. And we are aided, too, by the single exhibition broadsheets produced by community museums or interested dealers. For each of these documentary assets presents any number of dangling threads—interesting sidebars, undeveloped story lines, unanswered questions—that may one day entice another curious cultural scholar to pick up the trail and begin crafting a wholly new contribution to the whole.

This directory owes its substance and style to Holly Watters, who devoted the better part of a year to its organization, content, and presentation here—satisfying her curiosity, arduously applying her relentless sleuthing skills, and ruining her eyesight. She would ask, on our behalf, that you please contact the collection with any corrections or additions you can offer to the fluid, amendable version of the directory, which will be continually updated.

Artist	Life Dates	Associated With
Abbe, Elfriede/Alfriede Martha	b. 1919, Washington, DC; d. 2012, Washington, DC	DC
Abbott, Mary Lee	b. 1921, New York, NY	DC
Aboud, Victoria	b. 1915, KY; d. 1978, KY	KY
Acheson, Alice Stanley	b. 1895, Charlevoix, MI; d. 1996, Washington, DC	DC
Adams, Harriet Dyer	b. 1910, Urbana, IL; d. 2005, Albany, NY	NC
Adams, Katherine Langhorne	b. 1890, Plainfield, NJ; d. 1977, Annandale, VA	DC / VA
Adams, Margaret Graham Burroughs	b. 1882, Austin, TX; d. 1965, Austin, TX	LA
Adams, Virginia Elizabeth Quest	b. 1908, Louisville, KY; d. 1952, KY	KY
Ahrens, Ellen Wetherald	b. 1859, Baltimore, MD; d. 1935, Pennock Terrell, DE	MD
Aiken, Mary Augusta Hoover	b. 1907, Cuba, NY; d. 1992, Tybee Island, GA	DC / GA / SC
Ainslie, Maud/Maude	b. 1870, Louisville, KY; d. 1960, Louisville, KY	KY
Aked, Elizabeth Aleen	b. 1907, Yorkshire, England; d. 2003, Toronto, Canada	FL
Akers, Anne	d. 1960, Clearwater, FL	DC / FL
Akers-Peyton, Juanita	b. 1925, Charleston, WV; d. 2010, Lewisburg, WV	WV
Albaugh, Martha Hollis Page	b. 1912, French Creek, WV; d. 2004, Buckhannon, WV	WV
Alberga, Alta Clarence Wheat	b. 1905, Tuscaloosa, AL; d. 2004, Greenville, SC	AL / SC
Albers, Annelise Elsa Frieda Fleischmann	b. 1899, Berlin, Germany; d. 1994, Orange, CT	NC
Albers, Dorothy Lenore	b. 1924, Brooklyn, NY; d. 1996	NC
Albritton, Nina Bonner	b. 1881, Barclay Lake, KY; d. 1975, San Diego, CA	DC / KY / TN
Alderson, Nancy Jane Virginia	b. 1926, Washington, DC; d. 1956, Washington, DC	DC
Alexander, Frances Bexley	b. 1911, Moreland GA; d. 1990, Lithonia, GA	GA
Alexander, Mary Barton	b. 1828, Barren County, KY; d. 1904, Cumberland County, KY	KY
Aley, Janet "Bingo" Ramsey	Westport, CT	NC
Alford, Lillian May	b. 1900, Augusta, KY; d. 1998, Alexandria, KY	KY
Allan, Amey/Amy/Amie Nicholson	b. 1873, Charleston, SC; d. 1965, Charleston, SC	SC
Allen, Anna Elizabeth	b. 1879, Worcester, MA; d. 1959, Orange City, FL	FL
Allen, Erma Paul	b. 1897, Washington, DC; d. 1978, Washington, DC	DC
Allen, Hazel Leigh	b. 1892, Morrilton, AR; d. 1983, Milwaukee, WI	AR
Allen, Jane Potter Mengel	b. 1888, Jefferson County, KY; d. 1952, Louisville, KY	KY
Allen, Martha Francis	b. 1907, Appleton, TN; d. 1995	AL / TN
Allen, Pearl Olivia Wright	b. 1879, Kossuth, MS; d. 1973 Tulsa, OK	MS
Allender, Nina Alexander Evans	b. 1872, Auburn, KS; d. 1957, Plainfield, NJ	DC
Alsobrook, Anna Ruth {Poggenpohl}	b. 1911, Macon, GA; d. 2001, Amherst, MA	GA
Altvater, Catherine "Cathy" Tharp	b. 1907, Little Rock, AR; d. 1984, New Smyrna Beach, FL	AR / FL
Ames, Grace Greenwood	b. 1905, Brooklyn, NY; d. 1979, New York, NY	TN
Amis, Eleanor Spivey	b. 1903, NC; d. 1979, Durham, NC	NC
Anderson, Annette McConnell	b. 1867, New Orleans, LA; d. 1964, Ocean Springs, MS	LA / MS
Anderson, Bertha May Freeland	b. 1889, Wetzel County, WV; d. 1981, Clarksburg, WV	WV
Anderson, Ellen Graham	b. 1885, Lexington, VA; d. 1970, Lexington, VA	VA
Anderson, Jessica B.	b. 1890, San Rafael, CA; d. 1945, Richland County, SC	SC
Anderson, Loulie	b. 1887, Brownsville, TN	FL / MS / SC / TN
Anderson, Martha "Mary" Fannin Fort	b. 1885 Macon, GA; d. 1968, Mount Airy, GA	AL / GA
Anderson, Virginia Frances	b. 1893, Lexington, KY; d. 1990, Lexington, KY	KY

Artist	Life Dates	Associated With
Andrews, Marietta Fauntleroy Minnigerode	b. 1869, Richmond, VA; d. 1931, Falls Church, VA	DC / VA
Anshutz, Elsa Martin	b. 1882, PA; d. 1971, Pensacola, FL	FL / WV
Anthony, Mary B.	d. 1941, Washington, DC	DC
Appel, Carolyn J.	b. 1907; d. 1941	KY
Arbenz, Florence Bradshaw	b. 1873, England; d. 1939, Wheeling, WV	WV
Arbo, Aurelia Josephine Coralie	b. 1909, LA; d. 1993, New Orleans, LA	LA
Archer, Dorothy Bryant	b. 1919, Hampton, VA; d. 1980, El Paso, TX	VA
Archer, Eleanore Joicely	b. 1919, Roane County, WV	NC / WV
Archer, Hazel-Frieda Larsen	b. 1921, Milwaukee, WI; d. 2001, Tucson, AZ	NC
Arena, Lucia Cecelia	b. 1897, Italy; d. 1970, New Orleans, LA	LA
Arlt, Emilie M.	b. 1892, Philadelphia, PA; d. 1970, Sarasota, FL	DC / FL / VA
Armstrong, Bessie Butler Newsome	b. 1903, Brookhaven, MS; d. 1987, Little Rock, AR	AR / MS
Armstrong, Jane Taylor Bottsford	b. 1921, Buffalo, NY; d. 2012, Manchester, VT	NC
Arnold, Elizabeth A.	b. 1857, New York, NY	AL
Arnold, Helen Halsted	active in Washington, DC, 1904–1923	DC
Arnold, Laura Elizabeth	b. 1916, Montgomery, AL	AL
Arnold, Mary Daisy	b. about 1873, Washington, DC; d. 1955, MD	DC / MD
Aronson, Elizabeth "Lisa" Jalowetz	b. 1920, Prague, Czechoslovakia; d. 2013, Nyack, NY	NC
Arrington, Katherine Clark Pendleton	b. 1876, Warrenton, NC; d. 1955, Warrenton, NC	NC
Arthur, Anne Eastman	b. 1910; d. 1986 (buried in Arlington National Cemetery, Arlington, VA)	MD / NC
Arthur, Henrietta Charlezetta Hill	b. 1899, MD; d. 1993, Washington, DC	DC / MD
Asawa, Ruth Aiko {Lanier}	b. 1926, Norwalk, CA; d. 2013, San Francisco, CA	NC
Ashton, May Malone Stanhope	b. 1878, Fairfax, VA; d. 1976, Washington, DC	DC / VA
Askew, Elizabeth Hoevel [Joel Marhoe, pseud.]	b. 1893, Germany; d. 1983, Washington, DC	DC
Atkins, Minnie Evon Wooldridge	b. 1934, Isonville, KY	KY
Aud, Roxie Edith Hunt Walter	b. 1910, Menifee County, KY; d. 2001, IL	KY
Austin, Mary Fisher	b. 1868, Brookline, MA; d. 1951, Cambridge, MA	GA
Austrian, Florence Hochschild	b. 1889, Baltimore, MD; d. 1979, Baltimore, MD	MD
Avent, Mayna Treanor	b. 1868, Nashville, TN; d. 1959, Sewanee, TN	TN
Axe, Judy Shepard	b. 1922, Asheville, NC; d. 2013, Sarasota, FL	FL / NC
Ayme, Florence Harrison	b. 1859, Washington, DC; d. 1922, Washington, DC	DC
Baccich, Eunice	b. 1895, New Orleans, LA; d. 1981, New Orleans, LA	LA
Bach, Emilie Marie	b. 1911; d. 2000, Pensacola, FL	FL
Bache, Martha Moffett	b. 1893, Flint, MI; d. 1983, Washington, DC	DC
Backus, Josepha/Josefa Crosby	b. 1875, Brooklyn, NY; d. 1959, Washington, DC	DC / GA
Backus, Mary Chase Gannett	b. 1876; d. 1945	DC / NC / VA
Bacon, Frances Montgomery	b. 1906; d. 2003, Louisville, KY	KY
Badgley, Azalea Green	b. 1880, Bates County, MD; d. 1971, Washington, DC	DC / MD
Baekeland, Celine Swarts	b. 1868, Ghent, Belgium; d. 1957, Coconut Grove, FL	DC / FL
Baggerly, Elizabeth Frederick	b. 1901, Louisville, KY; d. 1988, Oak Ridge, TN	KY / TN
Bahan, Winifred Peters	b. 1919, Union, SC; d. 2007, Isle of Palms, SC	SC
Bahr, Florence Elizabeth Riefle	b 1909, Baltimore, MD; d. 1998, Elkridge, MD	MD

Artist	Life Dates	Associated With
Bailey, Caroline Baskerville	b. 1905, Baltimore, MD	KY / MD
Bailey, Ellen	b. 1867, Charleston, MS; d. 1922, Oxford, MS	MS
Bailey, Henrietta Davidson	b. 1874, New Orleans, LA; d. 1950, New Orleans, LA	LA
Bailey, Hilda "Peggy" Loram	b. 1910, South Africa; d. 2008	NC
Bailey, Ruth	b. 1914; d. 1975	NC
Baird, Myra Howard	b. 1865, Louisville, KY; d. 1954, Louisville, KY	KY
Baker, Doris Winchell	b. 1905, Washington, DC; d. 1987, Big Sur, CA	DC
Baker, Jessie E.	d. 1944, Washington, DC	DC / MD
Baker, Maria May	b. 1890, Norfolk, VA	DC / VA
Baker, Mary Frances	b. 1879, New Orleans, LA; d. 1943, New Orleans, LA	LA
Baker, Sarah Marindah	b. 1899, Memphis, TN; d. 1983, Ossining, NY	DC / MD / TN / VA
Baldwin, Amy	b. 1899, New London, CT; d. 1987, Chester, PA	DC / FL
Baldwin, Lois	d. 1993, Woodbine, MD	DC / MD
Ball, Alice Worthington	b. 1869, Boston, MA; d. 1929, Baltimore, MD	MD
Ball, Mary Wilson	b. 1892, Charleston, SC; d. 1984, Charleston, SC	DC / SC
Ballard, Mary Ruth	b. 1908, Logan, UT; d. 2004, Jupiter, FL	DC / FL / VA
Ballou, Adelaide/Adeline Jacobs	b. 1895, Fall Creek, WI; d. 1992, Kearney, NE	DC
Ballou, Julia Bertha	b. 1891, Hornby, NY; d. 1978, Spokane, WA	DC
Bane, McDonald "Mackey"	b. 1928, NC	NC
Bannister, Pati	b. 1929, North London, England; d. 2013, Gulfport, MS	LA / MS
Baringer, Mary Louise "Terry"	b. 1900, Louisville, KY; d. 1988	KY
Barker, Grace	active in Washington, DC, 1937	DC
Barkley, Florence Howell	b. 1880, Maysville, KY; d. 1954, East Northfield, MA	KY
Barnes, Dorothy Dyer	b. 1881, Charleston, WV; d. 1974, Sarasota, FL	FL / WV
Barnes, Elizabeth A.	active in Washington, DC, mid-1930s	DC
Barnes, Halcyone Drennan	b. 1913, Dallas, TX; d. 1988, Summit, MS	MS
Barnes, Jean Haskell Cattell	b. 1898, Chicago, IL; d. 1982, Bluefield, WV	DC / VA / WV
Barnes, Virginia "Vae" White	b. 1895, Livingston, AL; d. 1984	AL
Barney, Alice Pike	b. 1860, Cincinnati, OH; d. 1931, Los Angeles, CA	DC
Barnhill, Maybelle Roberson	b. 1901, Martin County, NC; d. 1970, Martin County, NC	NC
Barnum, Fayette	b. 1871, Louisville, KY; d. about 1960, Louisville, KY	KY
Barr, Clayre Lewis	b. 1913; d. 1980	LA
Barr, Leslie Beckwith	b. 1894, Nettie, WV; d. 1977, Richwood, WV	WV
Barret, Adele/Adela	b. 1876; d. 1959, St. Louis, MO	FL
Barrett, Elizabeth Hunt Amherst	b. 1863, New York, NY; d. 1955, New York, NY	VA
Barringer, Anna Maria	b. 1885, Charlotte, NC; d. 1977, Charlottesville, VA	LA / MS / NC / VA
Barth, Jane	b. 1922; d. 1975, Fort Mitchell, KY	KY
Bartle, Sarah Norwood	b. 1896, Washington, DC; d. after 1931, Washington, DC	DC
Bartlett, Annie Latham	b. 1865, Grafton, WV; d. 1948, Buckhannon, WV	MD / WV
Bartlett, Evelyn Fortune	b. 1886, Indianapolis, IN; d. 1997, Beverly, MA	FL
Barton, Maude E. F. Kingsbury	b. 1860, Cincinnati, OH; d. 1932, Natchez, MS	MS
Barton, Mettie Marie Taylor	b. 1904, Anderson, TN	TN
Baskerville, Mary Effie	b. 1874, NC	NC
Batchelor, Miriam "Mimi" French	b. 1922, Nashua, NH; d. 2000, Melbourne, FL	FL / NC

Artist	Life Dates	Associated With
Batchelor, Nina Gordon {Comtesse de Foiard}	b. 1861, Frankfort, KY; d. 1912	KY
Bauer, Marilyn Jean	b. 1924; Cleveland, OH	NC
Baughman, Mary Barney	b. 1874, Richmond, VA; d. 1956, Richmond, VA	VA
Bauman, Muriel Knowles	active in Charleston, WV, 1931	WV
Baxter, Eula Blanche McMichael	b. 1909, KY; d. 1981, Anderson County, KY	KY
Baxter, Margaret Cunningham	b. 1895; d. 1948, Washington, DC	DC
Beadenkopf, Anne	b. 1875, Baltimore, MD	MD
Beale, Bertha Fitzgerald	b. 1877, Arden, NC; d. 1942, Arden, NC	NC
Beall, Adelaide	b. 1845, Washington, DC; d. 1908?	DC
Beall, Kenna Dalton	b. 1924, Durham, NC; d. 1995, Greensboro, NC	NC / VA
Beall, Mary Jones	b. 1865, Davidson, NC; d. 1943, Wilmington, NC	GA / NC / VA
Beals, Callie	b. 1870, Monroe County, KY; d. 1958, Barren County, KY	KY / LA
Bean, Caroline van Hook {Blommers} {Binyon}	b. 1879, Washington, DC; d. 1980, Washington, DC	DC / FL / GA / LA
Beason, Sarah "Sadie" Willard	b. 1895, Union County, SC; d. 1976, Spartanburg, SC	FL / SC
Beatty, Barbara Ann	active in Washington, DC	DC / NC
Beaux, Cecilia	b. 1855, Philadelphia, PA; d. 1942, Gloucester, MA	NC
Beck, Minna McLeod	b. 1878, Atlanta, GA	AL / GA / KY / NC
Becker, Faye Graham	b. 1917; d. 1999, Elizabethtown, KY	KY
Becket/Beckett, Maria/Marie Graves	b. 1839, Portland, ME; d. 1904, New York, NY	FL / VA
Beckham, Eleanor Raphael	b. 1901, Frankfort, KY; d. 1987, Frankfort, KY	DC / KY / VA
Beckwith, Mary L.	active in Washington, DC, 1928–1929	DC
Beecher, Julia "Judy" Margaret Hull	b. 1920, Waterbury, CT; d. circa 1996–1998	NC
Begien, Jeanne Marie	b. 1913, Cincinnati, OH; d. 2001, Richmond, VA	VA
Belcher, Hilda	b. 1881, Pittsford, VT; d. 1963, Maplewood, NJ	FL / GA
Bell, Janet McLean	b. 1900	KY
Bell, Jeanie	active in Louisville, KY	KY
Bell, Wenonah Day	b. 1890, Trenton, SC; d. 1981, Alvaton, GA	GA / SC
Bellinger, Margaret Thomson	b. 1899, New York, NY; d. 1992, Bethesda, MD	DC / MD
Belt, Avis Rebecca	b. 1921, Washington, DC	DC / MD / NC
Benas, Bess	b. 1917; d. 1965	KY / TN
Benedict, Enella	b. 1858, Lake Forest, IL; d. 1942, Richmond, VA	VA
Benedict, Martha Milner	b. 1916, Birmingham, AL	AL / GA / LA
Benglis, Lynda	b. 1941, Lake Charles, LA	LA
Benjamin, Mary J.	b. 1863, Washington, DC	DC
Bennett, Emma Sutton	b. 1902, New Bedford, MA	DC
Bennett, Lyle "Leona" Hatcher	b. 1903, Beckley, WV; d. 1988, Riverside, CA	WV
Bensman, Marie E. Hansom	b. 1908, San Francisco, CA; d. 1992	FL? / KY
Benson, Marie Levering	b. 1877; d. 1958	DC / LA
Benton, Joy Kime	b. 1886, Guilford County, NC; d. 1957, Hendersonville, NC	NC
Bentz, Natalie Sawyier	b. Frankfort, KY	KY
Berchmans, Sister Agnes (nee Julia Alma Landry)	b. 1879, New Brunswick, Canada; d. 1973	VA
Berman, Eleanore Ruth	b. 1928, New York, NY	NC

Artist	Life Dates	Associated With
Bernard, Mary A.	b. 1865, Lenoir, NC	NC
Berresford, Virginia	b. 1902, New Rochelle, NY; d. 1995, Martha's Vineyard, MA	FL / MD
Berry, Camelia	b. 1918, Washington, DC	DC
Bessom, Florence Higgs	b. 1905, Marblehead, MA; d. 2008, Solomons, MD	DC / MD / VA / WV
Bethea, Florence Elizabeth	b. 1902, Birmingham, AL; d. 1973, Birmingham, AL	AL / LA
Bethel, Mary Eloise	b. Savannah, GA	GA / NC
Bettersworth, Beulah	b. 1894	MS
Betts, Mary Hall Stryker	b. 1903, VA; d. 1990, VA	VA
Betts, Virginia Battle	b. 1880, Yazoo City, MS; d. 1942, Dallas, TX	MS
Beyers, Bernice West	b. 1906, New York, NY; d. 1986	NC
Binckley, Ellen "Nella" Fontaine	b. 1877, Washington, DC; d. 1951, Washington, DC	DC
Bingham, Olivia Cochrane Gilmour	b. 1890, Scotland	DC
Bird, Esther Brock	b. 1888, Union Dale, PA; d. 1950, Warrenton, VA	DC / VA
Bishop, Dorothy Peyton Putzki	b. 1892, Washington, DC; d. 1960, Indianapolis, IN	DC
Bishop Emily Clayton	b. 1883, Washington County, MD; d. 1912, Smithsburg, MD	MD
Bishop, Mary Alice Fielitz	b. 1933, Elmhurst, IL; d. 2015, South Acworth, NH	NC
Bissell, Virginia	active in Louisville, KY, 1936	KY
Black, Eleanor Rose Simms	b. 1872, Washington, DC; d. 1949, Pittsburgh, PA	DC / VA
Black, Mary McCune	b. 1915, Broadwell, OH; d. 2011, West Chester, PA	WV
Black, Minnie	b. 1899; d. 1996, Laurel County, KY	KY
Black, Virginia Hutzler	b. possibly 1847, Flintstone, MD; d. 1924	MD / WV
Blackshear, Annie Laura Eve	b. 1875, Augusta, GA; d. 1967, Augusta, GA	GA
Blain, Julia	b. 1893, Ozark, MO	TN
Blaine, Nell Blair Walden	b. 1922, Richmond, VA; d. 1996, New York, NY	VA
Blair, Jeanette Kenney	b. 1922, Buffalo, NY; d. 2016, East Aurora, NY	LA
Blair, Nellie Elizabeth Walling	b. 1906, Great Falls, MT; d. 1987	KY
Blakely, Joyce Carol	b. 1929, New Orleans, LA	LA / NC
Blakeslee, Sarah Jane {Speight}	b. 1912, Evanston, IL; d. 2005, Philadelphia, PA	DC / NC / VA
Blanch, Esma Lucile/Lucille Lundquist	b. 1895, Hawley, MN; d. 1981, Kingston, NY	FL / KY / MS / SC / VA
Blanchard, Blanche Virginia	b. 1866; d. 1959, New Orleans, LA	DC / LA / MD
Blank, Ida	b. 1913, New York, NY; d. 1978	GA
Blankenship, Myrtle S.	b. 1889; d. 1962	WV
Bloch, Lucienne	b. 1909, Geneva, Switzerland; d. 1999, Gualala, CA	KY
Blount, Vincencia	b. 1924, Miami, FL; d. 2012, Atlanta, GA	FL / GA
Boal, Sara Metzner	b. 1896, Wheeling, WV; d. 1979	WV
Boas, Belle	b. 1884; d. 1953	NC
Boas, Isabelle Martine Simone Brangier	b. 1895, France; d. 1981, Philadelphia, PA	MD
Bodebender, Laura	b. 1900, New Orleans, LA; d. 1991	LA
Bogart, Harriet C.	b. 1917, Charlotte, NC; d. 1984, Charlotte, NC	NC / VA
Boler, Ruth Richardson	b. 1926, Washington, DC	DC
Bolin, Leone	b. 1893, Bluffton, IN	FL
Boll, Nancy	b. possibly 1860, Louisville, KY	KY
Bollen, Doris Margaret {Dippman}	b. 1925, Scranton, PA; d. 2012, Mine Hill, NJ	NC
Bond, Ella Tyler	b. 1854, Louisville, KY; d. 1935, Louisville, KY	KY

Artist	Life Dates	Associated With
Boney, Mary Lily Hussey	b. 1899, Duplin County, NC; d. 1974, Wilmington, NC	NC
Bongé, Eunice "Dusti" Lyle Swetman	b. 1903, Biloxi, MS; d. 1993, Biloxi, MS	MS
Boring, Mollie Day	b. 1925, Cambridge, MA; d. 2004	NC
Bornheim, Carrie	active in Washington, DC, 1911–1913	DC
Bornstein, Yetta Libby Frieden	b. 1913, Waynesboro, PA; d. 1968, Norfolk, VA	VA
Bose, Norma	b. San Francisco, CA; d. 1970	DC / VA
Bostick, Alma E.	b. 1891, Monroe County, AL	AL / DC
Bousman, Lou Tate	b. 1906, Bowling Green, KY; d. 1979	KY
Bowden, Beulah Beatrice	b. 1875, Townsville, NC; d. 1969	NC
Bowdoin, Annie S. Dodd	b. 1839, NC; d. 1903, Gordon County, GA	GA / NC
Bowers, Inez Hogan	b. 1895, Washington, DC; d. 1973, Provincetown, MA	DC / MS
Bowman, Jean Eleanor {Magruder} {Mackay-Smith} {Morgan}	b. 1917, Mount Vernon, NY; d. 1994, Middleburg, VA	VA
Boyd, Mollie	b. 1870, Rome, GA; d. 1928, Rome, GA	GA
Bradbury, Mattie Lou	b. 1899, Jackson, GA; d. 1977, Athens, GA	GA / SC
Bradford, Martha Jane	b. 1912, Guntersville, AL; d. 1993, Guntersville, AL	AL
Bradford, Myrtle Taylor	b. 1886, Indianapolis, IN; d. 1974, Miami, FL	FL
Bradley, Mary Parrish	b. 1911, DE; d. 1993	MS
Bradt, Delphine	b. 1887, Chattanooga, TN; d. 1927, Philadelphia, PA	TN
Bramlett, Betty Jane	b. 1925, Augusta, GA; d. 2015, Spartanburg, SC	GA / SC
Brandeis, Adele	b. 1885, Jefferson County, KY; d. 1975, Louisville, KY	KY
Brannigan, Gladys Ames	b. 1882, Hingham, MA; d. 1944, New York, NY	DC / VA
Braswell, Callie O'Kelly	b. 1883, GA; d. 1967, Greensboro, NC	GA / NC
Breckinridge, Mary Marvin Patterson	b. 1905, Manhattan, NY; d. 2002, Washington, DC	DC / KY / MD
Breeskin, Adelyn Dohme	b. 1896, Baltimore, MD; d. 1986, Washington, DC	MD / NC
Brennan, Arrah Lee Gaul (see Gaul, Arrah Lee {Brennan})		
Brigham, Gertrude Richardson [Viktor Flambeau, pseud.]	b. 1876, Boston, MA; d. 1971	GA
Britton, Faith Murray	b. 1922, Charleston, SC; d. 1983, Edisto Island, SC	NC / SC
Brody, Ethel Sobel	b. 1923, New York, NY; d. 2014, Columbia, SC	SC
Brooks, Billie	active in Louisville, KY, 1935	KY
Brooks, Miriam E.	active in Washington, DC, 1903–1913	DC
Brown, Amelia Ward	active in Washington, DC, 1895–1912	DC
Brown, Armantine	b. 1860; d. 1945, Mobile, AL	AL / LA
Brown, Gertrude Grant	b. 1880, Malden, WV; d. 1967, Malden, WV	DC / GA / WV
Brown, Helen Cheney	b. 1854, Canandaigua, NY; d. Carmel, CA	DC
Brown, Hilda Wilkinson	b. 1895, Washington, DC; d. 1981, Washington, DC	DC
Brown, Lillian Mason	d. 1924	FL
Brown, Lydia M.	b. about 1875, Watertown, NY	GA / LA
Brown, Mrs. Rhodes	b. Cincinnati, OH	LA
Brown, Ruth T.	b. 1924, Akron, OH; d. 1994, New Smyrna Beach, FL	FL
Brown, Sarah Nelson	active in Nashville, TN, 1916	TN
Browning, Ellen Guild	b. 1841, Tuscaloosa, AL; d. 1915, Anniston, AL	AL
Browning, Emma E. J. Donohoo	b. 1873, Muhlenberg County, KY; d. 1950	KY

Artist	Life Dates	Associated With
Browning, Louise Starkweather	b. 1878, New Bern, NC; d. after 1957	DC / NC
Bruen, Elizabeth Dorsey Keech	b. 1873, Baltimore, MD; d. 1951, Savannah, GA	GA / MD
Brundage, Frances Isabell Lockwood	b. 1854, Newark, NJ; d. 1937, Brooklyn, NY	DC
Bruner, Alice Craddock	b. 1920, Lexington, KY; d. 1999, Owensboro, KY	KY
Brunk, Anne	b. Harrisonburg, VA	VA
Bruskin, Kathleen Spencer	b. 1911, Omaha, NE; d. 2001, Port Townsend, WA	VA
Bryant, Maude Drein	b. 1880, Wilmington, DE; d. 1946, Wilmington, DE	MD
Bryant, Rebecca L.	b. 1903, Parkersburg, IA	NC
Bryce, Virginia Keane	b. 1861, Richmond, VA; d. 1935, Richmond, VA	VA
Buchholz, Emmaline Hardy	b. 1887, Ormondsville, NC; d. 1973, Gainesville, FL	FL / NC
Buckner, Barbara	active in Washington, DC, 1951	DC
Buell, Alice Standish	b. 1892, Oak Park, IL; d. 1964, New York, NY	FL / LA
Bugbird, Mary Bayne	b. 1889, Richmond, VA; d. 1981, Richmond, VA	VA
Bulliet, Katherine Adams	b. 1880, New Salisbury, IN; d. 1946, Chicago, IL	KY
Bullitt, Nora Iasigi	b. 1881, MA; d. 1976, Louisville, KY	DC / KY
Bullock, Mary Jane McLean	b. 1898, Ft. Worth, TX; d. 1978, Ft. Worth, TX	WV
Bulluck, Mary Bell Heyer	b. 1889, Wilmington, NC; d. 1980, Wilmington, NC	NC / VA
Burdell, Alice Marion	b. 1858, Charleston, SC; d. 1930, Columbia, SC	SC
Burdette, Hattie Elizabeth	b. 1872, Washington, DC; d. 1955, Washington, DC	DC
Burdwise, Alice	active in Washington, DC, 1920	DC
Burfiend, Blanche E.	b. 1872, MA	DC
Burgess, Mary Cotheal	b. 1910, Saco, ME; d. 2002, Fort Washington, PA	NC
Burke, Marjorie	active in Louisville, KY, 1933–1934	KY
Burke, Mary "Mollie" Lillian	b. 1879, Washington, DC; d. 1952, Leesburg, VA	DC / VA
Burke, Selma Hortense	b. 1900, Mooresville, NC; d. 1995, New Hope, PA	NC
Burkenroad, Flora Salinger	b. 1873, Lafayette, LA; d. 1963, New Orleans, LA	LA
Burkhard, Verona Lorraine	b. 1910, Paris, France; d. 2004, Grand Junction, CO	NC
Burnside, Katherine Talbott	b. 1904, Ft. Worth, TX; d. 1979, Parkersburg, WV	NC / WV
Burnside, Lucile Margaret Woolfolk Hitt/ Hiit	b. 1877, Augusta, GA; d. 1927, Washington, DC	DC / GA
Buros, Luella Gubrud	b. 1901, Canby, MN; d. 1995, Tucson, AZ	VA
Burroughs, Victoria Margaret Taylor {Goss}	b. 1917, Saint Rose, LA; d. 2010, Chicago, IL	LA
Burton, Gertrude	b. 1907, Hot Springs, AR; d. 1972	AR / MS
Burwell, Mary Alice Travis	b. 1869, Brunswick County, VA; d. 1962, Oxford, NC	NC / VA
Burwell, Saida Jones	b. 1878, Charlotte, NC; d. 1965, Charlotte, NC	NC
Busbee, Juliana Adeline Royster	b. 1876, NC; d. 1962, Seagrove, NC	NC
Bush-Brown, Margaret White Lesley	b. 1857, Philadelphia, PA; d. 1944, Philadelphia, PA	DC
Bush-Brown, Marjorie Conant	b. 1885, Boston, MA; d. 1978	GA
Butler, Abby Congar	b. 1862, Louisville, KY; d. 1960, Atlanta, GA	GA / KY
Butner, Kathryn "Kitty" Elizabeth Pittman	b. 1914, Philadelphia, PA; d. 1979	GA
Butts, Doris	active in Washington, DC, 1951	DC
Byram, Elizabeth Patterson	d. 2004	GA
Byrne, Ellen Albert	b. 1858, Fort Moultrie, SC; d. 1947, Washington, DC	DC / SC
Byrns, Cornelia Park	b. about 1904, AL	AL / TN

Artist	Life Dates	Associated With
Cabaniss, Lila Marguerite	b. 1874, Savannah, GA; d. 1969, Savannah, GA	GA
Cabaniss, Mary Hope	b. 1882, Savannah, GA; d. 1941, Savannah, GA	GA
Caffery, Bethia Richardson	b. 1881, Franklin, LA; d. 1957, LA	DC / FL / LA
Caldwell, Marjorie	b. 1907, Parkersburg, WV; d. 1968, Los Angeles, CA	WV
Caldwell, Mary A.	b. 1847, MS; d. 1929, Los Angeles, CA	MS
Caldwell, Mary Moss Brents	b. 1865, Glasgow, KY; d. 1930, Glasgow, KY	KY
Callender, Marjorie Bruce	b. 1901, New Orleans, LA; d. 1990, Jackson, LA	LA
Callery, Mary Kenna	b. 1903, New York, NY; d. 1977, Paris, France	NC
Callihan, Ann Worthington	b. 1880; d. 1964	KY
Callmann, Ellen	affiliated with Black Mountain College, 1947	NC
Calvert, Bertha Winifred	b. 1885, Nashville, TN; d. 1943, Nashville, TN	TN
Calvert, Elizabeth	b. 1921, Greenville, MS; d. 1977, Memphis, TN	LA / MS / TN
Calvert, Jennie Alston Cooper	b. 1878, Philadelphia, PA; d. 1951, Philadelphia, PA	DC
Calvin, Louise Deese	b. 1914, Lumberton, NC; d. 2002, Burnsville, NC	KY / NC
Campbell, Anne/Anna Baraud	b. 1879, Nelson County, VA; d. 1927, New York, NY	DC / VA
Campbell, Annie	b. 1862, Charleston, WV; d. 1951 Dayton, OH	WV
Campbell, Bessie Stuart	active in Washington, DC, 1921–1922	DC
Campbell, Dorothy Stokes Bostwick Smith	b. 1899, New York, NY; d. 2001, Sarasota, FL	DC / FL
Campbell, Georgine/Georgia	b. 1861, New Orleans, LA; d. 1931, Washington, DC	DC / LA
Campbell, Helena Eastman Ogden	b. 1879, Eastman, GA; d. 1934, Bronxville, NY	GA
Campbell, Pauline	active in Washington, DC, 1908–1924	DC
Cane, Alice Norcross	b. 1876, Louisville, KY; d. 1957, Jefferson County, KY	KY
Canipe, Margaret "Peggy" Jewell Copeland	b. 1881; d. 1956, Vale, NC	NC
Cannon, Beatrice	b. 1875, Louisville, KY	KY
Cantieni, Margaret A. Balzer	b. 1914, Newton, KS; d. 2002, Bethlehem, PA	NC
Cargill, Annelieu "Anne" Tignor	b. 1877, Muscogee County, GA; d. 1998, Muscogee County, GA	GA
Carl, Katharine Augusta	b. 1854, New Orleans, LA; d. 1938, Peking, China	LA
Carlisle, Mary Helen	b. 1869; d. 1925	SC
Carlstead, Helena	active in Washington, DC, 1918	DC
Carothers, Sarah Pace	b. 1910, Baltimore, MD; d. 1999, Catonsville, MD	MD
Carson, Caroline "CC" Petigru	b. 1820, Orangeburg, SC; d. 1885, Charleston, SC	GA / SC
Carter, Betty Miller	b. 1897, New York, NY; d. 1971	DC / GA
Carter, Martha Lee Pallett	b. 1866, Woodville, CA; d. 1955, Orange County, CA	DC
Casamer, Mabel	b. 1882?; d. 1969?	KY
Casey, Laura Welsh	b. 1866, Philadelphia, PA; d. 1951 (buried in Arlington National Cemetery, Arlington, VA)	DC / MS
Cashwell, Viola Hollifield Scarborough	b. 1913, Spruce Pine, NC; d. 2010, Wilmington, NC	NC / VA
Catlett, Elizabeth Alice {White} {Mora}	b. 1915, Washington, DC; d. 2012, Cuernavaca, Mexico	DC / LA / NC
Cauthen, Deloris Vaughan	b. 1906, Wilmington, NC; d. 1992, Columbia, SC	NC / SC
Chaffee, Olive Ruth Holbert {Gibson}	b. 1886, Woodville, KY; d. 1980, St. Louis, MO	AL / KY
Chalaron, Corrinne Marie	b. 1900, New Orleans, LA; d. 1977, New Orleans, LA	LA
Chamberlain, G. Hope Summerell	b. 1870, Salisbury, NC; d. 1960, Chapel Hill, NC	NC
Chamberlin, Helen	b. 1871, LA; d. 1914, San Francisco, CA	KY / LA
Chambers, Hallie Worthington	b. 1881, Louisville, KY; d. 1970, Louisville, KY	KY

Artist	Life Dates	Associated With
Chambers, Willie M.	b. 1865, GA; d. 1919, Monroe County, GA	GA
Chandler, Gabrielle	active in Washington, DC, 1926	DC
Chandler, Margaret Patterson	affiliated with Black Mountain College, 1943–1944	NC
Chant, Elisabeth/Elizabeth Augusta	b. 1865, Yeovil, Somerset, England; d. 1947, Wilmington, NC	NC
Chapman, Esther I. E. McCord	b. 1862, Richardson County, NE; d. 1952, Washington, DC	DC
Chase, Mary Agnes	b. 1869, IL; d. 1963, MD	DC
Chase, Susan Brown	b. 1868, St. Louis, MO; d. 1948, Clearwater, FL	DC / FL
Chesney, Letitia	b. 1875, Louisville, KY; d. 1939, Seattle, WA	KY
Child, Jane Bridgham Curtis	b. 1868, New York, NY; d. 1958, Boston, MA	DC
Chisholm, Margaret Sale Covey	b. 1909, Englewood, NJ	TN
Chisholm, Marie Margaret	b. 1900, Garnett, SC; d. 1994, Garnett, SC	SC
Chisolm, Valeria North	b. 1871, SC; d. 1949	GA
Chodorov, Rachel Mildred Katzin	b. about 1935, Winston-Salem, NC	NC
Choy, Katherine	d. 1958	GA / LA
Chrissinger, Mary Helen	b. 1877, Hagerstown, MD; d. 1968, Hagerstown, MD	MD
Christensen, Abbie/Abby Winch	b. 1887, Beaufort, SC; d. 1969, Beaufort, SC	SC / WV
Christoph, Willa Skipwith	b. 1930?, NY	NC
Churchill, Anna Eleanor Franzen	b. 1888, Washington, MN; d. 1981, Arlington, VA	KY / VA
Citron, Minna	b. 1896, Newark, NJ; d. 1991, New York, NY	TN
Clark, Adèle Goodman	b. 1882, Montgomery, AL; d. 1983, Richmond, VA	AL / VA
Clark, Constance Willis	b. 1914, NY; d. 2004, Natick, MA	KY
Clark, Elise Thomson	b. 1872, Brampton, Canada; d. 1941, Washington, DC	DC / WV
Clark, Georgia E. Belle Lawrence	b. 1869, Adams County, IA	DC
Clark, Kate Freeman [a.k.a. Freeman Clark]	b. 1875, Holly Springs, MS; d. 1957, Holly Springs, MS	MS
Clark, Margery Griffen	b. 1910, Brooklyn, NY; d. 2003, South Charleston, WV	WV
Clark, Marsha "Mattie" Elizabeth Goolsby	b. 1881, Abemarle County, VA; d. 1959, New Orleans, LA	LA / VA
Clark, Virginia Hynson Keep	b. 1878, New Orleans, LA; d. 1962, Winter Park, FL	FL / LA / MD
Clarke, Emily Ruth Abbott	b. 1909, Greensboro, NC; d. 1981, Greensboro, NC	NC
Clay, Emily Thomas	b. 1897, Summerville, GA; d. 1991, Augusta, GA	GA
Claypool, Naomi Segel	b. 1895, Bath County, KY; d. 1983, Memphis, TN	KY / TN
Clayton, Clara Zimmerman	b. 1936, Burlington, NC	NC
Clemens, Alethia Beatrice	b. 1874, Biloxi, MS; d. 1960, Pass Christian, MS	LA / MS
Clement, Shirley A.	b. 1922, New York, NY; d. 2002, Sarasota, FL	FL
Clements, Edith Gertrude Schwartz	b. 1874, Albany, NY; d. 1971, La Jolla, CA	DC
Clements, Gabrielle de Veaux/DeVaux/ DaVaux	b. 1858, Philadelphia, PA; d. 1948, Folly Cove, MA	DC / MD / NC / SC
Clements, Rosalie Thompson	b. 1878, Washington, DC; d. 1969, St. Petersburg, FL	DC / FL
Clendenin, Genevieve "Eve"	b. 1896, Baltimore, MD; d. 1974 (buried in Sleepy Hollow, NY)	MD
Clephane, Rosebud Almand	b. 1892, Atlanta, GA; d. 1972, Coral Gables, FL	FL / GA
Clinedinst, May	b. 1887, Brooklyn, NY; d. 1960, St. Petersburg, FL	FL
Cloyd, Mary Elizabeth Saylor	b. 1889, Washington County, TN; d. 1957, Boone, NC	FL / NC / TN
Coates, Caroline Pennock Spiller	b. 1917, Baton Rouge, LA; d. 2011, Ojai, CA	LA
Cobb, Katherine McKinley Treanor	b. 1887, Salem, GA; d. 1971, Athens, GA	GA
Cochran, Doris Mable	b. 1898, North Girard, PA; d. 1968, Hyattsville, MD	DC / MD

Artist	Life Dates	Associated With
Cochrane, Constance	b. 1888, Pensacola, FL; d. 1962, Chester, PA	FL / NC
Cochrane, Josephine Granger	b. 1864, Enfield, CT; d. 1953, Preston, CT	DC / MD
Cohee, Marion M.	b. 1896, Baltimore, MD; d. 1980, Philadelphia, PA	MD
Cohn, Mildred Amalie Hiller	b. about 1920; d. 2008, Birmingham, AL	AL / LA
Colborn, Eva Grace Bauman	b. 1878, Deal, PA; d. 1948, Washington, DC	DC
Colburn Helen Frances	b. 1868, Baltimore, MD; d. 1943, Takoma Park, MD	DC / MD
Colby, Alix Bettison	b. 1890, Brenham, TX; d. 1983, Ft. Lauderdale, FL	FL / LA
Cole, Annie Elizabeth	b. 1880, Providence, RI; d. 1932, Washington, DC	DC
Cole, Jessie Duncan Savage	b. 1858, Pass Christian, MS; d. 1940, Wellesley, MA	MS
Cole, Peggy Stallings	b. 1931, Wilmington, NC; d. 2012, Wilmington, NC	NC
Cole, Sallie Leigh	b. 1897, Petersburg, VA; d. 1976, Petersburg, VA	VA
Coleman, Laura Alexander	b. 1914, Boydton, VA	VA
Coler, Stella C.	b. 1892, Grand Rapids, MI; d. 1992, Indianapolis, IN	FL
Coles, Anne Cadwallader	b. 1882, Columbia, SC; d. about 1969, Columbia, SC	SC
Collier, Emily Alberta	b. 1911, Vicksburg, MS; d. 1985, New Orleans, LA	LA / MS
Collins, Corinne Cunningham	active in Washington, DC, 1915–1926	AL / DC
Collins, Elizabeth Madeline	b. 1879, Petersburg, VA; d. 1951, Petersburg, VA	VA
Collins, Florestine Perrault	b. 1895; d. 1988, LA	LA
Collins, Julia Alice	b. Savannah, GA; d. 1952, Savannah, GA	GA / NC
Collison, Helen F.	b. 1895, Washington, DC; d. 1981, SC	DC / SC
Collison, Marjorie/Margory Nelms	b. 1902, Washington, DC; d. 1983, Richardson, TX	DC / SC
Colton, Mary-Russell Ferrell	b. 1889, Louisville, KY; d. 1971, Phoenix, AZ	KY / NC
Colvin, Clara Stroud	b. 1890, New Orleans, LA; d. 1984, Ocean City, NJ	FL / LA
Coman, Charlotte Buell	b. 1833, Waterville, NY; d. 1924, Yonkers, NY	FL
Coman, Zoe Carnes	b. 1872, Benton County, TN; d. 1967, New York, NY	TN
Combs, Frances Hungerford	b. 1876, Washington, DC; d. 1973, Washington, DC	DC
Comegys, Margaret Lewis	b. 1884, MD; d. after 1947	DC / MD
Comer, Belle	b. 1878, GA; d. 1966, AL	AL / GA
Comfort, Katherine McIntosh	b. 1897; d. 1981, Atlanta, GA	GA / NC
Compton, Caroline Russell	b. 1907, Vicksburg, MS; d. 1987, Vicksburg, MS	LA / MS / VA
Compton, Dorothy Dumesnie {Stephenson} {Wearing}	b. 1917, Edgewater, AL; d. 1973, Deltona, FL	AL / FL
Condon, Florence B.	active in Washington, DC, 1919–1926	DC
Cone, Louise Austin Shaefer	b. 1888, Birmingham, AL; d. 1969, Birmingham, AL	AL
Conger, Hallie Ramsay	b. 1874, Alexandria, VA; d. 1977, Alexandria, VA	DC / VA
Conley, Sarah/Sara Ward	b. 1859, Nashville, TN; d. 1944, Nashville, TN	TN
Connell, Minnie Clyde Dixon	b. 1901, Belcher, LA; d. 1998, Elm Grove, LA	LA
Connell, Sybil	b. 1895, Dana, IN; d. 1983, Nashville, IN	NC
Conover, Alida Van Rensselaer	b. 1904, NY; d. 1981, Clearwater, FL	DC / FL
Conrad, Jenetta Emily	b. 1811, Harrisonburg, VA; d. 1898, Harrisonburg, VA	VA
Constable, Susan M.	d. 1913, Baltimore, MD	DC / MD
Converse, Lily Schierenberg	b. 1876, St. Petersburg, Russia; d. 1961, Philadelphia, PA	NC
Cook, Irma Virginia Howard	b. 1899, Ballston Spa, NY; d. 1984, Spartanburg, SC	SC
Cook, Mildred Taylor	b. 1917, Oberlin, KS; d. 2007, Paradise Valley, NV	NC

Artist	Life Dates	Associated With
Cooke, Honoré Guilbeau	b. 1907, Baton Rouge, LA; d. 2006, Summit, OH	DC / LA
Cooley, Ursula Dixie Cleveland	b. 1896, Hartwell, GA; d. 1956, Pinellas County, FL	FL / GA / TN
Coolman, Hundley Love Wells	b. 1890, New Albany, IN; d. 1973 (buried in New Albany, IN)	GA / KY
Coombs, Genevieve C.	active in Washington, DC, 1913–1914	DC
Cooper, Ann T.	b. 1935, New Orleans, LA; d. 2005, New Orleans, LA	LA
Cooper, Ellen	b. Columbia, SC; d. 1858	AL / SC
Cooper, Emma Esther Lampert	b. 1855, Nunda, NY; d. 1920, Pittsfield, NY	GA / MD / SC / VA
Cooper, Jane "Janie" James Farrow	b. 1861, Laurens, SC; d. 1950, Atlanta, GA	GA / SC
Cooper, Nettie Bartlett	b. 1879, Prospect Valley, WV; d. 1951, Harrison County, WV	WV
Cornish, Katherine Theodosia	b. 1864, Aiken, SC; d. 1948, Charleston, SC	SC
Corpron, Carlotta	b. 1900, Blue Earth, MN; d. 1988	LA
Costa, Elizabeth Petts	b. 1938, Dover, DE	FL
Costello, Helen	active in Washington, DC, 1945	DC
Coulon, Mary Elizabeth Emma	b. 1859, New Orleans, LA; d. 1928, New Orleans, LA	LA
Coulon, Mary-Paoline Casbergue	b. 1831, New Orleans, LA; d. 1914, New Orleans, LA	LA
Coulter, Mary Jencques	b. 1880, Newport, KY; d. 1966, Amherst, MA	KY
Couper, Emma Josephine Sibley [a.k.a. Mrs. B. King Couper]	b. 1867, Augusta, GA; d. 1957, Greenville, SC	GA / NC / SC
Cousins, Clara Lea	b. 1894, Halifax County, VA; d. 1991, Bremo Bluff, VA	VA
Covington, Wickliffe Cooper	b. 1867, Shelby County, KY; d. 1938, Bowling Green, KY	KY
Cox-McCormack, Nancy Mal {Cushman}	b. 1885, Nashville, TN; d. 1967, Ithaca, NY	TN
Crabtree, Donna Angeline Wilson	b. 1868, Nebraska City, NE; d. 1956, Washington, DC	DC
Crabtree, Nannie E. Chaney	b. 1893, Warren County, KY; d. 1981, Warren County, KY	KY
Craig, Margaret H.	b. 1852 or 1853, Westmoreland County, PA; d. 1951, Washington, DC	DC
Craig, Marie Jackson	b. 1906, Memphis, TN	TN
Craighill, Eleanor Rutherford	b. 1896, Fort Totten, NY; d. 1988, Newport News, VA	VA
Crane, Mary Florence Hedleston	b. 1888, Pleasant Grove, KY; d. 1973, Gulfport, MS	KY / MS
Crawford, Esther Mabel	b. 1872, Atlanta, GA; d. 1958, San Gabriel, CA	GA
Crawford, Josephine Marien	b. 1878, New Orleans, LA; d. 1952, New Orleans, LA	LA / MS
Crawford, Margaret	b. 1932	NC
Crawley, Ida Jolly	b. 1867, Pond Creek, TN; d. 1946, Asheville, NC	DC / NC / TN
Creecy, Emma Treynor	b. 1869, Washington, DC; d. 1964, Washington, DC	DC
Cresson, Margaret French	b. 1889, Concord, MA; d. 1973, Stockbridge, MA	DC
Critcher, Catherine Carter Coles	b. 1868, Westmoreland County, VA; d. 1964, Blackstone, VA	DC / VA / WV
Critcher, Louisa "Lulie" Kennon	b. 1866, Washington, DC; d. 1939, Washington, DC	DC / VA
Cron, Nina Nash	b. 1882, Spokane, WA; d. 1946 (buried in Arlington National Cemetery, Arlington, VA)	DC
Cross, Bernice Francena	b. 1912, Iowa City, IA; d. 1996, Washington, DC	DC / VA
Crowe, Amanda Marie	b. 1928, Cherokee, NC; d. 2004, NC	NC
Crozier, Katharine Sewall	b. 1896, Washington, DC; d. 1979, Washington, DC	DC
Crummer, Mary Worthington	b. 1878, Baltimore, MD; d. 1958, Pikesville, MD	MD
Crump, Kathleen Wheeler	b. 1884, Reading, England; d. 1977, Washington, DC	DC / MD
Cudlipp, Thelma Somerville {Grosvenor} {Whitman}	b. 1891, Richmond, VA; d. 1983, Greenwich, CT	VA

Artist	Life Dates	Associated With
de Creeft, Alice Robertson Carr	b. 1899, Roanoke, VA; d. 1996, Santa Barbara, CA	VA
De Ghize, Eleanor May Jenks	b. 1896, New York, NY; d. 1981, possibly Santa Fe, NM	MD
de Kooning, Elaine Marie Catherine Fried	b. 1918, Brooklyn, NY; d. 1989, Southhampton, NY	NC
De Lamotte, Caroline Jones	b. 1889, Pikesville, MD; d. 1947, Moss Point, MS	MD / MS
De Lappe, Phyllis Pele	b. 1916, San Francisco, CA; d. 2007, Petaluma, CA	DC
Deachman, Nelle Kerr	b. 1895, Prescott, AR; d. 1989, Downers Grove, IL	AR
Dearing, Mildred "Millie" Lyle(s)	b. 1906, Athens, GA; d. 1995, Athens, GA	GA
de Brennecke, Muriel "Nena/Nina" Jackson	b. 1888, Argentina; d. after 1957	NC
Decker, Dorothy Marie Horne	b. 1917, Red Springs, NC; d. 2005, Parkersburg, WV	NC / WV
Decker, Effie Bennett	b. 1869, Washington, DC; d. 1936, Washington, DC	DC
Degen, Mabel Hussey	b. 1885, Stoneham, MA; d. 1954, Louisville, KY	KY
Degener, Faustina Monroe	b. 1906; d. 1964	NC
Deike, Clara L.	b. 1881, Detroit, MI; d. 1964, Rocky River, OH	KY
Deikman, Etta Diane Mandelbaum	b. 1929, Lawrence, NY	NC
Del Mar, Frances/Francesca Paloma	b. 1869, Washington, DC; d. 1957, New York, NY	DC
Delaplane, Adele "Laddie" Sylvia Marshack	b. 1923, Chicago, IL; d. 2012, Sacramento, CA	NC
Demonet, Inez Michon	b. 1897, Washington, DC; d. 1980, Green Valley, AZ	DC
Dent, Dorothy	b. Washington, DC; d. after 1940, possibly in New York, NY	DC
Derryberry, Gertrude Joan Pitt-Rew	b. 1906, Torrington, England; d. 1994, Cookeville, TN	KY / TN
Derryberry, Mary Lou	b. 1901, Marshall County, TN; d. 1981, Chattanooga, TN	GA / NC / TN
de Saint Mart, Lucienne de Neuville	b. 1866, Laval, France; d. 1953, Laguna Beach, CA	LA / VA
Desport, Juliette Marie	b. 1895, Louisville, KY; d. 1985, Bowling Green, KY	KY / TN
Deweese, Harriet Ley	b. 1901, Titusville, PA; d. 1995, Philadelphia, MS	MS
Dick, Caroline L.	d. 1965, Birmingham, AL	AL
Didier, Rosaltha Kent	b. 1887, VA	DC / VA
Diebold, Henriette	b. 1894; d. 1973, St. Paul, MN	NC
Diecks, Lucy McGowan	b. 1907, Louisville, KY; d. 1998, Jefferson County, KY	KY
Dillaye, Blanche	b. 1851, Syracuse, NY; d. 1931, Philadelphia, PA	KY
Dismukes, Mary Ethel	b. 1870, Pulaski, TN; d. 1952, Biloxi, MS	MS / TN
Diuguid, Mary Sampson	b. 1883, Lynchburg, VA; d. 1968, Lynchburg, VA	VA
Dixon, Madeline Norris	d. 1988, Anniston, AL	AL
Dobson, Margaret Anna	b. 1888, Baltimore, MD; d. 1981, Los Angeles, CA	MD
Dodd, Marilee Beverly	b. 1907, GA; d. 1990, Chester, CT	GA
Dodge, Margaret "Peggy" Elizabeth Polsky	b. 1911, Akron, OH; d. 1985, Asheville, NC	NC
Dodge, Mary "Mamie" Lucinda Leftwich/ de Leftwich	b. 1838, VA; d. 1928, Italy	VA
Dodson, Nellie Plitt	b. 1906, Pilot Mountain, NC	NC
Doelckner, Dorothy	b. 1907, Jefferson County, KY	KY
Doherty, Lillian A. Cook	b. 1869, Washington, DC; d. 1927, Washington, DC	DC
Dohlgrin, Josephine	active in Washington, DC, 1907–1908	DC
Doke, Sallie George Fullilove	b. 1872, Keachi, LA; d. 1953, Pineville, LA	LA
Donahoo, Sara Freeman	active in Washington, DC, 1926–1927	DC
Donaldson, Elise	b. 1887, Elkridge, MD; d. 1980, La Jolla, CA	MD

Artist	Life Dates	Associated With
Donelson, Mary Hooper	b. 1906, Hermitage, TN; d. 2000, TN	TN
Donnally, M. Louise	active in Washington, DC, 1913–1914	DC
Donnelly, Hester Claire	b. 1912, Augusta, GA; d. 1992, New Hanover County, NC	GA / NC
Dorhauer, Marjorie Ruth	b. 1899, Gulfport, MS; d. 1994, Gulfport, MS	MS
Dortch, Elizabeth "Lizzie" Hogg	b. 1895, Goldsboro, NC; d. 1985, Raleigh, NC	NC
Dortch, Mary Louise Pegues	b. 1896; d. 1952, Oxford, MS	MS
Dotterer, Selma Tharin (see Tharin, Selma Marie {Furtwangler} {Dotterer})		
Doud, Isabel M. Cohen	b. 1867, Charleston, SC; d. 1945, Charleston, SC	SC
Dougherty, Bertha Hurlbut	b. 1883, Plainfield, NJ	VA
Dougherty, Jeanie Caldwell	b. 1842, Wheeling, WV; d. 1930, Florence, Italy	WV
Douglas, Laura Glenn	b. 1896, Winnsboro, SC; d. 1962, Washington, DC	DC / SC
Douglass, Lucile Sinclair	b. 1878, Tuskegee, AL; d. 1935, Andover, MA	AL
Downey, Mary Virginia Ryder	b. 1881, New York, NY; d. 1976, El Paso, TX	VA
Dreskin, Jeanet Steckler	b. 1921, New Orleans, LA	LA / SC
Drew, Antoinette Farnsworth	b. 1864, Fond du Lac, WI; d. 1941, Atlanta, GA	DC / GA
Driggs, Elizabeth "Elsie" H. Gatch	b. 1898, Hartford, CT; d. 1992, New York, NY	LA
Drinker, Catherine Ann {Janvier}	b. 1841, Philadelphia, PA; d. 1922, Philadelphia, PA	MD
Drummond, Sally Hazelet	b. 1924, Evanston, IL	FL / KY
Dryden, Helen	b. 1887, Baltimore, MD; d. 1982, Brentwood, NY	MD
Dryer, Della Frances	b. 1867, Tuskegee, AL; d. 1951, Mountain Brook, AL	AL
Dubé, Mattie	b. 1861, Florence, AL; d. 1944, Paris, France	AL
Dudley, Virginia Evelyn	b. 1913, Spring City, TN; d. 1981, Rising Fawn, GA	GA / TN
Duggan, Edith Boxer	b. 1878, New Orleans, LA; d. 1932, New Orleans, LA	LA
Duhamel, Elizabeth A.	b. 1862, Washington, DC; d. 1953, Washington, DC	DC
Dulac, Margarita {Walker}	b. 1922, Asheville, NC	NC
Dummett, Laura Dow	b. 1856, Allegheny, PA; d. after 1931, possibly in NJ	DC
DuMond, Helen Savier	b. 1872, Portland, OR; d. 1968, Alhambra, CA	FL
Duncan, Muriel Ethel Morrison	b. 1914, Charlotte, NC; d. 1984, Charlotte, NC	FL / NC / SC
Duncan, Virginia	active in Louisville, KY, 1934	KY
Dunlop, Anna Mercer	b. 1873, Petersburg, VA; d. 1957, Petersburg, VA	VA
DuPré, Grace Annette	b. 1894, Spartanburg, SC; d. 1984, Spartanburg, SC	SC
Dupuy, Laura Nevitt	b. 1893, Albany, NY; d. 1971, McLean, VA	DC / VA
Durieux, Caroline Spelman Wogan	b. 1896, New Orleans, LA; d. 1989, Baton Rouge, LA	LA
Dutheil, Anna	active in Washington, DC, 1909–1917	DC
Duval, Ella Moss	b. 1843, Pass Christian, MS; d. 1911, St. Louis, MO	LA / MS
Dwyer, Adelaide	b. 1896, Washington, DC	DC
Eagle, Clara M.	b. 1908, Columbus, OH; d. 1985, Columbus, OH	KY
Eanes, Susan Frances "Fannie"	b. 1884, Leesville, VA; d. 1974, Lynchburg, VA	DC / VA
Earle, Cornelia Thompson	b. 1859, Huntsville, AL; d. 1928, Richmond, VA	SC / VA
Ebersole, Mabel Helen	b. 1885, IA; d. 1969, Keokuk, IA	AR
Eckel, Julia E. Dibblee	b. 1870, NY; d. 1964 (buried in Arlington National Cemetery, Arlington, VA)	DC
Edell, Josie Van Gent	b. 1921, Amsterdam, Netherlands; d. 2006, Charleston, SC	SC
Edelman, Barcia Stepner	b. 1925, Boston, MA; d. 2009	NC

Artist	Life Dates	Associated With
Edgerly, Beatrice Edna {MacPherson}	b. 1898, Washington, DC; d. 1973, Tucson, AZ	DC
Edsall, Louisa Cabot Richardson	b. 1884, Chestnut Hill, MA; d. 1964, Cambridge, MA	NC
Edson, Millicent G. Strange	b. 1882, Nottingham, England; d. 1956, Rabun County, GA	GA
Edwards, Alice Elsie	b. about 1871; d. 1932, Washington, DC	DC
Edwards, Ethel Gonzales	b. 1914, Opelousas, LA; d. 1999, NY	LA
Edwards, Jane Sumner {Funston} {Miskie}	b. 1937; d. 2010, Franklinton, NC	NC
Edwards, Kate Flournoy	b. 1877, Marshallville, GA; d. 1980, Atlanta, GA	GA
Edwards, Mary Elizabeth	active in Louisville, KY, 1939	KY
Egan, Eloise Carpenter Jackson	b. 1874, IA; d. 1967, New York, NY	FL / SC
Egbert, Evelyn "Lyn" Loretta Forsyth	b. 1898, Oakland, CA; d. 1986, Dallas, TX	DC / NC
Eggemeyer, Maude Kaufman	b. 1877, New Castle, IN; d. 1959, Asheville, NC	NC
Ehrmann, Marli	b. 1904; d. 1982	NC
Eliot, Theresa Ann Garrett	b. 1884, Louisville, KY; d. 1981, Cambridge, MA	KY
Elkins, Mary Louise "Hallie" Davis	b. 1854, Washington, DC; d. 1933, Washington, DC	DC / WV
Elliott, Bertie Fredericks	b. 1862, Perry County, PA; d. 1952, Carlisle, PA	DC
Elliott, Hannah	b. 1876, Atlanta, GA; d. 1956, Birmingham, AL	AL / GA
Elliott, Jane S.	active in Washington, DC, 1920–1935; d. about 1946, Washington, DC	DC
Elliott, Martha Beggs	b. 1892, Birmingham, AL; d. 1987, Panama City, FL	AL / FL
Elliott, Sophia Appolina Hopkins	b. 1821, NY; d. 1885 (buried in Rockport, OH)	AR
Ely, Letitia Thompson Maxwell	b. 1886, Pottstown, PA; d. 1967, New Hope, PA	DC
Emery, Lin	b. 1928, Larchmont, NY	LA
Emmerich, Mary Ashburton Pew	b. 1864, Staten Island, NY; d. 1957, West Hazleton, PA	DC
Emmons, Chansonetta Stanley	b. 1858, Kingfield, ME; d. 1937, Kingfield, ME	SC
Emmons, Dorothy Stanley	b. 1891, Roxbury, MA; d. 1960, Kingfield, ME	FL / GA / NC / SC
Engelhardt, Harriett Pinkston	b. 1919, Montgomery, AL; d. 1945, France or Germany	AL / NC
Ennis, Marion Elizabeth Brower	b. 1896, Brooklyn, NY; d. 1979, Fairfax, VA	DC / VA
Enquist, Mary Bisbee	b. 1879, WI; d. 1953, Silver Bow, MT	DC
Erb, Daisy Erin	b. 1875, Canton, OH; d. 1959, Davenport, FL	DC / FL / NC
Erlanger, Elizabeth Nachman	b. 1890, Baltimore, MD; d. 1975, Goshen, NY	MD
Erskine, Emma Payne	b. 1854; Racine, WI; d. 1924, Tryon, NC	NC
Erwin, Elsie George	b. about 1883, PA	DC
Estabrook, Florence C.	b. Lowell, MA; d. about 1936, Washington, DC	DC
Estill, Elizabeth Ritter Savage	b. 1895, Charleston, WV; d. 1992, Vienna, WV	WV
Ettling, Ruth Lena Droitcour	b. 1910, Pittsburgh, PA; d. 2003, Huntington, WV	WV
Etz, Pearl Potter	b. 1875, Washington, DC; d. 1963, Tucson, AZ	DC
Evans, Elizabeth Dolbear Montgomery	b. 1898, Marysville, OH; d. 1988, Rockville, MD	DC / MD
Evans, Minnie Eva Jones	b. 1892, Long Creek, NC; d. 1987, Wilmington, NC	NC
Evans, Virginia Barger	b. 1894, Moundsville, WV; d. 1983, Wheeling, WV	FL / WV
Evatt, Harriet Torrey	b. 1891, Knoxville, TN; d. 1983, Worthington, OH	TN
Everett, Reaunette	b. 1924, GA	GA
Everhart, Adelaide	b. 1865, Charlotte, NC; d. 1958, Decatur, GA	GA / NC
Everhart, Florence Aurelia	b. 1893, Athens, PA; d. 1975, Alexandria, VA	DC / VA
Everton, Louise Woodson Smith	b. 1920, Birmingham, AL; d. 1995, Princess Anne, MD	AL / MD

Artist	Life Dates	Associated With
Ewald, Marion Butler	b. 1910, Meriden, CT; d. 1944, Fallston, MD	MD
Ewen, Carrie Douglas Dudley	b. 1894, Flemingsburg, KY; d. 1982, Louisville, KY	KY
Fahey, Esther Edmunds	b. about 1887, NY; d. 1976, Stockton, CA	DC / LA / MD / SC
Fahrenbruch, Lottie L.	b. about 1887; d. 1976, Washington, DC	DC
Falkner, Maud Butler	b. 1871, Oxford, MS; d. 1960, Oxford, MS	MS
Fant, Elizabeth "Lizzie Betty" Anderson	b. 1852, Holly Springs, MS; d. 1935, Holly Springs, MS	MS
Faris, Gladys Going	b. 1930, Greenville, SC; d. 2010, Wilmington, NC	NC / SC
Farnham, Jessica Shirley	b. 1882, New Rochelle, NY; d. 1956, Jefferson County, AL	AL
Farr, Dorothy Bruce	b. 1910; d. 1989	DC
Faulconer, Eleanor Tevis	b. 1894, Shelby City, KY; d. 1985, Danville, KY	KY
Faunce, Ethel A.	active in Washington, DC, 1915	DC
Fell, Amy Watson Wells	b. 1898, Lynchburg, VA; d. 1981, Morrisville, PA	VA
Fenerty, Agnes Lawson	b. 1885, Louisville, KY; d. 1974, Woodbridge, VA	KY / VA
Fenner, Martha Elizabeth	b. 1898, LA	LA / TN
Ferguson, Alice Leczinska Lowe	b. 1880, Washington, DC; d. 1951, Washington, DC	DC / MD
Ferguson, Jean	active in Louisville, KY, 1936	KY
Fernow, Bernice Pauahi Andrews	b. 1881, Jersey City, NJ; d. 1969	SC
Ferris, Bernice Marie Branson	b. 1882, Astoria, IL; d. 1936, Alexandria, VA	DC / VA
Ferris, Katherine Norris	b. 1916, Greenwich, CT	NC
Féry, Lucie-Louise	b. 1848, Metz, France; d. 1922, Charleston, SC	SC
Fiene, Alicia Weincek	b. 1918, Chicopee, MA; d. 1961, New York, NY	DC / NC
Figg, Fannie Emma	b. 1860, Louisville, KY; d. 1942, Louisville, KY	KY
Findley, Ila B.	b. 1900, Birmingham, AL; d. 1944, Tuscaloosa, AL	AL
Finkelstein, Maria Hamel	b. 1891, France; d. 1975, Bel Air, MD	DC / MD
Fischer, Mary Ellen Sigsbee Ker	b. 1876, New Orleans, LA; d. 1960, Shandaken, NY	LA
Fischer, Pansy	b. 1892; d. 1967	KY
Fisher, Elizabeth Patten Brewer	b. 1855, ME; d. 1927, Washington, DC	DC
Fisher, Jane Tucker	b. 1896, Columbia, SC; d. 1972, Columbia, SC	SC
Fitzgerald, Harriet	b. 1904, Danville, VA; d. 1984, Danville, VA	VA
Fitzgerald, Zelda Sayre	b. 1900, Montgomery, AL; d. 1948, Asheville, NC	AL / NC
Flanigen, Jean Nevitt	b. 1898, Athens, GA; d. 1994, Athens, GA	GA
Fleming, Margaret Doubleday Eddy	b. 1888, New York, NY; about 1977, La Jolla, CA	LA
Flemming, Jean Robinson	b. 1874, Charleston, SC; d. 1956, Charleston, SC	SC / VA
Fletcher, Anne Christine	b. 1876, Chicago, IL; d. 1955, Richmond, VA	VA
Fliege, Lillian	b. about 1880, Michigan; d. after 1940	WV
Flippin, Mary	b. 1848; d. 1945	TN
Flisher, Edith Ella	b. 1885, Cleveland, OH; d. 1936, Nashville, TN	TN
Fonville, Jean McIver Lane	b. 1909; d. 2008, Hickory, NC	NC
Forbes-Oliver, Harriet	b. 1908, Atlanta, GA	GA / LA
Ford, Celinda/Celeste W.	active in Washington, DC, 1901–1920	DC
Ford, Louisa Wright Neilson	b. 1866, Baltimore, MD; d. 1931, Baltimore, MD	MD
Forsdale, Elinor Wulfekuhler	affiliated with Black Mountain College	NC
Forsyth, Elizabeth Duverje Villere	b. 1911, New Orleans, LA; d. 1975, VA	LA / VA
Fort, Gladys Coker	b. 1891, Hartsville, SC; d. 1976, Gaffney, SC	NC / SC

Artist	Life Dates	Associated With
Fosdick, Gertrude Christian	b. 1862, Urbanna, VA; d. 1961, Manhattan, NY	VA
Foster, Alice	b. 1873, IL; d. 1927, Washington, DC	DC
Foster, Anne Bemister Dunn	affiliated with Black Mountain College	NC
Foster, Ethel Elizabeth	b. 1873, Washington, DC; d. 1968, St. Petersburg, FL	DC / FL
Foushee, Ola Maie Suttenfield	b. 1905, Rockingham County, NC; d. 1999, Chapel Hill, NC	NC
Fowler, Frances Herrick	b. 1864, Bowling Green, KY; d. 1948, Bowling Green, KY	KY / TN
Fowler, Mary Blackford	b. 1892, Findlay, OH; d. 1982, Findlay, OH	DC / VA
Fowler, Maud E.	b. 1890, Washington, DC	DC
Fowler, Rhoda Gibbs	b. 1869, WI; d. 1951, Petersburg, VA	VA
Fox, Margaret Mason Taylor	b. 1857, Philadelphia, PA; d. 1942, Thomaston, CT	DC
Frank, Alyce	b. 1932, New Iberia, LA	LA
Frank, Elise	b. 1891, Haarlem, Holland; d. 1981, Tampa, FL	FL
Frankenthaler, Helen	b. 1928, Manhattan, NY; d. 2011, Darien, CT	NC
Frankforter, Katharine Ann Swartzbaugh	d. 2006, Marin, CA; affiliated with Black Mountain College	NC
Franklin, Mary Jett	b. 1842, Athens, GA; d. 1928, Athens, GA	GA
French, Lillie Bell Harper	b. 1877, Southport, NC; d. 1944, Wilmington, NC	NC
Frishmuth, Harriet Whitney	b. 1880, Philadelphia, PA; d. 1980, Hampton, CT	SC
Frohock, Edith Mary Harker	b. 1917, Kansas City, MO; d. 1997, Birmingham, AL	AL / FL
Frost, Eda	active in Washington, DC, 1920–1935	DC
Fry, Francisca Negueloua	b. 1917, New Orleans, LA; d. 1972, New Orleans, LA	LA
Fry, Rowena C.	b. 1892, Athens, AL; d. 1990, Nashville, TN	AL / TN
Fuelling, Annie M. Schoenborn	b. 1870, Washington, DC; d. 1917, Washington, DC	DC
Fulda, Elizabeth	b. 1879, Berlin, Germany; d. 1968, New York, NY	DC
Fuller, Sue	b. 1914, Pittsburgh, PA; d. 2006, Southampton, NY	GA / NC
Fuller, Susan E. W.	b. 1831, New York, NY; d. 1907, Washington, DC	DC
Fulton, Antoinette Willner	b. 1882, Loudoun County, VA; d. 1940, Washington, DC	DC / VA
Fulton, Ruth McConnell	b. 1905, Rome, GA; d. 2003, Winston-Salem, NC	GA / NC / TN
Furr, Dani Hayes	b. 1928, Selma, NC	AL / NC
Gage, Ethel Allen	b. 1873, Louisville, KY; d. 1960, Louisville, KY	KY
Gailor, Charlotte	b. 1889, Sewanee, TN; d. 1972, Memphis, TN	TN
Gaines, Denise "Nina" Martin	affiliated with Black Mountain College	NC
Gallagher, Mary Ashton Cotton	b. 1890, Charleston, WV; d. 1968, Charleston, WV	WV
Galt, Mary "Mollie" Jeffrey	b. 1844, Norfolk, VA; d. 1922, Norfolk, VA	VA
Gamble, Rose Evelyn	b. 1871, England	DC / MD
Ganong, Valerie M.	b. 1909, Memphis, TN; d. 1966, Memphis, TN	TN
Gardner, Letitia Sellar	b. 1894; d. 1968, Lexington, KY	KY
Garesche, Marie	b. 1864, St. Louis, MO; d. 1951, Tampa, FL	FL
Garner, Dorothy T.	active in Washington, DC, 1920–1935	DC
Garner, Sara L.	b. 1927, Marietta, GA; d. 1976, Marietta, GA	GA
Garrason, Clara Brandon	active in Charleston, SC, 1922	SC
Garrison, Margaret Fielding Estey	b. 1911, Washington, DC; d. 1996, Bethesda, MD	MD
Gassman, Frances Josephine	b. 1907, NJ; d. 1981, Marietta, GA	AL / GA
Gatchell, Dorothy Glendenning	b. 1904, Washington, DC; d. 1976, Washington, DC	DC
Gates, Margaret Casey "M.C."	b. 1903, Washington, DC; d. 1989, Mitchellville, MD	DC / MD / NC / VA

Artist	Life Dates	Associated With
Gates, Mary Leonard	b. 1912, Charleston, WV; d. 1981, Miami, FL	FL / WV
Gatewood, Maud Florance	b. 1934, Yanceyville, NC; d. 2004, Chapel Hill, NC	AL / NC
Gath, Ethel Robertson	b. 1892; d. 1972, Buffalo, NY	DC
Gattinger, Minnie	b. 1857, Nashville, TN; d. 1944, Nashville, TN	TN
Gaul, Arrah Lee {Brennan}	b. 1883, Philadelphia, PA; d. 1980, Philadelphia, PA	FL
Gay, Helen Darrough	b. 1898, Greenwood, MS; d. 1987, Rosenberg, TX	MS
Gearhart, Shirlee Elaine Morton	b. 1939, Jacksonville, NC	NC
Gersdorff, Bertha D.	b. 1890, Washington, DC	DC
Getman, Ina	b. 1881, Columbia, NY; d. 1941, St. Petersburg, FL	FL
Gibbs, Jean Allen	b. 1911, Stearns, KY; d. 2006, Somerset, KY	KY
Giffen, Lilian	b. about 1874, New Orleans, LA; d. about 1946, Baltimore, MD	LA / MD
Gifford, Marguerite Peters	b. 1877, Louisville, KY; d. 1969, Louisville, KY	KY
Gilbert, Katharine	b. 1886; d. 1952	NC
Gilchrist, Emma/Emily Susan	b. 1862, Charleston, SC; d. 1929, Charleston, SC	SC
Gill, Mary Irvin Wright	b. 1868, Washington, DC; d. 1929, Washington, DC	DC / NC
Gill, Minna Partridge	b. 1896, Washington, DC; d. 1964, Boulder, CO	DC
Gill, Rosalie Lorraine	b. 1867, Elmira, NY; d. 1898, Paris, France	MD
Gillespie, Dorothy Muriel	b. 1920, Roanoke, VA; d. 2012, Coral Springs, FL	FL / MD / VA
Gillespie, Jeanette	b. about 1895, IL; d. 1976	TN
Gillespie, Manda E.	b. 1862, TN	TN
Gilliam, Lucille Moore	b. 1901, Crider, KY; d. 1997, Louisville, KY	KY
Givens, Fannie Rosalind Hicks	b. 1872, Chicago, IL; d. 1947, Louisville, KY	KY
Glazer, Nancy Wellman	b. 1913, Memphis, TN; d. 1995, Memphis, TN	TN
Glennan, Mary Emilie	b. 1855, NY; d. 1949 (buried in Arlington National Cemetery, Arlington, VA)	DC
Glinberg, Rose Jean Cohen	b. 1917, Milwaukee, WI; d. 1992, Milwaukee, WI	NC
Gloetzner, Josephine	b. 1877, Washington, DC; d. 1952, Washington, DC	DC
Gobble, Gwendolyn Fussell	b. 1935, Rose Hill, NC	NC
Goddard, Virginia Hargraves Wood	b. 1872, Washington, DC; d. 1941, Charlottesville, VA	DC / VA
Godding, Mary Patten	b. 1867, Washington, DC; d. 1948, Washington, DC	DC
Godfrey, Mary Jo Slick	b. 1924, Johnstown, PA; d. 2013, Farmington, AR	AR / NC
Godwin, Judith	b. 1930, Suffolk, VA	VA
Godwin, Maggie Lee Ripa	b. 1922, Ahoskie, NC; d. 2013, Wilmington, NC	NC
Goings, Martha Henderson	b. 1911, Birmingham, AL; d. 2004, Birmingham, AL	AL
Gold, Lenore Ellis	b. 1930; Chicago, IL; d. 1996, Sandy Springs, GA	GA / NC
Goldsborough, Lucinda Davis	b. 1906, New Orleans, LA; d. 1993, New York, NY	LA
Goldthwaite, Anne Wilson	b. 1869, Montgomery, AL; d. 1944, New York, NY	AL
Gonzales, Juanita	b. 1903, New Orleans, LA; d. 1935, New Orleans, LA	LA
Good, Maude M.	active in Washington, DC, 1920	DC
Good, Minetta	b. 1895, New York, NY; d. 1946, New York, NY	LA
Goodrich, Gertrude	b. 1914, New York, NY	DC
Goodwyn/Goodwin, Sallie Aylett	b. 1896, Washington, MS; d. 1975, Athens, GA	GA / MS / VA
Gordon, Emeline N. Hastings	b. 1877, Boston, MA; d. 1963, GA	GA
Gordon, Rebecca Wilson Carson	b. 1890, Spartanburg, SC; d. 1979, North Salem, NY	SC

Artist	Life Dates	Associated With
Gosman, Lillian May Briggs	b. 1889, NY; d. 1976, Ft. Lauderdale, FL	DC/FL
Goth, Marie	b. 1887, Indianapolis, IN; d. 1975, Nashville, IN	KY
Gotthold, Florence Wolf	b. 1858, Ulrichsville, OH; d. 1930, Wilton, CT	DC
Gotthold, Rose/Rosell/Rozel	b. 1884, New Orleans, LA; d. 1966, New Orleans, LA	LA
Gough, Agnes E.	b. 1903, Marshall County, KY; d. 1988, Benton, KY	KY/TN
Gould, Alice Dinneen	b. 1908, New York, NY; d. 1963	KY/NC
Gould, Zoe Aileen	affiliated with Black Mountain College	NC
Goulet, Lorrie Helen {de Creeft}	b. 1925, Riverdale, NY	NC
Gourevitch, Jacqueline Hermann	b. 1933, Paris, France	NC
Graham, Katherine Camille	b. Canton, MS	MS
Graham, Margaret Nowell	b. 1867, Lowell, MA; d. 1942, Winston-Salem, NC	NC
Gramling, Martha/Marta Johnson	b. 1912, Marietta, GA; d. 1990, Marietta, GA	GA
Granbery, Henrietta Augusta	b. 1829, Norfolk, VA; d. 1927, New York, NY	VA
Granbery, Virginia	b. 1831, Norfolk, VA; d. 1921, Norfolk, VA	VA
Grandy, Julia Selden	b. 1903, Norfolk, VA; d. 1962, Norfolk, VA	MD/VA
Grange, Jessie Cary Stangland	b. 1881, Kendall, NY; d. 1987, Washington, DC	DC
Grant, Dorothy Eleanor Louise Mengis	b. 1911, Belize (British Honduras); d. 2004, Sicily Island, LA	LA
Grauer, Natalie Eynon	b. 1894, Wilmington, DE; d. 1955, OH	WV
Gravatt, Sara Hoffecker	b. 1898, Ridley Park, PA; d. 1973, St. Petersburg, FL	FL/VA/WV
Graves, Hilda V.	b. 1902, Laurel Grove, MD; d. 1995, Clearfield, PA	DC/MD
Graves, Nell "Nellie" Cole	b. 1908, Moore, NC; d. 1997, Seagrove, NC	NC
Gray, Mary	b. 1890 or 1891; d. 1963 or 1964	NC
Gray, Sophia DeButts	b. 1854, Baltimore, MD; d. 1942, Jefferson County, KY	KY/LA/MD
Green, Anne Guerrant	b. 1908, Jefferson County, KY; d. 2000, Louisville, KY	KY
Green, Laura E. K.	active in Louisville, KY, 1931–1932	KY
Green, Lydia M.	active in Washington, DC, 1913–1914	DC
Green, Myra Hamilton	b. 1924, Fayetteville, TN; d. 2002, Jackson, MS	MS/TN
Greene, Anne Waite Bosworth	b. 1878, Chippenham, Wiltshire, England; d. 1961	NC
Greene, Virginia Owen	b. 1905, AL; d. 1981	AL/FL/GA
Greenman, Frances Cranmer	b. 1890, Aberdeen, SD; d. 1981, Long Lake, MN	DC
Greenwood, Marion	b. 1909, New York, NY; d. 1970, Woodstock, NY	TN
Greer, Blanche L.	b. 1881, Eldora, IA; d. after 1940	DC
Greer, Sarah	b. 1879, Denver, CO; d. 1969, Birmingham, AL	AL
Gregory, Angela	b. 1903, New Orleans, LA; d. 1990, New Orleans, LA	LA
Gregory, Barbara Delle Simmons	b. 1914, Fordyce, AR; d. 1994, Pine Bluff, AR	AR
Gregory, Mary Bland Rogers	b. 1839, Apalachicola, FL; d. 1919, Atlanta, GA	FL/GA
Gregory, Mary "Molly"	b. 1914, Woodmere, NY; d. 2006	NC
Gregory, Selina Elizabeth Bres	b. 1870, New Orleans, LA; d. 1953, Neuilly-sur-Seine, France	LA
Grey, Gertrude G.	active in Washington, DC, 1905–1920	DC
Grider, Dorothy	b. 1915, Bowling Green, KY; d. 2012, New Hope, PA	KY
Griggs, Martha E.	active in Washington, DC, 1905–1935	DC
Grippe, Florence Berg {Roseman}	b. 1910; d. 2010, New York, NY	NC
Griswold, Jennie Montague	b. 1858, CT; d. 1941, NY	DC
Groome, Constance A.	active in Washington, DC, 1925	DC

Artist	Life Dates	Associated With
Grose, Ruth Turner	active Washington, DC, 1928–1935	DC
Grosz, Louise	b. 1908, New Orleans, LA; d. 2003, New Orleans, LA	LA
Guermonprez, Gertrud "Trude" Jalowetz {Elsesser}	b. 1910, Danzig, Poland; d. 1976, San Francisco, CA	NC
Guignard, Caroline	b. 1869, Aiken County, SC; d. 1958, Columbia, SC	SC
Guillaume, Bertha	b. 1856, France; d. 1928, Washington, DC	DC
Gulledge, Josephine F.	b. about 1877, MS; d. 1945, Lexington, MS	DC / MS
Guthman, Belle	active in Washington, DC, 1915	DC
Gwathmey, Rosalie Hook	b. 1908, Charlotte, NC; d. 2001, Amagansett, NY	NC
Haden, Eunice Barnard	b. 1901, Washington, DC; d. 1995, Washington, DC	DC
Hadley, Mary Alice Hale	b. 1911, Terre Haute, IN; d. 1965, Louisville, KY	KY
Haggart, Winifred Watkins	b. 1911, Albany, NY; d. 2002, Pittsburgh, PA	KY
Hahan, Helen	active in Washington, DC, 1920–1925	DC
Hahn, Florentine I.	b. 1893, PA	DC
Haines, Marie Bruner Burt	b. 1881, Cincinnati, OH; d. 1979, Bennington, VT	FL / GA
Hale, Ellen Day	b. 1855, Worcester, MA; d. 1940, Brookline, MA	DC / SC
Hale, Lillian Coleman Westcott	b. 1880, Bridgeport, CT; d. 1963, St. Paul, MN	VA
Hale, Martha Jane	b. 1892, KY; d. 1984, Knoxville, TN	KY / TN
Hall, Dorothy	active in Louisville, KY, 1940	KY
Hall, Frances Devereux Jones	b. 1872, New Orleans, LA; d. 1941, Gwynedd Valley, PA	LA
Hall, Helena Jameson	b. 1902, Summit, NJ	VA
Hall, Lee	b. 1934, Lexington, NC; d. 2017, Northampton, MA	NC
Hall, Margaret "Peggy" Tannahill	b. 1910, Wilmington, NC; d. 1992, Wilmington, NC	NC
Hall, Mary Ed Mecoy	b. 1895, Clinton, KY; d. 1949, Murray, KY	AL / GA / KY / TN
Halper, Lorna Blaine Howard	b. 1924, New York, NY; d. 2012	NC
Haltiwanger, Helen Gertrude Walker {McKay}	b. 1918, Sumter, SC; d. 2014, Sumter, SC	SC
Haltiwanger, Laura	b. 1890, Richland County, SC; d. 1988, Columbia, SC	SC
Hamblett, Theora Alton	b. 1895, Paris, MS; d. 1977, Oxford, MS	MS
Hamel, Genevieve	b. 1902; d. 1976, Sarasota, FL	FL
Hamer, Lenore Kirby	b. 1884, Smiths Grove, KY; d. 1960, Walterboro, SC	KY / SC
Hamilton, Blanche	b. 1880, Washington, DC; d. 1951, Washington, DC	DC
Hamilton, Hildegarde Hume	b. 1898, Syracuse, NY; d. 1970, New York, NY	FL / DC / VA
Hamilton, Leone Bowers	b. 1903, Jefferson County, WV; d. 1981, Kearneysville, WV	GA / LA / WV
Hanaw, Alice Burkenroad	b. 1908, New Orleans, LA; d. 1968, New Orleans, LA	LA
Hanford, Joan L.	b. 1913, CA; d. 2005, Jacksonville, OR	GA / VA
Hankins, Sophia Maude McGehee	b. 1875, Fulton County, KY; d. 1968, Nashville, TN	KY / TN / VA
Hanley, Sarah Eileen	b. 1883, Sligo, Ireland; d. 1958, Laurel Hollow, NY	FL
Hannaford, Alice Steel Ide	b. 1888, Baltimore, MD; d. 1975	MD
Hannan, Katherine A.	b. 1920; d. 1987, KY	KY
Hanson, Berta Mork	b. 1876, Belmont County, OH	DC
Harding, Grace M.	active in Washington, DC, 1924	DC
Harmon, Adelaide Heinitah	b. 1897, Spartanburg, SC; d. 1988, Nashville, TN	SC / TN
Harmon, Harriet	b. 1891, Springfield, OH	GA / TN
Harper, Edith Irene Jones	b. 1925, Conway, AR; d. 2010, Brandon, MS	AR / MS

Artist	Life Dates	Associated With
Harper, Margaret Ellen	b. 1895, Caldwell County, NC; d. 1984, Lenoir, NC	NC
Harrell, Elizabeth Lambert Hatton	b. 1882, Prince George's County, MD; d. 1975, Silver Spring, MD	DC / MD
Harrington, Vary Barbour Thrower	b. 1892, MS; d. 1983, Madison, MS	AL / GA / MS
Harris, Beverly Humphreys	active in Washington, DC, 1920–1935	DC
Harris, Caroline Estelle	b. 1907, Junction City, AR; d. 1954, Jacksonville, AL	AL / MS / NC
Harris, Edith Maude	active in Washington, DC, 1911–1931 (buried in DC)	DC
Harris, Florence E.	active in Washington, DC, 1912–1920; d. 1926 (buried in Highland Hills, OH)	DC
Harris, Lorraine Beauchamp	b. 1904, Williamson, GA; d. 1998, Cheraw, SC	GA / SC
Harris, Margie Coleman	b. 1891, Washington, DC; d. 1968	DC
Harrison, Caroline Lavinia Scott	b. 1832, Washington, DC; d. 1892, Washington, DC	DC / KY
Harrison, Dorothy Van Houton	b. 1895, Brooklyn, NY; d. 1994, Hastings, NE	DC
Harrison, Edith Smith	b. 1879, Jacksonville, FL; d. 1963, Jacksonville, FL	FL
Harrison, Rosalind M.	active Washington, DC, 1915	DC
Hart, Justina C.	b. 1907, Clarksburg, WV; d. 2011, Clarksburg, WV	WV
Hart, Pearl A.	b. 1897, MA; active in Washington, DC, 1917	DC
Hartigan, Grace	b. 1922, Newark, NJ; d. 2008, Baltimore, MD	MD
Hartley, Rachel V.	b. 1884, New York, NY; d. 1955, Southampton, NY	FL
Hartman, Ethel B.	active in Washington, DC, 1912	DC
Harvey, Bessie Ruth White	b. 1929, Dallas, GA; d. 1994, Alcoa, TN	GA / TN
Hasselman, Anna	b. 1871, Indianapolis, IN; d. 1966, Delaware County, IN	DC
Hattorf, Helen A. King	b. 1900, Huntington, IN; d. 1977, Richmond, VA	VA
Haupt, Winifred Hope	b. 1891, Bijou Hills, SD; d. 1972, Natchitoches, LA	LA
Hauze, Margaret Brunan/Brennan	active in Washington, DC, 1913–1920	DC
Hawkes, Alice Silliman Belknap	b. 1878, Louisville, KY; d. 1972, Miami, FL	FL / KY
Hawkins, Eloise Oviatt	b. 1897, Montgomery, AL; d. 1973, Montgomery, AL	AL
Hawkins, Estelle Fleming	b. 1872, Shinnston, WV; d. 1965, Shinnston, WV	WV
Hawkins, Harriet Alma Chambers	b. 1890, Birmingham, AL; d. 1961, Sarasota, FL	AL / FL / DC / MD
Hawks, Rachel Marshall	b. 1879, Port Deposit, MD; d. 1964, Towson, MD	MD
Hawley, Margaret Foote	b. 1880, Guilford, CT; d. 1963, New York, NY	DC
Hayes, Marian Yancey	b. 1890, Chase City, VA; d. 1989, Rockville, MD	DC / MD / VA
Haynes, Anne Lee	b. 1896, Atlanta, GA; d. 1997, Brunswick, GA	GA / SC
Hays, Etta Hast	b. 1873, Louisville, KY; d. 1944, Louisville, KY	KY
Healey, Emily	active in Washington, DC, 1905–1923	DC
Healey, Mary	active in Washington, DC, 1902–1923	DC
Healy, Marion Maxon	b. 1890, Cincinnati, OH; d. 1983, Green Valley, AZ	AL
Heath, Louise	active in Washington, DC, 1905–1914	DC
Hebb, Mathilde Marie Mylander	b. 1911, Baltimore, MD; d. 1982, Baltimore, MD	MD
Heckert, Isabelle Louise	b. 1914 Harrisburg, PA; d. 1977, Roanoke, VA	LA / SC
Heidel, Edith Hope Ogden	b. 1871, St. Paul, MN; d. 1956, St. Paul, MN	DC
Heidrick, Madeleine Johnson	b. 1913, IL; d. 1982, Chapel Hill, NC	NC
Heintzen, Elizabeth Carter {Laughlin}	b. 1914, New Orleans, LA; d. 2010, Conway, AR	AR / LA
Heiss, Peggy	active in Washington, DC, 1923–1924	DC
Heitmuller, Marian Roeder	b. 1894, Washington, DC	DC

Artist	Life Dates	Associated With
Heldner, Dorothy Colette Pope	b. 1902, Waupaca, WI; d. 1990, New Orleans, LA	LA
Heller, Carolyn Frohsin	b. 1937, Alexander City, AL; d. 2011, Tampa, FL	FL / LA
Heller, Henrietta Blackburn	b. 1908, Panama Canal Zone; d. Louisville, KY	KY
Hellman, Bertha Louise "Liza" Rublee	b. 1900, La Grange, TX; d. 1976, San Antonio, TX	TN
Helm, Clara Ester Lucas	b. 1856, Bristol, KY; d. 1950, Bowling Green, KY	KY
Hemenway, Alice Spaulding	b. 1866, Dedham, MA	FL
Hemenway, Mary Louise Liddell Jordan	b. 1893, Birmingham, AL; d. 1970, Pineville, LA	AL / FL / LA
Henderson, A. Elizabeth	b. 1873, Ashland, KY	KY
Henderson, Isabelle Worth Bowen	b. 1899, Wilmington, NC; d. 1969, Raleigh, NC	NC
Henderson, Martha Goings	b. 1911; d. 2004, Birmingham, AL	AL
Henning, Henrietta Hunt	b. 1893, Louisville, KY; d. 1964, Louisville, KY	KY
Henning, Julia Duke	b. 1900, Louisville, KY; d. 1996, Louisville, KY	KY
Henriksen, Catherine Turner	b. 1915, Denmark, SC; d. 2010, Hickory, NC	NC / SC
Henry, Natalie Smith	b. 1907; d. 1992, Malvern, AR	AR
Hergesheimer, Ella Sophonisba	b. 1873, Allentown, PA; d. 1943, Nashville, TN	TN
Herschel, Sarah Frances	b. 1866, Boston, MA; d. 1937, Montclair, NJ	DC
Herzog, Betty Warren Lancaster	b. 1920, New York, NY; d. 1993, Albany, NY	FL / LA
Heustis, Louise Lyons	b. 1865, Mobile, AL; d. 1951, New York, NY	AL
Heyns, Cornelia "Nell" Goldsmith	b. 1924; d. 2011	LA / NC
Heyward, Elizabeth "Lille" Barnwell Rhett	b. 1900, Atlanta, GA; d. 1930, Charlotte, NC	GA / NC / SC
Heyward, Katherine Bayard	b. 1886, Lexington, VA; d. 1974, Columbia, SC	SC / VA
Hiatt, Bertha Mabel Slayton	b. 1881, CA; d. 1964, Burlingame, CA	MS
Higgins, Elizabeth Vitezy	d. 2008, NC	NC
Hill, Carolyn "Carrie" Lillian	b. 1875, Vance, AL; d. 1957, Birmingham, AL	AL
Hill, Clara P.	b. 1870, Hyde Park, MA; d. 1935, Washington, DC	DC
Hill, Edith L.	b. 1884, Ridgewood, NJ	DC
Hill, Hattie Hutchcraft	b. 1847, Bourbon County, KY; d. 1921, Paris, KY	KY
Hill, Kate	active in Washington, DC, 1905–1924	DC
Hill, Margaret Mason	active in Washington, DC, 1920–1935	DC
Hill, Pauline "Polly" Knipp	b. 1900, Ithaca, NY; d. 1990, St. Petersburg, FL	FL
Hill, Victoria	b. 1871, SC; d. 1968, Sharon, MS	MS / SC / TN
Hillsmith, Fannie Louise	b. 1911, Boston, MA; d. 2007, Jaffrey, NH	NC
Hinton, Josephine	b. 1908, Wilmington, NC; d. 1979, Wilmington, NC	NC / VA
Hite, Marcia Shallcross Warren	b. 1876; Louisville, KY; d. 1946, Jefferson County, KY	KY
Hobson, Margaret Morehead	b. 1890, Warren County, KY; d. 1987, Warren County, KY	KY
Hodge, Lena Murray	active in Washington, DC, 1927–1939	DC
Hodge, Margaret Whitehead Magill	b. 1863, Washington, DC; d. 1935, York, PA	DC
Hodges, Annie Ruth Bethea	b. 1916, Mount Olive, NC; d. 2012, Wilmington, NC	GA / NC / SC
Hoffman, Helen Bacon	b. 1930, San Antonio, TX; d. 2017, Jacksonville Beach, FL	FL / VA
Hogan, Fanny Dunaway	b. about 1875, AR; d. 1964, AR	AR
Hokinson, Helen Elna	b. 1893, Mendota, IL; d. 1949, Washington, DC	DC
Holbrook, Vivian Nicholas	b. 1913, Mount Vernon, NY; d. 1994, Gainesville, FL	FL
Holden, Jean MacLeod Stansbury	b. 1842, Pinckney, MI; d. 1934, Tryon, NC	NC / SC
Holden, Lephe Kingsley	b. 1881, Hadley, MA; d. 1973, Volusia, FL	FL

Artist	Life Dates	Associated With
Holl, Mirande Roxane Geissbuhler	b. 1928, New York, NY	NC
Holland, Marion L.	active in Washington, DC, 1920–1935	DC
Hollerith, Lucia Beverly	b. 1891, Washington, DC; d. 1982, Bethesda, MD	DC / MD
Holliday, Annie May	b. 1887, Athens, GA; d. 1972, Athens, GA	GA
Holliday, Roberta	active in Washington, DC, 1920	DC
Hollingsworth, Flora Campbell	possibly b. 1891, Augusta, GA; d. 1944, Augusta, GA	GA
Holloway, Virginia Hudson	b. 1928, Boston, MA; d. 1989, Wilmington, NC	NC
Holmes, Beverly Elizabeth Neal	b. 1922, Smiths Creek, MI; d. 2003, Oakland, MI	NC
Holmes, Kate Clifton Osgood	b. 1858, Ellsworth, ME; d. 1925, Washington, DC	DC / VA
Holmes, Ruth Miller Atkinson	b. 1910, Hazlehurst, MS; d. 1981 McComb, MS	LA / MS
Holt, Julia Samuel Travis	b. 1897, Hampton, VA; d. 1978, Hampton, VA	VA
Holt, Maud Spiller	b. 1866, Carbondale, IL; d. 1952, Little Rock, AR	AR
Honan, Mary Agnes	b. 1894, Fall River, MA; d. 1984, DC (buried in Arlington National Cemetery, Arlington, VA)	DC
Honour, Leila	unknown	SC
Hood, Ethel Painter	b. 1908, Baltimore, MD; d. 1982	MD
Hooper, Annie Miller	b. 1897, Buxton, NC; d. 1986, Buxton, NC	NC
Hoover, Marie Louise Rochon	b. 1898, Washington, DC; d. 1976, Washington, DC	DC
Hopkins, Claire Miller	b. 1939	SC
Hopkins, Edna Bois	b. 1872, Hudson, MI; d. 1937, New York, NY	DC
Hopkins, Elinor F.	b. 1901, Hot Springs, VA; d. 1995, Warm Springs, VA	VA
Hopman, Marcia Elizabeth Evert	b. 1920, El Paso, TX; d. 2013, Arlingon, IA	DC / NC
Horne, Kathleen Perkins	b. 1894, Washington, DC; d. 1984, Alexandria, VA	DC / VA
Horne, Laura Trevitte	b. 1891, Dalton, GA; d. 1958, Mt. Vernon, NY	GA
Horne, Nellie Mathes	b. 1870, Eliot, ME; d. 1950, Los Angeles, CA	DC
Horner, Elizabeth Antoinette	active in New Orleans, 1905–1916	LA
Hosmer, Madeline Rose Flint	b. 1890, St. Louis, MO; d. 1947, DeKalb, GA	GA / MD
Hosterman, Naomi/Naomie Louise Sunderland	b. 1903, Elkhart, IN; d. 1990, Los Alamitos, CA	WV
Hotchkiss, G. Elenora	active in Washington, DC, 1921	DC
Houston, Eleanora "Nora" Clare Gibson	b. 1883, Richmond, VA; d. 1942, Richmond, VA	VA
Houston, Ruth Richardson	b. 1869, Brooklyn, NY; d. after 1938, WV	WV
Hovenden, Martha Maulsby	b. 1884, Plymouth Meeting, PA; d. 1941, Philadelphia, PA	DC
Hovey-King, Rita Yokum	b. 1911, Charleston, SC; d. 1975, New Orleans, LA	LA / SC
Howard, Esther A.	active in Louisville, KY, 1936	KY
Howard, Marion P.	b. 1883, Roxbury, MA; d. 1953, possibly in North Conway, NH	DC
Howell, Millicent Merritt	b. 1927, Meridian, MS	MS
Howen, Effie Lillian Harris	b. 1903, Pine Bluff, AR; d. 1985, Riverside, CA	AR
Howland, Anna C. Goodheart Whittleton	b. 1871, Atchison, KS; d. 1943, Washington, DC	DC
Howorth, Emma Louis/Louise	b. 1868, Kosciusko, MS; d. 1923, Forest, MS	AL / DC / MS / TN
Hoyle, Annie Elizabeth	b. 1851, Charles Town, WV; d. 1931, Washington, DC	DC / MD / WV
Hoyt, Margaret Howard Yeaton	b. 1885, Baltimore, MD; d. 1943, Lexington, VA	MD / VA
Hoyt, Vivian Church	b. 1880, Walworth, WI; d. 1957, Clermont, FL	FL
Hubbard, Emma Eva Boyers	b. 1858, Des Moines; IA; d. 1947, Morgantown, WV	WV
Hubbert, Lily Saxon	b. 1878, MS; d. 1976, Lubbock, TX	MS

Artist	Life Dates	Associated With
Huddle, Nannie Zenobia Carver	b. 1860, Mobile, AL; d. 1951, Austin, TX	AL
Huffer, Cornelia Cunningham Schoolcraft	b. 1903, Savannah, GA; d. 1974, Dover, NH	GA
Huger, Emily Hamilton	b. 1881, New Orleans, LA; d. 1946, Lafayette, LA	LA
Huger, Katherine Middleton	b. 1858, Charleston, SC	SC
Hughes, Ethel Parrot	b. 1884, Lenoir, NC; d. 1986, Winston-Salem, NC	NC
Hughes, Nina V.	active in Washington, DC, 1914–1915	DC
Hughes, Philippa Swinnerton de Pearsall	b. 1824, South Gloucestershire, England; d. 1917, Oldland, South Gloucestershire, England	KY
Hull, Emily Marie Atkinson	b. 1890, Summit, MS; d. 1980, Jackson, MS	MS
Humphrey, Eleanor Silliman Belknap	b. 1876, Louisville, KY; d. 1964, Miami, FL	FL / KY
Hunt, Celestia M.	active in Louisville, KY, 1936	KY
Hunt, Mabelle/Maybelle Alcott	b 1898, New York, NY; d. possibly in Savannah, GA	GA
Hunt, Una Atherton Clarke	b. 1876, Cincinnati, OH; d. after 1934, possibly in NH	DC
Hunter, Anna Colquitt	b. 1892, Savannah, GA; d. 1985, Savannah, GA	GA
Hunter, Bertha Mae Carmack	b. 1899; d. 1974, Caldwell County, KY	DC / KY
Hunter, Clementine Reuben	b. 1886, Cloutierville, LA; d. 1988, near Natchitoches, LA	LA
Huntington, Anna Vaughn Hyatt	b. 1876, Cambridge, MA; d. 1973, Redding Ridge, CT	SC
Huntington, Priscilla Weld	b. 1922, Norwich, CT; d. 2015, Greenport, NY	NC
Huntley, Victoria Ebbels Hudson	b. 1900, Hasbrouck Heights, NJ; d. 1971, Chatham, NJ	FL
Hurd, Angela Mary Parker	b. 1898, Stafford, England; d. 1976, Escondido, CA	DC
Hurry, Lucy Washington	b. 1884, Hagerstown, MD; d. 1950, Mineola, NY	MD
Huston, Harriet Lawrence Cann	b. 1901, GA; d. 1989, Savannah, GA	GA
Hutson, Ethel	b. 1872, Baton Rouge, LA; d. 1951, Gulfport, MS	LA / MS
Hyatt, Anna Vaughn (see Huntington, Anna Vaughn Hyatt)		
Hyde, Della Mae Pascal Ravenscroft {Bell}	b. 1895, Oakland, MD; d. 1973, Los Angeles, CA	DC / MD
Hyde, Helen	b. 1868, Lima, NY; d. 1919, Pasadena, CA	SC
Hyland, Ruth Hibbs	b. 1907; d. 1973, Richmond, VA	KY / NC / VA
Hynes, Mary Helen	b. 1894, GA; d. 1976	FL / GA
Ingram, Virginia Stebbins	b. 1929, Winston-Salem, NC; d. 2015, Winston-Salem, NC	NC / VA
Ions, Estelle de Willoughby	b. 1881, New Orleans, LA; d. 1977, Richmond, VA	DC / LA / VA
Ireland, Ada "Addie" Rosalie	b. 1875, Pennsboro, WV; d. 1944, Shepherdstown, WV	WV
Irvine, Sarah "Sadie" Agnes Estelle	b. 1887, New Orleans, LA; d. 1970, New Orleans, LA	LA / MD
Jackson, Amy Miears	b. 1903, Caldwell County, TX; d. 1970, Lockhart, TX	LA
Jackson, Elizabeth Leslie	b. 1866, Rochester, MN; d. 1958, Amsterdam, NY	DC
Jackson, Emerine	b. about 1911, OK	GA
Jackson, Lily Irene	b. 1848, Parkersburg, WV; d. 1928, Parkersburg, WV	WV
Jackson, May Howard	b. 1877, Philadelphia, PA; d. 1931, DC or Long Beach, CA	DC
Jackson, Ruth C.	b. 1894, Washington, DC; d. 1977, Washington, DC	DC
Jackson, Zuleima Bruff	b. 1843, Washington, DC; d. 1915, Washington, DC	DC
Jacob, Mariette Handy Allen	b. 1894; d. 1970, Scottsdale, AZ	NC
Jacobs, Dorothy	active in Louisville, KY, 1936	KY
Jamar, S. Corinne	b. 1873, Elkton, MD	MD
James, Alice Archer Sewall	b. 1870, Glendale, OH; d. 1955, Columbus, OH	VA
James, Bess B.	b. 1897, Big Spring, TX	LA

Artist	Life Dates	Associated With
Jansen, Henrietta Beckwith	b. 1913, Louisville, KY; d. 1998, Louisville, KY	KY
Jaques, Bertha Evelyn Clausen	b. 1863, Covington, OH; d. 1941 (buried in Covington, OH)	GA / SC
Jardet, Florence Mary	b. 1882, New Orleans, LA; d. 1980, New Orleans, LA	LA
Jennerjahn, Elizabeth "Betty" Marie Schmitt	b. 1923, Wauwatosa, WI; d. 2007, Sedona, AZ	NC
Jennings, Louise Burridge	b. 1879, Tecumseh, MI; d. 1953, Summit County, OH	MD
Jett, Virginia Lee Knox	b. 1912, Pulaski, TN; d. 1999, Chattanooga, TN	TN
Jetton, Norma	b. 1932; d. 1959, Graves County, KY	KY
Johansen, Beate "Ati" Eveliene Gropius {Forberg}	b. 1926, Wiesbaden, Germany; d. 2014, Wellfleet, MA	NC
Johnson, Elena Mix	b. 1889, Nogales, Mexico; d. 1939, Raleigh, NC	DC / NC
Johnson, Irene Charlesworth	b. 1888, Gering, NE; d. 1973, Kingsport, TN	TN
Johnson, Iris Beatty	b. 1897, Hamburg, Germany; d. 1983, Takoma Park, MD	DC / MD
Johnson, Isabella D.	active in Washington, DC, late 1920s	DC
Johnson, Margaret "Maggi" F. Kennard	b. 1918; d. 2015, Princeton, NJ	NC
Johnson, Mary Carter "Maud" Craven	b. 1874, Philadelphia, PA; d. 1950, Annapolis, MD	MD / MS
Johnson, Nellie Guild Hall	b. 1864, Tuscaloosa, AL; d. 1924, Talladega, AL	AL
Johnston, Annie B.	active in FL, 1930s	FL
Johnston, Frances Benjamin	b. 1864, Grafton, WV; d. 1952, New Orleans, LA	DC / LA / WV
Johnston, Mary Gardner	b. 1872, Evansville, IN; d. 1966, Pewee Valley, KY	KY
Johnston, Mary Virginia del Castillo	b. 1865, Puerto Principe, Cuba; d. 1951, San Francisco, CA	DC
Jones, Anna "Annie" Weaver	b. 1858, Nashville, TN; d. 1917, Cook County, IL	TN
Jones, Cora Evangeline Ellis	b. 1875, Aurora, IL; d. 1932, Fairfield, AL	AL
Jones, Gladys Moon	b. 1892, Colfax, IL; d. 1981, Washington, DC	DC
Jones, Loïs Mailou	b. 1905, Boston, MA; d. 1998, Boston, MA	DC / NC
Jones, Nell Hinton Choate	b. 1879, Hawkinsville, GA; d. 1981, Brooklyn, NY	GA
Joor, Harriet Coulter	b. 1875, Houston, TX; d. 1965, Baton Rouge, LA	LA / MS
Jordan, Anita Phillips	b. 1902; d. 1980	SC
Josey, Atha Hicks	b. 1888, Wilmington, NC; d. 1979, Wilmington, NC	NC / VA
Joy, Sue	b. 1903, Nashville, TN; d. 1960, Nashville, TN	TN
Julian, Freida Catherine Mylius	b. 1902, Chattanooga, TN; d. 1991, Roanoke, VA	NC / TN
Junkin, Marion Montague	b. 1905, Chunju, Korea; d. 1977, Lexington, VA	VA
Junkin, Mary Moreland "Toya"	b. 1907, Chunju, Korea; d. 1960, Richmond, VA	VA
Kabacker, Elizabeth Balfour Raymond	b. 1904, New Orleans, LA; d. 1986, Orange County, CA	LA
Kaish, Luise Clayborn	b. 1925, Atlanta, GA; d. 2013, New York, NY	NY
Kalb, Dorothy Buhrman	b. 1885, Washington City, DC; d. 1963, Washington, DC	DC
Kalbfeld, Carol Harriet Singer	d. 2008	NC / GA
Kane, Theodora A.	b. 1907, Boston, MA; d. 1977, Washington, DC	DC
Kant-Glaser, Maria	affiliated with Black Mountain College	NC
Kantlehner, Laura Bruenger	b. 1892 or 1893, KY; d. 1981, Louisville, KY	KY
Karnes, Karen	b. 1925, New York, NY	NC
Karow, Anna Bell Wilson	b. 1863, Savannah, GA; d. 1924, Savannah, GA	GA
Katz, Nancy Louise Brager	b. 1916, Baltimore, MD; d. 2004, MD	MD / NC
Katzen, Lila Pell	b. 1932, NY; d. 1998, NY	MD
Kay, Alexandra	active in Washington, DC, 1943	DC

Artist	Life Dates	Associated With
Kaye, Elizabeth Gutman	b. 1887, Baltimore, MD; d. 1971, Jamaica, NY	MD
Keane, Lucina Mabel	b. 1904, Gross, NE; d. 1984, Charleston, WV	WV
Keane, Margaret "Peggy" Doris Hawkins	b. 1927, Nashville, TN	TN
Keely, Harriet Madeleine	b. 1871, Charleston, WV; d. 1961, Charleston, WV	WV
Keen, Lila Moore	b. 1903, Cleveland, GA; d. 1963, High Point, NC	GA / NC
Keffer, Frances Alice	b. 1881, Des Moines, IA; d. 1953, San Diego, CA	NC
Keith, Lila McDuffie	b. 1890, Wilmington, NC; d. 1954, Greensboro, NC	NC
Keller, Marie de Ford	b. 1860, Germany; d. 1962, Baltimore, MD	MD
Kelley, May McClure	b. 1864; d. 1963, Georgetown, DC	DC
Kellogg, Marguerite Henrich	b. 1894, Germantown, CA; d. 1988, El Cerrito, CA	DC
Kelly, Alice M.	d. 1933, Washington, DC	DC
Kelly, Grace	active in Washington, DC, 1915–1917	DC
Kemeys, Laura Swing	b. 1860, Cumberland County, NJ; d. 1934, Washington, DC	DC
Kendall, Joanna Gichner	b. 1899, Baltimore, MD; d. 1989, Atlantic City, NJ	MD
Kendall, Minerva	active in Washington, DC, 1918–1924	DC
Kendrick, Elsie L. Lowe	b. 1914, South Amboy, NJ; d. 1998, Wilmington, NC	DC / NC / VA
Kennedy, Dawn S.	b. 1887, Crawfordsville, IN; d. 1959, Seattle, WA	AL
Kennedy, Doris Wainwright	b. 1916, Bernice, LA; d. 1994, LA	AL / LA
Keplinger, Lona Inez Miller	b. 1875, Marion County, IN; d. 1956, Bethesda, MD	MD
Kercheville, Christina Johnson	b. 1906, Altus, AR; d. 1989, Bernalillo, NM	AR
Kernodle, Evelyn Pratt	b. 1917, Guilford County, NC; d. 2002, Greensboro, NC	NC
Kerr, Adma Green	b. 1878, Lone Oak, TX; d. 1949, Boulder, CO	DC
Kerr, Lucy Whitney	b. 1883, Independence, MO; d. 1976, Washington, DC	DC
Kerr, Viola C.	b. 1892, Canada; d. 1987, Fayetteville, AR	AR
Kershaw, Alice Farias	b. 1911, Uruapan, Mexico; d. 1968, Hendersonville, NC	NC / WV
Keshishian, Margaret	b. 1899, Turkey; d. 1982, Washington, DC	DC
Kettig, Dorothy	b. 1906, Birmingham, AL; d. 1972	AL
Key-Oberg, Ellen Burke	b. 1905, Marion, AL; d. 1983, San Diego, CA	AL
Khouri, Greta Matson	b. 1915, Claremont, VA; d. 2004, Norfolk, VA	VA
Kiah, Virginia Jackson	b. 1911, Baltimore, MD; d. 2001, Savannah, GA	GA / MD / MS
Kilpatrick, Mary Grace	b. 1879, Baltimore, MD	MD
Kimberly, Cara A. Draper	b. 1866, St. Louis, MO; d. 1961, Washington, DC	DC
Kimbrough, Charlotte Ann Gray	b. 1824, Columbus, MS; d. 1910, Carrollton, MS	MS
Kimbrough, Sara Pryor Dodge	b. 1901, New York, NY; d. 1990, Bay St. Louis, MS	MS
Kindler, Alice Riddle	b. 1892, Germantown, PA; d. 1980, London, England	MD / SC
King, Blanche Tuing Elliot	b. 1895, Washington, DC; d. 1975, Washington, DC	DC
King, Daisy Blanche	b. 1874, Washington, DC; d. 1947	DC
King, Eleanor	b. 1909, Marlow, OK; d. 2003, Elmhurst, IL	FL
King, Frances "Fanny" Mahon	b. 1865, Aiken, SC; d. 1952, Point Pleasant Plantation, Meggett, SC	SC
King, Janet Catherine	b. 1886, Regina, Canada; d. 1959, St. Petersburg, FL	FL
King, Mary Elizabeth Mayes	b. 1899, Springfield, MO; d. 1991, Washington, DC	DC
King, Myrtle Valdosta Braddy Jones	b. 1913, Cummings, GA; d. 2005, Savannah, GA	GA
Kinney, Belle Marshall	b. 1890, Nashville, TN; d. 1959, Boiceville, NY	TN

Artist	Life Dates	Associated With
Kinsey, Alberta	b. 1875, West Milton, OH; d. 1952, New Orleans, LA	LA
Kirby, Lenore Hamer (see Hamer, Lenore Kirby)		
Kirk, Lydia Chapin	b. 1896, PA; d. 1984 (buried in Arlington National Cemetery, Arlington, VA)	DC
Kirk, Mary Wallace Wyman	b. 1889, Tuscumbia, AL; d. 1978, Tuscumbia, AL	AL
Kirkham, Charlotte Burt	b. 1856, East Saginaw, MI; d. 1943, Springfield, MA	DC
Kirkup, Mary A.	b. Ft. Atkinson, IA; d. after 1940, possibly in Larchmont, NY	DC
Klitgaard, Georgina	b. 1893, Spuyten Duyvil, NY; d. 1976, Bearsville, NY	FL / GA / NC
Klutts, Ethel Lindsay	b. about 1872, AL; d. 1935, Gadsden, AL	AL
Knapp, Grace Adele Le Duc	b. 1874, MN; d. 1958, Pasadena, CA	DC
Knecht, Fern Elizabeth Edie	b. 1888, Du Bois, NE; d. 1979, Georgetown, TX	AR
Knee, Gina Schnaufer {Brook}	b. 1898, Marietta, OH; d. 1982, Suffolk County, NY	SC
Knerr, Sallie Elizabeth Frost	b. 1914, Plattsburg, MO; d. 1988, SC	SC
Knight, Gwendolyn Clarine {Lawrence}	b. 1913, Bridgetown, Barbados; d. 2005, Seattle, WA	LA / NC
Knight, Julia Murray	b. 1889, Frankfort, KY; d. 1977, Los Angeles, CA	KY
Knowles, Geral Marley	b. 1895, MS; d. 1978	MS
Knox, Martha Katherine Crane	b. 1899, Blackstone, VA; d. 1990, Wilmington, NC	GA / NC / VA
Knox, Susan Ricker	b. 1874, Portsmouth, NH; d. 1959, Concord, NH	FL
Kogler, Gertrud Du Brau	b. 1889, Germany; d. 1965, Tacoma, WA	MD
Kohlhepp, Dorothy Irene	b. 1907, Boston, MA; d. 1964, Louisville, KY	KY
Kohlmeyer, Ida Rittenberg	b. 1912, New Orleans, LA; d. 1997, New Orleans, LA	GA / LA
Kollock, Mary	b. 1840, Norfolk, VA; d. 1911, New York, NY	VA
Kopman, Katharine	b. 1870, New Orleans, LA; d. 1950, Biloxi, MS	LA / MS
Kormendi, Elizabeth	b. 1897, Budapest, Hungary; d. 1980, Washington, DC	DC
Kortheuer, Katheryn Woods	b. 1908, New York, NY; d. 1988, Charlotte, NC	NC
Kosinsky, Anna Matilda	b. 1889, New York, NY; d. 1961, Washington, DC	DC
Kottgen, Eve	b. 1903; active in MS, 1942	MS
Kramer, Perna Krick	b. 1909, Greenville, OH; d. 1991, Baltimore, MD	MD
Kremelberg, Mary A.	b. 1876, MD; d. 1946, Baltimore, MD	MD
Kroman, Secile	b. 1889; d. 1967	AL
Kron, Adelaide	b. 1828, NC (possibly in France); d. 1910, Stanly County, NC	NC
Kuck, Anne Catherine	b. 1885, Savannah, GA; d. 1965, Hendersonville, NC	GA / NC
Kumm, Marguerite Elizabeth	b. 1902, Redwood Falls, MN; d. 1992, Falls Church, VA	DC / VA
LaBruce, Flora MacDonald Bryce	b. 1852, NY; d. 1931, Charleston, SC	NC / SC
LaFrance, Helen (see Orr, Helen LaFrance)		
Lahey, Carlotta Alma Gonzales	b. 1910, Wilmington, NC; d. 1999, Fairfax, VA	DC / NC / VA
Lake, Grace M.	b. 1908, Providence, RI; d. after 2008, Naples, FL	FL
Lampert, Emma Esther (see Cooper, Emma Esther Lampert)		
Lane, Helen MacMillan	b. 1914, Wilmington, NC; d. 1987, Wilmington, NC	NC
Lane, Marian Ursula Margaret	b. 1874, England; d. 1963, Washington, DC	DC
Lane, Mary Comer	b. 1881, Savannah, GA; d. 1966, Savannah, GA	GA
Lang, Annie Traquair	b. 1885, Philadelphia, PA; d. 1918, New York, NY	NC
Lange, Dorothea	b. 1895, Hoboken, NJ; d. 1965, San Francisco, CA	SC

Artist	Life Dates	Associated With
Langsdorf, Martyl Schweig	b. 1917, St. Louis, MO; d. 2013, Schaumburg, IL	DC
Lanpher, Helen Fowler	b. 1904, Superior, WI; d. 1961	LA
Latimer, Glenna Montague {Davies}	b. 1886, Newport News, VA; d. 1980, Newport News, VA	VA
Lautenschlager/Lautenslager, Lena	active in Washington, DC, 1909–1912	DC
Lauterstein, Ingeborg Svarc	b. 1923, Vienna, Austria; d. 2012, Rockport, MA	NC
Law, Margaret Moffett	b. 1871, Spartanburg, SC; d. 1956, Spartanburg, SC	MD / NC / SC
Lawrence, Betty Conway	b. 1903, Vicksburg, MS; d. 1963, Shreveport, LA	LA / MS
Lawrence, Josephine	b. 1905, Sumter, SC	AL / SC
Lawson, Blanche Maretta Cleveland	b. 1904, Seward, IL; d. 1993, Pittsburgh, PA	WV
Lazard, Alice Abraham	b. 1893, New Orleans, LA; d. 1972, Highland Park, IL	LA
Lazzell, Nettie Blanche	b. 1878, Maidsville, WV; d. 1956, Provincetown, MA	FL / WV
Leader, Garnet Rosamonde	b. 1905, Bessemer, AL; d. 2002, Bessemer, AL	AL / MS
LeBlanc, Eileen	b. 1917, New Orleans, LA; d. 2004, New Orleans, LA	LA
LeBlanc, Emilie de Hoa	b. 1870, New Orleans, LA; d. 1941, New Orleans, LA	LA
LeBlanc, Marie de Hoa	b. 1874, New Orleans, LA; d. 1954, New Orleans, LA	LA
LeBrecque, Adele Suska	b. 1927, New York, NY	NC
LeBron, Warree Carmichael	b. 1910, Elba, AL; d. 1998, Rockford, AL	AL / GA
Ledbetter, Alice McGehee	b. 1891, Montgomery, AL; d. 1984, Montgomery, AL	AL
Ledford, Freda Bernice Widder	b. 1894, Harrisburg, PA; d. 1959, Charlotte, NC	NC
Lee, Angelica Bodky	b. 1929, Berlin, Germany; d. 2012	NC
Lee, Doris Emrick	b. 1905, Aledo, IL; d. 1983, Clearwater, FL	DC / FL / GA
Lee, Ida N.	active in Washington, DC, 1897–1911	DC
Lee, Mattie Crawley	b. 1858, Pine Bluff, AR; d. 1935, Buncombe County, NC	AR / NC
Lee, Musier Taintor	b. 1909, New York, NY; d. 1968, Pittsburgh, PA	VA
Lee, Rosa	b. 1866, Memphis, TN; d. 1936, Memphis, TN	TN
Lee, Ruth Hudson	b. 1885, Ellisburg, NY; d. 1973, Ellisburg, NY	DC
Lee, Sarah Concord Everett	b. 1908, Rockingham County, NY; d. 1997, Spruce Pine, NC	NC
Lee, Selma Van Praag	b. 1879, New York, NY; d. 1968, Sarasota, FL	FL
Leech, Dorothy Sherman	b. 1913, Pittsburgh, PA; d. 2013, Sarasota, FL	FL
Leet, Marie Elizabeth	b. 1916, Charleston, WV; d. 1978, Charleston, WV	WV
Lehman, Louise Brasell	b. 1897, Orwood, MS; d. 1987, Memphis, TN	MS / TN
Leighton, Clare	b. 1898, London, England; d. 1989, Woodbury, CT	MD / NC
Leisenring, Mathilde Mueden	b. 1870, Washington, DC; d. 1949, Washington, DC	DC
Leist, Doris K.	b. 1911, New Albany, IN; d. 2004, Louisville, KY	KY
Lemly, Elizabeth "Bessie" Cary	b. 1871, Jackson, MS; d. 1947, Gulfport, MS	LA / MS
Lemm, Adele Marion Gawin	b. 1897, Milwaukee, WI; d. 1977, Memphis, TN	TN
L'Engle, Lucy Stelle Brown	b. 1889, New York, NY; d. 1978, Truro, MA	FL
Leòn/Leon, Eleanor Robson Smith	b. 1925, Bay City, MI; d. 2015, Ann Arbor, MI	NC
Leopold, Helen	active in Louisville, KY, 1936–1937	KY
Lesch, Alma Wallace	b. 1917, McCracken County, KY; d. 1999, Paducah, KY	KY
Levy, Miriam Flora	b. 1895, Franklin, LA; d. 1975, New Orleans, LA	LA
Lewis, Lalla Walker	b. 1912, Greenwood, MS; d. 2006, Greenwood, MS	LA / MS
Lewis, Laura Blocker	b. 1915, Manila, Philippines; active in 1940, New Orleans, LA	LA
Lewis, Louise Garland	active 1897–1924	GA / TN

Artist	Life Dates	Associated With
Lewis, Louise "Lucy" Dabney	b. 1906, Tuscaloosa, AL; d. 1990, Louisville, KY	KY
Lewis, Samella Sanders	b. 1924, New Orleans, LA	LA
Liebman, Marjorie C.	b. 1911; d. 2007, Memphis, TN	TN
Lieutand, Louise G.	active in Washington, DC, 1920–1935	DC
Liles, Nonie Margaret Brown	b. 1922, Bigheart, OK; d. 2013, Lake Charles, LA	LA
Lilienthal, Jane Drexler Roth	b. 1914, IL; d. 1983, Monterey, CA	MS / TN
Lilly, Thelma Raybeck	b. 1903, Friendsville, MD; d. 1985, Beckley, WV	MD / WV
Lindenfield, Lore Kadden	b. 1921, Wuppertal, Germany; d. 2010, Princeton, NJ	NC
Linger, Barbara	active in Washington, DC, 1951	DC
Lippitt, Margaret Walthour	b. 1872, Clayton, AL; d. 1964, Wilmington, NC	AL / DC / GA / NC
List, Crystal W.	active in Washington, DC, 1920	DC
Little, Mamie Burkhalter	b. 1869, Warrenton, GA	DC / GA
Livingston, Virginia Budd	b. 1898, Baltimore, MD	MD / SC
Livingstone, Aline T.	b. 1915, Tamaqua, PA; d. 2004, Jenkintown, PA	VA
Lobeck, Priscilla	b. about 1921, NJ; active in Atlanta, GA, 1946–1949	FL / GA
Lobingier, Elizabeth Miller	b. 1889; d. 1975, Washington, DC	DC / GA / NC
Lockerby, Elma E. Le Gro	b. 1861, Waupaca County, WI; d. 1949, Orlando, FL	FL
Lockwood, Mary Murray	b. 1861, Annapolis, MD; d. 1945, Washington, DC	DC / MD
Logan, Grace Redfield Boynton	b. 1873, Sterling, IL; d. 1944, Washington, DC	DC
Logan, Josephine Maria "Lillie"	b. 1843, Charleston, SC; d. 1923, Richmond, VA	SC / VA
Logan, Velma Enslen Kidd	b. 1912, Birmingham, AL; d. 1991, Maitland, FL	AL / FL
London, Edith Caspary	b. 1904, Berlin, Germany; d. 1997, Durham, NC	NC
Long, Elizabeth	active in Louisville, KY, 1932	KY
Long, Gulnare Baker	b. 1884, KY; d. 1965, Louisville, KY	KY
Long, Marion Lee	b. 1898, Louisville, KY; d. 1994, Jefferson County, KY	KY
Long, Ollie Palmore	b. 1899, Marion, AL; d. 1988, Marion, AL	AL / DC
Longman, Sarah Fannie May	b. 1860, Liverpool, England	TN
Longwater, Eleanor M. Goldberg	b. 1915, Savannah, GA; d. 1997, Savannah, GA	GA
Lonnegan, Ada Wilt	b. 1874, New Orleans, LA; d. 1963, New Orleans, LA	LA
Lossen, Emma	b. 1892, Wilmington, NC; d. 1976, Wilmington, NC	NC
Lotterhos, Edith	b. 1888, Crystal Springs, MS; d. 1965, Crystal Springs, MS	MS
Lotterhos, Helen Jay	b. 1905, McComb, MS; d. 1981, Jackson, MS	LA / MS
Lotz, Matilda	b. 1858, Franklin, TN; d. 1923, Tata, Hungary	TN
Loughborough, Margaret McClelland	b. 1872, Montgomery County, MD; d. 1947, Washington, DC	DC / MD
Loury, H. Sophie	b. 1858, Dayton, OH; d. after 1915, possibly in San Diego, CA	DC
Love, Josephine Harreld	b. 1914, Atlanta, GA; d. 2003, Detroit, MI	GA / NC
Loveless, Joan Couch Potter {Sihvonen}	b. 1925, San Angelo, TX; d. 2009, Taos, NM	NC
Lovell, Caroline Couper Stiles	b. 1862, Etowah Cliffs, GA; d. 1947, Savannah, GA	AL
Lovick, Annie Laurens Pescud	b. 1882, Raleigh, NC; d. 1968, Raleigh, NC	NC
Low, Juliette Gordon	b. 1860, Savannah, GA; d. 1927, Savannah, GA	GA
Low, Rebecca Cordis	b. 1897, Asheville, NC; d. 1980, Summerville, SC	NC / SC
Lowe, Mary Elizabeth Apperson	b. 1873, GA; d. 1957, Caryville, TN	GA / TN
Lowe, Willa May	b. 1871, Shinnston, WV; d. 1947, Shinnston, WV	WV
Loyacano, Mary Katharine Knoblock	b. 1910, Forest, MS; d. 2009, Forest, MS	MS

Artist	Life Dates	Associated With
Lucas, Clara Ester	b. 1856, Warren County, KY; d. 1950	KY
Lucas, Essie Leone Seavey	b. 1872, VT; d. 1932, Oconomowoc, WI	KY / VA
Lucas, Jean Williams	b. 1873, Hagerstown, MD	MD
Lucky, Eliza J.	active in Washington, DC, 1907–1920	DC
Luebkert, Rosina Bakersmith	b. 1893, Washington, DC; d. 1951, Washington, DC	DC
Lugano, Ines Somenzini	b. 1886, Verretto, Pavia, Italy; d. 1983, New Orleans, LA	LA
Luke, Anna	active in Manatee County, FL, 1937	FL
Lundborg, Elsa Marie	b. 1902	SC
Luria, Corinna Morgiana	b. 1890, New Orleans, LA; d. 1987, New Orleans, LA	LA
Lutz, Adelia Armstrong	b. 1859, Jefferson County, TN; d. 1931, Knoxville, TN	TN
Lwenstein, Loretto Christine	b. 1876, Washington, DC	DC
Lybrand, Lulu M.	b. 1888; d. 1976, Bethesda, MD	DC / MD
Lyles, Dorothy C.	active in Washington, DC, 1915–1917	DC
Lynch, Mary Pascard	b. 1877	NC
Lynn, Katharine Evans Norcross	b. 1875, Philadelphia, PA; d. 1930, Switzerland	DC
Lyon, Elizabeth Reeves	b. 1917; d. 2008, Winston-Salem, NC	NC
Lytle, Emma Knowlton	b. 1910, Perthshire, MS; d. 2000, Gunnison, MS	MS
MacAtee, Mary-Lane	active in Washington, DC, 1945	DC
MacCandless, Mary Madeline	b. 1885, Jackson, GA; d. 1983, Washington, DC	DC
MacCrowe, Flora E.	d. 1947, MD	MD
MacDowell, Elizabeth Kenton	b. 1858, Philadelphia, PA; d. 1953, Roanoke, VA	VA
Mack, Marie Elizabeth Hamrick	b. 1909, Cleveland County, NC; d. 2002, Shelby, NC	NC
MacKubin, Florence	b. 1857, Florence, Italy; d. 1918, Baltimore, MD	MD
MacMillan, Jane Meares Williams	b. 1882, Wilmington, NC; d. 1964, Wilmington, NC	NC
MacNaughton, Mary Hunter	b. 1892, Lockhart, TX	LA / VA
MacQueen, Virginia Hamilton	b. Fries, VA; d. 1972, Jacksonville, FL	FL / NC / VA
Magafan, Ethel Currie	b. 1916, Chicago, IL; d. 1993, Woodstock, NY	AR / DC / GA
Mahaffie, Isabel Cooper	b. 1892, Tacoma, WA; d. 1984, Bethesda, MD	DC / MD
Maher, Virginia	active in Washington, DC, 1917	DC
Mahier, Edith Albina	b. 1892, Baton Rouge, LA; d. 1967, Baton Rouge, LA	LA
Mahier, Lois W.	b. 1906; d. 1996, Baton Rouge, LA	LA
Mahoney, Elizabeth DuBose Porcher	b. 1908, Porcher's Bluff, SC; d. 2001, Charleston, SC	SC
Mahood, Sallie Lee Blount	b. 1864, Lynchburg, VA; d. 1953, Lynchburg, VA	VA
Majette, Vara Anna Swinney	b. 1875, Duluth, GA; d. 1974, St. Simons Island, GA	GA
Mallalieu, Olivia Pohlman	b. 1896, Baltimore, MD; d. 1980, Culpeper, VA	KY / MD / VA
Mallison, Euphame Clason	b. 1874, Annapolis, MD; d. 1962, Charlottesville, VA	MD / VA
Mallory, Frances "Daisy" Blocker Neely	b. 1871, Memphis, TN; d. 1969, Memphis, TN	TN
Malone, Blondelle Octavia Edwards	b. 1877, Bostwick, GA; d. 1951, Columbia, SC	GA / SC
Mamlok, Ursula	b. 1923, Berlin, Germany	NC
Manasse, Marianne/Marianna Bernhard	b. 1911, Breslau, Germany; d. 1984, Durham, NC	NC
Mangum, Elsie R.	b. 1865, MS; d. 1912, Coats, MS	MS
Manigault, Mary Jane	b. 1913, Mt. Pleasant, SC; d. 2010, Mt. Pleasant, SC	SC
Mannakee, Sarah Nelson Dale	b. 1877, Paterson, NJ; d. 1983, Sandy Spring, MD	DC / MD / WV
Manning, Eva	active in Washington, DC, 1920	DC

Artist	Life Dates	Associated With
Manning, Kate Covington	b. 1840, Columbia, SC; d. 1926, Clio, SC	SC
Mansfield, Blanche McManus	b. 1869 or 1870, East Feliciana, LA; d. 1929, New Orleans, LA	LA
Mapes, Doris Genevieve Williamson	b. 1920, Russellville, AR; d. 2013, Little Rock, AR	AR
Marbain, Sheila Rivka Oline {Ravin}	b. 1927, London, England; d. 2008, Brooklyn, NY	NC
Marden, Helen Grace Wright	b. 1919, Concord, MA	NC
Margoulies, Berta	b. 1907, Poland; d. 1996, Walnut Creek, CA	AR / DC
Markell, Isabella Mozier Banks	b. 1891, Superior, WI; d. 1980, New York, NY	FL / MD
Markham, Margaret Joy Pratt	b. 1894, Washington County, AR; d. 1976, Fayetteville, AR	AR
Marley, Geral Knowles	b. Jackson, MS; active 1920s	MS
Marlin, Hilda Gerarda Van Stockum	b. 1908, Holland; d. 2006, United Kingdom	DC
Marquette, Lena Mitchell	b. 1902, Ellisville, MS; d. 1997, Louisville, MS	MS
Marshall, Katherine Mateline	b. Natchez, MS	MS / TN
Marshall, May Chiswell	b. 1874, Markham, VA; d. 1959, Markham, VA	DC / VA / SC
Marshall, Pearl McDermott	b. 1888, Goodman, MS; d. 1970, Quitman, MS	MS
Marsteller, Pauline	active in Washington, DC, 1920	DC
Martin, Emma Norris	active in Washington, DC, 1892–1935	DC
Martin, Willa Gray	b. 1911, Greenville, SC; d. 2006, Rye, NY	SC
Mason, Ella May	b. 1912, Brookhaven, MS; d. 2005, Siloam Springs, AR	AR / MS / VA
Mason, Mary Stoddert Winfield	b. 1850, Jackson, TN; d. 1934, Elmsford, NY	TN
Mason, Mary Townsend	b. 1886; d. 1964	MD
Mason, Maud Mary	b. 1867, Russellville, KY; d. 1956, New Canaan, CT	KY
Mason, Nan	b. 1896, Woodstock, NY; d. 1982, Manatee County, FL	FL
Mason, Nanee F.	b. 1896; d. about 1982	KY
Massie, Martha Willis	b. 1894, Three Springs, VA; d. 1986, Lynchburg, VA	VA
Massie/Massy, Julia M.	b. 1869, Jackson, MS; d. 1949, New Orleans, LA	LA / MS
Master, Mary	active in Washington, DC, 1923	DC
Mathewson, Lucy Madeleine Stickney	b. 1866, France; d. 1918, Hartford, CT	DC
Matthews, Doris M.	active in Washington, DC, 1943	DC
Matthews, Kate Seston	b. 1870, New Albany, IN; d. 1956, Oldham County, KY	KY
Matthey, Jacqueline Katherine Tankersley	b. 1922, St. Louis, MO; d. 2003, Webster Groves, MO	NC
Maury, Cornelia Field	b. 1866, New Orleans, LA; d. 1942, St. Louis, MO	LA
Maxwell, Virginia	b. 1870, Wheeling, WV; d. 1951, Wheeling, WV	WV
May, Florence Lister Land	b. 1870, Caddo Parish, LA; d. 1937, New York, NY	LA
Mayer, Bena Virginia Frank	b. 1898, Norfolk, VA; d. 1994, New York, NY	VA
Mayer, Franziska	b. 1914, Hamburg, Germany; d. 1995	NC
Mayo, Isabel Bingham Jones	b. 1889, Amelia County, VA; d. 1972, Richmond, VA	VA
Mayo, Reba Elizabeth Harkey	b. 1895, Bryant's Mill, TX; d. 1974, Lexington, KY	KY
McAdams, Gladys Wilson	b. 1889, Cynthiana, KY; d. 1958, Fayette County, KY	KY
McAllister, Ethel M.	active in Washington, DC, 1919–1921	DC
McArthur, Betty	b. 1866, Port Gibson, MS; d. 1945, Atlanta, GA	AL / LA / MS
McBryde, Cora Bolton	b. 1839, Richmond, VA; d. 1920, Blacksburg, VA	SC / VA
McCallum, Corrie Parker {Halsey}	b. 1914, Sumter, SC; d. 2009, Charleston, SC	FL / GA / SC
McCarl, Helen Weathers	b. 1900, Richmond, VA; d. 1985, Wilmington, NC	NC / VA

Artist	Life Dates	Associated With
McCarthy, Helen Mary Kiner	b. 1884, Poland, OH; d. 1927, Philadelphia, PA	NC
McCauley, Caroline Kaufmann	b. 1919, Savannah, GA; d. 1999, Decatur, GA	DC / GA / NC / VA
McClean, Roberta Fisk	b. 1882, Russellville, KY; d. 1975, Russellville, KY	KY
McClure, Dorothy Sue	b. 1934; d. 2008	NC
McClure, Flossie Sheriff	b. 1892; d. 1975, Lexington, KY	KY
McComb, Marie Louise	b. 1883, Louisville, KY; d. 1973, Winter Park, FL	FL / KY
McCoy, Daisy B.	active in Washington, DC, 1920s–1930s	DC
McCoy, Margaret	b. 1845, Grant County, WV; d. 1929, Franklin, WV	WV
McCravey, Mary Katharine Knoblock Loyacano (see Loyacano, Mary Katharine Knoblock)		
McCullough, Geraldine Hamilton	b. 1917, Kingston, AR; d. 2008, New Edinburg, AR	AR
McDavid, Mittie Owen	b. 1873, Madison, AL; d. 1948, Birmingham, AL	AL
McDowell, Magdalen Harvey	b. 1829, Fincastle, VA; d. 1918, Ashland, KY	KY
McFarland, Pearl	active in Washington, DC, 1920s	DC
McGavock, Bessie Hunter Dawson	b. 1889, Maury County, TN; d. 1982, Columbia, TN	TN
McGee, Olivia Jackson Parkhurst	b. 1915, Clemson, SC; d. 1987, Clemson, SC	SC
McGehee, Helen Mahood	b. 1892, Lynchburg, VA; d. 1980, Lynchburg, VA	MS / VA
McGinnis, Geraldine Gunter	b. 1921, Sanford, NC	NC
McGowen, Ruth	b. 1876, Milwaukee, WI; d. 1962, Fair Haven, CT	DC
McIntire, Katharine Angela	b. 1876, Richmond, VA; d. 1960, Charlottesville, VA	VA
McIntyre, Florence Makin	b. 1878, Memphis, TN; d. 1963, Memphis, TN	TN
McKee, Lena Meyler	b. 1874, Shepherdsville, KY; d. 1955, Warren County, KY	KY
McKenzie, Annie Cole Hawkins	b. 1848; d. 1917	TN
McKinstry, Grace Emmajean	b. 1859, Fredonia, NY; d. 1936, Minneapolis, MN	DC
McLaughlin, Willie Cyrene	b. 1878, Pinson, AL; d. 1967, Birmingham, AL	AL
McLaws, Virginia Randall	b. 1868, Augusta, GA; d. 1967, Savannah, GA	VA
McMahan, Melva Kirkpatrick	b. 1918, VA; d. 1999	NC / VA
McMahon, Charlotte L.	active in Washington, DC, 1914–1917	DC
McMillan, Mrs. George E.	active in Washington, DC, 1917	DC
McMullen, Lilie Haynes	active in Louisville, KY, 1936	KY
McNamara, Lena Randolph Brooke	b. 1890, Norfolk, VA; d. 1983, Norfolk, VA	VA
McNamara, Mary E.	active in Washington, DC, 1925	DC
McNett, Elizabeth Vardell	b. 1896, New Bern, NC; d. 1988, Laurinburg, NC	NC
McNulty, Agnes Gabrielle Tait	b. 1894, New York, NY; d. 1981, Santa Fe, NM	NC
McNulty, Kathryn Marie	b. 1897, Bakersfield, CA; d. 1993, Tazewell, VA	VA
McWhorter, Jean	b. 1932, MS; d. 2011, Columbia, SC	GA / MS / SC
Mead, Lucile Elliott	b. 1887, Bellefontaine, OH; d. 1944, Bradenton, FL	FL / VA
Meade, Mary Belle Long	b. 1910, Norfolk, VA; d. 2008, Richmond, VA	LA / VA
Means, Sarah Jane Henderson	b. 1826, Dresden, TN; d. 1924, Hopkinsville, KY	KY / TN
Meares, Mary Burkett	b. 1928, Salisbury, NC	FL / NC
Meegan, Beatrice	active in Washington, DC, 1913	DC
Meegan, Blanche Van C.	active in Washington, DC, 1896–1924	DC
Meetze, Sarah R.	active in Washington, DC, 1902–1920	DC
Melchers, Corinne Lawton Mackall	b. 1880, Baltimore, VA; d. 1955, Falmouth, VA	VA

Artist	Life Dates	Associated With
Melton, Catherine Parker	b. 1888, Nashville, TN; d. 1959, Nashville, TN	DC/TN
Menk, Hazel W. Cameron	b. 1888, St. Paul, MN; d. 1956, FL	DC/FL/VA
Mercer, Geneva	b. 1889, Jefferson, AL; d. 1984, Demopolis, AL	AL
Mercke, Evelyn Scales	b. about 1904, VA; active in Lousiville, KY, 1930–1939	KY
Merilh, Mathilde Olivia Marie	b. 1889, New Orleans, LA; d. 1934, Metairie, LA	LA
Merrill, Olive Katherine/Katharine Clapp	b. 1876, Milwaukee, WI; d. 1962, Fair Haven, CT	FL/SC
Meyer, Lillie Bennett	b. 1881, Taylorsville, KY; d. 1959, Charlestown, IN	KY
Meyer, Louise M.	active in Washington, DC, 1924	DC
Meyer, Mary Eno Pinchot	b. 1920, New York, NY; d. 1964, Georgetown, DC	DC
Middleton, Sallie Williamson Ellington	b. 1926, Washington, DC; d. 2009, Asheville, NC	DC/NC/SC
Mierisch, Dorothea	b. 1885, NY; d. 1977, Brielle, NJ	SC
Mignon, Josephine Cressy Faget	b. 1896, New Orleans, LA; d. 2000, New Orleans, LA	LA
Mikell, Minnie Robertson	b. 1891, Charleston, SC; d. 1987, Charleston, SC	SC
Miles, Emma Bell	b. 1879, Evansville, IN; d. 1919, Chattanooga, TN	TN
Miles, Jeanne Patterson	b. 1908, Baltimore, MD; d. 1999, Los Angeles, CA	MD
Miller, Bessie Alexander	b. about 1877, Cabell County, WV; d. 1959, Barboursville, WV	WV
Miller, Cora Ella	b. 1868, Jenkintown, PA; d. 1940, Pittsburgh, PA	DC
Miller, Eleazer Hutchinson	b. 1831, Shepherdstown, WV; d. 1921, Washington, DC	WV
Miller, Ellen W.	active in Washington, DC, 1918–1924	DC
Miller, Josephine Anne Braendle Traynor	b. 1892, Washington, DC	DC
Miller, Marguerite Cuttino	b. 1895, Charleston, SC; d. 1956, Charleston, SC	SC
Miller, Mariema	active in 1952	DC/GA
Milligan, Kizzie Gladys	b. 1892, LaRue, OH; d. 1973, Tryon, NC	DC/NC
Milner, Caroline Connelly	b. 1917, Raleigh, NC	NC
Miltenberger, Lucia A.	b. 1873, New Orleans, LA; d. 1955, New Orleans, LA	LA
Mims, Eliza	b. 1862; d. 1968, Edgefield, SC	SC
Minish, Mary Virginia Duncan	b. 1910, KY; d. 1997, Louisville, KY	KY
Minnich, Lenora Florence Linger	b. 1889, Lewis County, WV; d. 1963, Weston, WV	WV
Mitchell, Gladys Vinson	b. 1894, Albuquerque, NM; d. 1968, St. Augustine, FL	DC/FL
Mitchell, Sue Lavinia	b. 1922, Copperhill, TN; d. 2012, Copperhill, TN	TN
Mixter, Felicie Waldo Howell	b. 1897, Honolulu, HI; d. 1968	DC
Mize, Mary	b. about 1834	KY
Moffatt, Adah Terrell	b. 1881, Vincennes, IN; d. 1930, Fairfax, VA	DC/VA
Moffett, Mary Elvish Mantz	b. 1863, Perry, IL; d. 1940, Mt. Vernon, NY	LA
Mohan, Jennie Cramer	b. 1874; d. 1956, Huntsville, AL	AL
Moise, Alice Leigh	b. 1905, New Orleans, LA; d. 1997, New Orleans, LA	LA
Molinary, Marie Madeleine Seebold	b. 1866, New Orleans, LA; d. 1948, New Orleans, LA	LA
Moncure, Elise "Lisa" Vance	b. 1886, Gallipolis, OH; d. 1960, Aquia, VA	VA
Montague, Harriotte Lee Taliaferro	b. 1871, Gloucester, VA; d. 1947, Gloucester, VA	VA
Montgomery, Alberta	active in Washington, DC, 1920s	DC
Montgomery, Caroline "Carrie" Garland Lewis	b. 1865, Montevallo, AL; d. 1951, Birmingham, AL	AL
Moomaw, Catharine	b. 1912, Roanoke, VA; d. 2000, Madison, WI	VA
Moore, Mary Virginia	b. 1878, Brownsville, TN; d. 1934, Brownsville, TN	TN

Artist	Life Dates	Associated With
Moore, Ruth C.	active in Washington, DC, 1923–1924	DC
Moore, Ruth Huntington	b. 1866, New York, NY; d. 1936, Raleigh, NC	NC
Moore, Susan Elizabeth	b. 1926, Williamston, NC; d. 2013, Winston-Salem, NC	NC
Mora, Emma Gladys	b. about 1927	DC/NC
Morales, Desdemona Agnes Wade	b. 1927, Washington, DC; d. 1992, Washington, DC	DC
Moran, Mary Eulalie	b. 1865, Washington, DC; d. 1963, Washington, DC	DC
Morel, May Sydnor	b. 1885, New Orleans, LA; d. 1920, New Orleans, LA	LA
Morgan, Adelaide Baker	b. Cleveland, OH; active in Washington, DC, 1923–1924	DC
Morgan, Annie Germany Stephenson	b. 1859, Memphis, TN; d. 1944, Memphis, TN	TN
Morgan, Barbara Brooks Johnson	b. 1900, Buffalo, KS; d. 1992, North Tarrytown, NY	NC
Morgan, Florence Gross	b. Marietta, OH; active in Washington, DC, 1940s–1950s	DC
Morgan, Georgia Weston	b. 1869, Floyd County, VA; d. 1951, Lynchburg, VA	VA
Morgan, Gertrude Williams	b. 1900, LaFayette, AL; d. 1980, New Orleans, LA	LA
Morgan, Gladys Rowley Butler	b. 1899, Houma, LA; d. 1981, Shreveport, LA	LA
Morgan, Samantha Jane Atkeson	b. 1843, Buffalo, WV; d. 1926, Winfield, WV	WV
Morley, Margaret Warner	b. 1858, Montrose, IA; d. 1923, Washington, DC	DC/NC
Morrell, Cordelia D. Young	b. 1868, Buckeystown, MD; d. 1938, Washington, DC	DC/MD
Morrell, Imogene Robinson	b. 1828, Attleboro, MA; d. 1908, Washington, DC	DC
Morrell, Mary Ogden	b. 1874, TN; d. 1935, Knoxville, TN	TN
Morris, Helen V.	active in Washington, DC, 1904–1917	DC
Morris, Katherine	active in Raleigh, NC, 1940	NC
Morrison, Mary Coples	b. 1908, Petersburg, VA	DC/VA
Morriss, Mary Rachel	b. 1904, Memphis, TN; d. 1996, Shelby County, TN	TN
Morse, Ruth Eleanor	b. 1887, Watertown, MA; d. 1992	SC
Morton, Christina May Boles	b. 1878, Dardanelle, AR; d. 1957, Dardanelle, AR	AR
Morton, Louise E. Jennings	b. 1870, Nashville, TN; d. 1947, Winchester, TN	TN
Morton, Nancy Bowden	active in Louisville, KY, 1936	KY
Moseley, Alice Latimer	b. 1909, Birmingham, AL; d. 2004, Bay St. Louis, MS	MS/TN
Moseley, Glenna "Glennie"	b. 1876, Chattooga County, GA; d. 1972, Winnetka, IL	GA/MS
Moseley, Helen Allston DuPré	b. 1887, Spartanburg, SC; d. 1984, Spartanburg, SC	SC
Moser, Martha Ingersoll Scoville	b. 1857, Cornwall, CT; d. 1941, White Plains, NY	DC/GA
Moser, Sarah Jane Irby	b. 1842, Union County, NC; d. 1925, Kannapolis, NC	NC
Moses, Anna Robertson [a.k.a. Grandma Moses]	b. 1860, Greenwich, NY; d. 1961, Hoosick Falls, NY	VA
Mosher, Catherine "Kate" E. Perry	b. 1836, Warsaw, KY; d. 1926, Covington, KY	KY
Moshier, Elizabeth Alice	b. 1901, Utica, NY	NC
Moulton, Sue Buckingham	b. 1873, Hartford, CT; d. after 1956	DC
Muhlhofer, Mary Elizabeth	b. 1877, Baltimore, MD; d. 1950, Washington, DC	DC/MD
Muldoon, Hannah L.	b. 1868 or 1869, KY; d. 1959, Jefferson County, KY	KY
Mulford, Margarete Lent	b. 1896, Washington, DC; d. 1989, McLean, VA	DC/VA
Muller-Uri, Hildegarde Petronella Bernhardina	b. 1894, New York, NY; d. 1990, St. Augustine, FL	FL
Munch, Margaret Obee	b. 1884, Whitehouse, OH; d. 1961, Cary, NC	NC
Munger, Anne Wells	b. 1862, Springfield, MA; d. 1945, Gulfport, MS	LA/MS
Munn, Marguerite Campbell	b. 1886, Washington, DC; d. 1979, Charlottesville, VA	DC/VA

Munroe, Sarah Sewell	b. about 1870, Brooklyn, NY; d. 1946	DC
Munz, Edna Hammer	b. 1913; d. 1984, Louisville, KY	KY
Murdaugh, Ella Lee Johnson	b. 1877, Bartow, FL; d. 1966, Orangeburg, SC	FL / SC
Murdoch, Dora Louise	b. 1857, New Haven, CT; d. 1933, Baltimore, MD	MD
Murdoch, Eleanor P.	active in Washington, DC, 1910–1921	DC
Murphy, Lelia Mae	Laurens, SC	NC / SC
Murphy, Lucile Desbouillons	b. 1873, Savannah, GA; d. 1956, Savannah, GA	GA
Murphy, Margaret Augusta	b. 1908, Savannah, GA; d. 1991, Savannah, GA	GA
Murray, Faith Earnestine Cornish	b. 1897, SC; d. 1984, Taylors, SC	DC / SC
Murray, Rosa Rainold Graner	b. 1904, New Orleans, LA; d. 1962, New Orleans, LA	LA
Myrick, Ann L.	b. about 1910, Greensboro, NC	NC
Namias, Edith Paipert	b. 1909, Somerville, MA; d. 2003, Sharon, MA	VA
Nash, Anne	b. 1884, Warwickshire, England; d. 1968, Tryon, NC	NC
Nash, Anne Mauger Taylor	b. 1884, Pittsboro, NC; d. 1968, Savannah, GA	NC / SC
Nash, Diana Lillian	b. 1873, Warwickshire, England; d. 1952, Tryon, NC	NC / VA
Nash, Marguerite L.	active in Washington, DC, 1909–1917	DC
Nash, Mary Screven Arnold	b. 1876, Savannah, GA; d. after 1940	GA / NC
Nay, Mary Spencer	b. 1913, Crestwood, KY; d. 1993, Provincetown, MA	KY
Neilson, Louisa Wright (see Ford, Louisa Wright Neilson)		
Nell, Antonia "Tony"	b. 1881, Washington, DC; d. 1960, New York, NY	DC
Nelson, Belle E.	b. 1912–1914, Washington, DC	DC
Neville, Katherine "Kate" Young	b. 1876, Camden, AL; d. 1967	AL
Newberry, Florence C.	active in Washington, DC, 1920–1925	DC
Newby, Ruth Warren	b. 1886, Goff, KS; d. 1952, Tucson, AZ	FL
Newcastle, Lena May	b. 1867 or 1868, Pittsfield, MA; d. 1951, Mineral Springs, NC	FL / NC
Newell, Natalie	active in Miami, FL, 1922–1923	FL
Newhoff, Theresa C.	b. 1908, Versailles, KY; d. 1996, Lexington, KY	KY / NC
Newman, Irene Hodes	b. 1900, Cameron, MO; d. 1982, New York, NY	GA
Newman, Willie Betty	b. 1863?, Murfreesboro, TN; d. 1935, Nashville, TN	TN
Newton, Amanda A.	b. 1858, PA; d. 1943, Washington, DC	DC
Ney, Franzisca Bernadina Wilhelmina Elisabeth "Elisabet"	b. 1833, Münster, Germany; d. 1907, Austin, TX	GA
Nicholson, Leona Fischer	b. 1875, St. Francisville, LA; d. 1966, New Orleans, LA	LA
Nickels, Myrtle	b. 1871, Bristol, TN; d. 1948, Bristol, TN	TN
Nickerson, Jennie Ruth {Greacen}	b. 1905, Appleton, WI; d. 1997	NC
Nickson, Lia	b. 1924, Durham, NC; d. 2010, New York, NY	NC
Niles, Rosemond	b. 1881, Portsmouth, NH; d. 1960, Old Lyme, CT	VA
Ninas, Jane Smith	b. 1913, Fond du Lac, WI; d. 2005	LA
Nirenberg, Rosalind Abramson	b. 1901, Norfolk, VA; d. 1938, Albany, NY	VA
Nison, Jean	b. 1922, Egypt	NC
Nix, Frances Nimmo Greene {Pitts}	b. 1907, Montgomery, AL; d. 1982, Montgomery, AL	AL
Noble, Ida S. Chandler	b. 1865, Beech Grove, TN; d. 1947, Beech Grove, TN	TN
Nohowel, Margaret Lily Dressler	b. 1888, Leipzig, Germany; d. 1969, North Elba, NY	DC
Northrop, Christine	b. 1897, Pass Christian, MS; d. 1975, Pass Christian, MS	GA / MS / TN

Artist	Life Dates	Associated With
Norton, Effie C. Y.	active in Washington, DC, 1911–1922	DC
Norton, Jane Lewis Morton	b. 1908, Louisville, KY; d. 1988, Pittsfield, MA	KY / MD
Nottingham, Mary Elizabeth Day	b. 1907, Salisbury, CT; d. 1956, Staunton, VA	NC / VA
Nourse, Elizabeth	b. 1859, Mount Healthy, OH; d. 1938, Paris, France	TN
November, Sara D.	b. 1902, Richmond, VA; d. 1983, Richmond, VA	VA
Noyes, Bertha E.	b. 1876, Washington, DC; d. 1966, Washington, DC	DC
Nungester, Mildred Bernice (see Wolfe, Mildred Bernice Nungester)		
Nunnally, Catherine	b. 1919; d. 1984, Fort Gaines, GA	GA
O'Bannon, Hildegarde Whitney	b. 1897, IN; d. 1976, Louisville, KY	KY
O'Brien, Nell Louise Pomeroy	b. 1899, New Orleans, LA; d. 1966, New Orleans, LA	LA
Ochs, Camille Caheen Hagedorn	b. 1910, Birmingham, AL; d. 2000, New Orleans, LA	AL / GA / LA
O'Day, Caroline Love Goodwin	b. 1875, Perry, GA; d. 1943, Rye, NY	GA
Odom, Minnie Rae	b. about 1908, AL	AL
Odum, Martha Ann Huff	b. 1917; d. 1995, Athens, GA	GA
Oelschig, Augusta Denk {Petressen}	b. 1918, Savannah, GA; d. 2000, Savannah, GA	AL / GA
O'Fallon, Virginia	b. 1897	KY
Ogburn, Hilda Lanier	b. 1895, Guilford County, NC; d. 1984, Walnut Cove, NC	NC
O'Keeffe, Georgia Totto	b. 1887, Sun Prairie, WI; d. 1986, Santa Fe, NM	SC / VA
O'Keeffe, Ida Ten Eyck	b. 1889, Sun Prairie, WI; d. 1961, Whittier, CA	AL / NC / VA
O'Kelley, Mattie Lou	b. 1908, Maysville, GA; d. 1997, Decatur, GA	GA
Oliphant, Carol Elizabeth Stephens	b. 1898, Washington County, IA; d. 1964, Baldwin County, GA	GA / SC
Oliver, Annie McIntosh Petree	b. 1893, Franklin County, AL; d. 1985, Birmingham, AL	AL
Oliver, Edith Walker	b. 1889, Chicago, IL; d. 1979, St. Augustine, FL	FL
Oliver, Elisabeth Paxton	b. 1891, Rockridge County, VA; d. 1977, Tryon, NC	GA / MD / NC / VA
O'Meallie, Kate "Kitty" Morrison Chamness	b. 1916, Bennettsville, SC; d. 2014, Cary, NC	NC / SC
O'Neill, Mary H.	active in Washington, DC, 1915–1916	DC
O'Neill, Ruth Heilprin/Helprin {Hammerslough} [R. Ford Harper, pseud.]	b. 1883, Washington, DC; d. 1983, Santa Barbara, CA	DC
Oppenheimer, Selma Levy	b. 1898, Baltimore, MD; d. 1988, Baltimore, MD	MD
Orr, Helen LaFrance	b. 1919, Graves County, KY	KY
Orrick, Agnes Gertrude	b. 1880, Canton, MS; d. 1966, Gary, IN	MS
Ortmayer, Constance	b. 1902, NY; d. 1988, Morristown, TN	AL / FL
Osgood, Ruth L.	b. 1887, Minneapolis, MN; d. 1977, Alexandria, VA	DC / VA
Oudin, Dorothy Lyman Savage	b. 1898, Baltimore, MD; d. 1956, Cooperstown, NY	MD
Owen, Eva Vatter	b. 1917, LA; d. 2005, Tulsa, OK	LA
Page, Cordelia	b. 1878, MS	MS
Page, Josephine	active in Washington, DC, 1912–1932	DC
Page, Katherine Stuart	b. Cambridge, MA	DC / MD / VA
Pagon, Katharine Dunn	b. 1892, Chestnut Hill, PA; d. 1985, Baltimore, MD	MD
Paine, Mary "May" Williman	b. 1873, Charleston, SC; d. 1941, Savannah, GA	SC
Pajerski, Elizabeth Mitchell	b. 1915, Meridian, MS; d. 2003, Vicksburg, MS	MS
Palmer, Adaline Osburn	b. 1817, Rippon, WV; d. 1906, Rippon, WV	WV
Palmer, Pauline Lennards	b. 1867, McHenry, IL; d. 1938, Trondheim, Norway	SC

Artist	Life Dates	Associated With
Picken, Claire Deborah {Jaeger}	affiliated with Black Mountain College	NC
Pierce, Delilah Williams	b. 1904, Washington, DC; d. 1992, Washington, DC	DC
Pierce, Martha Lily	b. 1873, Cumberland, WV; d. 1948, Lincoln, NE	WV
Pinhey, Amy Victorina Putman	b. 1850, New York, NY; d. 1931, Geneva, Switzerland	DC
Pinkerton, Lewers Lucile Wilkinson	b. 1910, Washington, DC; d. 1995, Orleans, MA	DC
Pitkin, Anna Denio	b. 1844, Louisville, KY; d. 1929, Tryon, NC	KY/NC
Plant, Olive	active in Washington, DC, 1919–1924	DC
Platt, Ella M.	active in Washington, DC, 1897–1926	DC
Plotkin, Edna Hibel	b. 1917, Boston, MA; d. 2015, Palm Beach Gardens, FL	FL
Poe, Elisabeth Ellicott	b. 1888, Philadelphia, PA; d. 1947, Washington, DC	DC
Pollak, Theresa	b. 1899, Richmond, VA; d. 2002, Richmond, VA	VA/SC
Pollak, Virginia Leigh Morris	b. 1898, Norfolk, VA; d. 1967, New York, NY	VA
Pollard, Ann Carter	b. 1930, Winston-Salem, NC	NC
Pollard, Mabel Carpenter	b. 1878, Baltimore, MD; d. 1953, Baltimore, MD	GA/MD
Pollitzer, Anita Lily {Edson}	b. 1894, Charleston, SC; d. 1975, Queens, NY	SC
Pook/Pooke, Harriett E. F.	active in Washington, DC, 1923–1924	DC
Poor, Anne	b. 1918, New York, NY; d. 2002, Nyack, NY	DC/TN
Poppenheim, Mary Barnett	b. 1866, Charleston, SC; d. 1936, Charleston, SC	SC
Porter, Beata Beach	b. 1911, Rome, Italy; d. 2006, Putnam Valley, NY	FL/GA
Porter, Doris Lucile McLean	b. 1897, Norfolk, VA; d. 1994, Portsmouth, VA	VA
Porter, Laura Shaefer	b. 1891, Fort Edward, NY	DC/FL/GA
Porter, Vida L.	b. 1889, Sherman, TX; d. 1985, Washington, DC	DC
Postle, Joy	b. 1896, Chicago, IL; d. 1989, Orlando, FL	FL
Poteat, Ida Isabella	b. 1858, Forest Home, NC; d. 1940, Raleigh, NC	NC
Potter, Bertha Herbert	b. 1895, Nashville, TN; d. 1949, Santa Fe, NM	TN
Powell, Georgette Seabrook	b. 1916, Charleston, SC; d. 2011, Palm Coast, FL	SC
Powers, Harriet	b. 1837, Athens, GA; d. 1910, Clarke County, GA	GA
Prather, Winifred Helen Palmer	b. 1912, Plainfield, NJ; d. 1993, Bucks County, PA	LA
Pratt, Hazel M.	b. Frankfort, KS	MS
Pratt, Ruth C.	active in Tryon, NC, 1921	NC
Prejza, Deborah Evelyn Sussman	b. 1931, Brooklyn, NY; d. 2014, Los Angeles, CA	NC
Preston, Blanche Barger	b. 1873, Fayetteville, WV; d. 1934, Beckley, WV	LA/WV
Prewitt, Ella May	b. 1889; d. 1990, Danville, KY	KY
Price, Irene Roberta	b. 1900, Savannah, GA; d. 1971, Wilmington, NC	DC/GA/NC
Price, Lucie Harris Locke	b. 1904, Valdosta, GA; d. 1989, Santa Fe, NM	GA/LA
Price, Mary Elizabeth	b. 1877, Martinsburg, WV; d. 1965, Trenton, NJ	WV
Price, Rosalie Pettus	b. 1913, Birmingham, AL; d. 2003, Birmingham, AL	AL
Price, Sarah "Sadie" Frances	b. 1849, Evansville, IN; d. 1903, Bowling Green, KY	KY
Pride, Joy	b. 1909, Lexington, KY; d. 1998	KY
Prince, Ethel T.	active in Washington, DC, 1905–1935	DC
Prince, Lottie D.	active in Washington, DC, 1920–1935	DC
Protas, Helen Frank	b. 1908, Hamilton, Ontario, Canada; d. 1961, Hamilton, Ontario, Canada	FL
Pryor, Eleanor Hancock	b. 1874, Lexington, KY; d. 1966, Lexington, KY	KY

Artist	Life Dates	Associated With
Pugh, Sarah Mabel	b. 1891, Morrisville, NC; d. 1986, Raleigh, NC	NC
Purefoy, Heslope	b. 1884, Chapel Hill, NC; d. 1934, Asheville, NC	NC
Purser, Mary May	b. 1913, Chicago, IL; d. 1986, Gainesville, FL	AR / FL
Puryear, Jr., Mrs. B.	active in Washington, DC, 1920–1935	DC
Putnam, Brenda	b. 1890, Minneapolis, MN; d. 1975, Stamford, CT	DC
Putzki, Kate Stuart Stirling	b. 1859, Newfoundland, Canada; d. 1941, Washington, DC	DC
Pyle, Mrs. Frank Wilkes	b. 1878, San Saba, TX	DC
Quaintance, Helen M. Yocum	b. 1871, WI; d. 1940, MD	DC / MD
Quarterman, Leonora	b. 1911, Savannah, GA; d. 1979, Savannah, GA	GA
Radley, Rose Burr	b. 1866, MI; d. 1944, San Diego, CA	DC
Raffle, Mary E.	b. 1917, MD	MD / VA
Raines, Mary "Minnie" Lanier	b. 1862, Raines, TN; d. 1955, Memphis, TN	TN
Ramseur, Mary Dodson	b. 1864, Caswell County, NC; d. 1935, Deweese, NC	NC / SC
Rankin, Dorothy Taylor	b. 1889, PA; d. 1977, Alexandria, VA	DC / VA
Rannells, Doris Krumm Wilson	b. 1897, Columbus, OH; d. 1981, Lexington, KY	KY
Rathborne, Jean Mary	b. 1913, Mobile, AL; d. 2005, Franklin, TN	AL / GA / TN
Raul, Minnie Louise Pyles {Briggs}	b. 1886, Camp Springs, MD; d. 1955, Washington, DC	DC / MD
Ravenel, Pamela Hart Brown Vinton {Strunz}	b. 1883, Brookline, MA; d. 1955, Woodstock, NY	GA / MD
Ravenscroft, Ellen	b. 1876, Jackson, MS; d. 1949, New York, NY	MS
Rawlins, Arline McLean Perkins	b. 1899, Bowling Green, KY; d. 1962, Bowling Green, KY	KY
Raymond, Grace Russell	b. 1876, Mount Vernon, OH; d. 1967, Winfield, KS	DC
Raymond, Kathryn Tileston	b. 1983, MA; d. 1943, Pinellas County, FL	FL
Raymond, Madeline Gordon	b. 1928, Washington, DC	DC / NC
Reading, Alice Matilda	b. 1859, Shasta County, CA; d. 1939, Shasta County, CA	DC
Reath, Dorothy Fisher Foulke	b. 1916, Montchanin, DE; d. 1988, Easton, MD	MD / NC
Redfield, Mary Bannister	b. 1883, Newark, NJ	DC
Rees, Mary de Berniere Graves	b. 1886, Chapel Hill, NC; d. 1950, Chapel Hill, NC	NC
Reese, Anabel Hays	b. 1890, Petersburg, VA; d. 1973, Louisville, KY	KY / VA
Reeves, Elizabeth Lovejoy Street	b. 1910, MA; d. 1994, Chapel Hill, NC	NC
Regan, Kathyrine	active in New Orleans, LA, 1930s	LA
Regester/Regesteri, Charlotte	b. 1883, Baltimore, MD; d. 1964, Rockport, MA	MD
Reichle, Leona B.	b. 1904; d. 1969, Jeffersonville, IN	KY
Reichman, Josephine Lemos	b. 1864, Louisville, KY; d. 1938, Chicago, IL	KY
Reid, Bessie C. Beall	b. 1871, Lenoir, NC; d. 1963, Lenoir, NC	NC
Reid, Celia Cregor	b. 1895, Springfield, KY; d. 1956, St. Augustine, FL	FL / KY
Reid, Dorothy Buchanan	b. 1918, Tacoma, WA	NC
Reid, Florence Sims	b. 1891, Birmingham, AL; d. 1973, Richmond, VA	AL
Reilly, Elvira	b. 1899, Oak Ridge, NJ; d. 1958, Oak Ridge, NJ	FL
Reindel, Edna	b. 1894, Detroit, MI; d. 1990, Santa Monica, CA	GA
Reiss, Mary Alice Peak	b. 1909, LA; d. 1981, New Orleans, LA	LA
Rembert, Catharine Phillips	b. 1905, Columbia, SC; d. 1990, Tryon, NC	MD / NC / SC
Remsen, Helen Quarton	b. 1896, Algona, IA; d. 1975, Sarasota, FL	FL
Rendall, Theodora Vance	b. 1884, Bossier Parish, LA; d. 1966 (buried in Bossier Parish, LA)	LA

Artist	Life Dates	Associated With
Rennie, Helen Sewell	b. 1906, Cambridge, MD; d. 1989	DC / MD
Resnick, Elizabeth Cowles Gellhorn	b. 1927, Pasadena, CA; d. 2008, MA	NC
Rettstatt, E. Myrna	b. 1892, PA	DC
Reuer, Eleanor Griswold	b. 1929, Durham, NC; d. 2017, Raleigh, NC	NC
Rex, Edna Leroy Crenshaw	b. 1893, VA; d. 1972, Richmond, VA	VA
Rhett, Antoinette Francisca Guerard	b. 1884, Baltimore, MD; d. 1964, Charleston, SC	MD / SC
Rhett, Hanna McCord	b. 1871, Columbia, SC; d. 1940, Brevard, NC	NC / SC
Rhett, Mary Alicia	b. 1915, Savannah, GA; d. 2014, Charleston, SC	GA / SC
Rhoades, Katherine Nash	b. 1885, New York, NY; d. 1965, New York, NY	DC / TN
Rhoads, Katherine	b. 1895, Richmond, VA; d. 1938, Richmond, VA	VA
Rhodes, Jessie	b. 1900; d. 1972	AL / LA
Rice, Ann Louise O'Hanlon	b. 1908, Ashland, KY; d. 1998, Mill Valley, CA	KY
Rice, Barbara Stone	b. 1925, Brooklyn, NY; d. 2008, Topanga, CA	NC
Rice, Emma Deuel	active in Washington, DC, 1906–1935	DC
Rice, Jenny Eakin Delony [a.k.a. Jenny Delony; Jenny Meyrowitz]	b. 1862, Washington, AR; d. 1949, Little Rock, AR	AR
Richards, Ella E.	b. 1899, VA	MD / VA
Richards, Martha "Matsy" Wynn	b. 1888, Greenville, MS; d. 1960, Greenville, MS	MS
Richardson, Mrs. L. E.	b. 1898; d. 1940	VA
Ricketts, Agnes Edmund Fairlie	b. about 1880, Glasgow, Scotland; d. 1964	GA / MS
Riddle, Kate	b. 1866, VA; d. after 1930	VA / WV
Riley, Mary Gine	b. 1883, Washington, DC; d. 1939, Washington, DC	DC
Ritter, Marie Antoinette	b. 1901, Baltimore, MD; d. 1993, Baltimore, MD	MD
Rivers, Cornelia McIntire	b. 1912, Savannah, GA; d. 1999, Savannah, GA	GA
Rivers, Rosetta Raulston	b. 1865, Barnesville, GA; d. 1946, GA	GA
Rives, Sarah Landon	b. 1874, Mobile, AL; d. 1958, Castle Hill, VA	AL / VA
Robbins, Ellen	b. 1828, Watertown, MA; d. 1905, Boston, MA	FL
Robbins, Hulda Dornblatt	b. 1910, Atlanta, GA; d. 2011, Atlantic City, NJ	GA
Robbins, Jenny Loring	b. 1866; d. 1946	KY
Roberts, Dolly Anderson	b. 1916, Roanoke, VA; d. 2002, Clearwater, FL	AL / FL / VA
Roberts, Edith Lucille Howard	b. 1885, Bellows Falls, VT; d. 1960, Moorestown, NJ	NC
Roberts, Helen	active in Washington, DC, 1917	DC
Roberts, Janet Chloe Heling	affiliated with Black Mountain College	NC
Roberts, Lucille Elizabeth "Malkia" Davis	b. 1917, Washington, DC; d. 2004, Silver Spring, MD	DC / MD
Roberts, Violet Kent	b. 1880, The Dalles, OR; d. 1956, Suitland, MD	DC / MD
Robertson, Persis Weaver	b. 1896, Des Moines, IA; d. 1992, Bridgeport, CT	DC
Robinson, Margaret Frances	b. 1904, Hull, MA; d. 1985, New Orleans, LA	LA / MS
Roddy, Edith Jannette	b. 1878, Meadville, PA; d. 1957, Sarasota, FL	FL
Rogers, Juanita	b. 1934, Tintop, AL; d. 1985	AL
Rogers, Lois Pauline Cochran	b. 1896, WV; d. 1979, Parkersburg, WV	WV
Rogers, Louise de Gignilliat	b. Macon, GA; active 1917–1923	GA
Rogers, Mary "Maize" C. Gamble	b. 1882, Louisville, KY; d. 1920, NY	KY
Rogers, Venda L. Marcum	b. 1920, KY; d. 2005, Louisville, KY	KY
Rohland, Caroline Melvina Speare	b. 1885, Boston, MA; d. 1964, New York	GA / LA / SC

Artist	Life Dates	Associated With
Rolando, Virginia Moorhead	b. 1898, North East, PA; d. after 1976, Erie, PA	DC
Roller, Janet Worsham	b. 1887, Lynchburg, VA; d. 1975, Lynchburg, VA	VA
Roller, Margaret J. R.	active in Washington, DC, 1920–1924	DC
Rollin, Kate C.	active in Washington, DC, 1914–1920	DC
Roman, Marie Desirée	b. 1867, St. James Parish, LA; d. 1950, New Orleans, LA	LA
Roman, Marie Jeanne Amelie	b. 1873, St. James Parish, LA; d. 1955, New Orleans, LA	LA
Roper, Mathilde/Matilda Secor McCord	b. 1886, Morristown, NJ; d. 1958, Norfolk, VA	VA
Rose, Cornelia "Nellie" Woodward	b. 1882, Fernandina Beach, FL; d. 1967, Wilmington, NC	FL / NC
Rose, Ruth Starr	b. 1887, Eau Claire, WI; d. 1965, Alexandria, VA	DC / LA / VA
Ross, Margaret Lavinia Hudson	b. 1908, Owensboro, KY; d. 2004	KY
Rosser, Barbara Winston	b. 1896, Charlottesville, VA; d. 1984, Charlottesville, VA	VA
Roth, Jane Malone	b. 1837, St. Louis, MO; d. 1922, Knoxville, TN	TN
Rothschild, Amalie Getta Rosenfeld	b. 1916, Baltimore, MD; d. 2001, Baltimore, MD	MD
Round, Edith Dexter Rice	b. 1906, Columbus, GA; d. 1995, Manassas, VA	GA / VA
Roush, Dorothy Alexander	b. 1923, Atlanta, GA; d. 2015, Carrollton, GA	GA
Roush, Sara	b. 1920; active in Louisville, KY	KY
Rowe, Nellie Mae	b. 1900, Fayette County, GA; d. 1982, Fayetteville, GA	GA
Rowe, Willie Lucille Reed	b. 1914, Goliad, TX; d. 1986, Pecos County, TX	DC / LA
Ruckman, Grace Merrill	b. 1873, Buchanan, MI; d. after 1948	DC
Ruddick, Dorothy Lawrence Cole	b. 1925, Chicago, IL; d. 2010, Manhattan, NY	NC
Rudofsky, Berta	b. 1910; d. 2006	NC
Rudolf, Doris Hankee	b. 1917, Palmerton, PA; d. 2016, Wilmington, NC	NC
Rudulph, Rella Merriwether	b. 1906, Livingston, AL; d. 1988, Paris, France	AL
Ruellan, Andrée {Taylor}	b. 1905, New York, NY; d. 2006, Kingston, NY	GA / SC / VA
Ruff, Alice Isham	active in Washington, DC, 1912–1924	DC
Rule, Fay Shelley	b. 1889, Chattanooga, TN; d. 1974, Signal Mountain, TN	TN
Rule, Mary Heyward Shand	b. 1929, Columbia, SC; d. 2003, Arlington, VA	DC / SC / VA
Rumley, Mildred Louise McMullen	b. 1915, Beaufort, NC; d. 2002, Beaufort, NC	NC
Rumph, Alice Edith	b. 1877, Rome, GA; d. 1957, Tuscaloosa, AL	AL / GA
Russell, Irone Hancock Sessions	b. 1866, Philadelphia, PA; d. 1946, Los Angeles, CA	DC
Rust, Mildred Anderson	b. 1893, Brooklyn, NY; d. 1973, Washington, DC	DC
Ruysenaars, Marie Augusta	b. 1901, Louisville, KY; d. 1952, Louisville, KY	KY
Sachse, Janice Rubenstein	b. 1908, New Orleans, LA; d. 1998, Baton Rouge, LA	DC / LA
Saenger, Elizabeth "Betty"	b. 1899; d. 1945	LA
Safford, Ruth Appleton Perkins	b. 1897, Boston, MA; d. 1979 Washington, DC	DC
Saint-Gaudens, Marie	d. about 1947, GA	FL / GA
Salisbury, Alta West	b. about 1879, Darnestown, MD; d. 1933, New Rochelle, NY	DC / MD
Samuel, Hélène	b. 1894, Superior, WI; d. 1944, Paris, France	LA
Samuels, Jane Todd Holmes	b. 1866; d. 1963, Frankfort, KY	KY
Sanders, Arzada Brown	b. 1896, SC; d. 1989, York County, SC	SC
Sands, Anna M.	b. 1860, MD; d. 1927, Washington, DC	DC / MD
Sanford, Marion	b. 1904, Ontario, Canada; d. 1988	GA
Sansum, Edith M.	b. 1867, Evanston, IL; d. 1934, New Orleans, LA	LA
Sarrazin, Louise Angelique	b. 1888, New Orleans, LA; d. 1967, San Bruno, CA	LA

Artist	Life Dates	Associated With
Sato, Nathalie Georgia	active in NC, 1933–1936	NC
Saugrain, Joan Bredendieck [a.k.a. Joan Wadell; Joan Wadell-Barnes; Joan Bredendieck]	b. 1921; d. 2008	GA
Saugstad, Eugenie deLand	b. 1872, Washington, DC; d. 1961, Fairfax, VA	DC / VA
Saunders, Clara Rossman	b. 1874, Cincinnati, OH; d. 1951, Washington, DC	DC
Saunders, L. Pearl	b. about 1885, TN; active in Nashville, 1910–1940	NC / TN
Saunders, Mary Ann Parmelia Xantippe "Tip"	b. 1838, Adair County, KY; d. 1922, Louisville, KY	KY
Saunders, Rebekah	b. 1912 or 1913; d. 2009, Boston, MA	GA
Saussy, Hattie	b. 1890, Savannah, GA; d. 1978, Savannah, GA	GA
Savage, Augusta Christine Fells [Moore] [Poston]	b. 1892, Green Cove Springs, FL; d. 1962, New York, NY	FL
Savage, Marguerite Downing	b. 1879, Bay Ridge, NY; d. 1976, possibly in Worcester, MA	DC
Sawrie, Mary "Mamie" Bang	b. 1874, Nashville, TN; d. 1968, Nashville, TN	TN
Sawtelle, Alice Elizabeth	b. 1875, Washington, DC; d. 1956, Washington, DC	DC
Sawtelle, Mary "Daisy" Berkeley Blackford	b. 1871, Washington, DC; d. 1954, London, Ontario, Canada	DC / NC
Sawyer, Helen Alton Farnsworth	b. 1900, Washington, DC; d. 1999, Sarasota, FL	DC / FL
Saxon, Lulu King	b. 1852, LA; d. 1927, New Orleans, LA	LA
Sayre, Elizabeth Grace Evans	b. 1896, Fort Brady, MI; d. 1985, Washington, DC	DC
Sayre, Zelda (see Fitzgerald, Zelda Sayre)		
Scanland, Alice Scott	b. 1924, Columbia, SC; d. 2005, Charleston, SC	SC
Scaravaglione, Concetta	b. 1900, New York, NY; d. 1975, Bronx, NY	DC / NC
Schachner, Katherine Amann	d. 1906 (buried in Jefferson County, KY)	KY
Schachner, Mary Weller	b. 1869, Louisville, KY	KY
Schaeffer, Hilda V.	active in Washington, DC, 1923–1928	DC
Schanzenbacher, Nellie	b. 1866, Louisville, KY; d. 1961, Louisville, KY	KY
Scharf, Katherine	active in Louisville, KY, 1936	KY
Schauffler, Verna Edith Raattama	b. 1924, New York Mills, MN	NC
Scheibner, Vira Grace McIlrath	b. 1889; d. 1956, St. Augustine, FL	FL
Schevlin, Rubye Everts	b. 1892, Anthon, OH; d. 1956 (buried in Arlington National Cemetery, Arlington, VA)	DC
Schmidt, Agnes C.	active in Washington, DC, 1912–1939	DC
Schmidt, Katherine [Kuniyoshi] [Shubert]	b. 1898, Xenia, OH; d. 1978, Sarasota, FL	FL
Scholtz, Anita F.	b. 1902, KY; d. 1996, Corydon, KY	KY
Schowe, Lou-Ellen Chattin	b. 1891, Temple, TX; d. 1937 (buried in Indianapolis, IN)	FL
Schutt, Ellen Ischam	b. 1873, Oak Grove, VA; d. 1955, Falls Church, VA	DC / VA
Schwartz, Marjorie Watson	b. 1905, Trenton, TN; d. 1999, Memphis, TN	TN
Scott, Bertha E.	b. 1884, Frankfort, KY; d. 1965, Frankfort, KY	KY
Scott, Carrie D.	active in Washington, DC, 1919–1923	DC
Scott, Charlotte T.	b. 1891	WV
Scott, Dorothy Carnine	b. 1903, Hannaford, ND; d. 1993, Estes Park, CO	VA
Scott, Elizabeth Talford	b. 1916, Chester, SC; d. 2011	DC / MD / NC / SC
Scott, Mary Florence	b. 1872; d. 1959, Sanford, FL	FL
Searcy, Elizabeth	b. 1877, Memphis, TN; d. 1965	DC / TN

Artist	Life Dates	Associated With
Secker, Alvena Vadja	b. 1916, McMechen, WV; d. 2012, Pompton Lakes, NJ	WV
Seebold, Marie Madeleine (see Molinary, Marie Madeleine Seebold)		
Selden, Dixie	b. 1868, Cincinnati, OH; d. 1935, Cincinnati, OH	KY
Selden, Wautell Gray Lambeth	b. 1910, Graham, NC; d. 1948, Durham, NC	NC
Seldon, Isabel Virginia Hall	b. 1898, Washington, DC; d. 1985, Washington, DC	DC
Selian, Elsa Rose	b. 1896; d. 1980, Manatee County, FL	FL
Sellers, Anna B.	b. 1824, Philadelphia, PA; d. 1905, Chattanooga, TN	TN
Serven, Lydia Maria	b. 1898, Washington, DC	DC
Sewell, Annie L.	active in Washington, DC, 1912–1935	DC
Shafer, Marguerite Phillips Neuhauser	b. 1888, N. Arlington, VA; d. 1976, Washington, DC	DC / VA
Shanks, Louise Newhall Johnson	b. 1905, Newton Center, MA; d. 1977, St. Augustine, FL	FL
Shannon, Aileen M. Phillips	b. 1888, Gillsburg, MS; d. 1964, Doña Ana County, NM	MS
Sharp, Bernadine Custer	b. 1900, Bloomington, IL	SC
Sharp, Lucile Whitten	b. 1883, Oxford, MS; d. 1973, Jackson, MS	MS
Sharrar, Honoré Desmond {Zagorin}	b. 1920, West Point, NY; d. 2009, Washington, DC	DC / VA
Sharrar, Madeleine Ellen Sachs {Poland}	b. 1898, Colorado Springs, CO; d. 1988, Guilford, CT	LA
Sharrard, Alice Belle	b. 1867, Louisville, KY; d. 1921, Louisville, KY	KY
Shaw, Mrs. Kenneth A.	active in Washington, DC, 1924	DC
Shaw, Ruth Faison	b. 1888, Kenansville, NC; d. 1969, Fayetteville, NC	NC
Shea, Annie K.	active in Washington, DC, 1918–1923	DC
Shea, Eileen A.	active in Washington, DC, 1918	DC
Shea, Elizabeth K.	active in Washington, DC, 1918–1920	DC
Sheerer, Mary Given	b. 1865, Covington, KY; d. 1954, Cincinnati, OH	KY / LA
Shelby, Lila Norma	b. 1900, Simsboro, LA; d. 1994, Metairie, LA	LA
Shennan, Florence	b. 1921, Winchester, KY; d. 2009, Greenville, SC	KY / NC / SC
Sheridan, Blanche	active in Washington, DC, 1918	DC
Sherman, Ella Bennett	b. New York, NY; active in Washington, DC, 1890s–1913	DC
Sherratt, Margaret J.	active in Washington, DC, 1890s–1930	DC
Sherwood, Bette Wilson	b. 1921, Sheffield, AL	AL
Sherwood, Mary Clare	b. 1868, Lyons, NY; d. 1943, Vicksburg, MS	MS
Sherwood, Rosina Hubley Emmet	b. 1854, Lyons, NY; d. 1948, New York, NY	GA
Shewmake, Maria "Mitzi" Byrd	b. about 1926, New York, NY	NC
Shields, Anne Mercer Kesler	b. 1932, Winston-Salem, NC; d. 2012, Winston-Salem, NC	NC
Shipman, Mary P.	d. 1932, Washington, DC	DC
Sholl, Elizabeth L.	active in Washington, DC, 1922–1928	DC
Shrenk, Adele Rogers	b. 1861, Mount Vernon, NY	FL
Shulz, Alberta Rehm	b. 1892, Indianapolis, IN; d. 1980, Bloomington, IN	FL
Shumacker, Elizabeth Blair Wright	b. 1912, Chattanooga, TN; d. 1993, Chattanooga, TN	TN
Shute, Nell Choate {Plummer}	b. 1896, Athens, GA; d. 1966, Anniston, AL	FL / GA
Sibley, Emma Josephine (Couper) (see Couper, Emma Josephine Sibley)		
Siebenthal, Myrtle Madden	active in Washington, DC, 1904	DC
Siebert, Marie H.	active in Washington, DC, 1917	DC
Siegel, Ellen	active in NC, 1949–1950	NC

Artist	Life Dates	Associated With
Smith, Suzanne Parker	b. 1919, Ontario, Canada; d. 2005, Bay City, MI	NC
Snead, Louise Hammond Willis	b. 1866, Charleston, SC; d. 1958, Darien, CT	SC
Sneed, Mrs. Thomas	Chapel Hill, NC	NC
Sneeden, Lillian Vaught	b. 1930, Pittsburgh, PA	NC
Snowden, Elsie Brooke	b. 1887, Ashton, MD; d. 1945, Montgomery County, MD	DC / MD
Solari, Mary Magdelene	b. 1849, Calvari, Italy; d. 1929, Memphis, TN	TN
Solomons, Aline Esther	b. 1860, New York, NY; d. 1942, Washington, DC	DC
Sommer, Emmy	b. 1878, Copenhagen, Denmark; d. after 1940	DC
Sondheimer, Rosalee	b. 1910, Memphis, TN; d. 2000, Memphis, TN	TN
Sones, Harriett Sylvia	Dorchester, MA	NC
Sonnemann, Nell Battle Booker	b. 1918, Durham, NC; d. 2004, Chapel Hill, NC	NC
Sonntag, Pauline "Posey Polly" Kinkead	b. 1896, KY; d. 1984, Evansville, IN	KY
Souther, Mary Langhorne Tayloe	b. 1868, GA; d. 1945, Wilmington, DE	DC / GA
Southerland, Elizabeth Burke	b. 1913, Burlington, NC; d. 1992, Wilmington, NC	NC
Southerland, Genevieve McClure	b. 1895, East Liberty, PA; d. 1953, Mobile, AL	AL
Sowerbutts, Laura G.	active in Washington, DC, 1917	DC
Spaeth, Marie Haughton	b. 1870, Hanover, NH; d. 1937, Sarasota, FL	FL
Spain, Gladys J.	b. 1908, Louisville, KY; d. 1969, Louisville, KY	KY
Sparhawk-Jones, Elizabeth	b. 1885, Baltimore, MD; d. 1968, Philadelphia, PA	MD
Sparks, Lillian B.	active in Washington, DC, 1914–1917	DC
Sparrow, Louise Winslow Kidder {Gripon}	b. 1884, Malden, MA; d. 1979, Washington, DC	DC
Spalding, Elizabeth/Elisabeth	b. 1868, Erie, PA; d. 1954, Denver, CO	NC
Spear, Emma Annie Austin	b. England; d. 1935, Washington, DC	DC
Speed, Jessie Clark	b. 1908, Louisville, KY; d. 2001, Taos, NM	KY
Spicer-Simson, Margaret Schmidt	b. 1874, Washington, DC; d. 1968, Miami, FL	DC / FL
Spitzer, Rose H.	active in FL, 1950s	FL
Spong, Laura	b. 1926, Nashville, TN	SC / TN
Springer, Eva	b. 1882, Cimarron, NM; d. 1964, Las Vegas, NV	DC
Sproul, Avard Pauline	b. 1923, Bridgewater, CT; d. 1999, Wrightsville Beach, NC	NC
Spruill, Eleanor Humes Duvall	b. 1909, Columbia, SC; d. 1998, Cheraw, SC	SC
Squire, Eunice Clay Pritchett	b. 1894, Keeling, VA; d. 1949, Danville, VA	VA
Stacey, Lynn Nelson	b. 1903, Washington, DC; d. 1979	DC
Staley, May Evans	b. 1887; d. 1964, Lafayette Hill, PA	DC
Stanley, Blanche Huntington	b. 1871, Fort Sully, SD; d. 1951, Washington, DC	DC
Stanley, Caroline A.	d. 1919, Washington, DC	DC
Stanton, Lucy May	b. 1875, Atlanta, GA; d. 1931, Athens, GA	GA / LA / NC
Starr, Cornelia "Nina" Howell	b. 1903, Newark, NJ; d. 2000, New York	NC
Steadman, Lena Alice Tuttle	b. 1907, Stokes County, NC; d. 1984, Walburg, NC	NC
Stephenson, Elizabeth "Bessie" Keenan	b. 1891, SC; d. 1959, Greenville, SC	SC
Sternberg, Marie Ascher	b. 1892, Jackson, MS; d. 1966, Jackson, MS	AL / MS
Sternhagen, Gertrude F. Hussey	b. 1890, Asbury Park, NJ; d. 1976	DC
Sterrett, Charlotte Woodman	b. 1888, Charleston; WV d. 1973, White Sulphur Springs, WV	WV
Steuart, Emily Nourse	b. 1893, Washington, DC; d. 1990, Washington, DC	DC
Steuart, M. Louisa	b. 1852, Baltimore, MD; d. 1938	MD

Artist	Life Dates	Associated With
Stevens, Marian	b. 1885, Washington, DC; d. 1974, St. Leonard, MD	DC / MD
Stevenson, Florence Ezzell	b. 1894, Russellville, AL; d. 1974, Chicago, IL	AL
Stevenson, Nora Wright	b. 1889, VA	NC / VA
Stewart, Edith Hoyt	b. 1890, West Point, NY; d. 1971, Washington, DC	DC / MD
Stewart, Esther Roberts Lippincott	b. 1895, Moorestown, NJ; d. 1982, Quitman, GA	DC / GA / VA
Stewart, Josie	active in Washington, DC, 1920	DC
Stewart, Mary Alice Leath (see Thomas, Mary Alice Leath Stewart)		
Stewart, Mary Montgomery	b. 1918, Fayetteville, NC; d. 2011, Bremerton, WA	NC
Stewart, Sue Vashon	b. 1898, St. Louis, MO; d. 1988, Washington, DC	DC
Stillman, Emma Maynicke	b. 1852, Germany; d. after 1915	DC
Stinson, Alice E.	active in Washington, DC, 1920–1935	DC / VA
Stockwell, Catherine Haynes	b. 1895, Eustis, FL; d. 1983, Eustis, FL	FL
Stokes, Barbara Hoyt	b. 1912, Brentwood, NY; d. 1965, Riverdale, NY	NC
Stokes, Rhoda Belle Brady	b. 1901, Meadville, MS; d. 1988, Baton Rouge, LA	LA / MS
Stone, Agnes Harvey	b. 1873, Chesterfield, NH; d. 1958, Washington, DC	DC
Stone, Madeline Masters	b. 1877, Washington, DC; d. 1932, Washington, DC	DC
Stone, Ruth Andress	b. 1914, St. Louis, MO; d. 2006, St. Petersburg, FL	FL / MS
Stoney, Louise/ Louisa Cheves Smith	b. 1868, Charleston, SC; d. 1939, Charleston, SC	SC
Stonier, Lucille Holderness	b. about 1884, TX; d. 1966	FL
Storer, Frances Nell	b. 1917, Central City, KY; d. 2003, Louisville, KY	KY / TN
Stork, Cordelia Page Gaines	active in Louisville, KY; 1937–1940	KY
Stottlemeyer, Margaret A. R.	b. 1859, MD; d. after 1933	DC / MD
Stoval, Emma Serena "Queena" Dillard	b. 1887, Lynchburg, VA; d. 1980, Lynchburg, VA	VA
Strange, Millicent	active in Washington, DC, 1913–1915	DC
Stratton, Alza Jessamond Hentschel	b. 1911, Fayette, KY; d. 1982, Lexington, KY	KY
Stringer, Mary Evelyn	b. 1921, Huntsville, OH; d. 2005, Columbia, MS	MS
Strong, Beulah	b. 1866, New Orleans, LA; d. 1951, San Francisco, CA	KY / LA
Strong, Margaret L.	active in Washington, DC, 1916	DC
Stroud, Ida Wells	b. 1869, New Orleans, LA; d. 1944, Herbertsville, NJ	LA
Sturgis, Margaret	active in FL, 1958–1959	FL
Sturm, Dorothy May	b. 1910, Memphis, TN; d. 1988, Memphis, TN	TN
Suitt, Mary Ellen	b. 1918, Greenville, SC; d. 2013, Spartanburg, SC	SC
Sullivan, Elizabeth T.	active in Washington, DC, 1913–1925	DC
Summer, Emily Eugenia	b. 1923, Newton, MS; d. 2016, Columbus, MS	MS
Summy, Katherine J. Strong	b. 1888, Washington, DC; d. after 1967	DC
Sussler, Mary Ruth Lyford	affiliated with Black Mountain College	NC
Sutton, Cantey McDowell Venable	b. 1887, Chapel Hill, NC; d. 1983, Charlotte, NC	MS / NC / SC
Swaffield, Caroline "Carrie"	b. 1869, Columbia, SC; d. 1959, Columbia, SC	SC
Sweets, Douschka Martin	b. 1880, SC; d. 1971, Louisville, KY	KY / SC
Swiggett, Grace Margaret Kiess	b. 1871, Cincinnati, OH; d. 1947	DC
Swinburne, Anna Trimble	b. 1846, MD; d. after 1920	MD
Swope, Kate F.	b. 1879, Louisville, KY	KY
Sylvester, Sara "Sally" Natalie Dwight	b. 1912, Jacksonville, FL	FL / NC

Artist	Life Dates	Associated With
Symington, Leslie Paul	b. 1896, Bowling Green, KY; d. 1997, Jacksonville, FL	FL / KY / NC / TN / VA
Symmers, Agnes Louise Shuey	b. 1882, Charlottesville, VA; d. 1965, Chapel Hill, NC	NC / VA
Symmes, Elizabeth "Bessie" R.	b. 1881, Brunswick, GA; d. 1974, Wilmington, NC	GA / NC
Tabary, Céline Marie	b. 1908, Vermelles, France; d. 1993, France	DC
Taggart, Mildred Hardy	b. 1898, Corsicana, TX; d. 1983, Corsicana, TX	DC
Talbert, Katherine C.	active in Washington, DC, 1922–1924	DC
Taliaferro, Elizabeth Stewart	b. 1869, Newark, NJ; d. 1965, Gloucester, VA	VA
Tancredi, Chiyoko Sonai	b. 1929, SD; d. 1990, Wilmington, NC	NC
Tannahill, Mary Harvey	b. 1863, Warrenton, NC; d. 1951, Warrenton, NC	NC
Tarbell, Ruth Whittier Shute	b. 1802, Dover, NH; d. 1882, Middletown, KY	KY
Tate, Elmira	active in Washington, DC, 1920	DC
Taylor, Anna Heyward	b. 1879, Columbia, SC; d. 1956, Charleston, SC	SC
Taylor, Annie Hall	active in Washington, DC, 1926	DC
Taylor, Bertha Fanning	b. 1883, New York, NY; d. 1980, Norfolk, VA	VA
Taylor, Bessie Margaret Barrington	b. 1895, Rutledge, AL; d. 1941, Bradenton, FL	AL / FL
Taylor, Grace Martin Frame	b. 1903, Morgantown, WV; d. 1995, Charleston, WV	WV
Taylor, Harriet Catherine Dibble	b. 1873; d. 1918	SC
Taylor, Katherine	active in Washington, DC, 1902–1910	DC
Temple, Grace Lincoln	b. 1864, Boston, MA; d. 1953, Washington, DC	DC
Temple, Ruth Alice Anderson	b. 1891, Carlisle, PA; d. 1957, Boston, MA	MD
Temple, Ruth Hines	b. 1899, Warren County, KY; d. 2001, Bowling Green, KY	KY / TN / VA
Terra, Adelene Evans Richards	b. 1910; d. 1982, Evanston, IL	MS
Terrell, Elizabeth E.	b. 1908, Toledo, OH; d. 1997, Attica, IN	FL / GA
Terry, Marion E.	d. 1984, St. Petersburg, FL	FL
Tharin, Selma Marie {Furtwangler} {Dotterer}	b. 1904, Charleston, SC; d. 1995, Charleston, SC	SC
Tharp, Rose B.	active in FL, early twentieth century	FL
Thaw, Florence	b. 1864, New York, NY; d. 1940, Washington, DC	DC
Theard, Mary Reymond	b. 1902, Baton Rouge, LA; d. 1982, New Orleans, LA	LA
Thomas, Addie Ray	b. 1901, Crystal Springs, MS; d. 1991, Crystal Springs, MS	MS
Thomas, Alma Woodsey	b. 1891, Columbus, GA; d. 1978, Washington, DC	DC / GA
Thomas, Anne Wall	b. 1928, Wadesboro, NC	NC
Thomas, Elaine Freeman	b. 1923, Cleveland, IL; d. 2013, Tuskegee, AL	AL / KY / NC
Thomas, Ellen Polk	b. 1895, Augusta, GA; d. 1972, Augusta, GA	GA
Thomas, Florence Young	b. 1909, Ashe County, NC; d. 2007, Ashe County, NC	NC
Thomas, Lenore	b. 1909, Chicago, IL; d. 1988, Blue Hill, ME	MD / VA / WV
Thomas, Margaret Gray	b. 1871, GA; d. 1951, Savannah, GA	GA
Thomas, Mary Alice Leath {Stewart}	b. 1905, Hazlehurst, GA; d. 1959, Athens, GA	DC / GA / NC / SC
Thomas, Sue Betty Rex	b. 1914, Richmond, VA; d. 2003, Richmond, VA	VA
Thompson, Bertha	active in Washington, DC, 1915	DC
Thompson, Dora "Dody" Harrison {Diffenderfer} {Warren} {Weston}	b. 1923, New Orleans, LA; d. 2012, Los Angeles, CA	LA / NC
Thompson, Frances Louise	b. 1879, Hagerstown, MD	DC

Artist	Life Dates	Associated With
Thompson, Georgette Rosamond Mothersead	b. 1905, New Orleans, LA; d. 1980, New Port Richey, FL	FL / LA / MS
Thompson, Harriet Lathrop	b. 1889, Wilkes-Barre, PA; d. after 1962, possibly in Vineyard Haven, MA	DC
Thompson, Julia M.	active in Louisville, KY, 1931	KY
Thompson, Juliet Hutchings	b. 1873, Washington, DC; d. 1956, New York, NY	DC
Thompson, Louise B.	b. 1895, Washington, DC; d. 1961, Washington, DC	DC
Thompson, Lucy M.	active in Atlanta, 1903	GA
Thompson, Mary Tyson	b. 1909, Sewanee, TN	TN
Thompson, Mildred	b. 1936, Jacksonville, FL; d. 2003, Atlanta, GA	DC / FL / GA
Thompson, Nettie Fant	b. 1878, Terry, MS; d. 1960, Jackson, MS	MS
Thorpe, Hilda Gottlieb Shapiro	b. 1920, Baltimore, MD; d. 2000, Alexandria, VA	DC / MD
Throckmorton, Josephine Holt	b. 1886, MI; d. 1940 (buried in Arlington, VA)	DC
Throckmorton, Roberta Cowing	b. 1860, Rushville, IN; d. 1924, Washington, DC	DC
Thrush, Helen Alverda	b. 1903, PA; d. 2006, Montgomery County, PA	NC
Thum, Patty Prather	b. 1853, Louisville, KY; d. 1926, Louisville, KY	KY
Tibbs, Charlotte Eliza	b. 1878, Buffalo, NY; d. 1968, Grand Rapids, MI	MS
Tillery, Mary Hallie	b. 1899, Halifax County, NC; d. 1989, Scotland Neck, NC	NC
Tipton, Mary L.	b. 1873, Birmingham, AL	AL
Titlow, Harriet Woodfin	b. 1875, Hampton, VA; d. 1943, Springfield, OH	VA
Tobey, Edith M. McCartney	b. 1897, Boston, MA; d. 1981, Washington, DC	DC
Tolbert, Julia Elizabeth DeLoach	b. 1988, Abbeville County, SC; d. 1963, Ninety Six, SC	SC
Tolk-Watkins, Margaret "Peggy" Vaughan	b. 1921, New York, NY; d. 1973	NC
Tolman, Nelly Summerhill McKenzie	b. 1877, Salisbury, NC; d. 1961, Washington, DC	DC / NC
Tomkins, Florence Lusk	b. 1883, Washington, DC; d. 1963, Pasadena, CA	DC
Tompkins, Clementina M. G.	b. 1848, Georgetown, DC; d. 1931, Washington, DC	DC
Tompkins, Eunice W.	active in Washington, DC, 1916–1917	DC
Totten, Hedvig Erika "Vicken" von Post {Börjesson}	b. 1886, Stockholm, Sweden; d. 1950, possibly in Washington, DC	DC
Towery, Sarah Louise Carlisle	b. 1911, Alexander City, AL; d. 2007, Alexander City, AL	AL / NC
Townsend, Helen Elizabeth	b. 1893, Effingham, IL; d. 1980, Silver Spring, MD	DC / MD
Toy, Ruby Shuler	b. 1911, Corey, FL; d. 2002, Orlando, FL	DC / FL
Toy, Sarah Concord Everett Lee	b. 1908, Rockingham County, NC; d. 1997, Spruce Pine, NC	NC
Tracy, Lois Bartlett (Bartlett Tracy)	b. 1901, Jackson, MI; d. 2008, Englewood, FL	FL
Traister, Helen Wells	b. 1909, Wilmington, NC; d. 2012, Wilmington, NC	NC
Travis, Kathryne Bess Hail	b. 1894, Ozark, AR; d. 1972, Ruidoso, NM	AR
Trenholm, Jane Gordon Waties	b. 1837, Charleston, SC; d. 1936, Charleston, SC	SC
Tricker, Florence	b. 1892, Philadelphia, PA; d. 1979, New York, NY	NC
Triggs, Emilia "Mimi" Pirra Jennewein	b. 1920, Rome, Italy; d. 2006, Snowmass, CO	FL / NC
Troemel, Jean Wagner Willhite	b. 1921, FL	FL
Tropp, Mina Surasky	b. 1897, Poland; d. 1990, Aiken, SC	SC
Troubetzkoy, Amélie Louise Rives	b. 1863, Richmond, VA; d. 1945, Albemarle County, VA	VA
Trout, Elizabeth Dorothy Burt	b. 1896, Fort Robinson, NE; d. 1977, Washington, DC	DC
Troutman, Ann	b. 1897, MI; d. 1989	KY / TN
Trowbridge, Irene Underwood	b. 1898, Pittsburg, KS	DC

Artist	Life Dates	Associated With
Truax, Grace Hobbs	b. 1893, KY; d. 1986, Bardstown, KY	KY
True, Grace Hopkins	b. 1870; d. 1943, Brevard County, FL	FL
True, Marguerite Neale	d. 1964, Washington, DC	DC
Truitt, Anne	b. 1921, Baltimore, MD; d. 2004, Washington, DC	DC / MD
Trynz, Libbian	b. 1904; d. 2000	NC
Tuke, Eleanor Gladys	b. 1899, Mingo Flats, WV; d. 1982, White Sulphur Springs, WV	WV
Tullis, Octavia Gayden	b. 1881, LA; d. 1970, Baton Rouge, LA	LA
Turk, Sandra	b. 1923; d. 1986	SC
Turkenton, Netta Craig	b. 1884, Washington, DC; d. 1959, Washington, DC	DC
Turlington, Patricia Davis	b. 1931, Sampson County, NC; d. 2009, Durham, NC	NC
Turnbull, Grace Hill	b. 1880, Baltimore, MD; d. 1976, Baltimore, MD	MD
Turner, Frances Hopkins Lee	b. 1875, Bridgeport, AL; d. 1945, Oxford, GA	AL / DC / GA
Turner, Harriet French	b. 1886, Giles County, VA; d. 1968, Roanoke, VA	VA
Turner, Helen Maria	b. 1858, Louisville, KY; d. 1958, New Orleans, LA	KY / LA
Turner, Martha Bacon	b. 1900, Memphis, TN; d. 1974, Memphis, TN	TN
Tuthill, Corinne	b. 1892, Lawrenceburg, IN; d. 1978, Florence, AL	AL
Tuttle, Helen Norris	b. 1906; d. 1977 (buried in Bryn Mawr, PA)	NC
Tuverson, Audrey K.	b. 1921, MI; d. 2016, Eastport, ME	NC
Tyler, Margaret Yard	b. 1903, New York, NY; d. 1997, Montclair, NJ	DC
Tyler, Mary Ellen	b. 1846, IN; d. 1939, Pasadena, CA	TN
Uhler, Anne Fuller Abbott	b. 1886, Brandon, VT; d. 1973, Washington, DC	DC
Ulman, Elinor Elizabeth	b. 1909, Enumclaw, WA; d. 1997, Enumclaw, WA	MD
Ulmann, Doris May	b. 1882, New York, NY; d. 1934, New York, NY	GA / KY / NC / SC / TN / VA
Underhill, Georgia Edna	b. 1883; d. 1956	FL
Underwood, Elizabeth Kendall	b. 1896, Gerrish Island, ME; d. 1976, Arlington, VA	DC / VA
Updegraff, Sallie Bell	b. 1864, Belmont County, OH; d. 1947, Anderson, IN	DC
Upham, Elsie Dorey	b. 1907; d. 1991, Naples, FL	FL
Upshur, Annie E.	b. 1892; d. 1929, Norfolk, VA	VA
Upshur, Martha Robinson	b. 1885, Richmond, VA; d. 1963, Richmond, VA	VA
Urbain, Elaine Louise Schmitt	b. 1925, Wauwatosa, WI; d. 2004, Milford, CT	NC
Van Buren, Amelia	b. 1858, New York, NY; d. 1942, Tryon, NC	NC
Van Doren, Charlotte A.	active in Washington, DC, 1882–1920	DC
Van Hook, Nell	b. 1897, Richmond, VA; d. possibly in 1974, Birmingham, AL	GA / VA
Van Horn, Lucretia Blow Le Bourgeois	b. 1882, St. Louis, MO; d. 1970, Stanford, CA	GA
Van Natter, Hazel	b. 1895, OK; d. 1980, Ft. Lauderdale, FL	DC / FL
Van Wegenen, Elizabeth Vass	b. 1895, Savannah, GA; d. 1955, Philadelphia, PA	GA / VA
Van Zant, Lorene J.	b. 1896; d. 1947, Jackson, MS	MS
Vance, Eleanor Park	b. 1869, Mansfield, OH; d. 1954, Tryon, NC	NC
Vance, Lois Piper	d. 1979, Louisville, KY	KY
Vance, May Howard	b. Rushsylvania, OH; d. after 1977	DC
Vassey, Mary Paul Glenn	b. 1917, Madison, GA; d. 1987, Gaffney, SC	AL / GA / SC
Vawter, Mary Howey Murray	b. 1871, Baltimore, MD; d. 1950, Mathews, VA	MD / VA
Verner, Elizabeth Quale O'Neill {Myers}	b. 1883, Charleston, SC; d. 1979, Charleston, SC	SC

Artist	Life Dates	Associated With
Vernon, Berenice	active in Louisville, KY, 1936	KY
Vetsch, Edith Emily d'Hemecourt Hibbard	active in New Orleans, LA, 1923–1934	LA
Vinson, Marjorie Laura Greene	b. 1903, Sterling, IL; d. 1946, Savannah, GA	GA
Vismor, Dorothy Anita Perkins	b. 1911, Crown King, AZ; d. 1999	GA
Vosseller, Frances Marie Newbury	b. 1906, MO; d. 1998, St. Louis, MO	FL
Wachman, Henriette	b. 1851; d. 1954	MD
Wagner, Rosa A.	active in Washington, DC, 1910–1935	DC
Waite, Emily Burling	b. 1879, Worcester, MA; d. 1980, Worcester, MA	DC
Wakem, Mabel J.	b. 1879, Chicago, IL; d. after 1933, possibly in Chicago, IL	DC
Walcott, Mary Morris Vaux	b. 1860, Philadelphia, PA; d. 1940, New Brunswick, Canada	DC
Waldraff, Charlotte S.	active in Washington, DC, 1917	DC
Walker, Annie E. Anderson	b. 1855, AL; d. 1929, Washington, DC	AL / DC
Walker, Carolina Clifford	b. 1855, Charleston, SC; d. 1936, Charleston, SC	SC
Walker, Christine Burke	b. 1911, VA; d. 2009, Virginia Beach, VA	VA
Walker, Emma J.	active in Washington, DC, 1884–1920	DC
Walker, Margaret Beverly Moore	b. 1883, Darlington, SC; d. 1963, Greenville, SC	SC
Walkinshaw, Jeanie Mayer Walter	b. 1885, Baltimore, MD; d. 1976, Mercer Island, WA	MD
Wallace, Lysbeth Mai	b. 1919, Hopkinsville, KY; d. 2007, Hopkinsville, KY	KY
Walley, Jane "Jano"	b. 1912	NC
Walsh, Alice Henry	active in Gulfport, MS, 1920s	MS
Walsh, Christine	active in New Orleans, LA, 1930–1932	LA
Walsh, Helene "Nelly"	b. 1883, TN	TN
Walsh, Nellie B. Glasscock	b. 1888, AR; d. 1955, Los Angeles, CA	AR
Walter, Anne L.	active in Washington, DC, 1918–1935	DC
Walter, Martha	b. 1875, Philadelphia, PA; d. 1976, Philadelphia, PA	TN
Walter, Mildred	b. 1911	KY
Walter, Ruby M. C.	active in Washington, DC, 1920–1935	DC
Walter, Valerie Harrisse	b. 1892, Baltimore, MD; d. 1984, Baltimore, MD	MD
Walters, Doris Mae Lawrence	b. 1920, Sandersville, GA; d. 2003, Sandersville, GA	GA
Walton, Florence Louise Bryant {Condon} {Mackenzie}	b. 1890, Boston, MA; d. 1968, San Francisco, CA	DC
Wanneke, Jessie Gilroy Hall	b. 1889, Philadelphia, PA; d. 1982, Middletown, CT	DC
Ward, Cora Kelley	b. 1920, Eunice, LA; d. 1989	NC / LA
Ward, Hilda Jeannette	b. 1878, Annapolis, MD; d. 1950, New York, NY	MD
Ward, Irene Stephenson	b. 1898, Oakman, AL; d. 1976, Oakman, AL	AL
Ward, Mary Trenworth Duffy Hughes	b. 1908, New Bern, NC; d. 2000, New Bern, NC	NC
Ward, Nina Belle	b. 1885, Rome, GA; d. 1944, Kalamazoo, MI	GA
Ward, Valerie	b. 1898, Washington, DC; d. 1986, Washington, DC	DC
Ware, Ellen Coleman Paine	b. 1859, Jacksonport, AR; d. 1928, Memphis, TN	AR / TN
Warfield, Majel	b. 1905, New Orleans, LA	LA
Waring, Leila	b. 1876, Charleston, SC; d. 1964, Charleston, SC	SC
Warner, Margaret	b. 1892	DC
Warner-Jones, Margarita Rose "Pipsi"	b. 1931, Suffolk, England	NC
Warren, Elizabeth Boardman "E. B."	b. 1886, Bangor, ME; d. 1980, Bridgeport, MA	FL

Artist	Life Dates	Associated With
Warren, Helen	active in Washington, DC, 1918–1920	DC
Warriner, Susanne Gutherz	b. 1880, MO; d. after 1940	DC
Warthen, Ferol Katherine Sibley	b. 1890, Aberdeen, SD; d. 1986, Potomac, MD	DC / MD
Washburn, Ann Louese Bunnell	b. 1875, Dimock, PA; d. 1959, Jacksonville, FL	FL
Washington, Elizabeth Fisher	b. 1871, Siegfried's Bridge, PA; d. 1953, Devon, PA	SC
Washington, Mary Jeanne Parks	b. 1924, Atlanta, GA	GA / NC
Wasson-Tucker, Susanne	b. 1911, Vienna, Austria	NC
Waters, Lottie A.	active in Washington, DC, 1915	DC
Watson, Agnes "Nan" Patterson	b. 1876, Scotland, d; 1966, Washington, DC	DC
Watson, Amelia "Minnie" Montague	b. 1856, East Windsor, CT; d. 1934, Orlando, FL	FL / NC
Watson, Corrine Young	b. 1854, Lyons, NY; d. 1948, Louisville, KY	KY
Watson, Edith Sarah	b. 1861; d. 1943, South Windsor, CT	SC
Watson, Kathryn E.	active in Louisville, KY, 1930–1933	KY
Watson, Ruth Crawford	b. 1892, Decatur, AL; d. 1936, Decatur, AL	AL
Wauchope, Elizabeth Bostedo	b. 1877, Weyauwega, WI; d. 1972, New Orleans, LA	LA / SC
Way, Edna Martha	b. 1897	NC
Weaver, Beulah Barnes	b. 1882, Washington, DC; d. 1957, Washington, DC	DC
Weeden, Maria Howard [a.k.a. Howard Weeden]	b. 1847, Huntsville, AL; d. 1905, Huntsville, AL	AL
Weil, Susan {Rauschenberg}	b. 1930, New York, NY	NC
Weil, Susan Fenimore Cooper	b. 1922, NY; d. 2013, Cooperstown, NY	NC
Weill, Erna Helft	b. 1904, Frankfurt, Germany; d. 1996, Teaneck, NJ	NC
Weinbaum, Judith	b. 1895, NY; d. 1992, Bethesda, MD	DC / MD
Weinstein, Florence	b. 1895; d. 1989	NC
Weisman, Clara	active in Washington, DC, 1920–1925	DC
Weiss, Charlotte	active in Washington, DC, 1920	DC
Weiss, Sylvia Wald	b. 1915, Philadelphia, PA; d. 1989, New Brunswick, NJ	KY
Welch, Ludmilla Pilat	b. 1867, Ossining, NY; d. 1925, Jackson County, FL	FL / GA / LA
Wells, Lillian	b. 1896, Luxola, AR; d. 1986, DeLand, FL	AR / FL
Wells, Pearl Carney	b. 1918, Wilmington, NC; d. 2003, Wilmington, NC	NC
Wells, Sabina Elliott	b. 1876, Charleston, SC; d. 1943, Hendersonville, NC	NC / SC
Welty, Eudora Alice	b. 1909, Jackson, MS; d. 2001, Jackson, MS	MS
Wemyss, Cora M.	b. 1856; d. 1941	KY
Werten, Marya	active in AL, about 1940	AL
Weschler, Anita	b. 1903, New York; d. 2000	NC
Wesner, Janet Major Eldridge	b. 1917, Washington, DC; d. 2011, Gaithersburg, MD	DC / MD
West, Myrtice Snead	b. 1923, Cherokee County, AL; d. 2010, Cherokee County, AL	AL
Westfeldt, Martha Jefferson Gasquet	b. 1884, New Orleans, LA; d. 1960, New Orleans, LA	LA
Weston, Anne Howard Chapin	b. 1913, Great Neck, NY; d. 1992, KY	KY / NC
Wexler, Hannah Paipert	active in Washington, DC, 1937	VA
Whaley, Caroline "Callie" Tennent Baker	b. 1877, Augusta, GA; d. 1965, Charleston, SC	SC
Whaley, Edna Lyman Reed	b. 1884, New Orleans, LA; d. 1979 Edisto Island, SC	LA / SC
Wharton, Alene Gray {Conover}	b. 1909, Chicago, IL; d. 1998, Boulder, CO	TN
Wharton, Margaret Agnes Harper	b. 1943, Portsmouth, VA; d. 2014 Riverside, IL	NC / VA

Artist	Life Dates	Associated With
Wheeler, Frances W.	b. 1879, Charlottesville, VA; d. after 1948	DC / VA
Wheeler, Kathleen	b. 1884, England; d. 1977	DC
Wheelock, Beatrice McLeish	b. 1897, Denver, CO; d. 1980, Carmel-by-the-Sea, CA	DC
Whipple, Jane Randolph	b. 1910, Baton Rouge, LA	LA
White, Cherry Ford	b. 1875, UT; d. 1948, Arlington County, VA	DC / MD
White, Clara	active in Washington, DC, 1906–1923	DC
White, Constance	active in Washington, DC, 1903–1920	DC
White, Elizabeth	b. 1893, Sumter, SC; d. 1976	SC
White, Mabel Dunn	b. 1902, Charlotte, NC	FL / NC / SC
White, Margaret Screven {Tuck} {Duke}	b. 1902, Savannah, GA; d. 1964, Savannah, GA	GA
White, Ruth Shotwell Roudebush	b. 1862, Woodville, MS; d. 1949, Jackson, MS	MS / KY
White, Virginia Saunders	b. 1889; d. 1959	KY / SC
Whitefield "Whitfield," Emma Morehead	b. 1874, Greensboro, NC; d. 1932, Richmond, VA	NC / VA
Whitehan, Edna May	b. 1887, Scribner, NE	DC
Whitehead, Edith Hindela	active in Washington, DC, early 1920s	DC
Whitehurst, Camelia	b. 1871, Baltimore, MD; d. 1936, Guilford, MD	MD
Whitman, Sarah De St. Prix Wyman	b. 1824, Lowell, MA; d. 1904, Boston, MA	MD
Whitney, Anna Josepha Newcomb	b. 1872, Washington, DC; d. 1968, Washington, DC	DC
Whorton, Hattie Hays	b. 1882, Pratt City, AL; d. 1982, Winston-Salem, NC	AL / NC
Wiener, Rosalie Mildred Roos	b. 1899; d. 1983, New Orleans, LA	LA
Wightman, Emilie M.	active in Washington, DC, 1911–1924	DC
Wilbur, Dorothy Thornton	b. Fincastle, VA; d. after 1956	DC / VA
Wilcox, Lois Dorothy	b. 1889, Pittsburgh, PA; d. 1958, Tryon, NC	NC
Wildenhain, Marguerite Friedlaender	b. 1896, Lyon, France; d. 1985, Pond Farm, CA	NC
Wilder, Cornelia Maclean	b. 1884, Savannah, GA; d. 1967, Savannah, GA	GA
Wiley, Anna Catherine	b. 1879, Coal Creek, TN; d. 1958, Philadelphia, PA	TN
Wiley, Eleanor McAdoo	b. 1876, Coal Creek, TN; d. 1977, Knoxville, TN	TN
Wiley, Grace Kirby	b. 1877, Smiths Grove, KY; d. 1952, Smiths Grove, KY	KY
Wilkes, Susan Heiskell	b. 1888, Nashville, TN; d. 1969, Morgantown, WV	TN / WV
Wilkins, Emma Cheves	b. 1870, Savannah, GA; d. 1956, Savannah, GA	GA
Wilkinson, Edith Lake	b. 1868, Wheeling, WV; d. 1957, Huntington, WV	WV
Wilkinson, Louise Wilson	b. 1899, Harrodsburg, KY; d. 1984, Danville, KY	KY
Wilkinson, Sarah R.	active in Washington, DC, 1914–1933	DC
Willard, Elizabeth "Bessie" Taylor	b. 1861, Washington, DC; d. 1944, Kingston, WA	NC
Willard, Irma Rosalind/Rosaline DeBlieux Sompayrac	b. 1897, Natchitoches, LA; d. 1991, New York, NY	LA
Williams, Adele	b. 1868, Richmond, VA; d. 1952, Richmond, VA	VA
Williams, Ann	b. 1906, Clinton, KY	KY
Williams, Dorothea Rockburne	b. 1944, Montreal, Canada	NC
Williams, Ethel	b. 1913, Sanford, NC; d. 1951, Wilmington, NC	NC
Williams, Henrietta "Etta" Frizelle	b. 1884, Savannah, GA; d. 1965, Wilmington, NC	GA / NC
Williams, Frances T.	b. 1882, TX	TN
Williams, Jane Iredell Meares	b. 1855, Wilmington, NC; d. 1935, Wilmington, NC	NC
Williams, Julia Tochie	b. 1887, Americus, GA; d. 1948, Macon, GA	GA

Artist	Life Dates	Associated With
Williams, Lida	b. 1859, KY; d. 1949, Henderson, KY	KY
Williams, Louisa A.	b. GA; active early twentieth century	GA
Williams, Lucy O.	b. 1875, Forrest City, AR; d. 1958, Forrest City, AR	AR
Williams, Margaret Click	b. 1930, Surry County, NC	NC
Williams, Marion Mudgett	b. 1869, Mille Lacs, MN; d. 1958, Los Angeles, CA	GA
Williams, Mary Lyde Hicks	b. 1866, Faison, NC; d. 1959, Faison, NC	NC
Williams, Nelly Miller	Fort McPherson, GA	GA
Williams, Olga Crawley	b. 1898, Sweetwater, TN; d. 1978, Asheville, NC	AR / NC / TN
Williams, Ora Marie Garland	b. 1910; d. 1985	LA
Williams, Pauline Bliss	b. 1888, Springfield, MA; d. 1962, Daytona Beach, FL	FL
Williams, Susie Pearl {Jones}	b. 1892, Danville, KY; d. 1984, Greensboro, NC	TN
Williams, Vera Baker	b. 1927, Hollywood, CA; d. 2015, Narrowsburg, NY	NC
Willingham, Helen Pittard Armour	b. 1921, Abbeville, SC; d. 2002, Washington, GA	GA / SC
Willis, Constance Clark	b. 1914, New York, NY; d. 2004, Natick, MA	KY
Willis, Eola Henley	b. 1856, Dalton, GA; d. 1952, Charleston, SC	GA / SC
Willis, Mary Motz	b. 1875, Blytheville, VA; d. 1961, Abilene, TX	GA / VA
Willis, Patty	b. 1879, Summit Point, WV; d. 1953, Charles Town, WV	WV
Willoughby, Alice Estelle	b. Groton, NY; d. 1924, Washington, DC	DC
Wills, Mary French Motz	b. 1875, VA; d. 1961, Abilene, TX	GA / VA
Wilson, Alice Pratt	b. 1909; d. 1981, Carmel-by-the-Sea, CA	VA
Wilson, Alice Steer	b. 1926; d. 2001, New Jersey	NC
Wilson, Ashton	b. 1880 Charleston, SC; d. 1952, Beaufort, SC	SC / WV
Wilson, Ellen Louise Axson	b. 1860, Savannah, GA; d. 1914, Washington, DC	DC / GA
Wilson, Julia Homer	b. 1910, Griffin, GA; d. 2001, Penn Valley, CA	GA / SC
Wilson, Vylla E. Poe	b. 1883, NJ; d. 1969, Washington, DC	DC
Wiltse, Clara Eastman	b. 1904; d. 1974, IN	WV
Winningham, Alma M.	b. 1878; d. 1959, Greensboro, NC	DC / NC
Winslow, Marcella Rodange Comès	b. 1905, Pittsburgh, PA; d. 2000, Washington, DC	DC / MS
Winston, Naomi Rabb	b. 1894, Evergreen, AL; d. 1979, Virginia Beach, VA	AL / DC / VA
Wise, Edythe Laurell Stephenson	b. 1924, Sheridan, WY; d. 2015, Spartanburg, SC	SC
Wise, Vera	b. 1892, Iola, KS; d. 1978, Stockton, CA	AL
Witherspoon, Evelyn Ruth Gladney	b. 1902, Bastrop, LA; d. 1998, LA	LA / TN
Witherspoon, Margaret	b. about 1914, New Orleans, LA; d. 2005, New Orleans, LA	LA
Witman, Mabel Foote	b. 1884, Washington, DC; d. 1941, Charlottesville, VA	DC / VA
Woelffer, Rachel Diana "Dina" Anderson	b. 1907; d. 1990, Los Angeles, CA	NC
Wohl, Mildred "Millie" Rittenberg	b. 1906, New Orleans, LA; d. 1977, New Orleans, LA	LA
Wolcott, Marion "Mary" Post	b. 1910, Montclair, NJ; d. 1990, Santa Barbara, CA	LA / SC
Wolf, May V.	active in Washington, DC, 1910–1916, 1926–1937	DC
Wolfe, Mildred Bernice Nungester	b. 1912, Celina, OH; d. 2009, Jackson, MS	MS
Wolfson, Emily Wilson	b. 1915, Corydon, KY; d. 2015, Murray, KY	KY / LA
Wood, Ella Miriam	b. 1888, Birmingham, AL; d. 1976, New Orleans, LA	LA
Wood, Ethelwyn	b. 1902, Germantown, PA; d. 1995, West Palm Beach, FL	FL
Wood, Jessie Porter	b. 1863, Syracuse, NY; d. 1941, Washington, DC	DC
Wood, Lillian Lee	b. 1906, Richmond, VA; d. 1989, Richmond, VA	VA

Artist	Life Dates	Associated With
Wood, Margaret	b. 1893	MD
Wood, Memphis	b. 1902, Dacula, GA; d. 1989, Atlanta, GA	GA
Wood, Virginia Hargrave	b. 1873, Washington, DC; d. 1941, Charlottesville, VA	DC / VA
Wood, Virginia Maude	b. 1895, Glen Dale, WV; d. 1992, Clarksburg, WV	WV
Woodham, Jean	b. 1925, Midland City, AL	AL
Woodring, Merle Crisler Foshag	b. 1899, Spokane, WA; d. 1977, Bethesda, MD	DC / MD
Woodward, Laura	b. 1834, Mount Hope, NY; d. 1926 , St. Cloud, FL	FL
Woodward, Leila Grace	b. 1858, Coldwater, MI; d. 1949, Coldwater, MI	DC
Woodward, Louise Amelia Giesen	b. 1862, New Orleans, LA; d. 1937, Biloxi, MS	LA / MS
Woodward, Mabel May	b. 1877, Providence, RI; d. 1945, Providence, RI	SC
Woodward, Martha Dewing [a.k.a. Dewing Woodward]	b. 1856, Williamsport, PA; d. 1950, Miami, FL	FL / MD
Woodward, Mary Belle Johnson	b. 1862, New York, NY; d. 1943, New Orleans, LA	LA
Wooldridge, Julia Ann Stanard	b. 1869, VA; d. 1938	VA
Woolfolk, Fanny Omer Owen	b. 1856, Louisville, KY; d. 1936, Louisville, KY	KY
Woolley, Virginia B.	b. 1884, Selma, AL; d. 1971, Laguna Beach, CA	AL / GA
Woolsey, Elizabeth Elsa Gamel	b. 1895, Aiken, SC; d. 1968, Málaga, Spain	SC
Woolwine, Marie Sudekum	b. 1907, Nashville, TN; d. 1998, Nashville, TN	TN
Wootten, Mary Bayard Morgan	b. 1876, New Bern, NC; d. 1959, New Bern, NC	NC
Wragg, Eleanor Toomer	b. 1860, SC; d. 1940, Bradford, CT	SC
Wrenn, Elizabeth Jencks	b. 1891, Newburgh, NY; d. 1978, Norfolk, VA	MD / VA
Wright, Sarah Jane	active in Washington, DC, 1908–1935	DC
Wyatt, Nan R.	active in Washington, DC, 1915–1916	DC
Wynne, Evelyn Burman	b. 1896, New York, NY; d. 1969, Washington, DC	DC
Wynne, Lillian Nunn	active in Durham, NC, 1924–1928	NC
Wynne, Madeline Yale	b. 1847, Newport, NY; d. 1918, Asheville, NC	NC
Yaffee, Edith Widing	b. 1895, Finland; d. 1961, Freeport, ME	DC
Yaghjian, Dorothy Candy	b. 1919; d. 1980, Columbia, SC	SC
Yandell, Enid Bland	b. 1869, Louisville, KY; d. 1934, Boston, MA	KY / TN
Yeiser, Mary Belle	b. 1905, Paducah, KY; d. 2008, Bardstown, KY	KY
Young, Helen Walcott	active in Washington, DC, 1920s	DC
Young, Mary Elizabeth	affiliated with Black Mountain College, 1933–1935	FL / NC
Young, May Belle Jones	b. 1891, Charleston, SC; d. 1968	SC
Youngs, Amelia Loretta L.	b. 1838; d. 1920, Washington, DC	DC
Yuditsky, Cornelia R.	b. 1895, Upper Marlboro, MD; d. 1980, Upper Marlboro, MD	DC / MD
Zhitlowsky, Eva Carina {Milton}	Croton-on-Hudson, NY	NC
Ziegler, Jane	b. Lansing, MI; active in Sarasota, FL, 1947–1959	FL
Zimmele, Margaret Scully	b. 1872, Pittsburgh; d. 1964, Kenwood, MD	DC / MD
Zimmerman, Jane	b. 1871, Frederick, MD; d. 1955, MD	MD
Zorach, Marguerite Thompson	b. 1887, Santa Rosa, CA; d. 1968, Brooklyn, NY	TN

THE PEDESTAL HAS CRASHED

1. Nell Battle Lewis, "Incidentally," *Raleigh (NC) News and Observer,* May 1, 1925, quoted in Anne Firo Scott, *The Southern Lady from Pedestal to Politics, 1830–1930* (Chicago: University of Chicago Press, 1970), 225.

2. Maria Weeden to Miss Arrington, March 16, 1904, quoted in Sarah Huff Fisk, "Howard Weeden, Artist and Poet," *The Alabama Review* 14 (April 1961), 125. Maria Howard Weeden (1847–1905) created compelling portraits in sepia tones of older African American residents of her Huntsville, Alabama, community who worked as gardeners, cooks, and nannies. She typically posed them in profile or three-quarter views, obviating any confrontation between sitter and viewer. Weeden had visited the 1893 World's Columbian Exposition in Chicago, where she encountered stereotypical and unflattering images of former slaves; shortly afterward, she resolved to make more uplifting likenesses, some of which were exhibited in galleries in Berlin and Paris. Many were included in small volumes of poetry, and when Weeden could not find verses aligned with her imagery, she wrote her own.

3. See Martha R. Severens, "Who was Henrietta Johnston?" *The Magazine Antiques* 148, no. 5 (1995), 704–9; Forsyth Alexander, ed., *Henrietta Johnston: "Who Greatly Helped…by Drawing Pictures"* (Winston-Salem, NC: Old Salem, 1991); Henrietta Johnston quoted in Frank J. Klingberg, ed., *Carolina Chronicle: The Papers of Commissary Gideon Johnston, 1707–1716* (Berkeley: University of California Press, 1946), 31.

4. Brown advertisement, *Charleston (SC) Mercury,* February 28, 1825, quoted in Anna Wells Rutledge, *Art and Artists of Charleston through Colony and State from Restoration to Reconstruction* (Philadelphia, PA: Transactions of the Philosophical Society, 1949), 158.

5. Margaret Mitchell, *Gone with the Wind* (New York: Macmillan, 1936), 59, quoted in Elizabeth Fox-Genovese, "Scarlett O'Hara: The Southern Lady as New Woman," in *Half Sisters of History: Southern Women and the American Past,* ed. Catherine Clinton (Durham, NC: Duke University Press, 1994), 158.

6. Edward H. Clarke, quoted in Catherine Clinton, *The Other Civil War: American Women in the Nineteenth Century* (New York: Hill and Wang, 1984), 131.

7. Jane Swisshelm, quoted in Clinton, *Other Civil War,* 51.

8. Blanche Lazzell, Morgantown, WV, to Arthur Lee Post, Baltimore, MD, July 1902, quoted in Susan M. Doll, "Blanche Lazzell Biography," in *Blanche Lazzell: The Life and Work of an American Modernist,* ed. Robert Bridges, Kristina Olson, and Janet Snyder (Morgantown: West Virginia University Press, 2004), 12.

9. Anna Heyward Taylor to Nell Taylor, July 14, 1904, quoted in Edmund R. Taylor and Alexander Moore, eds., *Selected Letters of Anna Heyward Taylor: South Carolina Artist and World Traveler* (Columbia: University of South Carolina Press, 2010), 29; Lillian Baynes, "Summer School at Shinnecock Hills," *The Art Amateur* 34 (1894): 91–92, quoted in D. Scott Atkinson, "Shinnecock and the Shinnecock Landscapes," in *William Merritt Chase: Summers at Shinnecock, 1891–1902,* ed. Jane Swinney (Washington, DC: National Gallery of Art, 1987), 26.

10. William Howard Taft, quoted in Amy McCandless, *The Past in the Present: Women's Higher Education in the Twentieth-Century South* (Tuscaloosa: University of Alabama Press, 1999), 62.

11. Georgia O'Keeffe to Alfred Stieglitz, February 1, 1916, quoted in Jack Cowart, Juan Hamilton, and Sarah Greenough, *Georgia O'Keeffe: Art and Letters* (Washington, DC: National Gallery of Art, 1988), 150.

12. Robert Henri, quoted in Erika Doss, "Complicating Modernism: Issues of Liberation and Constraint Among the Women Art Students of Robert Henri," in *American Women Modernists: The Legacy of Robert Henri, 1910–1945,* ed. Marian Wardle (New Brunswick, NJ: Brigham Young University Museum of Art in association with Rutgers University Press, 2005), 135; and Henri, quoted in Ellen Wiley Todd, *The "New Woman" Revised: Painting and Gender Politics on Fourteenth Street* (Berkeley: University of California Press, 1993), 18.

13. Blondelle Malone, quoted in Louise Jones DuBose, *Enigma: The Career of Blondelle Malone in Art and Society, 1879–1951, as Told in Her Letters and Diaries* (Columbia: University of South Carolina Press, 1963), 8–9; William M. Chase in "Notes from Talks by William M. Chase, Summer Class, Carmel-by-the-Sea, California, Memoranda from a Student's Note Book," *American Magazine of Art* 8, no. 11 (September 1917): 436; Chase, quoted in Wardle, ed., *American Women Modernists,* 106.

14. Helen Moseley, in a statement for the alumnae office of Converse College, May 5, 1952, Moseley Archives, Spartanburg, SC; and James F. Byrnes, typescript of a speech at a banquet given by Spartanburg Post Office employees, July 10, 1956, Moseley Archives.

15. Barbara Buhler Lynes, "Georgia O'Keeffe and Feminism: A Problem of Position," in *The Expanding Discussion: Feminism and Art History,* ed. Norma Broude and Mary D. Garrard (New York: Icon, 1992), 442.

16. Nell Blaine, quoted in Eleanor Munro, *American Women Artists* (New York: Simon and Schuster, 1979), 263.

17. Elizabeth Verner Hamilton, *Four Artists on One Block and How They Got Along* (Charleston, SC: Tradd Street Press, 1986), 9.

18. Anne Goldthwaite, in a 1934 radio interview, quoted in Adelyn Dohme Breeskin, *Anne Goldthwaite: 1869–1944* (Montgomery, AL: Montgomery Museum of Fine Arts, 1977), 9.

19. Helen Turner's remarks appeared in "New Orleans Has One of Four Women in the National Academy," *New Orleans Item-Tribune,* February 1, 1931, quoted in Maia Jalenak, "Helen M. Turner: An Enduring

Impressionist," in *Helen M. Turner: The Woman's Point of View*, ed. Jane Ward Faquin (Memphis, TN: Dixon Gallery, 2010), 14.

20. "The Bachelor Maid in Art," *The Southern Magazine* 5, no. 29 (February 1895), 504–7, quoted in Judy L. Larson, "Three Southern World's Fairs: Cotton States and International Exposition, Atlanta, 1895, Tennessee Centennial, 1897, South Carolina Inter-State and West Indian Exposition, Charleston, 1901–2: Creating Regional Self-Portraits" (PhD diss., Emory University, Atlanta, GA, 1998), 82, and Savage in an unidentified newspaper interview, quoted in Romare Bearden and Harry Henderson, *A History of African-American Artists: From 1792 to the Present* (New York: Pantheon, 1993), 168.

21. Anne Higonnet, "Wild at Heart: Rediscovering the Sculpture of Anna Hyatt Huntington," *The Magazine Antiques* 181, no. 1 (2014), 179.

22. Hamilton, *Four Artists*, 5.

23. Andrée Ruellan, 1992 interview with Donald D. Keyes, quoted in Keyes, "Andrée Ruellan: A Biography," in *Andrée Ruellan* (Athens: Georgia Museum of Art, University of Georgia, 1993), 30.

24. "Laura Glenn Douglas," American Art at the Phillips Collection, www.phillipscollection.org/research/american_art/bios/douglas-bio.htm.

25. Erskine Caldwell and Margaret Bourke-White, *You Have Seen Their Faces* (1937; reprint, Athens: University of Georgia Press, 1995), 1.

26. Doris Ulmann to Averell Broughton, October 4, 1929, quoted in David Featherstone, *Doris Ulmann: American Portraits* (Albuquerque: University of New Mexico Press, 1985), 43.

27. Heyward, quoted in Valerie Suzanne Bowen, "Katherine Bayard Heyward, South Carolina Art Educator" (master's thesis, University of South Carolina, 1991), 17.

28. McCallum to Valerie Bowen, February 12, 1990, quoted in Bowen, "Katherine Bayard Heyward," 23.

29. For information on female artists' often overlooked contributions to this movement, see Joan Marter, ed., *Women of Abstract Expressionism* (New Haven, CT: Denver Art Museum in association with Yale University Press, 2016).

30. Lynda Benglis, quoted in Robert Pincus-Witten, "Lynda Benglis: The Frozen Gesture," *Artforum* 13, no. 3 (November 1974), 58.

31. Cecilia Beaux, Barnard College speech, 1915, Cecilia Beaux Papers, Archives of American Art, Washington, DC, quoted in Laura R. Prieto, *At Home in the Studio: The Professionalization of Women Artists* (Cambridge, MA: Harvard University Press, 2001), 149.

SISTERHOODS OF SPIRIT

1. R. L. MacMillan, in "Many Big Plans Are Made for the Approaching Club Year: Art Program Attracts," *Winston-Salem (NC) Journal*, August 8, 1926, 3-C.

2. "Oscar Wilde in America" tour itinerary, www.oscarwildeinamerica.org/lectures-1882/itinerary.html (accessed January 1, 2017), and Deborah C. Pollack, *Visual Art and the Urban Evolution of the New South* (Columbia: University of South Carolina Press, 2015), 4–6. William Morris was the primary proponent of the Arts and Crafts movement, an offshoot of Aestheticism that advocated for the use of arts and crafts in home decoration and functional objects, a tenet that was reflected in the Ideal Home exhibitions, held primarily in Britain. During his 1882 American tour, Wilde encouraged Southerners to incorporate their region's natural beauty in home decor.

3. Jane Cunningham Croly, *The History of the Woman's Club Movement in America* (New York: Henry G. Allen & Co., 1898), 210, 218, 365; Pollack, *Visual Art*, 53, 70, 183; Florence N. Levy, ed., *American Art Annual*, vol. 14 (Washington, DC: American Federation of Arts, 1917), 57, 80, 114, 159, 228, 266, 267, 274, 277; and history of the Woman's Club of Louisville on the club's website, www.wcl1320.com (accessed March 5, 2011).

4. Patty Thum, "At Louisville," *Cleveland Leader*, September 13, 1883, 6; and Pollack, *Visual Art*, 183.

5. In an inscription on the back of her photograph of *Pallas Athena*, Yandell noted that the sculpture stood forty feet tall. An advertisement for low roundtrip railroad rates to the May 1, 1897, opening of the exposition, as well as various promotional articles concerning the centennial, made the same claim. Enid Yandell Papers, reel 2768 (frame numbers illegible), Archives of American Art, Smithsonian Institution, Washington, DC.

6. Nancy D. Baird, "Enid Yandell: Kentucky Sculptor," *Filson Club Historical Quarterly* 62 (January 1988): 5, 18–19; Herman Justi, ed., *Official History of the Tennessee Centennial Exposition* (Nashville: Brandon, 1898), 123. See also *Exhibition of Fine Arts, Catalog, South Carolina Inter-State and West Indian Exposition* (Charleston, SC: Lucas Richardson, 1902), 32. Yandell also served as a commissioner of the Tennessee Centennial's Fine Arts Department.

7. Among Willis's exhibited monotypes and paintings, one watercolor, *A Windy Day*, earned an honorable mention.

8. In the 1920s Willis chaired the Carolina Art Commission and the associate members of the Carolina Art Association. See "Willis, Eola," in *The Artist's Yearbook*, ed. Arthur Nicholas Hosking (Chicago: Art League Publishing Association, 1906), 222; "Mayor Names Art Board," *Charleston (SC) Evening Post*, May 26, 1925, 2; "Associate Members Carolina Art Assn.," *Charleston (SC) Evening Post*, December 15, 1926, 6; J. C. Hemphill to Willis, March 28, 1901; James B. Townsend to Willis, December 10, 1901; honorable mention certificate, "Fine Arts Committee," clipping; Martha Washington (chair of the press committee) to Willis, March 18, 1901; Willis, "Our Great Exposition," *New York Herald*, clipping. These items are found in the Eola Willis Scrapbook, Container 21/71/1, Eola Willis Papers, South Carolina Historical Society, Charleston, SC (hereafter Willis Scrapbook, Willis Papers). "Paintings Exhibited by Miss Willis," *Charleston (SC) News and Courier*, April 12, 1932, 8; and "The Charleston Awards—Studio Gossip," *Philadelphia Inquirer*, May 25, 1902, 4.

9. Willis to John H. Averill, March 18, 1901, Willis Scrapbook, Willis Papers.

10. *Fine Arts, West Indian Exhibition of Fine Arts*, 8, 13, 19, 27; clipping, May 24, 1902, Willis Scrapbook, Willis Papers; advertisement, *Spartanburg (SC) Herald*, March 17, 1923; classified advertisement, *Charleston (SC) News and Courier*, October 6, 1903, 3; "The Social World," *Charleston (SC) Evening Post*, November 22, 1902, 6; Estill Curtis Pennington and Martha R. Severens, *Scenic Impressions: Southern Interpretations from the Johnson Collection* (Spartanburg, SC: Johnson Collection in association with University of South Carolina Press, 2015), 170; and Karen Towers Klacsmann, "Emma Cheves Wilkins (1870–1956)," *New Georgia Encyclopedia*, www.georgiaencyclopedia.org/articles/arts-culture/emma-cheves-wilkins-1870-1956 (accessed January 2, 2016).

11. Blondelle Malone to parents, October 4, October 13, and November 16, 1902, from California, Blondelle Malone Papers, South Caroliniana Library, University of South Carolina, Columbia, SC;

"Social Personal," *Columbia (SC) State*, November 3, 1901; and "The State Fair in Full Blast," *Columbia (SC) State*, October 30, 1902, 1–2.

12. Mary I. Wood, *The History of the General Federation of Women's Clubs: For the First Twenty-Two Years of Its Organization* (New York: History Department of the General Federation of Women's Clubs, 1912), 128–31.

13. Mary Church Terrell, *A Colored Woman in a White World* (Amherst, NY: Humanity Books, 2005), 100.

14. Mary Church Terrell, "What the National Association Has Meant to Colored Women," typewritten manuscript, Mary Church Terrell Papers, Library of Congress, Manuscript Division, Washington, DC, 1; John H. Bracey Jr. and August Meier, "Records of the National Association of Colored Women's Clubs, 1895–1992," 1, 14, 42, www.lexisnexis.com/documents/academic/upa_cis/1555_RecsNatlAssoc ColWmsClubPt1.pdf (accessed December 14, 2015); and Kibibi Voloria C. Mack, *Parlor Ladies and Ebony Drudges: African American Women, Class, and Work in a South Carolina Community* (Knoxville: University of Tennessee Press, 1999), 104–5.

15. Annie Somers Gilchrist, *Some Representative Women of Tennessee* (Nashville, TN: McQuiddy, 1902), 78.

16. Robert Underwood Johnson, "The Establishment of Art Museums," in *The Proceedings of the First Annual Convention of the American Federation of Arts*, in *Supplement to Art and Progress, Art and Progress* 1 (July 1910), 88.

17. Kathleen D. McCarthy, *Women's Culture: American Philanthropy and Art, 1830–1930* (Chicago: University of Chicago Press, 1991), xiii, xiv, 44, 69; Pollack, *Visual Art,* 53; and "History," Woman's Club of Richmond, Virginia, http://twcrichmond.org/the-womans-club/history/ (accessed October 30, 2015).

18. Mrs. E. R. Michaux, "Report to the General Federation of Women's Clubs," in Mrs. Everett W. Pattison, "Art and the Women's Clubs," *Federation Bulletin,* April 1910, 223; and Florence N. Levy, ed., *American Art Annual*, vol. 8 (Washington, DC: American Federation of Arts, 1910–1911), 344.

19. Sarah Visanska, "South Carolina," in General Federation of Women's Clubs, *Tenth Biennial Convention, May 11–19, 1910, Cincinnati, Ohio* (Newark, NJ: General Federation of Women's Clubs, 1910), 342.

20. Levy, *American Art Annual*, vol. 14 (1917), 57, 80, 114, 159, 228, 266, 267, 274, 277.

21. Catherine Wiley, "The Art Exhibit of the National Conservation Exposition," in *The First Exposition of Conservation and Its Builders*, ed. W. S. Goodman (Knoxville, TN: Press of Knoxville Lithographing Company, 1914), 280–82; Fine Arts Committee, Appalachian Exposition, *Catalogue of the Fine Arts Section of the Appalachian Exposition, Sept. 12 to Oct. 12, 1910* (Knoxville, TN: S. B. Newman & Co., 1910), 1–78. Levy, *American Art Annual*, vol. 8 (1910–1911), 105, lists Parrish's painting as *The Green Lampshade.*

22. Goodman, ed., *First Exposition of Conservation*, 131; Pennington and Severens, *Scenic Impressions,* 128, 181–182; "Art in the Tennessee State Fair," *American Magazine of Art* 11, no. 13 (November 1920): 484–85; Delia Gaze, "Augusta Savage," in *Concise Dictionary of Women Artists*, ed. Delia Gaze (New York: Routledge, 2001), 601; Florence N. Levy, ed., *American Art Annual*, vol. 30 (Washington, DC: American Federation of Arts, 1933), 478; and Peter Hastings Falk, ed., *Who Was Who in American Art: 1564–1975* (Madison, CT: Sound View Press, 1999), 2:1538. The *American Art Annual,* reporting on the 1910 fair, did not list Hergesheimer as a medal winner. Goodman and Wiley assert that Hergesheimer won the medal in 1911.

23. Alabama Federation of Women's Clubs, "Resolutions Adopted at Convention," November 18–20, 1920, *Year Book: Alabama Federation of Women's Clubs* (Montgomery, AL: Paragon, 1921), 48–50.

24. Carol M. Sax, "Club Members to See Exhibit Again," *Lexington (KY) Herald*, March 21, 1921, 12.

25. "Southern Art League Exhibit to Open Tuesday," *Charlotte (NC) Observer*, November 22, 1925, 23.

26. Ben Steelman, "Who is Elisabeth Chant?" StarNewsMedia, April 22, 2009, www.myreporter.com/2009/04/elisabeth-chant/ (accessed December 17, 2015).

27. "Give Prizes in Woman's Club," *Biloxi (MS) Daily Herald*, January 18, 1929, 8; "Art Department Meeting," *Biloxi (MS) Daily Herald*, April 8, 1926, 2.

28. "Local Artists Are Lauded," *Charleston (SC) Evening Post*, December 28, 1927, 11; Edmund R. Taylor and Alexander Moore, eds., *Selected Letters of Anna Heyward Taylor: South Carolina Artist and World Traveler* (Columbia: University of South Carolina Press, 2010), xxvi–xxvii.

29. Karen J. Blair, *The Torchbearers: Women and Their Amateur Arts Associations in America, 1890–1930* (Bloomington: Indiana University Press, 1994), 89, 90.

30. Grace King to Angela Gregory, June 26, 1929, and November 19, 1930, Angela Gregory Papers, Box 12, Louisiana Research Collection, Tulane University, New Orleans, LA; and "Stratford Club to Entertain Tonight Honoring Debutantes," *New Orleans Times-Picayune*, November 13, 1930, 19.

31. "Woman's Club Forecast," *Charlotte (NC) Observer*, March 8, 1931, 16.

32. Pennington and Severens, *Scenic Impressions,* 144–45.

33. Eola Willis, "South Carolina Federation of Women's Clubs," *Charleston (SC) News and Courier*, November 22, 1931.

34. Anne Cantrell White, "Mabel Pugh Is Versatile with Brush, Pencil, or Pen," *Greensboro (NC) Daily News*, October 18, 1931, Sec. 2–5; "Mabel Pugh's Block Prints to Be Shown for Woman's Club," *Greensboro (NC) Daily News*, March 8, 1932, 8; "Local People View Art Exhibit at Winston-Salem," *Greensboro (NC) Daily News*, May 6, 1932, 8.

35. Mack, *Parlor Ladies and Ebony Drudges,* 104–5; "History of Montgomery City Federation of Women's Clubs, Inc.," on the Jackson Community House website, www.jacksoncommunityhouse.org (accessed November 13, 2015).

36. "Works Chosen by Museum for Exhibit," *Richmond (VA) Times-Dispatch*, September 29, 1940, 18.

37. "Exhibit of Paintings to Open on Sunday at Woman's Clubhouse," *Columbus (GA) Daily Enquirer*, April 5, 1941, 10.

38. Sally Cline, *Zelda Fitzgerald: The Tragic, Meticulously Researched Biography of the Jazz Age's High Priestess* (New York: Arcade, 2012), xvii; Sally Cline, *Zelda Fitzgerald, Her Voice in Paradise,* e-book (London: Faber and Faber, 2013), loc. 11280, 11315, 11427, 11437; Mary Jo Tate, *Critical Companion to F. Scott Fitzgerald: A Literary Reference to His Life and Work* (New York: Facts on File, 2007), 304; Nancy Milford, *Zelda: A Biography* (1970; reprint, New York: Harper Perennial, 2001).

39. "Colonel Vaughan Heard by Club," *Charleston (SC) Evening Post,* January 28, 1943, 6.

40. Florence N. Levy, ed., *American Art Annual*, vol. 35 (Washington, DC: American Federation of Arts, 1944), 209, 360.

41. Florence N. Levy, ed., *American Art Annual*, vol. 37 (Washington, DC: American Federation of Arts, 1948), 62.

42. Maurice C. York, *The Privilege to Paint: The Lives of Francis Speight and Sarah Blakeslee* (Greenville, NC: Greenville Museum of Art, 2002), 67.

43. "Artist to Show Paintings Here," *Greensboro (NC) Daily News*, March 11, 1959, 7; Steve Gilliam, "Studio Arts Building Named for N.C. Artist Maud Gatewood," *University of North Carolina at Greensboro University News*, May 2006; Maud Gatewood obituary, *Washington Post*, November 12, 2004, www.askart.com/artist_bio/Maud_Florance_Gatewood/105684/Maud_Florance_Gatewood.aspx (accessed December 19, 2015).

44. Merry A. Foresta, *A Life in Art: Alma Thomas, 1891–1978* (Washington, DC: Smithsonian Institution Press, 1981), 40. In her chronology of the artist's life, Foresta notes that Thomas organized several student art clubs, as well as a "Saturday morning art appreciation club" and the YWCA Art Club (39).

SUFFRAGE, SOCIAL ACTIVISM, AND WOMEN ARTISTS OF THE SOUTH

1. Anita Pollitzer to Georgia O'Keeffe, December 1916, in Clive Biboire, ed., *Lovingly Georgia: The Complete Correspondence of Georgia O'Keeffe and Anita Pollitzer* (New York: Simon and Schuster, 1990), 225. It was at Pollitzer's prompting that O'Keeffe joined the National Woman's Party, and she maintained her membership as Pollitzer ascended its ranks. See Charles C. Eldredge, *Georgia O'Keeffe: American and Modern* (New Haven, CT: Yale University Press, 1993), 20. In the summer of 1918 Pollitzer, then teaching at the University of Virginia, organized the first suffrage rally at the university. See Amy Thompson McCandless, "Anita Pollitzer: A South Carolina Advocate for Equal Rights," in *South Carolina Women, Their Loves and Times*, vol. 2, ed. Marjorie Julian Spruill, Valinda W. Littlefield, and Joan Marie Johnson (Athens: University of Georgia Press, 2010), 171.

2. McCandless, "Anita Pollitzer," 166–89. Pollitzer was affiliated with Alice Paul, the founder of the radical National Woman's Party. See Christine A. Lunardini, *From Equal Suffrage to Equal Rights: Alice Paul and the National Woman's Party, 1910–1918* (New York: New York University Press, 1986).

3. "Woman's Party Asks Passage of Equal Rights Amendment," *Washington Post*, December 9, 1940, 9. Pollitzer remarked that the South Carolina member of Congress whom they petitioned for a meeting did not acknowledge their letter, thinking it "was a practical joker…he had no idea women really wanted any rights."

4. Besides parades, activists organized public pageants to promote their message. See "Pageantry and the Women's Rights Movement, 1905–1925," in Karen J. Blair, *The Torchbearers: Women and the Amateur Art Associations in American, 1890–1930* (Bloomington: Indiana University Press, 1994), 118–42; particularly see pages 137–39 for details regarding Hazel MacKaye's pageant for women's suffrage in March 1913, which coincided with Wilson's inauguration.

5. The name derived from the women's silent protest. See Belinda A. Stillion Southard, "Militancy, Power, and Identity: The Silent Sentinels as Women Fighting for Political Voice," *Rhetoric and Public Affairs* 10, no. 3 (Fall 2007): 405, 399–417. See also Belinda A. Stillion Southard, *Militant Citizenship: Rhetorical Strategies of the National Woman's Party, 1913–1920* (College Station: Texas A & M University Press, 2011).

6. For Reynau's political activism, see Katherine H. Adams and Michael L. Keene, *After the Vote Was Won: The Later Achievements of Fifteen Suffragists* (London: McFarland & Co., 2010), 58–59. American suffragists modeled much of their activity on that of their compatriots in England. British women artists established the Artists' Suffrage League and the Suffrage Atelier in 1909 to create visual materials and agitate for the cause. See Lisa Tickner, *Spectacle of Women: Imagery of the Suffrage Campaign, 1907–1914* (Chicago: University of Chicago Press, 1988), 13–26. Tickner suggests that "suffragists were interested in the woman artist because she was a type of the skilled and independent woman, with attributes of autonomy, creativity and professional competence, which were still unconventional by contemporary criteria" (14).

7. Many suffragists were jailed at Occoquan Workhouse in northern Virginia; conditions there and in the District of Columbia jail were abhorrent, and women suffered severe physical and mental violence. For a firsthand account, see Doris Stevens, *Jailed for Freedom: American Women Win the Vote* (New York: Boni and Liveright, 1920). A large photographic collection at the Library of Congress records a variety of advocacy events and includes individual portraits of the suffragists; see "Women of Protest: Photographs from the Records of the National Woman's Party," https://www.loc.gov/collection/women-of-protest/about-this-collection/ (accessed June 3, 2016).

8. Philip N. Cohen, "Nationalism and Suffrage: Gender Struggle in Nation-Building America," *Signs* 21, no. 3 (Spring 1996): 721. For Wilson's attitudes toward suffrage, see Sally Hunter Graham, "Woodrow Wilson, Alice Paul, and the Woman Suffrage Movement," *Political Science Quarterly* 98 (Winter 1983–1984): 665–79; and Christine Lunardini and Thomas Knock, "Woodrow Wilson and Woman Suffrage: A New Look," *Political Science Quarterly* 95 (Winter 1980–1981): 655–71.

9. Suffragists continued to picket the White House throughout 1918; for an autoptic account, see Inez Haynes Irwin, "Burning the President's Words Again: A Demonstration at the White House, 1918," in *Votes for Women!: The Woman Suffrage Movement in Tennessee, the South, and the Nation*, ed. Marjorie Spruill Wheeler (Knoxville: University of Tennessee Press, 1995), 174–80.

10. Adams and Keene, *After the Vote Was Won*, 19. For Havemeyer's activities, see entries for 1913, 1915, 1917, and 1919 in Susan Alyson Stein, "Chronology," in *Splendid Legacy: The Havemeyer Collection*, Alice Cooney Frelinghuysen et al. (New York: Metropolitan Museum of Art, 1993). Havemeyer's radicalism greatly displeased her socially privileged family, and she noted that given their reactions one might have surmised that she had "stripped the family tree…had broken its branches…had torn up its roots and laid it prostrate in the sorrowing dust." Cited in Adams and Keene, *After the Vote Was Won*, 29.

11. On the supportive networks that engendered fruitful cooperation, see "Female Support Networks and Political Activism," in Nancy Cott and Elizabeth Pleck, *A Heritage of Her Own: Toward a New Social History of American Women* (New York: Simon and Schuster, 1979).

12. Ellen W. Todd, *The "New Woman" Revised: Painting and Gender Politics on Fourteenth Street* (Berkeley: University of California Press, 1993), 1–38; and Laura R. Prieto, *At Home in the Studio: The Professionalization of Women Artists in America* (Cambridge, MA: Harvard University Press, 2001), 145–78. For the Southern context, see Anne Firor Scott, "'The New Woman' in the New South," *South Atlantic Quarterly* 61 (Autumn 1962): 473–83.

13. The literature on suffrage in the South is large and expanding. See Anne Firor Scott, *The Southern Lady: From Pedestal to Politics,*

1830–1930 (Charlottesville: University of Virginia Press, 1995); Marjorie Spruill Wheeler, *New Women of the New South: The Leaders of the Woman Suffrage Movement in the Southern States* (New York: Oxford University Press, 1993); and Anne Firor Scott, "After Suffrage: Southern Women in the Twenties," *The Journal of Southern History* 30, no. 3 (August 1964): 298–318.

14. My search for Southern women artists invested in suffrage is indebted to Deborah C. Pollack, *Visual Art and the Urban Evolution of the New South* (Columbia: University of South Carolina Press, 2015).

15. For Ney, see Emily Fourmy Cutrer, *The Art of the Woman: The Life and Work of Elisabet Ney* (Lincoln: University of Nebraska Press, 1988); and Alexandra Comini, "Who Ever Heard of a Woman Sculptor? Harriet Hosmer, Elisabet Ney, and the Nineteenth-Century Dialogue with the Three Dimensional," in *American Women Artists 1830–1930*, ed. Eleanor Tufts (Washington, DC: National Museum of Women in the Arts, 1987), 17–25.

16. Elisabet Ney, letter to Sara Underwood, March 14, 1886, cited in Cutrer, *Art of the Woman*, 176. Ney often flaunted masculine attire that, as a contemporary observer noted, consisted of "white trousers, a black 'Prince Albert' coat, and boots reaching her knees. She carried a cane." Henry B. Dielmann, "Elisabet Ney, Sculptor," *The Southern Historical Quarterly* 65, no. 2 (October 1961): 159.

17. Elisabet Ney to Mariana Folsom, December 3, 1898, at www.tsl. texas.gov/exhibits/suffrage/battle/ney-folsom-4.html (accessed May 28, 2016). Nannie Zenobia Carver Huddle (1860–1951) was born in Mobile, Alabama, but moved to Austin in her youth. She apprenticed with William Henry Huddle (1847–1892), whom she later married. Following his death she returned to painting, and she pursued her training further in the early 1900s. See various citations in Cutrer, *Art of the Woman*, and Patricia D. Hendricks and Becky D. Reese, *A Century of Sculpture in Texas, 1889–1989* (Austin: Huntington Art Gallery, University of Texas at Austin, 1989).

18. For Ney's attitudes toward women's rights, see Cutrer, *Art of the Woman*, 176–77 and 246, note 3.

19. Erika Doss, "Complicating Modernism: Issues of Liberation and Constraint among the Women Art Students of Robert Henri," in *American Women Modernists: The Legacy of Robert Henri, 1910–1945*, ed. Marian Wardle (New Brunswick, NJ: Brigham Young University Museum of Art in association with Rutgers University Press, 2005), 119.

20. The criteria for the ideal "Girl of To-Day," as published in the December 7, 1913, edition of the *New York Times*, were both vague and florid: "She best represents the elusiveness of the subject. She is To-day.…Her costume is purely modern, yet could almost be of another century. She is American, yet she suggests other races. She is neither gay nor sad. She is beautiful, but not oppressive with it. There is mystery in her eyes—there is mystery in the whole picture." The winner was eighteen-year-old Helen McMahon. She was of "Irish-English ancestry," had received a Catholic education, "earne[d] her own living," and was "fond of open air sports" ("About the 'Girl of To-Day,'" *New York Times*, December 8, 1913, 5:2). The rest of the story of McMahon's life reads like a soap opera; in 1920 she married James Cox Brady, one of the wealthiest men of the day, who unfortunately died young in 1924, leaving his widow and children an inheritance of 20 million dollars. McMahon later married C. Suydam Cutting, a wealthy and influential patron of Asian art. Helen McMahon Brady Cutting was the first white woman to visit the Dalai Lama ("C. Suydam Cutting, Who Made Historic Visit to Tibet, Is Dead," *New York Times*, August 25, 1972). For more information about the competition and for Henri's opinions, see "New Ideals Shown by 'Girl of To-Day,'" *New York Times*, October 29, 1913, 5. I am grateful to Alexis Boylan for alerting me to this competition and for sharing this article with me. Other artists in the Henri circle, including William J. Glackens (1870–1938) and John Sloan (1871–1951), were supportive of suffrage. Glackens and his wife, Edith Dimock (1876–1955), had participated in suffrage parades. John Sloan's wife, Dolly Sloan, joined the Woman's Suffrage Committee in 1910 and was very involved in suffrage activities as an extension of her commitment to Socialist ideals. See Alexis Boylan, "The Curious Case of the Two Mrs. Sloans," *Woman's Art Journal* 33, no. 1 (Spring/Summer 2012): 26.

21. For a discussion of these shows, see Charles Musser, "1913: A Feminist Movement in the Arts," in *The Armory Show at 100: Modernism and Revolution*, ed. Marilyn Satin Kushner and Kimberly Orcutt (New York: New York Historical Society, 2013), 169–79. Musser argues that because these events were held close to or concurrent with the Armory Show, they demonstrated women artists' dissatisfaction with the preponderance of male painters and sculptors at the larger exhibition. Exhibitions to benefit suffrage were also held in 1912 at the Knoedler Galleries, much to the consternation of anti-suffragists who threatened to destroy the artworks. See "Art for Woman's Suffrage: Exhibition of Goya and El Greco Paintings at Knoedler Galleries," *New York Times*, April 2, 1912, 12; and "Art Show Offends 'Anti,'" *New-York Tribune*, April 3, 1912, 7.

22. See Mariea Caudill Dennison, "Babies for Suffrage: The Exhibition of Painting and Sculpture by Women Artists for the Benefit of the Woman Suffrage Campaign," *Woman's Art Journal* 24, no. 2 (2003/2004): 25. In April 1915 Havemeyer exerted her influence in organizing an art exhibit at Knoedler Galleries, the proceeds of which enriched the coffers of the Woman Suffrage Campaign Fund; she also gave a talk on Mary Cassatt and Edgar Degas in connection with the show. See James Briton, "Old Masters for 'Suffrage,'" *American Art News* 33, no. 27 (April 1915): 1–2; and "Art Exhibit for Suffrage: A Rubens among Old Master's Paintings at Knoedler's" *New York Times*, April 6, 1915, 10. See also Rebecca A. Rabinow, "The Suffrage Exhibition of 1915," in Frelinghuysen et al., *Splendid Legacy*, 89–95.

23. For additional information on Anne Goldthwaite, see Mariea Caudill Dennison, "Art of the American South, 1915–1945: Picturing the Past, Portending Regionalism" (Ph.D. diss., University of Illinois at Urbana, 2000), 294–310. The Parisian sojourn left an indelible mark on Goldthwaite's art, as she met Gertrude Stein and was exposed to the radical experimentations in the work of Henri Matisse and Pablo Picasso.

24. For Wright's activism, see Betsy Fahlman, *Sculpture and Suffrage: The Art and Life of Alice Morgan Wright (1881–1975)* (Albany, NY: Albany Institute of History and Art, 1978). Already active in suffrage prior to her European studies, Wright galvanized her allegiance to the movement following her encounter with the English suffragist Emmeline Pankhurst (1858–1928). Her activism in London led to her arrest in 1912. For the experiences of artists at the American Girls' Club, see Emily C. Burns, "Revising Bohemia: The American Artist Colony in Paris, 1890–1914," in *Foreign Artists and Communities in Modern Paris, 1870–1914: Strangers in Paradise*, ed. Karen L. Carter and Susan Waller (Burlington, VT: Ashgate, 2015), 7–110; and Mariea Caudill Dennison, "The American Girls' Club in Paris: The Propriety and Imprudence of Art Students, 1890–1914," *Woman's Art Journal*, 26, no. 1 (Spring/Summer 2005): 32–37. For the educational opportunities available to women

artists in Paris, see Kristen Swinth, *Painting Professional: Women Artists and the Development of Modern American Art, 1870–1930* (Chapel Hill: University of North Carolina Press, 2001), 37–62.

25. Quoted in Adelyn Dohme Breeskin, *Anne Goldthwaite: A Catalogue Raisonné of the Graphic Work* (Montgomery, AL: Montgomery Museum of Fine Arts, 1982), 25. Goldthwaite described in detail the transformative impact of the Parisian experience on Ethel Mars and Maud Hunt Squire, two artists from the American Midwest who also participated at the 1915 Macbeth show.

26. Breeskin, *Anne Goldthwaite*, 21.

27. Mary Elinor Poppenheim, letter to Mary Poppenheim, February 6, 1884, cited in Joan Marie Johnston, *Southern Women at Vassar: The Poppenheim Family Letters 1882–1916* (Columbia: University of South Carolina Press, 2002), 38. Neither Mary nor Louisa married; following their return to Charleston they dedicated their lives to artistic pursuits, Southern heritage, and philanthropic associations. See Johnston, *Southern Women at Vassar*, 11–12. Kentucky artist Patty Thum (1853–1926) also studied at Vassar, at the Art Students League with Chase, and later with Thomas Eakins (1844–1916). A prolific writer and an advocate for the arts in her state, Thum was also a suffragist; see Pollack, *Visual Art*, 183. For the suffrage movement at Vassar, see "The Suffrage Movement at Vassar," Vassar Encyclopedia, http://vcencyclopedia.vassar.edu/interviews-reflections/the-suffrage-movement.html (accessed June 2, 2016).

28. See Grace Elizabeth Hale, "Painting in the South: Class, Gender, and Race in the Life and Work of Lucy M. Stanton" (master's thesis, University of Georgia, 1991), 65.

29. See Betty Alice Fowler and Andrew Ladis, *The Art of Lucy May Stanton* (Athens: Georgia Museum of Art, University of Georgia, 2002), 19. In Paris Stanton studied with James McNeill Whistler (1834–1903) and would later adopt his chromatic analogies in some of her portraits, such as her 1923 *Self-Portrait in Blue, Gray, and Purple*, illustrated in Fowler and Ladis, *Art of Lucy May Stanton*, 111. Stanton returned to Atlanta at the conclusion of her first trip to Paris in 1898, establishing her career as a watercolor miniature painter and an art teacher amid a coterie of other female artists, including portraitist and illustrator Adelaide Everhart (1865–1958).

30. Stanton further claimed that the restrictions of the home were injurious to young women because "it is when in the shelter of her family, off her guard, and listening perhaps to their advice and entreaty that she comes to harm. There perchance she sells her birthright for peace; there she lays down her ideals for others of their choosing." See Hale, "Painting in the South," 70–71.

31. For an excellent account of the Shinnecock Hills Summer School of Art, see Cynthia V. A. Schaffner and Lori Zabar, "The Founding and Design of William Merritt Chase's Shinnecock Hills Summer School of Art and the Art Village," *Winterthur Portfolio* 44, no. 4 (December 2010): 303–50.

32. Priscilla Cortelyou Little and Robert C. Vaughan, *A New Perspective: Southern Women's Cultural History from the Civil War to Civil Rights* (Charlottesville: Virginia Foundation for the Humanities, 1989), 45–46. Clark often signed her works "Freeman Clark," clearly capitalizing on the gender ambiguity to promote her career. See also Cynthia Grant Tucker, *Kate Freeman Clark: A Painter Rediscovered* (Jackson: University Press of Mississippi, 1981). Although she had successfully exhibited her work at national exhibitions, Clark returned to Mississippi in 1922 and abandoned painting.

33. Marietta Minnigerode Andrews, *Memoirs of a Poor Relation: Being the Story of a Post-War Southern Girl and Her Battle with Destiny* (New York: E. P. Dutton, 1927), 195. For more information on Andrews, see Barbara J. Griffin, "The Life of a Poor Relation: The Art and Artistry of Marietta Minnigerode Andrews," *Virginia Cavalcade* 40, no. 4 (Spring 1991): 148–59; and Barbara J. Griffin, "The Life of a Poor Relation: The Art and Artistry of Marietta Minnigerode Andrews," *Virginia Cavalcade* 41, no. 1 (Summer 1991): 20–33.

34. Grace Elizabeth Hale, "'Some Women Have Never Been Reconstructed': Mildred Lewis Rutherford, Lucy M. Stanton, and the Racial Politics of White Southern Womanhood, 1900–1930," in *Georgia in Black and White: Explorations in the Race Relations of a Southern State, 1865–1950,* ed. John C. Inscoe (Athens: University of Georgia Press, 1994), 192. According to Hale, Stanton was "very close" to her friend artist Polly Smith, who supported her financially while the two were in Paris; see Hale, "Painting in the South," 65–67.

35. For Stanton's involvement with suffrage, see Hale "Painting in the South," 74; and W. Stanton Forbes, *Lucy M. Stanton* (Atlanta: Special Collections Department, Emory University, 1975).

36. For the complexities of the suffrage movement in Virginia, see Sara Hunter Graham, "Woman Suffrage in Virginia: The Equal Suffrage League and Pressure-Politics, 1909–1920," *The Virginia Magazine of History and Biography* 101, no. 2 (1993): 227–50; and Charlotte Jean Sheldon, "Woman Suffrage and Virginia Politics, 1909–1920," (master's thesis, University of Virginia, 1969). In 1920 Tennessee became the thirty-sixth state to ratify the Nineteenth Amendment; Alabama, Delaware, Georgia, Louisiana, Maryland, Mississippi, South Carolina, and Virginia refused to ratify the amendment in 1920.

37. Winston Broadfoot, "Interview with Adele Clark," Southern Oral History Program, February 28, 1964, http://docsouth.unc.edu/sohp/G-0014-2/G-0014-2.html (accessed June 13, 2016).

38. In recognition of her social activism, Adèle Clark will be one of the women commemorated in bronze in the forthcoming Virginia Women's Monument; see "Women's Monument Commission," http://womensmonumentcom.virginia.gov/index.html. Two studies deal with aspects of Clark and Houston's careers and political activism: Amanda Garrett, "Adèle Clark: Suffragist and Women's Rights Pioneer for Virginia" (honor's thesis, University of Virginia, 1999); and Colleen Yoder, "Nora Houston: Artist and Activist" (master's thesis, California State University, 2010). For Houston, see also L. M. Simms, "Nora Houston: Richmond Artist," *The Richmond Literature and History Quarterly* (Summer 1979): 44–46.

39. For connections between the Art Club and the political activism of Clark and Houston, see Shirley Ann Showers, "Nora Houston: A Long Life of Service to Art in Virginia," unpublished essay, 1972, 7, Adèle Clark Papers, Box 16, James Cabell Library, Virginia Commonwealth University, Richmond, Virginia. Houston's mother, Josephine Dooley Houston, a devoted suffragist, served as the Art Club's secretary.

40. For the social and cultural activism in women's clubs, see Anne Ruggles Gere, *Intimate Practices: Literacy and Cultural Work in U.S. Women's Clubs, 1880–1920* (Urbana: University of Illinois Press, 1997). For the South in particular, see Mary Martha Thomas, *The New Woman in Alabama: Social Reform and Suffrage, 1890–1920* (Tuscaloosa: University of Alabama Press, 1992).

41. Broadfoot, "Interview with Adèle Clark," 2. At a later point, Clark castigated the militarism of the Woman's Party, favoring instead

the "educational" and "non-partisan" methods of the National American Woman Suffrage Association. Alice Dooley, Nora Houston's aunt, also asked her brother Major James Dooley, a board member at the club, to sign a petition to Congress. Major Dooley declined because his spouse, Sally May Dooley, opposed suffrage and was a member of the Virginia Association Opposed to Woman Suffrage, which had been formed in 1913. See Charles Caravati, *Major Dooley* (Richmond: Maymond Foundation 1978).

42. For the ideological underpinnings of the suffrage movement in Virginia and its distinctly racial overtones, see Suzanne Lebsock, "Women Suffrage and White Supremacy: A Virginia Case Study," in *Visible Women: New Essays on American Activism,* ed. Nancy A. Hewitt and Suzanne Lebsock (Urbana: University of Illinois Press, 1993), 62–100.

43. Broadfoot, "Interview with Adèle Clark," 20–21. Clark and Houston's efforts were not always unopposed. Clark attested that white activists were often accused of being "Negro-lovers" and at times were the target of "a certain veiled violence." When Houston spoke at a rally at Jefferson Park—located in a predominantly black neighborhood—"rocks were thrown" at her (Broadfoot, "Interview with Adèle Clark," 39). Both Clark and Houston were instrumental in interracial cooperation movements such as the Urban League and the Women's Section of the Commission on Interracial Cooperation. The Commission on Interracial Cooperation was founded in Atlanta in 1919, and by 1924 there were a number of state branches.

"OF THE SOUTH, FOR THE SOUTH AND BY THE SOUTH"

1. The states that constituted the Southern States Art League upon the ratification of its constitution in 1923 were Alabama, Arkansas, Florida, Georgia, Kentucky, Louisiana, Maryland, Mississippi, Missouri, North Carolina, Oklahoma, South Carolina, Tennessee, Texas, Virginia, and West Virginia, as well as the District of Columbia.

2. According to the bylaws of the organization, artists whose work was considered for exhibition had to list the art schools they had attended and the names of their teachers.

3. H. L. Mencken, "The Sahara of the Bozart," *New York Evening Mail,* November 13, 1917.

4. See Larry J. Griffin and Peggy G. Hargis, eds., *The New Encyclopedia of Southern Culture,* Vol. 20: *Social Class* (Chapel Hill: University of North Carolina Press), 201–9.

5. "Big Art Association Formed for the South," *American Art News* 19, no. 29 (April 1921): 4. These artists' names appear in the exhibition catalog as J. S. Couper, Marie Atkinson Hull, Margaret M. Law, Willie Betty Newman, Clara Weaver Parrish, and Alice R. Huger Smith. Law was awarded third prize in the oil painting category for her entry, *Feeding Chickens,* and Alice Smith was selected for second prize in the watercolor category for a set of watercolors. The jury of awards consisted of Birge Harrison, Alfred Hutty, Florence Makin McIntyre, and Mrs. Earle Sloan.

6. Birge Harrison, "The All-Southern Exhibition," *American Magazine of Art* 12, no. 5 (May 1921): 166–69.

7. Betty A. Fowler, "Lucy May Stanton (1875–1931)," *New Georgia Encyclopedia,* December 6, 2013, www.georgiaencyclopedia.org/articles/arts-culture/lucy-may-stanton-1875-1931 (accessed February 10, 2016).

8. For example, the region of sixteen states and Washington, DC, is larger than the Confederacy and more expansive than the definition of the South used by the Center for the Study of Southern Culture in Oxford, Mississippi or by the Southeastern College Art Conference.

9. See Amy Kirschke, "The Southern States Art League: A List of Members," *Southern Quarterly* 26, no. 2 (Winter 1988): 51–63; Southern States Art League Records, 1921–1950, Louisiana Research Collection, Manuscripts Collection 11, Howard-Tilton Memorial Library, Tulane University, New Orleans, Louisiana.

10. *Southern States Art League Newsletter* 22, no. 3 (Winter 1947).

11. The exhibition catalog *Second Annual Exhibition of Works by Southern Artists,* Brooks Memorial Art Gallery, Memphis, TN, April 15 to May 30, 1922, notes six photographs by Richards.

12. "Constitution and Bylaws of the Southern States Art League Incorporated." Article III concerns membership.

13. Ellsworth Woodward, "An Art League Extension," *Times-Picayune,* September 27, 1922.

14. Amy Kirschke, "The Southern States Art League: A Regionalist Artists' Organization, 1922–1950," *Southern Quarterly* 25, no. 2 (Winter 1987): 8.

15. J. Richard Gruber, "Ethel Hutson," *Know Louisiana: The Digital Encyclopedia of Louisiana,* www.knowlouisiana.org/entry/ethel-hutson, September 12, 2012 (accessed February 17, 2016).

16. Ethel Hutson, "Sixth Circuit Exhibit of Art Shown at Delgado," undated newspaper article, ca. 1928, Georgia Historical Society, Savannah, GA, Manuscript Collection 869, Folder 17.

17. Amy Roe, "Madeline McDowell Breckinridge," http://explore kyhistory.ky.gov/items/show/334. Additional information is found in the Madeline McDowell Breckinridge Papers, 1867, 1888–1923, 52M3, Special Collections, University of Kentucky, Lexington, Kentucky.

18. The 1921 annual exhibition was held at the Gibbes Memorial Art Gallery in Charleston, and the next three were held at the Brooks Memorial Art Gallery in Memphis, the Isaac Delgado Museum of Art in New Orleans, and Telfair Academy of Arts and Sciences in Savannah, in 1922, 1923, and 1924, respectively.

19. A bequest in Parrish's will established the Weaver-Parrish Charitable Trust, which continues to support needy children in and around Selma.

20. "Historical Sketch with Revised Constitution and By Laws for the Year 1929–1930," March 1930, 3, Frick Art Research Library, New York.

21. Not every exhibiting artist fit the dictates of active membership. The most notable exceptions were three members of the Santa Fe, New Mexico, modernist group Los Cinco Pintores whose work appeared in the 1923 annual exhibition: Frank Applegate, Jozef Bakos, and Walter E. Mruk.

22. "Article XI. Historical Sketch with Revised Constitution and By Laws for the Year 1929–1930," March 1930, 15.

23. SSAL exhibition host cities in the 1930s included repeat locations: New Orleans, 1930; Savannah, 1931; Birmingham, 1933; Memphis, 1934; Houston, 1936; and San Antonio, 1939. New art museums were used when available, such as the High Museum of Art in Atlanta in 1937 and the Montgomery Museum of Fine Arts in 1938, as were alternative venues such as the Highland Park Society of Arts in Dallas (1932) and the Parthenon in Nashville's Centennial Park (1935).

24. See Jonathan Martin, "Peace College," http://northcarolinahistory.org/encyclopedia/peace-college/. A program of art and painting, the first of its kind in the South, was established in 1875.

25. Charlotte Streifer Rubinstein, *America Women Sculptors* (Boston: G. K. Hall, 1990), 294, 296.

26. Although no exhibitions were held after 1946, the SSAL limped along for another few years. Ben Shute and Lamar Dodd each served as president for less than a year between this time and the organization's closure in 1950.

CONTRARY INSTINCTS

1. The title of this essay comes from Virginia Woolf's *A Room of One's Own* and is also used in Alice Walker's essay, "In Search of Our Mothers' Gardens: The Creativity of Black Women in the South." See Woolf, *A Room of One's Own* (New York: Harcourt, 1929), 49; and Walker, *In Search of Our Mothers' Gardens: Womanist Prose* (New York: Harcourt, 1983), 231–44.

2. Charles H. Russell, "An Interview with Loïs Mailou Jones," *Callaloo* 39 (Spring 1989): 359.

3. Ibid.

4. Alain Locke, ed., *The New Negro* (New York: Albert and Charles Bone, 1925); and W. E. B. Du Bois, "Criteria for Negro Art," *The Crisis* (October 1926): 290–97.

5. See, for example, Darby English, *How to See a Work of Art in Total Darkness* (Cambridge, MA: MIT Press, 2007).

6. Elise Johnson McDougald, "The Task of Negro Womanhood," in *The New Negro*, 74.

7. Betty LaDuke, "Loïs Mailou Jones: The Grande Dame of African-American Art," *Woman's Art Journal* 8, no. 2 (1987/1988): 30. Despite being repeatedly assigned to teach watercolor classes, Jones continued to work in oils.

8. Museum interest in self-taught art has been on the upswing since the 1970s and 1980s, especially with the 1982 exhibition *Black Folk Art in America, 1930–1980*, at the now defunct Corcoran Museum of Art and the Souls Grown Deep Foundation's gift of fifty-seven works by Southern African American artists to the Metropolitan Museum of Art in 2014. See Kinshasha Holman Conwill, "In Search of an 'Authentic' Vision: Decoding the Appeal of the Self-Taught African American Artist," *American Art* 5, no. 4 (1991): 2–9; Paige Williams, "The Met Embraces Neglected Southern Artists," *New Yorker*, December 4, 2014; and Roberta Smith, "Curator, Tear Down These Walls," *New York Times*, February 3, 2013, AR1.

9. A note on my use of language: I take my cue from Kinshasha Holman Conwill, who used the term *self-taught* to describe artists such as Clementine Hunter as it is, perhaps, more inclusive and less fraught with contention than adjectives such as *outsider*, *naïve*, *primitive*, or *folk*.

10. Katherine Jentleson observed that Evans's Whitney exhibition appeared during a moment of the art world's rupture of "underrepresentation and cultural patrimony." See Jentleson, "Cracks in the Consensus: Outsider Artists and Art World Ruptures," in *When the Stars Begin to Fall: Imagination and the American South*, ed. Thomas J. Lax (New York: Studio Museum in Harlem, 2014), 106–14.

11. "Beautiful Dreamer," *Newsweek*, August 4, 1969, 85.

12. See Conwill's 1991 essay "In Search of an 'Authentic' Vision" in *American Art* and its revision, "Feeling at Home with Vernacular African-American Art," in Kinshasha Conwill et al., *Testimony: Vernacular Art of the African-American South in the Ronald and June Shelp Collection* (New York: Harry N. Abrams, Inc., in association with Exhibitions International and the Schomburg Center for Research in Black Culture, 2001), 54–61.

13. This debate has been the subject of several scholarly essays, all of which serve as the basis for the current exploration. See Conwill, "In Search of an 'Authentic' Vision" and "Feeling at Home." See also Lowery Stokes Sims, "Self-Taught and Trained Artists: An Evolving Relationship," in *Souls Grown Deep: African American Vernacular Art*, vol. 2, ed. William Arnett and Paul Arnett (Atlanta: Tinwood, 2001), 92–97; Lowery Stokes Sims, "Artists, Folk and Trained: An African American Perspective," in *Passionate Visions of the American South: Self-Taught Artists from 1940 to the Present*, ed. Alice Rae Yelen (Jackson: New Orleans Museum of Art in association with University of Mississippi Press, 1993), 29–37.

14. Kerry James Marshall, "Sticks and Stones…, but Names…," in *Bill Traylor, William Edmondson, and the Modernist Impulse*, ed. Josef Helfenstein and Roxanne Stanulis (Champaign: Krannert Art Museum in association with University of Illinois, 2004), 123.

15. Conwill, "In Search of an 'Authentic' Vision," 7.

16. Theresa Leininger-Miller translated an interview Savage gave to a French writer in which Savage states that in the United States, "people of color, and in particular black models, refused to pose for her." Savage does not say why this was the case. See Theresa Leininger-Miller, "Augusta Savage's Daring Sculptures of Women, 1929–1930," in *Women Artists of the Harlem Renaissance*, ed. Amy Helene Kirschke (Jackson: University Press of Mississippi, 2014), 162. However, women artists of any race were regularly prohibited from accessing nude models. Linda Nochlin addressed this problem in her seminal essay, "Why Have There Been no Great Women Artists?" *ARTnews* 69, no. 9 (January 1971): 22–39. See also Paulette Nardal, "Une femme sculpteur noire," *La dépêche africaine* (August–September 1930): 4, cited in Leininger-Miller, "Augusta Savage's Daring Sculptures," in *Women Artists of the Harlem Renaissance*, 162.

17. Walker, *In Search of Our Mothers' Gardens*, 231–43.

18. Jennifer Moses, "Looking for Clementine Hunter's Louisiana," *New York Times*, June 16, 2013, TR1.

19. As a West Coaster, I have found Scott Romine's *The Real South: Southern Narrative in the Age of Cultural Reproduction* (Baton Rouge: Louisiana State University Press, 2008) to be useful in helping me articulate the often complex entity that is the South.

20. Romare Bearden and Harry Henderson, *A History of African-American Artists: From 1792 to the Present* (New York: Pantheon, 1993), 168; and "Mud Pies Gave Sculptress Her First Inspiration: Augusta Savage Made Clay Animals When a Mere Child," *Afro-American*, January 2, 1926, 11.

21. W. E. B. Du Bois wrote an editorial piece on the racism of the American sponsors for the French scholarship. W. E. B. Du Bois, "That Architectural Lie," *The Crisis* 37, no. 6 (June 1930): 209. The event was also heavily reported in the papers: "Negress Turned Down as Student because of Race," *Chicago Daily Tribune*, April 24, 1923, 2; "Negress Denied Entry to French Art School," *New York Times*, April 24, 1923, 8; "Color Line Drawn by Americans," *New York Amsterdam News*, April 25, 1923, 1; "Augusta Savage Opens Fight to Beat Prejudice," *Chicago Defender*, May 5, 1923, 9; "Appeal Artists' Race Ban," *New York Times*, May 11, 1923, 17; "Americans Have Prevented Negro Girl Entering Art School," *Wichita (KS) Negro Star*, June 15, 1923, 4; "To Enlist Aid of President in Savage Case," *Pittsburgh Courier*, June 23, 1923, 12.

22. "Miss Savage Tells Story at Lyceum," *New York Amsterdam News*, May 16, 1923, 7.

23. Ibid.

24. T. R. Poston, "Augusta Savage," *Metropolitan Magazine* (January 1935).

25. Seattle Art Museum, *Bridging Cultures: Map and Guide* (London: Scala, 2007), 18.

26. "Negro Students Hold Their Own Art Exhibition," *New York Herald Tribune*, February 15, 1935, clipping from the Collections of the Manuscript Division, Library of Congress, Washington, DC. This article includes a photograph of the artist and the bust. See also "Harlem Will See Self as Others See It at Novel Show," *New York Amsterdam News*, February 9, 1935, 9.

27. Theresa Leininger-Miller, *New Negro Artists in Paris: African American Painters and Sculptors in the City of Light, 1922–1934* (New Brunswick, NJ: Rutgers University Press, 2001), 162. In 1988, when the Schomburg Center for Research in Black Culture mounted an exhibition of Savage's work, only nineteen pieces were found. Deidre L. Bibby, *Augusta Savage and the Art Schools of Harlem* (New York: Schomburg Center and New York Public Library, 1988).

28. A newspaper article mentions her "curious soap models" carved into "tiny canoes, minute pygmies and the like." "Augusta Savage Gives Art Exhibit," *New York Amsterdam News*, July 11, 1928, 4.

29. *Exhibit of Fine Arts by American Negro Artists* (New York: Harmon Foundation, 1930), 10; and Alain Locke, "Enter the New Negro," *Survey Graphic* (March 1925).

30. "Noted Sculptress Expects Distinct, but Not Different, Racial Art," *Pittsburgh Courier,* August 26, 1936, 5.

31. Jacqueline Trescott, "Sculptor Selma Burke: A Life of Art, for Art," *Washington Post*, March 17, 1975, B2.

32. "Georgia O'Keef [*sic*] Gets Overdue Recognition," *Roswell (NM) Daily Record*, January 31, 1979, 10.

33. "Selma Burke," *Ebony* 2, no. 5 (March 1947), 34.

34. Jacqueline Trescott, "Words at the Library on Black Women's Art," *Washington Post*, February 2, 1978, D3.

35. James L. Wilson, *Clementine Hunter: American Folk Artist* (Gretna, LA: Pelican, LA, 1988), 29–30.

36. Leigh Pressley, "Angels by Her Side," *Wilmington (NC) Morning Star*, October 11, 1991, 1D.

37. Conwill, "In Search of an 'Authentic' Vision," 3.

38. Nina Howell Starr, "Minnie Evans—Innocent Surrealist," in *Minnie Evans: Artist*, ed. Charles Muir Lovell and Erwin Hester (Greenville, NC: Wellington B. Gray Gallery, East Carolina University, 1993), 27.

39. "Oils by Primitive Painter at Riverfront Art Gallery," *St. Louis Post-Dispatch*, November 17, 1952, 14.

40. Art Shiver and Tom Whitehead, *Clementine Hunter: Her Life and Art* (Baton Rouge: Louisiana State University Press, 2012), 103.

41. Michael D. Hall, "The Mythic Outsider: Handmaiden to the Modern Muse," *New Art Examiner* (September 1991), 16, cited in Sims, "Self-Taught and Trained Artists," 92.

42. In 1985 Northwestern State College presented Clementine Hunter an honorary doctorate.

43. See Jentleson, "Cracks in the Consensus," 106–14.

44. Ibid., 108–9.

45. That year the Whitney Museum purchased the first and second drawings Evans ever created.

46. Countee Cullen, "Elizabeth Prophet: Sculptress," *Opportunity* 8, no. 7 (July 1930): 204; Lisa E. Farrington, *Creating Their Own Image: History of African-American Women Artists* (New York: Oxford University Press, 2005), 111.

47. Samella Lewis, *The Art of Elizabeth Catlett* (n.p.: Hancraft Studios, 1984), 15.

48. Charles H. Rowell, "A Conversation with Gwendolyn Knight," *Callaloo* 37 (Autumn 1988): 689–96. See also Barbara Earl Thomas, *Never Late for Heaven: The Art of Gwen Knight* (Seattle: University of Washington Press, 2003).

49. Rowell, "Conversation," 689–96.

50. See Merry A. Foresta, *A Life in Art: Alma Thomas, 1891–1978* (Washington, DC: Smithsonian Institution Press, 1981), 36n14.

51. David Driskell, *Two Centuries of Black American Art* (New York: Alfred A. Knopf and Los Angeles County Museum of Art, 1976), 150.

52. H. E. Mahal, "Interviews: Four Afro-American Artists—Approaches to Inhumanity," *Art Gallery* 13, no. 7 (April 1970): 36.

53. David L. Shirey, "At 77, She's Made It to the Whitney," *New York Times*, May 4, 1972, 52. Shirey incorrectly noted Thomas's age in this article.

54. Ibid.

55. A recent exhibition, *Alma Thomas*, underscores the resurgence of interest in the artist's career; the presentation was on view at the Frances Young Tang Teaching Museum and Art Gallery at Skidmore College, Saratoga Springs, New York, February 6–June 5, 2016, and at the Studio Museum in Harlem, New York, July 14–October 30, 2016. See also "First Lady Michelle Obama Announces Opening of Old Family Dining Room on Public Tour Route," The White House, https://www.whitehouse.gov/the-press-office/2015/02/10/first-lady-michelle-obama-announces-opening-old-family-dining-room-publi (accessed March 30, 2017).

56. See Bernard L. Herman, ed., *Thornton Dial: Thoughts on Paper* (Chapel Hill: University of North Carolina Press, 2011), 27.

EYES WIDE OPEN

1. Simone de Beauvoir, *America Day by Day*, trans. Carol Cosman (Berkeley: University of California Press, 2000), 80.

2. Ibid., 82, 83.

3. Adelyn Dohme Breeskin, "Modern Art Is International," November 3, 1955, Lecture typescript, p. 1, Adelyn Dohme Breeskin Papers, Archives of American Art, Washington, DC. Breeskin gave the lecture at Miller and Rhoads department store, a hub of cultural activity in Richmond, Virginia, at the time.

4. Lin Nelson-Mayson, introduction to *Southern Women Artists* (Columbia, SC: Columbia Museum of Art, 1990), 3. See also Marilyn Laufer, *Modernism in the South: Mid-Twentieth-Century Works in the Morris Museum Collection* (Augusta, GA: Morris Museum of Art, 2002).

5. Anne Goldthwaite, quoted in Kirsten Swinth, *Painting Professionals: Women Artists and the Development of Modern American Art, 1870–1930* (Chapel Hill: University of North Carolina Press, 2001), 187.

6. Ida Kohlmeyer, introduction to *American Women: 20th Century* (Peoria, IL: Lakeview Center for the Arts and Sciences, 1972), 15, 17.

7. Southern women who also studied Impressionism in Paris include Clara Weaver Parrish, Willie Betty Newman, Blondelle Malone, and Emma Cheves Wilkins. For more on these artists see Martha R.

Severens, "Some Things that Are Charming," in Estill Curtis Pennington and Martha R. Severens, *Scenic Impressions: Southern Interpretations from the Johnson Collection* (Spartanburg, SC: Johnson Collection in association with University of South Carolina Press, 2015), 27–43.

8. Information on women artists' experiences in the late nineteenth and early twentieth centuries in the South can be found in Rick Stewart, "Toward a New South: The Regionalist Approach, 1900 to 1950," in Donald B. Kuspit et al., *Painting in the South: 1564–1980* (Richmond: Virginia Museum of Fine Arts, 1983), 105–43; Greenville County Museum of Art, *Eight Southern Women* (Greenville, SC: Greenville County Museum of Art, 1986); and Montgomery Museum of Fine Arts, *Daughters of the South: Clara Weaver Parrish and Anne Goldthwaite* (Montgomery, AL: Montgomery Museum of Fine Arts, 1989).

9. For more on Lazzell, see Robert Bridges, Kristina Olson, and Janet Snyder, eds., *Blanche Lazzell: The Life and Work of an American Modernist* (Morgantown: West Virginia University Press, 2004).

10. Other murals by Southern women artists in post offices in the South are: Ethel Edwards, *Life on the Lake* (1942), Lake Providence, Louisiana; and Margaret Gates, *Landscape Tobacco Curing* (1941), Mebane, North Carolina. Caroline Wogan Durieux directed the Federal Art Project in New Orleans.

11. The standard monograph remains Adelyn Dohme Breeskin, *Anne Goldthwaite: 1869–1944* (Montgomery, AL: Montgomery Museum of Fine Arts, 1977). Breeskin, one of the first women to direct a major American museum, dedicated much of her scholarship to the work of Mary Cassatt and Anne Goldthwaite, each a singular American artist.

12. Avis Berman, "Oral History Interview with Jacob Kainen," 1982. Archives of American Art, Smithsonian Institution, Washington, DC, www.aaa.si.edu/collections/interviews/oral-history-interview-jacob-kainen-12620.

13. Louise C. Hoffman, *Josephine Crawford: An Artist's Vision* (New Orleans: Historic New Orleans Collection, 2009).

14. Tabary entered Jones's work into juried exhibitions that had racial restrictions.

15. Women active in the Little Paris Group included Ruth Brown, Barbara Buckner, Barbara Linger, Delilah Pierce, Alma Thomas, Desdemona Wade, and Elizabeth (Betty) Williamson. For a more detailed study of African American women artists in the South, see Erin Corrales-Diaz's essay in this volume.

16. Quoted in Richard J. Powell, *Black Art and Culture in the 20th Century* (New York: Thames and Hudson, 1997), 102.

17. Other women associated with the Washington Color School were Anne Truitt, Hilda Shapiro Thorpe, and Mary Pinchot Meyer.

18. An exhibition of abstract art at the Little Gallery on Royal Street included works by thirty-four artists and was very popular. "Crowds came to the opening and general enthusiasm for the new art form was expressed," a critic noted. "Abstracts in South," *ARTnews* 44 (April 1945): 10–11.

19. Patti Carr Black, *American Masters of the Mississippi Gulf Coast: George Ohr, Dusti Bongé, Walter Anderson, Richmond Barthé* (Jackson: Mississippi Arts Commission and Mississippi State University, 2009), 14.

20. Lawrence Campbell, "Dusti Bongé," *ARTnews* 57 (June 1958): 15.

21. Michael Plante, *Ida Kohlmeyer: Systems of Color* (New York: Hudson Hills Press in association with Newcomb Art Gallery, Tulane University, 2004).

22. Martha R. Severens, *The Charleston Renaissance* (Spartanburg, SC: Saraland Press, 1998), 158.

23. The Woman's College of the University of North Carolina at Greensboro organized an exhibition of women painters and sculptors in December 1950. The Duke Woman's College Gallery organized "Women in Contemporary Art," which ran from February 19 through March 22, 1963.

24. Belle Krasne, "Weyhe's Watercolor Septet," *Art Digest* 24 (July 1950): 20.

25. Donald B. Kuspit, "The Post-War Period, 1950–1980: A Critic's View," in Donald B. Kuspit et al., *Painting in the South: 1564–1980* (Richmond: Virginia Museum of Fine Arts, 1983), 154.

26. Southern women listed as students in the 1948–1949 Black Mountain College bulletin include Anne F. Banks (Bristol, Tennessee), Charlotte Robinson (St. Francisville, Louisiana), Carol Singer (Atlanta, Georgia), and Doris Miller (Asheville, North Carolina). Archives of Black Mountain College Museum and Arts Center.

27. The memorial exhibition of Ward's photographs and paintings was held at the Greenberg Wilson Gallery, New York, in June 1990.

28. Adelyn D. Breeskin and Virginia M. Mecklenburg, *José de Creeft: Sculpture and Drawings* (Washington, DC: Smithsonian Institution Press, 1983); and Dorothy Peck, "Black Mountain Follies—1943," on Peck's blog *Nine Decades of Living*, https://ninedecadesofliving.wordpress.com/category/recollections/.

29. Lyle Bongé, "Some of the Greats and the Grands," in *Black Mountain College: Sprouted Seeds: An Anthology of Personal Accounts*, ed. Mervin Lane (Knoxville: University of Tennessee Press, 1990), 236.

30. Sidney Tillim, "Adele Lemm," *Arts Magazine* 36 (May 1962): 101.

31. Day's exhibition, *New South: An Exhibition of Paintings*, was held at the David Porter Gallery in Washington, DC, in March 1945.

32. Worden Day, quoted in Mary Frances Williams, *Catalogue of the Collection of American Art at Randolph-Macon Woman's College* (Charlottesville: University Press of Virginia, 1977), 71.

33. Martica Sawin, *Nell Blaine: Her Life and Art* (New York: Hudson Hills Press, 1998), 18.

34. Gavin Butt, *Between You and Me: Queer Disclosures in the New York Art World, 1948–1963* (Durham, NC: Duke University Press, 2005), 82.

35. Dorothy Seiberling, "Women Artists in Ascendance: Young Group Reflects Lively Virtues of U.S. Painting," *Life*, May 13, 1957, 74–77; Jean Lipman and Cleve Gray, "The Amazing Inventiveness of Women Painters," *Cosmopolitan*, October 1961, 62–69.

36. Sawin, *Nell Blaine*, 14.

37. Lawrence Campbell, "Dusti Bongé, Jesse Reichek," *ARTnews* 59 (October 1960): 61.

38. Robert Dash, "Worden Day," *ARTnews* 58 (June 1959): 19. Day herself wrote capsule reviews for *ARTnews*, the leading journal of the time. Her name was listed on the masthead as an editorial associate from December 1961 through October 1963.

39. Ann Eden Gibson, *Issues in Abstract Expressionism: The Artist-Run Periodicals* (Ann Arbor, MI: UMI Research Press, 1990), 12. Gibson discovered this information in interviews with Beaudoin, Oscar Collier, and Gertrude Barrer (63n9). This controversial practice continues in the twenty-first century. White male artist Joe Scanlan exhibited work in the name of the fictional artist Donelle Woolford, stating that she was born in Conyers, Georgia.

40. Larry Rivers, with Arnold Weinstein, *What Did I Do? The Unauthorized Autobiography* (New York: HarperCollins Publishers, 1992), 35.

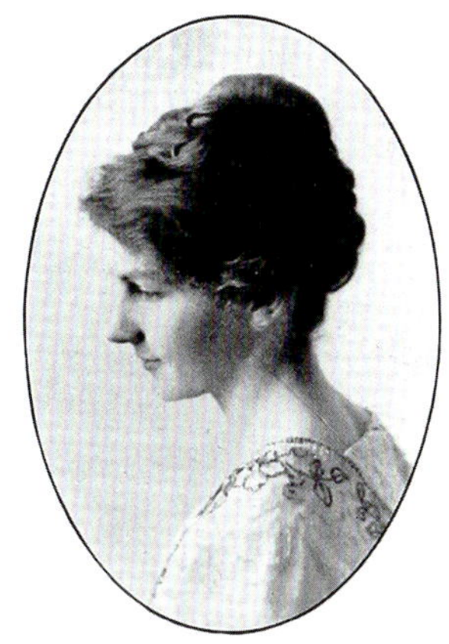

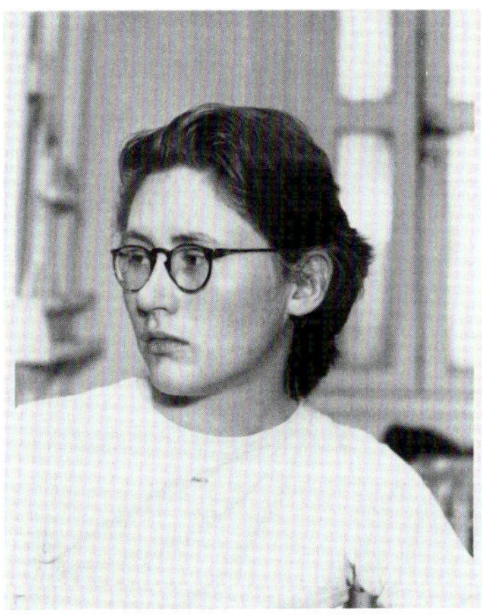

1. Wenonah Bell's father, James Austin Bell, held several pastorates in upstate South Carolina. Before settling in Gainesville, Georgia, in 1900, the family resided briefly in Spartanburg, Wellford, Taylors, and Gaffney. See the exhibition catalog Greenville County Museum of Art, *Work Song* (Greenville, SC: Greenville County Museum of Art, 1990), 7.

2. Ibid. Bell also attended the University of Pennsylvania and Columbia University Teachers College. Her advanced education in the North was made possible by financial assistance from a family member.

3. The Tappan Prizes were available only to students who had been awarded a Cresson scholarship. Wenonah Day Bell, *The Restless Bells* (New York: Vantage, 1973). See also *Work Song*, 7.

4. "Timeline," History of PAFA, www.pafa.org/history-pafa/timeline.

5. Scholars have attempted without success to identify the Spartanburg, South Carolina, farm or farming cooperative depicted in *Peach Packing*. It has been suggested that the B in question may refer to the artist's last name.

6. "Marketing Illinois Peaches," *Illinois Horticulture* 8, no. 4 (1922): 6.

7. Marilyn Neisler Windham, *Peach County: The World's Peach Paradise* (Charleston, SC: Arcadia, 1997), 32.

"Marketing Illinois Peaches," 7.

8. *Work Song*, 7.

9. Martha R. Severens, "Southern Scene," *American Art Review* 13, no. 1 (2001): 114.

10. According to the dust jacket copy of her memoir, *The Restless Bells*, the artist primarily resided in Hicksville, New York, between 1947 and 1973. During these decades, Bell spent approximately eleven years teaching at public schools and nine years at private schools, including her tenure at Parsons School of Design.

11. *Work Song*, 7.

Artist Image: *U.S. School Yearbooks, 1880–2012* (database online). Ancestry.com, 2010.

1. The other artists featured in the article were Helen Frankenthaler, Grace Hartigan, Joan Mitchell, and Jane Wilson; see "Women Artists in Ascendance," *Life*, May 13, 1957, 74–77.

2. For more on Nell Blaine's life and work, see Martica Sawin, *Nell Blaine: Her Art and Life* (New York: Hudson Hills Press, 1998).

3. Renee Arb, "They Are Painting Their Way," *Harper's Bazaar* (1947), 81, cited in Martica Sawin, *Image and Abstraction: Paintings and Drawings, 1944–1959* (New York: Tibor de Nagy Gallery 2007).

4. For a first-person account of Blaine's upbringing and career, see Nell Blaine, interview with Dorothy Gees Sackler, June 15, 1967, typescript, Archives of American Art, www.aaa.si.edu/collections/interviews/oral-history-interview-nell-blaine-12436.

5. Sawin, *Nell Blaine*, 22. For additional information on the Jane Street Gallery, see Jennifer Samet, *The Jane Street Gallery: Celebrating New York's First Artist Cooperative* (New York: Tibor de Nagy Gallery, 2003).

6. See "American Abstract Artists," http://americanabstractartists.org (accessed October 2016).

7. Clement Greenberg, "Art," *Nation*, April 7, 1945, 284.

8. See Siobhan Conaty, *Art of This Century: The Women* (New York: Stony Brook Foundation, 1997). For women artists and Abstract Expressionism, see Joan Marter, ed., *Women of Abstract Expressionism* (New Haven, CT: Denver Art Museum in association with Yale University Press, 2016).

9. Nell Blaine, interview with Dorothy Gees Sackler.

10. Ibid.

11. Roy Proctor, "'Green Thumb': Blaine's Vibrant Colors Grow," *Richmond (VA) News-Leader*, May 1, 1992. The exhibition referenced was held at the Reynolds Gallery in Richmond, Virginia.

Artist Image: Robert Bass, photographer, Nell Blaine, between 1942 and 1943. Nell Blaine Papers, 1930–1985, Archives of American Art, Smithsonian Institution, Washington, DC.

SARAH JANE BLAKESLEE

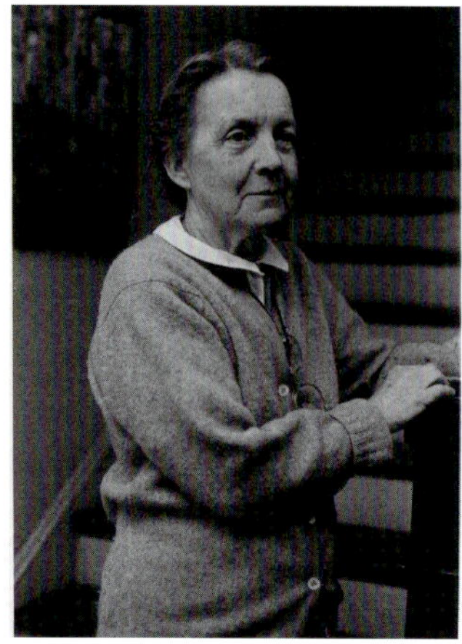

1. The story of the artistic and familial relationship between Francis Speight and Sarah Blakeslee is well documented in Maurice C. York, *The Privilege to Paint: The Lives of Francis Speight and Sarah Blakeslee* (Greenville, NC: Greenville Museum of Art, 2002).

Artist image: Sarah Blakeslee, 1978. East Carolina University Archives, Greenville, NC.

EUNICE "DUSTI" LYLE SWETMAN BONGÉ

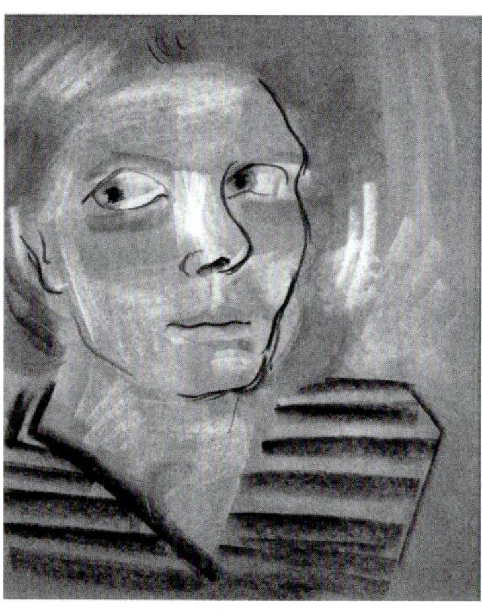

1. Patti Carr Black discusses the significance of Bongé's dreams in *American Masters of the Mississippi Gulf Coast: George Ohr, Dusti Bongé, Walter Anderson, Richmond Barthé* (Jackson: Mississippi Arts Commission and Mississippi State University, 2009), 43. Bongé tells her own life story in "Dusti Bongé," Mississippi Public Broadcasting video, http://dustibonge.org/early-personal-life (accessed June 1, 2016).

2. "Dusti Bongé."

3. Standing six feet, seven inches tall and hailing from Nebraska, Arch Bongé gained a reputation for painting cowboy scenes that were used as illustrations for book jackets. His death at the age of thirty-four was caused by amyotrophic lateral sclerosis, commonly referred to as Lou Gehrig's disease. See Black, *American Masters*, 36–37.

4. Dusti Bongé and Nancy Longnecker, *Dusti Bongé: The Life of an Artist* (Jackson: University Press of Mississippi, 1982).

5. Black, *American Masters*, 36.

6. *New York Herald Tribune*, 1960, as cited at http://dustibonge.org/reviews/ (accessed February 22, 2017).

7. Quoted in Black, *American Masters*, 43.

Artist image: Eunice "Dusti" Lyle Swetman Bongé (1903–1993), *Self-Portrait*, circa 1939, oil pastel on paper. Amanda Winstead Fine Art, New Orleans, LA, and the Dusti Bongé Art Foundation, Biloxi, MS.

SELMA HORTENSE BURKE

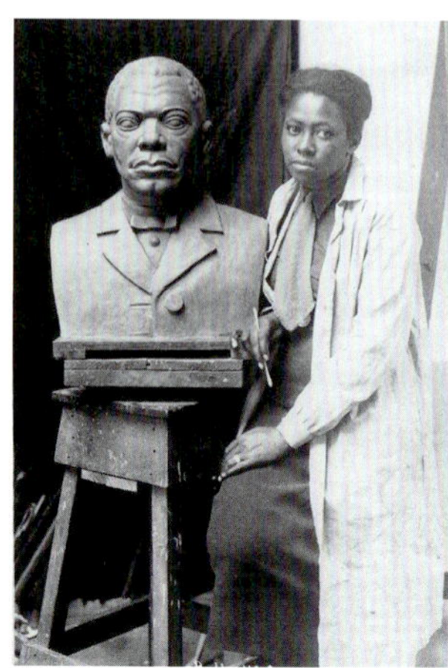

1. Andy Wallace, "Selma Burke, 94, Black Sculptor Whose Profile of FDR Graces Dime," *Seattle Times*, September 1, 1995.

2. Interview with Selma Burke conducted by Tritobia Hayes Benjamin, Pittsburgh, PA, March 21, 1970, from Lori Verderame, "The Sculptural Legacy of Selma Burke, 1900–1995," in *Masters of African American Art* (New York: Anyone Can Fly Foundation, 2003), 1.

3. Untitled article, *Washington Post*, April 2, 1961, G7.

4. Jacqueline Trescott, "Sculptor Selma Burke: A Life of Art, For Art," *Washington Post*, March 17, 1975, B1.

5. Lisa E. Farrington, *Creating Their Own Image: The History of African-American Women Artists* (New York: Oxford University Press, 2005), 110, 109.

6. *Congressional Record* 140, no. 150 (December 20, 1994). The Roosevelt dime was released on the late president's birthday, January 30, 1946.

7. Located on the campus of St. Augustine College (now University) in Raleigh, North Carolina, St. Agnes Hospital and Training School for Nurses was established in 1896 to provide medical care and education to the city's African American population. In the early twentieth century, it was considered a superior and progressive training ground within the Southern medical community. See W. Montague Cobb, "Saint Agnes Hospital, Raleigh, North Carolina, 1896–1961," *Journal of the National Medical Association* 53, no. 5 (September 1961): 439–46. St. Agnes Hospital closed in 1961, and its main structure, abandoned and dilapidated, was declared a Raleigh Historic Landmark in 1979. Scholars' accounts of Burke's education note that Burke also pursued nursing training in Philadelphia.

8. "N.Y. Woman to Sculpture Plaque for 15th Regiment," *Afro-American*, February 10, 1945, 15; "Most Exciting and Tragic," *Ebony* 2, no. 5 (March 1947): 34.

9. "Rosenwald Fund Announces Sixty-Eight Fellowships," *Atlanta Daily World*, May 1, 1940, 1; Farrington, *Creating Their Own Image*, 200, 108.

10. Charlotte Streifer Rubinstein notes that Burke exhibited at New York's Julien Levy Gallery in 1945 and Avant Garde Gallery in 1958; *American Women Sculptors: A History of Women Working in Three Dimensions* (Boston: G. K. Hall, 1990), 297. Burke exhibited at the Pennsylvania Academy of the Fine Arts in 1951, 1952, and 1958. See Peter H. Falk, ed., *The Annual Exhibition Record of the Pennsylvania Academy of the Fine Arts, 1914–1968* (Madison, CT: Sound View Press, 1989), 116–17.

11. Harry Schwalb, "Diary without Color," *ARTnews* 93, no. 7 (September 1994): 27.

Artist image: Pinchos Horn, photographer, Selma Burke, 193?. Federal Art Project, Photographic Division Collection, circa 1920–1965, bulk 1935–1942. Archives of American Art, Smithsonian Institution, Washington, DC.

ELISABETH AUGUSTA CHANT

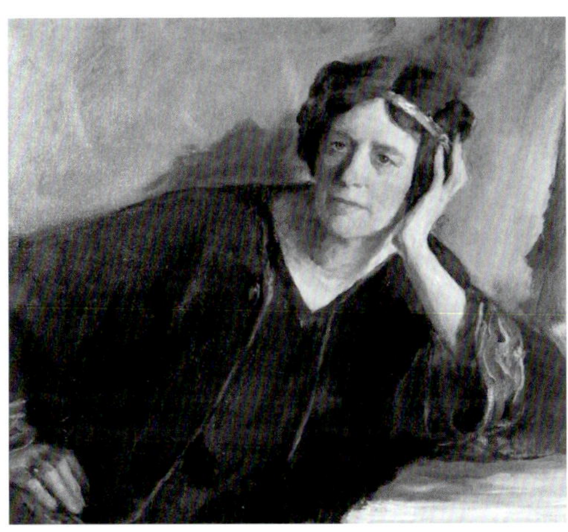

1. Henry MacMillan, *Violet and Gold: The Story of Artistic Activity on Cottage Lane in Wilmington* (Wilmington, NC: Lower Cape Fear Historical Society, 1991), 5.

2. Chant, quoted in Harriet S. Schmidt and Henry Jay MacMillan, *Elisabeth Augusta Chant, 1865–1947* (Wilmington, NC: St. John's Art Gallery, 1972).

3. Chant, quoted in Anne G. Brennan, *Elisabeth Augusta Chant, 1865–1947* (Wilmington, NC: St. John's Museum of Art, 1993), 12.

4. Howell, quoted in Brennan, *Elisabeth Augusta Chant*, 7.

5. Chant, letter to the editor, *Wilmington (NC) Morning Star*, July 17, 1938, quoted in MacMillan, *Violet and Gold*, 22.

Artist image: Henry Caliga (1857–1944), *Portrait of Elisabeth Chant*, 1925, oil on canvas, 26 × 28.675 inches. Cameron Art Museum, Wilmington, NC; gift of Hester Donnelly, 1972.2.28.

KATE FREEMAN CLARK

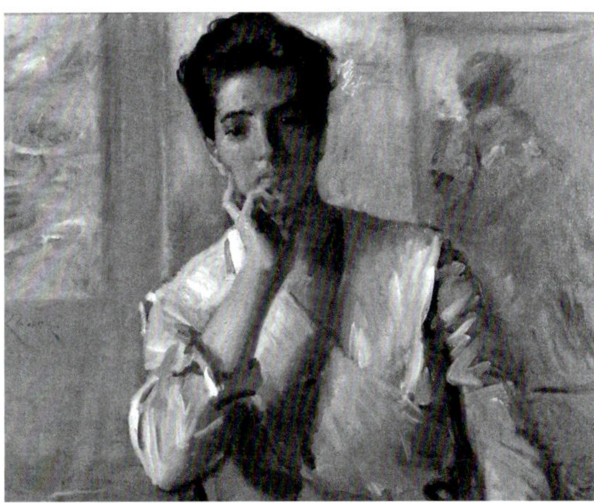

1. The phrase *Chase critique* is my own, coined after I read several accounts of William Merritt Chase's weekly reviews of his students' work at Shinnecock. These critiques were public spectacles, attracting area residents and students from other studios. Former Chase students, including Marietta Minnigerode Andrews and Rockwell Kent, wrote about their critique experiences, as did Kate Freeman Clark. Clark's account appears in its entirety in Carolyn J. Brown, *The Artist's Sketch: A Biography of Painter Kate Freeman Clark* (Jackson: University Press of Mississippi, 2017).

2. The Kate Freeman Clark Art Gallery continues to showcase the majority of the artist's work.

Artist image: William Merritt Chase (1849–1916), *Portrait of Kate Freeman Clark*, 1902, oil on canvas, 25 × 30 inches. Kate Freeman Clark Art Gallery, Holly Springs, MS.

EMMA JOSEPHINE SIBLEY COUPER

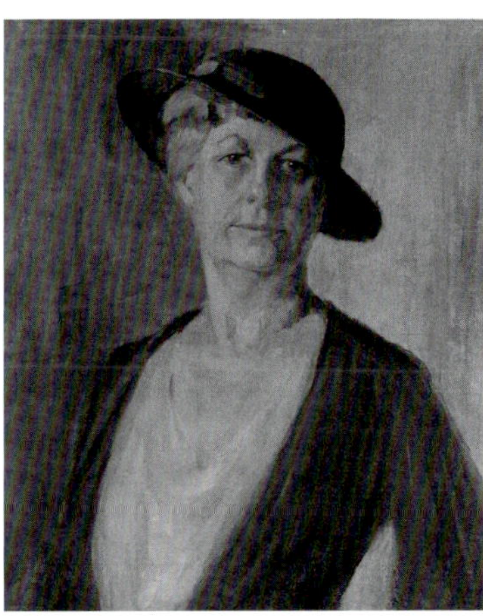

1. William Merritt Chase, quoted in Keith Bryant, *William Merritt Chase, a Genteel Bohemian* (Columbia: University of Missouri Press, 1991), 234.

2. Dorothy Joiner, "J. S. Couper: An Art Historian's Perspective," in *Josephine Sibley Couper: Daughter of the Old South*, ed. Suzanne Harper, Dorothy Joiner, and James Longstreet Sibley Jennings (Macon, GA: Museum of Arts and Sciences, 1992), 5.

3. James Longstreet Sibley Jennings Jr., "Emma Josephine Sibley Couper: A Family Perspective," in Harper, Joiner, and Jennings, *Josephine Sibley Couper*, 25.

Artist image: Emma Josephine Sibley Couper (1867–1957), *Self-Portrait*, circa 1935, oil on canvas 20⅛ × 24⅛ inches. Museum of Arts and Sciences, Permanent Collection, Macon, GA.

MINNIE EVA JONES EVANS

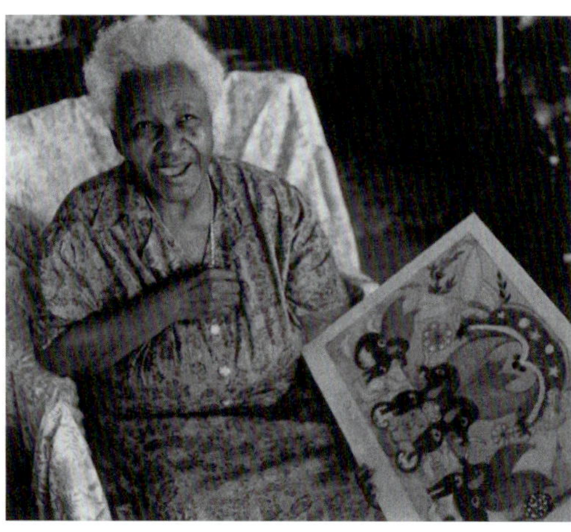

1. Typed transcript of an interview of Minnie Evans by Nina Howell Starr, Nina Howell Starr Papers, Archives of American Art, Washington, DC.

2. These two works, *My Very First* and *My Second*, are in the collection of the Whitney Museum of American Art. Evans referred to her calligraphic motifs as "ancient writing." See Nathan Kernan, "Aspects of Minnie Evans," *On Paper* 12 (July–August 1997): 13.

3. Charles Muir Lovell and Erwin Hester, *Minnie Evans: Artist* (Greenville, NC: Wellington B. Gray Gallery, East Carolina University, 1993), 11.

4. Typed transcript interview of Minnie Evans by Celestine Ware for radio station WBAI, New York, March 5, 1971, Archives of American Art, Washington, D.C.

5. I found Glenn Hinson's essay, "Thornton Dial's Journey of Faith," to be useful for thinking about the connection between Evans's drawings and her Christian faith. See Hinson, "Thornton Dial's Journey of Faith," in *Thornton Dial: Thoughts on Paper*, ed. Bernard L. Herman (Chapel Hill: Ackland Art Museum in association with University of North Carolina Press, 2011), 91–127.

6. Barbara Rogers, "To Draw or Die," *Wilmington (NC) Morning Star*, January 19, 1969; quoted in Lovell and Hester, *Minnie Evans*, 18.

7. Christian P. Daniel, *Minnie Evans' Art of Visions and Dreams: Inspired or Self-Taught?* (Wilmington, NC: Christian P. Daniel, 2008), 34.

8. Nina Howell Starr, "The Lost World of Minnie Evans," *The Bennington Review* (Summer 1969): 43.

9. It was in her capacity as Airlie's gatekeeper that Evans met graduate student Nina Howell Starr, who would eventually become the artist's gallery representative, spokesperson, and friend. Established in 1886, Airlie Gardens is a sixty-seven-acre public garden that hosts various events connected to the annual North Carolina Azalea Festival, held in Wilmington since 1948. North Carolina Azalea Festival, http://ncazaleafestival.org/about-us/mission-history/ (accessed March 30, 2017).

10. See for example, Sharon D. Koota, "Cosmograms and Cryptic Writings: 'Africanisms' in the Art of Minnie Evans," *The Clarion* (Summer 1991): 48–52; John Mason, "Old Africa, Anew," in *Another Face of the Diamond: Pathways through the Black Atlantic South* (New York: INTAR Latin American Gallery, 1988), 14–22; Lovell and Hester, *Minnie Evans*, 14; Gylbert Coker, "Elephants around the Moon: The Art of Minnie Evans," *Raw Vision* (Spring 1995): 28–35.

Artist image: Courtesy of Susan Mullally.

VIRGINIA BARGER EVANS

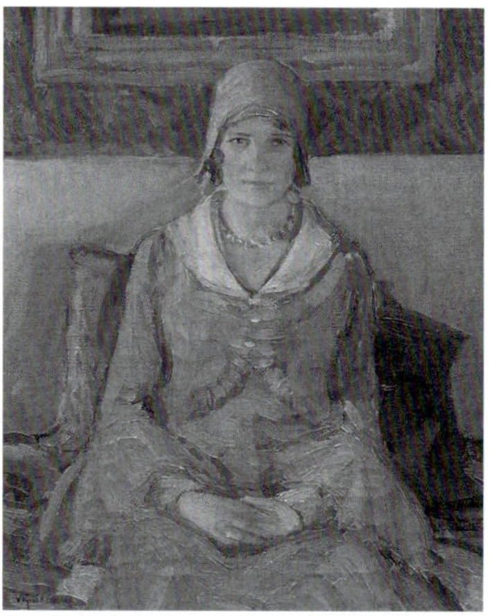

1. Virginia Evans fulfilled this commission with a landscape titled *The Remembered (The Devil's Elbow)*, circa 1972, oil on canvas, 36 × 40 inches, which remains in the collection of the West Virginia State Museum in Morgantown.

2. *Pittsburgh Sun-Telegraph*, March 6, 1934.

Artist image: Virginia Barger Evans (1894–1983), *Self-Portrait*, circa 1920–1925, oil on canvas, 20 × 16 inches. Private Collection.

ANNE WILSON GOLDTHWAITE

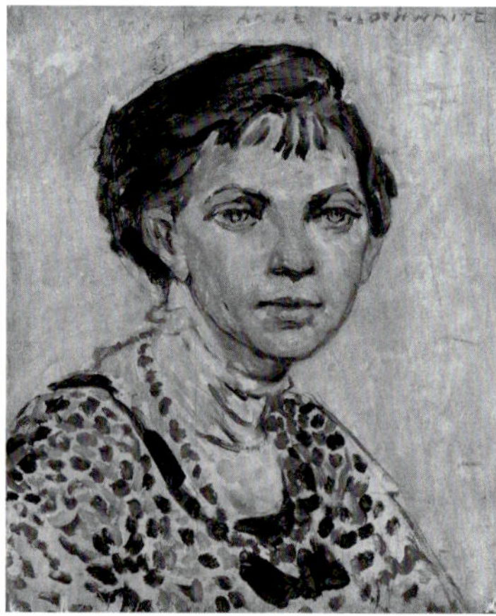

1. Adelyn Dohme Breeskin, *Anne Goldthwaite: 1869–1944* (Montgomery, AL: Montgomery Museum of Fine Arts, 1977), 9.

2. For a sustained analysis of the development of women's art in the United States during this era, see Laura R. Prieto, *At Home in the Studio: The Professionalization of Women Artists in America* (Cambridge, MA: Harvard University Press, 2001).

3. The artist was born in Montgomery, Alabama, to former Confederate captain Richard Wallach Goldthwaite and his wife Lucy Boyd Armistead Goldthwaite. She recounted her childhood in her unfinished memoirs, published in Adelyn Dohme Breeskin, *Anne Goldthwaite: A Catalogue Raisonné of the Graphic Work* (Montgomery, AL: Montgomery Museum of Fine Arts, 1982), 19.

4. Shirlaw and other members of the Society of American Artists were particularly invested in encouraging "women in Art-work." Lois M. Fink and Joshua C. Taylor, *Academy: The Academic Tradition in American Art* (Washington, DC: The National Collective of Fine Arts, 1975), 82.

5. Mariea Caudill Dennison, "The American Girls' Club in Paris: The Propriety and Imprudence of Art Students, 1890–1914," *Woman's Art Journal* 26, no. 1 (Spring/Summer, 2005): 32–37.

6. Goldthwaite had intended to visit New York for only a few months, but the outbreak of World War I prevented her return to Paris. Breeskin, *Anne Goldthwaite: A Catalogue Raisonné*, 30.

7. A. D. Defries, "Anne Goldthwaite as a Portrait Painter," *The International Studio* 59, no. 233 (1916): viii.

8. "Giants Aid Suffrage," *New York Times*, June 3, 1916, 8; Mariea Caudill Dennison, "Babies for Suffrage: The Exhibition of Painting and Sculpture by Women Artists for the Benefit of the Woman Suffrage Campaign," *Woman's Art Journal* 24, no. 2 (2003/2004): 24–30.

9. Goldthwaite's aunt Ellen Wallach Goldthwaite and her first cousin Annie Goldthwaite were members of the Montgomery anti-suffrage association. Elna C. Green, *Southern Strategies: Southern Women and the Woman Suffrage Question* (Chapel Hill: University of North Carolina Press, 1997), 75.

10. Goldthwaite's portrait of Nix dates to circa 1935–1940, a time period that dovetails with that of the Dixie Art Colony, which lasted from 1933–1945. See Mariea Caudill Dennison, "Summer Art Colonies in the South: 1920–1940," in *Crossroads: A Southern Culture Annual*, ed. Ted Olson (Macon, GA: Mercer University Press, 2004), 109–10; Dorothy B. Gilbert, ed., *Who's Who in American Art* (New York: R. R. Bowker, 1959), 423. Wayman Adams is also listed as one of Nix's instructors.

11. Frances Nix is listed as the director of the Montgomery Museum of Fine Arts in "Institution Members in the United States," *The Museum News*, June 15, 1949, 3; and Gilbert, *Who's Who in American Art*, 423.

12. Unlike most first ladies, Wilson refused to give up her career when her husband became president, and instead converted a room in the West Wing into a studio and continued to exhibit and sell her work. Lisa M. Burns, "Ellen Axson Wilson: A Rhetorical Reassessment of a Forgotten First Lady," in *Inventing a Voice: The Rhetoric of American First Ladies of the Twentieth Century*, ed. Molly Meijer Wertheimer (New York: Rowman and Littlefield, 2004), 94–95.

Artist image: Anne Wilson Goldthwaite (1869–1944), *Self-Portrait*, circa 1906–1913, oil on wood mounted on fiberboard, 15½ × 12⅜ inches. Smithsonian American Art Museum, Washington, DC; gift of Lucy Goldthwaite and Richard Wallach Goldthwaite; 1973.37.

ANGELA GREGORY

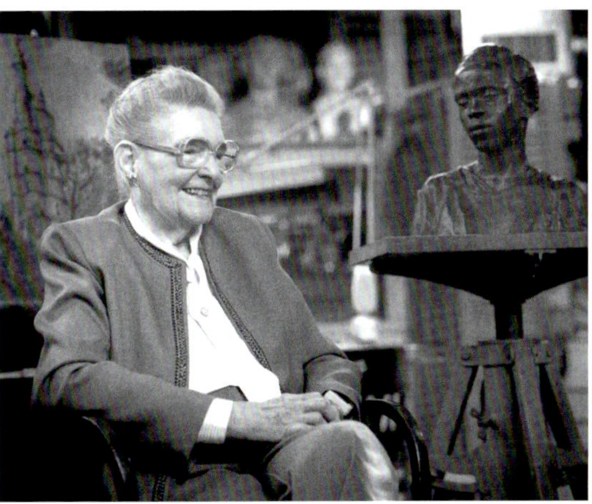

1. Angela Gregory to her father, William Gregory, June 17, 1918, Box 107, Folder 2, Angela Gregory Papers, 1784–1991, Howard-Tilton Memorial Library Special Collections, Tulane University, New Orleans, LA. For the most complete biographical information to date, see Suzanne Haik Terrell, *Angela Gregory: A Sculptor's Life* (New Orleans: Newcomb College, 1981); and Charlotte Streifer Rubinstein, *American Women Sculptors: A History of Women Working in Three Dimensions* (Boston: G. K. Hall, 1990), 293–96.

2. Suzanne Ormond and Mary E. Irvine, *Louisiana's Art Noveau: The Crafts of the Newcomb Style* (Gretna, LA; Pelican, 1976), 152.

3. Judith H. Bonner, "Angela Gregory," in *The New Encyclopedia of Southern Culture*, Vol. 21: *Art and Architecture*, ed. Judith H. Bonner and Estill Curtis Pennington (Chapel Hill: University of North Carolina Press, 2013), 322.

4. Ann Die, dean of Newcomb College, unpublished typescript of eulogy delivered at Gregory's memorial service, held on the Newcomb campus on February 17, 1990, artist file, Johnson Collection, Spartanburg, SC; and Angela Gregory, lecture, "Vocation and Avocation," Box 107, Folder 30, Angela Gregory Papers, Tulane University, New Orleans, LA.

5. Rubinstein, *American Women Sculptors*, 296.

6. Ibid., 294.

7. Leila Mechlin, quoted in "The Art Association of New Orleans," in *The Art Association of New Orleans Presents an Exhibition of Sculpture by Angela Gregory* (New Orleans: Isaac Delgado Museum of Art, 1933).

8. Michael Guttuso, who served as Gregory's studio assistant in the early 1980s, remembers that her Port Gibson sketchbooks contained numerous head and bust studies; he thinks that *Head of a Woman* could have been a part of that project. A glazed terra-cotta piece seems to be the same composition as the Johnson Collection's bronze (see Neal Auction catalog, February 7, 2004, lot no. 489). Guttuso posits that it was a maquette onto which she put a decorative finish. E-mail communication to the author, June 23, 2016.

9. Quoted in Robin Miller, "From Paris to Port Allen, Check Out Sculptor Angela Gregory's Exhibit," *The Advocate* (Baton Rouge), May 9, 2016; and Richard B. Megraw, *Confronting Modernity: Art and Society in Louisiana* (Jackson: University Press of Mississippi, 2008), 139.

10. Die, Gregory eulogy.

Artist image: Newcomb Archives and Vorhoff Library Special Collections, Newcomb College Institute, Tulane University, New Orleans, LA; and Gregory Art, LLC.

ELLA SOPHONISBA HERGESHEIMER

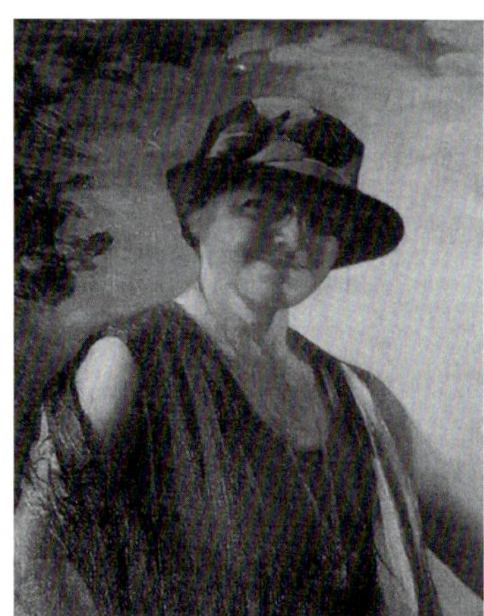

1. "Miss Hergesheimer's Portraits," *Harper's Bazaar* 46, no. 1 (January 1912): 15; and Clara Hieronymus, "Captivated by Mushrooms, Magnolias," *Nashville Tennessean*, January 6, 1957, 32.

2. Vincent Burton, "Some Portraits by Ella S. Hergesheimer," *International Studio* 37, no. 145 (1909): 32–33; and "Art School Notes and News," *The Art Amateur* 43, no. 2 (1900): 50. "Prize Winners," *Oakland (PA) Tribune*, August 2, 1902, 11; "Art Notes," *Biloxi (MS) Daily Herald*, September 23, 1902, 5; and "Strictly Personal," *Allentown (PA) Leader*, September 6, 1902, 6.

3. "Wanted in Allentown," *Reading (PA) Times*, December 26, 1905, 2; and Deborah C. Pollack, *Visual Art and the Urban Evolution of the New South* (Columbia: University of South Carolina Press, 2015), 47.

4. "State News Notes," *Philadelphia Inquirer*, January 24, 1907, 3.

5. "Address by Noted Artist," *Reading (PA) Times*, September 18, 1916, 8.

6. "Miss Hergesheimer Believes Nashville May Easily Become the Art Center of the South," *Nashville Tennessean*, March 2, 1908, 8.

7. Ibid.

8. Susan M. Doll, "Blanche Lazzell Biography," in *Blanche Lazzell: The Life and Work of an American Modernist*, ed. Robert Bridges, Kristina Olson, and Janet Synder (Morgantown: West Virginia University Press, 2004), 40.

9. Hieronymus, "Captivated by Mushrooms," 32.

10. For a biography on Breckinridge, see Melba Porter Hay, *Madeline McDowell Breckinridge and the Battle for a New South* (Lexington: University of Kentucky Press, 2009).

11. "Fine Art Lecture at Centennial," *Nashville Tennessean*, April 27, 1913, 10.

Artist image: Ella Sophonisba Hergesheimer (1873–1943), *Self-Portrait*, 1931, oil on canvas, 48¾ × 32¾ inches. Tennessee State Museum, Nashville; 2016.249.1.

EMILY MARIE ATKINSON HULL

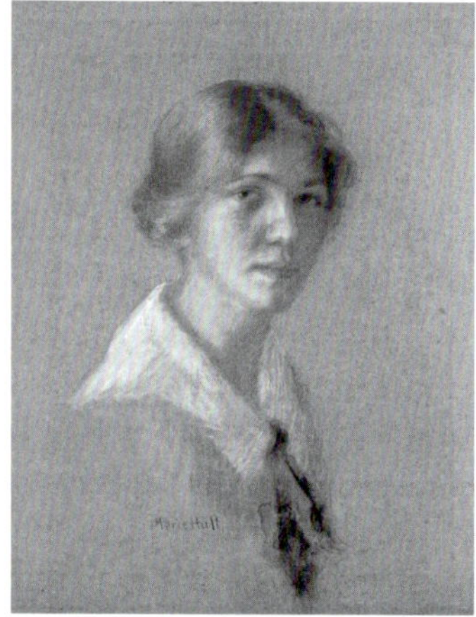

1. Although Marie Hull made generous gifts and bequests to several of her home state's university collections and museums, and left instructions for a voluminous bequest to the Mississippi Museum of Art in Jackson, only a small portion of her oeuvre is held by institutions. Drawings and watercolors from her loose-leaf portfolios and dismembered sketchbooks, which were plundered for sale and exhibition, have been thoroughly scattered and appear with some regularity on the art market. The lack of earlier documentation and the widespread dispersal of Hull's output into scores of private collections far beyond the borders of Mississippi mean that nobody has attempted anything like a systematic survey of it; nor has there been a definitive assessment of her place in the history of twentieth century American art. She and her oeuvre await the compilation of a well-deserved catalogue raisonné and appropriate critical evaluation. To date the best attempt at a comprehensive appreciation and art historical analysis of Hull's achievements is a publication by Bruce Levingston et al., created to accompany an exhibition of the same title: *Bright Fields: The Mastery of Marie Hull* (Jackson: University Press of Mississippi, 2015), in which *Red Parrots* is reproduced on page 46.

2. In addition to *Red Parrots*, the masterpieces in this genre are two three-panel folding screens: one featuring seven life-size scarlet macaws and the other depicting seven flamingos. Held by a private collection in Louisiana, these works were featured in the companion catalog to *Marie Hull: Visions of Color and Light*, an exhibition held at Hull's alma mater, Belhaven University, in Jackson, Mississippi, from May 20 through September 3, 2016. See pages 68–69.

3. *Blue Parrots, Florida* appears in Estill Curtis Pennington, *A Southern Collection* (Augusta, GA: Morris Museum of Art, 1992).

Artist image: Emily Marie Atkinson Hull (1890–1980), *Self-Portrait*, not dated, pastel on paper, 30 × 24 inches. Collection of the Mississippi Museum of Art, Jackson, MS; anonymous gift, 1996.019.

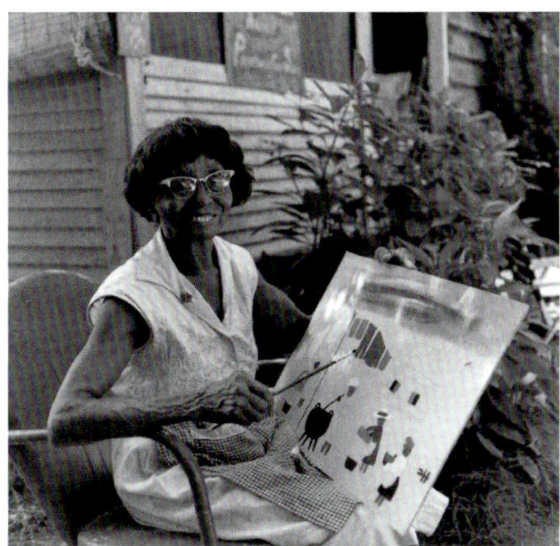

1. Shelby R. Gilley, *Painting by Heart: The Life and Art of Clementine Hunter, Louisiana Folk Artist* (Baton Rouge: St. Emma Press, 2000), 65.

2. Hunter's exact birthdate remains obscure. A baptismal record for Hunter notes that she was about three months old on March 19, 1887, and the artist herself declared that she was born around Christmastime. As a result, Hunter's birthdate is sometimes listed as late 1886 or early 1887. Art Shiver and Tom Whitehead, *Clementine Hunter: Her Life and Art* (Baton Rouge: Louisiana State University Press, 2012), 12–15.

3. Francois Mignon, *Plantation Memo: Plantation Life in Louisiana, 1750–1970, and Other Matter* (Baton Rouge: Claitor's Law Books and Publishing, 1972), 99–100; Charlotte Willard, "Innocence Regained," *Look*, June 16, 1953, 103–5.

4. For example, see Steven Morris, "The Primitive Art of Clementine Hunter," *Ebony* 24, no. 7 (May 1969): 144–48.

5. Cheryl Rivers, "Clementine Hunter and African American Catholicism," in *Sacred and Profane: Voice and Vision in Southern Self-Taught Art*, ed. Carol Crown and Charles Russell (Jackson: University of Mississippi Press, 2007), 151–55.

6. Mary E. Lyons, ed., *Talking with Tebé: Clementine Hunter, Memory Artist* (Boston: Houghton Mifflin, 1998), 27.

7. Laura Kathryn Lilley, "'Marking' Exodus: Death and Funerals in the Religious Paintings of Clementine Hunter" (master's thesis, University of North Carolina at Chapel Hill, 2008).

8. See Kenneth Chelst, *Exodus and Emancipation: Biblical and African-American Slavery* (New York: Urim, 2009).

9. Gilley, *Painting By Heart,* 126.

Artist image: State Library of Louisiana, Baton Rouge, LA.

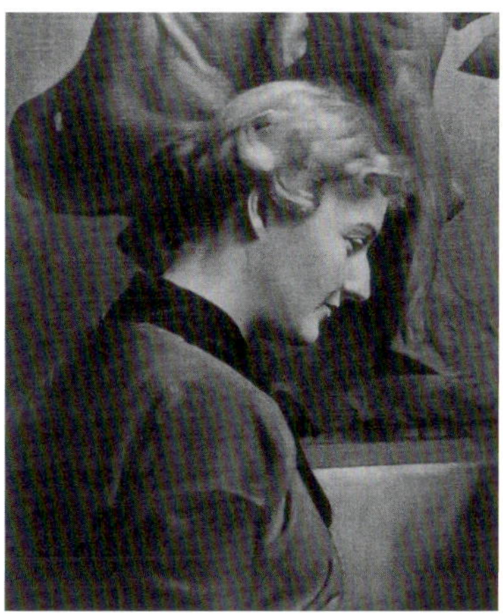

1. A. Hyatt Mayor, *A Century of American Sculpture: Treasures from Brookgreen Gardens* (New York: Abbeville, 1987), 24.

2. *New York Times*, December 31, 1905, quoted in Charlotte Streiffer Rubinstein, *American Women Sculptors: A History of Women Working in Three Dimensions* (Boston: G. K. Hall, 1990), 163.

3. Anne Higonnet notes that the $50,000 sum may have been exaggerated. When questioned about her income years later, Huntington is said to have conceded that perhaps the number was inflated, "but why spoil a good story?" Anne Higonnet, "Wild at Heart: Rediscovering the Sculpture of Anna Hyatt Huntington, *The Magazine Antiques* 181, no. 1 (2014), 179.

4. The first sculpture placements within the thirty-acre sculpture garden included important pieces by Anna Hyatt Huntington, as well as smaller works from the Huntingtons' personal collection, exhibited in a newly constructed and roofless Gallery of Small Sculpture. Forming the structural bones of the original sculpture garden, Huntington's bronze *Diana of the Chase* and numerous sculptures of wild animals, including the first aluminum castings in America, were placed throughout the property. Over the years, more of Huntington's works were placed on the spacious grounds, including the dynamic *Fighting Stallions*. Created in 1950 for the Brookgreen entrance, *Fighting Stallions* was the largest aluminum casting to have been made at that time. The artist located it to entice highway travelers to stop and see the treasures offered inside the gates. In 1992 Anna Hyatt Huntington's status as an artist and art patron was recognized when Brookgreen Gardens was named a National Historic Landmark and an important site for women's history in America.

5. Joseph Pijoan, "The Exposition of Contemporary Sculpture at San Francisco," *Parnassus* 1, no. 5 (May 1929): 11.

Artist image: Peter A. Juley & Son, photograph of Anna Vaughn Hyatt Huntington. ©Peter A. Juley & Son Collection, Smithsonian American Art Museum, Washington, DC.

LOÏS MAILOU JONES

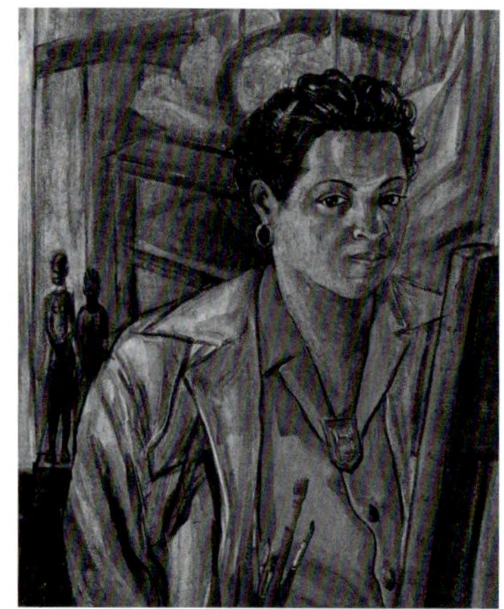

1. Tritobia Hayes Benjamin, "A Passionate Life in Art," *The International Review of African American Art* 15, no. 2 (January 1998): 39.

2. "Finding aid," Loïs Mailou Jones Papers, Moorland-Spingarn Research Center, Howard University, Washington, DC. See also Charles H. Rowell, "An Interview with Loïs Mailou Jones," *Callaloo* 39 (Spring 1989): 357–78; and Tritobia Hayes Benjamin, *The Life and Art of Loïs Mailou Jones* (San Francisco: Pomegranate Artbooks, 1994).

3. Pat Kirkham and Lynne Walker, eds., *Women Designers in the USA, 1900–2000: Diversity and Difference* (New Haven, CT: Yale University Press in association with Bard Graduate Center for Studies in the Decorative Arts, New York, 2000), 125. Jones was employed by the F. A. Foster Company and the Schumacher Company in Boston.

4. Polyxeni Potter, "…Myself That I Remake," *Emerging Infectious Diseases* 15, no. 2 (February 2009): 361.

5. Rowell, "Interview with Loïs Mailou Jones," 359.

6. Born in North Carolina, Brown was educated in Massachusetts, where, by chance encounter, she met Alice Freeman Palmer, who would later become the benefactor of the Palmer Memorial Institute. Brown founded the school in 1902 and remained its president until her retirement in 1952. For more information on the Palmer Memorial Institute and Charlotte Hawkins Brown, see Charles W. Wadelington and Richard F. Knapp, *Charlotte Hawkins Brown and Palmer Memorial Institute: What One Young African American Woman Could Do* (Chapel Hill: University of North Carolina Press, 1999).

7. For an in-depth analysis of Jones's trip to North Carolina, see Cheryl Finley, "Loïs Mailou Jones: Impressions of the South," *Southern Quarterly* 49, no. 1 (Fall 2011): 80–94.

8. David C. Driskell, "Loïs Mailou Jones: A Tribute," *American Art* 12, no. 3 (1998): 87.

9. "Artist of Sunlit Canvases: Loïs Pierre-Noël Explores Colors and Haitian Themes," *Ebony* 24, no. 1 (1968): 136.

10. Alain Locke, "The Legacy of the Ancestral Arts," in *The New Negro: An Interpretation*, ed. Alain Locke (New York: Albert and Charles Boni, 1925), 254–67.

11. Rowell, "Interview with Loïs Mailou Jones," 357.

12. Amy Helen Kirschke, "Laura Wheeler Waring and the Women Illustrators of the Harlem Renaissance," in *Women Artists of the Harlem Renaissance*, ed. Amy Helene Kirschke (Jackson: University Press of Mississippi, 2014), 111.

13. Benjamin, *Life and Art*, 6.

14. Cheryl Finley, "The Mask as Muse: Loïs Mailou Jones," *Nka: Journal of Contemporary African Art* 29 (Fall 2011): 142.

15. Betty LaDuke, "Loïs Mailou Jones: The Grande Dame of African-American Art," *Woman's Art Journal* 8, no. 2 (1987/1988): 32.

Artist image: Loïs Mailou Jones (1905–1998), *Self-Portrait*, 1940, casein on board, 17½ × 14½ inches. Smithsonian American Art Museum, Washington, DC; bequest of the artist; 2006.24.2.

NELL HINTON CHOATE JONES

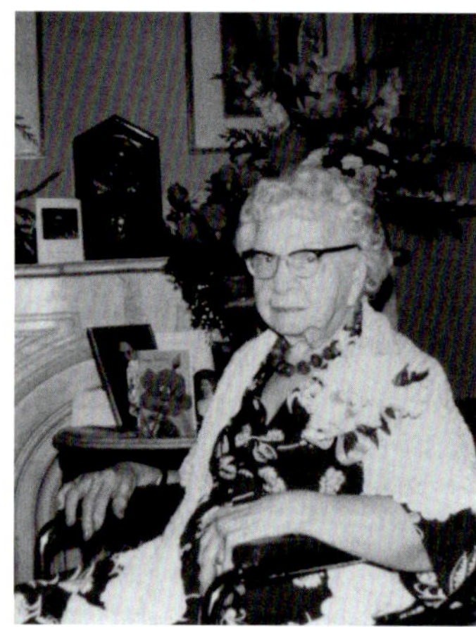

1. Randolph Delehanty, "Art and Artists" in *The Companion to Southern Literature: Themes, Genres, Places, People, Movements, and Motifs*, ed. Joseph M. Flora and Lucinda H. MacKethan (Baton Rouge: Louisiana State University Press, 2001), 68.

2. Nell Choate Jones, as quoted by reporter in "Confederate's Daughter Returns Home for Visit," *Hawkinsville (GA) Dispatch and News*, January 3, 1979.

3. Celeste Ray, "Ethnicity," in *The South*, ed. Rebecca Mark and Rob Vaughan, *The Greenwood Encyclopedia of American Regional Cultures* (London: Greenwood, 2004), 129.

4. Judith Linscott, "A Visit with Fort Greene's 98-Year Old Georgia Peach Turned Brooklyn Belle," *Brooklyn (NY) Phoenix*, April 14, 1977.

5. Ian Hancock, "Gypsies," in *The New Encyclopedia of Southern Culture*, Vol. 6: *Ethnicity*, ed. Celeste Ray (Chapel Hill: University of North Carolina Press, 1989), 432.

6. Ibid. Many Romani people, or gypsies, arrived in the United States in the mid-nineteenth century after five hundred years of gypsy slavery in the Balkan states ended.

Artist image: Nell Choate Jones, photographed on May 27, 1979, her one hundredth birthday, in New York City. Center for the Study of Southern Art, Morris Museum of Art, Augusta, GA; courtesy of Mrs. Thomas S. Potts.

IDA RITTENBERG KOHLMEYER

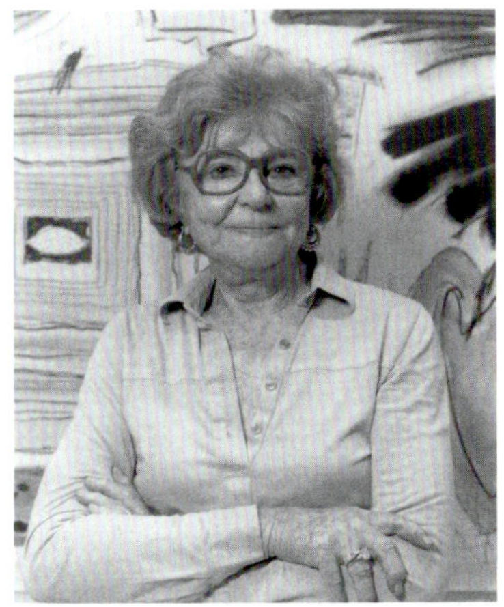

1. Ida Kohlmeyer, in *Panel Discussion: Pre-Pop Modernists*, video, Arthur Roger Gallery, September 12, 1989.

2. *Fantasy No. 1*, measuring 33 × 37 inches and horizontal in orientation, features primary paint colors of ochre, dark blue, blue, and violet, on light background. See copies of the artist's card catalog in the Ida Kohlmeyer Papers, Archives of American Art, Smithsonian Institution, Washington, DC.

3. Ida Kohlmeyer, *My Life as an Artist* (Columbus: Mississippi State College for Women, 1967), 7.

4. Ida Kohlmeyer, quoted in Whitney J. Engeran, *Ida Kohlmeyer: Thirty Years* (Charlotte, NC: Mint Museum, 1983), 104.

Artist image: Estate of Ida Kohlmeyer and Jerald Melberg Gallery, Charlotte, NC.

MARGARET MOFFETT LAW

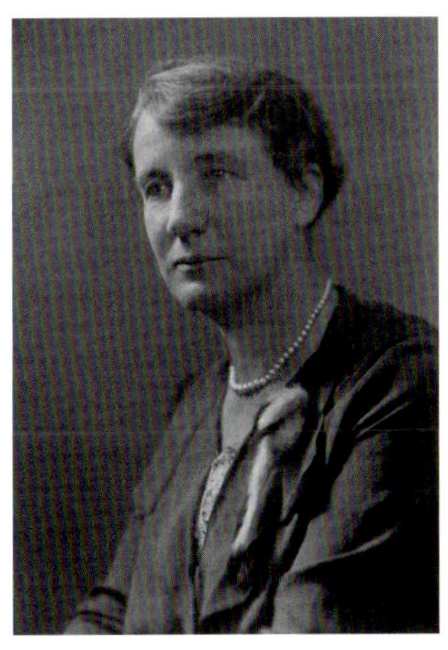

1. Dennis Taylor, *Rural Life in the Piedmont of South Carolina* (Chicago: Arcadia, 1999), 50. See also Charles Frank Kovacik and John J. Winberry, *South Carolina: A Geography* (Boulder, CO: Westview, 1987), 173; and Kim Severson, "Peach Rivalry Becomes War Between the Tastes," *New York Times*, July 27, 2011. As noted by Severson, the California peach crop now outpaces the combined Georgia and South Carolina harvests sixfold.

2. Zan Schuweiler-Daab, *From Fields to Mills: The Art of Margaret Law* (Spartanburg, SC: Regional History Museum of the Spartanburg County Historical Association, 2007), 5.

3. Zan Schuweiler-Daab, *Margaret Law: Painter of Southern Life* (Spartanburg, SC: Spartanburg County Museum of Art, 1999), 1. Henri organized independent juried shows to include women.

4. Henri outlined his approach to painting in his book, *The Art Spirit*, which was first published in 1923 and is still considered a seminal treatise.

5. Several sources were helpful in researching Spartanburg's peach industry, including the area's transition into a leading fruit producer after a boll weevil infestation destroyed local cotton crops. See Schuweiler-Daab, *From Fields to Mills*, 7; "The Commercial Peach Industry in South Carolina," *Spartanburg (SC) Herald-Journal*, January 11, 1921; "S.C. Peaches Best to Can: Processing Key to Better Market," *Spartanburg (SC) Herald-Journal*, June 30, 1946, sec. D.; and "The Orchard," *Farm Journal* 34, no. 9 (1910): 44–46.

6. Schuweiler-Daab, *From Fields to Mills*, 14.

7. Perhaps the best-known peach painting in Law's oeuvre is *The Legend of the Peach*, a monumental canvas measuring 72 × 107 inches. Inspired by Harry Russell Wilkins's poem of the same title, the work was commissioned in 1943 by Maurice Puckett, owner of the Cleveland Hotel in downtown Spartanburg. Completed in 1944, the painting was displayed in the hotel lobby until about 1964; it is now in the collection of the Spartanburg County Historical Association and on view at the Spartanburg Regional History Museum.

8. Mary Louise Dargan, "New Ideas Introduced in Teaching of Subject by Supervisor," *Spartanburg (SC) Herald-Journal*, and "Importance of Art in the Schools Told by Miss Law," *Anderson (SC) Daily Record*. Both undated clippings are in the Johnson Collection's file on the artist.

Artist image: Spartanburg County Historical Association, Spartanburg, SC; donation from the Law family.

NETTIE BLANCHE LAZZELL

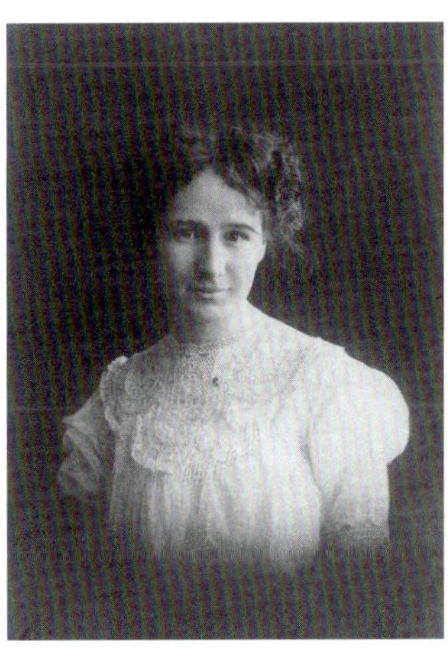

1. Lazzell's images painted between 1917 and 1918, following her study with William Schumacher, indicate her fascination with color analysis and broad color application that she undoubtedly learned at the Byrdcliffe Arts Colony. These works include: *Cornfield* (1917); *Landscape, Woodstock* (1917); *Hollyhocks* (1917); *Still Life with Fruit* (1917); and *Still Life with Jug and Oranges* (1918). To date, the most comprehensive introduction to the artist's career is Robert Bridges, Kristina Olson, and Janet Snyder, eds., *Blanche Lazzell: The Life and Work of an American Modernist* (Morgantown: West Virginia University Press, 2004).

2. Paintings by William Schumacher that may have influenced Lazzell include: *The Kiss* (1911); *Landscape, Moret* (1912); *Butterflies* (1913); *Cooper Lake, Woodstock* (1913–1915); *Tabletop Still Life* (1916); *Still Life with Flowers* (1916); and *Floral Landscape* (1916).

3. Having studied with one of Henri Matisse's teachers, Guérin had fauvist tendencies. The blue lines that Guérin used to outline his figures in *Nude* (1907) and *Le Modèle Debout* are replicated in Lazzell's paintings and ultimately in her woodcuts.

4. Lynn Proden, "The Decorative Work," in Bridges, Olson, and Snyder, eds., *Blanche Lazzell*, 95.

Artist image: West Virginia and Regional History Center, West Virginia University Libraries, Morgantown, WV.

ADELE MARION GAWIN LEMM

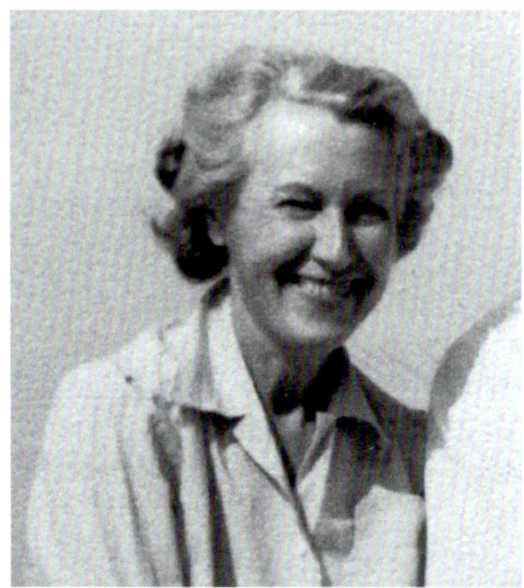

1. Sources inconsistently cite Lemm's birth year; some record the date as 1897, others 1904. In her November 21, 1977, obituary in Memphis's *Commercial Appeal*, her age is listed as seventy-three, indicating a 1904 birth year. This date is confirmed by members of her family. Yet all census records point to the earlier birth year of 1897. I am grateful to Jane Faquin, Marilyn Masler, and Kip Peterson for their assistance in my research.

2. See the 1900 Census: Year: 1900; Census place: Milwaukee Ward 14, Milwaukee, Wisconsin; Roll: 1804; Page 1B, in 1900 United States Federal Census Milwaukee Ward 14, District 0119: August Gawin cited his employer as Art Glass Works Manufacturing. An obituary for August M. Gawin noted that he had founded the Columbia Stained Glass Company in Milwaukee and had been active in state and city politics. *New York Times*, December 9, 1945.

3. A Catholic women's institution run by Dominican nuns, St. Agnes College opened in 1922. In 1939 its name was changed to Siena College to distinguish it from St. Agnes Academy, an elementary and high school located on the same campus. Siena College closed in 1972. In the 1940 census Lemm recorded that she had completed one year of college.

4. Lemm's work in watercolor, oil, and pastel garnered awards at the National Association of Women Artists exhibitions in 1954 (*Regatta*), 1959 (*Monhegan and Manana*), 1966 (*Horses in Meadow*), 1972 (*Dunelands*), 1974 (*Nesting Ground*), and 1975 (*Island Garden*). The NAWA permanent collection and archives are housed at the Jane Voorhees Zimmerli Art Museum at Rutgers University in New Brunswick, New Jersey.

Artist image: Courtesy of the Lemm Family, Memphis, TN.

EDITH CASPARY LONDON

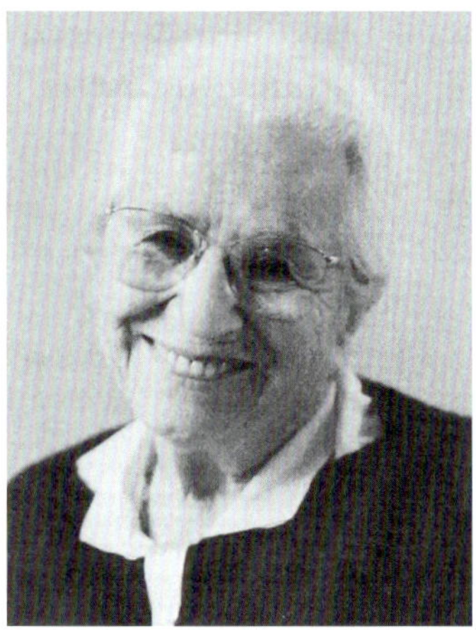

1. London, quoted in *The Work of Edith London* (Durham, NC: Duke University Art Museum, 1970), 9–10. This catalog accompanied an exhibition of the artist's work held from April 5 to May 30, 1970.

2. *Edith London: Collages* (Raleigh: North Carolina Museum of Art, 1988). The companion exhibition was held from October 22, 1988, through January 8, 1989.

3. London, quoted in *Edith London: A Retrospective: Selected Works from 1932–1992* (Durham, NC: Durham Art Guild, Inc., and Durham Arts Council, Inc., 1992), 59. The retrospective exhibition was held from March 8 through April 1, 1992.

4. London, quoted in *Work of Edith London*, 11.

5. London, "The Artist in the Crisis," in "Crosscurrents in Contemporary Life: A Commentary by Women," Duke University Symposium, March 13–17, 1963, Durham, NC.

6. London, quoted in an exhibition brochure foreword by William S. Heckscher. *Edith London: Paintings—Collages—Drawings* was presented by the Duke University Student Union Gallery from March 3 to March 31, 1968.

Artist image: North Carolina Government and Heritage Library, State Library of North Carolina, North Carolina Department of Natural and Cultural Resources, Raleigh, NC.

BLONDELLE OCTAVIA EDWARDS MALONE

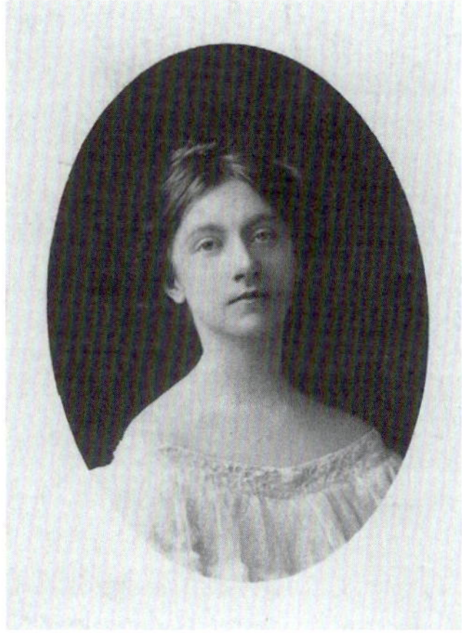

1. In *Enigma: The Career of Blondelle Malone in Art and Society, 1879–1951* (Columbia: University of South Carolina Press, 1963), author

Louise Jones DuBose identified Maryland native Anna Swinburne as both Mrs. A. H. and Mrs. H. H. Swinburne. The second name is correct because she was married to Henry H. Swinburne and is verified by the 1910 US Census for the Borough of Manhattan, which notes Anna Trimble Swinburne's given and maiden names. It seems probable that DuBose misread or was unable to decipher Malone's handwriting.

2. DuBose, *Enigma*, 126.

3. Ibid., 33–36. Malone's complex relationship—at times collegial, at times romantic—with the German-born, thrice-married Sickert lasted several years.

4. May Brawley Hill, *On Foreign Soil: American Gardeners Abroad* (New York: Harry N. Abrams, 2005), 61.

5. Sculptor Frederick MacMonnies and his wife Mary Fairchild MacMonnies became friends with Malone. See DuBose, *Enigma*, 63–68; and Hill, *On Foreign Soil*, 62–64.

6. "US Wildflower Database of Wild Flowers for Rhode Island," last modified April 18, 2015, http://uswildflowers.com.

7. This moniker for Malone was first used by Mary Taft, a critic for the *New York Times*, in 1920. As cited in Suzanne Kamata, "Blondelle Malone: The Sojourn of an American Garden Artist," *Sandlapper* (Summer 2008): 14.

Artist image: Blondelle Malone Papers, South Caroliniana Library, University of South Carolina, Columbia, SC.

there. In her letter Mason mentions Brangwyn and his school, which began informally in the London suburb of Kensington in 1903–1904. Ill health forced Brangwyn to give up teaching in 1907–1908.

5. Alsop-Robineau, "Miss Maud M. Mason," 160.

6. Ibid. See also Lowery, *Legacy of Art*, 148–149.

7. Peter Hastings Falk, ed., *Annual Exhibition Record of the National Academy of Design, 1901–1950* (Madison, CT: Sound View Press, 1990), 348.

8. Alsop-Robineau, "Miss Maud M. Mason," 160. Elizabeth Mason Vanderhoof also decorated porcelain and in 1918 was listed as president of the New York Society of Ceramic Arts. Florence N. Levy, ed., *American Art Annual*, vol. 14 (New York: American Federation of Arts, 1917), 206.

9. "Brooks to Have Preview of Mason Paintings," *Memphis (TN) Press-Scimitar*, September 27, 1957. Mason left almost her entire estate—which included paintings, ceramics, Japanese prints, and textiles—to the Brooks Memorial Art Museum in the hopes that proceeds from its sale would be used to establish a textile component at the institution.

Artist image: Archival photograph of Maud Mason at the Stork Club, New York, circa 1950. Memphis Brooks Museum of Art, Memphis, TN.

CORRIE PARKER McCALLUM

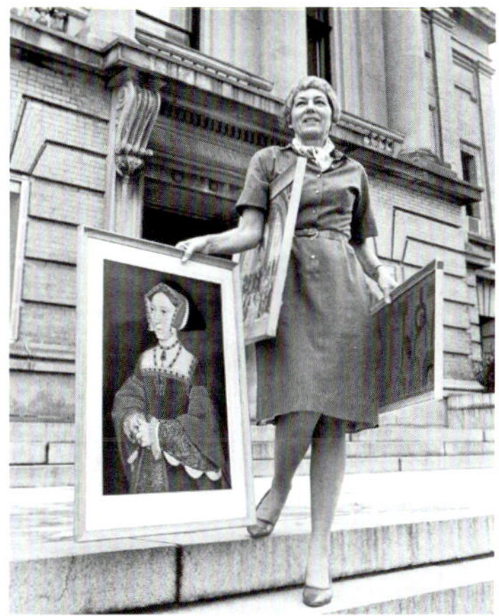

1. Corrie McCallum, 1976 South Carolina Arts Commission interview, quoted in Martha R. Severens, *Corrie McCallum: Take Note* (Greenville, SC: Greenville County Museum of Art, 2004), 34.

2. McCallum, quoted in Ann Hicks, "Woman of Goals," *Greenville (SC) News*, July 6, 2003.

3. McCallum, in "Dear Mother: Letters from Mexico, 1939–1941," typescript, Halsey-McCallum Collection, College of Charleston, Charleston, South Carolina.

4. McCallum, quoted in Jeffrey Day, "A Vibrant Colorful Life," *Columbia (SC) State*, May 4, 2003.

5. McCallum, quoted in Jeffrey Day, "McCallum's Long Career Gets a Gallery Look," *Columbia (SC) State*, August 22, 1999.

Artist image: Photograph of Corrie McCallum, 1967. Gibbes Museum of Art/Carolina Art Association, Charleston, SC.

MAUD MARY MASON

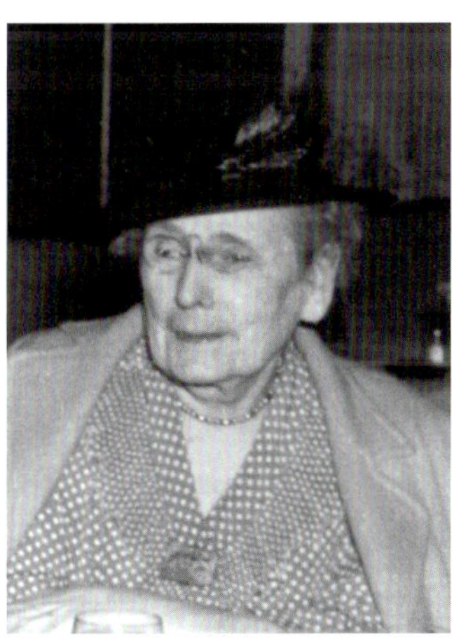

1. In the US Census of 1940, Mason said that her formal schooling ended in the second grade. See US Federal Census 1940, New Canaan, Fairfield CT, Roll: T67–496, page 62A, Ancestry.com (accessed June 6, 2016). The Masons lived in Kentucky until about 1890, when the family moved to Toronto, Canada. 1891 Census of Canada, St. Johns Ward, Toronto City, Ontario, Roll: T-6371, Family No: 68, Ancestry.com (accessed April 4, 2016).

2. Adelaide Alsop-Robineau, "Miss Maud M. Mason," *Keramic Studio*, 18, no. 4 (February 1917): 160.

3. Carol Lowery, *A Legacy of Art: Paintings and Sculptures by Artist Life Members of the National Arts Club* (New York: National Arts Club in association with Hudson Hills Press, 2007), 149.

4. Conversation with Jane Tisdale about Mason's time in Canada, April 4, 2016. The Archives of Mount Allison University, New Brunswick, Canada, contain correspondence, dated 1907, between Mason and a former student, Elizabeth McLeod, who later taught ceramics

WILLIE BETTY NEWMAN

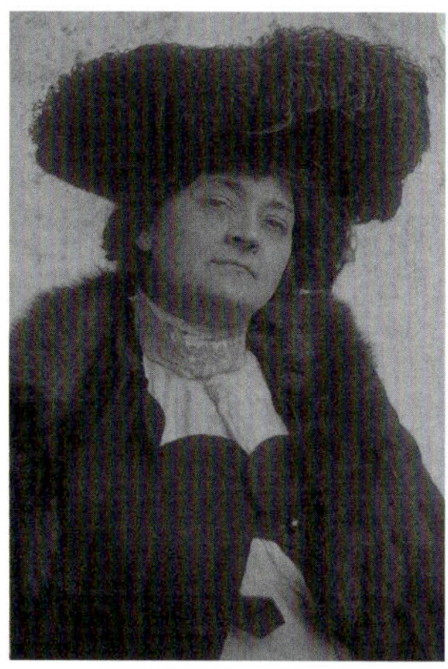

1. "Mrs. Willie Betty Newman, Artist," *Nashville (TN) American*, May 2, 1909.

2. Historical records cite Warren Newman as J. Warren Newman and alternatively as Isaac Warren Newman.

3. Newman, "Forum of the People: More about Art." Undated clipping, Newman files, Center for the Study of Southern Art, Morris Museum of Art, Augusta, Georgia.

4. Richard Folkard Jr., *Plant Lore, Legends, and Lyrics: Embracing the Myths, Traditions, Superstitions, and Folk-lore of the Plant Kingdom* (London: Sampson Low, Marston, Searle, and Rivington, 1884), 503.

5. "Mrs. Willie Betty Newman, Artist," *Nashville (TN) Banner*, August 26, 1905.

Artist image: Tennessee State Library and Archives, Nashville, TN.

AUGUSTA DENK OELSCHIG

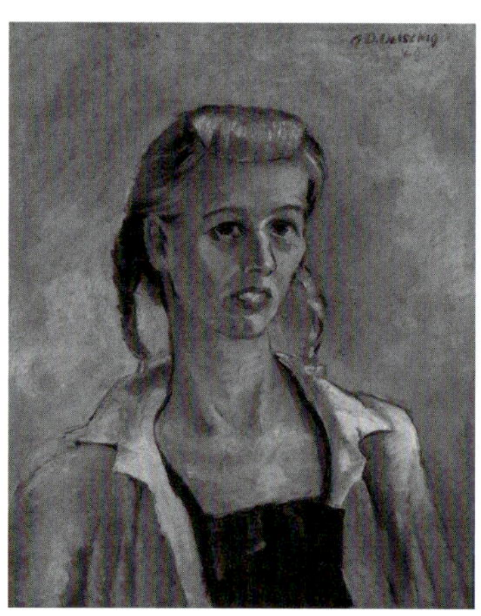

1. An Alabama native, Dodd was named the University of Georgia art department's first director in 1936 and is credited with establishing the department's robust framework and strong reputation. "Lamar Dodd School of Art, University of Georgia," http://art.uga.edu/about-us (accessed June 18, 2016).

2. Marty Shuter, "Savannah Native's Long Life Devoted to Art," *Savannah (GA) Morning News*, November 5, 1995, G1.

3. Lamar Dodd, foreword to *Exhibition of Paintings, Prints and Drawings by Augusta Oelschig, February 27–March 14, 1941* (Savannah, GA: Telfair Academy of Arts and Sciences, 1941).

4. "Miss Oelschig Wins Scholarship in Art: Savannah Artist to Study at Cincinnati Academy," *Savannah (GA) Morning News*, May 29, 1940, 14.

5. Shuter, "Savannah Native's Long Life."

6. Dodd's remarks continued: "We have a tradition of which we may well be proud. A tradition upon which to build the art of today and tomorrow. The artists of this state realize the particular opportunities that are theirs and with the whole hearted cooperation of the public, there is no reason that we should not take our place at the front ranks of American Art." Dodd, foreword to *Exhibition of Paintings*.

7. "A Will of Her Own: Telfair Exhibits Augusta Oelschig's Distinctive Art," *Savannah (GA) Morning News*, September 10, 2000.

8. *Portrait of a Young Man* was included in the 1940 exhibition of the Association of Georgia Artists, where it was awarded the Edward S. Shorter Purchase Prize.

Artist image: Augusta Oelschig, *Self-Portrait*, 1946, oil on canvas board, 20 × 16 inches. Morris Museum of Art, Augusta, GA; gift of the Robert Powell Coggins Art Trust.

CLARA MINTER WEAVER PARRISH

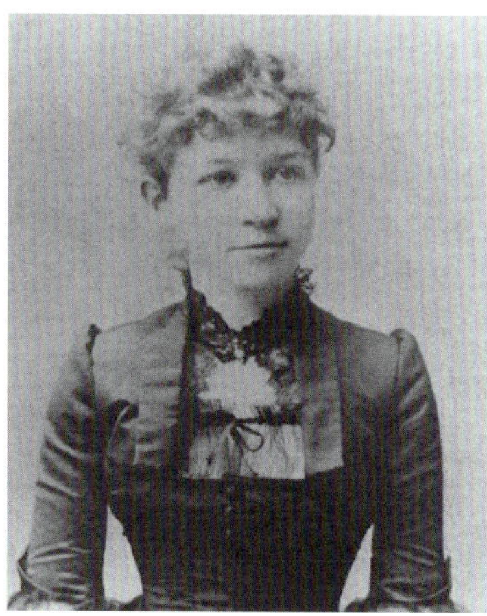

1. The legend of Tristan and Isolde has multiple iterations that vary across centuries and cultures. See Joan Tasker Grimbert, ed., *Tristan and Isolde: A Casebook* (New York: Routledge, 2002).

2. "The Lay Figure: On the Artistic Inspiration of War," *The International Studio* 57, no. 225 (1915): 76.

3. C. Reynolds Brown, *Clara Weaver Parrish* (Montgomery, AL: Montgomery Museum of Fine Arts, 1980), 7.

4. Ibid., 8.

5. Martha R. Severens discusses *The Red Lily* in "American Impressionism in Context," *American Art Review* 14, no. 1 (2002).

6. Estill Curtis Pennington, artist biography of Clara Weaver Parrish, in Pennington and Martha R. Severens, *Scenic Impressions: Southern Interpretations from the Johnson Collection* (Spartanburg, SC: Johnson Collection in association with University of South Carolina Press, 2015), 167. Another Pennington essay on Clara Parrish appears as the catalog entry on page 104.

7. "William Peck Parrish Dead," *New York Times*, May 1, 1901.

8. Pennington, in Pennington and Severens, *Scenic Impressions*, 168.

9. Brown, *Clara Weaver Parrish*, 12.

10. Donald B. Kuspit et al., *Painting in the South: 1564–1980* (Richmond: Virginia Museum of Fine Arts, 1983), 273.

Artist image: Weaver-Parrish Charitable Trust, Selma, AL.

THERESA POLLAK

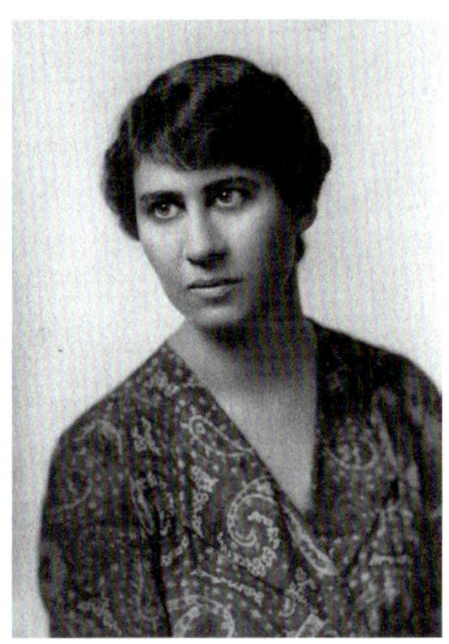

1. "Remembering Theresa Pollak: An Exhibition on the Founder of VCUarts," online exhibition, https://gallery.library.vcu.edu/exhibits/show/remembering-theresa-pollak.

2. Pollak supplemented her income by teaching art classes at the University of Richmond. In 1969 Virginia Commonwealth University's school of art published a brief memoir, *An Art School: Some Reminiscences*, detailing the artist's forty-year tenure at the institution. Two years later a new arts building on the campus was named in her honor.

3. The ninth installment of the institution's "Virginia Artist Series," an exhibition of fifty of Pollak's oil paintings, watercolors, and pen and ink drawings, was held at the Virginia Museum of Fine Arts from April 23 through May 12, 1940.

4. Pollak to the *Richmond (VA) Times-Dispatch*, quoted in Deveron Timberlake, "Icon—And Working Artist," *Shafer Court Connections*, Spring 2003, 23. https://archive.org/stream/shafercourt82spr2003virg/shafercourt82spr2003virg_djvu.txt.

Artist image: Special Collections and Archives, Virginia Commonwealth University Libraries, Richmond, VA.

SARAH MABEL PUGH

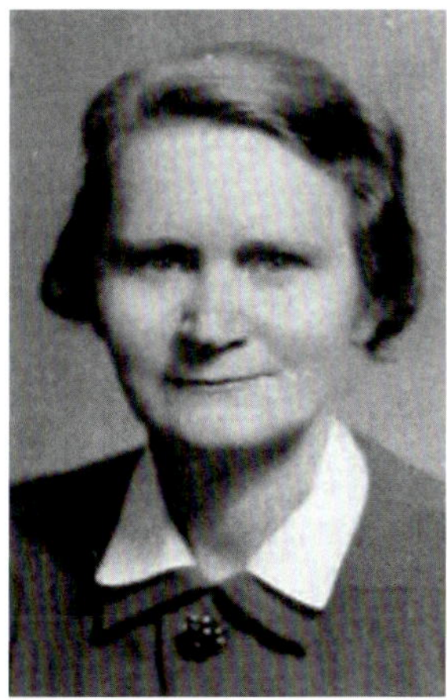

1. Pugh's later papers are in the archive of Walter Clinton Jackson Library at the University of North Carolina at Greensboro.

2. Karen Klacsmann has suggested that the sitter may be Glenna Collett Vare, who bears a strong resemblance to the woman portrayed.

Artist image: Yearbook photograph of art instructor Mabel Pugh. William Peace University, Raleigh, NC.

HATTIE SAUSSY

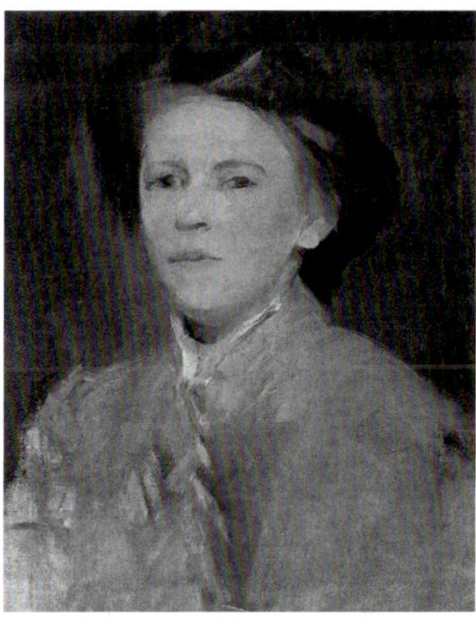

1. Cissy Fitzpatrick, "Fifty Years of Art and She's Still at It," *Savannah (GA) Morning News*, December 12, 1969, 2B.

2. Dinny Jones, "Art Association's Shows Opens." *Savannah (GA) Morning News*, September 3, 1974.

3. Ibid.

4. From 1923 through 1958, Saussy regularly exhibited with the Savannah Art Club at the Telfair Academy and likely served as the Art Club's president for several years; at the time of this printing, however, documentation can only be found of her presidency in 1936. Telfair Academy of Arts and Sciences, Proceedings, Sixteenth Annual Meeting, 1936, Telfair Museums Archives, Savannah, GA. She also served as vice president and president (1932–1934) of the Association of Georgia Artists. According to "A Short History of the Association of Georgia Artists, 1929–1962," Saussy "invited artists from several other Georgia cities to join them in showing at their annual exhibit. The response was so enthusiastic that shortly afterward this organization was formed." Saussy Family Papers, Box 5, Folder 32, Georgia Historical Society,

Savannah, GA. Hattie Saussy was a member of the Telfair Academy's board of trustees in 1933–1934.

5. Saussy built a home at 216 East 53rd Street, near Hull Park, in 1926 and resided there until her death on January 13, 1978. She is buried in Savannah's Laurel Grove Cemetery.

6. At Telfair Museums, Saussy exhibited *Wisteria Arbor* in 1932 (Assoc. of GA Artists, #39), *Wisteria* in 1939 (SAV Art Club, #10), and *Wisteria* in 1940 (Assoc. of GA Artists, #17). Telfair Museums Archives, Savannah, GA.

7. "Miss Saussy Exhibits Art Works," *Savannah (GA) Morning News,* October 24, 1960.

Artist image: Hattie Saussy (1890–1978), *Self-Portrait,* oil on canvas mounted on board, 20 × 16 inches. Charleston Renaissance Gallery, Charleston, SC.

AUGUSTA CHRISTINE FELLS SAVAGE

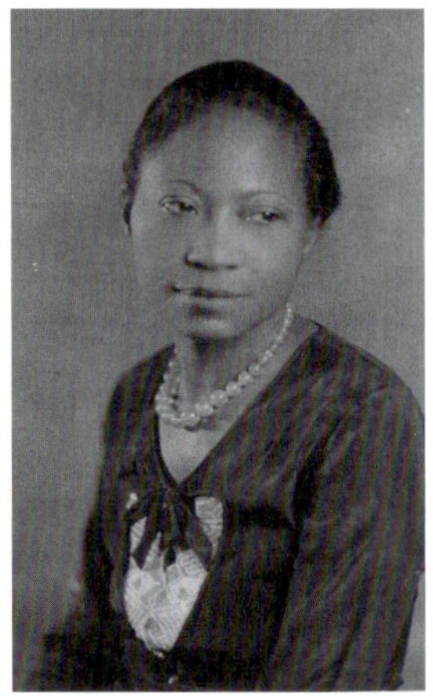

1. Savage was married three times. Her first marriage was in 1907 to John Moore, who died shortly after the birth of their only child, a daughter named Irene Connie Moore. She married a carpenter named James Savage on August 23, 1915. Though that union was short-lived, Augusta would keep his name for the remainder of her career. On October 27, 1923, she wed Robert Lincoln Poston, a journalist and activist for African American rights, who died just one year into their marriage, on March 19, 1924. In 1941 James Savage was granted a divorce from Augusta on the grounds of desertion.

2. Romare Bearden and Harry Henderson, *A History of African-American Artists: From 1792 to the Present* (New York: Pantheon, 1993), 168–80.

3. Quoted in Theresa Leininger-Miller, *New Negro Artists in Paris: African American Painters and Sculptors in the City of Light, 1922–1934* (New Brunswick, NJ: Rutgers University Press, 2001), 169, 171. See also "Appeal artists' race ban: Negroes to Ask Harding's Aid in Case of Augusta Savage," *New York Times,* May 11, 1923.

4. It is believed that Savage's first version of *Gamin* is the example in the collection of the Cleveland Museum of Art. See Augusta Savage, *Gamin,* circa 1929; Hand-painted plaster; 17½ × 9½ × 8 inches; Cleveland Museum of Art; purchase from the J. H. Wade Fund 2003.40. Accessed online at www.clevelandart.org/art/2003.40.

Artist image: Photographs and Prints Division, Schomburg Center for Research in Black Culture, New York Public Library, Astor, Lenox, and Tilden Foundations, New York, NY.

DIXIE SELDEN

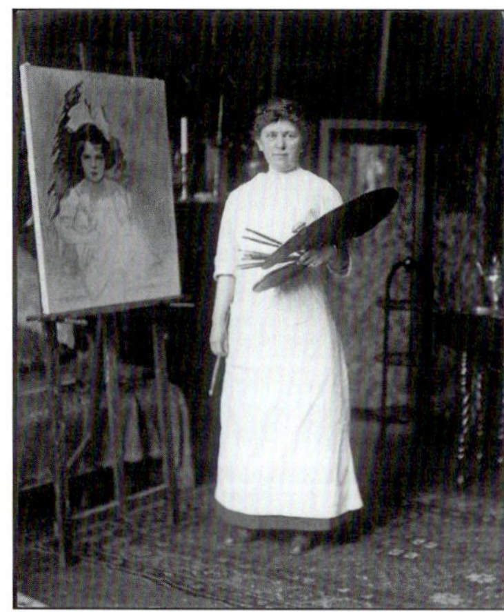

1. Herbert Greer French, *Memorial Exhibition of Paintings by Dixie Selden* (Cincinnati, OH: Cincinnati Art Museum, 1936). This exhibition was on view at the museum from March 5 to April 8, 1936.

2. Mary L. Alexander, "The Week in Art Circles," *Cincinnati Enquirer,* November 24, 1935, quoted in Genetta McLean, *Dixie Selden: An American Impressionist from Cincinnati, 1868–1935* (Cincinnati, OH: Cincinnati Art Galleries, 2001), 51.

3. "The Week in Art Circles," *Cincinnati Enquirer,* November 14, 1926, quoted in McLean, *Dixie Selden,* 77–78.

Artist image: Photographic portrait of Dixie Selden in her studio, 1913. Goldman Archives.

ALICE RAVENEL HUGER SMITH

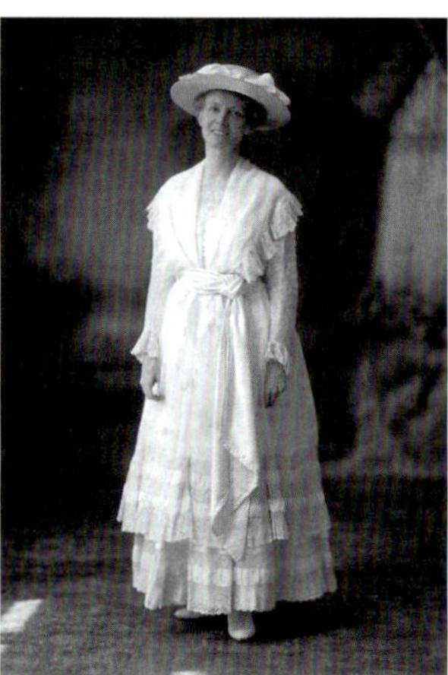

1. Alice Ravenel Huger Smith, "Reminiscences," in *Alice Ravenel Huger Smith: An Artist, a Place, and a Time,* ed. Martha R. Severens (Charleston, SC: Carolina Art Association, 1993), 90. In this memoir Smith recounts many details of her childhood, family milestones, pastimes, friendships, education, and career.

2. "The Fine Arts: Art Notes," in *The Critic: An Illustrated Monthly Review of Literature, Art, and Life* 9, no. 229 (May 19, 1888): 248. For more information about Smith's study with Féry, see also: "Among the Artists," *Charleston (SC) News and Courier,* May 6, 1888, 8; "A Capital Exhibit," *Charleston (SC) News and Courier,* April 22, 1895, 2; and "Miss L. Féry Will Have Her Out-of-Doors Sketching Class," *Charleston (SC) News and Courier,* October 29, 1893, 3.

3. Smith referred to these early works as "bright little sketches" several times, as noted in Severens, ed., *Alice Ravenel Huger Smith*, 31, 155. See also August P. Trovaioli and Roulhac B. Toledano, *William Aiken Walker: Southern Genre Painter* (Gretna, LA: Pelican, 2008) 53.

4. Smith, "Reminiscences," 120. This source cites Smith's teacher's last name as "Payer," an error likely due to transcription difficulties. See "Cecile E. Payen" in Ancestry.com, 1940 United States Federal Census, Provo, UT, 2012.

5. An inventory of Smith's work lists six watercolor landscapes created in 1906. *Alice Ravenel Huger Smith of Charleston, South Carolina: An Appreciation on the Occasion of Her Eightieth Birthday from Her Friends* (Charleston, SC: Privately Published by Her Friends, 1956), 41; and Dwight E. McInvaill, *Alice Ravenel Huger Smith: Photos and Sketchbooks*, filmed September 18, 2015, YouTube video, 35:55, posted September 30, 2015, www.youtube.com/watch?v=EkIGD2dxHlg.

6. Frederick W. Gookin was the curator of the Buckingham Collection of Japanese Prints at the Art Institute of Chicago; quoted in Severens, ed., *Alice Ravenel Huger Smith*, 40.

7. Severens, ed., *Alice Ravenel Huger Smith*, 4, 36. For more on Chinese landscape philosophies, see Ernest F. Fenollosa, *Epochs of Chinese and Japanese Art*, vol. 2 (New York: Dover, 1963), 10–19. To learn about Read's contributions to the *Dwelling Houses of Charleston*, see "Notes of Motte Alston Read, the Dwelling House Book," South Carolina Historical Society Archives, File #21/52/3, Alice Smith Papers, Charleston, SC. Smith, "Reminiscences," 122.

8. Read's collection included several examples by the Japanese artist Hiroshige.

9. Henry Timrod, "Carolina," in *Poems of Henry Timrod with a Memorial and Portrait* (New York: Houghton, Mifflin, 1899), 144.

10. Smith, "Reminiscences," 140.

Artist image: Charleston Museum, Charleston, SC.

GLADYS NELSON SMITH

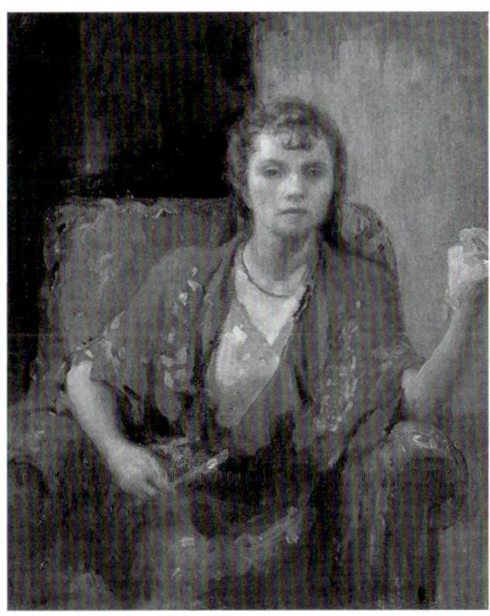

1. *Washington Star*, April 24, 1937, quoted in Linda Crocker Simmons, *Gladys Nelson Smith* (Washington, DC: Corcoran Museum of Art, 1985), 11.

2. Josephine Nelson to Alan Fern, director of the National Portrait Gallery, Washington, DC, December 26, 1984, copy in artist file, Johnson Collection, Spartanburg, SC.

3. Simmons maintained, to the contrary, that Smith painted *Time Out* at her Chevy Chase studio. See Simmons, *Gladys Nelson Smith*, 12.

4. Ilene Susan Fort and Michael Quick, *American Art: A Catalogue of the Los Angeles County Museum of Art* (Los Angeles, CA: Los Angeles County Museum of Art, 1991), 357.

5. *Washington Star*, February 11, 1940, quoted in Simmons, *Gladys Nelson Smith*, 16.

6. Smith to Josephine Nelson, March 16, 1939, copy in artist file, Johnson Collection, Spartanburg, SC.

Artist image: Gladys Nelson Smith (1890–1980), *Self-Portrait*, oil on canvas board, 15 × 12 inches. Johnson Collection, Spartanburg, SC.

ALMA WOODSEY THOMAS

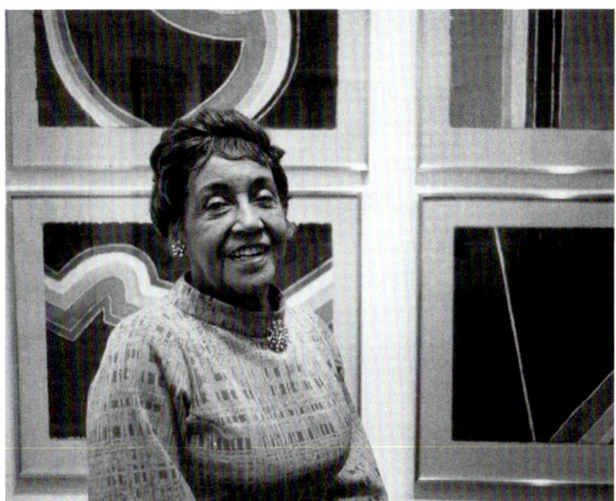

1. Eleanor Munro, "The Late Springtime of Alma Thomas," *Washington Post Magazine*, April 7, 1979, 24.

2. Ian Berry et. al., *Alma Thomas* (New York: Studio Museum in Harlem and the Tang Teaching Museum and Art Gallery, 2016), 227.

3. Romare Bearden and Harry Henderson, *A History of African-American Artists: From 1792 to the Present* (New York: Pantheon, 1993), 453.

4. As noted by Lauren Haynes in Ian Berry et. al., *Alma Thomas*, 18.

Artist image: Alma Thomas with her work at the Whitney Museum, 1972?, by unidentified photographer. Alma Thomas Papers, 1894–2000, bulk 1936–1982, Archives of American Art, Smithsonian Institution, Washington, DC.

MARY ALICE LEATH THOMAS

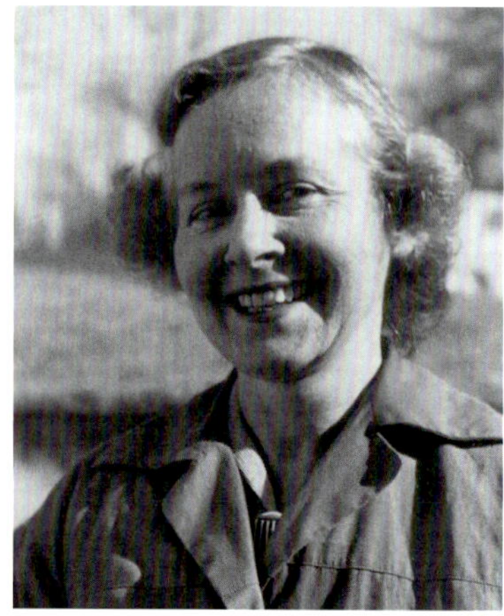

1. By the 1930s sign painters consumed approximately 40 percent of the palladium leaf produced. Louis S. Treadwell, *Annualog: A Cumulative Reference of Scientific and Other Useful Information*, vol. 8 (New York: Scientific American, 1933), 59.

2. Ivy, quoted in "Mary Leath Thomas (1905–1959)," Weaver Foundation website, http://weaverfoundation.com/mary-leath-thomas-1905-1959 (accessed January 26, 2017). Ivy was head of the art department at North Carolina's women's college (now the University of North Carolina at Greensboro) during Thomas's tenure there. Josephine Bloodgood, *A Pioneer in the Arts of the South: Mary Leath Thomas* (Athens: Georgia Museum of Art, 1996).

3. The artist was first married to a man with the last name of Stewart; some early works were signed with this name.

4. Thomas gave a small book of color reproductions of Klee's work to her friend and fellow teacher Jeffie Landers Rowland. She also mentioned Klee's *Pedagogical Sketchbook* repeatedly in conversations about visual principles taught at the Bauhaus. Bloodgood, *A Pioneer in the Arts*.

5. Bloodgood, *Mary Leath Thomas*.

Artist image: Lee Hansley Gallery, Raleigh, NC.

HELEN MARIA TURNER

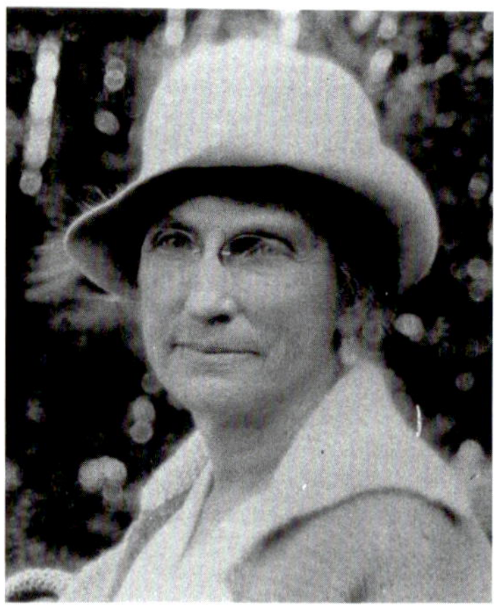

1. Helen Turner's works were acquired by such distinguished institutions as the Metropolitan Museum of Art, the Philadelphia Museum of Art, and the Detroit Institute of Arts, as well as by the great twentieth-century collector Duncan Phillips.

2. Ann Hall (1792–1863) was the first woman to become a full member of the National Academy of Design, in 1833. Cecilia Beaux (1855–1942) was elected in 1902, and Lydia Field Emmet (1866–1952) became a member in 1912.

3. Dorothea Storey Kelsey (1893–1980) also posed for Turner's 1914 *Girl with Lantern*, now in the collection of the Greenville County (South Carolina) Museum of Art. Kelsey later became a notable painter and printmaker and has works in the collection of the Connecticut Historical Society. Lewis Hoyer Rabbage, *Helen M. Turner, NA: A Retrospective Exhibition* (Cragsmoor, NY: Cragsmoor Free Library, 1983), 6; and Jane Ward Faquin and Maia Jalenak, *Helen M. Turner: The Woman's Point of View* (Memphis, TN: Dixon Gallery and Gardens, 2010), 45.

4. Lida Rose McCabe. "Some Painters Who Happen to Be Women," *The Art World* 4, no. 6 (March 1918): 491.

Artist image: Acc. No. 2004.0154. Historic New Orleans Collection, New Orleans, LA.

ELIZABETH QUALE O'NEILL VERNER

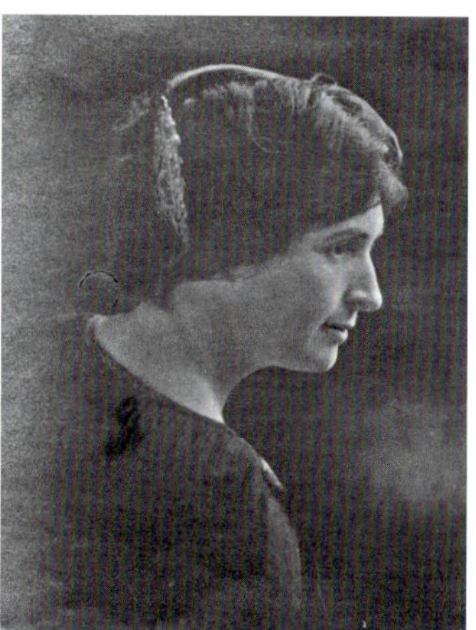

1. Martha R. Severens, *The Charleston Renaissance* (Spartanburg, SC: Saraland Press, 1998), 169; Elizabeth O'Neill Verner, *Mellowed by Time: A Charleston Notebook* (Columbia, SC: Bostick and Thornley, 1941), 7.

2. Student registration records in the archives of the Pennsylvania Academy of the Fine Arts show Verner was enrolled from 1901 to 1903 and studied drawing under Anschutz.

3. Lynn Barstis Williams, *Imprinting the South: Southern Printmakers and Their Images of the Region, 1920s–1940s* (Tuscaloosa: University of Alabama Press, 2007), 76; Marjorie Julian Spruill and Valinda W. Littlefield, eds., *South Carolina Women: Their Lives and Times*, vol. 2 (Athens: University of Georgia Press, 2010), 252–64.

4. For more on American Regionalism and Verner, see Patricia Phagan, ed., *The American Scene and the South: Paintings and Works on Paper, 1930–1946* (Athens: Georgia Museum of Art, University of Georgia, 1996); and Stephanie E. Yuhl, *A Golden Haze of Memory: The Making of Historic Charleston* (Chapel Hill: University of North Carolina Press, 2005), 56–57.

5. Verner, *Mellowed by Time*, 7.

Artist image: Elizabeth O'Neill Verner, circa 1917. Verner Gallery, Ltd., Charleston, SC.

ANNA CATHERINE WILEY

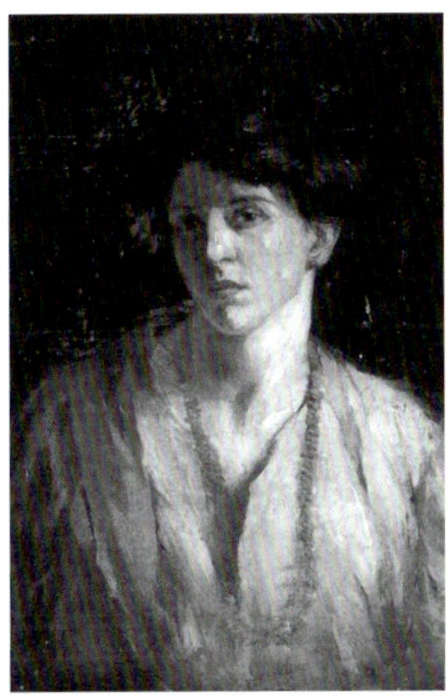

1. Wiley's *Willow Pond* (1914) is in the collection of the Metropolitan Museum of Art, while *A Sunlit Afternoon* (circa 1915) is owned by the Greenville County (South Carolina) Museum of Art. The artist's other parasol paintings include *The Green Parasol* (circa 1912, private collection) and *Two Girls with Parasol by Water (Summer at Newport)* (1913, collection of Mr. and Mrs. Edwin P. Wiley).

2. Anna Catherine Wiley, "Lecture XVIII, II—The Mind in Art; Modern Painting; Relations of Modern Painting to Personality and to Woman's Work in the Fine Arts," *Woman's Athenaeum* 10 (1912): 181.

Artist image: Anna Catherine Wiley (1879–1958), *Catherine Wiley: Self-Portrait*, oil on canvas, 23½ × 15 inches. Collection of David and Diana Wiley Blackledge; photograph courtesy of the Tennessee State Museum, Nashville, TN.

ENID BLAND YANDELL

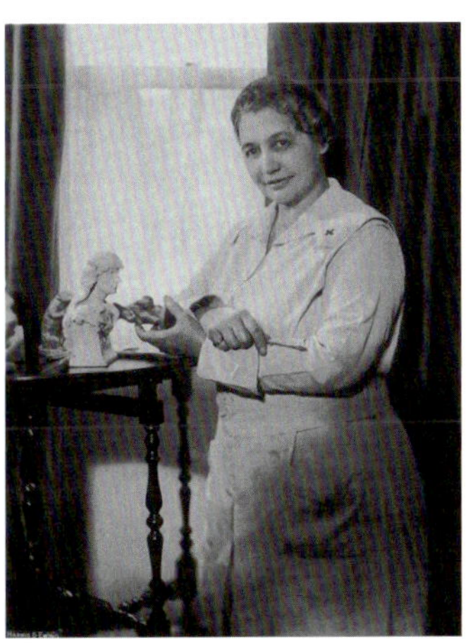

1. Charlotte Streifer Rubenstein, *American Women Sculptors: A History of Women Working in Three Dimensions* (Boston: G. K. Hall, 1990), 116.

2. The eldest child of Louise Elliston Yandell and Lunsford Pitts Yandell Jr., a surgeon, medical professor, and Civil War veteran, Enid Yandell was born in 1869. Verification comes in the form of Yandell's grave at the family plot in Louisville's Cave Hill Cemetery, as well as an entry in her father's diary for 1869–1871, in which he notes "Sunny's child born at 2 a.m." on October 6, 1869. See Filson Historical Society MSS A/Y21/Folder 53, Special Collections, Filson Historical Society, Louisville, Kentucky. Confusion as to the year emerged during the artist's lifetime, when exhibition records indicated a birth year as late as 1875. Other recent scholarship has mistakenly cited the year as 1870.

3. Given the sheer volume of work and limited timeline, Lorado Taft asked permission to hire a team of apprentices—specifically women sculptors—to assist him. The exposition's chief architect, Daniel Burnham, authorized Taft to "employ any one who could do the work—white rabbits, if they could help out." Quoted in Janet Scudder, *Modeling My Life* (New York: Harcourt, Brace, 1925), 58. The White Rabbits also included Ellen Rankin Copp, Helen Farnsworth Mears, Mary Lawrence, Carol Brooks MacNeil, Janet Scudder, Bessie Potter Vonnoh, and Julia Bracken Wendt.

4. See Filson Historical Society MSS A/Y21b/Folder 66.

5. Earlier renditions of Ariadne include several Roman copies of Greek sculpture, all dating to the second century CE: *Sleeping Ariadne* (Vatican Museums); the *"Medici" Sleeping Ariadne* (Uffizi Gallery Museum); the *"Wilton House" Ariadne* (San Antonio Museum of Art); *Sleeping Ariadne* (Prado Museum); and *Sleeping Ariadne* (Louvre Museum). See Brunilde Sismondo Ridgway, *Hellenistic Sculpture I: The Styles of ca. 331–200 B.C.* (Madison: University of Wisconsin Press, 2001), 331–332.

6. Yandell, quoted in "Sculptress Comes to Chicago to Help Orphans of War," *Chicago Tribune*, November 11, 1915, cited in Rubenstein, *American Women Sculptors*, 120.

7. "Listing 200,000 Wounded Doughboys," *New York Times*, July 6, 1919, 68. Based at the Red Cross's Debarkation Records Department in Hoboken, New Jersey, beginning in 1919 Yandell managed a staff of women charged with locating soldiers returned from the war—a role that garnered her the nickname "Aunt Enid" and "brought fame to the department." Under her authority, the office claimed never to have lost or misplaced a single name of the 200,000 listed. It is unclear how long she served in this position.

8. Yandell spoke frankly about the challenges she had faced as a professional artist and, in a 1903 interview, offered this advice: "Get married, girls. Success in other lines is hard won—too hard." "Get Married, Girls!," *Cincinnati Enquirer*, December 6, 1903, as cited in Rubenstein, *American Women Sculptors*, 120.

9. See "Bronze and Marble Worker Sun Dial's Enthusiastic Sponsor: Miss Enid Yandell, Sculptor, Has Done Meritorious Work, Gaining for Her Sex Recognition in This Field. Many of Her Best Known Pieces Are Designed for the Out-of-Doors," *New York Sun*, March 12, 1924, in Filson Historical Society MSS A/Y21b/Folder 95, between pages 4 and 5.

Artist image: Enid Yandell with small sculptures (987PC52x.08, Enid Yandell Collection). Filson Historical Society, Louisville, KY.

Contributors

SARA C. ARNOLD is curator of collections at the Gibbes Museum of Art in Charleston, South Carolina.

DANIEL BELASCO is the executive director of the Al Held Foundation and previously served as curator of exhibitions and programs at the Samuel Dorsky Museum of Art at the State University of New York at New Paltz.

LYNNE BLACKMAN is director of communications at the Johnson Collection in Spartanburg, South Carolina.

CAROLYN J. BROWN is an independent writer, editor, and scholar in Jackson, Mississippi.

ERIN R. CORRALES-DIAZ is the former curator of the Johnson Collection and the Johnson Collection Visiting Scholar at both Converse College and Wofford College in Spartanburg, South Carolina.

JOHN A. CUTHBERT is the director of the West Virginia and Regional History Center at West Virginia University in Morgantown.

JUILEE DECKER is an associate professor of museum studies at the Rochester Institute of Technology in Rochester, New York.

NANCY M. DOLL is director of the Weatherspoon Art Museum at the University of North Carolina at Greensboro.

JANE W. FAQUIN is the former curator of education at the Dixon Gallery and Gardens in Memphis, Tennessee, and now works as an independent curator and author.

ELIZABETH C. HAMILTON is an independent art historian.

ELIZABETH S. HAWLEY is a PhD candidate in art history at the Graduate Center of the City University of New York and teaches at Parsons School of Design and Pratt Institute.

MAIA JALENAK is the former museum curator at the Louisiana Art and Science Museum and associate director of the Louisiana State University Museum of Art in Baton Rouge.

KAREN TOWERS KLACSMANN, an independent art historian and author, served on the faculty of Augusta University and as curator for research at the Morris Museum of Art, both in Augusta, Georgia.

SANDY McCAIN, an independent art historian, served as the Johnson Collection's inaugural graduate fellow while completing her PhD at the University of Georgia.

DWIGHT McINVAILL is director of the Georgetown County (South Carolina) Library and an independent cultural historian.

COURTNEY A. McNEIL is chief curator of collections and exhibitions at Telfair Museums in Savannah, Georgia.

CHRISTOPHER C. OLIVER is assistant curator of American art at the Virginia Museum of Fine Arts in Richmond.

JULIE PIEROTTI is the Martha R. Robinson Curator of the Dixon Gallery and Gardens in Memphis, Tennessee.

DEBORAH C. POLLACK is an independent art historian, author, and art dealer in Palm Beach, Florida.

ROBIN R. SALMON is vice president of art and historical collections and curator of sculpture at Brookgreen Gardens in Murrells Inlet, South Carolina.

MARY LOUISE SOLDO SCHULTZ is a former member of the Honors College faculty at West Virginia University in Morgantown and is an independent art historian and author of historical fiction for children.

MARTHA R. SEVERENS, an independent art historian and author, has served as curator of the Greenville County (South Carolina) Museum of Art; the Gibbes Museum of Art in Charleston, South Carolina; and the Portland (Maine) Museum of Art.

EVIE TERRONO is professor of art history at Randolph-Macon College in Ashland, Virginia.

ROGER WARD, the former deputy director of the Mississippi Museum of Art in Jackson, is executive director of the Ann Norton Sculpture Gardens in West Palm Beach, Florida.

STEPHEN C. WICKS is the Barbara W. and Bernard E. Bernstein Curator of the Knoxville Museum of Art in Knoxville, Tennessee.

KRISTEN MILLER ZOHN is the executive director of the Costume Society of America, located in Columbus, Georgia, and is the curator of collections and exhibitions for the Lauren Rogers Museum of Art in Laurel, Mississippi.

Index

Page numbers indicating illustrations are given in **bold**.